INFANT
DEVELOPMENT
A Multidisciplinary Introduction

INFANT
DEVELOPMENT
A Multidisciplinary Introduction

Jean Mercer
Richard Stockton College of New Jersey

Brooks/Cole Publishing Company

I⊤P® *An International Thomson Publishing Company*

Pacific Grove • Albany • Belmont • Bonn • Boston • Cincinnati • Detroit • Johannesburg •
London • Madrid • Melbourne • Mexico City • New York • Paris • Singapore • Tokyo •
Toronto • Washington

Sponsoring Editor: *Jim Brace-Thompson*
Marketing Representative: *Jeff Wilhelms*
Marketing Team: *Lauren Harp, Christine Davis*
Editorial Assistant: *Terry Thomas*
Production Editor: *Keith Faivre*
Manuscript Editor: *Barbara Kimmell*
Permissions Editor: *May Clark*
Interior and Cover Design: *Sharon Kinghan*
Design Editor: *Roy R. Neuhaus*

Cover Photo: *David Young-Wolff/
    Tony Stone Images*
Art Editor: *Lisa Torri*
Interior Illustration: *LM Graphics*
Photo Editor: *Bob Western*
Photo Researcher: *Sue C. Howard*
Typesetting: *Carlisle Communications, Ltd.*
Cover Printing: *Phoenix Color Corporation*
Printing and Binding: *The Maple-Vail Book
    Manufacturing Group*

Credits continue on page 517.

For more information, contact:

BROOKS/COLE PUBLISHING COMPANY
511 Forest Lodge Road
Pacific Grove, CA 93950
USA

International Thomson Publishing Europe
Berkshire House 168–173
High Holborn
London WC1V 7AA
England

Thomas Nelson Australia
102 Dodds Street
South Melbourne, 3205
Victoria, Australia

Nelson Canada
1120 Birchmount Road
Scarborough, Ontario
Canada M1K 5G4

International Thomson Editores
Seneca 53
Col. Polanco
11560 México, D. F., México

International Thomson Publishing GmbH
Königswinterer Strasse 418
53227 Bonn
Germany

International Thomson Publishing Asia
221 Henderson Road
#05–10 Henderson Building
Singapore 0315

International Thomson Publishing Japan
Hirakawacho Kyowa Building, 3F
2-2-1 Hirakawacho
Chiyoda-ku, Tokyo 102
Japan

Printed in the United States of America.

10   9   8   7   6   5   4   3   2   1

Library of Congress Cataloging-in-Publication Data

Mercer, Jean.
    Infant development : a multidisciplinary introduction / Jean
Mercer.
        p.   cm.
    Includes bibliographical references and index.
    ISBN 0-534-33977-8 (alk. paper)
    1. Infants—Development.   I. Title.
RJ134.M47   1998
305.232—dc21   96-52400
                                                            CIP

With love for
Peter
who tolerated it
and Mike
who was enthusiastic

Brief Contents

Contents

CHAPTER 4   PRENATAL DEVELOPMENT   79

CHAPTER 5   BIRTH AND THE NEWBORN   113

CHAPTER 6   PHYSICAL GROWTH, NUTRITION, AND HEALTH   138

CHAPTER 7   THE DEVELOPMENT OF THE BRAIN AND RELATED STRUCTURES   173

CHAPTER 8   THE DEVELOPMENT OF SENSORY PROCESSES   199

CHAPTER 9   MOTOR DEVELOPMENT   230

CHAPTER 10   COGNITIVE DEVELOPMENT   255

CHAPTER 11   COMMUNICATION AND LANGUAGE   292

CHAPTER 12   EMOTIONAL DEVELOPMENT   328

CHAPTER 13   SOCIALIZATOIN AND PARENTING   358

CHAPTER 14   INFANT MENTAL HEALTH   387

CHAPTER 15   LAW, POLICY, AND ETHICS: EFFECTS ON INFANT DEVELOPMENT   421

Preface

TO THE STUDENT

You are about to begin the study of a period of life as fascinating and mysterious as any in human experience—a time that abounds in paradoxes. Infancy is a stage of development about which adults have powerful beliefs and strong emotional values that can motivate them to learn but that can also make objectivity difficult. It is a period we all have experienced but none of us can remember.

Infants are at a stage of enormous vulnerability, but, paradoxically, can show great resilience. Their memories are short, but they are learning attitudes and values that will be with them throughout their lives. Their vision is still in the process of developing, but they use it to recognize familiar people and to learn emotional connections that will be maintained at least into adulthood. Their ability to communicate is sophisticated, whereas their use of the spoken language is still primitive.

Infants are unique individuals, but are best studied and understood in the context of their families; to know the baby, we need to know the other family members as well. Powerful biological factors govern an infant's development, but they can do so only in conjunction with the environment. Similarly, the environment shapes many aspects of an infant's growth, but it does so by interacting with biological factors.

Infants have basic needs that must be satisfied to ensure survival and development, but those needs can be and are met in thousands of different ways. Most infants can signal and stimulate most adults to care for them lovingly and appropriately, but the combinations of some infants and some adults can lead to dreadful abuse or even the death of the infant.

Do these many paradoxes and apparent contradictions mean that it is impossible to understand how human babies develop? No, but they do mean that infant development is complex, with outcomes determined by multiple factors and processes. A real understanding of infant development comes slowly, with reading, observation, discussion, and more reading, observation, and discussion. There are few instant insights in the study of a subject with both intellectual and emotional complexity.

Scholars and clinicians who have spent their adult lives in the study of infancy are still learning, as new information is revealed every day. This book is an attempt to show the beginning student what those scholars and clinicians know today, but it should not be considered the end of what we can learn about infancy. I hope that some of you who are reading this preface now will be among those who will help us all advance our understanding of the first years of human life.

If you have the same ambition that I have for you (or even if you'd just like to make a good grade in the course), you can choose to start your work by using this book in the most effective way possible. The following features were designed to help you study, understand, and remember.

1. Vocabulary   As you learn this new subject matter, you will have to learn many new words to describe it. Students often make the mistake of thinking that they can figure out "generally" what a paragraph means without understanding the words that make it up. This just isn't possible.

The best way to learn new words is by *active* involvement, such as looking them up in a dictionary, asking your instructor for definitions, or using a definition given in the text. For this reason, this book does not provide a glossary of all terms; when students have a glossary, they are often unable to resist the temptation to memorize a definition without really understanding it. Keeping a dictionary nearby as you read will make it easier to acquire the vocabulary you need for the course.

If you understand the Latin, Greek, or other roots of words, you will be able to remember them better and to figure out the meanings of new words. On many pages of this book, you will see an explanation of the derivation of a word. Pay enough attention to the roots of the word, and you'll soon find that you can make sense of some unfamiliar words.

2. Problems   At the end of each chapter, you will find a set of problems to consider and discuss. Using these problems effectively is one of the best ways to study the material. Effective use means you have to be *active* in your response to the problems. Just glancing at them and saying, "Oh, I know that" won't do you much good. If you are in a class of people who like to discuss and argue points, that may be a good way to use the problems. If not, writing out your answer in essay form will be very helpful to you. Keep in mind that these are not short essay topics to be answered in a line or two. If you haven't produced 200 to 300 words in your answer, you probably have not done justice to the topic. Is your answer correct? Don't depend on your own judgment here; ask a fellow-student or, better yet, your instructor for feedback.

3. The integrated baby   One of the problems for students who are new to infant development issues is that they find it hard to remember how all the pieces fit together. How about that 8-month-old who's afraid of strangers? Can she crawl? Talk? Feed herself? At the end of most chapters in this book, a description of "the integrated baby" will remind you how all the details work together in an individual infant.

4. Applications & Arguments Each chapter in the book has two or three boxed sections titled "Applications & Arguments." Some of these are designed to shock you a bit, and others are simply to show the logical conclusions that can be drawn from common assumptions about infants. In either case, you can use these boxes for oral discussion or written commentary, which will help you organize information or realize that you need to learn more. If you find the statement shocking and disagree strongly, state the information you have that leads you to disagree. If you agree with what is said, try to restate the argument in a different way, or work only with information that seems to lead you to the opposite conclusion.

5. Finding more information If you want to find out more about a topic, you can look up the original work by noting the names of authors given in parentheses in the part of the text devoted to the topic. The reference section at the back of the book lists authors alphabetically. When you find the name or names you are interested in, you will also find where and when the original material was published. If your library does not have the work, it may be possible to get it through interlibrary loan service.

Watching films or videos about infant development can be an extremely helpful addition to your reading. Be aware, though, that most students do not learn or see all that a video has to offer after only one viewing. A video needs to be used the way a book is, with frequent reviews of important points—stopping, repeating a section of the video, and then proceeding to the next section.

Observing real babies is an invaluable help in learning, but many students may have access to few or none except in public places. Wherever you do get a chance to watch infants and parents, you ought to take it. Be careful, though, of what some have called the "vividness" problem (Stanovich, 1992). An isolated incident you experience for yourself may seem much more significant to you than less vivid statistical reports on many infants, whereas in fact a report about a large group of babies should be taken more seriously than an experience with just one. (If you have children yourself, you have probably learned that the vivid experiences you had with your first baby were contradicted by equally vivid but quite different situations with the second.)

6. Complexity The facts of infant development are far more complex than most beginning students can imagine. There are few simple questions and no simple answers in this field. Students who expect simplicity often react with anxiety when they discover the complex nature of the topic. They may think, "I must be awfully dumb if I have to think hard to understand something simple like a baby's life." On the contrary, even brilliant workers in this field must stretch their minds to understand how many factors work together to determine development.

Be careful not to give simple answers to complex questions. If you mention only one or two facts or ideas in an attempt to answer a question, you can be fairly sure that you haven't finished yet. Keep in mind, especially, that many different aspects of an infant's development work together. To understand an 8-month-old's tendency to follow her mother and a 4-month-old's tendency not to do so, you need to consider the babies' ability to move independently, their vision and hearing, their memories and experiences, and the emotions they are likely to have. Only at the end of the course will you really be able to pull all this information together.

ACKNOWLEDGMENTS

I would like to express my thanks to Jeff Wilhelms of Brooks/Cole, whose interest and support go back many years and whose arrival has always made a bright spot in my day; to Jim Brace-Thompson, whose intelligence and good humor carried me through various sloughs of despond; and to Keith Faivre, who recognized that I might not want to work on New Year's Day and whose baby should arrive a little while before this book. I am grateful, also, to the following reviewers whose comments helped me "find the range" for my work and who made some invaluable suggestions: Marguerite Barratt, University of Wisconsin-Madison; Joseph J. Campos; Les Cohen, The University of Texas at Austin; Dana Davidson, University of Hawaii; Saul Feinman, University of Wyoming; Alice Honig, Syracuse University; Jeanne Thibo Karns, University of Nebraska at Lincoln; Elizabeth Lemerise, Western Kentucky University; Carolyn Mebert, University of New Hampshire; Edith Sullivan, Portland State University; S. Kenneth Thurman, Temple University; Virginia Wyly, SUNY College at Buffalo.

Finally, I want to thank Theresa Steinke of Richard Stockton College, who made a neat production from long strips of taped-together handwritten sheets, and the library staff of the college, who were never stumped by my interlibrary loan requests for ever more obscure journal articles.

In a school in another country that I attended many years ago, we were sent to our classes in the morning with an injunction I would like to pass on to you: "Get knowledge, get learning; and, with all thy getting, get understanding." I hope my work on this text will foster in you the enormous satisfaction of understanding.

Jean Mercer

1

Thinking About Infant Development

Imagine you are watching three 12-month-olds as they separately experience a strange and somewhat frightening situation. Each is brought to an unfamiliar room by his or her mother. The room is pleasant but not very homey; it has simple furniture, big sunny windows, and a carpet with an uneven pattern that hides the effects of spills and other baby stains. There are baskets of toys that mother and baby can play with, if they choose. The room has two doors, and after a few minutes an unfamiliar adult comes through one of them. The stranger approaches the mother and baby. Soon, the mother gets up and leaves, closing the door after her. What happens when the mother returns? Each of our three babies acts differently.

Jamal is a big, robust baby who has not yet mastered walking alone, although he does well given a hand to hold. He can say a few words and can understand a dozen or more. When his mother returns to the room after a few minutes, Jamal crawls to her rapidly, crying and fussing. He pulls himself to a standing position while holding onto her leg and stretches one hand upward, asking to be picked up. His mother picks him up at once and speaks to him soothingly while she cuddles him. He quiets quickly and is soon ready to play with her.

Bobby is thinner and more "wiry" than Jamal. He has just started to walk alone and seems to understand some words but does not say many. His mother is about 6 months pregnant with an unplanned second child and is concerned about getting Bobby out of diapers soon. When his mother returns, Bobby scowls, fusses, and runs to her, but when she tries to pick him up he pushes her away. He stays near her and communicates his unhappiness, but she does not seem to be able to comfort him. It takes a long time for Bobby to settle down, although his mother keeps trying.

Tiffany is a small, thin, tense child who has already been walking well for several months. She does not use any words and does not seem to pay attention to other people's speech. When her mother returns, Tiffany suddenly freezes and stays in the same position for a minute or so. The expression on her mother's face seems to be more of fear than anything else.

What is the "moral" of this tale of three babies? Can it tell us anything about infant development? There are, in fact, several "morals." The first is that babies at a given age are both *similar to* and *different from* each other. Although

Jamal, Bobby, and Tiffany are at different points in the development of walking, they are all doing things in the same order, and we can predict what they are likely to do next.

A second "moral" is that some of the differences among the three seem to be *biological*. Jamal, Bobby, and Tiffany have different sizes and shapes and have been different since birth. Their biological differences may influence other aspects of development. For example, a thin child may find it easier to stand and walk than a heavier child does. This difference could in turn produce other differences, for example, by affecting an adult's attitude toward the child.

Our third "moral" is that these three babies seem to be living in different environments and having different experiences. Bobby's mother's new pregnancy has an effect on the whole family but affects Bobby in particular. Tiffany's mother's fearfulness gives Tiffany different experiences than Jamal has, whose mother is soothing and comforting.

A final "moral" may not be so obvious, but it will be a major concern of this book. It is the fact that biological and environmental factors work in *interaction* rather than in isolation. Each of the babies in our story—and every other baby—is a unique combination of the effects of biology and experience working together. Unraveling the effects of biological and environmental factors, and understanding how they interact, are the great challenges to the study of infant development today.

The tale of Jamal, Bobby, and Tiffany seems to have led us to more questions than explanations. The study of infant development is at a stage where, although some explanations exist, questions are multiplying faster than answers. It is a frustrating yet fascinating moment to begin a study of this important part of human development.

SOCIAL CHANGE, CULTURAL DIFFERENCES, AND UNDERSTANDING INFANT DEVELOPMENT

Why is it that we don't already know all there is to know about babies? One would think that after all these generations of human births, we would know a good deal more about infant behavior, even though some facts of physical development had to wait for modern scientific investigation. But, on the contrary, the study of many important aspects of infant development is just beginning.

infant mortality rate: the proportion of infants in a group who die before their first birthday; from the Latin *infans* (incapable of speech), *mors* (death), *rata* (proportion).

Historically, most cultures have considered the care of infants to be a private and a feminine matter. The first year or two of a child's life was viewed as a period not very different from pregnancy; the infant might or might not survive, he or she depended on the mother's body for nourishment, and the forces that determined the outcome were mysterious. The effect of the early years on emotional and intellectual development, if any, was seen as a minor concern compared to the fears engendered by a very high **infant mortality rate.**

The relationship between infant and parent is one of the most profound of all human experiences.

In recent years, changes in attitudes and lifestyles in developed countries have led to different views on infant development. Infants are expected to live (although they do not always do so), the birth rate is low, and there is an emphasis on the long-term effects of early development. Both individual families and society as a whole have concerns about infant development and infant care.

How did this change come about? Why did infant development become a matter of general concern? Why do we now dedicate money and trained research workers to the investigation of development, when in the not-too-distant past we left this concern primarily to mothers?

Part of this change dates back to the early 1960s, when there first arose the awareness that poor development in early life had multiple and expensive consequences, including the need for special education and, potentially, a lifetime on welfare or in prison. Programs like Head Start were initiated as an attempt to intervene in the preschool period and to correct problems that might have arisen in infancy. Although Head Start was successful in many ways, its results alerted us to the fact that even earlier **interventions** might be

intervention: action that either helps or hinders a later development; from the Latin *intervenire* (to come between).

needed and that there was not enough understanding of infant development to know how best to intervene.

Recent Social Change

Some social changes of the last 20 years also put the spotlight on issues of infant development. Changes in laws about gender discrimination, combined with economic recession, sent mothers back to work sooner and sooner after their babies were born. It was no longer unusual to see infants a few weeks old in day care, and it became clear that early development was not understood well enough to make it obvious how young infants should be cared for.

Other social changes led to an increased number of births to unmarried women, especially teenagers, and to a rapid shift from the traditional placement of babies in adoptive homes to the establishment of single-parent custody. Social services agencies were faced for the first time with large numbers of poor teenage mothers caring for their babies alone. Help was needed to determine when early development was proceeding normally and when it was not.

Another important social change involved the considerable increase in the use of alcohol and drugs by young women, particularly when "crack" became fashionable. We are still struggling for information about the effects of maternal use of alcohol and drugs on unborn infants and about the types of interventions that might help them.

Historical Change and Cross-Cultural Differences

culture: a set of learned and shared customs and attitudes; from the Latin *colere* (to cultivate).

Although recent social change has focused interest on infant development in a direct and practical way, it has also encouraged researchers to look at infant care practices in different **cultures** and at different points in history. This fascinating work by historians and anthropologists has shown how differently human babies can be cared for and yet still survive or even thrive. Understanding historical and cross-cultural differences should make us humble and diffident about declaring that certain infant care approaches should be required or others forbidden.

People new to the study of cultural differences may be used to assuming there is some sort of "traditional" or even "old-fashioned" infant care approach that mothers would give up if they learned about "modern" ways. This misunderstanding must be corrected if we are to understand cross-cultural differences. First, there is no single "traditional" approach. Cultural groups have always differed in infant care practices; some folkways resembled current practice in developed countries, and some did not. Second, there is no clear-cut difference between older and newer ways of doing things. Cultural change is gradual, not just a matter of dropping old baggage. Third, people in less developed countries are certainly not always eager to embrace "modern" ways. In fact, they are often horrified at the way babies are treated in the United States.

instinctive: based on an unlearned, hereditary capacity; from the Latin *instinctus* (impulse).

While thinking about cultural differences in infant care, we also need to keep in mind that *all* infant care practices are culturally determined. There is no such thing as "natural mothering" (Knauer, 1985) or an **instinctive** way of caring for a baby. All our care practices were learned from other members of our culture and are determined by that learning. (This is not to deny, of course, that there might be some practices that are especially easy for humans to learn because of certain characteristics of our species.)

Attitudes, Values, Resources, and Infant Care Practices

People see their infant care practices as ways to express their attitudes and confirm their values. Whereas many Euro-Americans and Europeans want to foster independence by having babies sleep alone, the Mayans and many other cultural groups want to increase family solidarity and bind the baby to the family emotionally; their co-sleeping practices are congruent with these values.

APPLICATIONS & ARGUMENTS
Have Times Really Changed?

It can be confusing to think about whether historical change really affects babies' experiences. In some ways, of course, it does not; although medical progress has relieved some birth difficulties, most babies are born in the same old way as our most remote ancestors were. The infant's need for warmth, contact, cleanliness, and particular types and frequencies of feeding dictates certain experiences no matter where or when she is born.

Some things actually have changed, though, at least in industrialized countries. The use of disposable diapers means that well-cared-for infants today rarely experience the severe diaper rash caused by cloth diapers, which were less absorbent and could harbor bacteria unless sterilized. Changes in attitudes over the last 40 years have meant that infants are likely to be fed "on request," rather than going hungry while they wait for a scheduled feeding. Compared to infants of other times and places, babies in the United States are less likely to sleep with their parents, although some middle-class parents are becoming more enthusiastic about the practice. Immunization for childhood diseases means that today's infants are far less likely than those in the past to suffer serious or fatal illness, such as polio. And the use of antibiotics has reduced the time they are sick with more minor problems. Finally, a dramatic recent change in infants' experience results from the enormous increase in early nonparental care, such as day care.

---

kibbutz: an Israeli collective farm or settlement; from the Hebrew *qibbus* (gathering).

Another example is the **kibbutz** culture in Israel, developed in part as a reaction against the self-described "overly emotional" nature of Eastern European Jewish groups (Bettelheim, 1969). The original kibbutzniks deliberately sought to break family ties, which they considered constricting. They designed infant care arrangements to avoid the development of infant-parent attachment and to create a commitment to the whole community; a second goal was to allow women full membership in the economic life of the community.

Not all infant care customs are necessarily an outcome of deep-seated value systems. Some arise out of a simple need to get things done. Where resources are scarce (as is the case for most of the world's people), some infant care approaches will develop just because they are functional. The babies don't suffer, and the mothers can work to bring in money or produce food for the family. If resources become scarcer or more abundant, we will probably see infant care change in response.

Historical Changes in Advice to Parents

Among literate people, written advice to parents provides an example of a society's prevalent values. A useful way of learning about historical changes in attitudes is to examine different eras' books and pamphlets on child-rearing.

European and U.S. attitudes toward infant care were strongly influenced in the 18th century by two major sources. The first was the Calvinist concept of juvenile depravity: the native guilt and inherent moral corruption of infants. This belief replaced the earlier Catholic view that unbaptized infants who died did not suffer actual torment in the afterlife, they were simply deprived of heaven. Calvinism stressed the idea of original sin and the necessity of early religious commitment. Because children were considered sinful and capable of damnation from birth, the parent's primary responsibility was to supervise the child's moral development. By means of scolding, whipping, confinement, and reward as well, parents were to ensure that the child became demure, obedient, and religious, even during toddlerhood (Slater, 1970). To carry out these responsibilities, parents had to attend closely to their children's behavior.

tabula rasa: a mind empty of thought or knowledge; from the Latin *tabula* (board), *rasa* (scraped or shaved).

A second 18th-century theme was the assumption that an infant at birth was like a **tabula rasa,** or "blank slate," knowing nothing and prepared to take in all impressions from the environment, as the 17th-century philosopher John Locke suggested in his essay "Some Thoughts Concerning Education." The tabula rasa concept clearly suggested that adult characteristics depended on the individual's previous experiences, including those of infancy and childhood. Providing appropriate experiences and associations would help guarantee the development of an adult mind of good quality. This idea implied that parents were to be responsible for a child's optimal development, because servants could not be expected to supervise the filling of the tabula rasa.

In the later 18th and the 19th centuries, the romantic period introduced a different attitude toward infants. Jean-Jacques Rousseau (b. 1712) suggested that children have a basic natural tendency to goodness that becomes distorted and perverted through their contact with civilization and education. If adults want to understand what is natural and good, they should learn from children, rather than trying to impose their ideas on the young. (Rousseau classed "primitive" peoples with children, a romantic idea we will see later in the work of Heinz Werner in the 20th century.) Romantic concepts of childhood had a real influence on New England Calvinism. By the 1830s, the theme of juvenile depravity had given way to the theme of "redemption of mankind through children properly raised by their parents" (Slater, 1970, p. 7). **Corporal** punishment began to receive less emphasis in child-rearing advice; instead, the recommendations for punishment stressed confinement and deprivation of toys or privileges.

corporal: having to do with the body; from the Latin *corpus* (body).

Historical Changes in Infant Care Practice: Economic Issues

Parents sometimes do follow the advice they are given, but their decisions about infant care are determined by multiple factors. The family's need for the mother's economic contributions is often a major determinant. Two historical examples of changes in infant care in response to economic considerations are the wet-nursing "industry" in 19th century France and the development of day care for infants and toddlers in the United States today.

wet-nursing: breast-feeding a baby in exchange for a fee; from the Latin *nutricius* (nourishing).

Wet-nursing, the breast-feeding of a baby by a paid nurse, has been practiced in many parts of the world and was the rule for the European aristocracy for several hundred years prior to the 20th century. But in 19th-century France, as Fildes (1988) has documented from contracts and legal records, the practice of wet-nursing among skilled workers greatly increased; almost 50% of infants born in Paris were placed in the homes of wet nurses in the first week of their lives, to be returned to their parents after 18 months or more. Wet nurses lived in the country and were brought to town to a central registration office to meet parents who needed to place their babies. A complicated system of record keeping and certification of the nurse's good character generated documents that allowed Fildes to give us a clear picture of the practice.

The economic situation that led to the French wet-nursing system involved increased urbanization, with many young people working in craft industries or retail trade and living in crowded conditions unsuitable for children. Women, who were employed along with men in the thriving weaving workshops, married in their late twenties after they had become skilled workers. After marrying another skilled worker, women continued to weave or to look after the retail side of the husband's trade. These families could not find a temporary employee as skillful as the wife, so putting the babies "out to nurse" was the only economically viable solution at a time when artificial feeding was not yet well developed. The poorer the parents were, the farther away they had to send the baby, because wet nurses who were near the city and easy to visit could command higher fees. The French wet-nursing system was eventually disrupted by travel restrictions during World War I and never really recovered (Fildes, 1988).

Day care in the United States has followed patterns of economic need, too. Orphanages and children's homes were initially more common than day care, and many children were placed not because they were orphaned but because both parents had to work. From 1942 to 1945, the Lanham Act day care centers provided child care in order to release mothers for war work, but federal funds for these centers were withdrawn within 6 months of the war's end.

An increase in the use of day care for preschool children began in the 1970s, and in the 1980s and 1990s came a rapid fall in the age at which placement in day care began. This change correlated with economic problems and the movement of more women into the labor force. Increased participation of women with babies in the workforce was, in part, due to the fact that Americans aged 35 to 44 were actually only half as wealthy as their parents had been at the same age (Phillips, 1993). Not all state laws have kept up with the social changes; some failed for years to institute specific regulations for children under the age of 2 (Schrag, 1984).

One of the consequences of economic difficulties and the increase in day care for infants has been the growth of an "underground economy" in day care (Richardson, 1993). Parents of infants often prefer to leave their babies at a caregiver's home rather than at a large day care center, and unlicensed family day care providers usually charge less than licensed facilities. The difference in price can be significant to poor parents; it has been estimated that families with incomes under $15,000 spend an average of 23% of their incomes on child care (Richardson, 1993). It is also estimated that in New York City there are 15 children under age 3 in illegal care arrangements for every 1 in a licensed day care setting (Richardson, 1993).

Changes in Demographics

Historical and cultural change may be driven by alterations in demographics—proportions of a population of particular ages, ethnic backgrounds, and so on. A complete description of recent demographic changes in the United States would be far beyond the scope of this book, but certain relevant points can be mentioned. Immigration has brought a wide variety of cultural groups to this country and has linked the West Coast to the Pacific Rim and the East Coast to Latin America with respect to infant care practices. The aging of the population has created competition between infants and the elderly for diminishing economic and medical resources. The tendency to delay childbearing until later in life has increased the rate of adoption and the numbers of couples seeking infertility treatment. Employment possibilities have decreased, as downsizing, cost-cutting, and computerization have eliminated management positions, but flextime and "telecommuting" have made it easier for women with babies to be employed (Calem, 1993; Noble, 1992).

Medical and technological changes have made possible the survival of infants who in the past would not have lived much beyond birth. They may be handicapped, however, so the proportion of individuals who need special care and services has increased.

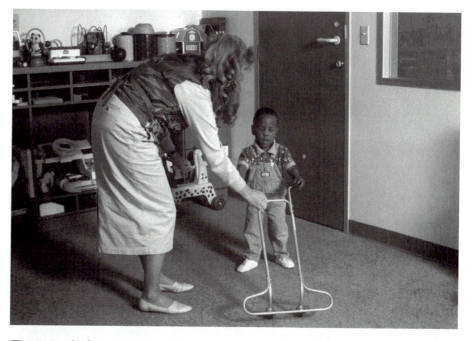

The study of infant development includes concerns with handicapping conditions and early intervention.

The Effect of Law and Policy on Infants

In any individual family, members may believe that their baby's development is a private matter and nobody else's business. As long as no problems develop, most of us would agree. However, as soon as the infant or the family runs into difficulty, it becomes clear that the state (its citizens) has an interest in the baby's welfare.

Many current national and state laws and policies affect infants. The availability of contraception and abortion makes a difference to the number of babies who are both planned and wanted. The setting of income levels that permit access to subsidized health care makes a difference to infants' health at birth and to their later immunization against childhood diseases. Laws about parental rights and adoption determine whether some babies will have stable homes and caregivers. The regulation of day care helps determine how well some infants are cared for while their parents work.

Laws about infants and children in the United States are in a process of slow change. The old common law of England, as well as many other ancient laws, treated children as property and stressed parental property rights rather than the children's developmental needs. Only in recent years have we begun to see legal decisions that showed concern for the facts of early development.

One goal of work on infant development is to provide a good foundation on which to base appropriate laws and policies. We have this foundation with respect to some aspects of development, but not for others. Even where the foundation exists, though, the law does not often take this information into consideration. Legal and policy decisions frequently flout knowledge of infant development that has been available for many years. It may be that real change will come about only when informed citizens act as advocates for infants and ask for judges who have some training in and awareness of developmental processes.

In sum, the result of work on social and cultural change is paradoxical: we know much more than we used to know about the different experiences infants can have, but we also have many new questions. As we see the enormous range of cultural differences in infant care, we can no longer assume that there will be any simple answers to questions about infant development. Certainly we cannot assume that there can be a useful, simple description of an infant's environment. Nor can we assume that there is a "best" method of infant care that works best for all babies. Research on infant development is more complex—and more interesting—than anyone thought in the past.

THE NATURE OF RESEARCH ON INFANTS

As social changes and awareness of cultural differences have made clear the importance of infant development, we have seen resources thrown into the investigation of both typical and atypical developmental changes. To understand how development proceeds, we first need to know how research questions are asked and answered. A fact by itself is often meaningless unless we know the context in which it was found.

Although certain foundations are common to all research enterprises, each discipline has its own specialized research approaches. This fact makes the explanation of research on infants especially complex, because the study of infancy has turned out to be a **multidisciplinary** affair. Information about infant development comes from neurologists, pediatricians, clinical psychologists, special education teachers, physical therapists, occupational therapists, speech pathologists, and many others, as well as from psychologists who use experimental methods to study infant memory or problem solving. Each discipline has only part of the information we need to create an accurate picture of the active, growing individual baby.

multidisciplinary: involving many fields of study; from the Latin *multus* (many), *disciplina* (teaching).

A genuine understanding of infant development requires a team approach. We cannot afford to ignore or reject findings from disciplines other than the ones we feel most comfortable with, and we will accomplish most when we use a blend of perspectives (Finney et al., 1992). But, on the other hand, as infant specialist Emily Fenichel has pointed out with respect to clinical treatment of early emotional problems, "No single professional can hope to absorb the full multidisciplinary literature, master the range of therapeutic techniques, and evaluate all promising conceptual and treatment hypotheses . . ." (1992, p. 3).

It would be equally impossible for this book to present to the student the full range of research approaches infant development workers use. It is possible, however, to describe some general ideas that are at the heart of much infant development work. Chapter 2 of this book is devoted to this topic, and further details about the study of specific issues (such as visual development or personality) can be found at the beginning of the appropriate chapters.

Some Assumptions of Researchers

Like all human understanding of the world, our understanding of infant development has to start somewhere. The starting places and assumptions we choose may or may not be "true" in any absolute sense, but we need them to begin with, nonetheless. To be able to use them rather than having them confuse us, however, we need to know what they are. Following are some assumptions that are often made in the study of infant development. As you will see, they are not always agreed on by everyone working in the field.

1. Babies exist in a family context   One of the most important ideas of modern infant development research was summarized in D. W. Winnicott's statement that "there is no such thing as an infant" (1965, p. 39). Winnicott meant, of course, that there is no such thing as an infant who grows and develops in isolation. All infants exist in the context of adult caregiving; they would not survive otherwise. Most aspects of infant development make sense

---

APPLICATIONS & ARGUMENTS
How Are Babies Different From Older Children?

When people try to understand infants' lives, they often attempt to imagine or remember their own early lives. Most of us, however, cannot remember much before our third or even fourth birthdays, and those seem to be the times "when we began." (It is hard to visualize a time when you existed but of which you have no memory.) When we think of day care, for example, we recall our kindergarten days, which are not at all the same thing.

Infants and toddlers have a number of characteristics that are different from our earliest memories of ourselves and that we need to keep in mind. They are *physically* different: smaller, weaker, less in control of their movements, and in need of more frequent sleep and feeding. They are *emotionally* different: intense and variable in their emotional reactions. Initially, they seem almost without fear, but toward the end of the first year they become very fearful, especially about separation from familiar people, which can have a profound effect on them. Finally, they are *cognitively* different: slow to learn and comprehend, and, at the first, lacking understanding of the world's simplest physical laws. With no, or little, comprehension of language, infants are profoundly different beings than the youngest "you" that you can recall.

only if we look at them in terms of the relationship between infants and adults. Parents and infants have mutual and constantly changing effects on each other.

2. Babies are already complex people when they are born   Modern work on infant development emphasizes that experience is not the only cause of differences in individual characteristics. Genetic and prenatal factors determine some individual differences before postnatal experience begins. The possibility of genetically based sex differences and differences between ethnic groups must be given serious consideration. Some infants are also more vulnerable than others and are more affected by poor environments.

3. Babies begin to learn very early   Modern work on language and emotional development stresses the idea that infants are already learning from their environments in the first days and weeks of life.

4. The infant's early experiences determine a good deal of the possibility of later development   The idea of the crucial importance of early experience is paramount in most intervention work with infants. The assumption is that

No matter how poor or stressed the family, a baby exists as a family member rather than as an isolated individual.

trajectory:
predictable
pathway or
pattern; from the
Latin *trans* (across),
jacere (to throw).

early experiences cause developmental events that set the infant on either an appropriate or an inappropriate developmental **trajectory;** if we are going to correct an inappropriate trajectory, we must intervene as early as possible. The longer we wait, it is assumed, the farther the child will move from the possibility of normal development.

We must realize, however, that not all infant development researchers hold this idea. Jerome Kagan (Kagan & Greenspan, 1986), for example, has suggested that experiences before 8 months of age may have less impact than those that occur later because the baby's capacity for memory changes at about 8 months.

5. Infants have a self-righting tendency   Although no one would argue that all babies can deal well with poor environments, most researchers accept the idea that babies have a tendency to recover by themselves from bad experiences. This idea of **self-righting** implies that bad early experiences do not always have serious long-term effects. It also implies that when we give some treatment to a baby who has problems, the improvement we see may have as much to do with self-righting as with our treatment.

self-righting:
recovering without
help from
problems or
injuries; from the
Latin *regere* (to lead
straight).

6. Many factors work together to determine how an infant develops   Most infant development researchers assume that multiple factors are at work in infant development and that each factor affects more than one infant characteristic. In addition, each factor usually needs to be considered on a continuum rather than in an either/or fashion. The infant's environment, for example, is not simply "good" or "bad" but is likely to be somewhere in between. Similarly, the baby itself is not simply "vulnerable" or "invulnerable" in relation to the environment but is likely to be between those extremes. Even factors that seem to be "all or nothing," like prenatal infection, have different effects depending on when they occur and on the child's particular genetic makeup.

This set of issues is important in understanding work on developmental problems. Each problem needs to be considered in its full complexity, not as an artificially simplified category. Single-parent families, for example, exist in many forms, ranging from the homeless adolescent girl with an infant to the affluent, well-educated widowed father of teenagers. Drug-exposed babies, too, can have many different experiences, from use of many drugs by a malnourished mother with AIDS to a single use of cocaine in late pregnancy that causes premature labor (Myers, Olson, & Kaltenbach, 1992).

7. A baby of any age is a complex person with many characteristics and abilities that cannot really be separated from each other   Infant development work in the 1960s and 1970s often dealt with isolated aspects of the infant, but more modern work tends to look at a variety of abilities and the way they function in the child's life. Language development, for example, is viewed as a way for the baby to interact socially, not simply as a cognitive function. Emotional development is understood as a foundation for learning. Although it is hard to comprehend all the characteristics of a complex individual, current infant development work attempts to move in that direction.

8. Although a baby's different characteristics function together, we may have to make different assumptions as we focus on each one   We may never be able to have a unified theory of infant development, because the different aspects of development do not necessarily follow the same developmental rules. It is not only possible that emotion and learning may develop differently; it may even be that learning about one set of events may work differently than learning about another set (Kagan & Greenspan, 1986).

UNDERSTANDING DEVELOPMENT

Underlying almost all issues in infancy research is a concern with developmental change. As time passes, an infant becomes more like an adult—she develops. What, if any, are the rules that govern developmental change?

The Nature of Development

development: to change through a process of natural growth; from the Old French *desvoloper* (to unwrap).

learning: change resulting from experience; from the Latin *lira* (furrow or track).

The term **development** refers to physical and behavioral changes that occur as a person gets older. Age is correlated with development, but age is just a way of describing the passage of time; age does not *cause* development. Development results from two major factors that can function both separately and together: learning and maturation.

Students need to be careful about the term **learning.** This word is used very loosely in everyday language. People say, for example, that a baby is learning to walk, but (as we will see later) learning does not have a great deal to do with early motor skills like walking. Learning is a change in behavior that occurs as a result of experience. It can be a simple change, like crying at the sight of a white coat after a painful experience at the doctor's office, or it can be a complex change, like mastering the pathway through a maze. It can be a matter of behavior changing because someone has deliberately instructed the baby on what to do, but is more likely (in infants) to involve discovery in the course of play or general observation. Sometimes learning involves physical movements and sometimes it involves symbols, but it can also involve emotional reactions; for babies, it is likely to involve all three. Although rewards and punishments may be connected with learning, they are not always present in any obvious way. Simple forms of learning can start even before birth. It is important to understand, however, that a baby is not equally ready to learn from every type of experience. At different points in development, different experiences are likely to attract the baby's attention and result in learning.

maturation: developmental change that occurs for biological reasons rather than through experience; from the Latin *maturus* (ripe).

Most students are quite familiar with the idea that babies develop as a result of learning. What is often harder to understand is that maturation makes a contribution to development. **Maturation** is the term used to describe the infant's genetically determined growth and change that will take place as long as the environment is good enough. The growth of an unborn baby is an obvious example: as long as the environment of the mother's body is reasonably adequate, the unborn baby will grow, change in proportions, and eventually become able to survive the transition to the outer world. After the baby is born, it is exposed to many more sources of learning, but much of its development is still determined by maturational factors. After birth, normal infants grow according to genetically determined guidelines as long as their environment is adequate. Their motor development, production of sounds, and even emotional responsiveness are under the control of genetic determination as well. However, an infant cannot learn to talk at age 4 months, no matter what her experiences are, because she is not maturationally ready to do so.

An old-fashioned debate used to argue for learning *or* for maturation, for nurture *or* for nature, for heredity *or* for environment. We know now that it is pointless to act as if one member of each pair could be separated from the other. Nobody could be born without the genetic material that organizes maturation, nor could any baby exist without an environment. Development always involves both experience and maturation. It is pointless, too, to get into general arguments about how much maturation contributes and how much nurture contributes to development. Different aspects of development have different maturational contributions. For example, the age at which a child is most ready to learn language seems to be largely maturationally determined, but which language is learned is entirely a matter of experience.

Rather than trying to separate maturation and learning, we need to think about how they work together and **interact** to bring about development. For example, the muscles and bones of a limb grow best when they are used, but large, strong bones and muscles can be used better and in different ways than can small, weak ones.

When we look at developmental changes, like language development, that go on over a long period of time, the term *transactional process* may be the best description of how maturation and learning work together. In this context, **transaction** (Sameroff, 1983) means that maturation and learning not only interact but also change in the way they do so over time. This concept may be easier to understand if we (1) think of the maturational factor as what the baby can do at a given point in development and (2) think of environmental factors as what the caregiver does (the rest of the baby's environment, mobiles or whatever, is insignificant compared to the caregiver). The baby makes a sound, and the caregiver responds in a certain way; the caregiver's response affects the baby's sound making, and the change in sound making causes the caregiver to respond differently. Meanwhile, of course, the baby is maturing and developing new abilities that are not based on learning, and those changes will also affect the caregiver and cause him or her to behave differently, thus changing the baby's experience. This concept of transactions in development is an extraordinarily important one, and we will see that it is useful for understanding many kinds of developmental change.

Even more complex than a transactional approach to development is one based on a dynamic systems perspective. General systems theory, initially

interaction: the combined effect of two or more factors operating simultaneously; from the Latin *inter-* (between), *actus* (doing).

transaction: in this context, changes in the nature of an interaction that occur over time as a result of the continuing interaction; from the Latin *trans* (across), *actus* (doing).

suggested by Ludwig von Bertalanffy in the 1930s, stresses the importance of interrelations between and among factors. As infancy researchers have realized the number of factors working together in development, they have been more and more attracted to a systems approach (Aslin, 1993; Marvin & Stewart, 1990).

dynamic: active and changing in energy; from the Greek *dynamikos* (powerful).

A **dynamic action system** is a group of factors that influence each other and that are in a constant process of change. One important characteristic of the system is that it is *self-organizing;* the components of the system work together according to their own rules, which may or may not be like those of other systems. Another characteristic of the system is its *variability.* Even though all the components are the same, the outcome (growth or behavior, for example) is not identical from one moment to the next. The variability is self-limited, however, and only certain outcomes are possible unless some components of the system are changed.

A dynamic action system has a capacity for *reorganization;* this is one of the most fruitful ideas of a dynamic systems perspective. The idea here is that a system may, under some circumstances, suddenly begin to work according to a new set of rules. The system may follow an old set of rules for a long time, even though some factors are changing; but when the change reaches a certain point, it triggers a reorganization and a new set of rules emerges.

The dynamic systems perspective may be more useful for some areas of infant development than for others (Aslin, 1993). Applications are frequent in the study of motor development and are also seen in cognition and in language development. They are less common in studies of emotional and social development, which seems strange because theorists of family relationships have used the approach (Marvin & Stewart, 1990). Perhaps the dynamic systems perspective is easiest to apply when it is obvious that "the whole organism is involved in changes in self-organization, not just the brain" (Butterworth, 1993, p. 174).

Patterns of Developmental Change

A major question in the study of development concerns the actual pattern of the process. It is easy to say that the average 12-month-old has grown to 3 times its birth weight, but we do not have a real understanding of this aspect of development unless we have more details about changes that occurred over shorter intervals. Does the baby simply grow a little bit, the same amount every day, until it arrives at about 22 pounds? Does the baby grow very slowly for 6 months and then put on weight rapidly when it starts to eat solid foods? Does the baby maintain its weight on a plateau for 28-day periods and then grow very fast for the last 2 or 3 days of each month? Does the baby alternately gain and lose but ultimately gain more rapidly than it loses? Each of these cases represents a possible growth pattern (although we will see in a later chapter that none of them is what really happens).

Different aspects of development show different patterns of change, and most do not involve a simple daily addition in size or ability. Many aspects of development show periods of time when a baby does one kind of thing and other periods where the baby's behavior is quite different. When we see a time period in which the baby's activity is qualitatively different from what it is at another period, we may refer to the two periods as stages. For example, a baby does not go on indefinitely getting more and more skillful at crawling; at some point, the baby begins to walk instead. If the baby just crawled more and faster, we would say there was a quantitative change. Because the baby actually begins to do something new and different, we say the change is **qualitative.**

Of course, babies can display qualitative differences in behavior in many ways. An 8-month-old might be crazy about sweet potatoes for a week, and then get tired of them and prefer green beans for a while. Although there are qualitative differences between these two time periods, we would not call them stages. The term *stage* is used when a period in development involves qualitative differences from other periods and when the period occurs in a particular order or sequence with respect to other periods. A **stage** then, is a period in development when behavior or physical characteristics are qualitatively different from what they are at other periods, and which occurs after certain developmental events and before others.

The concept of stage implies that all members of our species experience the same set and sequence of stages, although the stages do not necessarily occur at the same chronological age for every person. When we use the stage concept, then, we are often thinking in terms of maturation rather than of learning. Some aspects of physical development are obviously far more affected by heredity than they are by environment. But we have to be careful with the stage concept, because the existence of stages does not necessarily mean that all human beings have to develop in a certain way. It may be that most humans care for their babies in a way that causes them to show certain qualitatively different behavior at specific times in their lives. We have to be especially careful not to assume that every baby in the world develops through certain stages just because we see that the babies (usually white and middle-class) tested by "First World" researchers show stagelike development.

When we talk about stages, we are usually referring to the development of measurable behavioral or physical characteristics. However, the idea of a stage can be broadened to refer to internal changes that involve a readiness to be affected by experience. The term **critical period** (sometimes called sensitive period) is used to describe a stage of special readiness. A critical period is a time during development when events in the environment have an effect on development that they would not have had earlier and that they will not have later.

The idea of a critical period comes from ethological studies of animal development. Critical periods have been demonstrated to occur in a number of animals, but most—like the famous ducklings imprinted on Konrad Lorenz—are not genetically similar to human beings. Whether human beings really have critical periods for postnatal development in the exact sense is not clear; if we do, most periods are certainly not as short as a duckling's. Nevertheless, we will find the critical period concept useful for talking about

qualitative: relating to the type or kind of phenomenon under consideration; from the Latin *qualis* (of what kind).

stage: one of a sequence of periods in development, each of which is qualitatively different from the others; from the Latin *stare* (to stand).

critical: related to a turning point; from the Greek *krisis* (decision).

prenatal development, and we will return to it in our consideration of language and emotional development.

The dynamic systems perspective provides an interesting approach to stage issues. From this point of view, changes in experience or in maturation can lead to reorganization of an infant's functioning. Such a reorganization, leading to qualitatively different behavior, is referred to as a *phase shift*. A tendency toward a particular quality of functioning is termed an *attractor state* and is roughly equivalent to a stage. Dynamic systems theory assumes that a system tends to fall into certain modes of action because of its own internal rules, but it is not clear why a system should have particular stages or attractor states rather than others (Aslin, 1993).

One warning may help you understand a bit more about stages or attactor states: the fact that a baby moves into a new stage does not mean that the child's care gets easier for adults. Development involves moving toward a more adultlike status but not necessarily toward obviously adultlike behavior. A baby who is too young to care which adult is the caregiver is less developed than a baby who cries when strangers approach. Although harder to care for, the one who cries is more like an adult because adults care very much who they spend time with. No emotionally healthy adult behaves the same way toward strangers as toward intimate friends. Greater maturity means greater awareness of one's own feelings about the world, not necessarily a greater willingness to comply with other people's wishes.

ADULT DEVELOPMENT AND UNDERSTANDING INFANTS

If you have never spent much time with horses, you probably approach them with a little anxiety. If you have any sense, you do not assume that you and a horse necessarily think or feel the same way. The fact that horses are a lot bigger and stronger than humans encourages us to remember that we are different.

Unfortunately for babies, they are not bigger or stronger than adults, so adults do not always give much thought to the ways babies are different. One tendency adults often show in their approach to babies is called **adultomorphic** thinking. This invented word refers to the adult's tendency to assume that infants feel, think, and decide in exactly the ways that adults do and that infants understand and even anticipate or plan an adult's reaction to their behavior.

adultomorphism:
an invented word that refers to the tendency to ascribe adult characteristics to infants; from the Greek *morphe* (form).

To understand infant development, we need to become aware of and lose our tendency to think adultomorphically. Adult thinking is more complex and more culturally determined than that of any infant. It is also qualitatively different. As we will see in later chapters, infants solve problems differently than adults do, as well as being less successful at the task. Assuming that an infant thinks and feels the same way you do will blind you to the realities of infant development.

In addition to the tendency to think adultomorphically, adults may have some more subtle problems in their approach to early development. Because development does not stop until we die, we adults are embedded in our own process of developmental change. We have our own developmental concerns, and those concerns may either help us or hinder us as we try to comprehend what goes on with people at a different developmental stage. For example, parents of young children are often at a stage of development where they are especially concerned with forming close ties to other family members. When they think about a 12-month-old's need for strong emotional relationships, they feel very comfortable with the idea. On the other hand, a student of 19 or 20 years of age, unmarried and childless, may be most concerned with loosening the ties to his or her parents. The idea that we need to encourage a strong attachment between parent and child may not be a very comfortable one for this student to contemplate, and he or she may feel much more interested in the toddler's movement toward greater independence.

Finally, many of us bring to our consideration of infant development some aspects of personal history of the type that Selma Fraiberg called "ghosts in the nursery" (Fraiberg, Adelson, & Shapiro, 1975). This phrase refers to memories we may have of the death or serious illness of siblings, or sometimes of our own children. Those memories can have a powerful effect on what we remember or think about certain stages of infant development, and we may need to understand our own past in order to clarify our thoughts.

PROBLEMS TO CONSIDER AND DISCUSS

1. Describe how a family is an example of a dynamic action system. How does the birth of a new baby lead to reorganization of the family system? Give your reasons for your answer.

2. Do you think of infant care as a public or a private matter? Give your reasons for putting it in one category or the other.

3. Give an example of developmental change in yourself or another person, and describe the roles that learning and maturation played in it.

4. How do you think that your present developmental stage and your family history have influenced your attitudes toward infant development?

5. Give an example of an infant care practice you have seen or heard of that seemed culturally foreign to you. How did it make you feel to see or hear of the practice?

2

Research on Infant Development

SOME GENERAL COMMENTS

Research on infant development is fascinating, complex, and sometimes difficult. Like other research, it requires a systematic approach; in a sense, it is a game whose rules researchers have agreed upon. Those rules, which will be discussed in this chapter, are generally like those of any research endeavor. However, there are some ways in which research on infants is special.

Researchers working with infants are particularly careful to avoid doing any harm. The *ethical code* for dealing with people, like infants, who cannot make their own decisions is especially stringent. In addition to this ethical concern, there is a practical one; a baby who is miserable is not going to "cooperate" and show the researchers what they want to know. (Sometimes an investigator may want to study a baby's reaction to something unpleasant that is going to happen anyway, such as an inoculation, but that is a different matter.)

Much of the research on infants uses relatively few subjects rather than the large numbers required in some types of research. There is nothing wrong with using small groups as long as we understand that we cannot necessarily generalize from one small group to babies in general. It can be quite hard to get a large group of infants to work with, and even when this can be managed, quite a few of them will fail to do what the researchers require. In one study of infants' responses to sounds, for example, 100 out of 262 babies completed the task; 107 cried, 26 fell asleep, 24 would not do what they needed to do for the task, and 6 had to be left out because of errors the researchers made (Jusczyk, Pisoni, Reed, Fernald, & Myers, 1983).

Research on infants hardly ever uses a random sample or a representative sample from a larger group. In a random sample, every member of a larger group has an equal chance of being chosen as a research subject. Work on infants is more likely to involve an *incidental* sample—all healthy infants born in a given hospital on a particular day, for instance, or all 6-month-olds whose mothers answer an ad placed on a bulletin board. It is thus sometimes quite hard to argue that a group of research subjects necessarily represents babies in general.

The central problem of research on infant development involves our wish to get information from people who cannot understand our directions or tell us what they think or feel in any direct way. In some cases, they cannot even move or cry, and we have only physiological changes to indicate what is happening within them. In one study of premature babies' reactions to pain, for example, the investigators had to rely on changes in heart rate and amount of oxygen carried in the blood to show that painful stimuli actually affected the babies (Gonsalves & Mercer, 1993).

WAYS OF ASKING QUESTIONS ABOUT INFANTS

Experimental Work

experiment: a research approach that involves manipulation of variables; from the Latin *experiri* (to try).

placebo: an inactive form of a treatment used as a comparison to test the effects of the active form; from the Latin *placebo* (I will please).

Much research that looks at developmental change in infants and toddlers is nonexperimental in nature, although experimental work is sometimes carried out. People commonly use the term *experiment* to refer to almost any research, but the word should actually be applied to only one research category. An **experiment** involves some direct manipulation or treatment of the subjects; the researcher does something to the subjects, rather than just waiting to see what might happen. In a good experiment, the researcher randomly divides a group of people into two or more groups (that is, each subject has equal chances of being assigned to each group). The groups are given different experiences, and any changes that occur are measured. If the changes in a group that received one treatment are different than the changes in the other group(s), it is considered legitimate to conclude that the treatment *caused* the change. If we are investigating a treatment of some kind and want to compare a group of infants who receive the treatment to an untreated comparison group, we may need to make sure that the comparison group is given a **placebo** treatment: the infants go through everything the experimental group

Curiosity about early development is not new to human beings, but modern research approaches can answer some questions that were little understood in the past.

experiences except the actual "active" part of the treatment. If a drug treatment is being tested, for example, the comparison group will receive injections or oral "medication," but the substances given will not be pharmaceutically active.

Experiments on infants and toddlers are sometimes done in child care settings, where two or more instructional approaches might be compared. When the concern is with medical issues, an experimental test of a vaccine might be carried out.

Tests of interventions and treatments ideally should be experimental because only this approach, according to the rules of research, allows us to conclude that our treatment was the cause, and the only cause, of a change. In many cases, however, tests of interventions fail to follow the rules for a good experiment. An antidrug campaign in the mass media might be shown to be followed by a reduction in births of drug-exposed babies, but in the absence of an experimental comparison, we cannot know that the campaign caused the

APPLICATIONS & ARGUMENTS
Can You Learn About Babies by Watching Your Own?

Jean Piaget, probably the most famous of all students of infant development, collected his data on infants' lives by systematically observing his own babies. Such a research procedure is virtually unheard of today.

Modern researchers are concerned about the biases that might affect observations of a familiar and beloved infant. Every observer has to make some judgment calls about observed behavior: Does it or does it not fit a particular category? If it's at the edge of the category, do we count it as "in" or "out"? Surely there is a possibility that a parent, who naturally wants his or her baby to be intelligent and emotionally healthy, could make slightly different judgment decisions than a more objective observer would. To base research entirely on your own children seems to be asking for distorted data collection.

On the other hand, observing a familiar infant can be a wonderful way to start the research process. When the same behaviors are seen again and again, the observer can get past the details and begin to see patterns. For example, in investigations of language development, an observer may not be able to make any sense of a strange baby's vocalization, but a familiar baby's little tricks of pronunciation and vocabulary fall into place and allow the underlying communication to emerge.

There are probably many examples of research on infants that started with an observation of a familiar baby. But modern research standards require us to avoid the biases that would occur if that were our only source of information.

reduction. It might have been caused by many other events, such as a crackdown in Latin America that reduced supplies of drugs in this country, the end of a strike by policemen, or bad weather that kept potential drug customers off the streets.

Quasi-Experimental Work

quasi-experiment:
a research approach that does not involve manipulation of variables but that compares groups of subjects who have naturally experienced exposure to different variables; from the Latin *quam* (as), *si* (if), *experiri* (to try).

Research on infants and toddlers often asks questions about factors that cannot be manipulated experimentally. If we want to compare the effect of being male with the effect of being female, we cannot do an experiment because we cannot make one individual male and another initially identical person female. Similarly, we cannot work experimentally on ethnic differences or on stages of motor development; we cannot make a person a Samoan or a Navajo and we cannot control when a baby starts to walk.

What to do, then? Questions about gender differences, about maturation, and especially about age are at the heart of our study of infants and toddlers. We answer them through a group of approaches that are *quasi-experimental* in nature. A **quasi-experiment** involves comparison of groups that are naturally different in specific ways but similar in as many other ways as we can manage. Any study that compares males and females, 10- and 12-month-olds, or infants who can sit alone and those who cannot is a quasi-experiment.

Some infant behaviors occur spontaneously at home. Observing them can help researchers decide on topics for investigation.

prospective:
examining the later
effects of subjects'
particular earlier
experiences; from
the Latin *pro*
(forward), *specere*
(to look).

retrospective:
examining the
earlier experiences
of subjects who
show certain later
effects; from the
Latin *retro*
(backward), *specere*
(to look).

When quasi-experiments investigate issues like the effect of anaesthesia during childbirth on the infant's early development, we can take one of two approaches. In the first, the **prospective** study, we begin with two groups of babies at the time of birth: one born while the mothers were anesthetized, and the other born to unmedicated mothers. Six months later, we may locate the babies in the two groups and compare them on a series of potentially relevant factors (for example, weight, sleep patterns, and achievement of motor milestones).

In the second approach, the **retrospective** study, we select babies on the basis of some characteristic we might expect to relate to the experience of maternal anesthesia. Perhaps we choose sleep patterns as a factor that might be affected; we then select a group of 6-month-old babies whom we can classify as having less mature sleep patterns and another group we can classify as having more mature sleep patterns. We now examine the backgrounds of the babies in the two groups, asking whether a significantly greater number of those with immature sleep patterns had experience of maternal anesthesia.

Prospective studies give us a clear set of data about the infants' childbirth experiences but leave us in potential difficulty with respect to the later data collection. Even within 6 months, families may move away or withdraw from the study; babies may become too sick to participate or may even die. Retrospective studies have the opposite problem; information about the 6-month-olds may be available, but accurate information about the past may not be so easy to get. If "the past" is 6 months ago, and the factor under investigation was recorded in hospital notes, the situation is not bad; on the other hand, information from 20 or 30 years ago, where memories may be the only records, can be extremely difficult to pin down. (This is the problem with studies that seek to establish early childhood experiences of criminals or that ask whether abusive parents were themselves victims of abuse.)

A major problem with all quasi-experiments is the need to make as sure as possible that the groups we are comparing are really similar on factors that might confuse our results. This process is called *matching* the groups. If we wanted to compare baby boys' and baby girls' heart rates, for instance, we would want to make sure that the boys and the girls were similar in body size and general health, because those factors are also capable of affecting heart rate. In quasi-experimental work, because we can never be sure that we have managed to control all the variables that could influence the factor we are measuring, we cannot conclude, as we could from an experiment, that one single factor has directly caused any differences between the groups. This is frustrating but important to understand so we do not misinterpret quasi-experimental findings.

When the Question Is About Age

Investigations of development commonly focus on changes that are due to age or to maturational change. Studies of this type are not experiments because the researcher cannot control aging; all one can do is wait until the subjects get older.

Quasi-experimental research on maturation deals with several important questions. Do babies show specific maturational changes at specific ages? How big are the differences between infants of different ages? Do babies gradually become more mature, or do individuals experience times of dramatic change? Does maturation always involve improved abilities, or are skills lost through maturation, too?

Quasi-experimental work on maturation takes a number of different forms. The specific approach chosen by a researcher depends on the question at hand and the time and money available to deal with it.

Longitudinal:
involving repeated testing or examination of individuals; from the Latin *longus* (long).

Longitudinal studies are quasi-experiments that measure and remeasure characteristics of a group of subjects as they age. More than one measurement is made for each person, so it is possible to compare the person's characteristics at an early age to his or her characteristics at a later age (or ages). This technique is a good way to find out about patterns of maturation because it lets the researcher see whether each person changed gradually or whether some or all subjects experienced periods of rapid change interspersed with times of slow change.

Longitudinal studies may cover days, weeks, or years of subjects' lives, depending on the particular topic being studied. If the study retests the subjects every year, or less often, it may be hard to contact the subjects and arrange for their continued participation. Generally, longitudinal studies require a lot of clerical work and record keeping and can be quite expensive to do; however, they give us a great deal of useful information, even if it may take years before it is collected and available. Longitudinal studies are critical to our understanding of sequences in development, of **transitions** from one stage to another, and of **temporal** organization of events or sequences of events.

transition:
movement from one state to another; from the Latin *trans* (across), *ire* (to go).

temporal: having to do with time; from the Latin *tempus* (time).

cohort: a group of people born at about the same time; from the Latin *cohors* (throng).

When a less expensive and less time-consuming approach is desired, a *cross-sectional* study may be the form of quasi-experiment used to study maturation. In a cross-sectional study, a number of groups of subjects are selected. Each is a **cohort,** or group born at around the same time, and each cohort is at one of the ages the researchers want to test. For example, there might be a group of 14-month-olds, a group of 15-month-olds, and a group of 16-month-olds. Each group is tested, and the results for the three groups are compared with each other.

A cross-sectional approach allows quick data attainment and a quick analysis. A potential problem in this design, however, must be carefully dealt with before data collection begins: unless the groups resemble each other closely on all variables except age, we may accidentally conclude that age causes some effects that are really associated with other factors. Suppose, for instance, that we wanted to look at bone development as babies get older. Because girls and boys mature physically on different schedules and because girls tend to be advanced in bone development, we would have to be careful that each age group contained the same proportion of males and females. If all the 14-month-olds were females and all the 15-month-olds were males, we would get the mistaken impression that little change in bone development occurred between age 14 months and age 15 months.

To make sure that the age groups are similar, we attempt to match them on factors that might be associated with bone development (or whatever factor we are concerned with)—perhaps sex, ethnic background, health status, diet, and living conditions. If we had access to a very large population, we might also draw subjects at random from all the 14-month-olds, all the 15-month-olds, and all the 16-month-olds, but this is not usually possible.

Two major problems are associated with cross-sectional research. One is that *patterns* of maturation are very hard to find, because we have no way to see how individuals change over time. Unless every subject changed in just the same way at just the same age, which is unlikely, the pattern of changes will be blurred by the averaging process of our data analysis. The second problem has to do with *cohort differences*. (Remember, a cohort is a group of people—*not* one person—who are all born at about the same time and, naturally, continue to share age as they grow up.) Usually, cohorts born a few months or years apart will not have vastly different experiences, but it would be possible for one cohort of babies to be affected prenatally by an epidemic (of rubella, for example) and for a cohort born a month later not to be affected. Cohort differences may lead researchers to think that differences are due to maturation, when in fact they may be due to experiences one particular group has had.

A third quasi-experimental design investigates maturation in a way that tries to deal with cohort differences *and* with the fact that longitudinal and cross-sectional studies do not always come to the same conclusions (Mullis et al., 1992; Nesselroade & Baltes, 1984). *Sequential* designs are a way of combining several longitudinal and cross-sectional studies into one in order to investigate differences between individuals as well as differences between ages and cohorts. For example, a study could look at cohorts born in June, July, August, and September and could test each individual in October, November, and December. One group would be 4 months old when tested in October, one 3 months, one 2 months, and one 1 month. In November, each group would be a year older. Thus the researchers would be able to look both at the characteristics of infants of a given age and at the cohort effect—the effect of being at a given age at a given time.

As research funding has become scarcer, researchers have become more motivated to use these complex sequential designs, which provide much data. If a study is well designed, it can be used for multidisciplinary purposes, and many types of questions can be answered from work on a relatively small group of subjects. This is useful in dealing with infants, where a multidisciplinary approach has so many advantages.

Correlational Studies

When researchers study maturation or other topics that cannot be handled experimentally, they often ask whether two factors change together in a predictable way: for example, when one gets larger, the other does, too; or when one gets smaller the other also gets smaller; or when one gets larger, the other gets smaller, and vice versa. When there is a consistent, predictable relationship between two factors being measured, the factors are said to be *correlated.* If the factors increase or decrease together, the correlation is *positive;* if one increases while the other decreases, the correlation is *negative.* Thus, height and weight are positively correlated, as are age and grade level, but the temperature in New York City and the number of people going to the beach in Rio are negatively correlated.

Correlational studies can help us understand some patterns in infants' lives, but it is important to realize that a correlation between two factors does not show us that one necessarily causes the other. Sometimes there is a cause-and-effect relationship, but sometimes both factors are determined by a number of other factors. Young women who rate themselves as having happy marriages treat their babies with greater warmth and sensitivity (Cox, Owen, Lewis, & Henderson, 1989), but the rating does not cause the warmth. We could pay people to rate themselves as happy, but that would not *cause* them to treat their babies better. Both the ratings and the parenting are caused by multiple factors that we have not even mentioned.

Animal Studies, Experimentation, and Ethology

When a question about infants involves some possible danger or harm, one approach is to work with infants of other species rather than with humans. It is common to use species that are very similar to us genetically, such as chimpanzees. An important point to remember, though, is that many effects are *species-specific;* that is, what affects one species in one way may have very different, or no, influences in other species. For example, the drug thalidomide, which caused serious birth defects in human infants about 30 years ago, was carefully tested on other primates before it was used on humans. The other species did not develop birth defects, but it was a mistake to generalize those findings to humans.

The less a species is genetically like human beings, the less likely it is that we can safely generalize from that species' infants to ours. For example, you probably know that it is difficult to get a ewe to care for a strange lamb if her own lamb dies; but a ewe becomes ready to accept a strange lamb if her cervix is stimulated for 5 minutes with a vibrator (Keverne, Levy, Poindron, & Lindsay, 1983). Although no one has tried the experiment, it seems most unlikely that we could generalize from sheep to humans and eliminate maternal child abuse by investing in large numbers of vibrators!

lateralization: the association of a function with a particular side of the brain or body; from the Latin *latus* (side).

Although some work on animals is primarily descriptive, many studies attempt to consider evolutionary links to explain human development. For example, MacNeilage (1991) discussed the idea that human preference for using either the right or the left hand derives from our tree-dwelling ancestors. These primates needed to use one hand to hold on and one hand to reach for food, and complex communication began to develop at about the same time that **lateralization** was taking place.

ethology: the descriptive study of behaviors characteristic of a species; from the Greek *ethos* (custom or character).

The **ethological approach,** which derived from work on animals, is a potentially useful source of information about infant development. This primarily descriptive technique involves careful, detailed observations of infants and toddlers in their normal environments in order to collect information about spontaneous behavior patterns. This is very exacting work and requires careful training as well as many hours of observation and recording. An example of this kind of work is a study by Anderson (1972), in which he watched children between 15 and 30 months of age playing in a park with their mothers. Anderson reported that when a child raised one arm but did not point, the child then moved in the direction of the arm; if the child only pointed, no subsequent movement in that direction was made. The mothers, who probably could not have described what the children were doing, responded by smacking the children who raised their arms in a direction they were not supposed to go, but not smacking them if they pointed in the forbidden direction.

Qualitative Research

The research approaches we have discussed so far all involve some sort of quantification; events are counted or measured in some way, and the resulting numbers are given statistical analysis. *Quantification* is a technique characteristic of the physical sciences, and as such has been taken as a model by many researchers in the biological and social sciences.

In recent years, however, some researchers working on topics like infant development have expressed concerns that quantitative approaches are not the best way to answer their research questions. Instead, they have advocated using *qualitative,* descriptive approaches. Qualitative studies do not necessarily begin with a statement of hypotheses or predictions about outcomes; they do not use large or random samples of subjects, manipulate treatments, use standardized tests, or employ statistical analyses (Murray, 1992).

Qualitative research depends primarily on narrative descriptions based on field notes of *participant observers,* observers who do not try to be objective or avoid influencing what is happening. Qualitative investigation may also involve *case studies,* or detailed descriptions of specific individuals or situations (Murray, 1992).

Qualitative research is more likely to be found in evaluation studies than in basic "pure" research. Intervention programs, which attempt to improve the development of infants who are in difficulty, must be evaluated for a number of reasons. One reason is that it is essential to know what works and what does not—or whether something does more harm than good. At a more practical level, evaluation grants from government sources or from private foundations require that evaluation be built into any funded program. The intention is to make sure that money is spent as originally proposed, and not wasted on ineffective programs.

Some parts of program evaluation must involve quantitative work. Government or private funding assumes that there will be numerical reports, at least on topics like the number of people attending a program (some refer to this as "bean counting"). However, program staff often feel that quantitative feedback tells them little about how their programs are doing. They may be much more interested in formative evaluation or *project monitoring*—descriptions of the ways the program functions and the changes it goes through (Murray, 1992).

RESEARCH DIRECTIONS: SOCIETAL NEED, THEORY, AND THE ZEITGEIST

What makes a researcher choose a particular research topic? Why are research questions asked in one way rather than another? Although undergraduates in research classes often suspect that "magic" is the only answer to these questions, research topics and approaches actually emerge in a logical way from a combination of factors. Research is a social activity that depends on communication with other researchers and with the larger community, and communications from those sources help shape a particular investigator's work.

Societal Need

pathology: the study of disease processes; from the Greek **pathos** (suffering).

Current research on infants is sometimes driven by an interest in **pathology.** Our very real national concerns about educational success, health, and crime prevention have made it more likely that researchers will start with infants who are at risk of poor development rather than with infants who seem to be doing very well. This can be quite depressing for the beginning student, who gets the impression that all infants are doing pretty badly. The fact is, of course, that most babies do quite well, but the study of babies with problems is important not only because of its relevance to national issues but also because the study of pathology can often give us some insight into how normal development takes place.

Similarly, research on infants may test the outcome of early intervention programs. It is important to know whether such programs are effective, and both scientific considerations and the national interest require that we investigate whether our efforts to help are beneficial, irrelevant, or even harmful. In fact, when people in the helping professions ask for government grants to do early intervention, they must write into their proposals a description of the methods by which the outcome of the project will be tested.

Theory and Research

data: observations or measurements of events; from the Latin *datus* (given).

Whether or not there is a social need related to research, the formulation of research issues is driven by *theory*. Researchers planning an investigation base their thinking both on **data** (existing observations and measurements) and on theories that attempt to pull together data and make sense of the relationships between them.

APPLICATIONS & ARGUMENTS
Are Decisions About Babies Based on Research?

Some decisions about infants are based on systematic, formal research of the kind described in this chapter. For example, information about infant and toddler growth rates was derived from careful, systematic study, and the decision to give a baby special treatment because of slow growth is possible only because that research was done. Similarly, decisions about a baby's need for help with language development are based on meticulous collection of information.

In some areas of development, however, there is little crossover from systematic research to practical decision making. For example, there are research techniques for investigating a baby's emotional relationship with her parents, but decisions about therapy are more likely to be based on a therapist's own clinical experience. Clinical knowledge comes from observation, of course, but it is not necessarily systematic or formal observation.

Legal decisions, such as permission for adoption, are not usually research based. In the courtroom, research findings are sometimes attacked on the ground that "most babies" are not necessarily the same as the baby in question. Legal decisions tend to result from the judge's own experience; testimony of expert witnesses, who are usually clinically oriented; and negotiation with child protective services.

What about issues of practical parenting, such as the decision to breast-feed? It is doubtful that either parents or medical advisers pay much attention to formal research on this subject. Anecdotal evidence and personal experience and opinion receive much greater consideration.

Sometimes a theory is an elaborate, formal statement of the possible connections between observations and measurements. Other times, a theory is just a set of assumptions based on informal observations; and sometimes a researcher may not even be able to articulate the assumptions he or she is using. In either case, a theory is an abstraction based on concrete observations and real events. It is a framework that seems to fit existing data and allows us to make some guesses about the nature of observations we have yet to make. Sometimes theories outrun their data and stand on shaky ground, and sometimes data exist that do not seem either to fit into any existing theory or to suggest any new theoretical framework.

A theory allows a researcher to formulate a reasonable prediction about what might happen under certain circumstances—in other words, to create a *hypothesis*. Hypotheses are based both on data that already exist and on the theoretical framework of assumptions about relationships among data. To be investigated by a researcher, a hypothesis must be testable. It must be specific enough that we could reject it on the basis of contradictory data. It must also involve predictions about data of types we can measure (even if the only measurement we can manage involves counting how often the event occurs).

The useful hypothesis must also involve *operational definitions* of the events we are looking at—definitions of the ways we observe and measure occurrences. The need for operational definitions harkens back to the "social" nature of research we discussed earlier. Without operational definitions, we cannot communicate our research to other people, nor can we figure out whether other researchers' findings are similar to ours.

Operational definitions may involve qualitative measurements, quantitative measurements, or a combination of the two. A qualitative measurement looks at what a baby is doing and also describes the way the action is being done. For example, a qualitative study of reaching might investigate how often the baby appears to an observer to be trying to reach (as opposed to making some other arm movement), and it might describe the movement as fast, slow, hesitant, or vigorous. (Operational definitions of qualitative data collection can be difficult.) A quantitative study of reaching, alternatively, might measure velocity of arm movement at different times during the reach, changes in elbow angles as the reach proceeds, or finger positions in response to a moving object. Research topics once pursued in a qualitative fashion may become quantitative with technological advances, as is noted elsewhere in this chapter.

An important way in which theory can influence research involves theories of how research should be conducted. A school of thought that goes back hundreds of years suggests that experimental research is by far the most desirable because (1) it allows us to manipulate variables that do not necessarily occur independently in nature (Massaro, 1987) and (2) it allows us to understand cause-and-effect relationships. An alternative approach (see Brunswik, 1955) assumes that useful research examines events in the context of the many factors operating in the real world—in other words, nonexperimentally. The idea is that, however internally valid experimental results may be, they cannot be generalized to the real world, and ungeneralizable data cannot lead us to any real understanding of infant development.

The Zeitgeist

zeitgeist: the spirit or attitude of a historical period; from the German *Zeit* (time) and *Geist* (mind).

The **zeitgeist,** or "spirit of the times," is the set of basic assumptions behind the thinking of people alive in a given place and time. These assumptions are broader than theories, and theories develop and exist within their context. The zeitgeist takes a long time to change, but it may change a good deal faster in the thinking of theory makers than in that of the average person. Thus, the mass media and even textbooks may lag behind changes in experts' thoughts on a topic.

Throughout the 18th and 19th centuries, a major aspect of the zeitgeist in Europe and America was the assumption of *mechanism*. A mechanistic approach to development assumes that the environment controls development, providing experiences to learn from and rewards or punishments that govern the direction of change. This approach does not deny the existence of physical maturation, of course, but attributes language development, cognitive development, and emotional and personality development to external pressures.

The mechanistic viewpoint was very useful for researchers in the physical sciences and was later adopted by the biological and social sciences. Two highly influential, mechanistically inclined workers in the social sciences are John B. Watson (1878–1958) and B. F. Skinner (1904–1990), both of whom discussed infants as creatures shaped entirely by their environments. The behaviorist view espoused by Watson and Skinner has had a major impact on the U.S. educational establishment and on child guidance advice.

Although the mechanistic approach was dominant in U.S. infant development work for some time, an alternative viewpoint informed the work of Arnold Gesell (1880–1961) and became a more substantial part of the zeitgeist after about 1950. This viewpoint, which can be called the *maturationist* or *organismic* approach, stresses genetically determined, built-in tendencies for infants to develop along certain pathways. Although organismic thinkers cannot deny that the environment influences infants, they stress that organisms change developmentally in ways that are determined by their own nature, rather than by their experience. The analogy compares an infant to a flower growing from a seed rather than to a machine; a flower may grow more slowly in a poor environment, but it grows into a marigold if it comes from a marigold seed. The environment cannot make it into a nasturtium, nor can it make the flower grow faster than an upper limit set by the flower's own nature. Jean Piaget's (1896–1980) work on cognitive development is an example of an organismic approach that has strongly influenced U.S. educational and child-rearing approaches.

One real advantage of an organismic approach to infant development is the assumption that we do not need to explain why infants develop and change. The process of change is considered to be inherent in the organism. Thus, research can concentrate on factors that slow development or alter its outcome. The dynamics of the process, the motivation for development, are simply part of the living organism (Oyama, 1987).

In recent years, the zeitgeist of infant development work has come to emphasize an approach that looks simultaneously at maturational and environmental factors in development. This idea, which may be either a transactional (Sameroff, 1983) or a dynamic systems approach (for example, Butterworth, 1990a), stresses that an understanding of infant development will be based on examination of all the interrelated elements involved in an event, including mutual interaction between the infant and the environment. One element included in the dynamic systems approach is the idea that the organism's *purposes* must be considered, even if we can only infer them from behavior (Butterworth, 1990a; von Hofsten, 1990). This emphasis on purpose would have been considered quite unacceptable in a mechanistic approach and is a dramatic alteration in the zeitgeist (although you may well argue that it is exactly what your great-grandmother would have said).

Dynamic systems theorists have criticized earlier infant development work's tendency to stress the things young babies *cannot* do. For example, mechanistic thinkers essentially considered the baby as "empty" of abilities; they then found it difficult to relate the baby's initial condition to its later "fullness" of competence (Butterworth, 1990a). Work based on the dynamic systems viewpoint stresses the infant's initial positive, adaptive abilities and examines the infant's change toward even greater competence. This approach, then, has **heuristic** value; it helps the researchers ask progressively more complex and interesting questions.

heuristic:
valuable for empirical research; from the Greek *heuriskein* (to discover).

An example of the complexity of modern research on infant development is Fogel's (1990) work on the roles both mother and infant play in the development of visually guided reaching. Communication and social support are part of the process, and the infant becomes able to give an object to another person or to take something from another's hand. Similarly, Blass (reported by Kolata, 1987a) looked at the infant's capacity to learn from different kinds of sound signals; some sounds led quickly to anticipation (of a sugar solution), whereas others were ignored. Vinter (1986) investigated the contribution of movement an infant sees to the infant's tendency to imitate facial expressions. Balaban (1995) showed that the size of the eyeblink a 5-month-old baby made when startled by a sound depended on the slide the baby was looking at when surprised; blinks were smaller when the baby was inspecting a slide of a face with a happy expression, and larger when the face looked angry. Each of these studies examined the interaction of multiple and changing factors in the determination of development. (We may also note that the dynamic systems perspective's stress on multiple factors can lead to confusion and "analysis paralysis," not unlike that of the centipede who could walk quite well until asked which leg came after which—whereupon "he lay distracted in the ditch, considering how to run"!)

MEASUREMENTS, AVERAGES, AND VARIATIONS

Although different disciplines are interested in different kinds of *measurement* of infant development, all need to deal with measurement in some form. To tell someone else what we have observed about an infant, we need to be able to include measurement in our description, even if all we measure is how long an activity goes on. Communicating information to others is one of the critical parts of any modern research approach, and measurement is essential to accurate communication.

When we think about measurement, we are most apt to consider everyday physical measurements, like height or weight. Measurements of that type are sometimes called *ratio* measurements, and they have certain characteristics: there is a real zero point; and the numbers stand in certain relationships to each other, so that the difference between 2 and 3 is always the same as the difference between 4 and 5 and so on. Some aspects of infant development, such as some physical measures, do involve ratio measurement, but others do not. If we are looking at a baby's body temperature, for example, we are dealing with an *interval* measurement; the difference between 37°C and 38°C is the same as the difference between 38°C and 39°C, but there is no real zero

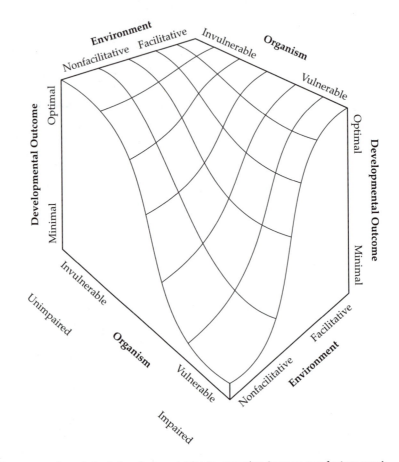

Modern research on infant development tries to examine how many factors work together, but these complex interactions may be difficult to describe. This three-dimensional graph shows how some factors interact. (Source: Horowitz, 1985)

point where there is no temperature at all. Other measures, like the Apgar test used to assess a newborn's condition, are *ordinal* measures; there is no guarantee that the difference between 8 points and 9 points is the same as the difference between 9 points and 10 points. The simplest kind of measurement is **nominal,** or category, measurement, where we simply classify the baby as belonging to one group or another (male or female, cocaine-exposed or not, bald or with hair).

nominal:
classified according to categories rather than amounts; from the Latin *nomen* (name).

The point of thinking about these forms of measurement is that the level of measurement determines what kind of statistical analysis we can do with our data. To understand measurements of babies' development or to tell other people about them, we have to do some arithmetic. No human being can understand at a glance what a large number of measurements mean. Even if only one baby is being observed, chances are that many measurements will be made.

There are three basic reasons for analyzing data we get from studies of infants. The first two we have already mentioned: to improve our own understanding of what we have found, and to communicate it to other people. The third reason is that research data about infant development are often used for purposes of *assessment*. In a medical or other clinical setting, research information is used as a standard of comparison to assess infants' development and decide whether a baby is or is not doing well. For purposes of assessment, the information needs to be presented in the form of a few simple numbers so that it is easy to use.

Without getting into calculations, we can look at some statistical approaches that are useful in understanding infant development. An *average* is a common way to present information about large numbers of measurements. There are three common forms of averages: (1) the *mean*, for ratio data, where all the measurements are added together and the result is divided by the number of measurements; (2) the *median*, for interval or ordinal data, where the measurements are arranged in order from the biggest to the smallest and the middle one is called the median; and (3) the *mode*, for nominal measurements, where the classification that occurs most frequently is considered to be a form of average.

Averages are useful ways to summarize a lot of measurements in a single number. It is important, though, to remember that *numbers* are what get averaged; there is no such thing as an "average baby." This expression is sometimes just shorthand for "a baby who has some measurement equivalent to the average of all babies' measurements." When we say the average newborn baby weighs 7½ pounds, what we really mean is that the average weight of all the newborn babies is 7½ pounds. In fact, there may be no baby in the group whose weight is exactly 7½ pounds. For example, if the weights of 10 babies were 7, 7, 7, 7, 7, 8, 8, 8, 8, and 8 pounds, the average would be 7½ pounds, but the actual weights would all be different from the average.

If we were assessing the weight of one newborn and deciding whether the baby was healthy, it would not make any sense to worry if the baby's weight was not exactly average. The average tells us only what happens if we do some arithmetic on all the measurements. We need to know more than the average if we are going to use the information in any practical way. We also need to understand the amount of variation in the measurements.

Variability is an essential concept for the understanding of infant development. Every biological phenomenon shows variation. If you go to the garden and pick pea pods, you will see that some pods have 5 peas in them, some 6, some 10, some none. If you weighed hens' eggs, you would find that even a single hen lays some light ones and some heavy ones. In the same way, human babies are different from each other in their height, weight, growth rate, length of sleep periods, and so on. Thus we can expect most babies' measurements to be somewhat different from the average; there will be some variation. The question then becomes not "Is this baby average?" but "How much different from the average is this baby, compared to the variability of all babies? Is it so different from the others that we can assume that something unusual is going on?"

A simple measure of variability is the *range*, which tells the difference between the largest and the smallest measurement. However, the arithmetic needed to calculate variability is usually more complicated than what is done to calculate averages, and a statistics course is the way you can best learn about this. For our purposes, we can simply say that we need to keep in mind variations as well as average measurements if we are going to understand infant development.

Understanding averages and variability will help us grasp some terms often used in assessing development, such as *above average, below average, normal, abnormal, typical,* and *atypical.* If you know what an average is, you will know that being above or below average on a measurement may be unimportant unless the baby is quite far above or below.

Understanding the nature of an average also should let you know that *average* and *normal* do not mean the same thing. Average is a statistical statement, whereas **normal** is an assessment and involves an evaluation about the need for special help. Since babies are so variable, there is no one score or measurement that is the normal one. Instead, there is a normal *range* of scores, above or below which there may be a need for help.

normal: within a range of variation that does not imply a need for intervention; from the Latin *norma* (a carpenter's square).

The normal range is often defined in terms of *percentiles,* which are calculated in much the same way as the median. Scores are arranged in order from the biggest to the smallest, and the lowest 10%, lowest 20%, and so on, of the scores are calculated. The normal range for birth weights, for example, is defined as every weight between the 90th percentile (the weight below which 90% of the babies' weights lie, about 8½ pounds) and the 10th percentile (the weight below which only 10% of the babies' weights lie, about 5½ pounds). Thus 80% of the babies have weights within the normal range of 5½ to 8½ pounds, and the 20% whose weights are less than 5½ or more than 8½ pounds are considered **abnormal** in size.

abnormal: outside the acceptable range of variation; or needing intervention; from the Latin *ab-* (away from), *norma* (a carpenter's square).

The terms *normal* and *abnormal* are used for assessment and evaluation, but we need to keep in mind that they are basically ways of comparing one baby to a large group of other babies. *Normal* does not mean "perfect", and *abnormal* can certainly have a variety of implications. Babies who have abnormally low birth weights are in much greater danger of dying than are babies whose birth weights are abnormally high, for example, although the latter are somewhat more likely to die than are babies whose weights are within the normal range.

typical: characteristic of a group; from the Latin *typus* (image).

atypical: uncharacteristic of a group; from the Latin *ab-* (away from), *typus* (image).

Sometimes there is so much variability in an aspect of development that even the calculation of a normal range does not make much sense. This is especially true if the variations are qualitative as well as quantitative. Cultural differences, for example, cause babies to have very different experiences in early life. Rather than saying a certain experience is normal or abnormal for babies, we may say that it is **typical** or **atypical.** These terms are an attempt to consider how common something is without placing a higher value on the more common event. It may be typical, for example, for U.S. babies to be exposed to a great deal of television, but this is not necessarily a good thing.

RESEARCH SUBJECTS AND GENERALIZATION

Only rarely do researchers want to find out about only one group of infants. Most of the time, the intention is to collect information about one group in order to generalize from that group to large numbers of other babies. But not all babies are alike, and generalization is not always possible.

When the research topic is biological in nature, generalization may not be an issue. In some ways, one human being is very like another. The process of circulatory system change following birth is very likely the same for a full-term baby born to middle-class parents in Paris as it is for a full-term baby born to upper-class parents in Calcutta and for a full-term baby born to lower-class parents in Newark. (It appears, though, that some aspects of early behavior result from genetic differences; Brazelton, 1990.)

When an aspect of development is affected by experience, it becomes much less likely that all humans are alike in that respect. There are enormous cultural differences in infant care techniques (although they all have to have enough in common to meet the baby's basic needs). Infants developing in different circumstances even experience different physical events, such as different foods, sleeping positions, or illnesses. It is not necessarily safe to assume that we can generalize from one group of babies to another in terms of language, personality, or even motor development.

Many infants who are research subjects are well-fed, well-cared-for children of educated, middle-class families of European descent. These families are easiest for researchers to reach and easiest to get informed consent from, and their children are the least likely to be withdrawn from a research project because of illness or legal problems. Even in a study that deals with drug-exposed babies, the mothers available for study are often the ones who are in good enough shape to get into a treatment program and to maintain some contact with their children.

We need to be careful about assuming that the results of studies on white middle-class infants in the United States can be generalized to other groups. Above all, we need to be careful about making recommendations about other groups of babies on the basis of middle-class life. Each infant's life needs to be understood within the context of its own family and its own cultural environment. These cultural differences themselves are an entire topic of study in themselves.

RESEARCH ON HISTORICAL AND CROSS-CULTURAL DIFFERENCES IN INFANT CARE

The term *culture* is commonly misused by people today, who often believe that it refers to a particular genetically defined ethnic group. Although genetically similar people may well share a culture, they do so because they have learned that culture's ways, not because their genetic material forces them to do so.

APPLICATIONS & ARGUMENTS
When Research Is Possible but Improbable: Infants' Sexuality

Certainly, research on infant development covers a wide variety of topics, but some aspects of infant life have been studied very little. Sometimes practical difficulties interfere, and sometimes the problem is with assumptions about the realities of infants' lives and with associated values.

A topic that has received little study is the role of sexuality in an infant's life. Late in the 19th century, Freud published the claim that the infant experiences wishes and sensations that are analogous to adult sexuality. (It is possible that, of all his ideas, this was the one people found most shocking.) Freud's claim, of course, was based on clinical work with adults rather than on studies of young children. Many similarly unsubstantiated statements about early sexuality have subsequently appeared. One example is the early 20th-century belief that an infant's touching of his or her genitals was a symptom of or would produce serious problems. Another is the more recent concern that a display of interest in sexuality must mean that a child has been abused.

It is well known that baby boys have erections. In cultures that consider it permissible, stroking an infant's penis has been used to calm and soothe him, so it seems reasonable to conclude that the sensation is pleasurable. However, our practice of using diapers makes it difficult for a researcher to determine how often a boy baby experiences an erection or how long it lasts. Gathering any similar material about girl babies would involve inserting a recording device into the vagina, which has not been done and probably never will be done. For good or ill, value judgments make it unlikely that we will see any systematic study of infant sexuality.

People who are genetically quite different may also share a culture if they have learned its ways, as we can see when a child of one ethnic group is adopted by a family of another group. A culture is a set of customs, attitudes, and values that are shared by members of a group and that are learned through a process of socialization beginning very early in life. Although members of a group share a culture, they are not likely to be identical in the way they think or do things. There is variability within a culture, just as there is genetic variability within a group. Phillips and Cooper (1992) offer some useful descriptive statements that help explain what a culture is:

1. A culture is a set of rules for behavior.
2. Cultures are shared by groups.
3. Culture is learned.

4. Individual members of a group are embedded in their culture to different degrees.
5. Cultures borrow and share rules.
6. Members of a culture may follow its rules but not be able to tell you what the rules are.

There are different infant care practices that all exist in the world at the same time and that can influence each other (cultural differences), as well as practices that existed in the past and do not necessarily exist today (historical differences). Even though both can be thought of as cultural in nature because they are ways different groups of people do or have done things, our ways of studying them are rather different.

The study of historical changes in infant care relies on written documents, folk songs and stories, paintings, and sculptures. Where people in the past could not write or did not represent infant care in any way, we have no way of knowing what a group's practices were. Even when we do have documentation, we do not know whether it is accurate or complete. The writings of a group of people may not mention a particular practice either because it never occurred or because it was so common and "obvious" that nobody needed to be told about it. Particular practices described may have been commonplace or amusing or horrifying to the writer, and that is why they were chosen for comment. The concept of variability, which has been discussed repeatedly in this book, is a rather modern one; writers discussing infant care before this century rarely concerned themselves with relative frequencies or individual differences.

In most cases, historical materials began with some actual observations, but the writer or the artist passed along the interpretation rather than the facts. We, in our turn, interpret the interpretation, which takes us one more step further from reality. For example, a pre-Columbian statuette of a woman giving birth was long displayed in a reclining position until someone reinterpreted the appropriate position as squatting (which the position of her toes indicates); the "modern" assumption that one gives birth lying down shaped the museum personnel's initial interpretation (Klaus & Kennell, 1982).

Investigations of infant-care practices in other cultures are especially difficult because they involve mothers as well as infants. It is very unlikely that a male researcher will get to ask Third World women about such intimate things as pregnancy, birth, and breast-feeding. Women researchers are essential for this kind of work, and even they must invest a great deal of time and energy in forming friendships before they can ask questions about private matters (Raphael & Davis, 1985).

Structured interviews and questionnaires used for cross-cultural research must be supplemented by observation, or interviewer and interviewee may find themselves at cross-purposes. For example, Super and Harkness (1982), studying infant temperament in a rural African community, asked whether a baby could entertain himself if left alone for half an hour. Many mothers said their babies could, but the researchers had noticed that the babies were hardly ever actually left alone. When the researchers questioned the mothers more

Historical and cultural factors affect the experiences of parents and infants alike.

aggressively and demanded to know why they said the babies would be happy alone, the mothers asked whether by "alone" they meant "with no one at all." They had assumed that of course a baby would be left with his sisters and brothers, not completely by himself.

TECHNOLOGICAL ADVANCES AND RESEARCH

Every area of research in infant development has its own techniques and equipment for data collection. These methods will be discussed in detail in the following chapters, but some general ideas about the role of technology in research may be useful here. Of particular note is technology's critical role in helping move infant development research from a qualitative to a quantitative approach.

Video recording has made possible remarkable advances in our understanding of early development. Behaviors that are too rapid and subtle for an observer to see and remember are revealed by video recordings. Examined frame by frame, these records allow us to measure small, quick movements and to examine events occurring in different parts of the body—for example, eye movement or facial expression occurring simultaneously with hand movement.

Video recording helps us see an activity in enough detail to develop a good operational definition for it. It provides us with a check on observers' reliability and allows for decisions when observers disagree on what has happened. Disagreement between observers can be dramatic. For example, in one study of toddlers following their parents at a shopping mall, the researchers were startled to find that some parents denied that their children had just been walking at a distance behind them—or, indeed, that the children had ever done so (Mercer & McMurdy, 1985).

The development of noninvasive techniques to record brain function has brought about advances in our understanding of fetuses, neonates, and older infants. Brain imaging techniques give us special insight into continuity of function from the prenatal to the postnatal period.

meta-analysis: a statistical test involving data collected in many separate studies; from the Greek *meta-* (among, with, after), *analyein* (to break up).

Finally, we must acknowledge the role of computer technology in infant development research. It would be impractical to analyze large numbers of data, or many simultaneous measurements of different factors, without computer facilities. In particular, the technique called **meta-analysis,** which examines data from large numbers of similar studies, requires computer analysis. Because individual studies on infants often use rather small numbers of subjects, meta-analysis is a way of strengthening research conclusions.

ETHICS AND INFANCY RESEARCH

Like other values, ideas about ethics in infant development research have changed over time. In John B. Watson's day, it was considered acceptable to pursue studies like the one in which "little Albert" was conditioned to be afraid of furry animals and even fur coats (Watson & Raynor, 1920). Today, human subjects protection rules are particularly stringent with respect to fetuses, infants, and toddlers. Research that might be considered suitable with adult subjects is often rejected when the proposed subjects are the very young. Ethical considerations in research are complex enough that students often need some guidance when they design or carry out research projects. A set of guidelines is included at the end of this chapter.

Today, it is against ethical codes to collect many kinds of information about human beings without their informed consent. Research subjects must be given some explanation of the research, and in many cases they must sign a consent form to permit use of their data. But an infant or toddler obviously cannot understand research issues and thus cannot give informed consent. Instead, parents or guardians are asked for permission to use infants as research subjects, especially if there is to be any experimental treatment or manipulation, no matter how harmless it might appear to be.

A second important ethical consideration involves confidentiality of information gathered through research. Researchers must guarantee that information about parents and infants will not be released in any way that would allow outsiders to identify parent or baby. This protection is intended not only to prevent embarrassing gossip but also to keep research information from negatively influencing the family's life through its effects on the attitudes of day care providers and teachers. Most important, confidentiality should protect subjects against legal proceedings when any material of a criminal nature has been revealed in the course of the research. Unfortunately, information collected in the course of most research does not have the legal status of a "privileged communication," and a researcher could be sent to prison for refusing to reveal information to a court or grand jury.

A third ethical consideration requires debriefing, or offering information to subjects at the conclusion of a study. Informed consent requires an initial explanation of the research, but in some cases a complete explanation may cause the family to change its behavior in some way, altering the research results. An example would be a study investigating the effect of sugar or preservatives on a toddler's behavior; if family members know what the child's diet involves, they may treat the child differently because their expectations are changed. When a complete explanation cannot be given initially, the family must be offered one after the data are collected. In any case, the family whose child has been a research subject must be given the name and phone number of an investigator, whom they can contact if there are questions or problems following participation.

Research on all humans, but especially on infants and unborn babies, is monitored by an institutional review board in the hospital or other institution. The institutional review board is charged with protecting human subjects and maintaining high ethical standards for research. A board has the power to waive the requirement for informed consent in certain cases, but the board requires very good reasons for doing so. Institutions must keep to high ethical standards to remain in compliance with directives of the Department of Health and Human Services, and those that fail to comply run a serious risk of losing all federal funding.

An ethical concern that is sometimes forgotten is the obligation to do only well-designed, meaningful research on infant subjects. Researchers do not have the right to use babies in research whose outcome is meaningless or untrustworthy, especially if there is any potential for harm in the study. A recent concern of medical research on human beings is that people involved in studies of treatments be part of a "meaningful partnership" with researchers (Heymann, 1995, p. 797). Research that makes parents of infants meaningful partners involves them in the design of the study and takes into account their ideas about the questions to be considered.

Inclusion of an appropriate comparison group is an important part of well-designed, meaningful research. But the issue of comparison groups in research design can be problematic in work that involves intervention or treatment of infant or family problems. Some researchers have serious concerns about the use of control or comparison groups that do not receive the treatment being tested, believing it is not fair or right to withhold treatment from infants who obviously need it and whose lives may be seriously affected if they are not given help soon (Murray, 1992). This empathetic response and desire to help are very understandable, but the fact remains that we do not know whether an untested treatment really does any good. It may either waste the subjects' time or actually hurt them in some way. Only the use of a

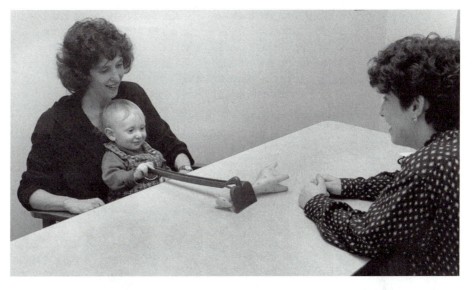

Being "tested" has to be fun for a baby. Otherwise, the researcher will not find out what he or she wants to know about many aspects of early development.

matched, untreated comparison group can tell us whether our treatment works. (Sometimes the matching of the groups needs to include a placebo situation for the untreated comparison group.) This is especially important when we are working with infants and toddlers, because they are always maturing and will be different at the beginning and the end of a month whether our treatment helps them or not. We need a comparison group to tell us whether the change in the treated babies is bigger than would have been caused by maturation alone, is the same (in which case our treatment did nothing), or is smaller (in which case our treatment actually interfered with development). Sometimes researchers argue that a comparison group is unnecessary because standardized tests give them a standard of comparison, but in some cases comparison groups and standardized tests give different results (Gross, Slagle, D'Eugenio, & Mettelman, 1992).

Ethical decisions may be needed in intervention research when it is decided that some members of the comparison group need treatment. For example, in one study of early physical therapy with high-risk infants (Piper et al., 1986), some infants in the comparison group had sufficient problems to be referred to other physical therapy programs before the initial study was completed. It was obviously ethically appropriate to give the babies the therapy they needed, but interference with the original design has the potential to destroy some of the meaning of the results.

A final special ethical issue involves research on infants in Third World countries. It is not infrequently the case that less developed countries have or enforce few regulations about protection of research subjects. Pharmaceutical developments and new medical technologies are sometimes tested in such situations precisely because there are few restrictions.

Students embarking on research are sometimes confused by human subjects protection requirements. Here is an example of a checklist aimed at protection of subjects. Note the circumstances when consent is not required, and the special concerns when subjects are minors.

Human Subjects Protection Checklist for Student Researchers

Student's name _____

Faculty member's name _____

Course name and number _____

Date _____

Research topic _____

PART I

In research using human subjects, we are required to protect our subjects by following *informed consent* procedures. These procedures ensure that subjects agree voluntarily to participate in a study and do so with a reasonable understanding of the nature and purpose of the work before participation. The procedures also provide subjects with sources of help in case they feel distressed following participation in the research. Evidence of informed consent is a *document* signed by the subject or guardian.

Subjects who are paid for research participation or who receive course credit for it have the same rights to informed consent procedures as do other subjects.

Some kinds of research are *exempt* from informed consent requirements because they create no risk for subjects. Examples are observations of public behavior where the subjects are not identified and use of existing medical or educational records that are available to the public. If your research is of this type, check the box on the right. You do not need to fill out the rest of the checklist. ☐

Some kinds of research are impossible if the subject is fully informed about the research before participation. Where *deception* is involved, you may request a waiver of the requirement for a complete description of the study. If you need to do this, check the box on the right and fill out the rest of the checklist. You will have to give your subjects a written statement with an accurate description of the study after they participate. ☐

Some kinds of research keep the subjects completely *anonymous* and include no way that subjects could be identified, directly or indirectly. When this is the case, you may request a waiver of informed consent of documentation but you must give your subjects a written statement *before* they participate. If this is your case, check the box on the right and fill out the rest of the checklist. Face-to-face interviews and experimental manipulations cannot be included here because the researcher can identify the subject. Questionnaires may be included. ☐

PART II

The statement or document you present to your subject should contain the following information where appropriate. Circle "yes" or "no" for each item to show whether you have included it.

1. Explanation of purpose; description of procedure   YES   NO

2. Description of any probable risks or discomforts to the subject   YES   NO

3. Description of benefits to subject or others   YES   NO

4. Disclosure of alternative procedures that might benefit subject   YES   NO

5. Statement of extent of confidentiality   YES   NO

6. If there is more than minimal risk, statement of compensation and   YES   NO
   treatment available if injury occurs

7. Name and telephone number of person to be contacted in case of   YES   NO
   questions about research or help in case of injury.

8. Statement that participation is voluntary and may be discontinued   YES   NO
   at any time without penalty.

Items 3 and 4 may not apply to your research unless you are looking at a topic like smoking.

PART III

Under some circumstances, you may ask your faculty supervisor for a waiver or alteration of the usual informed consent procedures. This may *not* be done, however, if you answer "yes" to any of the following questions; such alteration should be approved by an institutional review board.

1. Is the subject's identity known to you and sex-related material involved?   YES   NO

2. Is the subject's identity known to you and material related to drug or   YES   NO
   alcohol use involved?

3. Is the subject's identity known to you and material related to criminal   YES   NO
   acts involved?

4. Is the subject's identity known to you and other emotionally   YES   NO
   sensitive material (such as suicide) involved?

5. Is physical measurement involved?   YES   NO

If the subject cannot be identified and the research involves sex, drugs, alcohol, criminal acts, or other emotionally sensitive topics, you may ask for a waiver or alteration of informed consent procedures. But you must at the minimum provide your subject with a written statement, including the name and phone number of a person to talk to if he or she is distressed following participation.

PART IV

Under some circumstances, information about the research should be read to the subject or the subject's guardian, as well as being presented in written form. You should do so if you answer "yes" to any of these questions.

1. Are the subjects under 18?	YES	NO
2. Are the subjects elderly people?	YES	NO
3. Are the subjects prisoners?	YES	NO
4. Are the subjects of a low educational level?	YES	NO

PART V

Unless you have been given permission not to do so, your subjects or their guardians must sign a consent form, which you must keep on file with your data.

1. Are you planning to have your subjects sign the consent form?	YES	NO
2. Are you planning to have your subjects' guardians sign the form?	YES	NO
3. Are you requesting a waiver or alteration of informed consent?	YES	NO

4. Reason for request: _____

_____

_____

PROBLEMS TO CONSIDER AND DISCUSS

1. Why is it important to collect information about many infants before trying to generalize to all infants?
2. What areas of study other than infant development are limited in their use of experiments? Give reasons for your answer.
3. What factors make a researcher decide to ask a certain question in a certain way? Be complete, and be practical in your answer.
4. Could a study that compares the language ability of walking and nonwalking 12-month-olds be an experiment? Why or why not?
5. What are the advantages and disadvantages of longitudinal studies of development?

3

The Biological Beginnings of Development

heredity: the passage of individual characteristics from an earlier to a later generation by biological means; from the Latin *heres* (heir).

Even as children, most of us realize that family resemblances are not accidental. We expect babies to look like their parents, or at least like a grandparent, an uncle, or a cousin. Sometimes we even expect relatives to act similarly; a mother may express serious concern about a teenage son's drinking because "it runs in his father's family." We recognize that there is a factor—**heredity**—that makes related people resemble each other more than they resemble an unrelated passerby. In this chapter, we will examine the mechanisms of heredity and the rules that govern family resemblances—a set of rules of which little was understood before the 20th century and about which new information is pouring in every day.

Perhaps our first task should be to clarify the idea of family resemblances and note the wide range of individual characteristics that are partly determined by heredity. Family resemblances most obviously involve the aspects of appearance that help us tell one person from another: height, hair and eye color, nose and chin sizes, and so on. But family members also resemble each other in their likelihood of developing serious diseases, like cystic fibrosis and sickle cell anemia, and possibly in their probability of suffering allergies. It is even possible that the mother described in the first paragraph is right, that there are hereditary factors in alcoholism.

But as we look at how heredity works, we see an odd situation. An individual may have characteristics unlike anyone else's in the family, but the mechanism that produced those differences may be the same one that determines family resemblances. This is true, for example, of some forms of mental retardation. The paradox of there being some "hereditary" event that makes a person different from other family members shows us why we need to refer to **genetics,** rather than just heredity. The term *genetics* covers not only the transmission of individual characteristics one has as a result of family membership, but also the transmission of other characteristics whose origins are built into every cell.

genetics: the study of the mechanisms that determine heredity and other biological sources of variation; from the Latin *genesis* (birth).

Modern work on genetics has shown that every cell in an individual's body carries a code, or blueprint, that instructs the cell how to function and how to make a new cell. The most basic questions in genetics involve the nature of that blueprint and how it controls individual differences as well as family resemblances.

The ways in which these basic questions can be answered are quite technical in nature, as we will see in a little while. Whether they *should* be answered is an issue of more general concern. Every step that has led to improved understanding of the genetic code in recent years has also led to increased concern about the potential impact of genetic science on the human race. There are deep fears about a potential loss of freedom and the creation of "artificial" humans, enhanced by the manipulation of their genetic makeup. But such people would presumably be as happy or unhappy, as complex and as subject to the impact of experiences, as any of us who are accidental genetic combinations. Perhaps the real fear is that the less-than-perfect human being would no longer be acceptable, that even mild disabilities like nearsightedness would become grounds for rejecting, isolating, or even killing the imperfect individual. Both the 19th and the 20th centuries have certainly seen movements that attempted to improve our species. The **eugenics** movement initially stressed the idea that competent people should have more children, but the Nazi party under Hitler moved actively to eliminate the mentally retarded, the physically disabled, and members of particular ethnic groups. It is indeed frightening to think that genetic science might be put to such brutal use.

eugenics: the study of the improvement of the hereditary qualities of a group; from the Greek *eugenes* (wellborn).

The ethics of genetic testing and treatment are a very real concern, as we will discuss later in this chapter. But clarification of one point may help put this concern in perspective: human individuality is *not* the result of genetic blueprints alone. The genetic code guides the individual's development within the environment, and the environment can either permit the full expression of the genetic possibilities or place limitations on development. For example, a baby of highly intelligent parents may have the potential for excellent mental development, but an environment contaminated with lead will limit her intellectual achievement. Similarly, after World War II, Japanese children growing up in good conditions in California grew taller than their parents and taller than their cousins in Japan, who experienced poor conditions in the years right after the war. Thus, except for trivial issues like eye color or more serious but isolated ones like the elimination of certain diseases, genetic information alone cannot make it possible to redesign the human species.

RESEARCH METHODS
Breeding Studies

The oldest of all research methods in genetics is undoubtedly the study of inheritance in animals. *Selective breeding* of desirable characteristics in domestic animals has been carried out for centuries and is the source of much practical knowledge.

Domestic animals have obviously been bred for particular physical traits, such as the amount of beef on a steer or the size of a horse used to draw heavy wagons. But breeding for behavior traits has also been practiced. A cow that produces large amounts of milk is not very useful if she is so ill-tempered that nobody can get close enough to milk her! Dogs are particularly good examples of deliberate selective breeding for desirable behavior traits; traits desirable in a pet may be quite different from those desired in a working dog. Spaniels, for instance, were bred to crouch down when they saw a sudden movement because they were used to hunt ground-nesting birds, who were captured with a flung net. If the dog remained standing up, the net would be held up too, and the birds could simply walk out from under it. As a result of this breeding, the modern pet spaniel sometimes embarrasses its owner by cringing with little provocation. Terriers, too, were bred for a specific behavior; in their case, digging to find rabbits in their burrows was desired, but their genetically determined tendency to dig up the tulip bulbs is not much appreciated.

More recently, geneticists have used controlled breeding of laboratory animals like mice to study patterns of genetic transmission. Breeding litter-mates, or mating a parent and an offspring, can uncover patterns of inheritance that show up only when the mates are genetically very similar.

Family Studies

We human beings, of course, do not mate simply to answer geneticists' questions. We also have almost universal taboos against incest. Even if we were more cooperative, however, we would not make as good subjects for genetic research as laboratory mice do. We tend to be extremely outbred—that is, to have considerable genetic mixtures—and our pedigrees, unlike those of lab mice, may be falsified by the assumption that every baby is the child of its mother's legal husband.

Although controlled breeding of a small number of animals can reveal genetic information, *family studies* of human inheritance require large numbers of subjects. One reason is that outbreeding greatly increases the number of possible genetic combinations in humans, compared to those found in inbred laboratory animals. A second reason for using large numbers of human subjects is that genetic research on humans often focuses on unusual characteristics, such as physical diseases or behavior disorders that are rarely seen but are devastating when they do occur.

Twin studies are a specialized type of family genetic studies. These studies take into account the fact that there are two types of twins, with different levels of genetic resemblance. **Monozygotic** ("identical") twins develop from a splitting of a fertilized ovum into two separately developing individuals who have the same genetic makeup (this is true at least at the point where division occurs; it is possible for one of the individuals to experience certain genetic changes after that point). **Dizygotic** ("fraternal") twins result from the fertilization of two eggs by two sperm; each egg and sperm has its own genetic makeup, so the resulting individuals are genetically as different as nontwin siblings, sharing half their genes on average.

Twin studies look at rates of **concordance**, or resemblance on certain points, between members of twin pairs. If each twin has the same eye color as his or her co-twin, for example, the concordance rate for eye color is 100%.

monozygotic: developing from the division of a single fertilized ovum; from the Greek *monos* (single), *zygoun* (to join together).

dizygotic: developing from two separate fertilized ova; from the Greek *di* (two), *zygoun* (to join together).

concordance: in this context, the extent to which a characteristic of a twin is also shown by the co-twin; from the Latin *concordia* (agreement).

Specific behaviors, such as the upper-body "squeeze" shown here, may be part of a genetic disorder.

If a characteristic is genetically rather than environmentally determined, we would expect higher concordance rates between monozygotic twins (who share more genes) than between dizygotic twins (who share fewer genes). Looking at differences in concordance rates should then give us an idea whether a particular characteristic is genetically determined. The problem with this approach, however, is that it assumes that the environment is as similar for the two members of a dizygotic pair as it is for monozygotic twins. This is not necessarily true, especially if the dizygotic twins are of different sexes (Porges, Matthews, & Pauls, 1992).

Separation or *adoption studies* look for concordance rates between children and parents. These studies compare the resemblances between parent and child in three ways: (1) comparing children and their biological parents, who raised them; (2) comparing adopted children and their adoptive parents; and (3) comparing adopted children and their biological parents. Where the concordance rate is highest between adopted children and their biological parents, the characteristic is presumably *genetically* determined. Where the concordance rate is lowest between adopted children and their biological parents, the characteristic is presumably *environmentally* caused. Where the strongest resemblance is between nonadopted children and their (biological) parents, the characteristic is presumably brought about by *both* genetic and environmental factors.

General family studies consider all members of families over several generations. These studies look for familial occurrence of particular characteristics and may investigate a variety of potentially related traits. For example, families that have members with Tourette's syndrome (characterized by involuntary speech and noise making) also have members who show chronic tics and obsessive or compulsive behavior (Porges, Matthews, & Pauls, 1992).

Clinical Observation

syndrome: a group of symptoms that tend to be found together; from the Greek *syndrome* (combination).

Recognition of a **syndrome,** or associated pattern of symptoms, generally occurs long before an underlying genetic cause is identified, usually in the course of medical or psychological practice. The individual is seen by a clinician as a result of physical or behavioral problems. If a clinician sees or reads about a number of cases in which patients have similar physical or behavioral problems, the clinician may identify and describe a syndrome present in all the patients.

Today, identification of a syndrome may also involve analyzing possible genetic problems. For example, in a case history of a boy who walked late, had little facial expression, and at age 14 showed symptoms of mental retardation, autism, and epilepsy, the authors also reported genetic problems in an area of

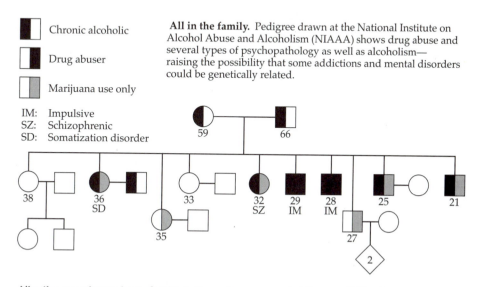

All in the family. Pedigree drawn at the National Institute on Alcohol Abuse and Alcoholism (NIAAA) shows drug abuse and several types of psychopathology as well as alcoholism—raising the possibility that some addictions and mental disorders could be genetically related.

Like the one shown here, family patterns have suggested the possibility that some undesirable behaviors may be genetically related to each other. (Source: National Institute on Alcohol Abuse and Alcoholism)

a chromosome that has been implicated in other genetic syndromes (Bundey, Hardy, Vickers, Kilpatrick, & Corbett, 1994).

Clinical identification of a genetic syndrome must be done with great caution, however. As we will discuss later in this chapter, people with the same genetic problems do not necessarily show exactly the same physical or behavioral characteristics. Early reports of associations between genetic makeup and physical or behavioral traits have often been exaggerated (Einfeld & Hall, 1994). To identify a genetically caused syndrome, researchers need to follow clinical observations with *case-control* research. This approach would take individuals with the cluster of symptoms under study and would match each with a person who did not show the symptoms but who resembled the patient in relevant ways (for example, sex, age, exposure to disease). Presence of a particular genetic makeup in the case group and its absence in the control group would confirm the existence of a genetically caused syndrome (Einfeld & Hall, 1994).

Physical Analysis of Genetic Material

Although the methods described above remain useful approaches to understanding human genetic transmission, work since about 1980 has concentrated on the development of methods for studying the genetic blueprint inside each cell. These more recent techniques allow for highly focused studies of the genetic blueprint, rather than a dragnet approach.

A later section of this chapter will discuss some details of the physical nature of the genetic material. For present purposes, we can simply note that the job of genetic transmission is carried out by deoxyribonucleic acid (DNA), a chemical compound whose pattern of molecules encodes the genetic information within a cell.

enzyme: a biochemical substance that acts as a catalyst and changes the speed of chemical reactions in the body; from the Greek *en-* (in), *zyme* (leaven).

Techniques used for the study of DNA are aimed at removing small segments of DNA and duplicating those segments for easier analysis. The removal of segments is done by means of restriction enzymes—bacterial **enzymes** (biological substances that influence chemical reactions) that cut a chain of DNA segments into smaller pieces. Duplication (cloning) of a segment is done by means of a polymerase chain reaction (PCR), a technique that can create millions of copies in a few hours. These techniques make possible genetic linkage mapping, or the study of the order of segments of genetic material as they exist in a living cell (Roberts, 1992b; van Dyke & Lin-Dyken, 1993). At a less detailed level, it is possible to do a *karyotype,* or photographic analysis of the chromosomes on which the genetic material is found.

The Human Genome Project

genome: the set of genetic materials found in a cell; from the Greek *genos* (birth, kind).

A **genome** is all the genetic information encoded in a complete strand of DNA as it lies coiled inside a cell. Organisms of different species have somewhat different genomes but not as different as you might suppose; the human and the chimpanzee genomes differ by only 1%, and the human and the mouse genomes differ by only 2% (Seabrook, 1994).

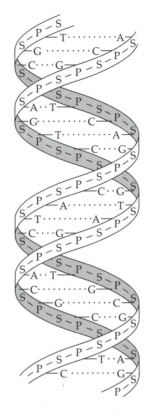

As this figure shows, genetic information is carried in the form of an orderly arrangement of nucleotides that form the spiral double strands of DNA.

The Human Genome Project is an organized effort to map the billions of chemical structures in the human genome. This project, funded by the U.S. government, has been described as "the most expensive and elaborate marriage of public policy and human genes since Nazi Germany" (Seabrook, 1994, p. 109)—a description that reveals the anxiety sometimes felt about the potential use of this kind of knowledge.

The Human Genome Project's initial goal is to map the genome by the year 2005, at a cost of about $3 billion. The progress that has already been made is due in large part to the assignment of specific mapping tasks to specific laboratories and to the use of electronic communication techniques. Without the latter, simple storage and sharing of information would be very difficult. For example, the draft map available on the Internet in 1993 would have used a pile of paper several hundred meters high if it were printed out (Nowak, 1993).

Anthropology, Diversity, and Genetic Research

As researchers have become able to describe human genetic material, questions have arisen about differences between and among specific population groups. Genetic differences between populations are much more complex than might have been guessed, and differences among individuals within a group are often greater than the differences between groups.

A *population* is a group of people whose ancestors have lived in a given area for some time. Members often resemble each other genetically in certain ways and may have some genetic characteristics that are not often found in other populations. Certain genetically caused diseases, for example, are more common among people from a Mediterranean group than among people of Siberian (or other) ancestry.

Although population differences certainly exist, there is no clear-cut genetic basis for the division of human beings into "races." Physical similarities and genetic similarities do not necessarily go together. For example, the Ainu of Japan used to be classified as Caucasian because of their eyelid structure, pale skin, and wavy brown hair, but genetically they have proved to be more like East Asians than like Europeans. Similarly, the Bushmen of southern Africa have flattened faces and yellowish skin characteristic of Asian peoples, but genetically the Bushmen resemble other Africans (Wills, 1994).

homogeneous: of a similar kind; from the Greek *homo* (same), *genos* (kind).

One important difference between population groups can be the amount of genetic variability that exists in each of them. A population can be genetically **homogeneous** (members resemble each other rather closely) or **heterogeneous** (members may show considerable genetic differences). Populations originating in Africa show a high degree of heterogeneity. Native Americans, on the other hand, are so homogeneous that the average two persons genetically resemble each other more closely than do siblings from an Old World population (Black, 1992). This matter of variability is more than just a genetic curiosity; it can influence resistance to disease. Viruses, for example, adapt to the genetic makeup of the infected person, so they are "preadapted" and more serious if passed on to a genetically similar person than to a dissimilar one. (A child who catches measles from a family member has twice the chance of dying from the infection as does a child infected by a stranger.) This appears to be a major reason for the large numbers of Native American deaths from diseases originally introduced by Europeans. As an infection was passed from one to another member of a genetically homogeneous group, the disease became more and more adapted to the population's narrow range of genetic makeups (Black, 1992).

heterogeneous: of dissimilar kinds or components; from the Greek *heteros* (different), *genos* (kind).

The Human Genome Project has made some efforts to include samples from diverse populations. In 1992, the Human Genome Organization (HUGO) asked anthropologists to suggest a sample of populations and chose about 500 out of the approximately 7000 defined populations (Roberts, 1992a.) However, organizations representing **indigenous** peoples soon accused HUGO of racism and of making their potential research subjects feel like experimental animals. Some expressed fears that the project could be used to develop biological weapons against specific populations, whereas others noted that many indig-

indigenous: native to a particular area; from the Latin *in* (in), *gignere* (to beget).

enous peoples consider taking blood, tissue, or fluid samples as desecrating the body (Kahn, 1994).

Unfortunately, genetic and other biomedical research that uses only Caucasian subjects may not benefit other populations. Tissue matching for organ transplants, for example, is less likely to be correct in populations that have not been studied much; indeed, there are lower success rates for organ transplants in African Americans than in European Americans (Kahn, 1994). A recent law, in fact, requires that medical research include diverse subjects unless there is a good scientific reason to do otherwise (Marshall, 1994b).

Cross-Cultural Issues in Genetics Research

Although the greatest proportion of work in genetics involves strictly biological factors, *cultural* factors also need to be considered for a full understanding of human genetic functioning.

As noted in Chapter 2, a cultural group is a group of people with similar practices and attitudes, not a group of genetically similar people. Nonetheless, because people tend to choose spouses from their own group, it is common to be genetically as well as culturally similar to people in your cultural group. Cross-cultural research sometimes runs into *confounded variables*, which make it impossible to tell whether something is caused by cultural forces or is a result of the group's genetic characteristics. And, of course, those variables interact with each other; a person with a particular genetic makeup may be more likely to marry and have children in one culture than in another, and infant care practices in a group may have been specialized to work best with babies who have a particular genetic makeup (cf. Brazelton, 1990).

Cultural differences play a major role in determining how matings and combinations of genes occur. For example, in most states in the United States, laws dating back to the 19th and early 20th centuries forbid the marriage of first cousins. In Asia and Africa, however, from 20% to 50% of marriages are **consanguineous** (involving second cousins or closer relationships). In Muslim groups, an especially popular arrangement is marriage of a boy to his father's brother's daughter. Very few such families seem to show adverse effects due to inbreeding. They have somewhat larger numbers of children but also a somewhat higher mortality rate, so the number of surviving offspring is about the same as in nonconsanguineous unions (Bittles, Mason, Greene, & Rao, 1991).

consanguineous: descended from the same ancestor; from the Latin *com-* (with), *sanguis* (blood).

The Ethics of Genetic Research

The fears expressed about the Human Genome Project are only part of the concerns people have felt about the potential ethical or unethical use of genetic research. One issue is about the increased use of abortion if an embryo does not suit the parents' wishes; in one survey, 11% of respondents said they would abort if a gene for obesity were present (Seabrook, 1994). Other concerns involve the availability of health insurance to people whose genetic makeup suggests an increased likelihood of cancer, and the reluctance of employers to hire those with an unusual genetic potential for health problems. Of the Human Genome Project's budget, 4% goes to study these and similar ethical problems (Seabrook, 1994).

Although legal restrictions vary from country to country, there seems to be consensus about certain ethical issues (Knoppers & Chadwick, 1994). There is agreement on the need for individual *autonomy*—the right to know and the right "not to know" one's genetic potential for serious disease, especially when testing reveals only the probability that disease will develop. Except when newborns are screened for treatable diseases, both informed consent and the availability of counseling should be involved in a person's decision to be tested (Knoppers & Chadwick, 1994).

A special aspect of autonomy comes from the fact that families share genetic characteristics. When one family member is tested, information that applies to other members may also be revealed. Should information garnered from testing one person be communicated to relatives who may also be at high risk for serious problems? If a newborn baby proves to have the genetic potential for serious illness, should his pregnant aunt be informed that her child may also be at risk, if no treatment or cure is available?

Policies and laws that relate to the autonomy issue vary from country to country. In France, for example, research on a hereditary form of blindness has shown that about 30,000 people who are descendants of a single couple in a 15th-century French village are at risk for the disease. Early treatment prevents this form of blindness, but French privacy law forbids the use of the available information to contact families at risk (Dorozynski, 1991).

MECHANISMS OF GENETIC TRANSMISSION

chromosome:
one of a set of threadlike bodies within a cell, on which the genetic material is carried; from the Greek *chroma* (color), *soma* (body)— because of the chromosome's response to the stains used by early researchers.

Although family resemblances were probably noticed as long ago as humans existed, real understanding of the mechanisms of inheritance was only hinted at in the 19th century and wasn't understood until the last half of the 20th. For all Charles Darwin's discussion of evolution, he had no concept of how characteristics could be inherited. Even the careful studies of the monk Gregor Mendel on the inheritance of characteristics of peas did not suggest a mechanism that could make one pea round and another wrinkled, although he assumed there must be a physical cause.

Understanding genetic mechanisms began with an observation made possible by the development of techniques for staining cells and studying them microscopically. In 1888, the biologist W. Waldeyer saw peculiar thread-like structures in the nuclei of cells he was examining. Because the structures were easily colored by the cell stains he was using, Waldeyer called them **chromosomes** (colored bodies). Although deoxyribonucleic acid, which makes up about 50% of the chromosome, was identified in 1944 as the material involved in genetic transmission, much was still unknown about the chromosomes. The number of chromosomes in human cells was not established until 1956, and identification of the chromosomal error associated with Down

---

APPLICATIONS & ARGUMENTS
Do You Want to Know Your Child's Genetic Makeup?

Concerns about genetic testing are often directed toward the decisions of insurance companies. Until legal changes have thoroughly covered this area, there will be some worries about denial of health insurance coverage to people with the genetic potential for health problems.

But what about the individual? What if you knew that you or your child had been identified as having a genetic makeup that would lead to untreatable problems? The information could be devastating, and many people feel that they would *not* want to know because they could not live a normal life with the anxiety hanging over them.

On the other hand, unpleasant as it might be, such knowledge could allow the individual to make appropriate life decisions. Parents who knew that genetic problems would lead to serious difficulties for their child could make an informed decision about having more children. They might decide to live near a city with excellent medical facilities, rather than live out in the country. Career plans could be made around the possibility that flexible schedules would be needed to care for a sick child. Networks and relationships with family and friends could be organized before a time of crisis. It is possible that previous knowledge could lead to more effective functioning instead of the crisis behavior that can compound a tragedy. Although the death of a child is perhaps the worst of all losses, there could be some satisfaction in knowing that the situation had been handled in the way that gave the child the best possible care.

---

syndrome did not occur until 1959 (Wagner, Maguire, & Stallings, 1993). Meanwhile, James Watson and Francis Crick had begun to show in 1953 how DNA in the chromosome was organized into chains of *genes*—the basic mechanisms of inheritance.

Chromosomes

karyotype: an analysis of an individual's chromosomal makeup; from the Greek *karyos* (nut or nucleus), Latin *typus* (image).

Every cell in the body—muscle cells, blood cells, hair cells—contains a specific number of chromosomes that is characteristic of the owner's species. In all the cells except the *gametes* (sperm or ova), the chromosomes normally exist in pairs in which one member of the pair came from the individual's mother and the other from his or her father. In human beings, the number of chromosome pairs in body cells is normally 23. (The gametes, as a result of a process to be described later, have 23 nonpaired chromosomes in humans.)

Examination of the chromosomes involves a process called **karyotyping,** in which photomicrographs of a stained cell show the actual shapes and sizes

autosome: any chromosome other than a sex chromosome; from the Greek *autos* (self), *soma* (body).

of the chromosomes arranged in pairs. Chromosomes in a karyotype are assigned to numbered positions from 1 to 22. These 22 pairs are known as **autosomes** and are associated with characteristics of the individual other than sex. The final pair consists of the sex chromosomes, which not only determine the individual's sex but also influence certain other characteristics. The two sex chromosomes differ in size; the smaller—the Y chromosome—is found only in males, whereas the larger—the X chromosome—is found both in males and in females.

The individual's sex is determined by the pair of sex chromosomes in each body cell. The XY individual, who has one of each type of sex chromosome, normally develops as a male; the XX chromosome pair determines development as a female. Because there are two possible sex outcomes, people often assume that the probability of having a baby boy or girl would each be 50%, but this is not correct. The sex ratio, or number of boys compared to the number of girls, is not 1 to 1; in fact, some estimates of the number of males and females *conceived* have been as high as 180 males to 100 females. By the

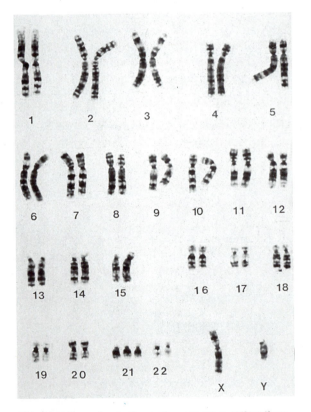

This karyotype shows three chromosomes rather than two on one of the sites (in this case, the site associated with most cases of Down syndrome). This child will probably show some degree of mental retardation and some physical problems.

time of birth, the sex ratio is about 106 to 100, indicating a much higher prenatal death rate for males.

Like the sex chromosomes, the autosomes have specific developmental jobs to do. In both cases, those jobs are determined by the genes carried on each chromosome.

Genes

Each chromosome is made up of a long, coiled chain of DNA. The order of molecules in DNA creates meaning, just as the meaning of the letters and words of this sentence is determined by the sequence in which they appear. The "letters" of the genetic code are four base molecules: adenine, cytosine, guanine, and thymine.

gene: a basic unit of genetic material; from the Greek *genos* (birth, kind).

nucleotide: chemical building block of a gene; from the Latin *nucleus* (kernel), the Greek *-ide* ("child of").

A **gene** is a repeating sequence of combinations of three **nucleotides,** structures made up of a phosphate, a sugar, and either adenine and guanine *or* cytosine and thymine. The information in the gene determines how the cell synthesizes specific proteins out of the 20 amino acids. Each human cell contains about 10,000 different types of proteins, most of which are **enzymes** that alter chemical reactions in the body. The timetable of development requires very specific speeds of chemical reactions at certain times; if these speeds are not correct, the coordination of events is disrupted and the formation of organs is disturbed (Abel, 1989). Thus, the formation of an eye, a

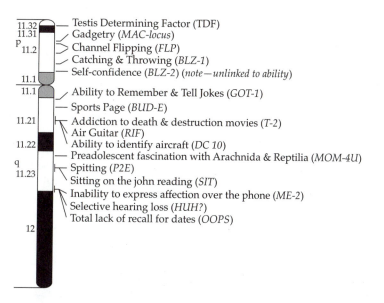

A growing interest in genetic factors in behavior led to this tongue-in-cheek suggestion about genes on the Y chromosome. Male readers should feel free to retaliate with speculation about the X chromosome! (Source: Jane Gitschier)

kidney, or a part of the brain is determined by the speed of chemical reactions, which in turn is determined by the presence of enzymes and the activity of genes that make production of the enzymes possible.

The physical analysis of a chromosome through genetic linkage mapping is an attempt to discover exactly where on each chromosome a gene that has a specific effect is located. Considerable information about the position of genes has already been uncovered. For example, we know that every mammalian Y chromosome carries the testis-determining gene designated as SRY, and that without the presence of this gene, the individual will not develop male gonads (Farr & Goodfellow, 1992).

Simple Genetic Transmission

Understanding that genes determine the production of enzymes gives some insight into genetic transmission, but the mechanism is so complicated that the student cannot use it to predict what will be inherited. Fortunately, there are rules to help us predict some characteristics of the offspring of known parents.

Genetic transmission involves two basic factors and the relationship between them: the **genotype,** or an individual's actual genetic makeup, and the **phenotype,** or physical and behavioral characteristics after development has occurred. The genotype is a matter of the genes themselves, whereas the phenotype consists of *traits,* like eye color or a dog's readiness to cringe. The gene involved in producing a blue eye color is not a "blue-eye gene" because blue eyes are a trait (part of the phenotype), not a characteristic of the gene itself.

genotype: an individual's genetic makeup; from the Greek *genos* (kind), the Latin *typus* (image).

phenotype: an individual's physical and behavioral characteristics; from the Greek *phainein* (to show), the Latin *typus* (image).

The relationship between genotype and phenotype is not the same for all genes and traits. Some genes act directly to determine a trait, as is the case for true blue or true brown eye colors. However, the expression of other genes in the phenotype depends on the environment in which development is taking place. For example, a child of tall parents may grow to be tall if well nourished and protected from injury and disease; but that child might not grow tall if born in a time of war and famine. The *genetic potential* for height is present, but it is only expressed in the phenotype when the environment provides the right conditions. Similarly, even if we could select for genes that would make for high intelligence, chances are that the phenotype would not be affected unless the environment was appropriate for intellectual development.

In a number of cases, however, there is a very direct relationship between genotype and phenotype. In one such case, inheritance follows the so-called dominant-recessive pattern.

To understand the nature of dominant and recessive genes, we need to remember that each gene is part of a chromosome and that chromosomes normally are found in pairs in body cells. A gene usually does not act alone but acts in cooperation with the gene in the same position on the other chromosome. The two cooperating genes are not necessarily identical, and in many cases they differ in a variety of ways. In the *dominant-recessive* pattern, however, there seem to be only two ways in which each of the pair of cooperating genes can function. The two possible genes are called *alleles* —alternative genes.

The pair of dominant-recessive cooperating genes can consist of two of the same allele or of one of each of the alleles. In the first case, the individual is said to be **homozygous** for the gene ("the same"); in the second case, the individual is said to be **heterozygous** ("different"). In the dominant-recessive inheritance pattern, the phenotype is determined by either homozygosity or heterozygosity.

homozygous: receiving the same allele from both parents; from the Greek *homo* (same), *zygoun* (to join together).

heterozygous: receiving different alleles from each parent; from the Greek *heteros* (different), *zygoun* (to join together).

How does an individual become heterozygous or homozygous in the first place? Part of the answer to this question will need to wait for a later discussion of how sperm and ova are produced, but part can be discussed here. Remember that only body cells have pairs of chromosomes. Having the full number of pairs is called the *diploid* condition. The gametes alone are *haploid;* they have only one member of each chromosome pair. When gametes combine at the time of fertilization, the *zygote* (fertilized ovum) is diploid, and the genes carried on its paired chromosomes can be either a homozygous or a heterozygous combination.

Examination of inheritance patterns shows that where a dominant-recessive pattern exists, the presence of one of the alleles in the genotype will completely determine the phenotype. That allele is called the *dominant gene;* whether the individual is heterozygous or homozygous for the dominant gene, the phenotype will be the same. The *recessive gene* is the allele that influences the phenotype only if the person is homozygous for that allele.

A *recessive trait* is a characteristic of the *phenotype* that is apparent only when the person is homozygous for the recessive gene. A *dominant trait* is one that is apparent in the phenotype as long as there is at least one of the dominant genes in the phenotype. A commonly used example is that of phenotypic true blue or true brown eye color; the recessive trait (blue eyes) is possible only in a person with a homozygous recessive genotype, and the dominant trait (brown eyes) is present whether the person is heterozygous or homozygous for the dominant allele.

Because a sperm and an ovum are both haploid, each is carrying only one of the alleles that will help determine a dominant or recessive trait. Which allele is carried depends on the genotype of the parent who produced the gamete. A homozygous parent can contribute only one allele, whereas a heterozygous parent can contribute either, and only chance will determine whether that parent's gamete will carry the dominant or the recessive allele. If both parents are homozygous for the same allele, all their children will also be homozygous and will share the relevant trait (such as eye color). If one parent is homozygous for the dominant gene and the other is homozygous for the recessive gene (in which case one will show the dominant trait and the other the recessive trait), all their children will be heterozygous and all will show the dominant trait (in the case of eye color, brown eyes). Two heterozygous parents will both show the dominant trait, but, through different combinations of sperm and ova, they may produce a child who is heterozygous (a probability of 50%), one who is homozygous for the dominant gene (a probability of 25%), or one who is homozygous for the recessive gene (a probability of 25%). The probability of the dominant trait (brown eyes) in their children is thus 75%.

A point about probabilities in genetics should be made here. Each time a gamete is produced, and each time fertilization occurs, the event is *statistically independent* of every other time. If the chances that a couple will have a brown-eyed child are 75%, the chances will be 75% at every conception whether the parents have had no children before or had 10 of them. There is certainly nothing unlikely about having 10 brown-eyed children even though the probability of brown eyes is only 75% each time; and although having 10 blue-eyed children in this case is less likely, it could well happen.

Except for aesthetic preferences or implications about parentage, eye color is a rather unimportant trait. More important for human health are genetically caused diseases that follow dominant-recessive inheritance patterns, especially those that are recessive traits. A number of genetically caused diseases, such as sickle-cell anemia, occur when an individual is homozygous for a recessive gene. The heterozygous parents show no sign of the disease and may even have some health advantages because of their genotypes; the recessive gene associated with sickle-cell anemia, for example, seems to confer some resistance to malaria. The occurrence, detection, and treatment of such diseases will be discussed later in this chapter.

Sex-linked inheritance is another situation in which the genetic material on one chromosome plays the more important role. In sex-linked inheritance, a gene is carried on one of the sex chromosomes, and its effect on the phenotype depends on whether the individual is male (XY) or female (XX). For example, hemophilia, a disease in which blood does not clot normally, results from a gene carried on the X chromosome. A female who has one X carrying the hemophilia gene is likely to have a normal genotype on the other X, and hemophilia is rarely expressed in the phenotype of a female. A male with the hemophilia gene on his X chromosome, however, has no other X to suppress expression of that gene, and he suffers from hemophilia. In other similar cases where a relevant gene is carried on the X chromosome, such as color blindness or male pattern baldness, the problem is far more likely to show up in the male than in the female phenotype.

Although the dominant-recessive inheritance pattern is important for the purposes of this book, it would be a mistake to suppose that all genetic transmission follows these rules. In fact, much inheritance involves a combination of effects from maternal and paternal genes, so the resulting phenotype (height, for example) is not exactly like that of either parent. It is also very common for genetic transmission to involve *pleiotropy*—the effects of many genes working in combination. One gene often influences many traits, and one trait is often influenced by many genes. Genes do not even have to be at the same loci, or positions, on the chromosome in order to interact. A pair of genes in one position may mask the effects of a pair in another position, an event known as *epistasis*. Although the presence of the SRY gene is essential to

APPLICATIONS & ARGUMENTS
Want a Boy or a Girl?

Occasionally couples really don't care whether a coming baby turns out to be male or female, as long as it's healthy. Certainly some couples do not want to know the sex of the fetus when it is determined prenatally; they don't want to "spoil the surprise."

Many parents-to-be, however, have a conscious sense of preferring one sex of baby over the other. Not only do they want to know the sex of the fetus, but in some parts of the world they may opt to abort the "wrong" sex so they can try again as soon as possible.

Preference for males is so strong the world over that there would probably be twice as many boys as girls if parents could choose. Boys may be wanted as inheritors of property or titles in some legal systems. They may be desired in anticipation of their physical strength, to be used for farming or fishing. The birth of a boy may also be seen as evidence of his father's virility (only a sissy produces gynosperm, it appears).

Girls are preferred sometimes, though. They are often thought of as easier to rear—less likely to fight, be noisy, and get into trouble. They may be wished for as helpers with younger children or as eventual nurses for elderly parents. Parents who are carrying certain sex-linked genetic defects may hope for a girl because, although she may carry the gene, she will not exhibit the defect.

Individual parents may have profound psychological reasons for preferences. A woman who has had traumatic experiences with men may irrationally fear the power of even an infant boy. Fathers have been known to express the idea that "no man will ever be good enough" for their 2-day-old daughter. Although social factors influence our preferences for boys or girls, the reasons for our wishes may go very deep indeed.

development of a male phenotype, the presence of other genes working in cooperation is necessary for normal male physical development to take place (Migeon, 1995). Indeed, the work of genes can be considered a dynamic action system, where an individual's pattern of genes organizes itself to create the set of rules that will determine development of the phenotype.

Recent work actually shows that in some cases inheritance patterns appear to work backward from the standard dominant-recessive model. For example, in a genetically determined pattern of fat accumulation in sheep, homozygous individuals do *not* show the phenotype. It appears only when the animal is heterozygous and received the gene through the father (Pennisi, 1996).

Complex Genetic Transmission and Genetic Change

The rules of the dominant-recessive inheritance pattern described above were known to Mendel in the 19th century. On the basis of these classical Mendelian rules, some assumptions about inheritance were made that have been questioned only recently. The most important assumption was that the genetic material on a chromosome functions in a very predictable way, almost as if it were a sealed package whose source and destination can have no effect on its contents. Under this assumption, it should make no difference whether a chromosome comes from the father or from the mother or how many times the genetic material has been passed along.

Recent work, however, shows that in some cases a gene's functioning is determined by whether it originates in the mother or in the father. In Fragile X syndrome, a cause of mental retardation, a gene on the X chromosome increases in size from generation to generation as it passes through the female, but does not do so in the male. In the Fragile X syndrome, the normal gene carries about 50 copies of a particular trinucleotide. At some point, the gene begins to expand, up to about 200 repeats, but the carrier is still healthy until the number of repeats becomes excessive. Children who inherit the gene and show severe symptoms may have thousands of repeats of the sequence where there should be only 50. Other disorders, such as muscular dystrophy and Huntington's disease, also involve genes that expand by adding extra copies of repeated DNA sequences (Morrell, 1993). When new cases of Huntington's disease occur in a previously unaffected family, the unstable gene apparently has passed through several generations before expanding into a sufficient number of repeats to cause the disease; in this case, the father's body seems to cause the gene's expansion (Morrell, 1993).

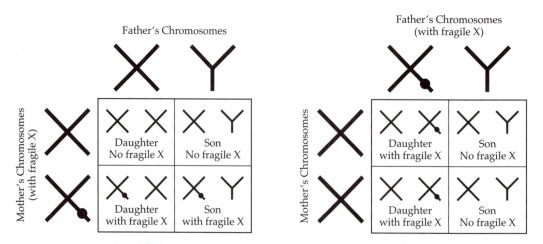

The expression of a gene can be altered in different ways while it is in the body of a parent. In Fragile X syndrome transmission, children who received the X chromosome from the mother will have a less normal gene than the mother had, whereas the X chromosome received from the father will be the same for father and child. (Source: Based on Freund, 1994)

It should also be noted that genes derived from the mother may have specific effects that differ from those of paternal genes. In humans, the maternal genes have a greater effect on the development of the embryo, whereas the paternal genes play a greater role in the development of the placenta and the tissues that surround the embryo (Abel, 1989). In the mouse embryo, the paternal genes have a greater effect on the skeleton, and the maternal genes have a greater effect on the brain (Hoffman, 1991).

An additional complexity of genetic transmission has to do with *mitochondrial DNA*. So far, our discussion of genetic transmission has been confined to the DNA found in the chromosomes and recombined during sexual reproduction. Some additional DNA, however, is found in the **mitochondria** (energy-producing organelles) of the ovum. This mitochondrial DNA (mtDNA) plays a role in inheritance and comes only from the mother. For example, one inherited form of deafness is carried in mtDNA from a female ancestor. Mitochondrially inherited diseases often cause general muscular or neurological symptoms as well as specific tissue problems (Prezant, Shohat, Jaber, Pressman, & Fischel-Ghodsian, 1992).

mitochondria: energy-producing parts of a cell; from the Greek *mitos* (thread), *chondros* (grain).

A final issue in complex genetic transmission involves the possibility of genetic and chromosomal change. Alterations in chromosomes may occur during sperm or ova production (see the section on "Genetic Diseases" for further discussion of this process). A portion of a chromosome may break, or chromosomes lying across each other may exchange segments **(translocation)**. It is also possible for a pair of chromosomes to fail to separate when a sperm or ovum is produced **(nondisjunction);** after fertilization, there may then be three chromosomes or only one where a pair should exist.

translocation: exchange of material between chromosomes; from the Latin *trans-* (across), *locus* (place).

Genetic change may occur through the process of *mutation*, as well. Mutations involve changes in a gene's structure and may be as simple as substituting one of the base molecules—adenine, cytosine, guanine, and thymine—for another, or changing the sequence of two of them. Mutations can be brought about by exposure to ultraviolet radiation, x-radiation, or chemical substances, and they occur in the natural course of events as well as in cases of unusual exposure, such as a nuclear explosion. A change due to mutation sometimes involves a very small alteration in the gene but may lead to major developmental differences. For example, one group of researchers described a family with a mutation in the gene that governs the production of a form of monoamine oxidase (MAO); some males of the family show a syndrome of borderline mental retardation and impulsive aggression, in acts such as arson and attempted rape (Brunner, Nelen, Breakefield, Ropers, & van Oost, 1993).

nondisjunction: failure of a pair of chromosomes to separate during meiosis; from the Latin *non-* (not), *dis-* (apart), *junctus* (joined).

GENETIC DISEASES, DETECTION, AND TREATMENT

Usually, the functioning of genetic transmission proceeds normally and leads to the development of a normal individual; when it does not, the result is often the death of the fertilized egg at such an early stage that the mother doesn't even know she has been pregnant. Sadly, however, genetic errors can lead to birth defects, problems that are already present when the child is born, or diseases that may not become apparent for years or even decades.

The development of a genetic birth defect should not be regarded as a simple matter. As soon as the fertilized egg begins to develop, it is exposed to *environmental* factors, as well as being guided by its genetic blueprint. In addition to the environmental factors, other genetic material the individual carries affects the expression of the genetic error in the phenotype; for example, girls often show less severe cases of genetically caused birth defects than boys do. Genetic information, whether normal or abnormal, functions as part of a dynamic action system. The abnormal genetic material, the rest of the genotype, and the environment interact with each other in ever-changing ways to produce the eventual phenotype.

It may not even be accurate to say that an abnormal genotype *causes* a particular abnormal phenotype. It has been suggested that the typical phenotype associated with Down syndrome, for example, is a result of the organism's reduced ability to resist the types of environmental problems to which all developing organisms are exposed (Shapiro, 1994). This view suggests that the genetic abnormality changes the functioning of the dynamic action system, rather than directly influencing all aspects of development.

One helpful approach to understanding interactions in development is the idea of the *epigenetic landscape,* first suggested by the geneticist Conrad Hall Waddington. This analogy compares development to a ball rolling down an undulating surface. Depending on the trough it is rolling in, the ball will end up at one endpoint or another; in the same way, the organism ends up with one phenotype or another, depending on the genetic "trough" it started in. An event in the environment, however, can make the ball skip to a different trough, so the organism ends with a different phenotype than might have been expected. Various characteristics of the genotype can make it more or less likely that the ball can be made to skip to a new trough; for example, a girl with a particular abnormal genotype is likely to show a less severe effect in the phenotype than a boy.

Thousands of problems associated with genetic errors are known to exist, and many more are being discovered each year. It is far beyond the scope of this book to deal with all of them. The following discussion will be limited to a small number of genetic problems, chosen because of their special significance for development or because of the light they shed on specific developmental mechanisms.

Genetic Diseases

Down syndrome Like many other genetic syndromes, *Down syndrome* is named after the first person to describe it in detail. The Down syndrome phenotype involves a number of characteristic traits, but it is notable that no one physical sign is present in all cases, and individuals who do not have Down syndrome can still have some of the symptoms considered part of the syndrome. In one study, in fact, 28 out of 150 children diagnosed with the

Down syndrome phenotype proved to have normal karyotypes (Shapiro, 1994).

Some traits included in the Down syndrome phenotype are more or less severe mental retardation, congenital heart disease, duodenal atresia (a defect of the digestive tract that prevents normal eating unless it is surgically corrected), short stature (especially shortened thigh bones), and a large tongue. About half of affected individuals have a single transverse crease on the palm of the hand, rather than the complex set of lines normally present on the palm. (This may also be found in genetically normal individuals.)

Like other genetic birth defects, Down syndrome is not correctable; every cell of the individual's body carries the same error. However, treatment can relieve or improve some of the most severe problems. Before antibiotics were invented, the majority of Down syndrome children died before age 12 from respiratory infections, but this is no longer the case. Also, surgical treatment of heart and duodenal problems can be life-saving. Intellectual and speech problems can be improved through excellent home care and therapy, although it would be irresponsible to claim that all Down syndrome children can function at even a relatively high level (in spite of some media representations to the contrary) (Burke, 1989). Treatment of the poor vision characteristic of Down syndrome infants and toddlers can also encourage intellectual, social, and motor development (Courage, Adams, Reyno, & Kwa, 1994).

How does Down syndrome come about? Its more technical name, trisomy-21, tells us that there are three chromosomes where the 21st pair should be. This situation arises as a result of *nondisjunction*, when a gamete (usually the ovum) is being produced. DNA probe analysis has shown that the extra chromosome comes from the ovum rather than the sperm in 94% of cases of Down syndrome (Van Dyke & Lin-Dyken, 1993). In nearly 75% of cases, nondisjunction has already occurred during the beginning of ovum production, while the mother herself is still unborn; the other errors occur in the mother's adulthood, when the ovum is being prepared for release.

The circumstance most closely correlated with Down syndrome is maternal age at the time of conception. Although it is not clear why this should be the case, older mothers are far more likely to conceive Down syndrome infants. The probability of having the syndrome is calculated by looking at the number of women who become pregnant at different ages and noting the number of Down syndrome babies conceived for each age group. When this is done, it is clear that the probability of a Down syndrome conception is much higher (1 out of 45) for a 45-year-old woman than for a 30-year-old (1 out of 3000). Paradoxically, however, *most* Down syndrome babies are born to younger mothers because younger women are much more likely than older women are to become pregnant. A case-control study showed no effect of the father's age on the risk of a Down syndrome conception (de Michelena, Burstein, Lama, & Vasquez, 1993).

Fragile X syndrome   *Fragile X syndrome,* discussed earlier as an example of complex genetic transmission, is associated with effects ranging from normal

IQ and subtle learning disabilities to severe mental retardation and the social and language difficulties called *autism*. Among the physical features sometimes associated with Fragile X are an elongated face and jaw, prominent and large ears, a high arched palate with malocclusion, flat feet, and large testicles (Freund, 1994). (All these features can also occur in the absence of Fragile X, of course.) Males with Fragile X show more serious problems than females do and may have unusual responses to sensory stimuli as well as social and communicative problems; however, 20% of males with the Fragile X karyotype have completely unaffected phenotypes. Fragile X girls are more likely to have IQs in the normal range but are at risk for math and language problems, short-term memory deficit, depression, and social withdrawal.

The gene involved in the Fragile X condition is designated as FMR-1; it is present in all humans and is needed for normal brain development. When the number of repeats goes beyond about 600, however, the functioning of the gene is "turned off," perhaps as a result of a mechanism in which physical arrangements of proteins are altered (see Matthews, 1996).

An interesting issue in the development of the Fragile X phenotype is that some of the traits may result from the environment *after* birth. If the mother has some degree of symptoms as a result of the number of repeats she is carrying, her handling of the child may be poor (Freund, 1994). If she has poor language ability, for instance, the mother will probably not be very effective in fostering her child's communication. The child's father may also be limited in his abilities and feel comfortable with the mother for exactly that reason. Fragile X syndrome may thus be an example of the *dynamic interaction* of genetic and environmental factors.

Phenylketonuria   *Phenylketonuria* (PKU) is a genetically caused disease characterized by a deficiency in an enzyme normally produced in the liver. This enzyme, phenylalanine hydroxylase, is responsible for breaking down phenylalanine, an amino acid found in many foods. When the enzyme is absent, phenylalanine that is ingested is not broken down, so it accumulates in tissue and begins to cause brain damage. The outcome is irreversible brain damage unless phenylalanine is barred from the diet from an early age. After brain maturation has progressed well, phenylalanine may be reintroduced into the diet. However, female PKU patients must again exclude phenylalanine from their diets before and during pregnancy. Even if the unborn baby does not have PKU, the collection of phenylalanine in the mother's tissues can damage the baby's developing nervous system.

PKU occurs when the individual is homozygous for the recessive gene, so both parents must be at least heterozygous for one of their children to have PKU. The frequency of PKU is about 1 in 10,000 for people of European descent but only 1 in 120,000 among the Japanese.

Sickle-cell anemia   Individuals with *sickle-cell anemia* experience problems when their red blood cells, which are normally oval, take on a curved "sickle" shape, which makes it difficult for the cells to move through the blood vessels. The sickle-shaped cells can lodge in small blood vessels, causing painful swelling of joints or even bleeding into the brain. It was long assumed that there was no point in diagnosing the sickle-cell disease early in a baby's life because no treatment was thought possible. More recently, however, it has been shown that babies with sickle-cell anemia are unusually vulnerable to bacterial infections; an overwhelming infection can be the first sign of sickle-cell disease, and it can occur as early as 4 months of age.

A special problem for sickle-cell babies is the fact that their condition may be mistaken for the results of child abuse. An enlarged spleen, a common sickle-cell symptom, could also result from a beating. Painful joints could result from abusive treatment, such as jerking an infant's arm or leg. Parents of sickle-cell babies have been accused of abusing their babies when they sought medical care for sickle-cell-related problems (Kolata, 1987a).

Sickle-cell anemia results from homozygosity for a recessive gene that is most common among non-Europeans, especially those of African descent. About 1 in 400 African Americans has sickle-cell anemia, and about 1500 African American babies are born with it each year (Kolata, 1987a).

Turner's syndrome and Klinefelter's syndrome   Turner's syndrome occurs only in females, and Klinefelter's only in males. Girls with *Turner's syndrome* are short as adults (rarely more than 5 feet tall) and are without sexual development; a web of skin also may be present on the sides of the neck. These girls are described as immature and unassertive. In one study that compared Turner's syndrome girls with chromosomally normal girls who were similar in height and verbal intelligence, the Turner's syndrome girls were shown to have particular trouble interpreting facial expressions and understanding emotional intentions (McCauley, Kay, Ito, & Treder, 1987).

Boys with *Klinefelter's syndrome* tend to be tall, with long arms and legs, and tend to have small, usually sterile, testicles. They sometimes have mental retardation, and they may be emotionally unstable.

Turner's and Klinefelter's syndromes result from nondisjunction of the sex chromosomes at the time a sperm or ovum is being formed. In Turner's syndrome, the girl's karyotype is XO rather than XX. The total number of chromosomes, of course, is 45 rather than 46. Klinefelter's syndrome boys have 47 chromosomes, with XXY where XY should be. Because Turner's syndrome girls are sterile and Klinefelter's syndrome boys are usually sterile, these syndromes are not passed on through generations.

Detection and Treatment of Genetic Diseases

Diagnosis or prediction of a genetically caused disease can occur before conception through genetic screening and counseling, prenatally as a result of tests of the embryo or fetus, or after birth. The present discussion will concentrate on prediction of problems before conception; the other issues will be discussed in Chapters 4 and 5.

Presymptomatic genetic testing, or *screening,* attempts to predict the possibility of later development of genetic problems when none are yet apparent. Before conception, such screening investigates whether the prospective parents are carriers of genetic problems whose gametes (sperm or ova) may combine to produce an individual who is homozygous for the recessive gene. In some cases, specific tests of the parents can reveal whether they are carriers.

Genetic counseling deals with the outcome of screening, but it also investigates a variety of family factors that have the potential for creating birth defects. The mother's age is taken into consideration, as is family history of birth defects, miscarriages, and early, unexplained deaths. Trained genetic counselors have been working with families since the 1970s. Their job is to pull together information and to help the couple in decision making. Genetic counseling does not stress medical issues, but instead focuses on the prospective parents' autonomy and their right to make decisions within their own value framework and with adequate information (Faden, 1991).

One of the problems confronting family counselors is a lack of family information. Birth defects, early deaths, and miscarriages are taboo topics in many families. Many couples who come for genetic counseling find that they do not know how a baby brother or sister died or whether their mothers and aunts had any miscarriages or stillbirths. A family medical record may be useful if genetic counseling is needed. The situation is especially difficult for a prospective parent who has been adopted and has no contact with his or her birth parents.

Prenatal genetic tests for many diseases already exist, and more are predicted for the near future (Faden, 1991). However, a test after conception may not be of much use for a couple opposed to abortion. Therefore, genetic counseling is initially directed at the decision to begin a pregnancy and risk genetic problems.

New reproductive technologies have made it possible to examine the fertilized egg itself. For example, screening for Tay-Sachs disease has been done when the newly fertilized egg has divided into a few cells. (In Tay-Sachs disease, the stakes are particularly high, for affected children are usually blind and paralyzed by age 2 and die by age 5.) This process involves in vitro fertilization, in which sperm and ovum are combined outside the parents' bodies. After a few cell divisions, one cell is removed (at this point, the removal does not affect development) and analyzed for Tay-Sachs. If the fertilized egg is healthy, it is then implanted in the mother's body and left to develop normally ("First pre-pregnancy screened," 1994).

What about *treatment* of genetic diseases? Does screening simply mean a choice to avoid pregnancy, or a choice about implanting a fertilized egg? A number of potential treatments for genetic problems have been envisaged (Wivel & Walters, 1993). For example, *somatic cell gene therapy* would involve inserting genes into cancer cells to provoke an immune response. Another possibility would be the transfer of properly functioning genes into gametes in order to prevent the development of problems after fertilization—so-called germ-line modification. Germ-line modification could occur either before or soon after fertilization. Most work has been done on the post-fertilization stage; **transgenic** mice are produced by introducing foreign genes into the fertilized egg, which is then replaced in the oviduct. Genes can be introduced

transgenic:
resulting from an exchange of genetic material between species; from the Latin *trans-* (across), *genesis* (birth).

Family Health History

Name

Date of Birth   Blood and Rh Type

Occupation

Please note any serious or chronic diseases you have experienced, with special attention to the following:

- [ ] Alcoholism
- [x] Allergies
- [x] Arthritis
- [ ] Asthma
- [ ] Blood diseases (hemophilia, sickle cell anemia, thalassemia)
- [ ] Cancer (i.e., breast, bowel, colon, ovarian, skin and stomach)
- [ ] Cystic Fibrosis

- [x] Diabetes
- [x] Epilepsy
- [ ] Familial high blood cholesterol levels
- [ ] Hearing defects
- [ ] Heart defects
- [ ] Huntington disease
- [ ] Hypertension (high blood pressure)
- [ ] Learning disabilities (dyslexia, attention deficit disorder, autism)

- [ ] Liver disease (particularly hepatitis)
- [ ] Lupus
- [ ] Mental illness (manic-depressive disorders; schizophrenia)
- [ ] Mental retardation (Down syndrome, fragile X, etc.)
- [ ] Migraine headaches
- [ ] Miscarriages or neonatal deaths

- [ ] Multiple Sclerosis
- [ ] Muscular Dystrophy
- [ ] Myasthenia Gravis
- [ ] Obesity
- [ ] Phenylketonuria (PKU)
- [ ] Recurrent or severe infections
- [ ] Respiratory disease (emphysema, bacterial pneumonia)
- [ ] Rh disease
- [ ] Skin disorders (particularly psoriasis)
- [ ] Thyroid disorders

- [ ] Tay-Sachs disease
- [ ] Tuberculosis
- [ ] Visual disorders (dyslexia, glaucoma, retinitis pigmentosa)

Other:

Please note names of your relatives below, along with indications of any illnesses, such as those above, which affected them. Also make note of lifestyle habits such as smoking.

Father

Mother

Brothers and sisters

Children of brothers and sisters

If deceased, age and cause

March of Dimes
Preventing Birth Defects

About the March of Dimes
The mission of the March of Dimes Birth Defects Foundation is to improve the health of babies by preventing birth defects and infant mortality. The March of Dimes carries out its mission through the Campaign for Healthier Babies, which includes programs of research, community service, education and advocacy.

March of Dimes Birth Defects Foundation
National Office
1275 Mamaroneck Avenue
White Plains New York 10605

To order additional copies:
Call: 1-800-367-6630
FAX: 717-825-1987
Or write:

March of Dimes Birth Defects Foundation
P.O. Box 1657
Wilkes-Barre, PA 18703

Check, VISA or MasterCard, Purchase Order accepted.

© March of Dimes Birth Defects Foundation, 1994   09-022-00   Join Our Campaign for Healthier Babies

This family health history form, developed by the March of Dimes, helps genetic counselors guide couples in their decisions.

by attaching them to *viruses* that enter the egg or by micro-injection—physical insertion.

Germ-line modification might be suitable when both parents are homozygous for a recessive disorder, such as sickle cell anemia or cystic fibrosis. This is an increasingly likely possibility, as new treatments prolong the lives of these disease sufferers and make them healthy enough to reproduce (Wivel & Walters, 1993). Although heterozygous parents would have only a 25% chance of conceiving an affected child, they too might prefer germ-line modification to selective abortion or to the risk of having a child with a serious illness, with its high economic and emotional costs and its potential impact on care of already-born children.

PASSING ON THE GENES: GAMETES AND FERTILIZATION

Our discussion of inheritance has concentrated up to now on the individual's chromosomal and genetic makeup. Except for noting that the gametes are haploid and somatic cells diploid, we have said little about the nature of sexual reproduction and the recombination of chromosomes that result.

Chromosomes obviously do not get together in new combinations by themselves. Their recombination depends on appropriate anatomy and function of the prospective parents' reproductive organs, appropriate hormone secretion, and, of course, suitable sexual behavior. If there is a problem in any one of these areas, reproduction may depend on new reproductive technologies that compensate for natural deficits.

gonad: an organ that produces gametes; from the Greek *gonos* (procreation, seed).

hormone: a chemical messenger that carries signals within the body; from the Greek *horme* (impulse).

hypothalamus: a part of the brain associated with the endocrine as well as the nervous system; from the Greek *hypo-* (under), thalamus (another part of the brain).

pituitary: the "master gland" of the endocrine system; from the Latin *pituita* (phlegm; it was once thought to be made by the pituitary!)

The **gonads**—the ovaries in the female and the testes in the male—have the job of producing gametes and secreting some of the reproductive **hormones.** The other structures in the reproductive tracts transfer gametes from the gonads and make it possible for ovum and sperm to meet and join at fertilization.

The individual's hormonal makeup is essential for the events of reproduction. Production of hormones in both sexes follows patterns of periodicity, in which larger amounts of certain hormones are produced at one point in the cycle than at others. This pattern is most strikingly obvious in the female's menstrual cycle, which is based on periodic alterations in hormone levels.

The menstrual cycle depends on changes in the hypothalamus, the pituitary, and the gonads—the so-called hypothalamic-pituitary-gonadic axis—which have a profound effect on body and behavior. The **hypothalamus** is responsible for production of luteinizing hormone–releasing hormone (LH-RH), which in turn acts on the **pituitary** and brings about production of luteinizing hormone (LH) and follicle-stimulating hormone (FSH), both of which affect the ovaries and the testes. Under the influence of LH and FSH, the gonads act as **endocrine glands:** The ovaries produce estrogen and progesterone, which circulate in the blood, and the testes produce testosterone. The functioning of these hormones is coordinated by melatonin, a hormone produced by the pineal gland, which is stimulated by darkness and inhibited by light. This responsiveness to light and dark helps establish well-timed cycles of reproductive functioning (Tamarkin, Baird, & Almeida,

endocrine:
referring to glands that secrete hormones to be circulated in the blood; from the Greek *en-* (in), *krinein* (to separate).

1985). Exercise levels also influence the production of LH and progesterone. The effects of exercise and training may be related to fat levels, for a certain minimum level of fat is necessary to maintain adequate estrogen levels. Use of alcohol can also influence hormone production; in experimental work with rhesus monkeys, habitual use of alcohol has been shown to lower LH levels (Mello, Bree, Mendelson, & Ellingboe, 1983).

Levels of reproductive hormones may be affected by the environment in more direct ways, too. Many synthetic substances now found in the environment are chemically related to estrogens and can bind to those cells affected by natural estrogens; DDT and dioxins are examples. It is possible that high environmental levels of estrogenlike substances are responsible for a change in average sperm count (the number of sperm present in an ejaculation) from 113 million/milliliter of ejaculate in 1940 to 66 million in 1990 (Stone, 1994b). Although it may be that this reduction is only apparent and has to do with an unusually high sperm count in the 1940 sample, there is certainly evidence that exposure to two or more weak environmental estrogens can have a much stronger effect than would be expected from the level of estrogen alone (Kaiser, 1996). This sort of interaction effect makes it quite difficult to ascertain the impact of substances in the environment.

Estrogen and progesterone levels change during the menstrual cycle. Low levels of both are present following day 1 (which arbitrarily designates the first day of menstruation). Estrogen levels rise and an ovarian follicle ripens until, at about day 14, the mature follicle bursts open and ovulation (the release of the ovum) occurs. The unhealed scar, where the ovum broke away from the ovary, is called the corpus luteum, and it produces the hormone progesterone. The level of progesterone rises after ovulation and then drops just before menstruation begins. The luteal phase, when the corpus luteum is present, is fairly constant at a length of 14 days; when the menstrual cycle is longer or shorter in length than 28 days, changes in the length of the preovulatory phase are responsible.

The effects of the reproductive hormones are far-ranging. Basal body temperature gives an indication of the levels of estrogen and progesterone in a woman's body. When the level of estrogen is high, basal body temperature is low; when the level of progesterone is high, basal body temperature is high. Because estrogen levels are high just before ovulation and progesterone levels are high between ovulation and the next menstrual period, body temperature can thus give some indication of whether ovulation has occurred. If the basal body temperature rises and remains high for several days, ovulation has occurred and will not happen again in that cycle. Intercourse between that time and the next menstrual period will thus not lead to conception.

It is important to realize, however, that what temperature level is considered high or low varies from individual to individual. A single temperature reading is meaningless unless it is compared to a series of readings taken from the same woman over several menstrual cycles. In addition, low temperatures cannot show how far away ovulation is; because they show only that it has not yet occurred, they do not indicate a "safe period" for intercourse. The only time a woman is infertile is after several days of high temperatures.

Gametogenesis

gametogenesis: the production of sperm or ova; from the Greek *gamein* (to marry), the Latin *genesis* (birth).

The production of the gamete itself (**gametogenesis**) requires special discussion because of its relationship with chromosomal reassortment. *Oögenesis*, the production of the ovum, has a somewhat different schedule than does *spermatogenesis*, the production of the sperm. The first steps in oögenesis occur before the potential mother has herself been born; in fact, each newborn girl baby already has in place in her ovaries all the ova she will ever produce. One of those ova will ripen and be released approximately once a month throughout her reproductive years, unless she is already pregnant or using contraceptive hormones that inhibit ovulation. Sperm production, on the other hand, takes only about 70 days and produces millions of sperm at a time.

The events of spermatogenesis occur from puberty, at roughly age 14 to 15 years, into old age; ovulation begins at about age 13 years on average and continues until *menopause*, generally between ages 45 and 55 among healthy women. As noted earlier, the events of oögenesis become less reliable with age, and after age 35 the chances increase that nondisjunction of chromosomes will lead to a Down syndrome conception.

mitosis: cell division resulting in new diploid cells; from the Greek *mitos* (thread).

meiosis: cell division resulting in haploid cells; from the Greek *meiosis* (diminution).

To understand spermatogenesis and oögenesis, it is necessary first to understand that cell division (the production of a new cell) takes two forms. The first form, **mitosis,** occurs in the production of all new cells except gametes. It begins with a diploid cell (in the case of humans, a cell containing 23 chromosome pairs) and, through replication of chromosomes, ends with two diploid cells. Gametes are formed through a different cell division process; **meiosis** or *reduction division,* begins with a diploid cell and ends with one or more haploid gametes.

In both males and females, meiosis begins with a diploid cell in a gonad. The female cell has 22 pairs of autosomes and two X chromosomes; the male cell has 22 pairs of autosomes and one X and one Y chromosome. The first division of the female cell (which occurs before the baby girl is born) doubles the number of chromosomes but puts half of them into a cell called the *first polar body,* which will not produce an ovum. The second division, which will not occur until after puberty, yields an ovum and another polar body, each of which is haploid and each of which carries an X chromosome. Only an error like nondisjunction will create an ovum that has more or fewer than one member of each chromosome pair.

In spermatogenesis, meiosis in a diploid cell leads to the production of two haploid sperm. Because the diploid cell had one X and one Y chromosome, the result will be one X-bearing sperm (*gynosperm*) and one Y-bearing sperm (*androsperm*). When a gynosperm fertilizes an ovum that has the normal single X, the resulting XX individual will develop with a female phenotype. When an androsperm fertilizes a normal ovum, the resulting XY individual will develop with a male phenotype.

Meiosis in either gamete depends on the appropriate pairing of chromosome "partners." Errors in pairing can lead to nondisjunction and inappropriate numbers of chromosomes in cells that should be haploid. The alignment of chromosomes may be regulated by heterochromatin ("junk" DNA), which is

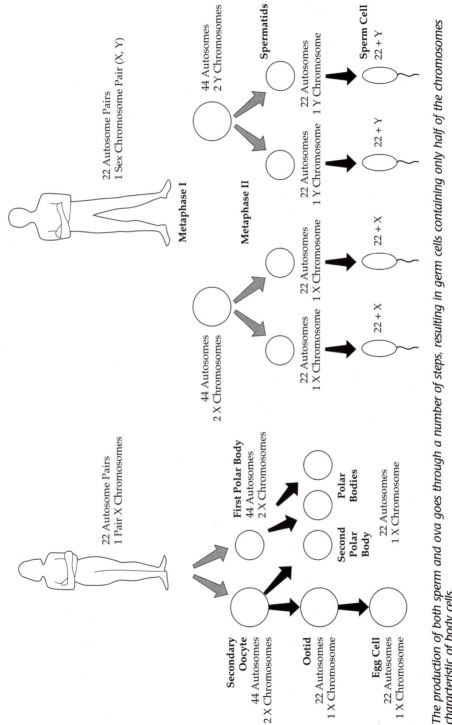

The production of both sperm and ova goes through a number of steps, resulting in germ cells containing only half of the chromosomes characteristic of body cells.

not organized into gene sequences and which is found at the chromosomes' centers and ends. These DNA sequences may align the chromosomes by pairing up, either directly or through indirect protein binding (Karpen, Le, & Le, 1996; Marx, 1996a).

When both sperm and ovum carry a normal chromosomal and genetic makeup, there is a good chance that normal development of the new individual will begin and proceed. However, 60% of very early pregnancies may be lost, and at least a third of embryos after implantation are obviously abnormal (Winston & Handyside, 1993). It is possible for a genetically normal sperm to carry into the ovum some other sources of developmental problems. For example, in laboratory studies, it appears that *cocaine* can bind to sperm in such a way that it is carried into the ovum, with a resulting potential ill effect on the development of the fertilized egg (Yazigi, Odem, & Polakoski, 1991).

Fertilization

For *fertilization* of the ovum by a sperm to occur, the two must get together in the right place at the right time. The right place is the Fallopian tube, into which the ovum is moved as it is released from the ovary. The sperm, deposited in the vagina during intercourse, must swim into the cervix and through several inches of uterus and Fallopian tube in order to encounter the ovum, which one of the sperm will fertilize. The actual entrance of the sperm into the ovum requires that the sperm pass the zona pellucida, a thin coating around the ovum. The acrosomal membrane on the head of the sperm contains a series of enzymes that apparently make a hole in the zona pellucida and allow a single sperm to pass through (Service, 1994b).

The right *time* for fertilization depends on ovulation. If intercourse occurs too long before ovulation—more than about 3 days—the sperm will have died before the ovum is released. If intercourse occurs more than about 12 hours *after* ovulation, the dying ovum is past the point where it can be fertilized. It is possible that the ovum releases some chemical signal that attracts the sperm up the Fallopian tube. In some mammals, sperm accumulate in the female reproductive tract and remain motionless for hours and move again only when ovulation occurs. Their movement may be influenced by a substance in the fluid from the ovarian *follicle* that released the egg (Roberts, 1991a).

Timing may also be related to the sex of the child conceived. The androsperm, which will produce boys, are slightly lighter than the gynosperm because the Y chromosome is smaller than the X. Androsperm are thought to swim faster than gynosperm, so that if intercourse occurs soon after ovulation, an androsperm may arrive at the egg before a gynosperm does. If intercourse is a couple of days before ovulation, however, the gynosperm will have had time to catch up and the androsperm may have started to die, so it is possible that the conception of a girl may be somewhat more likely.

Contraception and Fertility: New Technologies

fertility: the probability of reproduction; from the Latin *ferre* (to carry or bear).

Control over fertilization and birth have always been major concerns of human societies. In some times and places, the wish is for greater **fertility;** in others, the freedom to have sexual relations without conceiving a child is greatly desired.

Development of new contraceptive technologies depends on biological, social, and economic factors. Many couples wish to prevent conception at some points in their lives, but social and religious attitudes may limit their options for doing so. New contraceptive technologies must take social and religious attitudes into consideration, or the chances that they will be used are small. The cost of development must also be moderate compared to possible sales, or pharmaceutical companies will not be willing to put time and money into new contraceptive approaches. Contraceptive development has in fact been very slow over the last few decades (Service, 1994b). Manipulating hormones, such as testosterone, that are involved in sperm production is a possible route to blocking conception, but drug companies have avoided doing so because of the fear that they may be open to lawsuits if men experience impotence (failure to sustain an erection) and blame the hormone treatment.

One new approach to contraception involves immunizing women so that they produce an antibody that works against a hormone needed for implantation of the fertilized egg in the uterus (Aldhous, 1994). Four-fifths of the women in one study responded appropriately to the vaccine, and few of them became pregnant.

Although throughout history infertile couples the world over have longed to conceive, their problems are less frequent than the everyday need most couples today have to limit fertility. Few couples require the new reproductive technologies, and few of those have access to such reproductive help.

The technology of in vitro fertilization had its first success on July 25, 1978, with the birth of "Baby Girl Brown." *In vitro* ("in glass," as opposed to *in vivo*, "in the living") *fertilization* involves hormonal stimulation of the growth of an ovarian follicle, surgical puncture of the ovary and capture of the ovum, collection of the father's sperm, fertilization of the ovum outside the mother's body, and placement of the fertilized egg into the uterus (Thatcher & DeCherney, 1991). These events require precise control and timing if they are to result in a pregnancy. For example, the fertilized egg needs to be placed in the uterus 44 to 48 hours after it is removed from the ovarian follicle.

Although in vitro fertilization (IVF) offers real hope to infertile couples, it is expensive, time-consuming, and not invariably effective. The timing of IVF may produce chromosomal problems. Because several ova are usually fertilized and inserted into the uterus, multiple pregnancies, with their increased infant mortality rates, are not uncommon. The chances that IVF will lead to a pregnancy in a given cycle are only about 14% in the United States (Winston

& Handyside, 1993); and, as is the case with a natural conception, there is no guarantee that a pregnancy will result in a healthy, full-term baby.

The treatment cycle involved in IVF has been described as an "emotional roller coaster" (Adler, Keyes, & Robertson, 1991), with particular stress in the two weeks between the transfer of the fertilized egg and the confirmation of the pregnancy. Many IVF patients enter treatment already feeling distressed after years of infertility; they may unrealistically exaggerate the probability of a successful pregnancy, especially because the media tend to publicize successful IVF treatments rather than the many unsuccessful cases. When the treatment is not and cannot be successful, the couple's adjustment to the reality of infertility may be delayed by this last hope (Adler, Keyes, & Robertson, 1991). At this point in its development, IVF is certainly not suitable for every infertile couple.

PROBLEMS TO CONSIDER AND DISCUSS

1. Do you believe that there are more advantages or more disadvantages to further research on human genetics? Explain your answer.

2. What are the pros and cons of diagnosing a genetic problem when no treatment for it exists?

3. Describe the possible genotypes of the parents of a baby with sickle cell anemia.

4. Do you think that health insurance should pay for infertility treatment? Why or why not?

5. What factors determine whether gametes are healthy at the time of fertilization?

4

Prenatal Development

Sperm and ova have to pass through many dangers before fertilization takes place, but the newly created zygote is only at the beginning of a more perilous journey. It may already be carrying genetic defects that will soon halt its development, or it may not manage the trip down the fallopian tube to the uterus. Should the zygote reach and implant in the uterus, it will enter a stage where its development can easily be disrupted if the mother is exposed to—or exposes herself to—toxic substances.

The story of human prenatal development has several parts: the events in the growth of the new individual; the experience of the mother whose body nurtures the new organism; and the views of medical helpers, genetic counselors, and the father of the baby—people who can sometimes offer help and can sometimes only stand by and watch events unfold.

Prenatal development is a unique part of growth because it is the focus of deeply felt values and value conflicts. The rights of the mother, the rights of the developing individual, and the rights of society as a whole at times come into conflict during prenatal development. Can society prevent a mother from engaging in activities that might harm her embryo or fetus—especially if those activities are legal? Could a society demand that a pregnancy be terminated, if the costs of caring for a defective offspring would be very high? Is it not only legally but morally acceptable for a woman to abort a pregnancy simply because she prefers not to have a child? What if she knows the child will be severely handicapped? Does the stage in the pregnancy, or the circumstances of conception, make any difference here?

The present chapter will discuss the facts of prenatal development, but everyone will approach this material with values already firmly in place. We may not all agree on some of the issues, but we should all be able to tell the difference between value and fact.

RESEARCH METHODS

The wide variety of topics included in prenatal development means that an unusually wide range of research methods are related to this issue. Prenatal development includes normal development of the **embryo** and **fetus** and of specific organ systems; it includes nutrition and care of the pregnant woman;

embryo: the developing infant between implantation and day 56 of gestation; from the Greek *embryein* (to swell).

fetus: the developing infant between the end of the embryonic period and birth; from the Latin *fetus* (newly delivered).

sonography: the use of ultrasound to produce images of the unborn baby; from the Latin *sonus* (sound), the Greek *graphein* (to write).

congenital: occurring during prenatal development; from the Latin *com-* (with), *genesis* (birth).

it includes nongenetic birth defects. As of this writing, it also includes research on embryonic and fetal tissue and its possible application to treatment of disease. Each of these topics has its own set of methods and its own ethical issues.

The Study of Normal Development

To understand the normal prenatal development of the human being, it is necessary to have records of the developmental status of unborn babies at different times after conception. Historically, these records have been compiled by examining many embryos and fetuses of different ages, either after their deaths from induced or spontaneous abortion or after the death of the mother. Because it is not always possible to know when human conception took place, this approach was supplemented by comparative research, in which embryos and fetuses of other species were removed and examined at known times after they were conceived. A recent contribution to comparative work has been the study of the zebrafish larva, which is so transparent that changes in internal structures can be seen in the living organism (Nüsslein-Volhard, 1994).

A number of new techniques have made it possible to measure prenatal development with greater accuracy. Through **sonography** (ultrasound examination), we can measure the baby's length and head size and estimate its weight. Although we cannot measure events at the cellular level through sonography, new techniques in *magnetic resonance imaging* (MRI) allow us to do so. Use of the MRI with frog embryos shows the actual movement of groups of cells relative to each other in the living embryo. The process does not harm the embryo and can go on over a period of days (Jacobs & Fraser, 1994). It is even possible to use MRI to study mouse embryos within the uterus (Travis, 1994).

Problems in Prenatal Development

Not all embryos that are normal to begin with will continue to show normal development. Events during pregnancy may alter the course of development, leading to **congenital anomalies,** or birth defects. The investigation of causes of birth defects is complex, both conceptually and practically.

A study of the effect of maternal drug use on development, for example, would generally begin with case reports describing defective development and its possible causes in the cases under consideration. The next step would probably be a quasi-experimental approach, comparing drug-exposed babies and babies of nonusers. Such quasi-experiments are difficult to carry out, and they may be adversely affected by poor matching of groups and difficulty with confounding variables, like the families' socioeconomic status. There also may be no reliable way of identifying drug users and nonusers (Lester & Tronick, 1994). Drug users often use more than one drug and are commonly exposed to stress, poverty, and violence as well, so it becomes very difficult to know whether a particular drug event was the cause of a particular birth defect. In addition to all these problems, knowledge of the timing of drug use or other problems is essential, but it rarely can be accurately determined (Cohen & Roessmann, 1994).

One final difficulty in quasi-experimental studies of the causes of birth defects is that cultural factors may influence outcomes. For example, in a study of Jamaican babies whose mothers smoked marijuana during their pregnancies, the more heavily exposed babies did *better* as newborns than did those who had had less exposure (Dreher, Nugent, & Hudgkins, 1994). The Jamaican women who smoked a great deal of marijuana did so as part of a religious ritual, and they tended to be well-fed, stable, and competent people—all characteristics that make for better early development, and that are absent in most drug-using women in the United States.

It would be ethically out of the question to conduct *experiments* to study the effects of drugs or disease on human development. However, some research questions must focus on causes and effects of birth defects. For example, before a new medication is sold, its effect on the unborn baby needs to be known. Experimental investigations of this nature may be done on other species, such as mice, pigs, or chimpanzees (the last being genetically closest to human beings). Unfortunately, the effect of a medication on development may well be different for different species, as with the drug thalidomide (Taussig, 1968).

New Applications of Prenatal Research

Unlike most other research on early development, work on some aspects of prenatal life has potential applications for older human beings. Cells and tissues have unusual characteristics in the prenatal period. A wound to a fetus in the womb heals without a scar, for example. It is possible that cells from embryos, transplanted into older bodies, could treat diabetes, some forms of blindness, Alzheimer's disease, broken bones, and many other problems. However, there are ethical and religious objections to using actual cells from embryos in these applications. Fortunately, enough has been learned about some functions of embryonic cells to create synthetic forms of some substances made by cells (Nowak, 1994a).

Ethics of Research on Prenatal Development

Case reports and quasi-experimental or correlational studies of prenatal development involve no unusual ethical issues, although informed consent of the pregnant woman may be needed. Some research, in addition, has had to deal with a little-applied federal regulation dating from the 1970s requiring that the father as well as the mother give written permission for participation in any federally funded research. For example, in a study of drug treatment of the AIDS virus in pregnant women that aimed at preventing infection of the fetus, researchers ran into difficulty trying to locate the fathers and persuading them to give their written permission (Kolata, 1991).

Research on embryonic cells or fetal tissues has been the subject of many ethical questions. Fetal tissue research was banned for 13 years in the

United States, until the ban was lifted in January of 1993 (Anderson, 1993a), and there has continued to be disagreement about the ethicality of other specific types of research. It is probable that heated discussion of ethical concerns will continue as long as new technologies are developed.

In 1994, the Director of the National Institutes of Health convened a Human Embryo Research Panel to set guidelines for researchers. As of this writing, the panel had approved research in the following categories (Marshall, 1994c):

1. using existing embryos that were created in connection with in vitro fertilization but were not used
2. using a limited number of embryos fertilized specifically for research purposes, but only for gathering baseline information and only for "compelling" reasons
3. extracting cells from in vitro fertilized embryos before they are implanted (this does not lead to defective development if it is done early enough)
4. growing new cells from unused existing embryos
5. maturing unfertilized eggs for research (this involves an artificial stimulus that starts development; the ovum does not live long)

At present, work on embryos is to proceed only to the 14th day of development, but there is discussion of extending this period for several more days so that the important process of neural tube closure (discussed later in this chapter) can be studied. Unacceptable research work would include transferring human embryos to animals for gestation, implanting research embryos in humans, continuing research on embryos past the 18th day, or purchasing sperm, eggs, or embryos from donors.

NORMAL PRENATAL DEVELOPMENT: THE EMBRYO

The natural history of prenatal development of human beings has filled many books and will only be summarized here. In examining some of its complexities, however, we will gain better understanding if we recall the concept of the *dynamic action system*. The developing organism is guided by its genetic makeup, but at the same time it is either supported or interfered with by the environment. The relative importance of these two major factors changes from one time to the next, while simultaneous changes go on in the most influential environmental factors. These dynamic processes of change—their timing, patterns, and rates of speed—are as much a part of the equation as are the genes and the environment themselves (cf. Oyama, 1987).

Cleavage, Implantation, and Later Development

At the end of Chapter 3, we left the newly developing organism as a fertilized ovum. Now we need to look at the events that will make possible the growth and birth of living infants.

We have discussed the fertilization of one ovum by one sperm. How do multiple births come about? There are two possibilities: Two eggs may have been released and fertilized, producing genetically dissimilar *dizygotic* twins, or one fertilized egg may have split into two, producing *monozygotic* twins. When more than two babies are produced, there usually are more than two ova, but there may be one that divided after fertilization as well as one that did not. Congenital malformations are twice as common in twins as in singletons (babies who develop singly) (Greenhill & Friedman, 1974). Multiple births are considered to be an abnormal reproductive process.

Twin or singleton, the steps in development are the same. The fertilized egg, or zygote, begins the process of **cleavage** (cell division), which increases the number of cells present. Even as this process begins, so does cell organization. The internal organization of the ovum determines what the organization of the later embryo will be like (Cooley & Therkauf, 1994). The head-tail organization may depend on the presence of one protein from the mother at one end of the cell and another at the opposite end (Touchette, 1994). Concentration gradients of proteins—more at one part of the cell than at another—may "turn on" different genes in different parts of the embryo; the "turned on" genes can produce new proteins that activate other genes, which helps determine which part of the structure any new cell will become (Barinaga, 1994). One gene that helps establish the right-left and **anterior-posterior** pattern of the embryo's development has the surprising and once trendy name "sonic hedgehog" (Roush, 1995). Derivatives of vitamin A may also play a role here (Hoffman, 1991).

By day 4 after conception, the dividing ovum has reached the morula stage (from the Latin word for mulberry) and consists of 12 to 16 cells called **blastomeres.** Fluid inside the uterus now moves into the morula and separates the cells into an outer layer (the **trophoblast,** which becomes the placenta) and an inner cell mass (the embryoblast). As a fluid-filled central cavity is formed, the developing organism becomes known as a **blastocyst.**

By this point, the blastocyst should have moved along the fallopian tube and into the uterus, where the process of implantation begins. The blastocyst erodes the lining of the uterus, and by 9 to 12 days, the blastocyst is implanted or embedded in the thick wall of **endometrium,** which is present in the uterus during pregnancy. If it has not moved rapidly enough through the fallopian tube, however, the blastocyst may implant in the tube itself, creating an ectopic (outside the uterus) pregnancy, which must be ended surgically because it will lead to the rupture of the tube and the mother's death from internal bleeding.

Once implantation has occurred, the new organism is an embryo and the process of differentiation begins. Cell division now produces not only more cells but more new types of cells. By 14 days after conception, the embryo consists of two layers of cells, the *ectoderm* (outer skin) cells, which will become the skin and nervous system, and the *endoderm* (inner skin) cells, which will become internal structures like the intestines.

In the third week, a new cell layer, the *mesoderm* (middle skin) arises; this layer will give rise to bone and muscle. The mesoderm develops during the

cleavage: the division of the fertilized ovum; from the Old English *cleofan* (to split).

anterior: toward the front or head end of the body. From the Latin *ante* (before).

posterior: toward the rear of the body; from the Latin *post* (after).

blastomere: one of the cells produced during cleavage; from the Greek *blastos* (bud), *meros* (part).

trophoblast: the outer cell layer of the cleaving ovum, which becomes the placenta; from the Greek *trophe* (nourishment), *blastos* (bud).

blastocyst: the cleaving ovum after it has developed a fluid-filled central cavity; from the Greek *blastos* (bud), *kystis* (bladder).

endometrium: the lining of the uterus into which the blastocyst penetrates; from the Greek *en-* (in), *meter* (mother).

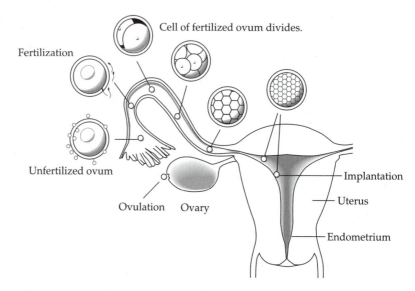

The fertilized ovum must travel down the fallopian tube before it can implant in the uterus. (Source: Zigler & Finn Stevenson, 1993)

gastrulation: the folding inward of the previously ball-shaped embryo; from the Greek *gastero-* (belly).

process of **gastrulation,** in which the ball-shaped embryo folds inward. The cells that move into the newly created cavity become mesoderm. The embryo becomes longer and less ball-like as cells move into a new orientation, squeeze between each other, and push each other apart (Barinaga, 1994).

Although cell differentiation and cell movement are important to the embryo's development, another mechanism shapes the organism. *Programmed cell death,* which we will discuss again in relation to the nervous system, allows the emergence of features such as fingers and toes; the death of certain cells creates the spaces between the digits (Barinaga, 1994). Programmed cell death may also play a part in kidney development (Raff et al., 1993).

organogenesis: the differentiation of cells that will develop into specific organs; from the Greek *organan* (tool), the Latin *genesis* (birth).

The embryonic period—from implantation to day 56 after conception—is a time of **organogenesis.** As cells differentiate, the foundations of tissues for all the organs are laid down in a predictable sequence. Events in this period can be thought of as a series of stages; the tissues developing at any point are qualitatively different from those at other points and the events occur in an orderly series. The timing of the development of specific tissues is genetically determined and follows a schedule characteristic of the species. However, characteristics present at any given stage are not necessarily obviously human; at one stage, for example, a tail is temporarily present.

NORMAL PRENATAL DEVELOPMENT: THE PLACENTA

As the embryo develops, a series of simultaneous events occur in the growth of the **placenta,** an organ the mother possesses only during her pregnancy.

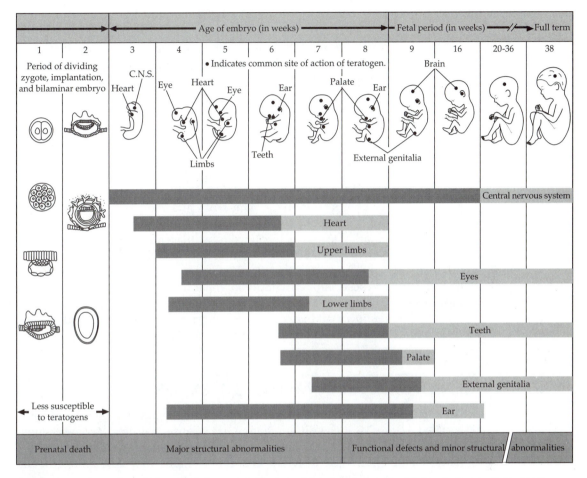

During the embryonic period, growth in complexity is rapid. Later, during the fetal period, growth in size is more evident. (Source: Moore, 1993)

placenta: the temporary organ that connects the bloodstreams of mother and unborn baby; from the Latin *placenta* (a flat cake).

The placenta performs a wide variety of functions as development proceeds, and the pregnancy could not continue without it.

Initially, the placenta and associated membranes arise from the trophoblast, the outer cell layer that develops as the blastocyst forms. All the cells involved are derived from the fertilized egg, so they are genetically identical to those of the embryo—a fact that will prove useful for prenatal diagnosis.

As implantation occurs, the trophoblast and other related tissue (together called the *chorion*) are in close contact with the endometrium. Together, the tissues of embryo and mother begin to form the placenta, in which small blood vessels of each individual come close enough together so that food, oxygen, and waste products can diffuse from one to the other. Both sets of blood vessels are functioning by day 17. At the same time, there develops the connection between embryo and chorion, which will become the umbilical

amnion: a thin membrane surrounding the embryo and fetus; from the Greek *amnion* (a caul).

cord. In addition, the **amniotic sac** has started to develop; it will become a membrane filled with amniotic fluid that completely surrounds the embryo (Wynn, 1975). (Beware of a common misunderstanding about the placenta: it does *not* surround the unborn baby, as is sometimes claimed in the media. This mistake seems to be traceable to a popular seventh-grade biology textbook that has confused many a student.)

The placenta serves as a supply line for the unborn baby, providing food and oxygen and removing waste products. It also serves a protective function, preventing some substances from crossing from the mother's to the baby's circulation. But it is far from a perfect barrier and has been described as more like a sieve than like a wall (Streissguth, 1983). The placenta has two immunologic functions as well; it transfers **antibodies** against disease and prevents the mother's immune system from attacking the baby as an "invader."

antibodies: globulins that defend the body against infection; from the Latin *anti-* (against).

A final remarkable characteristic of the placenta is its function as an endocrine organ that produces hormones. Whereas some endocrine organs produce only one hormone, the placenta produces a diverse group of hormones. One of these, human chorionic gonadotropin (HCG), is excreted in urine at a level that can be detected by home pregnancy tests. The placenta also produces *estrogen* and *progesterone*; they maintain the uterus and prevent new ovulation, and they prepare the breasts for lactation.

NORMAL PRENATAL DEVELOPMENT: THE FETUS

After the end of the embryonic period, at day 56, the developing human being is called a *fetus*. Most cell differentiation has occurred, although some changes are still going on in the nervous system. The basic tissues of organ systems are in place and a period of growth is beginning—first an increase in length, and later a gain in weight.

The fetus normally continues to develop in the uterus until about 40 weeks after the first day of the mother's last menstrual period (38 weeks from conception). A fetus born at 25 or 26 weeks gestational age may survive with a great deal of medical treatment, but it is likely to sustain some long-term problems in the process. Every week in the uterus means greater maturity of organ systems, a better chance of survival, and a better quality of life.

The development of the lungs is especially important for survival, as we will discuss later in this chapter. For breathing to be effective, the lungs must be able to secrete *surfactants*, which make oxygen exchange possible. Surfactants secreted by the lungs enter the amniotic fluid, which can be tested for an indication of the fetus' maturity.

The developing fetus is active in the uterus. It swallows amniotic fluid and it urinates; it moves, and it can be felt more and more strongly by the mother as the pregnancy advances. As the months pass, its movements usually turn it into a head-down position, which is ideal for birth. The eyes move (although, of course, there is nothing to see in the dark of the uterus) and there is electrical activity in the brain. Although the fetus may not be ready to do very well outside the uterus, there is a great deal of continuity in its activities before and after birth.

There is one major difference between the baby before and after birth, however: the pattern of *blood circulation.* After birth, blood must pass through the lungs in large quantities in order to pick up oxygen to carry to the cells. In the fetus, only a small amount of blood passes through the lungs; most of the blood bypasses the lungs through a short blood vessel called the ductus arteriosus. Blood also flows from the right atrium to the left atrium of the heart through an opening called the foramen ovale. As we will see in the next chapter, there are dramatic alterations in circulation shortly after birth.

Just as circulation is different in the fetus than in the newborn, components of the blood are also different. The hemoglobin in the red blood cells, which binds to oxygen molecules and carries them to other cells, is a different form in the fetus (fetal hemoglobin) than will be present later (mature hemoglobin). Fetal hemoglobin is less efficient at oxygen exchange than the mature form.

It would be a mistake to assume that the developmental events just described always yield a live, full-term baby. There are probably almost as many spontaneous deaths of embryos and fetuses as there are live births; a very large proportion die because of chromosomal abnormalities or implantation problems, and their deaths may occur so early that the mother is not aware of her pregnancy. When chromosomal problems are not responsible, deaths may result from maternal alcohol or drug use or tobacco smoking (Bloch, 1992). And, of course, the mother may choose to abort the pregnancy.

NORMAL PRENATAL DEVELOPMENT: SEX DETERMINATION

The development of the sex characteristics of the embryo and fetus involves a precise sequence of events at the molecular and cellular levels. The two sequences, culminating in either a male or a female fetus, begin with what has been called a "genetic switch"—the presence of a gene that determines the direction of development (Hagg et al., 1994). Errors in the sequence lead to abnormalities of the gonads and related structures.

Between the second and third months of gestation, the sexual organs of males and females are identical. In the abdomen, both have a structure with the potential for developing into male gonads (the *Wolffian duct*) and a structure with the potential to develop into female gonads (the *Müllerian duct*). Both males and females have a genital tubercle (a slight projection where the external genitalia will be) and a single external opening to both the bladder and the gonads (Money & Ehrhardt, 1972).

In the third to fourth month of gestation, sex differentiation begins to be evident. In the male, the Müllerian structures begin to diminish in size and the Wolffian structures begin to grow into testes—although they are still high in the abdomen where they began, not in the scrotum. The genital tubercle enlarges to form the penis. In the female, the reverse occurs; the Müllerian structures grow to form ovary and uterus, the genital tubercle enlarges slightly to form the clitoris, and the Wolffian structures shrink. Externally, the labia are relatively undeveloped. Only when the fetus is close to full term will the testes descend into the scrotum and the labia enlarge sufficiently to cover the clitoris.

What throws the genetic switch and causes development into a male or into a female? A specific gene is necessary. This gene, designated SRY, is found on the short arm of the Y chromosome. When SRY is present, differentiation in the male direction begins; when SRY is absent, the "default" development to the female form is initiated. Usually, of course, the absence of SRY means that the individual is a chromosomally normal XX female.

One interesting point about fetal sex development is that the female fetus at 5 months gestational age already has in her ovaries all the ova she will ever produce. They are not, of course, mature ova, ready to be released at ovulation or ready to be fertilized. However, they have taken the first step in their development and are waiting to mature under the influence of reproductive hormones when the female reaches puberty.

NORMAL PRENATAL DEVELOPMENT: THE NERVOUS SYSTEM

The prenatal development of the nervous system has some unusual characteristics compared to development of other systems. One is its extraordinary importance with respect to complex postnatal functions like learning, perceiving, and language. The other is the continuity it shows between the prenatal and the postnatal period. Nervous system development is not nearly over at birth; it proceeds postnatally for weeks, months, or even years for some functions. Only after the first month of postnatal life is a real transformation of neural functions seen (Cioni & Prechtl, 1989). (The processes involved in brain and nervous system development will be discussed in some detail in Chapter 7. The present section offers a brief summary.)

During the embryonic period, billions of neurons (nervous system cells) begin to grow and make the contacts (synapses) with each other that will allow communication in the system. Cells proliferate, differentiate, and grow in size according to patterns that initially are determined by specific genes but that later involve the influences of hormones and contact with other cells (Kolata, 1983; Rubenstein, Martinez, Shimamuru, & Puelles, 1994).

Cells in the nervous system also move during the embryonic and fetal periods. Some are moved by passive cell displacement, in which newly produced cells push the older ones away from the area of proliferation. Other cells move actively by migration, traveling in waves to the areas that will form the higher brain centers. (If these patterns for migration do not occur normally, the result is a neuronal migration disorder, involving a variety of behavioral and intellectual problems.) Axons, the long "arms" that grow out of the cell body of the neuron, then extend to make contact with other neurons, guided by "pioneer" neurons that die once mature organization of the brain is achieved (McConnel, Ghosh, & Shatz, 1989). The final shaping of the system occurs through programmed cell death; more neurons are made during the embryonic period than are needed, and where there are too many or they are in the wrong places, they die off in large numbers (Barinaga, 1993b).

During the third week of embryonic development, some of the ectoderm cells transform into nerve cells and form the neural plate. This transformation occurs through induction; some ectoderm cells are induced to change by their contact with certain other tissues, whereas those ectoderm cells that do not have such contact become skin cells (Prechtl, 1984a). Contact with a protein called a *neural inducer* may be responsible for the change.

During days 18 to 26, the neural plate folds inward and then closes up the back to form the neural tube, the basis of all further development of the spinal cord and the brain. Any problems in this process may lead to neural tube defects such as *spina bifida* (an opening in tissue over the spinal cord) or *anencephaly* (failure of the brain to develop), which will be discussed in later sections on problems of development and prenatal diagnosis.

In weeks 4 through 10 of gestation, the formation of the brain and face proceed. It should be noted that this process and later events extend beyond the 56-day point that ends the embryonic period.

During months 2 through 4 of gestation, neuronal proliferation produces rapid development of new neurons, and during months 2 to 5, neuronal migration carries neurons to higher brain areas and organizes them into layers and patterns (Nickel, 1992).

During this period of development, as well as later, the nervous system functions as a dynamic action system with self-organizing properties. Small changes in the system can sometimes trigger reorganization according to new rules, resulting in major developmental differences. For example, a slight change in activity at one point in development can result in four layers of cells where six would normally occur. As Stryker (1994) has pointed out, "Just as crystals grow, with new molecules fitting precisely onto only certain specific points of the surface formed by their predecessors, so too may portions of the nervous system.... Prominent and precise features may result from quite limited and apparently minor singularities" (pp. 1244–1245).

A period of organization goes on from 6 months gestational age until sometime after birth; neurons are grouped, synaptic connections are created, and excess neurons die off. Beginning at about the same time but continuing until adulthood, the process of myelination covers axons with a fatty myelin sheath, which helps them function more efficiently (Nickel, 1992).

THE EFFECT OF THE ENVIRONMENT ON PRENATAL DEVELOPMENT

One hundred or even fifty years ago, it was commonly believed that a mother's experiences during pregnancy could influence her unborn baby—so-called maternal impressions. According to such folklore, a baby whose mother was frightened by a dog might be born with a doglike face, or a mother who longed for strawberries might give her unborn baby a "strawberry mark."

These beliefs are less common today, and certainly no one who is educated about prenatal development believes in such simple connections between environmental events and the baby's development. (Although, of course, if the mother is frightened by the grizzlies at the zoo, the baby *will* be born with bare feet!)

Some of our current questions about the effect of the environment on the unborn baby are concerned with the possibility of prenatal learning. Many new parents buy cassette tapes of heartbeat sounds on the assumption that the unborn baby found the sound familiar and soothing. (Actually, it would probably be more realistic to use recordings of intestinal gurglings—and even less romantic sounds that can be left to the reader's imagination.)

What the unborn baby might or might not ordinarily learn is not very clear, but there is some evidence that taste preferences may develop prenatally from flavors of food eaten by the mother and detectable in the amniotic fluid (Mennella & Beauchamp, 1993).

As for other environmental effects on the embryo and fetus, it seems that normal development can take place in a fairly wide range of environmental conditions. The mother's body buffers the unborn baby against extremes of heat or cold and can protect it against many potentially harmful substances. There certainly does not seem to be any unusual substance or condition that makes development *better* than it would be in the ordinary environment. Unfortunately, however, there are substances and conditions that can interfere with normal development and lead to congenital anomalies, or birth defects. These substances are called **teratogens,** and their effects on the unborn baby are complex.

teratogen: a substance or event that can cause birth defects if present during the embryonic period; from the Greek *teras* (marvel, monster), *genos* (kind, birth).

Critical Periods

To understand how teratogens work, we must first understand that the developing baby is not equally vulnerable to potentially harmful events at all times. There are points during prenatal development at which a particular teratogen would cause no harm at all, and other points at which it would cause a serious birth defect. As development proceeds through the sequence of stages described earlier, there are times when critical periods occur.

A *critical period* is a time during development when an event in the environment can have an effect it could not have had earlier and will not be able to have later. Some critical periods after birth involve the need for an environmental event that will produce a good outcome, but critical periods during gestation involve a disturbance of development that leads to a birth defect.

Except for periods affecting some aspects of brain development, prenatal critical periods occur during the embryonic stage. Different times in this stage are critical periods for the development of different organs; a time that involves a critical period for the heart does not necessarily involve one for the liver or kidneys.

Why are most critical periods for organ development in the embryonic stage? The vulnerability of this time in gestation comes from the occurrence of cell differentiation. The timing of differentiation of specific cells is genetically determined; cells cannot differentiate earlier than their proper time, *nor can they differentiate later.* If something happens to disrupt differentiation, whatever should be happening at that time is simply skipped. The embryo cannot go back and "pick up a stitch in its knitting" or otherwise redo a lost step in differentiation. It goes on with its development after the disruption is over, and the steps in differentiation that should have occurred, never happen. Instead, the embryo continues its growth without the foundation for a structure that may be extremely important.

Before implantation, cleavage occurs but cell differentiation does not. If the mother is exposed to disease or toxic substances at this point, the zygote could be killed, but if it survives it does so intact, without any harm from the experience. After day 56, most cell differentiation is complete, although some important developments in the nervous system are still in progress. Exposure to teratogens in the fetal period can slow growth or cause brain damage, but there are no obvious, easily detectable birth defects that result from events at this time.

Critical periods for the differentiation of particular cells often overlap during the embryonic period. For example, in nervous system development, parts of the brain and parts of the *face* develop at the same time. Exposure to a teratogen at this point could thus lead to multiple birth defects. For example, defects of the mid-facial area, such as a cleft or "hare" lip (a split in the upper lip) are often accompanied by hearing loss because parts of the inner ear are differentiating at the same time that mid-facial structures are developing.

Understanding Teratogens

Identifying teratogens and understanding how they work is an extremely complex task. One reason for this difficulty was mentioned in the last paragraph; the effect of a teratogen on development depends to a considerable extent on the *timing* of exposure. It is rare for a teratogen to produce a single, unique birth defect; the same teratogen can produce different defects depending on the time of exposure, and different teratogens can produce the same defect.

Teratogens do not function simply and independently. The creation of a teratogenic birth defect is not a simple matter of pressing a specific button and producing a specific outcome. On the contrary, teratogens function as part of a dynamic action system, and the impact of a teratogen on the embryo changes with the timing of exposure and with some additional factors.

The effect of a teratogen on the embryo depends in part on the embryo's genetic makeup. Different embryos exposed to the same teratogen at the same point in development may show different severities of birth defects, and some may be completely unaffected. A litter of puppies whose mother is exposed to a teratogen will not all show the same birth defects (they are not identical genetically, even though they are born at the same time). The effect of a teratogen may also be altered by the mother's previous exposure; for example, later babies of alcoholic mothers are more likely to have birth defects than are earlier ones.

A final factor in the complex functioning of teratogens is the interaction between different environmental factors. A teratogen might have a specific effect only if another potentially harmful situation exists at the same time. In the real world, there are usually simultaneous exposures to many sources of harm. A mother working on a farm is probably exposed to more than one pesticide; a woman who lives in substandard housing and is exposed to lead paint may also have unusual exposure to sexually transmitted diseases and a poor diet as well. Drug-using mothers almost invariably are multidrug users; although it is common to talk abut the "drug of choice," the drug of choice among serious users is "whatever you got."

Thus, the identification of a teratogen is no simple matter, and a birth defect is not clearly labeled "caused by cocaine" or "caused by syphilis." For every birth defect, there are many possible teratogens, and for every teratogen, there are many possible birth defects. To make the matter even more complex, we must remember that not all birth defects result from teratogens. As we saw in the previous chapter, some birth defects are genetic in origin, and they may appear to be exactly the same as those caused by teratogens.

SOME TERATOGENS AND THEIR EFFECTS

A survey of teratogens may seem intended just to horrify and to make one decide never to have a baby. However, the bright side is that there is a possibility of avoiding teratogens, the success of which depends on public education and appropriate public health approaches.

Teratogens occur in a startling number of forms. Sometimes they are manmade, like alcohol and chemical pesticides. Sometimes they are naturally occurring organic substances that contaminate foods. Sometimes they are diseases, and sometimes they are events like radiation. Some teratogens are easy to avoid if the mother knows she should do so, whereas others are difficult even to be aware of.

Alcohol As a Teratogen

The mother's consumption of alcohol during pregnancy is one of the leading causes of mental retardation in the Western world, yet not all alcohol-exposed infants show clear-cut effects, and of those who do show effects, only half show retardation (Olson, Burgess, & Streissguth, 1992). As many other teratogens do, alcohol operates in unpredictable ways, but there is no question that it has the potential for doing serious harm to the unborn baby.

The effects of alcohol during gestation may come in the form of full-blown *fetal alcohol syndrome* (FAS), or the less serious *fetal alcohol effects* (FAE). An absolute line between the two is hard to draw. As infants, alcohol-exposed babies may be jittery, tremulous, excitable, and irritable. They may suck weakly and sleep fitfully. There may be congenital anomalies, such as a small head, an odd face shape, and low birth weight. As preschoolers, FAS/FAE children are typically short, skinny, alert, talkative, and friendly. Many are

hyperactive: impulsive and showing an abnormally high activity level; from the Greek *hyper* (above), the Latin *actus* (doing).

hyperactive and oversensitive to touch. They frequently have eye problems and difficulties with ear infections (although, of course, there may be many other causes for those problems). They often have attention deficits, fine motor problems, and developmental delays, but because alcohol-exposed children are small, adults may respond to them as if they are younger children whose development is on time (Olson, Burgess, & Streissguth, 1992).

Fetal alcohol syndrome occurs about 1 to 3 times in every 1000 live births in the United States—about twice the frequency of Down syndrome and almost 5 times that of spina bifida. Fetal alcohol effects may be 3 times as frequent as FAS (Olson, Burgess, & Streissguth, 1992). There is probably an even broader range of alcohol-related birth defects (ARBD). Full-blown FAS may be only one extreme of a continuum of damage that parallels the amount of alcohol ingested. Subtle molecular changes in the brain may affect later learning and memory. In one experiment, in which pregnant rats ingested the equivalent of 2 to 3 drinks per day, the offspring did no worse than controls did on easy mazes but had great difficulty on harder tasks (Braun, 1996).

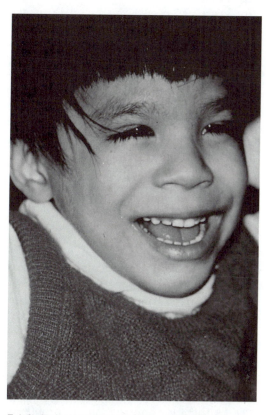

Fetal alcohol syndrome has continued to have an effect on this child's behavior and abilities, even though he has been reared in an excellent foster home.

African Americans are diagnosed with FAS 7 times as often, and Native Americans 30 times as often, as are those of European descent, but this may result in part from using European-based norms for the comparison. The annual cost of treating FAS was estimated in 1991 at $75 million, most of which was directed toward individuals with mental retardation (Abel & Sokol, 1991).

FAS and its associated problems are absolutely preventable; if no alcohol is ingested during pregnancy, there are no alcohol effects on the baby. There is no documented safe level of drinking during pregnancy, and recommendations such as "only three drinks a week" are based entirely on guesswork. It is often difficult for women to accept these facts, however, because people tend to believe their own experience in preference to statistics. If a woman knows someone who drank during pregnancy and whose baby had no apparent problems, or if she herself drank during a previous pregnancy, she may be very likely to deny the possibility of FAS. Only about 6% of infants of heavy drinkers show FAS (Braun, 1996), so most women who drank during pregnancy are likely to have personal experience of good outcomes. A woman who for years has been accustomed to using alcohol for self-medication and for mood change when she is uncomfortable may drink even more in early pregnancy, when she feels tired, "flu-ish," and queasy.

hypoxia: having a low level of oxygen; from the Greek *hypo* (under) (plus part of *oxygen*).

Research on animals suggests that one of the direct causes of FAS is the collapse of the umbilical veins within 15 minutes after the mother ingests alcohol, leading to severe **hypoxia** (lack of oxygen) and other chemical changes in the fetus' blood (Mukherjee & Hodgen, 1983). A direct effect on the developing nervous system also occurs as the alcohol crosses the placenta and enters the body of the embryo or fetus. In the rat study described above, researchers found that a process called *long-term potentiation* (LTP) in brain cells was reduced and an important neurotransmitter was not released in the brains of affected animals; both of these changes would lead to learning problems (Braun, 1996).

Tobacco Use

Tobacco smoking is particularly hard to assess for teratogenic effects because smokers commonly are exposed to other potential teratogens, like alcohol, as well. Cigarettes are suspected of being one of the causes of ectopic pregnancies, where implantation takes place outside the uterus; women who smoke are two or three times as likely to have an ectopic pregnancy as those who do not, and the fourfold increase of ectopic pregnancies since 1970 has followed the increase in women's smoking. Experimental work with hamster oviducts has shown that tobacco smoke slows or stops the motion of the cilia, which normally move the ovum along toward the uterus (Nowak, 1994b).

Although some cognitive problems have been attributed to prenatal exposure to tobacco smoke (Abel, 1989), the most serious well-documented effect of the experience is a reduction in birth weight of about half a pound. Pregnant women who quit smoking have babies with higher birth weights compared to babies of women who only reduce the amount of smoking; and the latter have heavier babies than do those who continue to smoke without cutting back at all (Li, Windsor, Perkins, Goldenberg, & Lowe, 1993).

A final issue about smoking during pregnancy involves sudden infant death syndrome (SIDS), the unexpected, unexplained death of an apparently well infant. SIDS is second only to birth defects as a cause of infant deaths in the United States (Schoendorf & Kiely, 1992). Unfortunately for our understanding of the effects of tobacco smoke on development, it is almost unheard of for a woman to smoke only during pregnancy and not after the baby is born, so there is no way to separate the effects of exposure during gestation from those of secondary smoke inhalation during infancy. However, there is an association between SIDS and *either* smoke exposure during infancy or smoke exposure during both gestation and infancy with the latter being higher, suggesting a possible effect during gestation (Schoendorf & Kiely, 1992).

Recreational Drugs

Again, recreational drugs such as cocaine and heroin are unlikely to be the sole potential teratogens a woman ingests. Most drug users are polydrug users; they use alcohol and tobacco as well as illegal drugs; they often have poor diets and untreated health problems; they get little prenatal care; and they often suffer from sexually transmitted diseases that may be teratogenic. Isolating teratogenic effects of recreational drugs in human beings in the real world is a daunting task.

Although the precise details of the effects of specific recreational drugs remain unclear, here are some apparent outcomes of exposure:

1. *Heroin:* Rather than showing specific birth defects, heroin-exposed babies have low birth weights. The babies are addicted at the time of birth and go into withdrawal soon after, exhibiting fever, feeding problems, and irritability.

2. *Tranquilizers:* As do other substances that affect the mother's nervous system, tranquilizers affect that of the unborn baby as well. Withdrawal symptoms are seen soon after birth, with poor sucking, breathing problems, and low body temperature. There may be congenital anomalies associated with some tranquilizers.

3. *Barbiturates:* Sudden withdrawal for infants can lead to seizures and possibly death. The withdrawal symptoms are similar to those of heroin-addicted babies, but are more severe ("Drug abuse's most innocent victims," 1989).

4. *Cocaine:* Maternal cocaine use can restrict the oxygen the fetus receives by cutting down blood flow to the uterus. Low birth weight and high frequency of strokes (burst blood vessels in the brain) in infants are associated with exposure to cocaine. Premature labor can be brought on by maternal cocaine use, contributing greatly to the problems of cocaine-exposed babies.

In the late 1980s and early 1990s, much media attention was focused on prenatal drug use, especially use of cocaine in its "crack" form, which was particularly common among women. The media presentation implied that specific relationships between cocaine use and birth defects were well known, and that exposed babies were "born addicted" to cocaine. This exciting but simplistic presentation was not well supported by the research literature—although this is certainly not to suggest that anyone thinks cocaine is *good* for unborn babies!

Concerns about so-called crack babies were intensified by the number of drug-exposed babies abandoned by their mothers. The foster care systems of many cities became overwhelmed during the late 1980s. In a number of cases, drug-exposed babies stayed on as "boarder babies" in hospitals because there was nowhere else for them to go. The drug-involved mothers dropped out of sight, the fathers were unknown, and—even had adoptive parents been available—the legal complications of adoption were (and are) enormous.

The fetal brain is exposed to concentrations of cocaine much higher than those in the blood (Mayes, 1994). Some studies have suggested motor problems in cocaine-exposed babies, including stiffness (Dixon, 1994). Subtle differences may also be present in the cocaine-exposed baby; for example, an analysis of the baby's cry shows different characteristics for exposed than for nonexposed infants (Corwin et al., 1992). Whether the concepts of withdrawal or addiction make sense with cocaine-exposed babies is questionable (Dixon, 1994; Myers, Olson, & Kaltenbach, 1992); it may be more useful to think of these infants as experiencing an *abstinence syndrome*—a set of symptoms that accompany the absence of some accustomed event.

An estimated 11% to 44% of deliveries in different parts of the United States involve prenatal cocaine exposure (Behnke & Eyler, 1994). Whether it is suitable to treat the mothers as criminals remains an arguable point, which will be discussed further in Chapter 15. A real continuing concern about the many cocaine-exposed babies is that they should not be regarded as irrevocably damaged by cocaine alone; such a conclusion leads to the assumption that it is pointless to attempt to help them (Mayes, Granger, Bornstein, & Zuckerman, 1992).

Medications

analgesic: a pain-reducing medication or practice; from the Greek *ana*- (back, backward), *algos* (pain).

The fact that a drug is used for treatment of an illness rather than for entertainment does not rule it out as a possible teratogen. For example, one study has associated use of **analgesics** and decongestants with a rare but serious congenital defect of the abdominal wall (Werler, Mitchell, & Shapiro, 1992). The drug Accutane, which is used to treat acne, is associated with congenital deformities such as low-set, deformed, or absent ears; mental retardation; and damage to the brain and heart.

Teratogenic Diseases

Infectious diseases have the potential for causing birth defects if the mother is exposed during the embryonic period of gestation. A number of teratogenic diseases have been identified, but a compete list is quite difficult to achieve.

Because these diseases often have few or no obvious symptoms in adults, the pregnant woman is not likely to seek medical care; thus there is no clear record that she was infected, and she may not even recall the event after the baby is born. Probably at least 40,000 infants born in the United States each year are affected by teratogenic diseases (Williamson & Demmler, 1992).

1. *Toxoplasmosis:* This disease involves infection with the intracellular parasite *Toxoplasma gondii,* and abnormalities of the eyes and brain are common effects. The frequency is about 2.3 per 1000 live births in the United States and higher in Europe and South America. The severity of the effects, of course, is much higher if the infection occurs during the embryonic period. About 75% of infected babies are born without evident symptoms, but only 8% to 16% are still normal at age 4 years (Sever, 1983; Williamson & Demmler, 1992).

APPLICATIONS & ARGUMENTS
The Effects of Postnatal Drugs and Alcohol

When pregnant women use alcohol and drugs, their infants can experience some serious teratogenic effects. However, the effects of maternal drug and alcohol use do not end at birth. Women who have been involved in substance abuse while pregnant care are quite likely to continue the practice after the baby is born (although a small number are sufficiently concerned that they try to get "clean" at the end of the pregnancy).

Drugs and alcohol interfere seriously with a parent's ability to do a good job with an infant or toddler. In the early months of a child's life, a caregiver needs to put a great deal of energy into nurturing and comforting. Caregivers must be alert and mentally competent in order to decide what the baby needs, to try different solutions to problems, and to figure out what works and what doesn't. The intoxicated parent is not alert and may be too numbed to care what the baby's problem is. Energy that should go to the baby may be expended on the search for the next drug or alcohol dose.

From about age 2 to 12 months, the baby's great need is for a sensitive, responsive, interactive caregiver. Substance abuse interferes with the parent's capacity for responsiveness, even at such a simple level as eye contact and the exchange of smiles. The impact on emotional and communicative development can be serious.

The crawling or toddling child needs to be protected from household safety hazards like unguarded stairs. Anticipating accidents can be difficult enough for a sober parent, let alone an intoxicated one.

Finally, where drugs and alcohol are used, an infant can inhale crack smoke, swallow pills, or drink alcohol left within reach.

Toxoplasma gondii is found in uncooked meat and in animal feces, so pregnant women should avoid rare meat and should have someone else clean the cat's litter box or do gardening where neighborhood cats have defecated. Antiparasitic drugs can be used when infection has already occurred.

2. *Cytomegalovirus:* A member of the herpesvirus family, cytomegalovirus is also known as CMV. It affects 0.5% to 2.5% of U.S. births, but only about 10% of babies are identified as affected at birth. These babies have small head circumferences, eye problems, and low birth weight. Infants without symptoms at birth may still have long-term problems like hearing loss.

Because the virus is shed in urine, pregnant women are sometimes advised to avoid diapering babies (for example, if working in a day care center), but the actual risk from handling diapers is not clear. There has been some experimental use of antiviral drugs to treat CMV (Williamson & Demmler, 1992), and work is in progress on a vaccine (Plotkin, 1994).

3. *Rubella:* In the first 12 to 14 weeks of gestation, rubella, or German measles, has a serious potential for causing birth defects. The developing baby contracts the disease from its infected mother in 67% to 80% of cases (Williamson & Demmler, 1992). Common effects of rubella are multiple organ involvements, low birth weight, heart defects, and problems with vision and hearing, as well as many cases of mental retardation.

A vaccine against rubella makes it possible to remove this cause of teratogenic birth defects, but the vaccine cannot be used during pregnancy. Because recent immigrants and disadvantaged girls may not have been immunized, a number of women enter the childbearing years still susceptible to rubella. Delays in immunization of young children due to lack of education or economic resources may mean that the children pass the virus to pregnant women.

4. *Syphilis:* Although the venereal disease syphilis was at one time thought to be almost wiped out in the United States, it has come back to a considerable degree. The spirochete, the infectious organism of syphilis, crosses the placenta and infects the child. About 40% of affected babies are stillborn if untreated, and damage to teeth, bones, and the nervous system is common. Treating the mother also treats the unborn baby and arrests the disease, but of course it cannot undo any damage that has already occurred. Because the initial symptoms of syphilis are painless and difficult to detect in women, good prenatal care is needed to prevent damage to the unborn.

5. *Chickenpox:* Varicella-herpes zoster, better known as chickenpox, is contracted by many children, who become immune as a result. However, about 15% of U.S. women of childbearing age are susceptible (Sever, 1983). About 2% of babies infected in the first 16 weeks of gestation show teratogenic effects such as cataracts, other eye problems, brain damage, skin scars, and poorly developed limbs and trunk. Infection of the mother is most dangerous if it occurs a few days before delivery; the infection of the baby may then be very severe. A significant number die, and the survivors may have small heads and mental retardation.

Although a vaccine against chickenpox has been under development for many years and is used in other countries, it is not presently widely used in the United States, and there is some debate about whether it is necessary (Plotkin, 1994).

6. *Herpesvirus:* Genital herpesvirus (HSV) infections are the second most common venereal disease in the United States, but an unborn infant is rarely exposed unless the membranes surrounding it have torn. HSV and gonorrhea are ordinarily contracted at the time of birth and will be discussed in greater depth in Chapter 5.

7. *HIV:* The human immunodeficiency virus (HIV), the cause of acquired immunodeficiency syndrome (AIDS), is easily passed by "vertical transmission" from mother to fetus. About 30% of infants born to infected mothers are HIV-positive, and without treatment about 50% of them will develop AIDS within 2 years (Cohen, 1992). The disease has not been reported to cause specific birth defects.

8. *Other teratogenic diseases:* The list of teratogenic diseases is certainly not complete. Some recent additions are parvovirus B19, which causes a rash in early childhood and is suspected of teratogenic effects, and other viral infections like influenza. One study of an influenza epidemic speculated that **schizophrenia** in later life might result from influenza infection in the 16th to 24th weeks of gestation (Mednick, Machon, Huttunen, & Bonnet, 1988).

schizophrenia: a psychotic condition in which there is a loss of contact with reality and a split between emotion and cognition; from the Greek *schizein* (to split), *phren* (mind).

Other Teratogens

A variety of other factors that are neither diseases nor drugs, have been implicated as teratogens. For example, exposure to electromagnetic fields from power lines has been discussed as a possible cause of childhood leukemia (Stone, 1992b). Research is in progress about the effects of cosmic radiation and other factors on babies of female flight attendants (Stone, 1993b).

Environmental pollutants such as lead and mercury are known to cause prenatal nervous system damage. Chemicals such as dioxin, DDT, and PCBs have estrogenlike effects and may be associated with the rise in reproductive system anomalies in the last 50 years (Holden, 1993; Stone, 1994b).

Naturally occurring food contaminants, such as fungi that make aflatoxins (carcinogenic substances), are other possible environmental teratogens. As these funguses grow on grain, they may be consumed directly by humans or be concentrated in milk after cows are fed the grain.

A last possibility currently under consideration is that hot tubs, which actually raise the bather's core body temperature, when used by pregnant women, may be associated with neural tube defects such as spina bifida (Sandford, Kissling, & Joubert, 1992).

BECOMING A PARENT

A person's capacity to function as a parent does not emerge suddenly after the baby is born. It develops slowly during the pregnancy and continues to develop for months and years after the birth. During the pregnancy, a person's self-identification as a parent will contribute to the quality of prenatal care, diet, and the taking of precautions. The pregnant woman's concept of herself as a mother directly affects her behavior; her partner's concept of himself as a father can make it easier or more difficult for the woman to choose good health practices.

crisis: a point at which old ways of functioning no longer work; from the Greek *krisis* (decision).

Pregnancy is a **crisis,** a transitional period that requires serious changes in the parents as individuals and as a couple. Coping with the crisis depends on the current life situation and lifelong personality patterns. For women, difficulty in coping may emerge from past losses and failures as well as from lack of support at the time. For men, problems often arise from unfulfilled early dependency needs; they increase their demands on their wives for attention and nurturance (Osofsky, 1983). Both men and women have to rethink their senses of autonomy (separateness from other people) and of affiliation (relatedness to other people) (Grossman, Pollack, Golding, & Fedele, 1987).

The first psychological task of pregnancy is pregnancy validation—ascertaining that the pregnancy is real and accepting the implications of the fact (Clark, 1979). Women often have ambivalent or even negative feelings at this point, especially if they are tired and nauseated; they are more focused on themselves than on the baby. The second task is fetal embodiment—making the fetus part of the mother's own body image and reworking her relationships with her husband and with her own mother (Clark, 1979). This occurs in

trimester: a 3-month period; from the Latin *tri-* (three), *mensis* (month).

the second **trimester,** or 3-month period, of pregnancy. The woman is more introspective, more dependent on her husband, and worried about miscarriage or injury to the baby. The third task, in the third trimester, involves fetal distinction, a progressive psychological separation from the fetus and the beginning of thinking of the baby as a separate person (Clark, 1979). The mother is actively interested and preparing for the birth.

Accomplishing these psychological tasks and coping with the crisis of pregnancy will lead to the mother's increased ability to monitor her own health. But not every mother has the same skills or problems of health management.

Adolescent mothers have some of the greatest difficulties adjusting to their (usually unplanned) pregnancies and managing health concerns. They are twice as likely as older women are to give birth prematurely, and their babies are too often of low birth weight. The pregnant girl's age is not as important a factor as her initial weight and height, her weight gain during pregnancy, and her health habits (for example, substance abuse and sexually transmitted disease) (McAnarney, 1985). Teenagers' educational levels may limit their understanding of pregnancy. Although there had been decreasing alcohol, tobacco, and other drug use by adolescents in the 1980s, there is in the 1990s a trend toward increasing use (Battle, 1994; Mason, 1992).

Older parents may be very pleased with a pregnancy and have the knowledge and resources for good health care, but they may find pregnancy more physically demanding than they expect and may have special health concerns, particularly about the conception of a Down syndrome baby. If the pregnancy has to be achieved through in vitro fertilization, questions arise about the appropriateness of this use of scarce, expensive technology.

APPLICATIONS & ARGUMENTS
How Does It Feel to Be Pregnant?

Pregnancy is a process of development, so it should not be surprising that different parts of the process feel different. Hormonal, physiological, and anatomical alterations will influence the mother's sensations throughout pregnancy.

Occasionally, women say that they knew they had become pregnant within a day or two of fertilization, but this is presumably because they were aware of what had probably occurred rather than because of altered sensations. Most women go for some weeks or even longer without being aware of new sensations.

The first sensation of pregnancy may be some cramping without bleeding at the time the first period is missed. Soon, some flulike symptoms of easy fatigue and loss of appetite may appear. Often foods smell and taste funny and unappetizing, whether there is actual nausea or not, and these sensations continue until the third or fourth month.

By about the fourth month, most women feel good and recover their energy and spirits—especially when they see their sparkling eyes and pink cheeks in the mirror. They feel the baby move, a tiny fluttery or scratchy sensation low in the abdomen. Although this feeling may be startling at first, most women soon find it exciting and gratifying.

By the seventh or eighth month, the baby is getting heavy. The mother must change her posture to balance its weight and her back and legs may ache. Heartburn and constipation may come along as the baby fills more and more of the abdomen. The mother may feel that she is trudging along on a journey whose end is finally in sight.

A prospective parent's habits of alcohol or drug use can interfere with proper health management during pregnancy, as well as with the psychological tasks of the period. Uncontrolled alcohol or drug use can produce added complications by leading to behavior that puts the woman at risk for contracting sexually transmitted diseases ("Drinking, female sexuality, and AIDS," 1994).

THE EXPERIENCE OF PREGNANCY
Symptoms of Pregnancy

The most obvious symptom of pregnancy, which would lead any reasonable adult to suspect that conception might have occurred, is **amenorrhea,** or failure to menstruate. Although obvious, this symptom is not absolutely definitive of pregnancy, for it may be caused by many other factors such as

amenorrhea: failure to menstruate; from the Greek *an-* (not), *men* (moon), *rhein* (to flow).

sudden weight loss or serious athletic training. Then, too, a pregnant woman may have a few monthly episodes of vaginal bleeding that resemble menstruation but that are progressively shorter in duration.

Some of the common ailments of pregnancy are also symptoms. A few weeks after she misses a period, the woman may experience morning sickness—queasiness and nausea that can actually occur at any time of day and is better termed "pregnancy sickness." The pregnant woman may find that everything "smells funny," and cooking odors that would normally be appetizing are quite revolting. (This change in smell sensitivity is based on actual hormonal changes.)

Pregnancy sickness generally occurs at the same time that cell differentiation is going on, and some researchers have suggested that pregnancy sickness helps protect the embryo against teratogens. The tastes and smells that seems so revolting to the pregnant woman are often those associated with toxins or with spoiled foods, such as bitterness and pungency. Some women show **pica,** the desire to eat nonnutritive substances such as laundry starch. In the past and in rural areas, pica involved eating clay, which in fact can bind or detoxify some dangerous substances (Profet, 1992).

pica: a desire to eat nonnutritive substances; from the Latin *picus* (woodpecker).

The pregnant woman may also experience frequent urination as the uterus begins to enlarge. And, for the first few months, many pregnant women are constantly tired and feel they could sleep anywhere, any time.

Combined with amenorrhea, these symptoms suggest pregnancy, but they could be caused by other factors such as illness. A woman in early pregnancy may be convinced that she has the flu. Tests that show the presence of human chorionic gonadotrophin (HCG) or ultrasound pictures of the fetus in the womb are needed for accurate diagnosis of pregnancy.

Changes During Pregnancy

The average pregnancy lasts for 10 lunar months: 280 days from the first day of the last menstrual period to the day of birth. During that time, a series of changes occurs in the mother's body, but except for the changes we have already described as symptoms of pregnancy, most do not become very apparent until after the first trimester.

Weight gain is a feature of the vast majority of pregnancies. At 13 weeks, the embryo is still very small, weighing about 1 ounce, whereas the average mother has already gained 2 pounds. The mother's weight gain continues to be more rapid than the baby's throughout pregnancy. In addition to accumulated fat and water, her weight gain includes the enlargement of her breasts, the growth of the uterus, an increase in her blood supply, the placenta, and the amniotic fluid.

ketonuria: the presence of ketones (organic compounds) in the urine; from the Greek *keton* (acetone), *ouron* (urine).

Some years ago, pregnant women were placed under a great deal of pressure to limit their weight gain. It is now thought that only obese women should restrict their weight gain, because the practice limits fetal growth too. For underweight or normal women, each kilogram of maternal weight gain significantly increases the baby's birth weight (Abrams & Laros, 1986). In addition, it is easy for pregnant women to develop **ketonuria,** a chemical

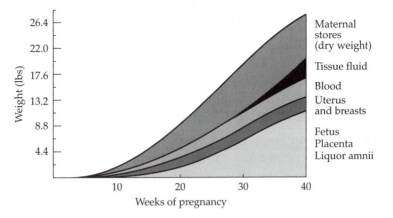

The weight a woman gains in pregnancy is not "all baby," as this chart clearly shows. (Source: National Research Council, 1970)

condition of the blood resulting from calorie restriction that may impair fetal neural development (Shaver, 1979).

As pregnancy progresses, more physical changes become apparent. The breasts become tender and increase in size. Skin pigmentation changes, so that a dark vertical line often develops on the abdomen. Some women develop chloasma, sometimes called the "mask of pregnancy"—an increase in pigmentation on the upper lip and cheeks. The joints become more flexible under the influence of the hormones of pregnancy. The pituitary gland enlarges and presses on the optic nerve, narrowing the visual field. Increased fluid behind the lens of the eye may alter focus and impair the women's judgment of short distances, making her clumsy. (Fortunately, the estimation of long distances is not affected, so driving is not a problem.) In a few cases, increases in fluid create pressure on the nerves of the hands and wrists, leading to numbness and the carpal tunnel syndrome (Wiggins, 1979).

The mother's posture changes during the course of pregnancy. As her center of gravity moves forward with her growing belly, she has to lean backward to offset the tendency to fall over. High-heeled shoes become very difficult to walk in as the pregnancy progresses.

Some gastrointestinal changes occur as a result of pregnancy. Some of these changes are simply anatomical and are caused by the growing uterus, which pushes the digestive organs out of their normal positions. Others are actual physiological changes, in which functioning alters as a result of hormonal change.

Quickening is an exciting and sometimes unnerving event for the pregnant woman. At around the 16th week of pregnancy, the mother feels the baby move for the first time. (It has been moving earlier, but the movements were too small and weak for the mother to detect.) The movement is light and fluttery and feels very much like some movements of intestinal gas. Over the course of gestation, the movements become far stronger. They can eventually be seen and felt through the mother's abdominal wall and can even push off an object like a book which she has rested on her belly. Depending on how the baby is lying, its kicking can be quite uncomfortable; some seem able to get their feet under the mother's ribs and push much harder than she cares for.

PRENATAL CARE

For most of the history of our species, prenatal medical care was no different from care at any other time of life. Although concepts of prenatal care had certainly developed by the 1930s, such care was not sought by or available to every pregnant woman. In the 1970s, it was fashionable in some circles to stress pregnancy and birth as natural processes that required little supervision.

A more balanced attitude seems to prevail today. Pregnancy is certainly a natural process, but there is nothing "unnatural" about birth defects, miscarriage, or stillbirth. Good prenatal care makes a distinct difference in the prevention of these natural but undesirable events. When prenatal care is rare or absent, outcomes are more often poor than when it is present. In this section, we will discuss a variety of issues relevant to prenatal care.

What should the pregnant woman do that is different from her nonpregnant daily life? Is she a fragile creature who needs to be helped to an overstuffed chair? (She would probably prefer a straight one, because standing up from a soft chair in advanced pregnancy is a real gymnastic feat.) Is she tough and healthy, resilient as ever? To some extent, the answers to these questions depend on the individual. Some women do feel ill during pregnancy, and their physical condition could affect fetal development. Most feel fine most of the time; some say they never felt or looked better than when pregnant. As pregnancy advances, though, the physical changes described earlier do make it more difficult for many women to perform a lot of physical work without tiring.

Working During Pregnancy

Most women in most jobs can continue working safely right until labor begins. Office jobs, teaching, law practice, and most medical or dental work are not any more dangerous for a pregnant woman than they are when she is not pregnant. If her job involves heavier work, she can still lift whatever she could lift before pregnancy. As one discussion has noted, pregnant workers probably lift just as heavy loads outside of work, carrying heavy bags of groceries into the house and lifting a 35-pound child out of his crib (Carney, Freeman, McMurrain, Slavin, & Ueland, 1980).

Some jobs, however, do involve occupational hazards for the pregnant woman. Exposure to anesthetics or to other chemical agents is potentially dangerous for the unborn baby. Pregnant women also should not work around radiation without protective clothing.

What about exercise during pregnancy? Let us note, to begin with, that the vast majority of pregnant women will not be in peak athletic condition. Even trained athletes usually need to cut down on exercise to become pregnant, because serious training often causes irregularities in the menstrual cycle (Estok & Rudy, 1984). When we talk about exercise during pregnancy, then, we are referring to several games of tennis or to running 2 or 3 miles several times a week, not to the intense exercise of the serious athlete.

There are contradictory answers to the exercise question. One recent study reported that at 20 and at 32 weeks of gestation, the fetal heart rate rose significantly after the mother ran (Clapp, 1985). This increase was interpreted as a fetal recovery response following prolonged oxygen deprivation. Another study, however, reported no increase in uterine activity or in fetal heart rate following running or stationary bicycle exercise in the last 8 weeks of pregnancy (Veille, Hohimer, Burry, & Speroff, 1985). The effect of exercise on the fetus is thus not clear.

aerobic: using oxygen; from the Greek *aer* (air), *bios* (life).

Exercise has some advantages and some disadvantages from the mother's point of view. It helps maintain her circulation, especially in her legs, where difficulties are likely to develop. It maintains the muscular strength she will need in labor and delivery. However, the pregnant woman experiences a decrease in the reserve of air in the lungs and thus may have problems with **aerobic** exercise (Artal, Wiswell, Romem, & Dorey, 1986). Because she is clumsier than usual, too, she is more likely to injure herself in a game like tennis. Moderation in exercise seems to be the best approach during pregnancy.

Sex and Pregnancy

Unless there are physical problems with the pregnancy, there is probably no reason to limit sexual activity at any point between conception and the beginning of labor. But, like birth and lactation, sexuality among human beings is not simply a physical event. Social pressures, learning, and expectations all enter into our sexual behavior.

libido: sexual desire; from the Latin *libido* (desire).

Some anatomical and physiological changes in the pregnant woman have the potential to make an impact on the couple's sexual relationship. As the uterus grows and changes in the first and second trimesters, the blood supply to the pelvic organs increases. For some women, this results in easier sexual arousal and an increase in **libido,** especially in the second trimester (the nausea and fatigue of the first trimester are "anti-erotic" for many women).

If both husband and wife agree that particular sexual practices are acceptable during pregnancy, they can avoid conflicts that would otherwise develop during the pregnancy. They will thus arrive at the crisis of birth and early care of the newborn with relatively happy, satisfied feelings about each other. In addition, their continuation of mutually satisfying love-making during the pregnancy will help maintain their interest in each other and keep them from turning to outsiders for romance. Their continued attachment to each other will help them weather the frustrating, difficult early months of child care.

Diet

As noted above, the pregnant woman needs to consume an adequate number of calories to gain weight. She needs sufficient protein and fats, particularly for the development of the baby's nervous system. Although protein, fats, and calories are easiest to acquire from animal foods, they can be managed by a knowledgeable person from vegetable sources alone. The U.S. government supplemental food program for women, infants, and children (WIC) helps provide cheese, milk, and similar calorie-protein sources for poor pregnant women, but it also has been criticized as contributing to obesity; protein-calorie malnutrition is rarely a problem in the United States, although it is in many parts of the world (Holden, 1991).

After some disagreement, the U.S. Public Health Service recommended in 1992 that pregnant women take appropriate amounts of folic acid, one of the B vitamins (Palca, 1992b). Addition of folic acid to grain products has occurred more recently, and folic acid supplementation has been reported to reduce the frequency of neural tube defects. However, folic acid can mask other problems, especially among women of African descent, who rarely have babies with neural tube defects (Herbert, 1994). Leafy green vegetables, legumes, whole grains, and oranges are natural sources of folic acid. Beta-carotene, which is converted to vitamin A in the body, has also been suggested as a preventer of neural tube defects (Sandford, Kissling, & Joubert, 1992). Recent research also indicates that vitamin A may help prevent the transmission of the human immunodeficiency virus (HIV) from an infected mother to her unborn baby (Service, 1994a).

Adequate levels of iron in the blood are essential for the health of both mother and baby. The baby needs to store iron in the liver for use in the months after birth when iron intake will be low. And anemia, or lack of iron in the mother's blood, has been associated with premature birth.

Although a certain level of vitamin C is needed for good health, excessive use during pregnancy may make the baby less able to utilize the vitamin after birth.

Special Maternal Health Problems

The mother's health may have a serious effect on the pregnancy, especially in the later months. Diabetic mothers are prone to infection, especially of the urinary tract, and tend to have problems with high blood pressure. Although many deliver healthy babies, there is an unusually high frequency of heart and skeletal defects in babies of diabetic mothers. Some infants of diabetic mothers are very large, with large visceral organs but with lungs that may still be poorly developed. Because these fetuses may die shortly before birth, labor is often induced early. Some women (about 1% to 3% of pregnancies) who have not been diagnosed as diabetic when not pregnant develop gestational diabetes in the later part of the pregnancy (Keohane & Lacey, 1991).

Preeclampsia and **eclampsia** in the third trimester involve rapid and dangerous physiological changes. Sodium and water retention in the mother's

eclampsia: a toxic state during pregnancy, leading to convulsions; from the Greek *eklampsis* (sudden flashing).

body results in rapid weight gain, swelling, and high blood pressure. The woman may experience double vision and blind spots, and retinal detachment may even occur. The mother may die of bleeding into the brain or swelling of the lungs if the baby is not delivered. Preeclampsia and eclampsia are most common in young women in their first pregnancy. Preeclampsia may result from abnormal connections of blood vessels at the time the placenta is forming (Cross, Werb, & Fisher, 1992).

Mothers who have phenylketonuria (PKU), a genetic problem described in Chapter 3, have a special health issue during pregnancy. Although their brains are too mature to be damaged by phenylalanine, the brains of their fetuses are vulnerable. Even if the fetus does not have PKU, it depends on its mother's body to metabolize phenylalanine. If she cannot perform this metabolic task, the fetus needs to be protected by a phenylalanine-free diet. The mother needs to go on the diet several months before conception and to remain on it throughout the pregnancy.

One final health issue toward the end of pregnancy is Rh incompatibility. Blood types are characterized by the presence or absence of the Rh factor. Those who have the factor are said to be Rh-positive (Rh+), and those without it are termed Rh-negative (Rh−). The Rh+ trait is determined by a dominant gene, so the Rh+ individual can be either homozygous dominant or heterozygous; the Rh− person is homozygous recessive.

When blood containing the Rh factor comes in contact with Rh− blood, as, for example, in a transfusion, the Rh− individual's body reacts by attacking the "invading" Rh+ blood cells. As pregnancy progresses, very small numbers of fetal blood cells cross the placenta to the mother's circulation. If mother and fetus are of the same Rh type or if mother is Rh+ and fetus is Rh−, there is no problem. However, if the mother is Rh− and the fetus is Rh+, Rh incompatibility exists. The mother's body responds to the fetal blood by mobilizing against the invader. In the first pregnancy, there will probably be little effect on the fetus, but each successive pregnancy with an Rh+ fetus will make the mother's body more sensitized, and the attack on the fetal blood will be earlier and more severe. Later pregnancies with Rh+ fetuses are likely to end in miscarriage unless there is treatment. Fortunately, treatment with gamma globulin at the end of each pregnancy prevents this unpleasant scenario by tricking the mother's immune system. (And, of course, she would never have a problem carrying an Rh− baby.)

Pregnant women may be unusually susceptible to certain contagious diseases. In Third World countries, malaria has a powerful impact on women in their first and second pregnancies, even though they have acquired immunity to the disease earlier. Infected red blood cells bind to particular proteins in the placenta, resulting in preterm births, retarded fetal growth, increased infant mortality, or maternal anemia and death (Fried & Duffy, 1996).

Stress is often thought of as a potential problem in pregnancy, but there is little specific research evidence on the subject. One study looked at stressful events such as marital discord, death of a close relative, and job loss and found slower fetal growth in the offspring of stressed mothers (Low et al., 1994).

GENETIC COUNSELING AND PRENATAL DIAGNOSIS

In the previous chapter, we discussed issues about conceiving a baby that some couples have to deal with. When genetic problems are in a family's background, avoiding conception or using in vitro fertilization techniques may be the only ways to prevent gestation of a defective zygote. But what if the genetic problem is one of low probability, like Down Syndrome? Or what if the concern is whether a teratogen has caused problems of development?

Prenatal diagnosis is carried out after conception and implantation, sometimes in the embryonic and sometimes in the fetal period. Only rarely does the diagnosis lead to repair of problems. In most cases, prenatal diagnosis is done to permit abortion if a serious problem exists or to allow the parents to plan how to deal with an infant with a disability.

Blood Testing

Alpha-fetoprotein (AFP) is a substance that normally circulates in the fetal blood and normally is excreted into the amniotic fluid. AFP in the mother's blood has crossed the placenta from the fetus, so the mother's AFP levels indicate something about the fetus. If there is an abnormal opening in the fetus—as in the case of spina bifida, for instance—extra AFP leaks into the amniotic fluid and can be detected in the mother's blood. Low levels of AFP indicate an increased probability of Down syndrome, although the reasons for this are not clear.

The AFP test can be done through a blood test at about the 16th week of pregnancy. It can screen out pregnancies where levels are normal and thus prevent many people from having to go through more invasive procedures, but it does not definitely confirm that an abnormality exists.

Testing for several blood factors at once can be more accurate than testing for AFP alone. In one study, 75% of Down syndrome fetuses were detected using a combination of AFP, a subunit of human chorionic gonadotropin (HCG), information about the mother's age, and a marker called dimeric inhibin A (Aitken et al., 1996).

Ultrasound

Ultrasound examination, or sonography, can show the existence of a neural tube defect. In cases of sex-linked genetic defects like hemophilia, sonography can show whether the fetus is a boy who is likely to have the hemophilia phenotype. There is also some evidence that an ultrasound picture can detect Down syndrome by revealing an unusual ratio of upper-leg to lower-leg length.

Through ultrasound examination, one can estimate the size of the fetus. When the size is compared to the norms for fetuses of the same gestational age, intrauterine growth retardation (IUGR) can be diagnosed. IUGR can be a clue to a number of genetic syndromes, various teratogenic effects, and some maternal health problems, among other things (Allen, 1992). It has also been suggested that movement patterns of the fetus, recorded through sonography, can give an early indication of brain defects (Prechtl, 1990).

Amniocentesis

If a chromosomal analysis is necessary for prenatal diagnosis, more invasive procedures must be used. The process cannot be done without some cells from the fetus or from related tissues.

amniocentesis: puncturing of the amniotic sac and removal of fluid for diagnostic purposes; from the Greek *amnion* (a caul), *kentein* (to prick).

Amniocentesis is the process of removing a sample of amniotic fluid by inserting a hollow needle through the mother's abdomen into the amniotic sac within the uterus. The fluid contains cells that have sloughed off the fetus. This procedure can be done only when enough amniotic fluid has developed, which is not until 16 to 18 weeks of pregnancy. The process of karyotyping may then take 3 to 4 additional weeks, bringing the pregnancy very close to the usual legal limit for abortion.

Amniocentesis followed by karyotyping gives a clear genetic diagnosis of Down syndrome and other genetic problems and identifies the sex of the fetus. Although there is a small danger (about 0.5%) of miscarriage, the procedure has become safer as it has become more routine, and it is now

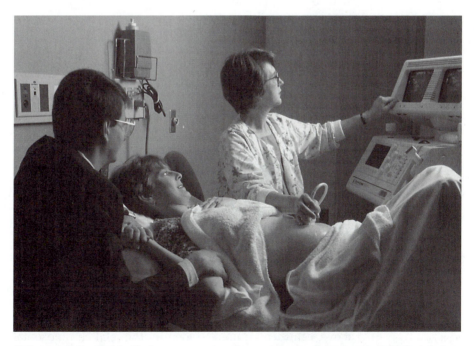

Tests during the first half of pregnancy can diagnose many, though not all, birth defects.

widely used for women over 35 and women with reason for concern about genetic problems.

The length of time for karyotyping has been so great because of the need to culture the fetal cells and grow larger numbers. However, a process called FISH (fluorescent in situ hybridization) examines only the specific sites on five chromosomes that account for 90% to 95% of all chromosomal abnormalities. This process can be done rapidly and with a small number of cells (Roberts, 1991b). An advance on FISH called spectral karyotyping involves combinations of dyes and can answer multiple questions simultaneously, rather than requiring a new analysis for each question (Marx, 1996b).

Amniocentesis can also be done later in pregnancy to assess the baby's maturity, in cases where early delivery may be necessary.

Chorionic Villus Sampling

Because the chorion develops from the fertilized ovum, its chromosomal makeup is the same as that of the fetus, and analysis of chorion cells will reveal the fetus' karyotype. Chorionic villus sampling (CVS) is a procedure, done at about the 9th week of pregnancy, in which an instrument passed through the vagina and cervix removes some tissue from the chorion.

Karyotyping following CVS can be done within a week or so, so the diagnosis is complete much earlier in the pregnancy than is the case with amniocentesis. However, the rate of miscarriage is higher (1% to 2%), and there is some possibility of damage to the fetus, which might result from infection or hemorrhage.

Early reports (such as Kaplan, Normandin, Wilson, et al., 1990) suggested no difference in birth defects following CVS and amniocentesis, but more recently (Burton, Schulz, & Burd, 1993) an unusual anomaly has been associated with CVS. The defect involves absence or shortening of fingers and toes and problems in the development of fingernails and toenails. This is a rare occurrence, but it seems more frequent when CVS is done before 10 weeks of gestation.

Flow Cytometry: A Developing Technique

It would be very desirable to be able to diagnose the fetus by means of a maternal blood test. The mother's blood needs to be tested at times during pregnancy in any case, and the process cannot cause miscarriage, as the invasive CVS or amniocentesis can.

cytometry: procedure for counting certain types of cells; from the Greek *kytos* (hollow vessel), *metron* (measure).

A test currently under development is based on the fact that a very small number of fetal cells cross the placenta and circulate in the mother's blood— about 1 fetal cell to 20 million maternal cells. A process called **flow cytometry,** which uses laser light to sort out particular cells, can pick out the fetal cells and leave most of the maternal cells behind. The FISH technique, described above, can then be used to identify the fetal chromosomal makeup (Roberts, 1991b).

Genetic Counseling

Detection of a genetic or teratogenic abnormality in the fetus usually means that the father and mother face an agonizing decision. Although prenatal treatment of the fetus is occasionally possible, the choice is usually whether to allow the pregnancy to continue or to terminate it by abortion. Genetic counseling is one source of help with the decision.

Genetic counselors play a critical role in supporting parents who must deal with serious birth defects. The parents' stress and anxiety make it very difficult for them to comprehend information, most of which is new to them, or to make serious decisions. Yet those decisions need to be made.

Abortion

conceptus: the zygote and, later, the blastocyst; from the Latin *conceptus* (taken in, conceived).

When a fetal abnormality leads to a decision to terminate the pregnancy, the procedure to be followed depends on the stage of gestation. During the first three months (trimester) of pregnancy, abortion is carried out by a suction procedure or by dilation and curettage, where the **conceptus** is surgically removed from the uterus. The procedure does not take long, but some pain may be involved, and complete recovery takes a month or so. In 1996, the Planned Parenthood Federation began the use of a combination of two drugs to produce abortion before the ninth week. Most women aborting an unwanted pregnancy at this point feel little emotional distress, but there is more sadness and more physical complaints following abortion of a wanted pregnancy (Adler et al., 1990).

Abortion in the second trimester is a more complicated matter. Labor is induced with hormones such as prostaglandins or oxytocin. Laminaria, which swell with exposure to moisture, are inserted into the cervix, where their slow expansion causes the cervix to dilate gradually. The woman may experience nausea, vomiting, sweating, diarrhea, and pain during the hours needed to accomplish the delivery of the fetus. She is grieving, even if the pregnancy was not wanted, and is concerned about her ability to become pregnant again. It is a good idea to offer the mother the chance to see the fetus, because what she can imagine about it is usually far worse than the reality; if she declines, photographs can be taken and kept for her (Williams, 1994).

In the United States, abortions in the third trimester are legal in about 50% of states, although most doctors refuse to perform them. Only one-tenth of 1% of abortions in this country are carried out so late. One procedure involves an injection into the fetal heart to stop it from beating, followed by induction of labor. Decisions to have such late abortions are often related to late detection of defects, coupled with the understanding that, if delivered alive, even a very severely handicapped baby may not be allowed to die (Kolata, 1992). This last issue will be discussed in some detail in Chapters 5 and 15.

Just as individual beliefs help determine whether a person will seek contraception or abortion, cultural differences have a strong effect on such choices. Kojima (1986) has discussed ancient and modern Japanese attitudes toward reproduction. In the past, as poems and popular songs reveal, the Japanese sometimes chose infanticide when a baby was born; they referred to the act by a horticultural term used to describe the "thinning" of plants. Today, abortion is widely practiced in Japan as a birth control technique, and oral contraceptives are illegal (Jitsukawa & Djerassi, 1994). (Surviving Japanese infants, both in the past and today, are treated with great tenderness and concern.)

In any country, deliberate policy decisions may work together with culture to determine the frequency of abortion. China's "one-child" policy has produced a remarkable reduction in the birth rate through severe penalties for having a second child (Kristof, 1993; Porter, 1993; WuDunn, 1993). An unusually high ratio (118 to 100) of boy to girl babies has also been reported (Kristof, 1993). The traditional Chinese preference for sons may account for this imbalance, through differential abortion rates for male and females and female infanticide (historically common in China, according to Sidel, 1973). Another factor could be the practice of hiding girls from census takers so the mother will not be forced to be sterilized (Porter, 1993). Girl babies are also abandoned and given up for adoption. This action affects U.S. **demographics** as well, because the Chinese authorities readily permit adoption of the abandoned girls by foreigners (Porter, 1993).

demographics: the statistical study of human populations; from the Greek *demos* (people), *graphein* (to write).

PROBLEMS TO CONSIDER AND DISCUSS

1. Discuss the idea that teratogens function as part of a dynamic action system.

2. Argue for and against the idea that research on embryos should be extended to include the period of neural tube closure. (You may want to look ahead at Chapter 15 to see how the "personhood" of the unborn infant has been viewed.)

3. How does cell differentiation lead to critical periods for the effects of teratogens?

4. Why is it difficult to get a compete list of teratogenic diseases?

5. If a couple were completely opposed to abortion, would there be any point to prenatal testing? Why or why not?

CHAPTER

5

Birth and the Newborn

Most of the topics discussed in this book involve slow, gradual developmental change. In this chapter, however, we will look at several abrupt and dramatic transitions as the developing individual moves from the status of fetus to that of neonate. As we will see, these transitions involve considerable changes in the baby's physical functioning, as well as a change in its immediate environment and sensory experience. The infant reorganizes and begins to function in new ways.

The most important transitions in functioning occur within hours or even minutes after birth. The terms *neonate* or *newborn*, however, are usually applied throughout the first month or so of the baby's life—a period during which the parents may be even more aware of their own transitions than of the baby's.

RESEARCH METHODS

Much of our information on the birth process and on the newborn has come from *clinical observation*—observation of a formal and systematic nature for a century or two and of an informal nature for thousands of years before that. The signs of beginning labor, for example, are known because of the experiences of women and their helpers in childbirth as far back as the human race goes. The understanding of the relationship between the mother's skeletal dimensions and the ease of the birth, on the other hand, had to wait for systematic observation and formal analysis of information.

Modern clinical research on birth and the newborn tends to take a different time perspective than used to be the case. Previously, work was most concerned with the infant's condition shortly after birth; if the baby survived the birth and seemed normal, few further questions were asked. Today we tend to take a longer view. An infant may seem to be doing well in early life, but problems may show up in the toddler or preschool periods. The issue of *quality of life* has become a concern in addition to that of simple survival.

Advances in technology are in many cases responsible for research questions about quality of life. New techniques have made it possible to salvage many infants who would have died not long ago, but questions need to be asked about long-term disabilities that may arise as a result of the very treatments that saved the babies' lives. With every technological advance comes a host of research questions.

Interest in long-term quality of life has prompted attempts to create standardized tests to assess a baby's condition. Such tests ask an examiner to follow specific rules rather than give a global evaluation based on his or her previous experience. Valuable though the judgment of the experienced observer may be, there is a great deal more value to a test that (1) can be used effectively by even inexperienced observers and (2) whose scores mean the same thing to every knowledgeable person.

Standardized tests of infants, like those for older people, must meet certain criteria in order to be acceptable. They must be *reliable*; that is, if a baby were to be given the test on several occasions or by several different people, the scores produced would have to be very similar to each other. The tests must also be *valid*; they must measure what they are supposed to measure and must thus show a high correlation of scores with some other type of assessment. To be useful, standardized tests for infants should also be reasonably quick to administer, because a young baby does not stay "in the mood" to be tested for very long.

One aspect of test standardization is the publication of *norms*, information about large numbers of tested infants that allows a tester to compare a baby or babies to other infants. It would appear that the existence of norms would allow a researcher to do without a comparison group, but this may not be a good idea. Changes in the population may occur over a period of years, or testers themselves may become more skillful and elicit better performances from infants than before (Gross et al., 1992).

objective: relating to the aspects of reality that are separate from personal perspectives or feelings; from the Latin *objectum* (thrown in the way).

subjective: relating to reality as perceived rather than independent of thought or feeling; from the Latin *subjectus* (one under authority).

Although many researchers have emphasized quantitative and **objective** measurements of the type stressed by standardized tests, other researchers still stress the need to look at qualitative and **subjective** judgments of the infant. Prechtl (1990) has reported that experienced observers could pick out abnormal qualities in the movement patterns of preterm infants and that their evaluations were reliable and valid.

Much research on birth and the newborn has focused on average differences between groups, or on *correlation* between one measure and another. Some recent work has begun to focus on variability as a way to assess maturity. For example, some research suggests that preterm babies who show more variation in heart rate are in better shape than are those who show less (Porges, Matthews, & Pauls, 1992).

Research on birth and the newborn often involves questions about parental attitudes and behavior as well as questions about the infant alone. Such information may be collected through interviews, standardized observations (which need to satisfy the same requirements as the standardized tests discussed before), and questionnaires. Good questionnaire research is remarkably difficult and time-consuming, contrary to the assumptions of many people who have never tried to do any. Questionnaire research starts with some careful interviews, proceeds through careful construction and testing of questions, and concludes with elaborate statistical analysis. Research on parental attitudes and behavior may also involve medical and judicial opinions about negligent or abusive treatment.

Informed consent is, of course, a necessary component of research on birth and the newborn. It can be particularly tricky in this context, because the pain and crisis atmosphere of even a normal birth may make it extraordinarily difficult for parents to think about information they are given. Before consent can be truly "informed," a patient or research subject must have substantial understanding of what is happening and must be operating in a substantial absence of control by others. The person must then intentionally authorize the beginning of medical treatment or research participation (Faden, 1991). Whether an 18-year-old mother of a sick, premature baby can satisfy these requirements is a very difficult question to answer.

LABOR AND DELIVERY

The birth process is influenced by a number of psychological, biological, and physical factors. The mother's level of control and cooperation, the hormonal and muscular activities of her body, and the characteristics of the baby itself all affect the speed and success of the birth. Once again, we are dealing with a complex dynamic action system, in which changes in apparently small factors can have a great deal of impact on the outcome.

It has been said that the birth process depends on the *powers*, the *passages*, and the *passenger* (Greenhill & Friedman, 1974)—that is, the muscular contractions of the uterus, the mother's soft tissues and the bony structures behind them, and the baby's size and position. If special problems exist in any of these factors, the birth may be slowed and the baby may be endangered.

Changes During Pregnancy

The uterus changes dramatically during pregnancy. By the end of gestation, it is ready to exchange its role as container of the fetus for that of expeller. From a weight of 3 or 4 ounces and a length of about 4 inches in the nonpregnant state, the uterus has grown to about 4 times that length and about 1½ pounds in weight. Its muscle fibers are much larger than they were before. The cervix, the opening of the uterus through which the baby will move down into the vagina, has become softer and somewhat effaced (thinned out), so it no longer protrudes from the uterus. Even before labor begins, **dilation** or widening, of the cervix may have started.

dilation: enlargement of an opening; from the Latin *dilatare* (to spread wide).

ligament: a structure that connects one bone to another; from the Latin *ligare* (to tie).

The mother's muscles and other soft tissues change during pregnancy in preparation for their role in birth. The bones of the pelvis, on the other hand, do not change (although the relaxation of **ligaments** alters their relations a bit). The pelvic bones are like a funnel through which the baby must pass during the birth process. The soft tissues can move, stretch, or even tear to allow the baby to pass, but the bony structure behind them cannot.

The Beginning of Labor

Toward the end of the pregnancy, a number of signs indicate that the birth process will soon begin. *Lightening* involves the movement of the baby's head downward into the pelvis, with an accompanying lessening of pressure in the mother's upper abdomen, and an increase in the lower. The mother may also be aware of irregular contractions of the uterus (Braxton-Hicks contractions), which may or may not be painful but that do not increase in frequency as the contractions of true labor do.

The onset of labor is still not completely understood. Throughout most of the pregnancy, progesterone helps relax the muscular fibers of the uterus, and, although contractions do occur, they are generally weak and irregular. At some point, however, the contractions become strong, regular, and increasingly frequent, and true labor has begun.

The pituitary hormone *oxytocin* is a well-known cause of uterine contraction; it is used to induce labor and to cause the uterus to stay contracted after childbirth. However, levels of oxytocin circulating in the blood do not seem essential for labor. Instead, oxytocin seems to be produced in the uterus itself, even before labor begins, at the same time that the uterus increases its number of oxytocin receptors (which must be present for the hormone to affect the muscles) (Lefebvre, Giaid, Bennett, Larivière, & Zingg, 1992). Prostaglandins may also be involved in the process.

Hormones released by the fetus' maturing pituitary and adrenal glands, at a signal from the developing brain, also may be involved in causing the changes that lead to the beginning of labor (Palca, 1991a). Another substance that may be involved in the onset of regular uterine contractions is *fetal fibronectin,* a protein that attaches the membranes surrounding the fetus to the wall of the uterus. Separation of the membranes from the wall occurs during labor and may further stimulate the uterus (Radetsky, 1994).

Gap junctions are structures in the uterus that have also been associated with the timing of labor. These are membrane structures that carry electrical messages between cells. They are absent during most of gestation and appear soon before labor begins (Garfield & Daniel, 1977). It is possible that the gap junctions help the uterine muscle fibers contract in a coordinated way, thus initiating the regular and powerful contractions of labor (Radetsky, 1994).

Much current work on the onset of labor is concerned with prediction and prevention of premature births, with their many dangers for the child. Some related issues will be discussed in a later section of this chapter.

The Stages of Labor and Birth

The processes of labor and the actual birth of the baby are usually divided into three stages. Stage I begins when the uterus starts to show regular, repeated contractions; it ends when the cervix is completely dilated to a width of 10 cm and forms a continuous channel with the vagina. This stage is quite variable in length, although the average duration is about 12 hours for women having their first baby and about 8 hours for those with second or later babies. Stage

II begins when dilation of the cervix is complete and ends when the baby is born. Ordinarily, it takes from one-half to two hours. Stage III involves the expulsion of the placenta and of the torn membranes that surrounded the baby.

During Stage I, there is little the laboring woman can do to hasten the process. She experiences contractions every 15 or 20 minutes at first, and the frequency increases to every 2 minutes or so by the end of this stage. Most women experience the contractions as painful, some as extremely so; there is no evidence that "primitive" women experience less pain in labor than do modern women in industrialized societies. Because the contractions last only for a minute or so, however, the pain is much more manageable than it might otherwise be. The woman's primary job during Stage I is to try to stay relaxed and to save her strength for Stage II.

Pain management is often a concern during Stages I and II, and women experience the contractions of labor as painful in varying degrees. Tissue damage, a cause of pain, certainly occurs as the cervix opens and other soft tissues are stretched or even torn. But tissue damage is not the only factor to be considered. A certain amount of the mother's discomfort is what we might call "suffering" rather than pain. It comes from fear, tension, and anticipation of difficulties to come.

Pain management during childbirth needs to focus on the relief of suffering as well as of pain due to tissue damage. A mother who does not know what to expect seems to experience increased suffering, a fact that led to the development of preparatory classes for expectant parents. During the pregnancy, the parents-to-be go to a series of weekly classes that give instruction on the events of childbirth and how they can be handled. The classes often include a tour of the hospital labor and delivery rooms, so the physical environment will not be completely unfamiliar while birth is going on.

hyperventilation: rapid breathing that upsets the body's balance of oxygen and carbon dioxide; from the Greek *hyper-* (over), the Latin *ventus* (wind).

Most classes that prepare expectant parents for childbirth stress the use of *breathing techniques* to diminish discomfort. When used properly, these techniques help keep the mother from either **hyperventilating** or getting out of breath during labor. They also help her control her pushing during delivery. Their main function may be to serve as a distraction, for the woman who is concentrating on breathing properly cannot be agonizing over how much longer a contraction can go on. People helping the laboring woman also can use her breathing pattern as an index of her feeling of control over her sensations. Different breathing techniques are used for different stages of labor and for different levels of discomfort. If a woman's breathing pattern seems irregular or inappropriate, she may need guidance to maintain her concentration.

Laboring women often seem to be much more distressed if left alone during labor. A supportive companion, whether husband, mother, or friend, can greatly reduce anxiety and suffering.

The most common approach to alleviating the pain that results from tissue damage involves drug treatment. A wide variety of *analgesics* (which reduce pain sensations) and *anesthetics* (which reduce all sensations) are available that can generally be used quite safely. However, they can also reduce the mother's alertness, her control over her actions, and her ability to follow instructions.

APPLICATIONS & ARGUMENTS
Is Birth Painful to a Baby?

If we imagine our adult selves in the place of a baby, we are likely to think of birth as a painful process. How could it help being unpleasant if your body is folded up and crammed through a small opening? What about having your head jammed repeatedly up against a ring of muscle until the muscle is at last forced to stretch open? And, after all, babies do cry right after they are born, and they often look red, bruised, and battered. It seems logical to assume that birth is painful and traumatic.

We can never really know what the infant experiences, because babies do not have the words to tell us at the time or the memory to tell us later. We do know, however, that the infant experiences a surge of hormones during a vaginal birth. One hormone, adrenalin, is associated with feelings of well-being in adults when present in levels equivalent to those in newborn babies. If infants' sensations are anything like those of adults (and, of course, we have no way of knowing whether they are), this hormone's functioning suggests that by the time the birth is over, the baby is feeling good rather than traumatized.

Whether or not the squeezing and pushing of birth is painful, the process seems to play a role in readying the infant for life outside the mother's body. Babies born by Caesarean section experience little squeezing and have lower hormone levels; they also have more difficulty breathing. The surge of hormones during vaginal birth seems to alter blood flow to the lungs and make the lungs do a better job of oxygen exchange. Even if the baby does experience pain during birth, the effect on the body seems to be worth it.

Pain due to tissue damage can also be reduced by techniques associated with the *gating theory* of pain (Melzack & Wall, 1965). The idea of gating is that pain messages can get through to the brain only when the proper neural pathways are open. When other sensory information is being transmitted to the brain at the same time, pain messages may be "closed out." When we scratch a mosquito bite or rub a bumped shin, for example, we are sending sensory messages that temporarily close the gate and prevent pain messages from getting through. Some of the pain of childbirth can thus be prevented by offering competing sensations: back rubs, cool moist cloths, or **effleurage** (a light fingertip massage of the abdomen during a contraction).

effleurage: a light, fingertip massage; from the French *effleurer* (barely to touch).

Birth

During Stage II, the woman can work to move the process onward. Now the reasons for the term *labor* become apparent, as the mother throws all her physical strength into her efforts to expel the baby. She experiences a sensation comparable to the need for an enormous bowel movement (unromantically put, but accurate), and she holds her breath and presses downward by contracting the abdominal and diaphragmatic muscles while the uterus contracts.

The mother's position during Stage II makes a difference to the effectiveness of her pushing, although there is no one best position for her to be in. We usually think of birth taking place with the mother in the **lithotomy** position—on her back, with legs spread and raised and feet in "stirrups." Although the laboring woman is most often placed in this position for delivery, it is not the most efficient one for her work, and it only became common in the late 17th century. When the woman is in a vertical position, her contractions are more efficient and she reports decreased pain (Romond & Baker, 1985). Squatting to give birth is probably an excellent approach in normal births, because it enlarges the pelvic outlet and makes bearing down easier. A birthing chair serves the same purpose.

lithotomy: surgical incision for removal of a bladder stone; from the Greek *lithos* (stone), *temnein* (to cut).

This statue of an ancient Mexican goddess shows the squatting position for giving birth. This very effective position was common to many traditional cultures.

During Stage II, the characteristics of the "passenger" (as Greenhill and Friedman call the unborn baby) become important factors. A large baby with a large head is harder to push out than a small one is. The position in which the baby lies in the uterus is also influential. The ideal and most frequent position for the baby is head down, the **vertex** presentation. A much less common and more difficult position is the **breech** presentation, where the baby's buttocks or legs pass through the cervix first. The most difficult position is a transverse or sideways position; a baby lying this way probably cannot be delivered vaginally.

Ideally, as the baby descends into the vagina headfirst, it will turn through a process of *internal rotation* until it is lying face down (that is, face toward the mother's back). This moves the head into a position that lines it up best with the mother's pelvic bones and from which it can move through the pelvic outlet most effectively. For the shoulders to pass through the bony structure, however, they need to be perpendicular to the mother's hips, so the baby at this point has the head turned to one side rather than straight relative to its shoulders. Once the head is born, the head rotates back to its own "straight ahead" position, so the baby is looking to one side as the shoulders are emerging.

This description shows how tight the fit is between the baby and the passage it must negotiate. Indeed, the fit is so tight that the baby's head is actually reshaped temporarily by the pressures it experiences. This is possible because **ossification** of bones is not complete in the infant; rather than a hard, bony skeleton, the child's skeleton is largely cartilage with relatively little mineral content. In addition, the bony plates of the skull are unfinished at the

vertex: the head-downward position of a fetus; from the Latin *vertere* (to turn).

breech: the buttock-downward position of a fetus; from the Middle English *brec* (leg covering).

ossification: the process of mineral deposit by which cartilage becomes true bone; from the Latin *os* (bone), *ficare* (to make).

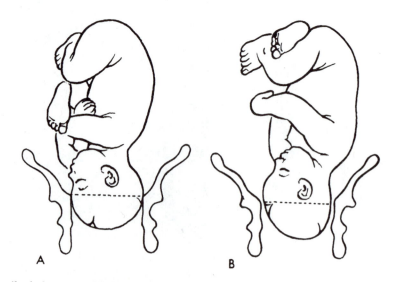

A   B

When the baby moves his head into a more flexed position, the birth process becomes easier because the tilted head fits more easily through the mother's pelvic outlet.

suture: the line of union between the bones of the skull; from the Latin *sutura* (seam).

fontanel: one of the "soft" areas of a baby's head where the skull bones have not yet grown together; from the Middle English *fontinelle* (a bodily hollow or pit).

Caesarean section: a surgical opening of the uterus for the purpose of delivering a baby; possibly named after Julius Caesar, who is said to have been born in this way, but possibly from the Latin *caedere* (to cut) and *secare* (to cut).

time of birth and have not completely formed the **sutures** that will later link them into a continuous structure. At several points, the bones do not even touch each other but instead surround openings called **fontanels,** the well-known "soft spots" on the baby's head. The fontanels and incomplete ossification allow the forces of labor to mold the baby's skull into a shape that more easily passes through the pelvic outlet. (If the baby is in a breech position, however, the pressures will not be on an area that is easily molded.)

If the baby becomes physiologically distressed by the birth process, changes in its heart rate indicate that there is a problem. In recent years it has become very common for the laboring woman to wear a fetal monitor, a beltlike sensor device that records the baby's heart rate and displays it on a bedside television monitor. Sometimes the infant's distress can be relieved if the mother simply moves into a different position; sometimes the distress is serious and delivery by **Caesarean section** is needed to save the baby. As some workers in this area have noted, the fetal monitor may actually give an oversupply of information. Physicians' fears of harm to the baby, as well as fears of malpractice suits, are among the factors that have caused a 25% increase in the rate of Caesarean sections in the United States since fetal monitors came into use, with no associated change in infant mortality (Crease, 1993).

Caesarean section   The Caesarean section, or C-section, operation is a surgical delivery of the baby through the mother's abdomen, rather than through the cervix and vagina. It is performed under a number of circumstances, such as when the fetus is in distress or when the mother's pelvic outlet is too small for the fetus to pass through. As with any surgical operation, delivery by C-section is more dangerous to mother and baby than is a nonsurgical birth.

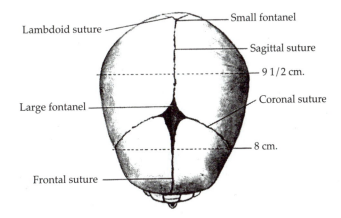

Lambdoid suture

Small fontanel

Sagittal suture

9 1/2 cm.

Large fontanel

Coronal suture

8 cm.

Frontal suture

The fontanels, or "soft spots" in a baby's head, are at the crossings of sutures where the skull plates will eventually join. This diagram indicates the positions and names of the fontanels and sutures.

After the Birth

Once the baby is expelled from the mother's body, care must be taken to ensure the health of both mother and baby. The expulsion of the placenta in Stage III must be complete, because any parts left in the uterus can cause bleeding and infection. The uterus should contract to close off torn blood vessels and prevent blood loss; if it does not do this automatically, the uterus may be massaged through the abdominal wall, or oxytocin may be injected, or the baby may be put to the mother's breast to suck—all actions that cause contraction of the uterus.

Immediate care of the infant is first directed toward making sure that the baby can breathe on its own. Techniques to help clear the airway and allow independent breathing to begin include suctioning mucus and fluid from the baby's nose and mouth, and tilting the baby with head down to allow drainage. The baby also needs to be kept warm. The baby cannot yet maintain its body temperature well, it is wet and can lose heat through evaporation, and chilling can worsen or create problems at this time. Putting the baby on the mother's abdomen allows it to share her body heat and allows the mother her first "external" contact with her child.

At this point, the umbilical cord is still attached to the placenta, and, if Stage III is not complete, the placenta is still inside the mother. Within a few minutes after birth, the cord is compressed with two clamps spaced close together and then cut between the clamps with scissors. The sterility of scissors or other cutting edges is very important; a cause of infant death in underdeveloped countries is tetanus contracted from a contaminated implement used to cut the cord. There is no sensation in the cord, so cutting it does not hurt the infant or mother.

A final step in the immediate care of the newborn is to apply antiseptic or antibiotic treatment to the baby's eyes. Gonorrhea or other infections present in the vagina at the time of birth can cause serious eye infections that can lead to blindness unless this precaution is taken. A detailed physical examination of the baby is also carried out soon after birth. (This process will be described in the section "Examining the Newborn.")

neonate: an infant in the first month after birth; from the Greek *neos* (new), the Latin *natus* (born).

Depending on the family's wishes, the infant's health, and hospital policy, the baby may at this point be taken to the **neonatal** nursery or, if it is ill, to the neonatal intensive care unit (NICU). Ideally, though, the parents and the baby will be given an hour or so to make each other's acquaintance in a recovery room, where their progress can be carefully monitored. Telephone calls are made to family and friends, the mother drinks thirstily, and the baby may be put to the breast and suck for the first time.

The immediate recovery period, which lasts for an hour after the expulsion of the placenta, can be considered Stage IV of labor and delivery. During this time, a mother who has not been medicated is alert, excited, and talkative. She wants to see her baby and ideally will be able both to see and to nurse the infant. This period may be one in which the process of emotional attachment of the mother to the baby naturally begins. The mother usually desires and appreciates the presence of the baby's father or other family members during Stage IV.

After their period in the recovery room, mother and baby may be separated or they may both go to a "rooming-in" unit, where the mother will do most of the infant care. In the 1970s, most mothers and babies stayed in the hospital for 5 to 7 days, but in the mid-1990s many hospitals switched for a time to a "short stay" policy for healthy mothers and newborns, who went home within 24 hours after vaginal delivery. This insurance-driven change was welcomed by some mothers but was rather frightening to others, and it prevented them from attending hospital education programs. As for the infant, the short stay was probably not a life-or-death matter; of infants who die in the neonatal period, 99% of them have already shown symptoms by 18 hours after birth and so would not have been sent home (Beebe, Britton, Britton, Fan, & Jepson, 1996). Federal legislation in 1996 required insurance companies to provide for a minimum 48-hour stay.

THE INFANT IN TRANSITION: FROM FETUS TO NEWBORN

A few hours before birth, the fetus is *anatomically* the same as it will be after delivery, but it is *functionally* somewhat different. The birth and the period soon after birth lead to some remarkable reorganizations of the baby's physical processes.

Before birth, the fetus' response to stress (such as the need for more oxygen) is an *inhibition* of behavior. The so-called paralysis reflex (Lagerkrantz, 1989) is very different from the neonate's usual agitated response to stress. The difference between the two states may have to do with levels of neurohormones that inhibit activity before birth. After birth, there is a surge of excitatory neurohormones called catecholamines. Catecholamines seem to be released especially during vaginal delivery and may be stimulated by the pressure on the fetus' head; babies delivered by Caesarean section have much lower catecholamine levels (Lagerkrantz, 1989). When adults are given large amounts of these hormones, they become alert and experience a sense of well-being, which may also be what the neonate experiences soon after birth.

The fetus' physical functioning is different in many ways from that of the infant after birth. All the tasks the mother's body did for the fetus—consumption of food, digestion, elimination of waste products, and so on—must now be accomplished by the baby's own body. Breathing must become independent within a very few minutes or the baby will not survive without help. Changes in the circulatory system should also occur almost immediately. Consumption and use of food can take more time, and some functions, like that of the immune system, will need years of development before they are complete.

In the fetus, the lungs do not provide oxygen to the body or dispose of carbon dioxide; the placenta does these jobs. Only the amount of blood needed to carry in oxygen is circulated to the fetal lungs; most of the blood is

---

APPLICATIONS & ARGUMENTS
How Does a Baby's Birth Affect the Parents' Marriage?

Common sense alone tells us that a baby in the house changes the parents' lives. Three people create a different situation from two, no matter who the third one is. The birth of a child brings about specific changes different from those that would occur if Uncle George moved in.

Pregnancy and childbirth alter the couple's sexual relationship. The woman's enlarged body in the last months of pregnancy may make it difficult to find a mutually satisfactory position for intercourse. In the weeks after birth, the mother's need for physical recovery makes it advisable to postpone the resumption of sexual relations. Even when healing is complete, the new mother's fatigue and preoccupation with the baby may diminish her interest in sex. It is not unusual for the father to feel somewhat displaced and to withdraw emotionally. If the basic relationship is good, the marriage can reorganize with a new set of boundaries and expectations, but this does not happen instantaneously. In fact, the marriage may need to continue reorganizing as the baby's needs and abilities change and as more children are born.

Some changes in the parents' lives are simple but stressful. For example, parents may have depended on Saturday morning as a time to sleep late, make love, talk, and catch up with each other after a busy week. But babies don't sleep late, nor do they know the difference between Saturday and any other day. The parents need to find new ways to confirm their relationship as a couple.

Finally, caring for infants and toddlers takes a lot of work. Laundry, dishes, cooking, and food shopping all multiply at the same time that sleep and energy levels are reduced. It should not be surprising that many couples experience early parenthood as a time of crisis.

---

diverted away from the lungs through the ductus arteriosus. In *fetal circulation*, blood inside the heart moves from right to left through the foramen ovale, an opening in the wall between the two sides of the heart.

At birth, the baby's lungs must begin the job of exchanging oxygen and carbon dioxide. During prenatal life and at the time of birth, however, the lungs are filled with fluid and mucus. The pressure of a vaginal delivery helps squeeze out some of the lungs' contents. Turning the baby head downward and suctioning out the fluid also helps empty the lungs and prepare them for the inflation with air that must occur within a few minutes. Lung inflation is almost completely accomplished "with the first good cry" (Avery & Fletcher, 1974, p. 33).

With the first cry, the alveoli of the lungs expand and there is a decrease in the resistance to blood flow of the pulmonary blood vessels. This is followed by a decrease in pressure in the right atrium of the heart, as more blood flows to the lungs, and an increase in pressure in the left atrium from increased blood flow back from the lungs. The direction of blood flow through the heart becomes left to right in *neonatal circulation.* The foramen ovale begins to close, and a muscular contraction then closes the ductus arteriosus and forces blood to flow to the lungs by way of the pulmonary artery.

If all has gone well, the blood now circulates past the lungs, where it picks up oxygen and eliminates carbon dioxide and is then pumped to all parts of the body, providing all cells with sufficient oxygen. A successful transition in breathing and circulation will be shown in the baby's pink or reddish skin; the bright red, oxygenated blood shows through the skin even in infants with dark skin pigmentation. Problems in the transition cause bluish or ashy lips and nailbeds, or, more severely, a bluish skin tone all over. The Apgar test, an examination of a newborn baby that will be discussed in the next section, focuses on the baby's color as one of five particularly important points to assess.

Within two or three days after birth, another transition process involving the blood becomes apparent. In addition to changing its route around the body, the blood is changing its **hemoglobin** and red blood cell content. Hemoglobin in the red blood cells carries oxygen in both the fetus and the newborn, but fetal hemoglobin functions somewhat differently from the mature form. Fetal hemoglobin does not give up oxygen to the tissues as readily as adult hemoglobin does. The fetus also has a problem with oxygenation because it cannot breathe more rapidly or deeply when more oxygen is required. A greater number of red blood cells in circulation helps the fetus overcome these problems, but the cells are not needed in such quantities after birth. These extra cells are broken down by the liver and their byproducts are excreted from the body.

hemoglobin: the protein in red blood cells that transports oxygen; from the Greek *haima* (blood).

When the immature liver does not break down the red blood cells completely, a byproduct of the breakdown is bilirubin, a yellow pigment that can temporarily color the eyes and skin (and which is seen in the coloration of healing bruises). Neonatal or physiological jaundice is a yellowish cast to the skin that reflects the presence of bilirubin in circulation, and it often appears on the second or third day of life. When **hyperbilirubinemia,** an unusually high level of bilirubin in the blood, is present, treatment may be necessary to prevent brain damage. Exposure to ultraviolet light helps break down bilirubin, as the light passes through the skin. Making sure that the baby consumes plenty of fluids increases blood volume and thus decreases the proportion of bilirubin in the blood. Hyperbilirubinemia is most likely to occur in preterm babies and will be discussed in more detail in a later section of this chapter.

hyperbilirubinemia: an excessive amount of bilirubin in the blood; from the Greek *hyper-* (over), the Latin *bilis* (liver), *ruber* (red), the Greek *haima* (blood).

Consuming and digesting food involve less complex transitions than breathing and circulation do. The baby's rooting and sucking reflexes are normally strong, and the neonate readily turns toward a potential food source, mouths it, and begins to suck and swallow. The baby frequently swallowed

meconium:
material inside the bowel of a fetus, which forms the neonate's first feces; from the Greek *mekonion* (poppy juice).

colostrum: the first fluid to form in the breast as a preliminary to lactation; from the Latin *colostrum* (the fluid produced by a cow at the same point).

amniotic fluid during the fetal period, and many also sucked their thumbs, so these functions are well established in the full-term baby.

Bowel movements do not ordinarily occur before birth in a healthy baby but usually take place in the first 24 hours after birth. The newborn's lower intestine contains **meconium,** a dark, sticky, unattractive substance that comes from sloughed-off cells and other material swallowed with the amniotic fluid. Urination, which takes place regularly in the fetus, should occur in the first 48 hours.

The neonate has trouble maintaining its body temperature and has a limited capacity to fight infection by means of the immune response. The baby depends on clothing, artificial heat, and contact with the bodies of its caregivers to keep it warm enough. (A sick or preterm baby may develop serious problems if it becomes chilled.) The baby is born with a supply of antibodies that it received through the placenta, and it receives another dose if allowed to ingest the **colostrum** the mother's breasts are producing at this point.

EXAMINING THE NEWBORN

Some characteristics of a newborn baby obviously show the need for immediate help. Failure to breathe or a failing heartbeat are clear indications that resuscitation is necessary. Serious birth defects such as the development of the heart or intestines outside of the body are also readily apparent.

Some aspects of the baby's condition, on the other hand, are subtle and could easily be missed, yet they may be essential to evaluating the newborn's condition in the critical period of adjustment right after birth. Standardized techniques like the Apgar test have been developed to allow rapid assessment.

Developed by and named after Dr. Virginia Apgar, the *Apgar score* is an assessment almost invariably used in U.S. hospitals. It is a "quick and dirty" test, rapidly administered but yielding only rough estimations of the baby's condition. Given at 1, at 5, and sometimes at 10 minutes after birth, the Apgar test is intended to identify babies who need special observation or help. It does not identify the more intelligent babies or correlate with success in life; it simply shows which babies should be all right with ordinary care and which may not.

To conduct the test, an examiner follows specific criteria, such as promptness of crying and heart rate measures, to assign points on the Apgar score. Each of the five categories on the test can receive a maximum of 2 points, so the highest possible score is 10. If the baby's score is from 7 to 10, no special help is needed; a score from 4 to 6 indicates the need for observation and assistance with breathing; a score from 0 to 3 indicates that measures to resuscitate the baby are needed if it is to survive (Keller & Sandelski, 1994).

Examination of the baby's weight and certain physical characteristics give further information about the need for special care. In the past, the terms *premature* and *low-birth-weight baby* were used almost synonymously, but today two separate classifications have emerged from the old categories.

The first category that relates to the baby's need for special care is that of *gestational age:* the length of time the baby has been developing. The expected date for a baby's birth is 40 weeks after the first day of the mother's last menstrual period; a baby born at that point is at 40 weeks gestational age (GA). Any baby born between 38 and 42 weeks GA is considered to be a term baby and to have no special risk factors based on gestational age alone. A baby born at more than 42 weeks GA is designated as *postterm* and has a somewhat higher risk of dying soon after birth than a term baby has.

The gestational age classification associated with the greatest risk is *preterm;* these babies are born at less than 38 weeks GA and may survive when born as early as 25 weeks. The lower the GA, the greater the risk for death or severe handicapping conditions. The risks for these babies and the special care they need will be discussed later in this chapter.

How is the baby's gestational age determined? Records of the pregnancy, including the date of the mother's last menstrual period, are helpful, but the baby's physical development is most informative. Scales like the Dubowitz Scale (Dubowitz, Dubowitz, & Goldberg, 1970) look at specific features that change predictably as gestational age increases. The baby's nipples are flat during the early preterm period and increase in size and protrusion as term approaches. The ears initially have incompletely formed cartilage and will stay folded in any position they are put into, but in the term baby they will snap back into their normal position if folded over. The genitals are immature in the preterm infant; the testes have not descended into the scrotum, and the labia have not grown sufficiently to cover the clitoris. Whereas the term infant has many lines and wrinkles on its palms and soles, the preterm infant has few. The preterm infant has a great deal of a white, greasy substance called **vernix caseosa** on its skin, whereas in the full-term baby the vernix is only in skin folds. These and a number of other features allow an accurate assessment of gestational age.

vernix caseosa: a cheeselike substance found on the skin of the newborn; from the Latin *vernix* (varnish), *caseus* (cheese).

Once gestational age is established, it is possible to look at the baby's size for gestational age rather than its weight category alone. A growth chart shows the percentages of babies of different GAs who have achieved particular weights by the time of birth. A baby whose weight lies between the 10th and the 90th percentiles for its gestational age is considered to be within the normal range and is designated *appropriate for gestational age* (AGA) in weight. If the baby's weight is above the 90th percentile, it is considered *large for gestational age* (LGA), and a baby whose weight is below the 10th percentile is said to be *small for gestational age* (SGA). The mortality rate for LGA babies is higher than that for AGA babies, but that of SGA babies is highest of all. The SGA condition is often associated with genetic defects or with exposure to teratogens.

Babies can thus be placed into nine subcategories as a result of assessing gestational age and size for gestational age. The full-term AGA baby has an excellent chance of survival without handicaps and very probably needs no special care, whereas the preterm baby of 25 or 26 weeks GA, who is also SGA, is in very serious trouble indeed.

A scale intended for assessment of more subtle differences between babies is the Neonatal Behavioral Assessment Scale, or NBAS (Brazelton, 1984). The

NBAS involves 28 behavioral items and 18 neurologic reflex items placed into 7 categories (Lester, Als, & Brazelton, 1982). The habituation category addresses the infant's lessened response to stimulation as a stimulus becomes familiar; the orientation category has to do with alertness and responsiveness to stimulation; autonomic regulation involves signs of stress; range of state refers to the baby's transitions from one state (such as calm alertness) to another; regulation of state has to do with efforts the baby makes to control its own state. The reflex and motor performance categories are self-explanatory. The NBAS is a highly standardized assessment, but there is a good deal of variability in an individual baby's responses to it (Cioni & Castellacci, 1990). An interesting use of the NBAS is as an intervention that teaches parents about their baby.

When indicated, screening for physical problems is carried out during the first few days after birth. Some tests, such as blood tests for phenylketonuria and for thyroid problems, are conducted on most babies in the United States, because treatment exists that can prevent developmental problems. Testing for sickle cell anemia is becoming more common as treatment becomes better understood (this will be discussed in detail in Chapter 6). The ethics of mandatory testing for the presence of genetic diseases that are not presently curable have been questioned, however, on the grounds that parents' attitudes toward the child may be adversely affected by the information (Marshall, 1993).

When a concern about brain damage exists, problems can be assessed through a variety of noninvasive techniques such as ultrasound and magnetic resonance imaging. If there is reason to suspect exposure to AIDS, the newborn can be tested for human immunodeficiency virus (HIV). Similarly, if there is reason to think the mother used drugs within a few days before giving birth, the baby can be tested for the presence of drug residues. Urine to test the presence of cocaine in the baby can be taken directly from a diaper, for example.

PRETERM BIRTH

The preterm birth of more than 10% of U.S. babies is a serious problem. In recent years, 85% of all deaths in early infancy have been associated with prematurity (Radetsky, 1994). Preterm babies are likely to suffer from multiple problems, and high-tech care of a severely preterm baby may add up to a quarter of a million dollars before the baby is ready to go home. And, contrary to folklore, problems increase in number as gestational age goes down.

The traditional approach to premature labor has been to use medication to try to stop the contractions after they have begun. Nonpharmaceutical interventions have included having the mother (1) lie down on her left side, (2) drink 4 to 5 cups of water (the increased fluids cause greater uterine blood flow and decreased contractions), (3) avoid orgasm, and (4) avoid stimulation of the nipples, which could cause the release of oxytocin (Talley-Lacy & McCarthy, 1994).

At this writing, efforts to deal with premature labor focus on identifying and treating *bacterial infections,* which some researchers consider to be the major cause of preterm birth. Bacteria may cause *premature rupture of mem-branes* (PROM), which may trigger the beginning of labor; antibiotic treatment of women in premature labor has been shown to delay the birth significantly (Radetsky, 1994). For vaginal infections, antibiotic treatment before labor begins can help prevent preterm delivery. Bacterial infection of the placenta is a more difficult problem because the drugs used to combat it would be teratogenic; screening and treating both parents before conception would be the best approach (Roush, 1996).

Another predictor of preterm labor may be the presence of fetal fibronec-tin in vaginal fluids. This substance seems to be released as the membranes pull away from the wall of the uterus. Testing for fetal fibronectin seems to be a way to tell true preterm labor from other contractions (Lockwood et al., 1991). Finally, electrodes on the abdomen can detect the electrical activity of the gap junctions discussed earlier in this chapter. Nitric oxide apparently reduces this electrical activity and can prolong pregnancy (Radetsky, 1994).

Other factors associated with preterm labor are multiple gestations and the mother's age. Twins and larger groups are rarely carried to term, and mothers over age 40 and under age 18 are more likely to give birth prematurely (Talley-Lacy & McCarthy, 1994). Mothers under the age of 15 are especially likely to have preterm or SGA babies (McAnarney, 1985).

THE PRETERM INFANT

Concerns about preterm infants focus first on their increased death rate and second on serious problems that will need treatment in the first months of life. Long-term effects, such as motor and visual-motor problems that will be present at school age, are also of interest (Herrgard, Luoma, Tuppurainen, Karjalainen, & Martikainen, 1993). Blindness due to **retinopathy** of prematu-rity may be another long-term result (Gibson, Sheps, Schechter, Wiggins, & McCormick, 1989); researchers are currently working on isolating a protein factor that could be responsible for this disorder (Barinaga, 1995).

retinopathy: damage or disease of the retina; from the Latin *rete* (net), the Greek *pathos* (suffering).

For the purposes of this text, the problems of the preterm infant and their treatment in the first months of life are of greatest importance. Preterm infants, with their immature lungs, are likely to suffer from *respiratory distress syn-drome*. They experience periods of **apnea**, where breathing stops temporarily for no obvious reason, and disorganized breathing, where the chest rises and falls but no air passes through the nostrils (Lucey, 1984).

apnea: failure to breathe for a period of time; from the Greek *an-* (not), *pnein* (to breathe).

As mentioned before, preterm babies are also likely to have dangerously high bilirubin, which can often be treated with medication and with **phototherapy** using ultraviolet light (Valaes, Petmezaki, Hensche, Drum-mond, & Kappas, 1994). They tend to experience bleeding into the brain, with resulting brain damage. They may spend many weeks in the neonatal intensive care unit (NICU), where they are subjected of necessity to many invasive procedures; they must often be fed by a tube through nose or mouth, have their breathing artificially assisted, and receive medications or fluids intravenously.

phototherapy: treatment of neonatal jaundice with ultraviolet light; from the Greek *phos* (light), *therapeuein* (to treat).

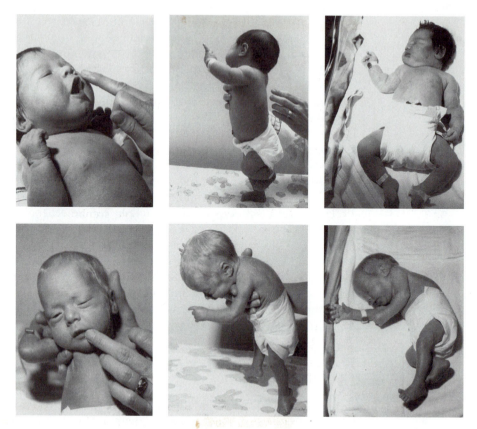

The behavior as well as the appearance of preterm babies causes difficulties for their parents. The baby on the top, who is full-term, can suck well and hold his head up, whereas the preterm baby on the bottom is much less competent.

Other treatments attempting to ease the physical stress on preterm babies and to help maintain adequate breathing and circulation have included the use of water beds (Korner, 1984b) and massage (Field & Schanberg, 1990).

Brain damage as a result of brain bleeds can be related to the difficulties the preterm baby has in breathing and in blood circulation. A number of physical functions affect each other, and when one goes wrong a whole cascade of difficulties may follow. For example, at times of *hypoxia*, the infant's body directs blood to the brain and away from the lower part of the body. As a result, the poor supply of blood to the intestines may lead to **necrotizing enterocolitis**—essentially, gangrene of the intestines—which must be treated surgically. Damage to the *kidneys* and to the *heart* may also occur.

An interesting point about brain bleeds is that they occur more often and cause more damage in the preterm babies of mothers who use alcohol during pregnancy (Holzman et al., 1995). Infants whose mothers have used cocaine during pregnancy seem to have some advantage in terms of survival after

necrotizing:
involving the localized death of living tissue; from the Greek *nekroun* (to make dead).

enterocolitis:
inflammation of the intestines; from the Greek *enteron* (intestine), *colon* (large intestine).

premature birth (Sumits, Bennett, & Gould, 1996), although presumably not in other ways.

Earlier in this chapter, we discussed how, at birth, the infant makes a transition from *fetal* to *mature circulation* of the blood; blood flow through the ductus arteriosus is reversed and soon ceases, and the foramen ovale closes. In the preterm baby, who is really still a fetus, *persistent fetal circulation* (PFC) may occur; the ductus arteriosus and foramen ovale remain open and hypoxia becomes more severe. The baby's reaction to decreased oxygen is to lessen the blood flow to the lower part of the body, sending most of the blood and oxygen to the brain. But the sudden increase in pressure can tear the fragile blood vessels, leading to bleeding and consequent destruction of nerve cells (Lou, 1989). Difficulty in breathing, as in respiratory distress syndrome, increases hypoxia and makes the whole scenario more likely to occur. The outcome of these incidents of brain damage may involve difficulties of motor control or other problems, such as decreased intellectual ability.

Respiratory distress syndrome (RDS) arises when the infant's lungs are too immature to produce the surfactants that facilitate the exchange of oxygen and carbon dioxide. The lungs do not provide sufficient oxygen to the body without help. Mechanical ventilation, which essentially blows air under pressure into the lungs, can easily cause irritation and long-term lung damage. Modern attempts to assist the RDS baby without using mechanical ventilation have included the use of artificial surfactants and of liquid perfluorocarbon, which expands the lungs and helps with oxygen exchange. Nitric oxide has also been used in these cases.

A procedure that has greatly reduced the mortality rate in babies with RDS is **extracorporeal membrane oxygenation** (ECMO), which is essentially a modified heart-lung bypass. Blood is removed through vessels in the infant's neck, sent through a device where oxygen is added and carbon dioxide removed, and returned to circulation (Hunter, Zwischenberger, & Bhatia, 1992). The baby stays on ECMO for 5 to 10 days and is awake and alert. When some improvement has occurred in the lungs, the infant is gradually "weaned" by taking less blood into the ECMO circuit and letting more pass the lungs. Unfortunately, the fragile blood vessels of the younger preterm babies make ECMO impossible for very small infants or for those less than 35 weeks of GA.

More subtle problems for the preterm baby may result from the difficulty of interaction between parent and infant. In an earlier section of this chapter, we looked at the influence of the baby's alertness and responsiveness on the parents' emotional involvement. We also noted how the infant's good or poor health could influence parental attitudes. A small, sick, severely preterm infant does not present the ideal stimulus for parental bonding. The child is in a small crib in the NICU and may hardly be visible because of a crib cover that helps regulate oxygen and warmth. The baby may have ventilation apparatus in place, feeding tubes in nose or mouth, intravenous needles, and a heart monitor. This is not a baby who can be picked up and cuddled, or even looked at without wincing until it becomes more familiar (Mercer & Gonsalves, 1992). Emotional withdrawal is a way of self-defense for the parent who is up against a very frightening situation.

extracorporeal: outside the body; from the Latin *extra* (outside), *corpus* (body).

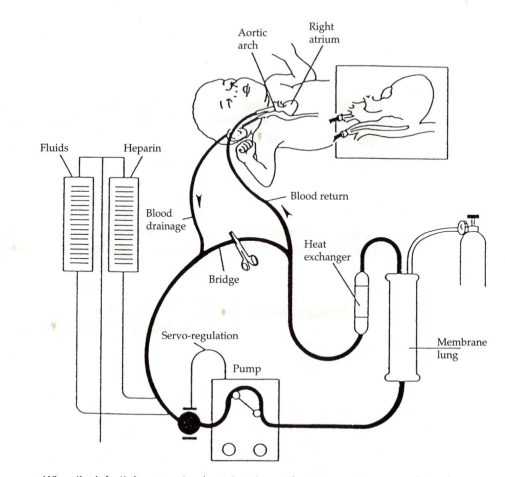

When the infant's lungs are too immature to supply oxygen, extracorporeal membrane oxygenation (ECMO) can be used temporarily. Blood from the baby's neck flows through a line to absorb oxygen and then returns, carrying the oxygen into the infant's body. (Source: Based on Hunter, Zwischenberger, & Bhatia, 1992)

Whereas a healthy, full-term baby responds to the parent and gives some clear signals in return, a preterm baby's social signals are hard to read. A parent may try especially hard to get the infant's attention but succeed only in overwhelming the baby, who will look away as if uninterested (Thurman & Gonsalves, 1993). Once again, the parent may withdraw emotionally in self-defense, thus beginning a poor relationship with an infant who needs unusual amounts of care and attention.

The High-Risk Infant and Decision Making

The birth of a baby is most often an occasion for joy, even when the pregnancy was unplanned. When a baby is extremely preterm, is very sick, or has severe

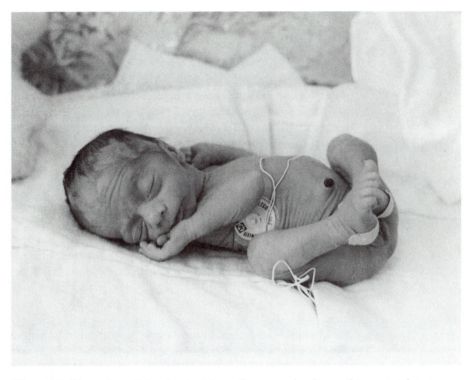

The small, thin preterm baby does not have the same visual appeal to a caregiver as does a more robust, full-term infant.

disabilities, however, the birth may be the beginning of a series of agonizing decisions for parents and medical staff.

Technology has become so advanced that most infants could be kept alive indefinitely with assistance in breathing, artificial feeding, and even kidney dialysis. When this is done, however, the hospital space, the staff, and the money involved are not available to other babies who might benefit from them. Where there are limited resources, some decisions must be made about how these resources are allocated.

These issues have become increasingly difficult as it has become possible to salvage preterm babies of 25 or even 24 weeks GA, but it has become clear that many survive with severe damage to vision and brain functioning, as well as other disabilities. The question of allocation of resources now turns on a very basic value issue: Is life alone the highest priority, or is *quality of life* a greater concern? Are there times when it would be most ethical to withhold treatment, let "nature take its course," and allow the baby to die? And who makes the decision?

As we will discuss in Chapter 15, for a short time in the 1980s, rules of the U.S. Department of Health and Human Services required that hospitals post notices stating that all infants were to be treated, whatever the severity of their problems. Under these "Baby Doe" rules, actions by state child protective services were ordered if treatment was withheld. Subsequently, the Supreme Court ruled against this simplistic approach to a complex issue (Holden, 1986).

The Child Abuse Amendments of 1984 mandate certain standards of care for infants with disabilities but also allow for failure to provide treatment under certain conditions. All infants must receive "comfort care" as well as food, fluids, and medication. They are also to be given medically indicated treatment except under two circumstances: (1) when the judgment of the treating physician is that the infant is irreversibly comatose; or (2) when treatment would merely "prolong dying" and would be futile in terms of the infant's survival (Bopp & Nimz, 1992).

Although it is assumed that decisions about treatment are made in consultation with the infant's parents, this does not necessarily happen. The parents of a very sick infant may be in shock, very angry, or still denying that there is anything really wrong with their child. Their emotional state interferes with their ability to deal with new, complicated information. The medical staff cannot make an absolute prediction about a baby, but when staff members provide information about the *probabilities* of certain events, the parents often have great difficulty understanding it (see Tversky & Kahneman, 1974).

Medical staff do not always agree about the appropriateness of continuing treatment for a given baby. Medical training has traditionally emphasized the absolute value of saving life. Before the developments of modern technology, there were no dilemmas about treatment of high-risk babies and no need to make decisions together with parents. Some physicians remain extremely uncomfortable with the decision-making process and prefer to deal only with the mechanics of treatment, whereas others are genuinely concerned about "overtreatment" (Silverman, 1992).

Nursing staff in the NICU, on the other hand, may be deeply concerned and distressed about the ethics of questionable treatment. As one nurse has written, "the amendments, which supposedly protect infants from child abuse, may in some cases actually be the instrument for child abuse in the form of prolonging dying under conditions of a brutal intensive care from which there is no escape" (Penticuff, 1992, p. 273).

A special concern for parents, NICU nurses, and increasing numbers of physicians is the availability of pain relief for the preterm or other high-risk infant. As we will see in Chapter 8, medical practitioners assumed for many years that neither preterm nor full-term neonates were capable of feeling pain; both major and minor surgeries were carried out without anesthesia. New understanding of infants has led to much greater use of anesthesia and analgesia, but high-risk infants in the NICU experience frequent painful stimulation such as a heel-lance for a blood sample, in which adequate blood may be obtained only after several sticks. The use of medications such as analgesic cream to reduce pain before such procedures is, fortunately, becoming more common.

As we will discuss in a later chapter, laws, policies, and ethics surrounding the treatment of high-risk infants remain uncertain. The uncertainty will probably continue as long as the development of new technology creates new dilemmas. One approach that some parents take is to try to circumvent anticipated problems by signing a document like the following, which was circulated to prospective parents in France by the *Association Pour la Prévention de l'Enfance Handicappée* (*"A 'declaration of intent,' "* 1987):

> We consider that life is good but that the chances to lead a happy and productive life with others rests on being structurally normal. I request that my physician give me all examinations and tests that would permit me to know that my infant does not have significant risks of abnormality. In the case that a significant risk is noted, my physicians should provide me or refer me to someone who will perform a therapeutic interruption of pregnancy.
>
> At the time of delivery, if by chance my infant is not normal, I ask formally that the doctors do not resuscitate him. If the baby is structurally normal but fails to breathe appropriately, I ask that the doctors do everything possible so that the baby will live, but that they continue the resuscitation only as long as they can be reasonably sure that his brain will stay intact and function normally.
>
> I wish to assure all of you who will execute my wishes that I understand fully the implications and I hope that no one will contradict them.

_____

_____

Signature of Prospective Parents

Although the death of an infant is agonizing to parents and can be devastating to families, there may be still greater agony in treatment that prolongs a life with pain and serious handicaps. One mother of preterm triplets who survived with multiple handicaps wrote about her experiences: "We had no choices, could give no input. Neither our concerns, nor our values, nor the impact on our lives, nor the quality of our children's lives were ever considered valid information in the decision-making process. Only those with no stake in the outcome of these decisions were allowed to be a part of the process. We entered the health care system believing we were consumers. We left it feeling we were victims. People who have been victimized never forget" (Thorson, 1994, p. vii).

EARLY EMOTIONAL CHANGES: THE BONDING ISSUE

Much has been written on the subject of maternal-infant (or parental-infant) *bonding* in the hours or days soon after a baby's birth—and probably as much has been exaggerated or misunderstood. This topic needs careful attention, for popular preconceptions often lead to confusion. Ideas based on animal behavior are not necessarily useful here; for example, recent work showing a failure of maternal care in mice with a missing gene (Cohen, 1996a) is not likely to be directly relevant to the complexities of human parenting.

Before trying to understand the bonding issue, it is important to keep in mind that parents have almost always gone through some emotional changes in anticipation of contact with the baby. The pregnant woman in particular carries out a psychological task called *fetal distinction*. She progressively begins to view the fetus as a separate individual (particularly if prenatal tests have revealed its sex or any other characteristics) and to identify herself as a mother. She may be tired of being pregnant and eager to know the baby. The mother and father may seek clues about the baby's personality, for example, whether it kicks hard or squirms quietly; they try to think of suitable names.

Although it is easy to see how the months of pregnancy are a time of preparation for the relationship with the child, adoptive parents too have anticipated their child's arrival, usually for far more than nine months. Adoptive parents have often gone through years of infertility diagnosis and treatment and may have spent further years on an adoption agency's "waiting list." They have many expectations and fantasies about their baby.

The general idea of bonding is that parents of a newborn are especially ready to develop positive emotional feelings about (to "fall in love" with) their baby. The newborn, in the first hours after its birth, is especially lovable and stimulates the parents to respond. It is more awake, alert, and responsive than it will be the next day, and its bright eyes and incredibly soft skin are very appealing. Parents who get to spend some time with their baby in the first hours after birth are most often captivated and become deeply preoccupied with the baby and its needs.

Unfortunately, two serious misunderstandings have developed about parental-infant bonding. One is that bonding must occur through extended contact soon after birth or it will never occur at all. It is probably ideal, and it is wonderfully exciting for the parents, to have that early time with the baby, but all evidence tells us that is is quite possible for bonding to occur later. Many (if not all) adoptive parents feel strong love for their children, even though they did not have early contact, and even parents whose babies need weeks of intensive medical care frequently form a genuine bond.

The other misunderstanding is that parental-infant bonding involves love on the part of the baby as well as on that of the parent. It is a grave mistake to suppose that a newborn infant is capable of a strong preference for one person over another, much less that a baby's love has the powerful self-sacrificing drive of a parent's. As we will see in later chapters, the infant can tell a stranger from a familiar person within a few weeks, but it will be many months before a strong preference is apparent—and years before love can be anything but self-centered.

Why the concern with bonding? Parents certainly experience this "falling in love" with the baby as exhilarating and emotionally dominant over all other feelings. It is genuinely comparable to romantic love without the erotic component. But there is more to it than that. The parents experience a change in *attitude*, a "readiness to respond." Behavior changes when attitude changes. In the case of "bonded" parents, all the changes are positive ones with respect to good care of the infant. Bonding makes it easier to care for the infant well because it makes the parent preoccupied with the infant. Satisfying the baby's needs becomes much more important than satisfying one's own needs; the parent will find it truly more painful for the infant to be hungry than to be hungry him- or herself. Bonding probably also decreases the chances of physical abuse of the infant. It is likely that the vast majority of parents feel an occasional impulse to attack a crying baby, but most never do so; bonding may help prevent the parent from carrying out the (momentary) wish to stop the crying by hurting the baby.

Bonding certainly exists as a set of feelings and attitudes held by most parents. The problem with the concept comes when it is oversimplified. This is not a matter of a simple equation in which contact with the newborn equals powerful emotional changes in all cases. Like other emotional responses, bonding involves a complex dynamic action system in which many factors interact to produce an outcome. The emotion resulting from the interacting factors may be very powerful, moderate, or almost nonexistent.

The factors that interact and influence bonding are in the parents and in the situation as well as in the child. *Parental* factors include recent losses of close relationships and the grief that results; a parent who is mourning and "giving up" a lost person is not in an emotional state that encourages bonding. This is especially true when the lost person is a child—a miscarriage or stillbirth within the previous year, or the death of a twin while the co-twin survives. Fears that this baby will die interfere with bonding, and they may come either from past experience or from real or imagined health problems in the baby.

Situational factors could include early or delayed opportunities to hold and interact with the baby, as well as privacy for the early interactions. If a baby is in intensive care or behind a nursery window, neither privacy nor real interaction is possible.

Characteristics of the *baby* that may affect bonding are the baby's health, alertness, and responsiveness. A limp, drowsy, uninterested baby does not easily catch the parent's attention. Physical defects in the baby are important primarily when they interfere with eye contact or with facial expression, two essential pathways of interaction.

Further discussion of the role parental bonding plays in an infant's emotional development will be postponed to a later chapter.

PROBLEMS TO CONSIDER AND DISCUSS

1. What would you have to do to be sure that a standardized test of newborns was reliable?
2. What characteristics of the baby in the process of birth ("the passenger") help determine whether or not the process ends with a healthy newborn?
3. How is the newborn 5 minutes after birth different from the fetus 5 minutes before birth?
4. What problems are likely in a preterm, SGA baby?
5. When does the process of bonding begin and end, or is it impossible to tell?

6

Physical Growth, Nutrition, and Health

Physical growth, health, and nutrition are the foundation of all other aspects of infant development. Poor growth and poor health are not only symptoms of problems but also potential causes of other problems.

Poor growth patterns generally indicate some nutritional deficiencies. These deficiencies may result from or may lead to a vulnerability to infection and subsequent disease processes. The sick child has a poor appetite and a lowered activity level, and the poorly nourished child is more likely to become sick.

Poor growth and health patterns also influence adults' responses to infants. The bright-eyed, responsive, active infant attracts attention, care, and interaction, whereas the chronically **apathetic,** small, sickly child is easier to ignore. An infant with a poor appetite may actually be offered food infrequently because she displays little interest or even aversion to it. Where food is scarce and in demand by other children, such an infant may slowly starve. She certainly is less likely to receive the attention and care that are critical to cognitive and emotional development.

apathetic:
without interest or feeling; from the Greek *an-* (without), *pathos* (suffering).

Poor growth and health are signals of the need for early intervention. If these problems are not corrected, the infant may start on a developmental pathway that will move progressively further from normal levels. Once severe damage has been done, it may be impossible to return the individual to normal health and development.

RESEARCH METHODS

Work on growth and health issues rarely involves experimental manipulation because some factors are impossible to control and others are potentially very dangerous to the infants involved. As noted earlier, correlational studies can examine relationships between environmental factors and health or growth status. Quasi-experiments allow comparison of groups with different experiences (for example, children exposed to secondhand smoke compared with those from nonsmoking families).

Recall that quasi-experimental research requires extensive matching of subjects in order to isolate the effect of a factor; otherwise, confounding variables may confuse the outcome. For example, in a study that compared breast-fed and bottle-fed babies on the number of ear infections they experienced, some possible confounding variables were ethnicity, use of day care, number of siblings, and parental smoking (Duncan, Ey, Holberg, Martinez, & Taussig, 1993).

If *growth* is the topic under study, longitudinal research is an appropriate quasi-experimental approach. In this form of research, a group of infants are measured or weighed repeatedly over a period of time. Each infant's size at a given age is compared to its size at other ages, and the same is done for all the members of the group. The longitudinal approach allows an understanding of individual patterns of growth. A *cross-sectional* comparison, on the other hand, would average periods of slow growth for some babies with periods of rapid growth for others and would make it appear that all the infants had the same rate of growth. One issue about studies on growth is the *frequency* with which measurement should be done. For example, measurement every 60 days would not reveal whether rapid spurts of growth occurred at long intervals (Raloff, 1992).

Studies of growth also require precise measurement techniques. Until the child is 2 years old, measurements of length are taken with the child supine. The head must be held in such a position that the imaginary line from eye to ear is vertical. According to Tanner's directions on supine measurement, the "ankles are gently pulled to stretch the child, the legs are straightened, the feet are turned up vertically, the [measuring] triangle brought up against them and its position . . .marked" (1978, p. 175).

Testing of vaccines or other medical treatments is a difficult matter because of the potential for harm to infants. In most cases, the issue is not potential illness from a vaccine but a failure to protect the vaccinated child. In other cases, unpredictable harm seems to occur. Tests of one experimental measles vaccine were stopped because children who had received it, especially girls, died in unusually high numbers of other common diseases (Weiss, 1992). Some parents in the United States avoided immunizing their children against pertussis (whooping cough) after it was shown that between 5 and 20 out of 3.5 million children each year die following immunization (Sun, 1985); it was impossible to detect whether those particular children would have died at that point anyway, whether they had received the vaccine or not.

compassionate: merciful; from the Latin *com-* (with), *pati* (to suffer).

Testing of vaccines or medications requires informed consent from parents or guardians and is properly done by assigning children randomly to either a medication or a placebo group. Treatments that have not been thoroughly tested may nevertheless be provided to desperately ill infants on a **compassionate use** basis (see, for example, Thompson, 1992).

The study of particular diseases in early life (AIDS, for example) depends largely on *statistical* data gathered by the Centers for Disease Control (CDC). The CDC collects information about reported diseases from thousands of sources, collates the information, and publishes analyses of changes in disease occurrence. Data gathering and analysis are extremely time consuming, so the most recent available data are usually from 3 or 4 years in the past.

EARLY DEATHS

The number of deaths in infancy is an indication of the state of health in a population of babies. As health care improves in a population, the infant mortality rate (proportion of babies dying before age 1) drops. Between 1980 and 1991, for example, the infant mortality rate for U.S. babies dropped from 12.6 per 1000 live births to 8.9 per 1000 live births.

Looking at the infant mortality rate for a large mixed group does not give us the entire picture, however. Characteristics of specific babies affect the probability of their early deaths. Males are more likely to die in the first year than females are, for example (Naeye, Burt, Wright, Blanc, & Tatter, 1971). Disadvantaged populations can show considerably higher mortality rates than advantaged populations do; when the figures for U.S. infant mortality are examined by racial groups, remarkable differences appear. The infant mortality rate for African Americans was 17.6 per 1000 live births in 1991, compared to 7.3 per 1000 for European Americans. The African American figure was down 20% from a rate of 22.2 per 1000 in 1980, but the European American rate fell 33% in the same time period. If these trends continued, African American infants in the year 2000 would be three times as likely to die in the first year as would European Americans ("Black infant mortality," 1994).

A poorly understood cause of early death is *sudden infant death syndrome* (SIDS), the most common cause of death between age 1 month and 1 year (Lamont, Sachinwalla, & Pamphlett, 1995). Deaths considered to be due to SIDS generally occur before the baby is 8 months old. The infant has seemed healthy or perhaps has had a slight cold or stuffy nose. The baby is put to bed for a nap or to sleep at night and is found dead some time later. No obvious cause of death is present.

Many possible causes of SIDS have been investigated. Secondhand tobacco smoke (discussed later in this chapter) appears to be one of the factors involved in SIDS. The chances of SIDS are more than twice as great for an infant in a household where one person smokes than for a baby who is not exposed to smoke, and they are more than three times as high if more than one adult smokes (Klonoff-Cohen & Edelstein, 1995).

Some research has triggered concern about the roles bedding and sleeping position play in SIDS. Recommendations in other countries that babies not be placed prone for sleeping have been followed by reductions in SIDS rates, and similar recommendations are being made in the United States. Soft bedding, into which the baby's face can press, may be a problem, and it may be that countries where SIDS was reduced when infants did not sleep prone were also countries where soft bedding was more common than it is here.

SIDS has been discussed as the result of a congenital abnormality in breathing control. Infants whose older sibling has died of SIDS are at greater than average risk. Use of a breathing monitor while the baby sleeps can be effective under these circumstances (Hunt, 1995).

It is possible that problems of the development and functioning of the nervous system are responsible for SIDS. The medulla of the brain, which is associated with the regulation of physical functions like breathing, may have poor development of an area called the *arcuate nucleus* in infants who die of SIDS (Kinney et al., 1995). The arcuate nucleus is thought to help regulate breathing responses to high carbon dioxide levels.

A final issue about SIDS involves the possibility that sudden unexplained deaths are actually murders. A small proportion, certainly less than 10%, of such deaths may be due to deliberate suffocation. One mother has recently confessed to and been convicted of murder in the deaths of five of her children who had been diagnosed as SIDS victims more than 20 years ago (Pinholster, 1995). In the great majority of these cases, though, there is no wrongdoing by the parents, and their anguish is dreadful if in addition to losing their child they are accused of murder.

GROWTH PATTERNS

Hormones

pulsatile: with rhythmic repetition; from the Latin *pulsus* (beating).

Physical growth is under the control of specific *hormones,* products of the endocrine system. Hormones are carried by the bloodstream from the cells that produce them to the cells that are influenced by them. Although many hormones are related to growth processes, three hormone categories are most relevant to our concerns (Tanner, 1978): the growth, thyroid, and adrenal cortical hormones.

Growth hormone itself is needed for growth to occur. This pituitary hormone is secreted in a **pulsatile** pattern; that is, rather than a slow, continuous secretion into the bloodstream, there are bursts or "squirts" of hormone several times a day. One such burst comes an hour or so after the beginning of sleep (so your mother was right; children do grow because of sleep). But growth hormone is not the direct cause of physical growth. To affect bone growth, for example, growth hormone works through a second hormone called *somatomedin.* Somatomedin is produced in the liver in response to a pulse of growth hormone and remains at high levels for 24 hours after a single pulse. The growing cartilage cells at the ends of bones are affected by somatomedin, and so are muscle cells, which are also directly influenced by growth hormone (Tanner, 1978).

Thyroid hormone is also involved in growth. Its effect, however, has been called a "permissive" action (Tanner, 1978); a normal level of thyroid hormone allows cells to behave normally, whereas low levels slow the functioning of cells, like the ones in the pituitary that secrete growth hormone.

adrenal: an endocrine gland located adjacent to the kidney; from the Latin *ad* (to), *renes* (kidney).

The outer part, or cortex, of the **adrenal** gland also produces hormones that are relevant to growth. Unusual amounts of *cortisol,* which may be used to treat asthma or other diseases, will slow growth in height and bone maturity and will increase fat levels. This hormone appears to block production of somatomedin, which would normally occur in response to growth hormone (other adrenal cortical hormones are related to growth that occurs years after the infant and toddler periods).

An interesting question involves *stopping* growth. If hormones are necessary to cause growth to occur and if a hormone like cortisol can slow growth, is there a mechanism that stops cell division from occurring? So far, this question has been pursued with respect to development in the embryo, where it appears that specific genes are responsible for production of *cell cycle inhibitors* that stop cell division (Marx, 1995).

The Speed of Growth

An essential measurement in the study of growth is the *growth rate,* or speed at which weight gain and increases in length occur. Growth rates are charted in the form of growth curves—graphs that display changes in size as they relate to increasing age.

It is much easier to assess a baby's health when the child's growth rate is compared to a standardized growth chart. Growth charts show standards of weight and height based on data from thousands of children. A baby's individual growth curve, plotted on the chart, shows whether growth is following a normal pattern. A baby whose birth weight was at the 40th percentile (that is, 60% of newborns were heavier) would be expected to be at the 40th percentile or higher when weighed in later months. If the infant's weight were at the 30th percentile at 2 months and at the 20th percentile at 3 months, it would be clear that normal growth was not occurring and the reason would have to be investigated.

The growth rate is sensitive to illness, injury, poor nutrition, and poor general care. This is one reason well baby care—physical examination of apparently healthy babies at regular intervals—can make such a difference to infant health and development. Early detection of the slowing of growth rates will allow intervention to correct problems before they have had a chance to become serious (Brams & Coury, 1985).

A rough, rule-of-thumb statement about growth curves is that a baby is expected to *double* the birth weight by age 4 months, to *triple* it by age 12 months, and to *quadruple* it by age 24 months. Notice that the growth curve has a *decelerating velocity;* although the baby grows much faster than a 10-year-old does, the growth rate slows down as the child gets older. The infant takes 4 months to gain an amount equal to the birth weight, then 8 months to gain the same amount again, and then 12 months to gain the third birth-weight equivalent.

A glance at a growth chart suggests that growth is gradual and uniform, with the same small amount gained every day. This impression is deceiving, however. The appearance of uniformity results from the fact that the chart is based on the *average* weight and height gains of many babies and does not reveal individual differences or daily variations. In fact, according to some research, physical growth in a single individual occurs in a **saltatory** fashion. Periods of days go by without any growth; then a spurt of growth leads to an increase in length of about 1 centimeter in a 24-hour period (Raloff, 1992). We should note, however, that there are some contradictions in this research; some work supports the saltatory model (Lampl, Cameron, Veldhuis, &

saltatory:
proceeding by a series of rapid changes rather than gradually; from the Latin *saltire* (to leap).

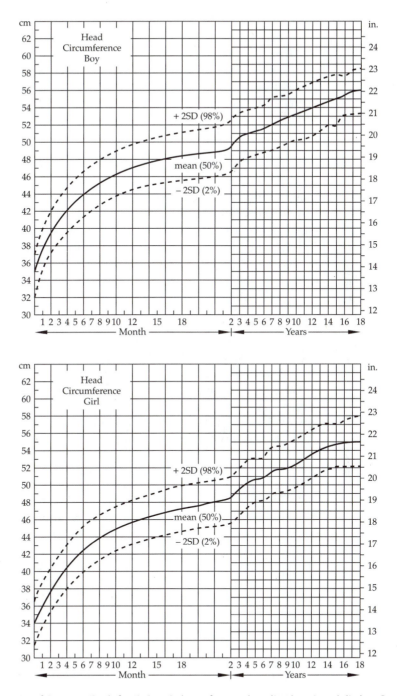

By the age of 2 years, the infant's head circumference is quite close to adult size. Separate growth charts for boys and for girls allow us to compare an infant's head size at any age to those of other infants and can alert us to growth and neurological problems. (Source: Nelhaus, 1968)

insult: in this context, an assault or injury; from the Latin *insultare* (to jump upon).

Johnson, 1995), whereas some suggests that slow, gradual continuous growth is the rule (Heinrichs, Munson, Counts, Cutler, & Baron, 1995).

Irregularities in growth also show up when illness, injury, or poor nutrition (so-called environmental **insults**) have temporarily prevented growth from occurring. *Catch-up growth* occurs when the illness is over or the injury heals. An example of catch-up growth is the rapid growth in the weeks after birth of the child who is genetically "programmed" to be large but who was born to a small mother. Catch-up growth is rapid and returns the infant to the point on the growth chart where he or she presumably would have been had the environmental insult never occurred.

canalization: channeling of development along predictable pathways; from the Latin *canalis* (channel, pipe).

The occurrence of catch-up growth is considered to be evidence for **canalization:** the tendency to follow a certain growth pattern even though the environment occasionally disrupts the pattern (Waddington, 1971). The basic idea of the canalization concept is that an individual has a genetically determined growth pattern that is powerful enough to provide some resilience in the face of environmental insult. When growth is slowed by environmental factors, the genetically determined growth pattern counters by pouring energy into catch-up growth until a correction has been achieved.

Every baby will suffer some environmental insults in the forms of colds, diarrhea, bumps, bruises, and so on, and canalization prevents these from having a permanent effect on growth. However, canalization has its limits, and an excessive number of problems will ultimately result in smaller size than we would predict on the basis of genetic background alone. What are these limits? What is an excessive number of problems? There seem to be great individual differences; some babies are unusually **vulnerable** and others are highly **resilient,** and at this point we cannot predict which is which. Protecting all infants from environmental insult as much as possible seems to be the best approach.

vulnerable: in this context, easily moved from a normal developmental pathway; from the Latin *vulnerare* (to wound).

resilient: recovering easily from environmental insults; from the Latin *resilire* (to jump back).

Failure to Thrive

When a baby's growth is seriously retarded and weight drops to the 5th or 3rd percentile or below, the child may be designated as a *failure to thrive* (FTT) baby. Failure to thrive may occur as a result of organic or nonorganic (environmental) factors, or, of course, as a result of an interaction between the two. *Nonorganic failure to thrive* (NOFT) is a far more complex matter than the simple forms of malnutrition we will discuss later in this chapter.

NOFT, which has accounted for as many as 5% of hospital admissions of infants, is the result of many possible problems, usually in combination (Frank, Allen, & Brown, 1985). Many infants diagnosed with NOFT were of low birth weight. In addition, they may have experienced poor nutrition, which increased the effects of exposure to lead and decreased resistance to disease. These factors may depress the infant's appetite and interfere with the use of nutrients, producing more complications and the irritability and hyperactivity that can harm the interactions between parent and infant (Frank, 1985). Children who experience severe NOFT may show delayed development and small stature even 10 years after the diagnosis (Altemeier, O'Connor, Sherrod, Yeager, & Vietze, 1985).

Treatment of NOFT has to focus on all the multiple factors that have brought about the child's condition. Providing appetizing and digestible food at appropriate intervals is a beginning, as is treating infectious disease and countering the effects of lead exposure. The resulting improvement in the child's appearance and responsiveness may help stimulate the parent to feed and nurture the child more appropriately, leading in a "benign circle" to increasing improvement (Altemeier et al., 1985). If poor caregiving has resulted from maternal depression or from drug or alcohol use, of course, there will be no solution until those problems are dealt with.

APPLICATIONS & ARGUMENTS
The Feeding Relationship

Feeding a baby is not a simple matter of moving food into a passive mouth and down a passive esophagus. Instead, it involves a reciprocal set of actions in which both feeder and baby take active roles.

Even the adult spoon-feeding a baby of a few weeks of age must take the baby's responses into account. Unless the spoon goes far enough into the baby's mouth, the tongue-thrust reflex will unintentionally push the food out again. Only the proper placement of the spoon, gauged to coordinate with the baby's reflexes, will lead to swallowing.

As the baby gets to an age at which feeding nonmilk foods might be more appropriate, her physical control has advanced so that she takes a major role in the feeding process. An open mouth and excited expression signal to the caregiver the child's desire for food. Averted head and tightly closed mouth show refusal, and if the caregiver insists, the infant can simply let the food dribble out of the corners of the mouth rather than swallowing it. By 12 months or so, the baby signals food preferences as well as hunger in these ways.

The feeding relationship thus involves communication from adult to infant and vice versa. The satisfaction of the feeding partners depends in large part on their success in sending and receiving messages.

Unfortunately, one of the messages sometimes sent in the feeding relationship has to do with power rather than food. This message is carried by the parent, because the infant initially has no concept of power over another person—especially not power to be valued for its own sake. The baby may learn in the course of meals that one or the other person must take all control. This experience interferes with the development of cooperative, empathic behavior. It also sets the stage for serious eating disorders.

REORGANIZATION AND GROWTH

Physical growth is not just a matter of becoming uniformly blown up to a larger size. It involves changes in physical proportions, the remodeling of body parts, and continued maturation of function, as well as the increase in physical size. Growth between birth and age 2 years involves *reorganization* of anatomy and of function.

Changes in Proportion

If a baby simply grew at the same rate all over, the result would be an exceedingly strange-looking adult. A newborn baby's head makes up about one-fourth of its length, whereas that of an adult accounts for only about one-tenth of height.

cephalocaudal:
from the head end of the body downward; from the Greek *kephale* (head), the Latin *cauda* (tail).

The change in proportions with growth illustrates two important principles of growth patterns. First, the baby's growth follows a **cephalocaudal** pattern; the head end of the body initially grows fastest and reaches mature size earliest, whereas the "tail" end takes longer to develop. The second principle of growth involves a **proximodistal** pattern; areas closer to the center of the body, like the shoulders, grow and mature earlier than do more distant parts, like the hands. (These principles will come up again when we discuss motor development in Chapter 9.)

proximodistal:
from the midline of the body outward; from the Latin *proximus* (near), *distare* (to be distant).

For a rough demonstration of these growth principles, try to get a 2-year-old to reach across the top of his head and touch his left ear with his right hand. He will probably try to reach around the back of his head to touch the ear. He cannot reach across the top of his head because his head is already close to adult size but his arms are proportionately much shorter.

Specific body parts may show their own patterns of developmental change. The infant's chest, for example, is different in shape as well as size from an adult's. The infant's chest is circular in cross section, whereas the adult's is elliptical; the infant's lower chest is very round and is wider than the upper chest, whereas the areas are consistent in width in the adult. The infant's ribs are evenly horizontal, whereas the adult's ribs are progressively more diagonal as they go down the trunk (Massery, 1993).

Skeletal Development

The infant's skeleton is in a very incomplete state at the time of birth. Many parts that will later be bone are only cartilage at birth. This fact has many advantages for the birth itself, for the baby's body is relatively soft and flexible. Babies' body parts bend rather than break under the pressures of birth.

The skull gives the most important example of the body's malleability. A completely hard skull the size of a normal baby's head simply could not be born by the normal route. The incomplete skull of the newborn is able to mold and change shape under pressure because it consists of a number of incomplete, unfused bony plates that can move. Thus, the skull becomes long and narrow enough to pass through the mother's pelvic outlet. It is easy to find the fontanels (spaces between the bony plates) by running your hands over a young baby's head. The most conspicuous fontanel, on the top of the head, is usually at least the size of the ball of your thumb. (The brain under the fontanel is well protected by tough membranes, so you cannot injure the baby by feeling its fontanel, although it may tickle the baby.)

The anterior fontanel may not close until the baby is 18 months old or more. This time frame allows for further growth of the brain, which is rapidly moving toward adult size. Too rapid a closing of the fontanel is of much greater concern than a late closing.

The cartilaginous areas of the infant's skeleton develop into bone by incorporating calcium and other minerals. This process of *ossification* occurs first at the ends and in the middle of the long bones. Because ossification of bones occurs in a predictable order, it is possible to judge a child's physical maturity in terms of skeletal age. Bone growth is regulated by genetic activity that keeps bones from growing too fast and too long. Proteins whose production is induced by a specific gene modulate the differentiation of cells and maintain an appropriate bone-growth rate (Roush, 1996; Vortkamp et al., 1996).

A lack of calcium or vitamin D in the diet obviously affects ossification. It is less obvious that a lack of calories or protein may also have an effect on skeletal development. A deficiency of calories in the diet slows bone growth and produces bone that appears normal but may be thinner than it should be. Protein malnutrition has a similar effect, but it too may alter the sequence of ossification (Pipes, 1977).

Ossification and growth at the ends of the long bones do not tell the whole story of skeletal development, however. A bone that changed only at the ends would become longer and longer but remain thin (and weak) in the middle of the shaft. In fact, the growing bone is constantly being broken down and replaced as layers of new bone are deposited. It is being remodeled, rather than just growing longer. The pull of muscles on bones as the limbs are used guides bone development and results in the shape of the mature bone years after infancy (Tanner, 1978).

Dentition

dentition: the development of teeth; from the Latin *dentire* (to cut teeth).

Dentition, the eruption of the teeth from the gums, is an anatomical change that leads to altered functioning and is essential to good nutrition. Although much development of the primary teeth occurs during the prenatal period, the enamel is not fully developed until weeks or months after birth. In fact, the tooth is not complete when it erupts; root development of the primary teeth does not finish until the child is age 18 months or older.

It is obvious that during prenatal development tooth growth will be dependent on the mother's nutrition. However, we can see that postnatal nutrition can have a serious impact on the tooth's final form. Wei (1974) noted that "[a]lmost all of the most caries-susceptible areas of the primary dentition

TABLE 6.1 _Several years of development must pass before all the primary teeth have come in._

Tooth	Age enamel completed	Age of eruption	Age root completed
Maxillary (upper)			
Central incisor	1 ½ months	7 ½ months	1 ½ years
Lateral incisor	2 ½ months	9 months	2 years
Cuspid	9 months	18 months	3 ¼ years
First molar	6 months	14 months	2 ½ years
Second molar	11 months	24 months	3 years
Mandibular (lower)			
Central incisor	2 ½ months	6 months	1 ½ years
Lateral incisor	3 months	7 months	1 ½ years
Cuspid	9 months	16 months	3 ¼ years
First molar	5 ½ months	12 months	2 ¼ years
Second molar	10 months	20 months	3 years

Source: Based on Wei, 1974.

are calcified after birth" (p. 339). This means that the use of fluoride to produce decay-resistant teeth is effective when the chemical is added to the young baby's diet, but it is not effective when introduced in the diet of the pregnant mother.

Protection of the primary teeth from decay is important for a number of reasons. The capacity for chewing is important for the development of good nutritional habits. Teeth play an important role in clear speech, which the child is just developing at the end of infancy. In addition, decay of primary teeth may cause abscesses that can lead to defects in enamel in underlying permanent teeth. It is clear that the common belief that baby teeth may safely be neglected is not correct.

caries: decay of the tooth or bone; from the Greek _ker_ (death).

For many years, parents were told that decay of the first teeth resulted from letting the baby have a bottle in bed—what was called "nursing bottle **caries.**" More recent work suggests that this is _not_ a major cause of early tooth decay.

CIRCADIAN RHYTHMS AND OTHER ENVIRONMENTAL INFLUENCES

circadian: over a 24-hour period; from the Latin _circus_ (circle), _dies_ (day).

Physical growth and development are accompanied by reorganization of functioning into new patterns. **Circadian rhythms,** alterations in functioning over the course of each 24-hour period, begin to emerge. The kidney, for example, develops a circadian rhythm that causes less urine production during the night (Moore, 1972). The kidney also improves in its ability to

dehydration: loss of water from the tissues; from the Latin *de-* (down, away), the Greek *hydor* (water).

conserve water and prevent **dehydration,** thus tailoring functioning to environmental conditions. In the first months, the kidneys throw off water in the urine at the same rate of speed regardless of whether or not there is plenty of water in the body. This means that diarrhea or vomiting can quickly lead to dehydration and even to death if treatment is not available. During infancy and toddlerhood, however, there is a gradual change so that water loss is followed by a reduction in urine production.

Circadian rhythms of sleep do not have much relationship to an infant's health or growth, but they can be of crucial concern to exhausted parents. The neonate may sleep for no more than an hour or two at a time, waking to eat and then sleeping again. Parents look forward to the time when the baby will "sleep through the night" and are disappointed when they find that this term only means sleeping from midnight to 5 A.M.! About 70% of babies sleep through the night in this sense by the age of 3 months; another 10% never do so during the first year. Of those who have begun to sleep through by 3 months, half of them begin to wake up during the night between 5 and 9 months (Anders, 1975). Breast-fed babies sleep less than others and continue to wake frequently into the second year, if they have not weaned by that time (Elias, Nicolson, Bora, & Johnston, 1986). Babies who are put into their cribs while they are still awake and who suck thumbs or pacifiers are more likely to go back to sleep on their own if they wake in the night (Anders, Halpern, & Hua, 1992).

BIOCHEMICAL CHANGE: STRESS RESPONSES AND THE IMMUNE SYSTEM

Growth in size and change in proportions are affected by the environment, but they show a high degree of canalization. This suggests that the body has capacities to buffer or minimize the effects of environmental insults and thus to allow growth to continue along its genetically determined pathway.

The buffering process is largely dependent on internal biochemical changes that preserve much of the body's functioning in spite of illness, injury, or emotional distress. The *immune* system fights infection and works to restore the organism to normal functioning, and one of the tasks of the *endocrine* system is to mediate protective stress reactions. As we will see, the two are not independent. Overwhelming stress reduces the immune system's coping capacity.

Immune Reactions

antigen: a substance that stimulates the production of an antibody; from the Latin *anti-* (against), *genesis* (birth).

The immune system defends the body against "foreign" protein molecules like those present when infectious agents invade the body. The two parts of the system in mammals are the B cells and the T cells. The B cells produce immunoglobulins (protein molecules often called antibodies) after "recognizing" circulating **antigens**—infectious agents or other foreign molecules. The T cells' cooperation is necessary for antibody production because T cells must be activated and must provide signals for the B cells to proliferate and make appropriate antibodies. In their resting, unstimulated state, the B cells are able to make only one type of antibody (Marx, 1993).

Five classes of immunoglobulins are present in normal adult serum (Wagner, Maguire, & Stallings, 1993). Of these, immunoglobulin M (IgM), immunoglobulin A (IgA), and immunoglobulin G (IgG) are of the greatest interest to us. Generally speaking, IgM protects against gram-negative bacteria entering the bloodstream, IgA protects against gastrointestinal infection, and IgG protects against many bacterial and viral diseases. Within each class of immunoglobulins, specific antibodies protect against specific diseases.

The newborn infant's body has a different way of acquiring each of these immunoglobulins (Stiehm & Fulginiti, 1973). Because IgG crosses the placenta from the mother's blood, the infant is ordinarily born with a good supply of IgG. This gives the infant passive immunity against bacterial and viral diseases (to which the mother has been exposed) for a period of about 6 months. By the time the infant is 9 months old, all the maternal IgG has disappeared, and the baby is producing its own IgG at almost 60% of the adult level. The baby has its lowest level of IgG between 2 and 4 months of age.

IgM does not cross the placenta, but it is the first immunoglobulin to be produced by the baby, beginning before birth and reaching 75% of the adult level by the age of 1 year. IgM levels are lowest at birth.

synthesize: to combine or produce from parts or elements; from the Greek *syn* (with), *tithenai* (to put, lay down).

IgA also does not cross the placenta, but it occurs in the infant's body in two possible ways: self-production and through breast milk. IgA is **synthesized** by the baby, but it reaches only 20% of the adult level by 1 year of age. The breast-fed infant receives an additional supply of secretory IgA through its mother's milk. The level of secretory IgA is especially high in colostrum.

gastrointestinal: involving the stomach and intestines; from the Greek *gaster* (stomach), *enteron* (intestines).

Clinical observations suggest that IgA received from the mother plays an important role in protecting the baby from infection. The importance of IgA in preventing **gastrointestinal** infections is especially important in light of the infant's susceptibility to dehydration from diarrhea and vomiting, noted earlier. IgA is also instrumental in preventing other serious diseases that are contracted through the gastrointestinal tract, such as diphtheria and poliomyelitis.

auxiliary: offering or providing help; from the Latin *auxilium* (help).

The secretory IgA found in colostrum is related only to immunities the mother possesses a day or two after giving birth. As breast-feeding continues, however, the mother acts as an **auxiliary** immune system for the baby. If mother and baby are exposed to a new infection of the IgA class, the mother's body will quickly begin to produce the appropriate antibody and will pass it on to the baby in her milk.

allergy: an exaggerated or pathological response to substances that have no such effect on the average person; from the Greek *allos* (other), *ergon* (work).

A final point about the immune system involves **allergies.** Allergic reactions occur when a foreign protein (from food, for example) triggers the production of an immunoglobulin E (IgE) antibody. Once such a reaction has occurred, the body is sensitized to the protein and will more and more readily respond to it with itching, wheezing, sneezing, and so on. Although there appears to be a genetic factor that predisposes a baby to allergies (Seachrist, 1994), the developmental timing of exposure can also make a difference.

Exposure to a foreign protein early in the first year is much more likely to cause sensitization than is exposure after 12 months. Cow's milk and wheat products are common causes of allergic sensitization when fed to an infant too early. A mother's milk does not cause allergies in her own infant, however.

Stress Reactions

Immune reactions are less likely to occur at a normal level when *stress* conditions—continuing pain, anger, or fear—are present. Infant monkeys, for example, reduce their production of antibodies when separated from their mothers in a strange environment (Coe, Rosenberg, Fischer, & Levine, 1987), and clinical observation suggests the same happens with humans.

These alterations in immune functioning are a symptom of the biochemical changes of the *stress reaction*. Stress reaction involves a number of steps: (1) secretion of releasing hormones from the hypothalamus; (2) secretion of adrenocorticotropic hormone (ACTH) into the bloodstream by the pituitary; (3) a rise in the release of glucocorticoids by the adrenal glands; and (4) an increase in the availability of energy to help deal with the stress situation. Without the stress reaction, the individual would find it difficult to mobilize extra energy to either fight or flee when threatened.

An example of the benefits of the stress reaction occurs at the time of birth, when a vaginally delivered baby shows a considerable rise in stress hormones. The stress reaction helps facilitate the beginning of breathing, enhances the flow of blood to major organs, and increases metabolism so more stored energy is available to cells. Stressful situations for infants could include frequent illnesses, injuries, abusive treatment, and separation from familiar people after the first months of the first year (see Elkind, 1981).

PLASTICITY: HOW THE ENVIRONMENT SHAPES EARLY DEVELOPMENT

The concept of canalization emphasizes the role a genetic blueprint plays in determining patterns of growth and development, and the phenomenon of catch-up growth shows that there is a blueprint at work. Nonetheless, it is also clear that some aspects of physical development show a great deal of **plasticity;** these aspects are guided by environmental factors.

plasticity: the extent to which development is guided by experiences with the environment; from the Greek *plassein* (to mold or form).

It is important to understand that different aspects of growth show different levels of canalization and of plasticity. As Tanner (1978) points out, for example, the upper jaw is strongly influenced by genetic factors, whereas the lower jaw is shaped by the muscular stresses of biting and chewing so it fits appropriately with the upper jaw.

Some environmental factors work to guide development by more or less chance exposure. For example, the number of functioning sweat glands in an adult depends on his or her exposure to a hot climate during the first 2 or 3 years of life. When Japanese adults who were born in Japan and later emigrated to the tropics are compared to Japanese who were born in the tropics, the latter have many more functioning sweat glands (Diamond, 1991). The early experience of climate determines how many functioning glands develop.

Environmental factors can also be put to work deliberately to guide development. For example, *massage,* which influences production of stress hormones, is used to help speed up preterm infants' growth rates (Field & Schanberg, 1990). Probably the most significant example of the deliberate use of environmental factors is immunization. In the natural course of events, an individual may or may not be exposed to certain infections; if exposed, an individual may or may not develop an infection, and if infected, an individual may or may not survive with a new resistance to the disease. Immunization manipulates exposure in such a way as to create maximum immunity with a minimum number of deaths from infection. These goals can be achieved with small, repeated exposures; with **attenuated** or weakened viruses; and, in some cases, with killed viruses. Immunization also has the advantage of

attenuate: to lessen; from the Latin *attenuare* (to make thin).

Good health care includes providing comfort measures and building good relationships, as well as immunizing against infection.

producing immunities early in life, before the individual is likely to be exposed to large numbers of people and potential infections.

Most vaccines involve the injection of antigens, which trigger the production of specific antibodies by the B cells. These antibodies remain in circulation and confer a long period or even a lifetime of immunity. New research on immunization, however, is focusing on the *mucosal immune system.* This system produces about 70% of antibodies and is part of the mucous membrane that lines the respiratory, digestive, and reproductive tracts (Service, 1994c). This system produces immunoglobulin A, which we discussed earlier. The mucosal immune system is especially relevant to infant health because of its influence on gastrointestinal ailments that may kill a baby through dehydration.

Vaccines that stimulate the mucosal immune system would be especially important for child health because they are easy to administer and do not use **hypodermic** needles, which can transmit disease if not sterile. Some mucosal vaccines presently under development target cholera, diarrhea, meningitis, and tooth decay—all particularly relevant to infants and children. A possible AIDS vaccine is also in the works (Service, 1994c).

hypodermic: an instrument for injecting substances under the skin; from the Greek *hypo-* (under), *derma* (skin).

NUTRITION AND MALNUTRITION

The ultimate measure of good nutrition is the arrival of appropriate calories, protein, vitamins, and minerals at the child's cells, where they can be used for functioning and for growth. That ultimate goal will obviously not be reached unless the food available contains the required nutritional elements. Many other factors, however, can determine whether available nutritious food actually produces a well-nourished child.

Food consumption by an infant or toddler often depends on the ways the food is prepared and offered. Without a full set of teeth, a baby cannot handle tough meats, partially cooked root vegetables, or coarse grains. A baby under 6 months of age does not have the ability to finger-feed, and a toddler cannot spoon up thin soups with any skill.

As mentioned before, the child's consumption of food can also be influenced by the feeding relationship. Some parental concerns and attitudes may make food consumption a "battle of wills" that can lead to actual growth disorders (Chatoor, Schaefer, Dickson, & Egan, 1985).

The food available to a given child may depend on cultural assumptions. In many parts of the world, high-protein foods are given to adult males first, and any leftovers go to the women and children. Because a boy baby takes precedence over a girl of the same age, he will often be substantially better nourished than she is.

Finally, actual nutrition can depend on differences in the *absorption* of nutrients from different sources. Zinc, for example, is absorbed better from human milk than from cow's milk and is least well absorbed from soy formulas (Casey, Collie, & Blakemore, 1985).

APPLICATIONS & ARGUMENTS
Why Is Self-Feeding Important?

One of the most common stereotypes about infant care is that spoon-feeding an infant is an arduous task. The baby doesn't want to eat and must be persuaded by imitations of airplanes or games in which the spoon-train goes into the mouth-tunnel. She wants to grab the spoon, and if she gets it she will throw it on the floor in order to produce a confrontation—or she will get food on her hair and face, which is disgusting and intolerable to any good parent. But what's the reality behind these beliefs?

First, a hungry baby does not need to be persuaded to eat, an infant or a young toddler does not anticipate or want a confrontation with a parent, and food on the face or hair washes off quite easily. Encouraging the baby to feed herself as much as possible from 6 or 7 months on is the real solution here. Self-feeding gives the baby the sense of mastery over the environment, which is probably the foundation for later hard work. It removes the sense of imminent confrontation that the parent—not the infant—may bring to the feeding situation. It's messy, but learning to tolerate a mess is something the parent will need to survive this child's teenage years! Self-feeding is also excellent practice in hand-mouth and hand-eye coordination.

Part of "encouraging" self-feeding is simply permitting it, but part is providing suitable food. Finger foods such as cooked peas, carrots, or potatoes can be eaten without mastery of the spoon. The novice spoon-eater may be able to manage thick, sticky rice cereal but cannot cope with chicken noodle soup.

omnivore: a member of a species that eats both animal and vegetable foods; from the Latin *omnis* (all), *vorare* (to devour).

Listing the factors that help determine nutrition points up some of the difficulties in ensuring a child's nutritional status. On the positive side, we should note that humans are **omnivores.** Because we eat many different kinds of foods, we can achieve a good diet in many different ways. Except (as a general rule) for milk, there is no single food that *has* to be in a child's diet to guarantee good nutrition. People of different cultures feed their babies differently, and if the parents can provide food in the way they consider ideal, the baby will generally be adequately nourished.

marasmus: the effects of deficiency of all calorie sources in the diet; from the Greek *marasmos* (wasting away).

Malnutrition

The greatest concern for most of the world's families is not providing some ideal diet for their children but preventing actual *malnutrition*—dietary deficiencies that lead to specific disease processes. If an infant simply does not get enough *calories*, the resulting form of malnutrition is called **marasmus,** which involves severe wasting of muscle and subcutaneous tissue. Another serious

kwashiorkor: the effects of protein deficiency; from a West African language: "the sickness a child gets after the birth of a second baby."

edema: swelling of body parts; from the Greek *oidema* (swelling).

keratomalacia: softening of the cornea as a result of a vitamin A deficiency; from the Greek *keras* (horn), *malakos* (soft).

Beikost: a food used during weaning from a milk diet to a solid diet; from the German *Beikost.*

premastication: chewing of food by an adult before it is fed to a baby; from the Latin *prae* (before), *masticare* (to chew).

form of malnutrition is **kwashiorkor,** which results from a deficiency of both calories and protein and commonly occurs when a baby is weaned from the breast but appropriate nonmilk foods are not offered. Kwashiorkor is characterized by **edema** (especially a tightly swollen potbelly), changes in the liver, and loss of hair pigmentation. Of course, growth slows or stops in both cases.

Deficiency diseases result from the absence of specific components in the diet. Rickets, a failure of normal bone development, results from the absence of vitamin D, necessary for the absorption of calcium. **Keratomalacia,** a softening of the cornea of the eye that can lead to permanent blindness, occurs because of a deficiency in vitamin A, of which milk is a major source for children. Some deficiencies have complex outcomes. A lack of zinc, for example, reduces taste sensitivity and interest in eating (Casey, Collie, & Blakemore, 1985), and thus may lead to deficiencies in other nutrients.

Genetic conditions can lead to nutritional problems even when a "normal" diet is consumed. The phenylketonuric child, for example, cannot consume foods containing phenylalanine without incurring brain damage, so dairy products and meats, as well as other foods, must be excluded from the diet.

A condition that results from an interaction of genetic and environmental factors involves milk tolerance. Infants and children who have had milk (whether human or that of another mammal) in their diets produce the enzyme *lactase,* which is necessary for the digestion of the milk sugar *lactose.* A small proportion of the world's people, mainly those of European ancestry, continue to produce lactase throughout their lives, but most humans begin to lose the ability after they are weaned and have no milk in the diet. The latter, larger group are said to be *lactase insufficient* and suffer much gastrointestinal distress if they consume milk.

For most of the world's children, the great danger of nutritional deficiencies arises after weaning from the breast. If the mother is well-nourished, human milk provides protein, vitamins, and minerals sufficient to support a baby up to about the age of 6 months. After that point (or earlier if the mother's nutrition is poor), the milk needs to be supplemented with suitable weaning foods; no common term exists for these words in English, but the technical term *Beikost* can be used to describe foods that an infant or toddler can consume before the child is able to eat the foods adults do. These foods have become especially important as "modernization" has encouraged Third World women to wean their babies earlier and earlier. *Beikost* generally must be cooked a long time or mashed so it can be eaten by a young child. Another traditional and very effective approach is **premastication;** an adult chews the food until it is soft, moist, and warm, and then passes it directly from his or her mouth to the child's. (This practice will be discussed further in the section on cross-cultural differences.)

A final addendum to the question of early nutritional difficulties involves pica, the eating of nonfood substances. Infants and toddlers, who commonly put everything into their mouths, are likely to swallow some nonfood items, especially things that have a sweet taste, like chips of lead-based paint. Such toxic substances can have a profound impact on the child's health and are even more harmful if the child is already malnourished.

Breast-Feeding

Until the 20th century, breast-feeding was the only healthy and reliable way to nourish infants. Even today, artificial feeding with cow's milk and other formulas is safe and healthy only in literate populations who have access to clean water and sterile containers. In many parts of the world, a failure to breast-feed still condemns the infant to poor health and an early death.

The process of breast-feeding involves a fascinating series of biological and behavioral interactions between mother and infant. The members of the nursing couple influence each other in a way which changes over time—another *transactional process*. The success of breast-feeding depends on the contributions of both mother and child.

An initial series of biological events are necessary in order for breast-feeding to occur. The process of **lactation** (production of milk in the mammary gland tissue of the breast) usually depends on hormonal stimulation by estrogen and progesterone during pregnancy, although it is possible for humans to lactate without having been pregnant. Following the infant's birth,

lactation: the production of milk in the breasts; from the Latin *lactare* (to secrete milk).

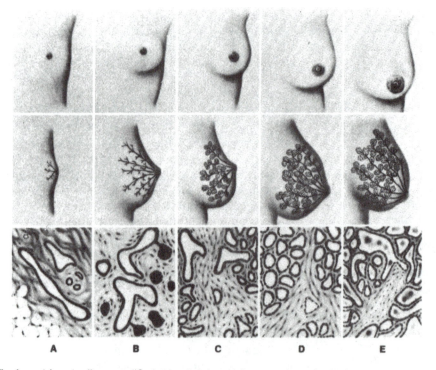

The breast is actually a modified skin gland, and the secretion of milk is parallel to the function of a sweat gland. The pictures here show how the breasts develop from infancy to lactation, with the corresponding cross-sections and duct structures. (Source: U.S. Department of Health and Human Services, 1984)

levels of the mother's pituitary hormone prolactin rise, and the readiness for lactation becomes established.

At this point, however, behavior and experience become essential parts of the process. The mother's prolactin levels will return to the prepregnant state within 14 days unless the baby stimulates the nipple by sucking. For the baby to suck, of course, it must be lifted to the breast and held in an appropriate position; when it is very small, the mother may need to press a finger against the breast to provide an air pocket so the baby can breathe.

Although the baby depends on the caregiver to position it to suck, it is far from passive at this point. The baby responds to the nipple with two **reflexes** that are essential to the breast-feeding process: the rooting and the sucking reflex. (The nature of reflex activity will be discussed in more detail in Chapter 9, but for present purposes we can simply note that reflex movements are automatic, unlearned, and involuntary.) The *rooting reflex* is a response to a touch on the baby's cheek; the baby turns toward the touch and moves the face as if to find and mouth an object. When an object of the right size enters the baby's mouth and penetrates to the right distance, the *sucking reflex* is released; the baby's lips seal around the object, negative pressure is created in the mouth, and a "chomping" motion of the jaws occurs.

The baby's sucking reflex is perfectly coordinated with the mother's *let-down*, or ejection, *reflex,* which causes the milk to be actively squirted out of the nipple. The infant's sucking releases the let-down reflex by producing sharp pressure just behind the nipple. For the pressure to be at the right point, the nipple must be inserted into the baby's mouth just to the point where the nipple's touch will release the sucking reflex. The let-down reflex occurs as a result of the stimulation of production of a pituitary hormone, oxytocin, which is produced in response to sucking stimulation of the nipple. Oxytocin is rapidly carried to the breast in the bloodstream, and it causes muscular cells to contract and eject milk. (Remember from Chapter 5 that oxytocin is also involved in contracting the muscles of the uterus.)

Ordinarily, the interaction between mother and baby will regulate the hormones needed for lactation and let-down. A preterm baby, who does not suck well and who especially needs breast-feeding, may not be able to stimulate the breast sufficiently. In such cases, human growth hormone administered to the mother can cause a significant increase in milk production (Gunn et al., 1996).

One more clearly biological factor needs to be considered: the nature of the fluid produced by the breast. The fluid produced in the first 2 or 3 days is not true milk, but *colostrum*—a thin, sticky yellowish fluid that does not contain much protein. As we discussed earlier, colostrum conveys a real benefit to the infant because it contains a large dose of antibodies. It also works as a mild laxative to clear the infant's bowels. Only after several days does the true milk "come in"—white, opaque, and with plenty of protein and lactose for the growing baby.

The transition from colostrum to milk and the amount of milk subsequently produced are under strong behavioral influences. Nursing the baby soon after the birth speeds the development of true milk, and delay in putting

reflex: an automatic movement in response to a specific stimulus to the nervous system; from the Latin *reflectere* (to reflect).

the baby to the breast can slow it by several days (Mercer & Russ, 1980). Timing is crucial to the amount of milk produced, too; the more frequent the nursing in the first few weeks, the more quickly the milk supply builds up. Even after lactation is well established, the amount of milk the mother makes will depend on the amount the baby takes. The baby who is having a growth spurt will want to nurse more frequently, and, in response, the mother's milk production will build up to provide the amount of food the baby needs.

Although biology obviously plays a powerful role in breast-feeding, it is crucial to understand the behavioral aspects of the process. A lethargic baby may suck too weakly to stimulate the mother's let-down reflex, and an anxious, impatient, or inexperienced mother may not hold the baby in a good position or be sure the nipple is far enough into the baby's mouth. Babies who later develop feeding problems have often sucked poorly from birth, and this problem may exist among healthy babies more often than it was once thought (Ramsay & Gisel, 1996).

Babies in industrialized societies today can be nourished quite adequately and safely with infant formulas. Nevertheless, where there are different consequences to breast- and bottle-feeding, the advantages are with the breast. Bottle-feeding is associated with a higher frequency of ear infections and with allergic reactions. It is also considerably more expensive. The traditional question about the comparative advantages of breast- and bottle-feeding is harder to answer when we take the needs of the whole family into consideration. Because every family is different, the best choice of feeding may be different too.

A more interesting question may be how breast- and bottle-feeding are *different*, especially in terms of the baby's experience. Because the baby cannot describe its experiences, our answers are purely speculative, but breast-feeding and bottle-feeding do involve somewhat different events. The bottle-fed baby, for example, gets milk as soon as it begins to suck, whereas the breast-fed infant may wait 30 to 45 seconds for the milk to let down. The bottle-fed baby is usually fed facing "straight ahead" and most often remains in the same position throughout the feeding, whereas the breast-fed baby has its head turned toward one side and usually has its position switched to the other breast once during each feeding. The breast-fed baby experiences skin-to-skin contact while nursing, whereas the bottle-fed baby generally does not. The breast-fed baby's mother will teach him not to bite the nipple, whereas the mother of the teething bottle-feeder may even encourage biting. The list could go on, but we should note that there is little or nothing to say about differences in bonding or attachment. The popular idea that the nursing mother makes constant eye contact with her baby (thereby enhancing bonding) is not accurate and in fact could be true only for women whose breasts are conical rather than spherical in shape.

wean: to gradually alter the type of food an infant consumes; from the Old English *wenian* (to accustom).

Weaning the baby, whether from breast or from bottle, is a matter of gradually or abruptly changing the baby's main source of food. A breast-fed baby may be weaned to a bottle, to a cup, or directly to nonmilk foods. In most times and places, human beings have weaned to nonmilk foods when the toddler was about 18 to 30 months old. In industrialized societies today, weaning generally occurs much earlier, when milk is still a crucial part of the baby's diet. Abrupt weaning from the breast can be very uncomfortable for the mother who has been nursing frequently, but a gradual weaning, over 6 weeks or so, creates a slow and painless reduction in milk production.

Because breast-feeding is so strongly behaviorally influenced, feeding practices can be very different from time to time and place to place. The popularity of breast-feeding was so low in the United States in 1971 that only about 25% of babies were ever put to the breast at all (Martinez, 1984), and only 9% were breast-fed for 3 months or longer. The trend reversed after the low point in 1971, but it is still quite unusual for babies to be breast-fed beyond 6 or 8 months. Toddler nursing is very rare in the United States and seems to shock many observers. Ethnic and educational differences are also related to breast-feeding choices, with well-educated European American women choosing to nurse most often and weaning latest.

Cross-Cultural Differences in Feeding Practices

Cross-cultural comparisons are not usually cross-national comparisons. Most countries today have many subcultural groups in their populations rather than a single uniform culture. And within a subculture, of course, there is individual variation. In one discussion of cultural dimensions of feeding relationships within the United States (Phillips & Cooper, 1992), an educated Chinese American woman said she didn't know anyone who didn't breast-feed; a young African American woman said she gave her baby solid foods at age 2 months because her mother said it would be all right, although her doctor had said to wait; and a European American husband and wife expressed quite different feelings about toddlers' messy self-feeding. Similarly, in a study of mothers in an Iranian city (Simpson, 1985), most women said colostrum was "dirty" and should be discarded, but a number of them let the baby suck a bit of colostrum just to pacify it.

Most people in the history of the world have breast-fed their infants for at least a few months because they have had little access to other suitable infant foods or to effective techniques for feeding other than suckling.

Many cultures have traditions about the treatment of new mothers that help lactation get established in the critical first 2 weeks after the birth. Spanish-speaking women in the Western Hemisphere may practice *la cuarantena*, a 40-day rest period in which the woman is to abstain from sexual relations, stay away from cold water (and therefore do no laundry), and avoid heavy work (Zepeda, 1982). Iranian city women are also given a 40-day rest (Simpson, 1985). These practices are ideal in allowing recovery from childbirth, extended interaction with and frequent nursing of the infant, and improved lactation. It would not be surprising to see more successful breast-feeding in women whose cultures enjoin rest than in a U.S. professional woman who may feel she has to be back at the office 2 weeks after the birth.

Weaning, the accustoming of an infant to foods other than its mother's milk, is a part of infant and toddler life in all cultures, often starting a few days after birth. Pediatricians in the United States today often advise mothers to delay introducing any nonmilk foods until the baby is at least 6 months old, but an examination of other cultures suggests that this practice is a rarity (and, in fact, most parents in the United States probably do not comply with the instructions they are given).

The timing, types, and amounts of weaning foods *(Beikost)* offered to the infant depend on a variety of factors. Many cultures do not include animal milks among their weaning foods because of religious beliefs (McDowell, 1979), because the culture's cuisine does not use them at all (Chung, 1979), or because of the belief that babies brought up on animal milks will be stupid and brutish (DiDomenico & Asuni, 1979). Most commonly, the weanling child is offered a cereal preparation, which may be presented in paste form on the mother's fingers or may be patted into a cone, inserted between the baby's lips, and gradually pulled into the baby's mouth by gravity (Bateson & Mead, 1942). In some areas where the nursing mother goes to work in the fields when the baby is a few months old, cereals may be the major form of nourishment for the baby until the mother returns to nurse it.

Many foods in adult diets are not consumable by infants unless they are cooked thoroughly (involving expenditures of scarce water, firewood, and time) and then mashed or unless they are prechewed by adults. Premastication, as we mentioned earlier, has been used to prepare food for infant use in most cultures and has disappeared only recently in developed countries (Platt & Ginn, 1938; Radbill, 1945; Whiting & Child, 1953). Premastication is an excellent example of an infant care practice that has a very real value in some cultural contexts but whose value is altered when the context changes. Prechewing mechanically reduces the size of food particles and moistens them, and the ptyalin in the adult's saliva begins the digestive process of converting starches to sugars, making the food more palatable to the infant. The practice also has the potential for colonizing the infant's body with benign microorganisms, thus preventing infection with virulent strains (Shinefield, Ribble, Borrs, & Eichenward, 1963). But premastication of food may become less beneficial when diseases such as AIDS are introduced into a population.

Although most cultures complete weaning from the breast much later than is common in the United States, there is a good deal of variation across cultures, and multiple factors in a culture determine the weaning decision. The family's need for the mother's financial contributions makes a difference, as does the type of work the mother does. A woman who may need to pick up domestic jobs at a moment's notice (as on St. Kitts in the West Indies) is likely to stop breast-feeding after a few months (Gussler, 1979), whereas Yoruba women who are market traders can take their children to the market with them and continue to nurse (DiDomenico & Asuni, 1979). The age of final weaning can also be affected by beliefs about what "nursing too long" can do to the baby (although "too long" is not usually less than 18 months). Nursing past the time when the child talks is sometimes thought to make the child naughty and difficult (Gonzales, 1963), but many groups have no such belief and may occasionally breast-feed the last child in the family until the age of 8 or 9 years. The most common practice is to wean a baby when a new pregnancy is confirmed.

polyphasia: having many short periods of sleeping and waking each day, as well as eating and eliminating frequently; from the Greek *poly* (many), the Latin *phasis* (the appearance of a star or a phase of the moon).

aversion: a sense of repugnance or distaste; from the Latin *avertere* (to turn away).

Some Special Issues About Nutrition

Even when appropriate foods are offered in the context of a good feeding relationship, food consumption by infants and toddlers does not follow exactly the same rules that apply to adults. Here are some points for which there are differences between the very young and older people.

1. *Frequency of meals and amount eaten:* Infants' food, sleep, and elimination patterns are characterized by **polyphasia;** that is, they eat or sleep frequently but briefly. Although this tendency is lessened as the child moves toward the toddler and preschool stages, frequent small meals are still the norm. The child's stomach size remains relatively small and energy requirements remain relatively large, so it is impossible for the stomach to hold more than a small amount of the day's food needs at one time.

2. *Food preferences:* As we will note in Chapter 8, infants are sensitive to tastes, but they do not show much in the way of food preferences until around the first birthday. This is when they begin to show some food **aversions,** and

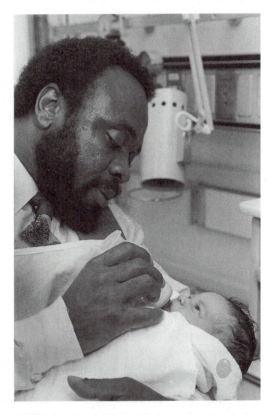

Physical caregiving is the first way for parents to get to know their baby and is the foundation of the parent-child relationship.

they much prefer foods that are familiar and foods that are calorie-dense. Aversion to a particular food may be overcome by allowing time for it to become familiar or by making it more calorie-dense—for example, by adding butter and sugar (Menella & Beauchamp, 1993).

3. *Appetite changes:* The amount of food an infant or toddler desires is primarily determined by its energy needs. These, in turn, depend on growth rate, health, and other determinants of energy expenditure. In a healthy infant or toddler with free access to food, the growth rate is the major factor affecting appetite.

Because the growth rate is very rapid in the first months, the appetite is ravenous and the baby is too hungry to show food preferences. As growth slows, however, especially after the first year, appetite also diminishes. The toddler may not be especially hungry at some meals and will sometimes accept only the most preferred foods. If given the opportunity, the child at this age may "fill up" on junk food and reject more nutritious offerings.

4. *Creating feeding problems:* The loss of appetite just described is a natural outcome of a change in growth rate and is not itself a feeding problem. However, at this point in development, inappropriate handling can create long-term difficulties with eating. As mentioned before, such problems occur, for example, when eating becomes a battle of wills and is determined by emotional issues rather than by a sense of hunger. Less eating comes to mean more attention from mother, which is more gratifying at this point than is satisfaction of the physical appetite (Chatoor et al., 1985).

SPECIAL HEALTH ISSUES OF INFANTS AND TODDLERS

The implications of ill health for the very young are more complex than for older children or adults. Serious health problems in the infant and toddler years interfere with development, and the child's future health is compromised. Assuring good health in early life is the best way to give long, productive lifetimes for the majority of the population.

The Third World

Although most of this book focuses on infant development in industrialized countries like the United States, our understanding of infant health issues requires some consideration of the health status of all the world's babies. Infant and child mortality rates in the Third World are enormously higher than those we are accustomed to. For example, in 1985, Afghanistan, the country with the highest reported infant mortality rate, had 189 deaths for each 1000 children under one year of age; the same year, the United States had 11 deaths per 1000 and Sweden had 6 (Grant, 1987).

These high Third World infant mortality rates are due to a combination of malnutrition and infectious disease. Many diseases, such as malaria, are more likely to kill children than older people. The most common killers of infants, however, are diseases that cause dehydration—cholera and diarrhea of all types.

Although death rates are still unacceptably high, the development in the 1980s of an inexpensive treatment for dehydration has saved the lives of many Third World infants. Oral rehydration therapy (ORT) is a simple and inexpensive treatment that restores fluid levels following diarrhea. A packet of salts costing about 7 cents, combined with clean water, is fed to the child with spoon or cup in order to replace lost fluid and electrolytes. If the salts are not available, sugar or rice can be combined with table salt and water to produce the same effect. ORT has the potential to save 3 million children each year from dying of dehydration following diarrhea (Grant, 1987).

Provision of immunization is another factor that has begun to reduce Third World infant mortality rates and that has the potential to change the world health picture greatly. For example, immunizing pregnant women against tetanus allows them to pass antibodies to their unborn infants and to guarantee that the babies will not die of tetanus contracted when the umbilical cord is cut with a contaminated knife or machete.

The Children's Vaccine Initiative began in 1990 with the intention of developing a single "supervaccine" that could immunize against all the major childhood diseases in one dose, but the program remains badly underfunded. The current regimen of at least six doses of vaccine before the age of 2 is not a real possibility in most Third World countries (Gibbons, 1994).

Vaccine Development and Immunization

As noted earlier in this chapter, current research on vaccines is proceeding rapidly. It is possible that by the end of the 20th century we will have vaccines against such varied diseases as AIDS and ear infections. After many years of development and use in other countries, a vaccine against chickenpox recently became available.

Some of the issues that have slowed vaccine research and development are policy matters, which will be discussed in Chapter 15. A curious sidelight on vaccine production is that whereas fetal tissue research was long banned and is still a topic of much disagreement, vaccines against polio, rubella, and rabies are produced with fetal cells derived from surgical abortion (Hayflick, 1992).

The present recommended schedule of immunizations is as follows. At 2 months of age, vaccine against poliomyelitis and combined vaccine against diphtheria, tetanus, and pertussis (DTP) should be given. Second doses of both are to be given at age 4 months, with a third DTP dose at 6 months. At 15 to 18 months, there should be additional doses of polio and DTP vaccine and a first dose of the combined vaccine for measles, mumps, and rubella (MMR). (Repetition of these vaccines is needed by kindergarten age.) Unfortunately, many U.S. children are not receiving a full schedule of immunizations while they are infants and toddlers. Twenty-five percent of children 19 to 35 months old are not fully vaccinated ("Key facts about children," 1996).

The Vaccines for Children program, which began in 1994, was a plan for providing free immunizations to uninsured, Medicaid-enrolled, and Native American children. Many states and municipalities have some similar programs as well. However, major obstacles to immunization may be transportation, record keeping, and bureaucracy. A mother who takes a day off work to take her infant by bus to a clinic, where she is told she has to reschedule, may simply give up the effort (Marks, 1993).

The Environment and Infant Health

The health of infants and toddlers is influenced by a variety of environmental factors as well as by nutrition and infection. Accidental injuries are of special concern because they are often preventable. Injury and death as a result of car accidents, for example, can be reduced to much lower levels by appropriate use of car seats from the time the baby is brought home from the hospital.

Accidental burns, even when not fatal, can cause devastating injuries followed by painful treatment, disfigurement, and physical disability. Although the source of the most severe burns is house fires, the most common cause of burns in young children is scalding. Scalding often occurs because water heaters are set too high; temperatures that would burn an adult in 2 to 5 seconds will burn an infant in a much shorter time. Although scalds are usually unintentional, they may result from abusive treatment. In either case, an infant cannot escape from immersion in hot water (Athey & Kavanagh, 1991).

Careful supervision is the key to accident prevention, but baby gates and other locking devices can help a great deal.

Exposure to lead, mercury, and other environmental pollutants has a potential for damaging the growing brain (this will be discussed in detail in Chapter 7). At particular risk are infants and toddlers of migrant workers, who may be taken into the fields with their parents and exposed to pesticides (Greenberg, 1991).

The effects of exposure to environmental tobacco smoke (ETS) are most obvious in the first year of life. ETS impairs lung development and is associated with asthma as well as with respiratory infections and ear infections (Bloch, 1992). As mentioned earlier, there is also a connection between ETS and increased risk of SIDS (Greenspan, 1991).

Even though other aspects of the environment are good, an infant's health status may be affected by care arrangements. Infants and toddlers who spend their time in large day care groups may experience increased rates of infection as a result of exposure to other children and to caregivers. Gastrointestinal infections due to rotaviruses (Butz, Fosarelli, Dick, Cusack, & Yolken, 1993) or to parasites are a common problem in day care; they are easily passed from infant to caregiver and vice versa. Because of this concern and because of present worries about transmission of the human immunodeficiency virus (HIV), many day care centers today employ universal precautions, such as using rubber gloves when handling babies.

otitis: inflammation of the ear; from the Greek *otikos* (ear).

acute: having a sudden onset and rapid increase; from the Latin *acer* (sharp).

effusion: in this context, the collection of fluid in the middle ear; from the Latin *ex* (out of), *fundere* (to pour out).

Infants in day care also experience increased rates of ear infections. **Otitis media,** inflammation of the middle ear, is most common among infants and toddlers because of the size and position of their eustachian canals (see Chapter 8 for a fuller discussion). There are two categories of otitis media: **acute** otitis media (AOM), which involves infection as well as fluid in the middle ear, and otitis media with **effusion** (OME), in which there is fluid without infection. Although AOM can be treated in a short time with antibiotics, complete drainage of the fluid may take weeks or months (Roberts, Wallace, & Zeisel, 1993).

Factors other than day care are also related to the occurrence of AOM and OME. Exposure to tobacco smoke increases the number of ear infections. Feeding techniques are also relevant; babies who are exclusively breast-fed for at least 4 months have been reported to have a lower rate (Duncan et al., 1993). Bottle-feeding in a supine position seems to be a particular problem.

A final comment on the relationship between the environment and infant health concerns poverty. The environment of the low-income family is especially likely to include serious health risk factors: an unpredictable water heater or old wiring that can cause burns, a neighborhood where physical violence is common, unregulated day care, and lack of transportation to medical care. Death from dehydration occurs not just in the Third World but also among the very poor of U.S. cities (Klass, 1992).

CHRONIC HEALTH PROBLEMS

In earlier chapters, we referred to disease processes that result from genetic syndromes, from teratogens, and from prenatal infection. We also discussed serious problems which can result from prematurity. Some of the infants affected by such problems die at a very early age. Others, however, live on with a range of more or less serious handicapping conditions.

Whether children with chronic health problems are cared for at home, by foster parents, or in institutions, the cost of their care is very high. When intensive care is necessary, a figure of $1600 *a day* would not be unusual, and months of such care may be necessary in the first year. Even for people with health insurance, lifetime caps can be reached rapidly. A family's income may also be reduced because of the difficulty of finding outside care for the sick child.

Preterm babies can have long-term breathing problems, and they may require an *apnea monitor*—a device worn by the child that sounds an alarm when the child's breathing stops. Weeks or months on mechanical ventilation may produce a chronic lung problem called bronchopulmonary **dysplasia,** with reduced breathing capacity and vulnerability to respiratory infections. Infants and toddlers with these problems may need frequent suctioning of mucus to keep the airway clear.

dysplasia: abnormal growth or development; from the Greek *dys-* (bad, difficult), *plassein* (to mold or form).

Genetic problems present two issues that we've already discussed: genetic screening and prejudicial knowledge. Early genetic testing is clearly useful when treatment of a condition is possible, but there are fears that parents who know that an infant has untreatable, possibly fatal, genetic problems may in some sense "give up" on that baby (Marshall, 1994a). There are also concerns about the response of insurance companies (Marshall, 1994a) to early diagnosis of genetic problems that will require expensive treatment.

Treatment of genetically caused problems is sometimes a clear-cut matter of medical intervention. For cystic fibrosis, for example, drugs or even gene therapy have the potential for thinning out the choking mucus in the respiratory tract (Marx, 1989; Thompson, 1993). In other cases, the medical intervention is not the complete answer to the problem. In phenylketonuria, a special diet helps protect the developing brain, but some cognitive functions may still be affected and may require special educational intervention (Welsh, Pennington, Ozonoff, Rouse, & McCabe, 1990).

Sickle-cell anemia is a genetically caused problem for which drug treatments are currently being developed, but the drug presently in use is approved only for adults. Appropriate care for sickle cell babies requires education of parents as well as suitable medical treatment. Infants who are homozygous for the sickle cell gene are often unable to fight off bacterial infections and have a 15% chance of dying from infection in the first few years. Their infections progress extremely rapidly; there may be only 6 hours between the first sign of infection and the infant's death. Family members need to know how to read a thermometer and to understand that a temperature of 101°F (no problem in a normal baby) means a real emergency for the sickle cell infant, who should be hospitalized. Hospital staff should also be aware that a baby's painful joints or swollen spleen do not necessarily indicate that there has been abusive treatment; these symptoms can result from sickle cell anemia (Kolata, 1987a).

Congenital infections such as cytomegalovirus are not all identified at birth. As they are diagnosed, they may be treated with antiviral or other drugs. Some effects may be reactivated and need new treatment months or years later; an example is eye damage from toxoplasmosis (Williamson & Demmler, 1992).

cerebral: related to the brain; from the Latin *cerebrum* (brain).

palsy: trembling or lack of control of movements; from the Latin *paralysis*.

Some forms of brain damage that occur around the time of birth result in various motor development problems categorized as **cerebral palsy.** The symptoms of these problems are often not obvious at the time of birth and are gradually revealed as deviations from normal motor development show up. Early diagnosis and physical therapy, sometimes in association with surgical treatment, can reduce the eventual seriousness of the motor handicap.

In Chapter 5, we discussed difficult decisions about nontreatment of newborns with very serious medical problems. When treatment has begun, it becomes even more difficult to decide to stop it unless the child's condition has taken a dramatic turn for the worse. However, an infant or toddler may be the subject of a "do not resuscitate" (DNR) order. This is a written order from a physician, requested by the child's guardian, specifying that there will be no attempt to use *cardiopulmonary resuscitation* (CPR) if the child stops breathing or the child's heart stops beating (Brown & Valluzzi, 1995). A DNR order for an infant or toddler who is in a child care or therapeutic setting gives rise to some complex legal concerns.

A final comment on infants with chronic health problems involves pain. Appropriate intervention for relief of pain is always indicated, from birth on. (This topic will be discussed in some detail in Chapter 8.)

AIDS AND INFANTS

A particularly tragic health problem in infants is infection with human immunodeficiency virus (HIV). As is the case for older people, HIV-positive babies will eventually develop AIDS (acquired immunodeficiency syndrome) and will die as a result of a variety of infections they cannot resist.

Exact counts of numbers of HIV-positive infants are almost impossible because only cases of AIDS itself are reported to many local health authorities, and because (as we will note later) diagnosis in an infant may be difficult. However, it is clear that HIV infection is moving away from being a "disease of gay men" and is becoming a disease of women and young children. This is the case in the United States, but is particularly true in a number of African countries, where local customs put women in an especially vulnerable position for infection (Eckholm & Tierney, 1990).

The great majority of HIV infections in infants occur because of *vertical transmission;* the mother's infection crosses the placenta to the unborn baby (Modlin & Saah, 1991). The chances are about 25% to 30% that the baby will be infected. Infection may also occur from contact with the mother's fluids at the time of birth, and when twins are born, the first-born is considerably more likely to be infected than is the second-born (Palca, 1991b). If the membranes surrounding the fetus rupture more than 4 hours before delivery, the chances of infection of the infant increase significantly (Landesman et al., 1996). In the United States, the infected mother is most often an intravenous drug user or has had intercourse with one.

Prenatal treatment of the mother can cause a significant reduction in vertical transmission. One study showed a two-thirds reduction in infection of infants when the mothers received oral drug treatment during the pregnancy and intravenous treatment during labor, and the babies received oral treatment for the first 6 weeks of life (Landers & Sweet, 1996). Unfortunately, as Landers and Sweet point out, most HIV-positive pregnant women are not even tested, much less treated.

Diagnosing HIV infection in the young infant is not a simple matter. Neither mother nor baby may show any symptoms at this point. Tests for HIV look for antibodies in the blood, and, as you recall, the young infant has antibodies that crossed the placenta from the mother before the baby was born. A number of tests are available to detect the presence of antibodies, but they do not show whether the antibodies come from the mother or have been made by the baby in response to infections. Not until the baby is about 15 months old is such a test considered to show that the baby itself is HIV-positive (Modlin & Saah, 1991). There have been cases of detection in children as old as 9 years who had had repeated negative test results in early life (Long, 1996). To add to the confusion, a small number of infants who initially tested HIV-positive on apparently accurate tests later tested negative. Whether this means that the tests are not accurate or that some infants can clear the virus from their systems is not clear (Thompson, 1996).

It is possible to diagnose HIV by culturing the virus, but this test may show false negatives for infants under 6 months of age and is very expensive to do. A test involving the polymerase chain reaction (PCR), which was discussed in Chapter 3, can detect a single copy of the viral genome, but it is also extremely expensive and is not always applicable (Modlin & Saah, 1991).

Symptoms of AIDS may appear at various times during infancy, but because they are also symptoms of other diseases, they do not make a clear-cut diagnosis possible. The baby's symptoms may be the first indication that the mother is infected.

As is the case for adults, the course of the disease varies from one infant to the next. Some infants become ill by 2 months, whereas some have lived to school age. About 60% develop symptoms in the first 12 months, and 75% by 2 years (Modlin & Saah, 1991). The first serious sign of infection may be pneumonia caused by *Pneumocystitis carinii* (PCP) (Hutton & Wisson, 1991). Infections like PCP in the first year usually mean that the baby will not live much more than another 6 months (Modlin & Saah, 1991). About 25% of HIV-positive infants have developed AIDS by age 1 (C. Johnson, 1993).

In addition to contracting respiratory and other infections, HIV-positive infants are likely to experience developmental delays. They may lose abilities that were previously achieved or go through long plateaus of development with increasing motor difficulties and slow growth (Barnes, 1986; C. Johnson, 1993). The emergence of expressive language (speech, as opposed to the understanding of language) is especially affected because of the disease's impact on brain development (Wolters, Brouwers, Moss, & Pizzo, 1995).

As of this writing, treatment of the HIV-positive baby involves several medications. Some cognitive improvements have been reported to result from medication, but the drugs are also potentially toxic (C. Johnson, 1993). A potential treatment approach involves attempts to fight a cofactor that must be present for HIV to enter a cell. Blocking this membrane protein (called *fusin*) might prevent the spread of the virus through many cells (Cohen, 1996b).

Adults who work with HIV-positive infants and toddlers need to use universal precautions, and many child care settings now do so even when the children are not known to be HIV-positive. Universal precautions are intended to prevent transmission of any disease, as much as to prevent the spread of HIV. Such precautions include avoiding contact with blood or other bodily fluids. They also include hand-washing routines as well as the use of gloves (Rathlev, 1994).

Chances are high that the socioemotional life of the HIV-positive baby has been or will be disrupted. It has been estimated that 125,000 to 150,000 children will have been orphaned by AIDS by the end of the century (Caldwell, Fleming, & Oxtoby, 1992). Not all of these children will be infants, of course, and only about 25% of those will be infected themselves. Nonetheless, it is clear that the HIV-positive baby is unusually likely to have a sick, dying, or already dead mother. As a result, the HIV-positive baby is unusually likely to be a candidate for adoption or foster care, but is not likely to be seen as a very desirable choice by most adults (see Dix, 1990). A disrupted family life, frequent illness, and painful treatment add up to increased stress for the HIV-positive child and thus to potentially even greater difficulties with immunity.

It is notable that the rate of infection of women in sub-Saharan Africa is especially high; it is expected to reach 3.5 million women by the year 2000. In some cities of sub-Saharan Africa, an estimated 40% of the women aged 30 to 39 are already infected (Preston, 1993). The possible consequences in terms of orphaned children are almost incomprehensible.

CHILD ABUSE AND VIOLENCE

When we are dealing with older children, definitions of *child abuse* are sometimes a matter of argument. Abusive treatment is usually considered to be the deliberate infliction of physical or mental trauma on a child. But how much trauma is trauma? To what extent does the adult's intention make a difference? Is physical punishment a form of abuse? The majority of U.S. parents appear to believe that spanking or slapping an older child can be an appropriate disciplinary measure, and the courts have generally supported that view.

Whether physical punishment is appropriate or abusive for toddlers is a matter on which parents have differing opinions. Some approve of spanking on the grounds that the toddler needs discipline but is too young to understand an explanation; others believe that physical punishment is abusive because it is frightening and incomprehensible to the toddler. The majority of U.S. parents probably do not approve of physical punishment of infants. They are aware of the baby's physical vulnerability and the very serious harm a blow can do. A baby who is shaken as a punishment, for example, can easily sustain serious brain and spinal cord injury. The American Academy of Pediatrics has recommended that pediatricians give guidance about discipline for babies from 9 months on up. This suggests that the committee making the recommendations did not anticipate forms of discipline at earlier ages (Committee on Psychosocial Aspects of Child and Family Health, 1988).

Defining abusive treatment of infants is an easier matter than defining abuse of older children because issues about physical punishment are less likely to arise. Although some parents would argue that they need to inflict

APPLICATIONS & ARGUMENTS
The Impulse to Harm a Baby

For many U.S. mothers and fathers, one of the most shocking experiences of early parenthood is the realization that they can feel an impulse to hurt a baby. They may always have assumed that only an evil person could harm a child, especially an infant. But now the baby won't stop crying, and inside the parent wells up the horrible impulse to lash out, to slap, even to throw the baby against the wall. Even though the parent resists the urge, he or she feels like an evil being. How could any decent person feel like hurting his or her own baby?

Most "decent" parents have felt such an impulse, and it may be their capacity to be aware of their feelings that allows them to avoid doing any harm. The feeling acts as a warning device that allows time to call a friend, ask for the other parent's help, or just leave the room for 10 minutes.

Another person's distress is a very complex stimulus for us, especially when there seems to be nothing we can do to stop it. If we can help, we often do; but when we cannot, we may respond in startling and inappropriate ways. Laughing at a funeral or at someone else's bad news is not uncommon (much slapstick comedy plays off this tendency). Anger against the distressed person may be displayed, especially if we believe that we have caused their unhappiness.

Parents want to soothe the infant, but the continuing wail proclaims that they are failing in their responsibilities. The cry itself, designed to bring help for the child, is almost impossible to ignore. There may be no other adults to help, or, if they are present, they may attack and criticize the parent. The surprise may be not that so many feel the urge to attack their babies, but that so few actually do so.

pain on an infant for disciplinary reasons, most of the population seems to feel that *any trauma deliberately inflicted on an infant* constitutes abusive treatment. There is somewhat less agreement regarding toddlers. [There are, however, groups of parents who consider physical punishment appropriate for infants under 1 year as well as for 1- to 3-year-olds. In one study of inner-city mothers, 19% said that at times it is appropriate to spank a child who is less than a year old, and 74% felt it was appropriate if the child was between 1 and 3 years old (Socolar & Stein, 1995).]

The relatively clear definition of infant and toddler abuse makes all the more startling the number of deaths and serious injuries caused by abusive treatment of babies. Many may think of child abuse as treatment given by an exasperated parent to a rebellious schoolchild or teenager. The distressing fact, however, is that infants are more likely to be physically abused than older children are, as well as more likely to die as a result of abuse. One-third of physically abused children are *less than 1 year old*. In 1990, 53% of those who died from abuse or neglect were younger than 1 year (noted by Osofsky, 1994).

trauma: a physical or psychological injury; from the Greek *trauma* (wound).

A form of infant and toddler abuse that deserves special attention is **abusive head trauma.** This form of injury is similar to the shaken baby syndrome mentioned earlier, but it has been renamed because of the possibility that babies injured by shaking also have been hurt by impact to the head. In one study (Starling, Holden, & Jenny, 1995), more than 60% of babies injured in these ways were boys, and the average age of the victims was a little over 6 months. About 23% of the victims died. Mothers committed the abuse in only 12% of the cases, whereas fathers, stepfathers, and mothers' boyfriends did so in 60% of the cases. Baby-sitters were the abusers in a surprising 20% of the cases.

An advertising campaign is currently aimed at educating adults never to shake a baby, but the action can be an immediate and thoughtless one in people who have often seen others do the same. Some adults, indeed, may believe that shaking is "less violent" than slapping, although shaking can actually do much more harm. A baby who is shaken because it is crying becomes quiet because of the trauma, and this may be reinforcing to the adult. Eradicating shaking may be a rather difficult job.

It is startling and shocking to realize that infants and toddlers may be the victims of sexual abuse, but this is unfortunately the case. In a child too young to speak clearly, evidence of sexual molestation may be very uncertain unless there has been physical penetration. And where physical penetration has occurred, as in anal intercourse, the injuries to the child may be very serious indeed.

With sexual molestation that involves fondling or oral sex, it may not be at all clear whether marks on the infant were caused by sexual activity or by diaper rash or other irritations (Frasier, Bachman, & Alexander, 1992). There may be no injury at all and no physical evidence of the abuse. A further complication is that physical examination may not yield clear evidence, because there are normal variations in the appearance of the infant's hymen, vulva, and anus. Considerable work has gone into mapping normal genital variations in children (Frasier, Bachman, & Alexander, 1992), but, without signs of injury, there is still no way of telling by sight that sexual molestation has occurred.

One piece of evidence of sexual molestation is the existence of sexually transmitted disease (STD) in an infant or toddler. This may show up because of throat or genital inflammation or may be investigated in the course of examination of a molested child.

Sexual abuse of infants or toddlers is most commonly committed by a man or boy in the child's own household: father, stepfather, older brother. It is rarely committed by women, by strangers, or by people in child care facilities. Indeed, most accusations of the latter have turned out to be groundless. Like other types of sexual abuse, molestation of infants and toddlers is not under good voluntary control; the abuser behaves impulsively and finds the temptation almost irresistible. Treatment of an adult who has sexually molested infants is not likely to be successful.

A final comment on child abuse and violence must include the injuries and deaths that occur as a result of war and civil unrest. The infant or toddler is sometimes deliberately attacked under these circumstances, especially if the war is **genocidal** in nature. During civil strife and urban violence, the baby may simply be in the wrong place at the wrong time, unable to flee the attack aimed at a parent or caught in random gunfire. Even when there is no specific injury, **posttraumatic** stress disorders may result from these experiences.

genocide: the destruction of an entire population; from the Greek *genos* (birth, kind), the Latin *caedere* (cut, kill).

posttraumatic: following a trauma; from the Latin *post* (after), the Greek *trauma* (wound).

PROBLEMS TO CONSIDER AND DISCUSS

1. Do you think that people make different assumptions about the personality of a large, robust baby than they do about a small, thin one? How do they do so? May the babies be treated differently?

2. How do young children come to enjoy the foods that their parents eat? Be complete in your description of the ways in which the child experiences the foods.

3. What are the ways in which babies' experiences change as they begin to get teeth?

4. In the previous chapter, we discussed teratogenic diseases. What is the relationship between that source of birth defects and the immunization of infants and toddlers?

5. How does natural immunity change during the first year or so of life?

7

The Development of the Brain and Related Structures

What is the brain for? The average person's comprehension of the brain's functions stops at the awareness that it is somehow connected with thinking and is reflected in the statement that "we only use 10% (or some similar proportion) of our brains."

To understand how brain functions develop, we need to know the sorts of functions that this complicated organ actually has. In a brief overview, we will see that the activity of the nervous system influences all other body functions. The rest of the body can be seen as existing to maintain and reproduce the brain.

Some brain functions are vegetative. They include maintenance of body temperature and blood pressure, initiation and cessation of eating and drinking, and control of breathing. Although some development takes place after birth, these functions must be reasonably mature, or the neonate would not survive.

Some brain functions are endocrine. Signals from the brain cause glands to release hormones that respond to stress or take part in reproductive processes, among other things. The endocrine hormones in turn influence immune system reactions.

Some brain functions are sensory. The eye and ear do not see or hear on their own; unless their information reaches the brain, there is neither conscious awareness or unconscious response to stimulation.

Some brain functions are motor functions. Although some control over movement comes from the spinal cord, much of it results from activity at the level of the brain.

Some brain functions involve emotion. Certain areas of the brain are activated during emotional arousal. In addition, the brain produces chemical substances, such as endorphins, that modulate the pleasantness or unpleasantness of experiences.

And finally, of course, brain functions can be cognitive—involved in attention, thinking, remembering, language, and problem solving.

BASIC BRAIN STRUCTURES AND FUNCTIONS

To describe the brain is a task as complicated as describing a city of many millions right down to the appearance and personality of every inhabitant.

Like the citizens, the cells of the brain have their individual functions, their dwelling places, their communications with other cells, their diseases and injuries, and their developmental changes.

There are many excellent books that discuss the details of brain anatomy. For the purposes of this chapter, we need deal with only a few of the brain's structures and discuss some of the characteristics of the cells that make up those structures.

subcortical: beneath the cortex of the brain; from the Latin *sub-* (under), *cortex* (bark).

An important structural and functional characteristic of the brain involves the division between the *cortex,* or outer part of the brain, and the **subcortical** areas below it. Much of the developmental change we will discuss occurs in the cortex, which has the responsibility for conscious awareness. Particular areas of the cortex are primary centers for specific functions, such as hearing. This relationship between area and functions is called *cortical localization.* Of the subcortical areas, the one of greatest interest to us is the **thalamus,** the body through which most sensory information is conveyed to the cortex.

thalamus: the part of the brain that routes sensory messages to the cortex; from the Greek *thalamos* (chamber).

An important anatomical characteristic of the brain is its functional and structural division into right and left halves, or hemispheres. Although the two hemispheres look like mirror images, their functions differ from each other more and more in the course of development. The name given to this developmental change is *lateralization.*

The *pituitary* gland affects and is affected by brain functioning. This so-called master gland of the body lies directly under the brain and is in part controlled by the hypothalamus, a subcortical structure that is influenced by sensory experiences like smell and length of daylight. The sense organs include nerve cells, which connect the sense organs to the brain and develop in the embryo at about the same time as the brain. Developmental changes in sensory structures (for example, the length of the eyeball) influence the information the organ can send to the brain.

The brain and other structures involved in the nervous system are made up of *neurons*—specialized nerve cells that have the capacity to pass messages from one to another. Other cells, like the glial cells, support and nourish the neurons.

NEURON STRUCTURES AND FUNCTIONS

The basic function of a neuron is to allow an electrical charge to move from one end of the cell to the other and to cause the next neuron in line to do the same thing. This simple activity, which takes place in an organized fashion in billions of neurons, encodes incoming information from the sense organs and outgoing commands to muscles.

dendrite: a fine projection from the cell body of a neuron that receives stimulation from neighboring neurons; from the Greek *dendron* (tree).

The movement of the electrical charge, or *action potential*, involves rapid transfer of ions across the cell membrane of the neuron. The action potential moves in only one direction: from the soma or cell body along the axon. The action potential may occur because the **dendrites** of the soma have been stimulated by sensory input, or it may occur spontaneously. At the end of the axon is a space called the *synaptic cleft,* which separates the axon from the dendrites of neighboring neurons. Neurotransmitter chemicals are secreted by the axon into this cleft, stimulating an action potential in the next neuron through chemical stimulation of its dendrites. Each neuron may synapse with many others; visualizing the process as involving a single line of neurons is just a useful simplification.

The functioning of the brain always involves many neurons acting simultaneously. As Merzenich, Schreiner, Jenkins, & Wang (1993) have pointed out, "neurons are directly inter-connected to thousands to ten thousands of other neurons, and indirectly to millions or tens or hundreds of millions of others" (p. 6). The timing and sequence of action potentials in a group of neurons probably does as much to encode information as does their position within the brain. **Oscillation,** or self-organized changes in the timing of action potentials in a group of neurons, is an essential part of brain functioning. Timing and other aspects of the relationships between cells can change as a result of experience.

Although all neurons probably act together with other nerve cells, some neurons, especially those in the cortex, have highly specialized functions. A cell in the visual areas of the cortex, for instance, may respond only to very specific visual stimuli, such as an object moving to the right but not to the left,

oscillation: variation, fluctuation; from the Latin *oscillare* (to swing).

APPLICATIONS & ARGUMENTS
Poverty and the Nervous System

"Those that's got shall get, those that's not shall lose"—an old idea that seems tragically more applicable as time passes and that is true even of the physical health of infants. In particular, the health and functioning of the nervous system seem to suffer the ill effects of poverty.

The infant from a poor family is more likely to have been born without prenatal care, to lack immunization, and to go without medical care for infectious diseases. The resulting infections and high fevers have the potential to cause serious brain damage.

Poverty, overcrowding, and hopelessness are associated with excessive drug and alcohol use. Damaging to the nervous system prenatally, drugs and alcohol also dull adults' responsiveness to the baby so that accidents may happen or medical care go unsought.

Old housing in poor condition may be all that is available to the poor family. Flaking lead paint, which falls into food or is picked up from the floor and consumed by the crawling baby, can quickly raise blood lead levels to the point where brain damage begins. Rickety stairs and insecure windows can lead to falls that damage the brain and spinal cord.

It may well be that poverty is the single factor with the greatest influence on an infant's nervous system.

or a line tilted clockwise but not one tilted counterclockwise. These specialized neurons, called *feature detectors*, may do much of the work of perception.

Many explanations of the nervous system compare the functioning of groups of neurons to other systems—to computers, for example. A comparison of the brain to an orchestra (Holden, 1996) is probably more accurate, because it points up the need for organized activity and coordination of different areas. However, the brain follows its own rules, and any analogy is of only slight help. This is particularly true with respect to the development of brain functions during infancy.

RESEARCH METHODS

How is brain development investigated? A variety of techniques have existed for many years, and new approaches are coming into use at a considerable rate. Some methods concentrate on the development of particular structures in the nervous system; others look at functioning as a clue to development; some recent additions try to look at the two simultaneously. As Riesen (1971) pointed out, there may be a need for a structure before there can be a function, but the two may mature at different rates of speed, and one does not necessarily tell us all about the other.

Some of the oldest techniques involve work directly on nervous system structures. Measurement and description of parts of the brain at certain stages in development are among these. Staining techniques show smaller details of development and reveal the shapes of neurons at particular points in development. Electron microscopy can give similar information. Analysis of parts of the brain for neurochemical content gives information about developmental events. These techniques, of course, are not done on living brains, and they presuppose either the deaths of infants of a variety of ages or the use of animals as research subjects.

paradigm: a model or pattern; from the Greek *paradeiknynai* (to show side by side).

When animals are used as subjects, a tracing **paradigm** can be used to investigate developing connections in the nervous system. In this technique, chemicals are injected into particular areas of the young animal's brain. After further development takes place, the animal is killed and the cells examined for evidence of transport of the chemicals from the area of injection. The pattern that emerges demonstrates how connections have developed between one area and another (Schwartz & Goldman-Rakic, 1987).

Events of normal development can sometimes pinpoint a time when changes in the nervous system may be taking place. For example, there are several abrupt developmental changes in vision, including the onset of the use of both eyes in depth perception at about age 3½ months (Held, 1993b).

Some techniques allow direct recording of some events in the brain of the living infant. Electrical activity of the brain in response to sensory stimulation can be recorded from the scalp in the form of event-related potentials (ERPs). ERPs show where in the brain the activity is occurring and how it changes over milliseconds of time.

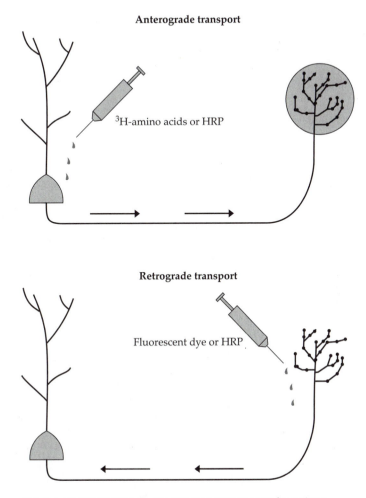

Tracing of connections in the nervous system may be antero-grade, *where dyes are injected into cell bodies and can be traced to the ends of the cells' axons, or* retrograde, *where dyes are injected into axons and can be traced back to the cell bodies.*

There are also a variety of imaging techniques that allow us to take "pictures" of the living brain. Ultrasound pictures can show harmful events like bleeding into the brain. Ultrasound has the advantage that it does not take long, does not require sedating the baby, and can be done at the bedside (Mantovani, 1994). It works best when the fontanels of the skull are still open. Positron emission tomography (PET) can record processes like glucose utilization, blood flow, oxygen use, and protein synthesis in different brain areas. Brain electrical activity mapping (BEAM) allows measurement of brain activity and mapping of specific active areas. Computed tomography involves the use of a rotating X-ray beam and detectors around the patient that record the amount of radiation that passes through different parts of the head.

Magnetic resonance imaging (MRI) is the best of the current techniques and can pick up small differences in tissue density. As Mantovani (1994) described it, the process involves

> images of protons (the positively charged, spinning nuclei of hydrogen atoms), which are abundant in all living tissues. Because of their spin and charge, protons are affected by a magnetic field and can change their alignment with respect to the direction of the field. In MRI, radio frequency energy is applied to the patient to reverse the alignment of protons within the magnetic field. The protons then 'relax' back to their original direction, producing a 'magnetic resonance signal' that is received by a radio antenna . . . surrounding the patient. This signal is then used to produce a visual reconstruction . . . [and] provides . . . dramatically improved pictures of the brain. (p. 64)

However, sedation is usually needed for children under age 6 years, and the process may not give a good image for infants under 6 months because of their poor myelination. In addition to their use in research, imaging techniques can be used to educate parents whose children are injured or have problems of brain development (Mantovani, 1994).

Clinical examination of a baby is generally done when a medical problem is suspected, but information from the examination can also be used for research purposes. The examiner looks at head circumference and compares it to standard head charts and examines the fontanels and sutures of the skull. Attention is also paid to the baby's sleep patterns, alertness, muscle tone, and reflex reactions. Convulsions, poor sucking, abnormal crying, unusual eye movements, and unusual posture may indicate nervous system injury or developmental problems. Old-fashioned but still useful clinical techniques include transillumination, examining the diffusion through the skull of a light source held behind the head; and auscultation, listening to sounds made by the circulation of blood in the head (Amiel-Tison & Grenier, 1986).

A serious issue in research on brain development involves the choice of research subjects. Medical and legal changes over the years have made it unlikely that some earlier work done on human infants will ever be duplicated (Hunter-Duvar, 1985). Noninvasive techniques like BEAM may be used, but staining techniques and other methods used on autopsy are relatively rare today. The use of animal subjects is also problematic in a number of ways. Colin Blakemore, a British researcher who has worked on early visual development in animals, has been the target of a great deal of pressure from animal rights groups. The differences between animal and human development also raise questions about generalizing from animal data to human infants. The rates of brain growth before and after birth differ a good deal from one species to another, and the human brain has a higher metabolic rate than do brains of other primates (Dienske, 1984).

One recent approach to the study of the brain involves computer modeling (Stone, 1993a). It remains to be seen how helpful this technique will be with respect to understanding nervous system development.

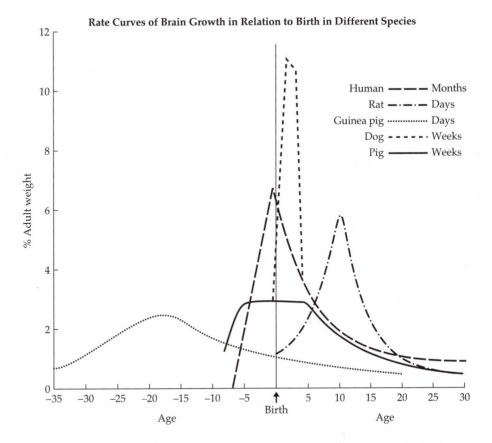

Rate Curves of Brain Growth in Relation to Birth in Different Species

Human ——— Months
Rat —·—· Days
Guinea pig ·········· Days
Dog - - - - Weeks
Pig ——— Weeks

Different mammals have their peak rates of brain growth at different points in development. As this figure shows, humans have a very rapid phase of brain growth right before birth. However, poor prenatal care and nutrition or preterm birth may disrupt this rapid growth. (Source: Dobbing, 1968)

THE DEVELOPING BRAIN

General Changes

myelin: a fatty coating surrounding the axons of some neurons; from the Greek *myelos* (muscle).

The brain and nervous system change in a number of ways during the course of development. The size of the brain grows rapidly after birth, and the shape and depth of its folds and convolutions become more complex. **Myelination** occurs—that is, neurons develop a fatty coating called *myelin*—which improves the speed and specificity of message conduction. The neurons mature and they also increase the number of synapses, or connections, they can make with each other. Parts of the brain increase their internal organization; for example, the cortex becomes more clearly defined into layers of cells.

At the time of birth, the average brain weighs about 335 g (0.75 lb). Some of its convolutions are still poorly defined. The nerves carrying olfactory messages are unmyelinated, the optic nerves and optic tracts are partially myelinated, and some other nerves of the head are well myelinated. The cortex shows lamination into layers, but the layers are poorly defined (Dekaban, 1970).

In the average 3-month-old, the brain weighs 516 g, which shows a growth rate less rapid than that of the whole body. The olfactory areas have just begun myelinating, whereas other areas are more advanced. By 6 months, brain weight has reached 660 g, about double what it was at birth (although the baby probably doubled its body birth weight by 4 months). Myelination continues to advance, and although some areas of the cortex have made a good deal of progress, others still show only slight myelination.

At 9 months, brain weight has increased to 750 g. All the nerves of the head are well myelinated, and the cortex has advanced, but the myelin sheaths are thin. The brain of the average 12-month-old weighs 925 g, not quite triple the weight of the neonate's brain, although the body has tripled its birth weight.

By 24 months, brain weight has reached an average of 1064 g, and the body has quadrupled its birth weight. Most structures are well myelinated, but some additional myelination may continue for many years (Dekaban, 1970; Gottlieb, 1971). An additional change in the brain during this period is *corticalization;* a shift in control occurs, with the cortex taking over from the subcortical structures (Muir, Clifton, & Clarkson, 1989).

Changes in Connections

The complex changes that occur in the neurons and structure of the brain after birth will be discussed later in this chapter. At this point, we should simply note that several kinds of connections between neurons come into being in the months after birth.

topography: the study of the configuration of a surface; from the Greek *topographein* (to describe a place).

Some changes in connections involve **topography** (Blakemore, 1989). The positions of neurons in relation to the neurons they synapse with are orderly and organized. Two neurons that carry messages from adjacent spots in the eye, for example, will pass on their messages to adjacent points in the cortex.

Some changes in connections involve *registration* (Blakemore, 1989). When there are two sets of neurons that carry messages to the same structure, the two sets remain unmixed. In the optic nerves, for example, axons from the right side of an eye stay on the right and those from the left side stay on the left.

Finally, some changes in connections involve *specificity* (Blakemore, 1989). Neurons in the cortex in particular become able to respond only to certain kinds of messages. For instance, some neurons in the visual cortex will respond only to the sight of a line tilted in a specific direction.

How Does the Brain Develop?

There is no question that the human brain continues to develop for many years after birth, even beyond the point at which the individual has reached reproductive maturity (Oppenheim, 1984). The processes through which brain development takes place are less clear, but information combined from many different research approaches has given us some ideas of the steps involved. As we noted in Chapter 4, brain development functions as a dynamic action system, with reorganizations that alter its activity. A small change during development can lead to major differences in structure and function later on (Stryker, 1994).

PROTEIN

neurogenesis: the production of nerve cells; from the Greek *neuron* (nerve), the Latin *genesis* (birth).

1. Neurogenesis   **Neurogenesis,** or the proliferation of cells that will become new neurons, occurs after birth as well as before—at least in the species that have been studied. Neurons in some parts of the brain continue to form after the first year of life in humans (Altman, 1970).

passive: acted upon, rather than acting; from the Latin *passus* (suffered).

2. Migration   Most neurons begin their lives in a limited area of the brain and actually move to the place where they will function. Sometimes this movement occurs by **passive** cell displacement, whereby neurons are pushed away from the proliferative area by newly produced cells; other times, an active process of neuronal migration takes place (Nowakowski, 1993), in which the cells move in amoeboid fashion (Bray & White, 1988). Although cell migration has been found to still take place in adult rodents (Lois & Alvarez-Buylla, 1994), it is most important because of its critical function in the shaping of the human infant's brain. The development of the six layers of the cortex and their organized interrelations depend on correct timing, direction, and speed of migration.

3. Axon growth and guidance   To carry messages appropriately, the axon of a neuron needs to grow toward the "target" neuron with which it will synapse. Axon guidance occurs as a result of chemical substances that attract or repel growth, causing the growth cone of the axon to change the direction of growth. These chemicals are examples of neurotrophic factors, which will be referred to again later in this chapter.

4. Neuron maturation   Although neurons are migrating, they have yet to reach their mature form. This does not mean that they cannot function at all (Scheibel & Scheibel, 1971), but it probably does signify that the cells' activity patterns are not what they will be later.

synaptogenesis: the development of synaptic connections between neurons; from the Greek *synaptein* (to fasten together), the Latin *genesis* (birth).

5. Synaptogenesis   The development of synaptic connections between neurons is called **synaptogenesis.** The early stage of this process has been described as exuberant and redundant; that is, many synapses develop rapidly, and there are more of them than are necessary for mature communication within the nervous system. It is as if too much material is provided so some can be trimmed away, as a sculptor removes excess stone or a dressmaker cuts away extra fabric.

6. Reducing the number of synapses   Although synapses are initially created in great numbers, they soon begin to disappear. In the visual area of the cortex, for example, a newborn baby has 10% of the maximum number of synapses he or she will ever have; and by the age of 8 months, the baby has the maximum. But by the age of 11 years, the boy or girl has only 50% to 60% of the synapses that were in that area at age 8 months (Huttenlocher, 1993). Presumably, the synapses that remain are the ones that are most useful. But what happened to the others? Some of the axons may simply have been withdrawn from inappropriate targets (Blakemore, 1989); others, however, are gone because of cell death.

The idea that cells die without disease or injury seems strange to most people. We expect cells to survive and function until the organism itself dies, and it seems that the death of brain cells in particular should mean the loss of intelligence or personality. But cell death is one of the ways the nervous system is "pruned" or "sculpted" into the form that functions most effectively (Blakemore, 1989). Programmed cell death, or **apoptosis,** is under genetic control (White et al., 1994) and is related to the presence or absence of neurotrophic factors that support the cell's life (Nishi, 1994). When such factors are lost, the result has been described as "a complex cascade [of events] leading to . . . cell death (Gluckman & Williams, 1992, p. 1010).

Not all changes in the number of synapses are genetically preprogrammed. Some occur because of the activation of neurons before and after a particular synapse, possibly because of sensory stimulation (for example, Hata & Stryker, 1994).

Activity in the nervous system can lead to "pruning" of synapses. Although this may create permanent changes in the system, it may also be related to a shorter-term alteration called *long-term potentiation* (LTP)—an increase in the strength of a synapse that results from a high frequency of nerve impulses (Kandel & O'Dell, 1992). The activity of a neuron can thus depend on its recent history of activation (Turrigiano, Abbott, & Marder, 1994).

There is also some evidence that a neuron can lose its membership in one network of neurons because of changes in sensory stimulation and can begin to work with a different network (Hooper & Moulins, 1989). These types of changes in the developing nervous system will be discussed further in the section on plasticity.

7. Myelination   After neurons and synaptic connections develop, the axons gradually acquire a coating of a fatty substance called myelin. A myelin coating is characteristic of more mature cells, and it improves the efficiency of their conduction of nerve impulses. Some parts of the nervous system are fully myelinated before birth, whereas others do not even begin the process until the baby is born. Although immature neurons can certainly function, the development of the myelin coating alters the process of neural conduction.

apoptosis: programmed cell death, which shapes the body prenatally and the brain both before and after birth; from the Greek *apo-* (from, away), *ptosis* (falling).

THE ENVIRONMENT AND BRAIN DEVELOPMENT

The Reorganizing Brain

Until rather recently, most brain researchers assumed that the brain was largely "hard-wired"—had unchanging synapses and pathways—from soon after a baby's birth (Barinaga, 1992). It has become clear, though, that the brain is constantly remodeling itself even after the individual reaches adulthood. Although changes during infancy place some limits on the brain's capacity to reorganize, remodeling can still occur after damage (Barinaga, 1992) or even during a temporary alteration by anesthesia (Pettit & Schwark, 1993). If changes in stimulation like these can cause the adult brain to reorganize, it seems likely that the same will be true of the infant brain—and that does turn out to be the case.

The Concept of Plasticity — *Force of Environment in dev. feature*

A good deal of the development of the brain is genetically determined. But when the course of brain development is altered by nongenetic factors, we say that plasticity has been shown. The term *plasticity* refers to structural and/or functional changes produced by **endogenous** (internal) or **exogenous** (environmental) influences (Buchwald, 1987).

The concept of plasticity does not necessarily imply change for the better or for the worse, although in some situations one or the other will be obvious. Plasticity is simply a matter of alterations in developmental events as a result of experience. Sometimes those alterations involve putting more energy into certain aspects of development, sometimes less. As one writer put it, "early transactions with the environment partition neural resources, allocating them to systems involved in those transactions at the expense of other systems. Abilities and disabilities are created simultaneously" (Spinelli, 1987, p. 26).

A number of possible mechanisms for plasticity were discussed earlier in this chapter. The internal and external environments apparently can influence **neurotrophic** factors, proliferation of neurons, cell migration, and synaptogenesis, as well as the long-term potentiation that may be involved in learning.

Critical or Sensitive Periods

As we noted earlier in this book, a critical period is a time during development when the environment can influence the direction of development in a way that would not have been possible earlier and will not be possible later. (Note that this definition, like our earlier definition of plasticity, does not say that the influence is necessarily for good or necessarily for ill.) The idea of critical periods implies a limitation on plasticity; it suggests that there are times when environmental influences on an aspect of development are strong, and other times when they are weak. Why is this the case for brain development? The reason probably has to do with the fact that different parts of the brain are developing at different times.

An example of a critical period study is an investigation of the changes in kittens' visual cortex that result when the animals are prevented from seeing with one eye (Olson & Freeman, 1980). It has been known for some years that keeping one of a kitten's eyes closed will cause an almost complete loss of neural connections from the closed eye to the cortex (Wiesel & Hubel, 1963). Olson and Freeman investigated the possibility that the effect can occur only

endogenous: occurring for reason of internal activity; from the Greek *endon* (within), *genos* (birth).

exogenous: occurring because of external stimulation; from the Greek *exo-* (outside), *genos* (birth).

neurotrophic: guiding the growth of a neuron; from the Greek *neuron* (nerve), *trophe* (nourishment).

during a limited time during development—the critical period. The researchers' technique involved suturing one eyelid closed so that the kitten could see only with the other eye. They subsequently studied connections in the nervous system between the eyes and the appropriate part of the brain after 10 to 12 days of deprivation. The researchers used kittens of a variety of ages, from 10 days to 109 days. The greatest effect was shown in kittens between 28 and 38 days; older and younger kittens were less affected, demonstrating that there is a critical or sensitive period for the effect of visual experience on this aspect of brain development.

Some authors (for example, Greenough, Black, & Wallace, 1993) have suggested that critical periods are a demonstration of one type of plasticity called *experience-expectant* plasticity. The changes seen in critical periods involve information from the environment that is normally experienced by all members of the species at a particular age and that has been experienced throughout the species' evolution. This sort of plasticity shapes all members of a species in similar ways. A second type of plasticity, *experience-dependent* plasticity, shapes the individual. Learning is an example of experience-dependent plasticity; it involves experiences that may occur at many times and in many ways, so the individual needs to be capable of adapting all the time, rather than only during limited periods.

Structural and Chemical Plasticity

The plasticity of the nervous system shows up at the neuron level as well as in connections between neurons. In cats whose vision has been restricted to one eye (like those in Olson's and Freeman's work described above), there were actually changes in the arrangements of axons after only two or three days (Antonini & Stryker, 1993). In rabbits, visual deprivation leads to reduction in dendrite structures (Globus, 1971). Rabbits also show changes in the proportions of amino acids in the visual system after only 3 days of visual deprivation.

Deprivation and Distortion of Vision

There is much evidence that deprivation of some aspect of visual experience or distortion of vision (such as by the use of special lenses) affects both connections in the brain and visual functioning. The experimental work in this area has naturally concentrated on animal rather than human subjects. For instance, when infant monkeys wear prism lenses that distort their experience of visual depth, they lose particular neurons from the cortex and fail to respond adequately to stimuli that are usually seen as three-dimensional (Crawford, Smith, Harwerth, & von Noorden, 1984.) Kittens kept in the dark except when they were looking at stripes moving in a single direction showed an increase in the numbers of certain neurons; the kittens also were clumsy when trying to catch a moving object and bumped into stationary objects (Tretter, Cynader, & Singer, 1975)—they were probably not good mousers, either!

amblyopia: loss of vision in one or both eyes because of a lack of appropriate visual experience; from the Greek *amblys* (blunt), *ops* (eye).

STRIBISMUS

1 hr. / week
=
NO AMBLY.

Some of the studies on sight in animals were prompted by special issues about human infants. When certain problems are present, humans may develop **amblyopia**—a loss of ability to see with one eye even though it is structurally perfect. Work on monkeys has shown that when one eye is kept closed between birth and 9 weeks of age, the vision in that eye is irrecoverably lost (von Noorden, 1973). The same experience after 12 weeks had no effect on vision.

Clinical work on humans has shown a similar critical period for amblyopia in humans, although it is a good deal longer than the period in monkeys (von Noorden, 1973; von Noorden & Maumenee, 1968). If cataracts (opaque lenses) develop in the eye between birth and 2 years, amblyopia is likely to result even after the cataract is surgically removed. Similarly, patching an infant's or toddler's eye during medical treatment may lead to amblyopia if the eye is covered for more than a week at a time. (This should not be confused with the use of a patch to try to force the use of a less functional eye in an older child.)

Learning

Experience involving learning also seems to affect brain development. For instance, when monkeys were trained for a year on shape discrimination, they showed an increase in one part of the brain from 9% of the cells showing a response to the shape to 39% showing such a response (Tanaka, 1993).

Lateralization

Both genetic factors and plasticity undoubtedly contribute to the development of brain *lateralization*—the specialization of one or the other side of the cortex for control over specific functions. Because the left side of the brain controls the right side of the body and the right side of the brain controls the left side of the body, it is easy to connect lateralization with hand preference, but there are many other issues involved as well. (Hand preference development will be discussed in Chapter 9.)

To understand lateralization, we must avoid the old-fashioned assumption that each hemisphere of the cortex functions separately. The two halves of the brain work in cooperation, and they cannot perform in the same way if separated from each other (Gazzaniga, 1989). The tasks of the left and the right hemispheres are often quite clearly parts of the same job. For instance, the right hemisphere deals with the recognition of a face's emotional expression, but the left hemisphere is needed to provide a verbal label for the expression (DeGangi & Greenspan, 1991).

Some lateralization is already present at birth (see Chapter 9). The right hemisphere develops a bit faster than the left (Changeux, 1985). The development of postnatal lateralization may depend in part on the differences in the speed of the hemispheres' development. One study of lateralization focused on the greater specialization of the right hemisphere for face recognition (de Schonen, et al., 1990). The researchers trained 4-month-old infants to discriminate between their mother's face and a stranger's face (see Chapter 10 for a discussion of this operant conditioning technique). The faces were shown either on the left side, where the image would be received by the right hemisphere, or on the right side, where it would be received by the left hemisphere. Much better discrimination of the faces was shown when the right hemisphere was at work. What does this have to do with the more rapid development of the right hemisphere? The researchers suggest that, among other things, the hemisphere that learns a task first can inhibit or suppress similar learning for a time in the other hemisphere, even though each hemisphere could do the task alone if the other did not interfere.

Lateralization of language functions is a complex issue that will be discussed in detail in Chapter 11.

BRAIN DAMAGE

In our discussion of plasticity in brain development, we looked at situations in which the brain's resources are reorganized in specific ways in response to environmental influences. When there is brain damage, however, the reorganization has to occur using diminished resources. It was once thought that the young nervous system had such a high degree of plasticity that it could recover from almost any damage, but this is no longer assumed (Prechtl, 1984b). Diminished resources appear to lead to diminished functioning no matter how the reorganization is carried out. When brain damage has occurred, therapy may help a child do many tasks, but these tasks cannot necessarily be done in the "normal" way (Farel & Hooper, 1995).

transient:
temporary; from the Latin *trans-* (across), *ire* (to go).

An awkward aspect of the diagnosis of infant brain damage is that many clinical signs are **transient.** The baby in the first year may show symptoms suggesting that there is brain damage, but the symptoms may disappear with time (Amiel-Tison & Grenier, 1986). Although the baby may then appear to be perfectly normal, cognitive problems may show up at school age.

The most useful studies of early brain damage involve information about other physical phenomena in addition to symptoms of brain damage. These studies may measure blood lead levels or evidence of trauma, for example. However, there are many possible causes of brain damage, and not all are simple to assess.

Traumatic Injury

Brain damage may occur as a result of a physical injury to the head or spinal cord. Accidental injuries from car accidents have diminished since protective car seats have come into use, but a number still occur when an adult holds an infant in the lap or when a car seat is not used or positioned appropriately for the baby's age. Child abuse remains a cause of brain damage; shaking an infant can easily cause serious brain injury or even death. Advertising programs are currently trying to combat the belief that shaking is somehow "less violent" than spanking.

TABLE 7.1   *Motor problems resulting from damage to the nervous system: changes in the first year.*

Problem	Time frame	Changes
Imbalance between extensor and flexor muscles of neck	First 2 months	Normalizes by 3 months in many cases; head control achieved
Stiff, unrelaxed legs	First 7 months	Legs relax
Falls backward when sitting	First 7 months	Normal sitting
Persistent straightening of legs and trunk	First 7 months	Normal posture
Cerebral palsy, spastic conditions, involuntary movements	Persists through first year	

Source: Based on Amiel-Tison & Grenier, 1986.

[handwritten: fetal hemoglobin]

[handwritten: Billirubin levels - UV light, fluids]

Oxygen Deprivation and Brain Bleeds

Lack of oxygen to the brain causes the death of neurons, which are not ordinarily replaced. There are a number of ways in which this can occur before or during birth. Following birth, choking accidents may occur when the baby gets an unmanageable piece of food or another object stuck in the throat; this can certainly happen when an infant or toddler bites a balloon, which bursts and hurls fragments into the child's throat. Hanging accidents can occur when loose clothing or jewelry gets caught on furniture. In both cases, the breathing blockage may be relieved before the child dies, but not before brain damage is done. Near-drowning accidents can have the same effect.

Where there is *hypoxia* (a diminished oxygen level), an increase in blood flow to the brain may occur, with the high pressure causing rupture of capillaries and bleeding into the brain (Lou, 1989). The **asphyxiated** baby may have this additional cause of brain damage (as was discussed in Chapter 5).

asphyxiate: to damage or kill by depriving of oxygen; from the Greek *a-* (not), *sphyzein* (to throb, pulse).

Chemical Causes of Brain Damage

Chemical substances that can damage the brain can come either from environmental pollution or from an inappropriate internal environment resulting from metabolic problems. Infants are far more vulnerable than adults to such sources of damage. Their gastrointestinal membranes are more permeable than adults'; their kidneys are less capable of detoxifying chemicals; and their blood-brain barriers, which serve to reduce danger to the brain, are less developed (N. Greenspan, 1991).

There has been much controversy in recent years about the level of lead required to do serious brain damage. The Centers for Disease Control have progressively lowered the blood lead level (BLL) used to identify a child's need for treatment. In 1987, it was estimated that 3 to 4 million U.S. children had BLLs higher than the allowable maximum, which is currently set at 10 mg/dl of blood. At levels between 10 and 35 mg/dl, the expected symptoms are intellectual and behavioral problems; with levels between 36 and 50 mg/dl, irritability, lethargy, and abdominal pain result; with BLLs at 51 to 69 mg/dl, there is general fatigue, inattentiveness, tremors, and headache; BLLs greater than 70 mg/dl can result in paralysis and possible coma (Benson & Lane, 1993).

Control over leaded gasoline has removed much of the organic lead from the environment. The remaining levels of inorganic lead are especially dangerous because the substance is not metabolized in the liver and so is readily available to the rest of the body. Lead-based interior paints, although their manufacture was banned in 1977, are still found in millions of homes. Removal of lead-based paints is difficult and expensive, and if done improperly, it can distribute the lead as a fine dust. Lead solder and lead material in plumbing, banned from public water supplies in 1988, are still present in many older houses (Benson & Lane, 1993). Toddlers are at particular risk because they pick up and mouth objects like paint flakes and because they may teethe on painted furniture or window sills.

Treatment of lead poisoning can be done through chelation therapy, in which drugs redistribute lead from bone to other tissues where it is more easily excreted. However, the damage that has already been done to the nervous system is not reversible and it may lead to mental retardation, learning disabilities, and hearing impairment (Benson & Lane, 1993; Pear, 1992).

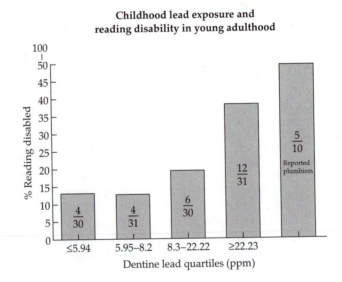

The proportion of children with reading disabilities in elementary school increases with lead exposure (plumbism is the term for lead poisoning). This graph shows the relationship to amounts of lead in tooth dentine. (Source: Needleman, 1991)

Mercury poisoning used to result in part from the use of the chemical in teething powders and in cures for intestinal worms. Exposure to high levels of mercury can lead to severe retardation. Mercury was an ingredient in about 30% of all indoor latex paint until 1990 and is still used in spackling compounds, joint compounds, and glues used in building (N. Greenspan, 1991).

Chemical substances may be ingested as part of the diet when they are used as food preservatives. Sodium nitrite, used to prevent botulism in foods, can lead to reduction of the brain's oxygen supply through a complicated chain of events. Although red blood cells normally contain hemoglobin, which carries oxygen to other cells, sodium nitrite alters the iron in the cell to create methemoglobin, rather than hemoglobin. Methemoglobin cannot give up oxygen to tissues, so hypoxia results. Nitrites are occasionally found in very high levels in foods, even in foods labeled "no preservatives added" (Isaacson, 1987).

Chemical causes of brain damage are found in the internal environment, too. Genetically caused problems of **metabolism** can create a dangerous chemical environment within the body. In phenylketonuria (PKU), for example, the individual lacks an enzyme that breaks down the amino acid phenylalanine, normally an essential component of the diet. The accumulation of phenylalanine in the blood causes gradual brain damage; motor problems and apathy are noticeable by the time the baby is a few weeks old. If phenylalanine is removed from the diet, development is much closer to

metabolize: to carry out the processes in cells that use energy; from the Greek *metabole* (change).

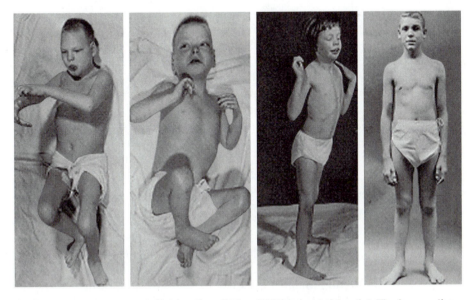

The three children on the left show the effects of PKU untreated by diet. The boy on the right had a phenylalanine-restricted diet but still shows some mental retardation.

normal (Dekaban, 1970). Even after phenylalanine is removed from the diet, however, preschool children with PKU seem to show some cognitive problems (Welsh et al., 1990).

Disease Processes and Brain Damage

High fevers associated with childhood diseases such as measles, mumps, and rubella can cause serious damage to the brain. A more direct effect is produced by acquired immunodeficiency syndrome (AIDS). Babies infected with AIDS have poor development and damage to specific brain areas. They show regression in mental functioning, sometimes slowly and sometimes very quickly (Barnes, 1986).

APPLICATIONS & ARGUMENTS
"Patterning" and the Brain-Damaged Child

It is not surprising that parents of children with disabilities have their eyes open for every new therapy that could possibly be helpful. When a child has suffered brain damage, the parents' longing for a treatment is desperate because their child's problems may be so serious—motor problems, intellectual retardation, even a permanent absence of conscious awareness. Unwilling or unable to accept the nature of the child's problems, the parents are eager to try the most unorthodox measures.

One such measure that emerged in the early 1970s was called *patterning*. This technique was offered as a way to guide the damaged nervous system through the steps of normal development, with the goal of retraining the system to a level of normal functioning. For minor problems, this might take the form of making the child crawl even though he or she had been walking for some time. For very serious brain damage, however, patterning involved repeated passive movements of arms, legs, and head, designed to initiate early reflexive movement patterns. Five adults were needed, one to move each body part in a synchronized pattern as the child lay prone. This was repeated several times a day for months and years and usually required volunteers from the neighborhood, as well as the parents and friends. The patterning procedure took up much of the parents' time and energy.

Sadly, there is no evidence that patterning helped the damaged nervous system. Some children showed improvement as they got older, but, of course, this could have been caused by development alone; development does not stop completely with injury. Patterning did seem to help prevent the muscle contractions that occur when the child lies unmoving for extended periods. Unfortunately, though, the treatment did not and does not do what the family so desperately wants.

Malnutrition

The brain's rapid growth and development require adequate amounts of proteins and fats in the diet. Malnutrition produces apathy as well as poor physical growth. Brain and head growth are certainly reduced. Problems occur with cell division, myelination, and so on (Altman, 1971). It was assumed for some years that intellectual development was affected in exactly the same way as the physical aspects of the brain (Jacobson, 1970), but more recent work has shown that good caregiving can help the child's mental ability recover even though head size does not (Winick, 1980)—evidence that plasticity involves the entire organism, not the brain alone.

Treatment for Damaged Brains?

Although it has long been assumed that central nervous system neurons could not recover from damage, hope for effective treatments is growing. One of the causes of long-term damage may be the accumulation of zinc in traumatized neurons, and there is some evidence that chemical agents that remove zinc could prevent serious effects (Koh et al., 1996). Regeneration of neurons in the spine may also be achieved through surgery that bridges damaged areas with parts of peripheral nerves and uses a "glue" impregnated with a nerve growth factor to stabilize them (Young, 1996).

SENSE ORGANS AND SENSORY SYSTEMS

During the development of the embryo, the sense organs and the neural systems related to them grow and mature in close conjunction with each other. The development of each is understandable only with respect to the development of the other, both pre- and postnatally; and the activity of each may drive some of the development of the other, as we saw in the earlier discussion of plasticity.

The sense organs and the neurons associated with them act as a unit in most ways. The sense organs are not simply image-catching or sound-catching machines that pick up information to be read elsewhere. Analysis of information starts at the receptor level. An eye is really no more like a camera than a refrigerator is like a shoebox.

Physical growth in each sensory system follows a particular schedule, so one system may be mature while another is still developing. The development of the auditory system, for instance, is faster than that of the visual system.

The Eye

The eyeball itself at the time of birth is not very far from its adult size. The length of the newborn's eye is about 16 to 17 mm, growing to 20 to 21 mm at 1 year and 23 to 25 mm in adulthood. The shorter eye produces a smaller image on the retina (Banks & Shannon, 1993).

accommodation: in this context, the change in the thickness of the lens that allows adjustment for vision at different distances; from the Latin *ad* (to), *commodare* (to make fit).

retina: the surface at the rear of the eyeball that contains light-sensitive receptor cells; from the Latin *rete* (a net).

The lens of the newborn eye does a poor job of **accommodation**—the adjustment of its thickness to bring images of near or far objects to a focus on the retina. Control of the muscles that adjust the lens' thickness comes about gradually over the first months (Atkinson & Braddick, 1981).

The **retina,** which contains the rod and cone receptor elements, is a delicate structure and is difficult to prepare for study. Postmortem examination of infant retinas has shown that their structures continue to change into the third and possibly the fourth year of life (Hendrickson & Yuodelis, 1984); receptor cells continue to move toward the center of the eye, creating a greater density of cells there.

The layer of receptors in the retina is initially only 1 or 2 cells thick (Abramov et al., 1982). The cone cells, which later have two functioning segments, are short and broad and do not collect light very effectively. The actual areas where light can enter the receptor cell are about 68% of the cell's area for adults, 28% for 15-month-olds, and only 2% for newborns (Dobson, 1993). The outer segments of the receptor cells are much bigger in the adult, which makes it much easier for the receptor to absorb the photons or "light particles" that will trigger the cell's response to light. It has been estimated that 350 photons are absorbed by an adult eye for every one absorbed by a young infant (Banks & Shannon, 1993).

The failure of the receptor to absorb light does not mean that it is completely inactive, however. All receptors and nerve cells show spontaneous

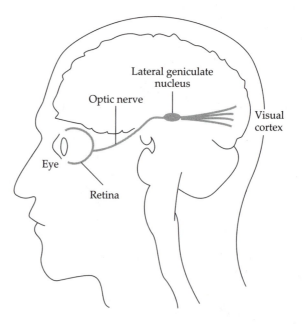

This diagram shows the primary visual pathway from the eye to the cortex. (Source: Goldstein, 1996)

electrical activity, and cells in the developing retina of mammals have been shown to carry on not only activity but *patterned* activity, even before the retina has been stimulated with light (Meister, Wong, Baylor, & Shatz, 1991).

A curious interaction between the characteristics of the eyeball and the activity of the retina can have a long-term effect on vision. One type of amblyopia (distortion or loss of vision because of a lack of appropriate visual experience) appears to result from irregularities in the shape of the eyeball. The eyeballs of 20% to 60% of infants and toddlers are asymmetrical, leading to *astigmatism*—the inability to form on the retina a clear image of all the lines in a scene at the same time. Depending on the shape of the eyeball, some lines will be blurred, perhaps horizontal ones, perhaps vertical ones, or perhaps those tilted 5° clockwise. Most children lose their astigmatism as they grow toward adulthood, but quite a few adults show the effects of early astigmatism in *meridional amblyopia*—the inability to get a clear image on the retina of all the lines in particular orientations, even with the help of corrective lenses. The timing of the astigmatism seems critical; if it is gone before the baby is 6 to 8 months old, meridional amblyopia does not result, but its presence between 8 months and 2 years creates later visual problems (Gwiazda, Bauer, Thorn, & Held, 1986).

Nerve impulses carrying messages to the subcortical areas and the cortex from the retina need to operate at a mature level in order for visual functioning to be good. In kittens, the rates of neural firing diminish greatly as they get closer to the cortex; the change is not so great in adult cats. Kittens, then, experience a smaller amount of meaningful activity in the visual system compared to the accidental or spontaneous activity; in other words, the signal-to-noise ratio is decreased. This would lead to information loss in the immature visual system (Banks & Shannon, 1993).

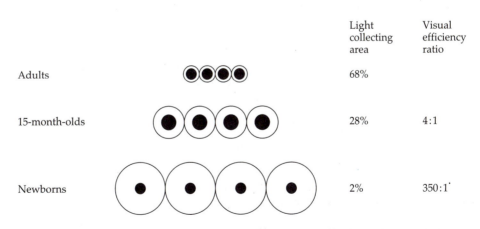

	Light collecting area	Visual efficiency ratio
Adults	68%	
15-month-olds	28%	4:1
Newborns	2%	350:1

The white circles represent the distances between receptor cells in the retina; the dark circles show the size of areas that respond to light. Newborns do not do a very good job of responding to the light that enters the eye. Fifteen-month-olds are much better but not nearly as efficient as adults are.

Some visual information is carried from the thalamus, in the subcortical area of the brain, to the cortex by two separate pathways: the magnocellular and the parvocellular systems. These systems develop at different rates of speed and do different jobs. The **magnocellular** system carries information about slight differences in brightness; about large, broad images with few details; and about rapid changes. The **parvocellular** system, on the other hand, deals with high-contrast dark and light images; with small details; and with still or slowly changing scenes, like those involved in reading (Lovegrove, 1993). In older children and adults, problems with the magnocellular system seem to be connected with *dyslexia,* a type of reading disability.

The Ear

Although the outer ear and the auditory canal do not reach their full size until adulthood, the bony inner parts of the ear begin to develop long before birth and are almost fully developed at birth (Bredberg, 1985). Myelination of the auditory nerve also occurs early.

One part of the ear, the eustachian canal, takes extra time to develop. This canal connects the middle ear to the back of the mouth and allows air to move back and forth, adjusting the air pressure behind the eardrum so it is equal to the pressure on the outside. In infants, the eustachian canals are almost horizontal, and it is difficult for fluid to drain out of them. As the face and jaw grow downward, so do the eustachian canals, and ear infections become less frequent as drainage becomes easier.

One developmental change in processing of sounds by the auditory system is shown by the emergence of the *precedence effect.* Older children and adults show the precedence effect when listening to two sounds that come from different places and occur at slightly different times (from 4 to 40 msec. apart); they notice only the sound that occurred first. It seems that the more mature nervous system can suppress the later sound as if it were an echo that would confuse the listener. Babies under 5 months do not show the precedence effect (Clifton, 1985).

For a long time, it was thought that damage to receptor cells in the ear could never be repaired. Receptor injuries due to infection or other problems would lead to permanent impairment. Recent research, however, suggests that it may be possible for auditory receptor cells to regenerate after they are damaged (Forge, Li, Corwin, & Nevill, 1993; Warchol, Lambert, Goldstein, Forge, & Corwin, 1993).

magnocellular: having to do with a system of neurons that carries information about large, rapidly changing visual images with few details; from the Latin *magna* (large), *cella* (a small room).

parvocellular: having to do with a system of neurons that carries information about slowly changing visual images with many details; from the Latin *parva* (small), *cella* (a small room).

NEUROCHEMICAL ACTIVITY

The functioning of the nervous and sensory systems depends on the effects of neurochemicals, specialized chemical substances that are the foundation of activity in nerve cells. Neurochemicals form both the environment of the neuron and its means of communication with other cells. The nervous system

*Infants and toddlers seem to seek the visual stimu-
lation they need to guide the development of the
visual system. Unfortunately, mouthing the window
sill while looking out may be a source of lead
poisoning.*

produces some neurochemicals and stimulates the endocrine system to produce others. It also develops and changes in response to neurochemical
stimulation.

Neurotransmitters

Specialized neurochemicals called *neurotransmitters* carry a nerve impulse
from the end of one neuron across the synapse to another neuron. A wide
range of neurotransmitters such as acetylcholine, noradrenalin, and glutamate
have been known for many years, but others such as nitric oxide and carbon
monoxide have only recently been identified (Barinaga, 1993a).

The amount of specific neurotransmitters in parts of the brain changes in
the course of development. A neurotransmitter that is at particularly high
levels in the infant and toddler period may be involved in assuring plasticity
(Court et al., 1993).

Endocrine Hormone Production and the Nervous System

The endocrine system produces chemical messengers called *hormones.* As they circulate in the blood, hormones affect cells of the nervous and other systems, encouraging or discouraging growth and functioning.

testosterone: a male hormone produced primarily in the testes; from the Latin *testis* (testis).

Although the reproductive hormones are obviously necessary for conception and pregnancy, there would seem to be little use for them in a baby's life. It is thus surprising to find that the level of the male hormone **testosterone** is higher in early infancy than it will be for many years. Testosterone levels in umbilical cord blood are significantly higher in boys than in girls, and the difference increases over several months. The boy babies' testosterone levels have been reported to increase significantly until between age 1 and 3 months, after which they decrease over several more months until they reach the level found in boys before puberty. The girls' testosterone levels, by contrast, decrease rapidly from their already lower level following birth (Forest, Cathiard, & Betrand, 1973).

It has been suggested that testosterone has a slowing effect on the "pruning" of synapses, which helps structure the nervous system (Held, 1989). The beginning of binocular vision, which requires that some synapses disappear and some survive, appears at a time that is related to testosterone levels (Gwiazda, Bauer, & Held, 1989).

Other endocrine glands, such as the thyroid, also produce hormones that affect the nervous system. Thyroxin, for example, is necessary for normal growth and development of the cortex in mammals (Jacobson, 1970).

Endocrine Hormones and Stress

The endocrine system is under the control of the pituitary gland, the so-called master gland of the body. Hormonal signals from the pituitary cause other endocrine glands to change their levels of hormone production. The activity of the pituitary gland is especially important with respect to stress. When unusual demands are placed on the body by pain, hunger, fear, or fatigue, the pituitary helps mobilize the body's resources.

The pituitary is especially suited for this job because of its relationship both to the nervous system and to other glands. The hypothalamus, part of the subcortical brain, responds to sensory stimulation both inside and outside the body by secreting chemical releasing factors. These are rapidly circulated in the blood to the nearby pituitary, which pours increasing amounts of its own hormones into the blood. The pituitary hormones are carried in the blood to the adrenal glands, which in turn release hormones such as cortisol that help make energy sources more available to the cells. This set of connections, referred to as the *hypothalamic-pituitary-adrenal (HPA) axis,* is especially responsive to stress and changes in activity as stress increases or decreases. The stress response is present at birth in humans (Anand, Brown, Christofides, Bloom, & Aynsley-Green, 1985).

Work on animals has demonstrated that early experiences of stress help determine whether the older organism will deal effectively with stressful situations. When rat pups are systematically handled by a researcher (an experience that seems to be stressful for them), they recover from stress in later life more easily than do rats that have not been handled. This plasticity in the development of stress responses may occur as a result of the following events: (1) handling the pup causes its body temperature to drop slightly; (2) the hypothalamus and pituitary become activated and affect the thyroid gland; (3) thyroid hormones affect the response of cells to cortisols produced by the adrenal glands; and (4) the changes in response to cortisols become permanent (Meaney et al., 1990).

Stress, Pain, and Neurochemicals

Responses to stress and other stimulation include the secretion of pain-controlling substances by the brain itself; morphine and codeine are among these substances. Ingestion of sugars and fats, as well as soothing touch, reduces stress reactions in ways that suggest neurochemical changes (Blass, 1989).

One very stressful experience for most young mammals is deprivation of contact with the mother, which results in slowing of growth (Schanberg, Kuhn, Field, & Bartolome, 1990) and reduction of immune reactions (Coe et al., 1987; Reite, 1990). How could maternal deprivation have such a powerful impact on the infant? Work with rat pups suggests that the effect occurs as a result of a change in the brain's production of beta-endorphins. Normally, the mother's touching and licking of the pup prevent the release of large amounts of beta-endorphins; tactile sensory stimulation results in nerve impulses that are carried to the brain and affect beta-endorphin production. When the sensory stimulation is reduced, the amount of beta-endorphins produced increases and triggers the release of other neurochemicals, either from the brain or from the pituitary. These, in turn, expend food energy in the stress reaction, rather than using it for growth (Schanberg et al., 1990). These neurochemicals also suppress the activity of the immune system (Meaney et al., 1990).

THE INTEGRATED BABY

Imagine a 6-week-old baby boy lying on his mother's lap, gazing at her face as music plays from stereo speakers. Making eye contact and moving in response to the music, he appears superficially to be doing things much as he will a few months hence. At the level of the nervous and sensory systems, however, this baby is much less developed than we might guess. Because his body is producing testosterone, the "pruning" of synapses has been slow, so he does not yet have the clear organization of nerve cells that would allow him to use information from both eyes in a mature way. The eyes themselves are likely to have asymmetrical shapes, so all parts of a picture are not equally clear. The receptor cells of the eyes are not well developed anyway, so they cannot send a detailed message to the brain. The music from the stereo speakers may seem to have a bit of an echo in it, because the brain is not yet able to deal with slight differences in timing of two sounds.

Plasticity is still at a high level in this baby. His head is still growing, and his brain can change in order to continue to interpret differences in the distance between the eyes or the ears. If he experiences a slightly scratched eye and has it protected by a patch for a week or two, plasticity may unfortunately also lead to a loss of functional vision. It is possible that his experiences with mild stress may also show some benefits of plasticity, as they make him more competent to deal with stress in the future. (Too much stress, especially lack of social contact, may lead to poor immune reactions to infection right now.)

Although the 6-week-old can do a great deal, the facts about his young nervous system tell us that his functioning remains immature and vulnerable. In many ways, he remains more like a still-developing fetus than like an older infant.

PROBLEMS TO CONSIDER AND DISCUSS

1. What techniques could you use to decide what proportion of the human brain is used in thinking?

2. Describe how one cell in the nervous system communicates with another.

3. Discuss how both good and harm can be done to a developing individual as a result of cell death in the nervous system.

4. What changes in the developing nervous system could lead to amblyopia?

5. How are neurochemicals affected by the baby's experiences?

8

The Development of Sensory Processes

Sensation, perception, cognition—these are three traditional terms that describe some of a person's reactions to the environment. Unfortunately, each term conveys somewhat different ideas in its everyday sense than it does in its technical sense. *Sensation* and *perception* are especially confusing words, because most people are not certain whether or not they imply that an individual is conscious of the processes. Can there be a sensation or a perception without awareness? On the face of it, it seems improbable that such a thing could be; yet there are certainly reactions to the environment that occur without conscious awareness.

To escape this semantic trap, this chapter will avoid both *sensation* and *perception* and will focus on *sensory processes*. A sensory process is a chain of events triggered by an alteration in some sort of energy the environment is sending toward the individual. The change in energy affects receptor cells and the associated neurons that carry messages to some higher part of the nervous system. Some change in nervous system functioning follows and may be accompanied by a change in behavior. There may or may not be conscious awareness that the sensory process is going on, but there must be some sort of measurable change in the individual. Each type of sensory process, involving a specific type of environmental energy, specific receptor cells, and specific neural or behavioral changes, is referred to as a *sensory modality,* or a *sense.*

FUNCTIONS OF THE SENSES

To understand the functioning of the senses, it is important to keep in mind that conscious awareness may be, but is not necessarily, part of the sensory process. In some cases, a person may be quite *aware* of sensory information and may deliberately try to collect it for cognitive purposes, such as to solve a problem, to recognize something, or to anticipate an event.

What do the senses accomplish when sensory processes occur with little or no awareness?

1. They may establish the safety or desirability of an action or event. Smell and taste, for example, often lead to immediate emotional reactions of attraction or repulsion.

2. They may function as organizers of behavior; for example, a toddler may walk effectively as long as he can make eye contact with his mother, but he falls when she turns away. One important organizing mode is that of the *Zeitgeber* (time-giver), in which stimulation such as light at regular intervals causes bodily processes to match the interval pattern of the stimulation (Moore-Ede, Sulzman, & Fuller, 1982).

modulate: to adjust; from the Latin *modulari* (to play, sing).

3. Sensory processes can function to **modulate** action. For example, a person picking up a squirming cat shifts and alters finger pressure in response to sensory messages about the cat's movement against the hands. The same person picking up a teddy bear will do little modulation of pressure, because the toy does not move of its own accord.

4. Vision seems to have a particular role as part of a social signaling system. When given the chance, infants spend time looking at people's eyes. Although this is probably a matter of a preference for a certain type of pattern, adults interpret the infant's gaze as indicating interest and affection. As a result, they spend more time interacting with the infant.

THE SENSES AS A DYNAMIC ACTION SYSTEM

It is commonly said that the eye is like a camera. This sort of simple statement about vision completely misses the point that each sensory modality acts as a dynamic action system, as indeed do all the senses working together.

In a dynamic action system, a change in the nature or functioning of any of the parts can change the outcome. Human sensory processes, unlike most cameras, involve many constantly changing components that interact to produce a specific reaction to an environmental stimulus. For example, brain and receptor cells both must function appropriately for a sensory process to occur, but both are constantly fluctuating in their readiness to be activated.

The senses act as filters of relevant information rather than as passive recipients of stimulation (Van Essen, Anderson, & Felleman, 1992). A visual receptor cell responds to one type of light (a particular color, for instance) at one level of brightness, but another type responds only when the brightness is much greater. All colors are not equally visible.

The senses influence each other, too, and act as a larger system. People judge where a sound is coming from on the basis of what they see as well as what they hear. Similarly, a vertical line can look tilted if it is surrounded by a tilted frame. Infants and toddlers can lose their balance if they see an artificial wall move, even though the floor below them is perfectly stable (Lee & Aronson, 1974).

AGE AND SENSORY CHANGES

Development with age is an important source of change in sensory processes. As we have discussed before, development occurs in part as a result of maturation and in part as a result of experience. Depending on the sensory process under consideration, either or both may play a powerful role in determining sensory development.

It is impossible to make a general statement about the sources of sensory development because each sensory modality follows its own developmental rules. Some sensory processes are fully developed and in place at birth; others are immature at birth and show high plasticity as their development is guided by experience with the environment. For some processes, plasticity comes to an end as a critical period concludes, whereas others remain malleable throughout life. All, of course, are susceptible to disease and injury, which may have an effect even before birth.

The gradual emergence of vision as the *dominant sense* can give us a clear view of sensory processes as a dynamic action system capable of reorganization. Mature humans are strongly visually oriented, as are some (but not all) other species; we trust information from vision even though our other senses contradict it. Early in life, however, vision is the least developed of the senses, and most of the individual's responses are to nonvisual sensory stimulation.

Sensory deficits—and losses, too—show us the functioning of the senses as a dynamic action system. Problems with vision or with hearing affect movement, social interaction, and emotional development. Rather than simply missing a part of sensory functioning, the individual reorganizes development completely.

RESEARCH METHODS

It may seem that it would be more difficult to study the sensory processes of infants than those of adults, but the basic issues are really the same for the young and the old. How do we manage to know how an environmental stimulus affects another person? It does not really matter whether the person can talk to us or not, because even the most articulate subject cannot explain what is happening in his receptor cells and in his nervous system; he may not even be able to give a name to a taste or a smell or to describe what a pain feels like. Adult subjects participating in research on the senses may be asked only whether they hear something or nothing, whether they see a light or not, or whether one liquid is sweeter than another.

In many sensory situations, babies can tell us whether they can tell the difference between two things. They do this not with words but with eye or head movements or with changes in sucking on a nipple.

Preferential looking is one technique that allows us some understanding of what babies see or sense in other ways. The baby is presented with two images, two sounds, or two scents, and an observer decides whether the eyes or the whole head turns toward one stimulus or the other. The assumption is that a baby who cannot tell the difference between two stimuli will spend approximately equal amounts of time turned toward each. If the baby spends a significantly greater amount of time turned toward or looking at one of the stimuli, the conclusion is that the baby can **discriminate,** or tell the difference, between the two. When testing preferential looking, one of the experimenters has the job of judging in which direction the baby is looking or turning, and

discriminate: in this context, to perceive the distinguishing features of something; from the Latin *discernere* (to distinguish between).

that person must not be able to tell which stimulus is on which side. (This technique requires a large number of trials or measurements in order to calculate whether there is significantly more time spent turned toward one stimulus than toward the other. It also requires that each of the two stimuli appears on the right or on the left in random order, because babies have position preferences, which can make them turn in one direction more than the other no matter what stimulus is there.)

Operant conditioning techniques are based on the baby's capacity to learn; if the baby can learn to behave differently in the presence of each of two different stimuli, we can conclude that he or she can tell the difference between them. For example, a baby can be given a nipple connected to a milk supply via a long tube. The experimenter can either let milk flow through the tube when the baby sucks or prevent its flow. If we want to know whether the baby can tell the difference between red and green, we might let the milk flow when the baby is looking at green but turn it off when the baby looks at red. A pressure-sensitive device inside the nipple can record the amount of sucking; if the baby soon stops sucking when looking at red, we can conclude that the two colors look different to her.

Habituation (Fantz, 1964) is a third useful technique for exploring babies' sensory abilities. This approach makes use of the fact that a baby who has scanned, or visually explored, a stimulus for a while will gradually look at it less and less. The reduction in looking at the stimulus is called habituation. If the stimulus picture is taken away and then put back where the baby can see it, the baby will briefly dishabituate and scan the picture once more, but habituation will quickly recur. Only a novel picture will lead to longer dishabituation and active scanning until the stimulus picture becomes familiar and habituation sets in once more.

If the baby treats the new picture as if it were the old familiar one—by a brief dishabituation followed by reduced interest—we conclude that the baby cannot tell the difference between the two stimuli. A long period of scanning before habituating to the new picture tells us that the baby can discriminate between the two.

optokinetic nystagmus: involving a reflexive eye movement in response to a moving visual stimulus; from the Greek *ops* (eye), *kinetos* (moving), *nystagmos* (drowsiness).

Sometimes reflex responses to stimulation can allow us to measure sensory abilities. In the study of vision, for example, **optokinetic nystagmus** can show whether a baby can detect fine details. This phenomenon involves a reflexive eye movement, nystagmus, which consists of a slow drift of the gaze in one direction followed by a quick eye movement that snaps the gaze back to the straight-ahead position; this movement occurs in response to certain images moving across the visual field (this is the "optokinetic" part of the phrase). A moving canopy above the baby's crib provides the moving images, such as a set of stripes, and an observer watches to see whether nystagmus occurs. A set of stripes that are too narrow for the baby to see will not produce nystagmus, but the reflex will occur if the stripes are large enough for the baby to detect.

Exploration of sensory abilities can also include observation of specific behaviors. Does the baby willingly crawl out onto a transparent surface that looks as if she might fall through? Does she reach accurately for objects? Does she make a face when given one food to taste but look pleased with another? Sometimes observation arises in clinical settings. Does the baby behave as if she is in pain when certain treatments are done? Does she seem to enjoy some forms of touch but resist others? In these clinical situations, researchers may find themselves paying attention to factors other than specific behaviors: for example, whether a sick baby gains weight more rapidly when given one set of sensory experiences than with another.

A very promising method for studying infant sensory processes involves *evoked potentials*. These are measurements of electrical changes in nervous system activity that result from specific forms of sensory stimulation. They may be used to test an infant for sensory problems or to explore the sensory capacities of normal infants.

Our discussion of research methods used in work on infant sensory processes needs to include a discussion of the subjects to be studied. Not every baby is equally likely to be a participant in sensory research. In one study of newborn habituation to colors, for example, the subjects chosen were those infants who stayed awake after feeding and did not cry or fuss (Slater, Morison, & Rose, 1984). Some techniques, such as habituation, work a bit differently with newborns than with older babies (Slater, Morison, & Rose, 1984). After age 8 to 10 months, many babies become shy with strangers and do not do so well in a testing situation. And because much sensory research involves repeated testing, many studies report data from only a small number of subjects (this is true about work on adults, as well).

Clinical work that is relevant to sensory processes necessarily focuses on babies who are sick or have disabilities. One problem with drawing conclusions from such work is that the subjects may not have resembled each other very closely, so many individual differences may affect the data. Most babies who are at risk have multiple problems, not all of which may have been diagnosed at the time of the study. However, many clinical studies report information about large numbers of subjects because the data are drawn from city- or statewide screening programs; the numbers certainly make such studies useful and worthwhile.

Animal studies can be useful additions to the understanding of infant sensory development. Experimental work with animals can explore issues like the relationship between the taste of the amniotic fluid and the taste preferences of the young after birth (Mennella & Beauchamp, 1993). However, the timing of development is obviously different from species to species, and we cannot assume that the sequence or the events are necessarily the same. Even different breeds of one species may show differences in adulthood (for example, some breeds of dogs hunt by sight, whereas others hunt by scent).

ONTOGENY AND THE UNDERSTANDING OF SENSORY PROCESSES

Ask most healthy adults which sense they would *least* like to lose and chances are excellent that the reply will be "vision." Mature humans are so strongly

ontogeny: the development of the individual; from the Greek *einai* (to be), *genos* (birth).

oriented to vision that we naturally consider it to be the most important of the senses. But the course of **ontogeny,** the development of the individual, shows us that vision is relatively late to develop and is probably far less significant to the newborn than are the other senses (Gottlieb, 1971).

Sensory systems develop in a predictable sequence. The infant's experience of the world at any given time is presumably dependent on her stage in the developmental sequence. Vision takes about 6 months after birth to develop to an adultlike level, so for younger babies, the sensory world may be richest in nonvisual areas. The next sections of this chapter will summarize current understanding of infant sensory abilities in the order of the ontogenetic sequence.

THE SKIN SENSES

The *cutaneous,* or *skin,* senses are usually considered to comprise touch, pain, warmth, and cold. Little is known about the development of the latter two, and much of our knowledge about touch and pain comes from clinical situations.

Not all parts of the body are equally sensitive to touch. The mouth is the first part of the body to show touch sensitivity prenatally, and it remains one of the most sensitive areas, partly because of the high frequency of receptor

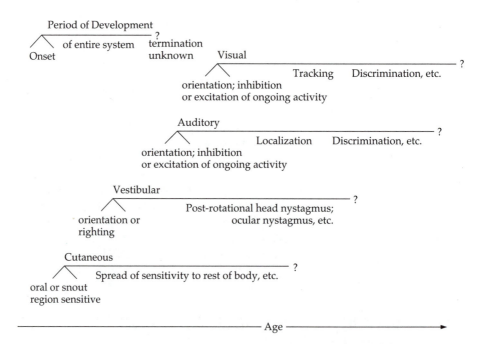

The sensory systems do not all develop simultaneously. Here we see that touch is the first and vision the last of the senses to begin to develop. (Source: Gottlieb, 1971)

organs for touch in the skin of the mouth area. These receptors are tiny end organs found on the small, branching nerve endings that connect the skin to the central nervous system. They respond to changes in pressure exerted against the skin.

Some studies with rats show a strong relationship between touch experience and growth. Reduced growth of rat pups follows even a short-term interruption of maternal care, but growth is restored by stroking the pups with a dampened paintbrush at a frequency like that of the mother's licking (Schanberg et al., 1990). In fact, most young mammals depend on the mother's licking, especially around the anal area, to foster digestion and elimination. The touching and handling of young rats have also been shown to affect the development of their responses to stress (Meaney et al., 1990).

Fortunately for adult sensibility, human infants do not need to be licked in order to digest their food. However, stimulation through touch has been shown to increase weight gain in preterm babies (Field & Schanberg, 1990a; Field et al., 1986). A possible link with the development of the immune system has also been suggested (Reite, 1990).

Many cultures deliberately stimulate infants with touch through massage. Daily infant massage with oil following a bath is common in Nigeria, Uganda, India, Bali, Fiji, New Guinea, Venezuela, and Russia (Field, 1993; Landers, 1990). In recent years, a movement to teach infant massage has begun in the United States (Evans, 1990). There has been no research to test whether massage has a particularly positive effect on growth and development of full-term infants, but it probably comes under the heading of "couldn't hurt." As long as the masseur or masseuse responds to the infant's responses of pleasure or discomfort, massage is probably one of many positive face-to-face interactions between infant and caregiver.

The concept of sensory defensiveness, especially with respect to touch, has become increasingly popular with clinicians who take a *sensory integration* perspective (for example, Anzalone, 1993; Sears, 1994). The sensory integration approach assumes that infants can normally organize all the information that comes from their bodies and the environment, but that injury, unpleasant experiences, or less specific factors may make it difficult for a baby to use information from one modality. The baby becomes defensive for that modality, avoids that type of stimulation, and feels uncomfortable when forced to experience it.

tactile: related to the sense of touch; from the Latin *tactus* (touched).

Tactile defensiveness is thought to involve avoidance of light touch rather than of deep pressure. Unfortunately, that type of avoidance sends highly negative social signals to caregivers and may disrupt their relationship with the baby. Many of our affectionate or playful bids to a baby involve light touches: stroking, tickling, hair rumpling, or kisses. Many everyday care routines also contain light touches, such as undressing and dressing the baby, bathing, applying oil or powder, brushing hair. A baby who resists all those activities may well be thought of as cold, aloof, distant, and difficult.

It is clear that unusual or uncomfortable touch experiences can make an infant respond negatively to some tactile experiences. This is especially

APPLICATIONS & ARGUMENTS
What Sensory Stimulation Does a Drug-Withdrawing Baby Need?

An infant who has been exposed to drugs during gestation may or may not suffer long-term problems; short-term effects are extremely likely, however. These might involve the need for specific medical treatment but almost certainly will include the need for comfort care. These babies tend to be easily startled and upset. Their jumpiness interferes with sound sleep, eating, and digestion. The input into their senses needs to be carefully regulated.

Sometimes drug-exposed babies need medication, but other techniques are useful too. These babies benefit from a quiet, dim environment but not from dead silence or complete darkness. A low level of sensory stimulation helps maintain the baby's level of arousal and helps override the tendency to twitch and startle. Slow, gentle rocking and patting work better than the more vigorous approach a healthy baby might need. A pacifier is one of the most calming devices for the drug-exposed infant, but the baby may not be able to keep it in the mouth for long without accidentally thrusting it out; the caregiver needs to be responsive and help with this until the infant develops some skill with the pacifier. Swaddling and firm but gentle holding also help. Calming the drug-exposed baby before and during feeding can be especially important, because the baby's distress and jumpiness interfere with food intake and digestion alike.

Caring for a drug-withdrawing baby is an exhausting task. The caregiver will need help and respite as well as emotional support when the infant seems impossible to comfort.

noticeable when the baby has had abnormal experiences of touch around the mouth (Morris, 1989). As Morris points out, a baby normally receives "a continuous bombardment" of various kinds of stimulation of the mouth; this occurs through feeding, finger sucking, chomping on toys, and so on (p. 136). A sick or preterm baby who has been too weak to suck and swallow has usually been fed by means of a *gavage tube* passed to the stomach through the nose or mouth. The placement of the tube is not a pleasant experience, and it is one of the few experiences of oral touch the baby may have, especially if physical disabilities make it difficult for her to bring her hand to her mouth. The mouth becomes hypersensitive and the baby resists any touch there, which further reduces the baby's chances of experiencing a normal level of stimulation.

Anxiety about sexual abuse of children can make caregivers or even parents afraid to do a lot of touching, but all young mammals need it to thrive. Touch and sexuality are not the same thing. (Source: Early Childhood Development Centre, Bristol, 1995)

Touch gives important information about the need to modulate action. For example, touch information about the hardness or softness of an object tells the infant about the *affordances* of the object—what can be done with it (Gibson, 1962). One study on this topic measured the pressure infants exerted on soft or hard objects they were mouthing or grasping (air pressure tubing attached to the objects allowed assessment of the pressure). Even in newborns, pressure is exerted differently by both mouth and hand on soft objects than on hard ones (Rochat, 1987). If we consider an infant sucking at the mother's breast as opposed to one sucking an artificial nipple, we can see that the two sucking patterns will be different simply because of the affordances of the two nipples. No wonder an infant who has been breast-fed for 6 months cannot figure out how to drink from a bottle; the habits developed as a result of the affordances of the mother's nipple do not work well with the bottle.

kinesthesis: the awareness of limb movement and position; from the Greek *kinein* (to move), *aesthesis* (perception).

A sensory modality that is related to touch is **kinesthesis,** the sense of limb movement and position. This sense depends on receptors such as muscle spindles, Golgi tendon organs, and joint receptors, which respond to changes of tension in muscles and ligaments. This sense is difficult to test in infants, but is still developing in the early school years (Bairstow & Laszlo, 1981). Presumably, the information from the receptors alters in meaning if not in content as the baby grows taller and heavier. The center of gravity needs to be over the feet in order to maintain a standing posture, and the center of gravity moves lower as the individual grows. With increasing size, then, there are changes in the pressure on receptors in the joints and the vertebral column (Dietz & Horstmann, 1991).

interoception: the awareness of events internal to the body; from the Latin *inter-* (between), *capere* (to take or capture).

It is possible that interoception should be counted as a relative of the skin senses. **Interoception** is the ability to process internal sensations that monitor bodily processes, such as blood pressure (Porges, 1993). Few of us have any conscious awareness of this sense, but the fact that biofeedback training helps people reduce their blood pressure suggests that some such sensory process exists. Some recent researchers have suggested that interoception is related to the ability to regulate emotional responses and may, therefore, be involved in some early emotional disorders (Porges, 1993).

Shockingly, the study of pain in infants is a very recent phenomenon. It was once generally believed that infants experienced no pain at all, or were at least not very sensitive to it. Because physicians generally assumed that preterm babies and full-term newborns were without pain sensation, many surgical procedures, even open heart surgery, were performed on infants without any anesthetic whatsoever (Lawson, 1988). In 1988, a new policy on anesthesia of young infants was adopted by the American Academy of Pediatrics and the American Society of Anesthesiologists. The policy statement set the rule that decisions about anesthesia of infants should follow the same rules as decisions about anesthesia of adults.

One of the reasons for the assumption that infants did not feel pain was our lack of complete understanding of pain receptors and pathways in the nervous system. Although the general stimulus for pain is destruction of tissue, there are no specific receptor cells that can be designated as responding to pain. Transmission of messages about pain in the nervous system is an extremely complex matter that appears to involve proportions of activities of different parts of the system, rather than specific pathways. Ordinarily, it is assumed that a sensory message must be carried to the cortex before awareness can occur, and certainly the newborn's cortex is functioning at a very immature level. But the extent to which the cortex is involved when even an adult senses pain is quite unclear.

Another reason for assuming that infants did not experience pain was a behavioral one. Generally, we expect a person who is in pain to *act* as if he or she is in pain. Crying, complaining, grimacing, rubbing the painful place or trying to get away from the cause of the pain—these are all cues that convey to us that someone is hurting. But very sick or preterm babies may be too weak or immature to show any behavioral reaction to pain. During surgery, infants are given muscle-relaxing agents to keep them lying still—whether or not an anesthetic is also given—so infants are not able to show their pain behaviorally. In addition, of course, babies do cry often, and they may cry whether they are experiencing pain or not (although there is a characteristic "pain cry," as we will see in Chapter 11).

How can we know whether a weak or sick baby is in pain? How can we tell crying in pain from other crying? Can we measure pain in any meaningful way? A number of attempts at answering these questions have been made in recent years (see McGrath, 1990). A good example is a rating scale that takes crying, facial expression, consolability, and so on into account as the infant's pain is assessed. One goal of this sort of rating, of course, is to determine whether particular medications or treatments are actually effective for relief of infants' pain; medications that are safe and effective for adults are not necessarily so for infants.

physiological: relating to the functioning of the body; from the Latin *physika* (natural science).

When infants are unable to express pain behaviorally, monitoring **physiological** changes may be the best way for us to assess their experience. In preterm babies, changes in blood oxygen level, heart rate, and breathing rate appear to be correlated with the severity of the procedure they are experiencing (Gonsalves & Mercer, 1993).

In spite of a new awareness of infant pain, many procedures, like heel-lancing for a blood sample, are performed repeatedly on sick babies without medication or other techniques (like pacifier sucking) that have been shown to reduce pain responses (Field & Goldson, 1984). Circumcision of baby boys is still frequently done without a local anesthetic, although educational programs for physicians have brought about some changes (Ryan & Finer, 1994).

All infants, term or preterm, well or sick, experience pain at times. There may be a reaction to immunization as well as the "shot" itself, or accidental rough handling, or a stomachache. Measures that can relieve the baby's pain are beneficial for many reasons, including some aspects of emotional development (to be discussed in Chapter 12). Such measures are especially helpful to the parents' view of their own competence and thus to their relationship with the baby.

Campos (1988) has suggested a number of principles that govern comfort techniques for uncomfortable babies.

1. The *principle of constancy of stimulation* notes that rhythmic, repetitive stimulation works better than a small number of pats followed by 1 minute in a rocking chair followed by a brief song. Often caregivers stop what they are doing because the baby keeps crying; they conclude that the activity "must not be what he wants." Calming takes time, however, and an agitated baby may not pay attention to a comfort measure until it has been going on for a while.

2. The *principle of additive effects of constant stimulation* suggests that two comfort measures may work better than one; rocking *and* singing may soothe a baby who goes on crying in response to rocking alone or singing alone.

3. The *principle of tactile stimulation* emphasizes the importance of touch as a comfort technique but notes that the broader, deeper pressure of a palm may soothe a baby who is aroused and annoyed by a light fingertip massage (whether or not the infant can be classed as showing tactile defensiveness).

4. The *principle of vestibular stimulation* stresses a sensory modality that will be discussed a bit later in this chapter. Rocking, jiggling, and similar movements all provide stimulation to the vestibular sensory system and are useful comfort measures.

5. The *principle of distraction* suggests that giving the baby a stimulus to focus on, like a pacifier to suck, can interfere with her attention to pain.

6. Finally, the *principle of arousal transfer and relaxation* notes that the infant who is hungry, tired, or otherwise stressed will react more intensely to pain than one who is relaxed and calm. To help a baby cope better with necessary discomfort, we can try to confine uncomfortable activities to times when the child is well-fed and rested. This principle calls into question the common hospital practice of "cluster care," in which multiple procedures and treatments are done in a short time and the baby is then left alone to "rest" (Cole,

TABLE 8.1   *Some factors that can indicate the level of an infant's postoperative pain.*

Sleep (inability to sleep indicates more pain)

Facial expression of pain

Amount and quality of crying (constant high-pitched cry indicates more pain)

Spontaneous motor activity (thrashing and agitation indicate more pain)

Excitability and responsiveness (trembling and spontaneous reflex movements indicate more pain)

Flexion of fingers and toes (constant tight flexion indicates more pain)

Sucking (no sucking, or disorganized sucking, indicates more pain)

Muscle tone (excessive muscle tension indicates more pain)

Consolability (lack of response to comforting for more than 2 minutes indicates more pain)

Sociability (lack of eye contact in response to voice or smiling face indicates more pain)

Source: Based on McGrath, 1990.

Begish-Duddy, Judas, & Jorgensen, 1990). It also suggests that parents may be wrong to bathe or dress an infant who dislikes those experiences at times when she is already upset, which they may choose to do on the grounds that they may as well deal with only one crying period, rather than two or three.

THE VESTIBULAR SYSTEM

Development of *vestibular* functions follows that of the skin senses in the developmental sequence of the individual. This sensory modality involves sensitivity to changes in head position relative to the pull of gravity and to rotary acceleration and deceleration, as well as acceleration and deceleration while traveling in a straight line. In other words, the vestibular system is stimulated by moving the head up, down, forward, backward, or sideways; by changing the velocity or direction of rotary movement (for example, when a race-car driver goes around a curve); and by changing velocity while traveling in a straight line (for example, coming to a halt after moving in a car or an elevator). If there is constant velocity and neither acceleration nor deceleration, there is no awareness of movement, because the sensory process proceeds exactly as it would if the person were sitting still.

The receptor organs of the vestibular system are in the head and are closely associated with the middle ear and inner ear. Information about vestibular activity and about hearing are carried to the central nervous system by way of the same nerve. Diseases or injuries that affect the vestibular system often affect hearing, and vice versa.

Stimulation of the vestibular organs produces the sensation of movement through space. Older infants and toddlers (as well as preschool and older children) often show tremendous excitement and pleasure over vestibular stimulation and beg for more swinging, sliding, or being thrown up in the air. Most playground devices are designed to give specific vestibular stimulation. As noted earlier, the unhappiness and discomfort of the infant can often be soothed away by gentle, repeated vestibular stimulation. (Unfortunately, as we mature, most of us come to respond to vestibular stimulation with boredom, at best, and with nausea, at worst.)

In addition to conscious awareness of vestibular activity, stimulation of the system results in systematic changes in muscle tension and posture, as well as in alterations in the responsiveness of the other sensory modalities. One important question has been whether deliberate vestibular stimulation would be good for the development of hospitalized babies. Korner (1984b) and her colleagues tried caring for preterm babies on waterbeds that oscillated intermittently. Sleep rhythms, visual alertness, and auditory responsiveness were all improved by using the stimulating waterbeds.

Vestibular stimulation is also frequently used in the treatment of older infants and children with organic brain damage (for instance, cerebral palsy). The goal can be cognitive as well as physical growth. Parents and caregivers often believe they see marked improvement in children following this sort of treatment, but evaluation of research on the topic has not supported the idea

Some parents replace this "hands-on" stimulation with a mechanical swing, but the original version provides touch and social stimulation as well as movement.

that it is effective (Cratty, 1981). Whatever effect the treatment may have, it is certainly not a simple question of stimulating the vestibular organs. The child also experiences social interaction, excitement, and fun. We should remember, too, that an infant or toddler will continue to mature even if a disability is present. There will be change over a period of time, whether treatment is occurring or not, unless the treatment actually delays development.

THE CHEMICAL SENSES

Smell and *taste*, the so-called chemical senses, are present at birth. Taste is probably experienced well before birth, when the fetus swallows amniotic fluid. Because the unborn baby does not breathe and there is normally no air in the uterus, smell as it is usually defined is not likely to occur before birth.

Study of the chemical senses is difficult even when adults are the subjects of the research. The receptor cells are difficult to stimulate separately, and subjects must be well trained to give the kinds of responses that are needed. Work with infants generally focuses on behavioral indications: facial expression in response to a taste or smell, turning toward or away from a stimulus, or drinking or eating food items. Toddlers may be asked what food they like better out of two choices. Animal work is also carried out to determine the reaction of the nervous system to smell or taste stimulation.

Some aspects of developmental change in the chemical sensory processes remain a matter of speculation. Smell experiences may alter as breathing patterns change and the position of the larynx in the throat alters during the first year (as is discussed in Chapter 11). One route for odorants, through the nostrils during inhalation (orthonasal), is most likely to be affected by changes in breathing pattern. The other—from the back of the nasopharynx to the nasal cavity during sucking, chewing, and swallowing (retronasal)—would obviously be more affected by changes in those patterns (Mennella & Beauchamp, 1993). Newborns' mouths and throats have more taste receptors that respond to sweet tastes than do older babies. Their patterns of sucking and swallowing are immature and may pull substances across the tongue at different rates than older children experience. Because of the tongue-thrust reflex, infants of less than 6 months do not easily move food around in the mouth so that it contacts different receptors.

Odor receptors are located high up inside the nose, so that a sniff is needed to draw large amounts of odor-laden air into contact with them. Receptor proteins on the surface of nerve cells bind odorous molecules to them, creating the stimulus for a sensory message. There are probably at least 10,000 different odorants, each a particular type of small, volatile, fat-soluble molecule (Barinaga, 1991).

A remarkable characteristic of the smell receptors is that they show *stimulus-induced plasticity;* the particular set of odorants an individual responds to is at least partially determined by experience with those odorants. Mice who are insensitive to a particular odor can be made sensitive by repeated exposure. Their changes in sensitivity are demonstrated by changes in recordings of electrical activity of the olfactory receptors (electro-olfactograms, or EOGs) (Wang, Wysocki, & Gold, 1993). Humans who are insensitive to a particular odorant can also begin to smell it after sufficient exposure. The plasticity of the receptors may be related to the fact that they are continually dying and being replaced, and therefore could mature in ways determined by the environment (Wang, Wysocki, & Gold, 1993). Rapid early learning of odors has been reported; for example, breast-fed infants turn their heads toward pads that have touched their own mother's milk rather than toward pads that smell of another woman's milk (Schaal et al., 1980).

Taste receptors are found in association with the taste buds on the tongue and inner cheek surfaces and inside the throat. Four taste sensations—sweet, salty, sour, and bitter—have traditionally been listed, but a fifth, "savory" (like monosodium glutamate), has recently been suggested (Mennella & Beauchamp, 1993).

Studies of the development of responses to these "primary tastes" have measured infants' facial expressions, sucking activity, and actual intake of flavored liquids. Sweet substances are preferred by preterm and newborn babies and continue to be preferred up to age 24 months. The response of preterm babies to sour substances is not known, but they are rejected from the newborn period up to 24 months of age. For bitter substances (like quinine or

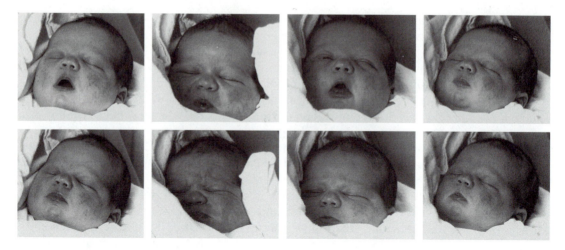

From left to right, these 3-day-old babies are responding to sweet, sour, bitter, and salty tastes.

urea), newborns show rejection or indifference, depending on the substance and the measure; rejection is the response from age 1 month to age 24 months. As for salty substances, newborns' sucking rate suggests rejection, but their facial expressions and intake seem to mean that they are indifferent to the taste. At about age 4 months, infants begin to prefer salty tastes over plain water. From the newborn period to age 24 months, babies prefer soup with MSG in it to plain soup but prefer plain water to water with MSG (Mennella & Beauchamp, 1993).

Two-year-olds' food preferences are clearly related to the familiarity of the food (Birch & Marlin, 1982). In fact, their resistance to unfamiliar foods is so great it has been called **neophobia**—a fear of the unfamiliar. It has been suggested that there are survival advantages to avoiding unfamiliar foods. A toddler in a hunter-gatherer group, for example, might risk illness or death if she ate unfamiliar roots or berries. Toddlers' willingness to consume foods is much increased if they get to see the food daily for some period of time.

neophobia: an intense fear of the unfamiliar; from the Greek *neos* (new), *phobos* (fear).

The link between flavor preferences and experience becomes more obvious when we realize that both amniotic fluid and breast milk take on the flavors of food the mother consumes. Thus, both the unborn and the nursing baby experience the flavors most common to the cuisine of their parents' culture. In animal studies, the young prefer the flavors of foods eaten by the nursing mother and accept unfamiliar foods better if the mother has had a variety of foods while suckling them—which raises some questions about the influence of the constant flavor of infant formulas on children's food preferences. Mennella and Beauchamp (1993) suggest that the taste of amniotic fluid may act as a "flavor bridge" that enhances appetite for breast milk, flavored as it is by similar foods in the mother's diet. The milk in turn acts as a "flavor bridge" to the solid foods themselves.

Sweet tastes appear to play a role in calming distressed babies; sucrose, for example, has been reported to reduce by 50% the crying of babies experiencing heel-lancing or circumcision (Blass & Smith, 1992; Smith, Fillion, & Blass, 1990).

HEARING

The sense of *hearing* has begun to function before birth. However, human ears are specialized to respond to sound waves passing through air. Sound waves travel more rapidly through the mother's body and through the amniotic fluid than through air, so the stimulus situation before birth is not exactly the same as it will be later. Some manufacturers produce recordings of mothers' heart sounds, which parents play for their new babies in the hope that they will be soothed by the sounds they have listened to for so long. But the sound of the heartbeat is different when it passes through flesh and fluid. For that matter, the position of the unborn baby seems to suggest that the sound of gurgling intestines would be more familiar than that of a beating heart!

The environmental stimulus for hearing, the *sound wave,* is basically a rapid alternation from high to low air pressure and back again. When a sound wave enters the ear canal, it causes the eardrum to move rapidly inward and outward with the same rhythm as the sound wave. This movement is indirectly passed on to receptor cells inside the cochlea. The movement of parts of the receptor cells causes nerve impulses that carry messages about the sound to the brain.

When a normal, full-term baby is born, many hearing functions are already in place. The baby can hear a variety of pitches and loudnesses. Those aspects of hearing will not be shaped into maturity by the environment, although they may be damaged in various ways.

One alteration in pitch sensitivity is seen when we compare babies' and adults' responses to high-frequency sounds; adults are more sensitive to moderately high frequencies (10,000 cycles per second) than infants are, but they are equally sensitive at quite high frequencies (19,000 cycles per second) (Schneider, Trehub, & Bull, 1980). The equality at the higher frequency exists in part because the adult has *lost* sensitivity to those sounds.

There is, however, a function of hearing that shows a high degree of plasticity. This is *sound localization,* the capacity to detect accurately where a sound is coming from. Sound localization is based on a comparison of sounds as they arrive at the left and at the right ears. If the sounds at the two ears are the same, the source of the sound is straight ahead (or straight behind, or somewhere else in the midline). If a sound is louder at the left ear and reaches the left ear before it is heard in the right, the source of the sound is on the left side (and so on).

Wertheimer (1961) reported that his child turned toward a sound at the age of 8 minutes, but further study (Muir, Clifton, & Clarkson, 1989) has shown an unusual change in the ability to localize sound, rather than maintenance of the early performance. The head-turning response diminished between the ages of 1 and 3 months and improved once again by 4½ months, as if some shift in brain functioning was occurring.

Why is plasticity necessary for sound localization? The reason is that the baby's head is going to continue to grow slowly for many years. As the head gets larger, a particular difference between the sound at the right ear and the sound at the left will mean a different sound position than it did when the head was small. If the individual's response to sound differences remained exactly what it was at birth, she would make frequent mistakes in sound localization.

The topic of sound localization has implications for much more than the ability to figure out where an ambulance siren is coming from. Sound localization is essential for the understanding of *speech* when it is heard against a background of other sounds. Think about a noisy party where you are trying to understand what someone is telling you. The sound waves from that person's voice mix with those from the voices of the other guests, from the music, from the air conditioning, and from the traffic outside. Your ability to pick out the direction a sound is coming from allows you to separate that person's voice from all the other sounds in the room, and (sometimes, at least) to understand what is said.

HEARING LOSS

The abilities to respond to different pitches and loudnesses and to localize sounds are essential for language development and for related social and communicative functions. As we will see in Chapter 11, good hearing is a starting point for development of language. When infants' hearing is poor, they are at risk for a number of developmental problems unless intervention occurs early.

How can we tell whether an infant has congenital poor hearing, or whether hearing loss begins during the infant and toddler period? There are a number of ways to assess hearing; some of them are highly accurate and specific, whereas others are of the "quick and dirty" type that look for general problems as an indication of the need for careful evaluation.

entrainment: a coordination of one rhythm with another, particularly of an infant's movement pattern to adult speech; from the Middle French *entrainer* (to pull or drag).

Some aspects of behavior can indicate whether an infant can hear. For example, **entrainment** of a newborn's movement to the rhythms of adult speech occurs when a baby hears adults talking. The changes in the baby's limb movements are hard to see except on film, but they reproduce the emphases and rhythmic patterns that he hears (Condon & Sanders, 1974). An older baby will look in the direction of speech, especially if his name is spoken. As the infant develops, his vocalizations will normally follow a developmental pattern based in part on hearing. Parents and caregivers can monitor the baby's sounds from about 6 weeks on as a way to detect hearing impairment (Butterfield, 1981). (This issue is discussed further in Chapter 11.)

Assessment of hearing loss on the basis of behavior is not very accurate, which probably accounts for the fact that the average age at which hearing loss is diagnosed in the United States is 2½ years (Clarkson et al., 1994). Many hearing-impaired infants are also overlooked when a *high-risk registry* for deafness is used. A high-risk registry looks for infants whose history contains a number of factors that show which babies are at risk for hearing problems.

Although only about 3% of newborns in the United States have their hearing tested (Clarkson, Vohr, Blackwell, & White, 1994), there are several tests available for use with the very young infant. The Crib-o-gram records and correlates infants' body movements with predetermined sounds, but it is not a very effective test. The ABR (auditory brain stem response) test records electrical activity in the nervous system as messages from the ear are carried toward the brain. This test requires placing electrodes on the baby's head (painless, but awkward), is expensive, and requires a trained tester. A recent development is the TEOAE (transient evoked otoacoustic emissions) test. In this test, a tiny microphone placed in the ear canal records an "echo" of sound that is emitted by the receptor cells and travels back through the middle ear. If hearing impairment is above a certain level, the "echo" will not be present (Clarkson et al., 1994).

There are many reasons that congenital, severe hearing loss is found in 1 or 2 infants out of every 1000 in the United States. We discussed a number of these reasons in earlier chapters (for instance, cytomegalovirus, genetic hearing-loss syndromes, and fetal alcohol syndrome). Although some of the causes are preventable, others are difficult to predict or prevent.

Unfortunately, having normal hearing at the time of birth is no guarantee that hearing will remain adequate long enough for good language development to occur. Some causes of hearing impairment occur soon after birth (for example, hyperbilirubinemia and effects of prematurity or low birth weight); the impairment may be anywhere from mild to profound, but it is permanent.

For many infants and toddlers, hearing impairment is not permanent but is intermittent, fluctuating, recurring, and temporary. Such hearing loss results from otitis media, an infection of the middle ear, and generally occurs following a cold. The baby may or may not experience pain with otitis media, but the associated hearing impairment, if it occurs frequently, can be enough to cause problems with language development.

The anatomy of the middle ear is the reason that babies' colds often lead to ear infections. The middle ear space behind the eardrum is normally filled with air. For best hearing, the air pressure in the middle ear needs to be about the same as the air pressure outside the head. When the atmospheric air pressure changes, the middle ear air pressure is altered as air passes either in from or out via the mouth by way of the eustachian canals. The eustachian canals ordinarily do an excellent job of equalizing air pressure, but unfortunately they also provide an easy route for bacteria to take into the middle ear. When bacteria-laden mucus secretions from a cold are in the mouth and throat, they are very close to the openings of the eustachian canals in the back of the mouth.

If an adult has a cold, bacteria that get into the eustachian canals tend to drain out easily because of the downward-slanted position of the mature canal. In an infant or toddler, however, the position of the canals is closer to horizontal, making drainage much more difficult. The baby's canals are also very narrow, and the irritation caused by infection can quickly make them swell closed. Drainage becomes impossible; the bacteria grow rapidly in the warm, moist middle ear; and an ear infection is well underway.

In acute otitis media (AOM), the infection is active. The middle ear begins to fill with fluid containing bacteria. Treatment with antibiotics gets rid of the bacterial infection, but the fluid remains in the middle ear for as long as several months; and as long as the fluid is there, some hearing impairment will be present. This condition, otitis media with effusion (OME), may need to be treated by placing a tympanostomy tube in the eardrum, which allows fluid to drain through the ear canal. About 10% to 20% of children experience repeated episodes of alternation between AOM and OME, with associated hearing impairment. The average hearing loss during OME is about what you will experience if you use your fingers to press the little triangles of cartilage in front of your ears down into the opening of the ear canal (Roberts, Wallace, & Zeisel, 1993).

Not all infants are at equal risk of developing AOM and OME. Exposure to secondhand tobacco smoke increases the rate, as do attendance at day care centers and membership in a large family (Bloch, 1992; Roberts, Wallace, & Zeisel, 1993). Babies with fetal alcohol syndrome (Olson, Burgess, & Streissguth, 1992) are more

TABLE 8.2   *Indicators of risk of hearing impairment in neonates and infants.*

Neonates (birth to 28 days)	Infants (29 days to 2 years)
Family history of childhood sensorineural impairment	Parent or caregiver concern about hearing, speech, developmental delay
Consanguinity with deafness	Bacterial meningitis
Congenital infection such as toxoplasmosis, rubella, cytomegalovirus, herpes	Head trauma
	Otitis media with effusion
Malformations of ears; cleft palate; low hairline; other midfacial malformations	Certain childhood diseases (e.g., measles, mumps)
	Ototoxic medications
Birth weight below 1500 g	Lack of speech
Hyperbilirubinemia at level requiring exchange transfusion	"Autistic" behavior
Ototoxic medications such as streptomycin	
Bacterial meningitis	
Poor condition at birth, including very low Apgar score, delay in breathing, hypotonia	
Prolonged mechanical ventilation	
Characteristics associated with certain genetic syndromes	
Failure to pass hearing screen	

Source: Based on Diefendorf, Reitz, & Cox, 1992; and Rapin & Ruben, 1981.

susceptible, as are Native Americans. African American babies and those who are exclusively breast-fed for at least 4 months have been reported to be less vulnerable (Duncan et al., 1993; Roberts, Wallace, & Zeisel, 1993).

Treatment of AOM and OME is aimed at restoring hearing. But what if there has been significant hearing loss, congenitally or from frequent infections? Amplification of sound by means of a "hearing aid" can be useful for certain kinds of hearing losses. Another, less widely known approach is the *tactual vocoder,* a device that translates sound stimuli into touch (Oller, 1990). The tactual vocoder takes sound through a microphone, divides it into frequency bands (groups of pitches), and uses the information from each band to drive a particular stimulator against the skin, producing painless, ticklelike sensations. A set of stimulators can be worn on the arm, leg, abdomen, hand, or forehead, and the movement of each one against the skin indicates a particular part of a sound. The wearer has to learn that each skin sensation has a particular sound meaning. Training has been done with babies as young as 6 months in a parent-infant program, but even the best of the stimulators are not completely comfortable for babies.

It was long thought that damage to hearing receptor cells was irreversible, but some recent work (Forge et al., 1993; Warchol et al., 1993) suggests that the receptor cells may be able to regenerate themselves. We are still very far from being able to apply this information to help infants with hearing impairments, however.

VISION

The last of the sensory processes to develop in the growing infant is, paradoxically, the one on which adults place the most reliance: *vision.* The late development of vision may be associated with the need for plasticity. Some aspects of vision, especially those involving the coordination of images from the two eyes, must be fine-tuned as the head grows and the distance between the eyes changes. Animal studies (for example, the work of Hubel & Wiesel, 1963) have stressed the idea of a critical period during which stimulation with patterned light must occur if vision is to develop normally. Studies of humans have shown that abnormal visual experience because of strabismus ("crossed eyes") in infancy leads to subtle errors in visual detection of motion even in adulthood (Tychesen, Rastelli, Steinman, & Steinman, 1996).

One remarkable and poorly understood characteristic of visual development is the occurrence of sudden changes or reorganizations of function in vision—at about 6 weeks, the emergence of the "oblique effect" (better sensitivity to horizontal or vertical lines than to diagonals) and of discrimination of changes in line slant, and at about 3½ months the emergence of depth perception using the eyes together (Held, 1993a, 1993b).

The anatomy and functioning of the visual system are far too complex to discuss in any detail. Very simply, we may say that the receptor cells for vision are found in the retina in the back of the eye. Each receptor cell contains molecules of visual pigments that absorb light that falls on them. Absorption of light causes the visual pigment molecules to change shape; this alters the electrical activity between receptor cell and neighboring nerve cells and sends sensory messages to appropriate parts of the nervous system. Some receptor cells respond in a similar way to all wavelengths of light, so the sensory messages they send carry no information about color. Other receptor cells respond very differently to different wavelengths of light and so are responsible for color vision.

The rest of the eye is organized to allow light to reach the retina and to focus, or bend light rays, so the image on the retina is a sharp, clear one. This process allows us to look at objects at a variety of distances and to have a clear image of each. Focusing occurs when the lens of the eye becomes temporarily thicker or thinner, thus bending light rays more or less. The changing of the thickness of the lens is called *accommodation,* and it is very poor in newborn babies. The newborn cannot focus on objects at a variety of distances, instead having a fixed focal distance of about 8 to 12 inches from the eye. Only objects within that distance range can be seen with any clarity. Interestingly, this best viewing distance is about equal to the distance between an adult's face and an infant's when the adult is cradling the infant in his arms. Thus, a caregiver's face may be the newborn's clearest visual experience. (By 3 or 4 months, though, the baby can easily focus on an object across the room.)

Another, less well-understood limitation on newborn vision is body position. Young infants are not usually visually alert, or attentive to visual stimulation, unless they are upright—for example, when they are picked up and held close to an adult's shoulder. This maneuver has been reported to make babies "bright-eyed, alert, and visually scanning about" (Korner, 1984a, p. 1). As the baby reaches 1 month of age or more, she will more and more frequently be seen to be visually alert when supine.

As is the case for all research on infants, of course, the baby's comfort affects the collection of information about visual development. In one study, the researchers started by putting the babies in infant seats; later, they found they could do many more test trials each day if they had someone hold the baby, change her position between trials, and give her back to her mother to hold while the apparatus was being adjusted (Teller, Morse, Borton, & Regal, 1974).

Aspects of Vision

Information gathered through vision is very complex, and the ways in which visual development is measured are many. Most research on vision attempts to limit the number of factors being studied. Rather than using a complex stimulus from the real world, like a picture of a face or a flower, vision researchers use simplified stimuli, such as checkerboards with squares of two colors, geometric shapes, or narrow dark lines on a neutral background. The stimuli are generally planned to be relevant to only one of the visual abilities the infant may be expected to have. When it is not possible to omit visual factors other than the one being studied, researchers attempt to hold them *constant.*

The rest of our discussion of vision will be an overview of the most frequently investigated aspects of visual functioning.

acuity: in this context, ability to discriminate fine details visually; from the Latin *acutus* (sharp).

Acuity   The term **acuity** of vision refers to the ability to discriminate fine details of an image. An infant who can tell the difference between a blank page and another page with very fine stripes is displaying a high level of acuity. Another baby, who acts as if the blank page and the narrow stripes look alike but who can discriminate a blank page from one with broad stripes, is showing lower acuity.

An adult's visual acuity is usually tested by asking the person to read letters of different size from an eye chart. The smaller the letter the person can read, the better the visual acuity. The level of an adult's acuity is commonly stated as a ratio. For example, 20/20 means that acuity is exactly what would be expected of an adult; 20/200 means that the person has to be 20 feet away from an object to see the details a "normal" eye would see at 200 feet.

Testing an infant's acuity can be done with preferential looking techniques, mentioned earlier. Two cards with different sizes of stripes are shown to the baby a number of times; a random order determines when a particular card will be on the right or on the left. An observer judges which direction the baby looks in on each trial. The baby is considered to have good enough acuity to tell the difference between the cards only if he looks at one significantly more than at the other.

Optokinetic nystagmus (OKN) is another approach to the measurement of acuity. As we discussed in Chapter 7, this reflex eye movement occurs when a visible pattern moves across the baby's visual field. If the stripes on a pattern are too narrow for the baby to see them (that is, the baby's acuity is not good enough), there will be no OKN. The reflex occurs only if the stripes are seen.

The visual evoked potential (VEP) measures electrical changes in the nervous system that occur when sensory messages are sent from the receptor cells. The VEP occurs when the baby's acuity is good enough to detect the stimulus stripes.

The reported acuities for babies of varying ages differ a bit as a result of different testing techniques (Dobson & Teller, 1978). One estimate is that at age 1 month, the infant's acuity is 20/250; at two months, 20/215; and at 3 months, 20/150 (Banks & Salapatek, 1978). An estimate of acuity at 6 to 7 months, using VEP, placed the acuity level close to 20/20 (Sokol, 1982), but an estimate using another technique did not show 20/20 vision until the child was 7 years old (Reuben, 1981). Unlike adults, whose acuity is better for horizontal and vertical than for diagonal lines, young infants have similar acuities for lines of different orientations.

It seems, then, that fine details are largely missing from the very young infant's visual world, with details gradually becoming clear over a period of months. From the functional point of view, we need to remember that there is little the infant can do to improve the clarity of his vision. An adult who is not seeing clearly can move closer to the object or hold it up to his eyes, and an adult can turn on a brighter light or change the angle to prevent glare. A precrawling infant is in no position to do any of these things.

Contrast sensitivity functions   Tests of acuity usually involve bright illumination and dark shapes contrasting sharply with a light background—the kind of visual situation found in reading. In the ordinary visual world, of course, there are many times when lights are dim or when the shape we look at is not much darker than the background. A face, for example (except for the eyes), has lights and shadows that are not very different from each other. The contrast between the nose and the cheeks is quite small, but we manage to tell them apart. This aspect of our vision is not based on acuity in the usual sense.

Work on human vision has shown that the ability to detect a visual stimulus can depend on two factors: (1) *contrast,* or the difference in brightness between shapes and their background, and (2) *spatial characteristics* of the stimulus, such as the distance between shapes. To simplify the study of spatial characteristics, researchers use figures called *gratings,* which are essentially dark and light stripes. The grating can be different in spatial frequency (the number of lines in a grating of a given size) and in wave form (whether there is a sharp boundary between dark and light lines, or whether one gradually blurs into the next). Gratings can also differ in contrast, with black and white lines, pale grey and paler grey lines, or any other combination. A viewer's ability to detect the lines on a grating is influenced by *all* the factors just discussed—contrast, as well as the width and blurriness of the lines.

Even if you have borne with all these details, you are probably exasperated by now. "What's to study?" you may be saying. "Of course it's easier to see black on white than grey on grey, and of course it's easier to see fat stripes than thin ones!" The surprise, however, is that it is *not* necessarily easier to see fat (low spatial frequency) stripes than thin (high spatial frequency) ones. In fact, to see really broad stripes, humans have to have quite high contrast, whereas moderate-sized stripes can be seen with lower contrast. A pattern can actually be too big to see easily. The relationship between the size of the stripes (or other details of a pattern) and our ability to detect them is called a *contrast sensitivity function,* and the function changes in the course of infant development.

At the age of 1 month, the baby seems to have as much trouble seeing broad as medium lines (Banks, 1982), but soon sensitivity becomes greater for medium than for coarse patterns, as is the case for adults. The infant's contrast sensitivity function at 2 or 3 months limits his visual world to large, high-contrast objects (Pirchio, Spinelli, Fiorentini, & Maffei, 1978). Because even a large object at a distance creates a small image on the eye, the infant's visual world is limited to near objects, too. The baby cannot yet crawl toward an object and make its image larger, so he may have little awareness of some objects unless an adult accidentally carries him toward them. The details the baby can see in daylight are about the same as what an adult can see in moonlight. Contrast sensitivity continues to rise from 1 to 3 months (Banks & Salapatek, 1978), although infants are not sensitive to nearly as wide a range of spatial frequencies or of contrasts as adults are (Banks & Salapatek, 1981).

Because young infants need high contrast to see narrower lines, we can provide them with more to look at if we avoid pastels and go for dark colors on a white background. Black on white gives the highest possible contrast, whereas pale pinks or blues against white are low in contrast. A black-and-white crib or crib bumper will shock the parents' friends, but either provides plenty for the baby to see. (Whether this is *necessary* is quite another question.)

Shape   Several approaches have been taken toward understanding the development of responses to the shape or form of objects. One approach has involved habituation and has shown that infants do habituate to a stimulus of one shape, but they pay attention to a new stimulus of a different shape (Cook & Birch, 1984).

holistic: emphasizing the relationship between the parts and the whole; from the Greek *holos* (whole).

analytical: emphasizing separate parts rather than the whole; from the Greek *analyein* (to break up).

A second approach has looked at the eye movements of infants as they scan a shape. How do infants recognize a shape? Is recognition **holistic,** so one glance gives an idea of a square or a rectangle? Or is it **analytic** and cumulative, so that the baby essentially counts the corners of a triangle before recognizing the shape? The youngest babies tend to scan the edges of a form, even when looking at a human face. Between the ages of 5 and 7 weeks, they increase the number of fixations on parts of the face, and after 7 weeks look at the eyes most (Haith, Bergman, & Moore, 1977). This suggests development through an analytic approach to shapes toward one that gives a more immediate recognition of the whole. On the other hand, reports of very early responses to faces have implied that even young infants can recognize a face as a face *and* look at individual details within it. Carpenter (reported by Bower, 1982) showed that 2-week-olds looked longer at their mothers' faces than at strangers' faces, and Meltzoff and Moore (1989) reported that newborn infants would imitate a person who protruded his tongue. Clinical work with newborn infants and mothers has led to many suggestions that the adult's eyes hold a special interest for the very young baby; Robson (1967), for example, has referred to the unusual visual interest of eyes, noting their shininess, the many contours and contrasts, the movements of the eye itself, and the movements of the dilating and contracting pupil.

The development of responses to shape will undoubtedly be understood better when more work has been done on the way shapes are represented in the nervous system. Work on monkeys suggests that a small number of cells in the cortex represent particular shapes as the eye "sees" them (Sary, Vogels, & Orban, 1993). Recognition of faces may depend on *sparse population coding;* that is, a few tens of cells respond to a particular face, with their response determined by physical characteristics of the face (Young & Yamane, 1992). But what experience leads to these events in the cortex—or whether experience is involved at all—remains unknown.

Color   When adults with normal vision look at light of different wavelengths, they experience different colors. Although the viewer is not usually aware of it, more than the color experience is affected by the wavelength of light. Adults are most sensitive to lights in the blue-green range; that is, we can detect light of those wavelengths even when its intensity is very low. A red light, on the other hand, must be quite intense for us to notice it.

Of course, we cannot test infants in ways that will communicate their color experiences to us, nor can we get them to name colors as older children can. Work on infant color vision has concentrated on the baby's capacity to discriminate between two colors and on her sensitivity to different wavelengths of light.

In one preferential looking study, newborns were shown checkerboards that combined yellow and grey, red and grey, green and grey, or blue and grey squares. Each color combination was presented along with another checkerboard that combined dark grey and light grey squares. The amount of time spent looking at each checkerboard indicated that the infants were able to tell the difference between yellow, red, green, and gray. However, there was no difference in the time spent looking at the blue-grey checks and at the grey-grey checks (Adams, Maurer, & Davis, 1986).

Tests of infants' sensitivity to different wavelengths can be done with a visual evoked potential technique. Light of different wavelengths is shown to the baby at a variety of intensities, and the VEP shows the lowest intensity the baby can detect at each wavelength. Infants are less sensitive than adults for all wavelengths; that is, the light must be brighter for an infant to detect it.

Different methods give different results at times, but in general we can say that infants in the first month show little color discrimination (Clavedetscher, Brown, Ankrum, & Teller, 1988; Varner, Cook, Schenck, McDonald, & Teller, 1985). By about 8 weeks, however, babies show evidence that they can discriminate some colors, but there may still be a weakness in their response to blue, indigo, and violet light (Allen, Banks, & Norcia, 1993; Banks & Shannon, 1993; see also Chapter 7 for related events in receptor development).

In sum, infants do seem to be able to discriminate some colors, but they experience more color when an object is not a pastel. The actual functioning of infant color vision is probably also affected by contrast sensitivity functions, so that the color and brightness of the background contribute to visual experience of an object.

Depth   One of our most useful sensory abilities is the capacity to judge *depth*—the distance between the eye and the object being looked at. Judgment of depth is based on two kinds of information, or depth cues. When only one eye is being used (the **monocular** condition), depth cues include the size of the image; whether one object partly covers the image of another; whether one image seems to move more than another when the head moves; and so on. These monocular depth cues give some ability to judge distance, but not nearly the accuracy one has when using **binocular** information. When both eyes are used in judging distance (the binocular condition), information about retinal disparity can be used. Retinal disparity refers to the fact that the images of an object on the right and the left retina are slightly different simply because there is a space between the eyes. The closer an object to the eyes, the greater the **disparity** or difference between the images; the farther the object, the less the disparity.

To use information about retinal disparity, the baby has to be able to use both eyes together; to **converge,** or move the lines of sight together so that both eyes are looking at the same object. Convergence (fixation of both eyes on

monocular: using one eye; from the Greek *monos* (alone), the Latin *oculus* (eye).

binocular: using both eyes; from the Latin *bi-* (two), *oculus* (eye).

disparity: difference; in this context, difference between the images on the left and on the right retinas; from the Latin *disparare* (to separate).

converge: to move toward each other or toward the same point; from the Latin *com-* (with), *vergere* (to bend, incline).

APPLICATIONS & ARGUMENTS
Are Mobiles Useful?

The mobile hanging over the crib has become a standard feature of early infancy for European and North American babies. Hung with silhouettes of animals, often painted in pretty pastels, it may be wound up to turn around by itself and even to play music while it revolves a couple of feet above the infant's head. The parents' intention is usually to provide stimulation for the young baby—yet the mobile is too far away to be seen clearly, the pastels give too little contrast, and the animal silhouettes are generally hung vertically so the infant sees only their feet!

Is there any point to this? There probably is, but it is not a matter of direct stimulation of the infant. The greatest effect of the mobile may be that the parents use it to send themselves a message that says they are doing a good job. They know that a baby ought to have a mobile. That belief may be a way to help themselves actually do well with their infant, for it energizes and comforts parents; the sense that they are doing poorly discourages and depresses them and makes them withdraw from the baby, who is a reminder of their "failure." The mobile may thus lead indirectly to more stimulation and better care by helping parents feel more comfortable about their important and difficult task.

the same object) does not occur consistently for near objects until the baby is about 2 months old, and it does not occur without delay until about age 3 months (Aslin, 1977).

The baby's difficulty with control over convergence suggests that monocular depth cues will be used before binocular cues. But even the use of monocular cues does not seem to be very good in the first months. For instance, in one study (Yonas, Granrud, & Pettersen, 1985), babies were allowed to reach for one of two objects; the objects were the same distance

TABLE 8.3   *Both infants and older people use monocular and binocular cues for depth.*

Monocular cues (looking with one eye)	Binocular cues (looking with both eyes)
Size of visual image	All monocular cues
Overlap of images	*and*
Texture	Retinal disparity
Movement cues	
Familiarity with size of object	

away, but one was larger than the other. With one eye covered (the monocular condition), 5-month-olds reached indiscriminately for either object, but 5½- and 7-month-olds reached for the larger one as if they were using size as a cue for distance. (The babies showed no preference when looking with both eyes, so this was not a matter of simply coming to prefer big objects.) The same group of researchers (Granrud, Yonas, & Petterson, 1984) also tested 5- and 7-month-old babies with pairs of objects, where one was within reach and the other was not but the sizes of the images were the same. At both ages, the babies reached for the near object much more consistently when they could look at it with both eyes.

When reaching for an object is the measure of depth judgment, of course, there is the possibility of confusing the baby's understanding of depth with her ability to reach accurately. With one preferential looking technique used to overcome this problem (Shea, Fox, Aslin, & Dumais, 1980), babies looked at a random-element stereogram on a color TV monitor; this pattern gave an impression of depth (binocularly, but not monocularly) when the babies wore goggles with one red lens and one green lens. The part of the pattern that seemed to have depth was moved around the screen and an observer judged whether the babies' gaze followed the moving 3-D area. The average performance of the infants suggested that binocular depth judgments are made after about 3½ months of age.

How does depth judgment work in infants' real-life functioning? Anyone who has been around crawlers and toddlers knows that they fall off things with alarming regularity—a tendency that has received the name "the Geronimo response." If babies can see depth, why don't they always avoid it? Work on this topic has used a device called the *visual cliff* (Gibson & Walk, 1960), where the illusion of a drop is produced by a sheet of transparent Plexiglass strong enough to bear the baby's weight. The baby's parent stands on the opposite side of the "drop" and tries to get the baby to crawl across. Infants who have only recently started to crawl will cross the "deep" side, but experienced crawlers refuse except under certain circumstances. Some back out onto the "deep" side as if going down a step. Babies who avoid the "drop" when crawling are willing to cross it in a walker (Rader, Bausano, & Richards, 1980). Other work (to be discussed in a later chapter) has shown that the parent's facial expression has a strong effect on the baby's willingness to cross.

Once again, as was the case for shape discrimination, a real understanding of distance judgments may have to wait until more is known about the brain's analysis of depth cues. Studies of animals have certainly suggested that some brain cells respond specifically to certain depth cues (Frost & Nakayama, 1983; Georgopoulos, Schwartz, & Kettner, 1986; Ohzawa, de Angelis, & Freeman, 1990). One confusing fact about depth perception is that baby girls show one type of response to depth at the age of 95 days, on the average, whereas boys do not show a similar response until the average age of 111 days (Bauer, Shimojo, Gwiazda, & Held, 1986). Earlier development for girls has also been shown on one measure of acuity (Held, Shimojo, & Gwiazda, 1984).

Implications of Visual Development

As vision develops, its role becomes primary in the control of attention, in social communication, and in cognitive advances, such as the understanding of cause and effect. The infant's responsiveness to visual events encourages adults to play, to show the baby interesting things, and generally to increase their sense of the baby as "a real person." The baby's visual interest in the world helps organize and sustain difficult activities. In physical therapy with a Down syndrome baby, a therapist may use the baby's visual interest in his face to help her develop head control (Williamson, 1988).

Visual Impairment

One of the most obvious relationships between developmental change and impairment of vision has to do with depth judgment. The capacity to judge depth on the basis of retinal disparity appears to grow as a function of experience with differences between the left-eye image and the right-eye image; this experience, in turn, affects the use of specific cells in the nervous

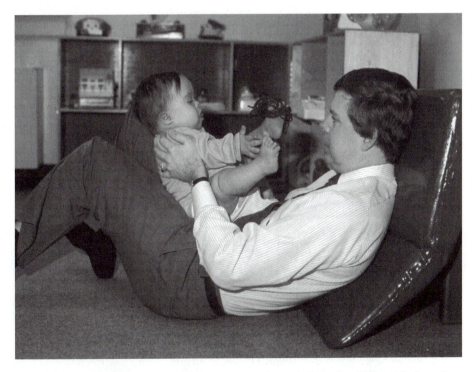

Therapist Gordon Williamson uses this Down syndrome baby's visual interest to keep her involved in the therapeutic technique.

strabismus: a lack of coordination between the directions of gaze of the eyes; from the Greek *strabismos* (squinting).

system (see Chapter 7 for a fuller explanation). When an infant has **strabismus,** or "crossed eyes," there can be interference with the development of retinal disparity judgments; this has been corroborated by experimental work with monkeys (Crawford, Smith, Harwerth, & van Noorden, 1984). It seems that appropriate experience with retinal disparity must occur within a critical period. Surgical correction of strabismus after the preschool period will improve the child's appearance, but binocular depth judgments will not be possible.

A similar issue involves amblyopia, the loss of vision in an eye as a result of temporary disuse. It has been suggested that even a week of eye patch treatment (for example, because of an eye injury) may lead to functional blindness in one eye if the baby is under 2 years of age (von Noorden, 1973). (This issue was also discussed more fully in Chapter 7.)

Work with visually impaired infants shows the extent to which vision serves as an organizer for other aspects of development. For example, Als (1985) described a baby girl born without eyes. At age 4½ months, she played sound and touch games with her mother, vocalized, smiled, laughed, and reached for her mother's face—but she would scream inconsolably if anyone else tried to play with her. This would certainly not be the response of a sighted child of this age. Peabody (1981) noted that the blind child walks late and may show "blindisms" (stereotyped body movements like head shaking, hand shaking, rocking, swaying, and eye poking) that interfere with normal interaction with the world. Blind infants have a limited number of behaviors they can use for starting a social interaction, and parents may assume incorrectly that this difficulty means a lack of interest or affection (Erwin, 1994).

THE INTEGRATED BABY

Discussing the details of each sensory process often makes it sound as if the baby experiences only one sense at a time. This illusion results from our difficulty in considering how all these complex events work together, not from the reality of the baby's experience.

Imagine a baby of 6 months who has just begun to crawl and who is placed on the "shallow" side of the visual cliff. Her experience includes the colors of the visual cliff pattern, the shape of the checks that make up the pattern, and the apparent distance of the "shallow" side's drop and the "deep" side's drop. To judge the distance effectively, the baby must have developed binocular motor control, so the eyes can converge.

As the baby rocks on all fours while examining the visual cliff, she feels tactile sensations, including deep pressure on her palms and the knees and lighter touch from clothing and from her arms and legs rubbing together. Smell sensation probably results from disinfectant sprayed on the apparatus after the last baby wet on it. The recently fed baby may spit up a little in the excitement, leading to the taste of the regurgitated milk and the touch of spit-up trickling down her highly sensitive mouth and chin area.

As the baby looks up to see her father on the far side of the visual cliff, she changes convergence and also accommodates by changing the muscle pull on the lenses, so she can see and recognize her father's face. (Activity of cortical neurons using sparse population coding may underlie recognition of the father.) As the father calls out, the baby's hearing analyzes not only the sounds themselves but the fact that they come from a single source. Continuing to hold her head up (using information from the vestibular system and the muscle spindles of the neck), the baby goes on looking at the father and crawls out onto the "deep" side of the visual cliff. Kinesthesis and intermittent pressure on the palms and knees help guide her crawling action. As the baby reaches her father, Dad holds out a toy, and the baby, precariously balancing on one arm and her knees, *reaches* for the object accurately, using retinal disparity as well as monocular depth cues like size to make her reach accurate. When she gets the toy, her grasp and her "chomp" take into account the affordances of the object—its size, slipperiness, and hardness.

PROBLEMS TO CONSIDER AND DISCUSS

1. What would the room you are in look like to a newborn baby?

2. What research approach would you take to find out whether vestibular stimulation actually helps infants who have brain damage?

3. How would you use sensory stimulation to calm a distressed baby? (Be complete in your answer.)

4. Discuss depth perception in the infant as a dynamic action system.

5. How do you think an infant's responses to sights and sounds would influence a parent's feelings about the infant?

9

Motor Development

flexion: moving the limbs toward the body; from the Latin *flectere* (to bend).

extension: moving the limbs away from the body; from the Latin *ex-* (out), *tendere* (to stretch).

The development of basic control over the body's movements proceeds throughout infancy, toddlerhood, and early childhood. The first and most important aspect of the development of motor control is simply an increase in the ability to lift and move body parts, to bring them toward the torso **(flexion)** and away from it **(extension).** The second part—and one that will be much less important for us—is the later learning of specific skills, such as cutting with scissors.

Motor development is critical to other aspects of the infant's and toddler's developmental progression. The capacity for movement allows the child to understand something about cause-and-effect relationships. It helps produce a sense of mastery as the child experiences control over the environment. Movements of the head and body contribute to the child's ability to judge the distance and direction of sights and sounds. Gesture and facial movements are among the child's first communicative techniques and are a foundation for the development of language. The development of control over the mouth and tongue is critical to the achievement of spoken language. The sense of being a "self" is partly based on experiencing the results of intentional movements.

One particular aspect of motor development is the foundation for everything the baby does in the course of development. The maintenance of posture within the gravitational field (called *anti-gravity reactions*) is necessary for the achievement of sitting, reaching, creeping, and all other motor abilities. The issue here is not just working against gravity but also adjusting the amount of muscle tension necessary when moving opposite to the pull of gravity, in the same direction as the pull, or at an angle to it. What a baby can do depends in part on whether she is in the prone position (belly down) or is supine (lying on the back).

COORDINATION AND FUNCTION

To have a genuine understanding of motor development, we need to keep firmly in mind that movement involves the coordination of multiple factors. These factors include the weight of a body part, its muscular strength, and the position of the rest of the body (as pointed out by Bernstein, 1967). Less obviously, coordination involves awareness of characteristics of the environ-

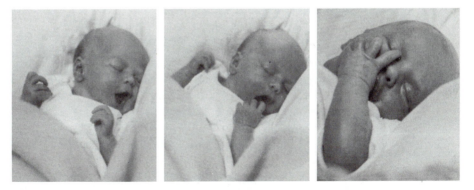

This 5-day-old baby struggles and finally succeeds in getting his thumb to his mouth. Without this motor skill, he would be very limited in his ability to try to comfort and calm himself.

ment, such as the movement of objects in the visual field and the baby's intention—for example, to chew on an object rather than to explore it with the mouth.

This chapter will focus primarily on the development of specific aspects of motor control in the form of muscle and joint movement. Please remember, though, that movement of the body would not be possible without appropriate functioning of the nervous system; it may help the student occasionally to go back to Chapter 7 to review how development of the nervous system proceeds. Modern research suggests that the brain makes complex computations about the movements of a body part and sends signals to muscles accordingly (Gomi & Kawato, 1996). Similarly, coordination of movement requires sensory information: **proprioceptive** and kinesthetic information about muscle contraction and joint position; and vestibular, visual, and tactile information about the position of body parts in space.

Lack of movement coordination might threaten life itself; too much flexion of the infant's neck and trunk can close off the upper airway and seriously interfere with breathing (Soltesz & Brockway, 1989). On the other hand, not all coordinations of movement have obvious value. Lifting of the big toe precedes urination in fetuses and neonates (Meizner & Bar-Ziv, 1985), and the usefulness of such a coordination certainly escapes this writer.

Guiard (1991) pointed out that even the simplest attempt to reach for an object involves coordination of movement of the shoulder and the elbow joints, as well as the wrist if the hand needs to be turned. If the baby succeeds in grasping the object, he or she will use at least two fingers, each of which has at least two segments, and each of the joints involves at least two antagonist muscles or muscle groups to move it—as well as the parts of the nervous system that signal the muscles to change tension. Similarly, the amounts of rotation in the ankle, knee, and hip joints of a kicking infant are coordinated with respect to each other throughout the kick. These coordinations remain similar for babies in different positions, although the different directions of

proprioceptive: relating to the sense of muscle stretching tension, or relaxation; from the Latin *proprius* (own), *capere* (to take, capture).

the pull of gravity mean that the muscles must function differently to produce the same movement (Thelen, et al., 1991).

Babies have differently coordinated movements as a result of their body type. One researcher described an observation in this way: "At a party for toddlers, I saw an 8-month-old youngster running around the room with perfect ease, while his host had not yet begun to try to walk at the age of 13 months (and would not do so until 18 months). The bodies of the two children were very different. The 8-month-old was slender and beautifully coordinated; he had no trouble coping with his weight. In contrast, his host was heavy, with a low center of gravity, and it was not easy for him to stand up. However, he had beautiful fine muscle coordination and could thumb the pages of a magazine like a grown-up" (Murphy & Small, 1991, p. 2).

Coordination of environmental information with body information is essential if movements are to accomplish anything. Objects need to be grasped differently if they are hard than if they are soft (Rochat, 1987). Walking on a rug requires different techniques than does walking on a sidewalk or on a lawn, as we see when a new walker trips over the grass on his first expedition outdoors. The characteristics of objects that allow us to do one thing with them and prevent another are sometimes called *affordances*. To show yourself how affordances contribute to movement coordination, try the following: spoon a few scoops of ice cream into a bowl, and then try to do exactly the same movements without either spoon or ice cream. You will find that part of the organization of your movements depends on the size and shape of the spoon and on the resistance of the ice cream (Reed, 1989).

A baby's motor acts also depend on the chances to do things the social environment offers. In traditional Bali, babies were not allowed to crawl because they were considered to be still close to the divine (Bateson & Mead, 1942). In many parts of the world, babies were swaddled or wrapped in long strips of cloth most of the time until they were as much as a year old; this practice persisted until well into the 20th century in Russia (Gorer & Rickman, 1962). One infant seen by this author did not sit alone at 7 months because his baby-sitter had only a carriage for him to nap in, and she would push him down each time he tried to sit up so he would not fall out. He was capable of sitting but had learned to "not sit."

The timing of some later motor milestones, like walking, also depends on what else the baby is doing. Infants do not seem to be able to put a large amount of energy into more than one developmental process at a time. Early speakers are said to tend to be late walkers, and vice versa.

precocious: developing unusually early; from the Latin *praecox* (early ripening).

Although it is not easy to see how an infant's emotional life is one of the factors coordinated to direct movement, it has been suggested that emotional deprivation can lead the baby to become **precociously** invested in motor activity (Lieberman & Birch, 1985). Anxiety resulting from separation from familiar people reduces a baby's movement and exploration.

Given the list of factors related to motor performance just discussed, it is not surprising that motor development can be analyzed as a dynamic action system. Without such an approach, it is difficult to conceptualize how movement patterns coordinate with the environment as well as with each other. One suggestion is that the various factors determining a movement pattern are coordinated by the *purpose* of the movement (Butterworth, 1990b). Body parts move together in different ways when they are used in different tasks.

Both normal and abnormal motor development can be considered in terms of dynamic systems principles (Darrah & Bartlett, 1995). Self-organization of the system, a principle we discussed in earlier chapters, works around the intended task, so development proceeds in terms of whole functions rather than isolated exercises.

We have not yet discussed two dynamic systems principles that are considered important in motor development. One of these principles is the idea that in the course of development there are *transition states*, periods of destabilization that occur as subsystems change. During these states, there is increased variability in movement; the infant experiments with new movements and new forms of movement are likely to begin (Darrah & Bartlett,

---

APPLICATIONS & ARGUMENTS
Emotional Support and Motor Performance

As a baby's control over her body develops, many factors work together to determine what she can do at a given time. Body type, health, cephalocaudal development of the nervous system, and the mastery of flexion and extension are all important determinants.

A less obvious factor in what the infant actually does may be the emotional support of a parent or caregiver. The Russian psychologist Vygotsky described what he called a *zone of proximal development*—a level of performance that is new to the child and that is successfully demonstrated only when an attentive, affectionate adult is nearby. According to this idea, the fact that an infant carried out an action while a parent was watching does not necessarily mean that she will be able to do the same thing when alone, with a stranger, or even if the parent stops looking. For instance, the 12-month-old who was successfully walking around the living room while exchanging smiles and looks with his mother may fall down as soon as his mother gets up to answer the phone.

What is actually accomplished by this affectionate attention? In the case of the toddling 12-month-old, it may provide a visual focal point to guide movement. Just as a spinning ice skater tries to maintain visual fixation on an object that is not moving, the baby may need the parent's interested, smiling face as a steady point to move toward or away from. The ice skater can fall if a flashbulb blinds her briefly. The baby's fall may occur for the same reason—the loss of a reference point as the parent looks away.

1995). A second principle we have not previously discussed is the principle of *rate-limiting* factors. These are factors in the organism or the environment that may slow change, such as body type or opportunity to perform an act (Darrah & Bartlett, 1995).

RESEARCH METHODS

Observational studies are the foundation of our comprehension of motor development. Careful longitudinal work on changes in infants' movements has given us a great deal of information about sequences of events. Many movement patterns are easy to see and describe; they last long enough for the observer to get a clear picture of what is happening. There are also many standardized tests of motor development that can help the observer.

Some movements, however, are quick, complex, and small in size. Observation by eye alone does not allow us to pick these up. We may be looking at the right time, but the impression we get is of random, formless motion. Modern technology allows us to record these small movements. When the visual record is slowed down and observed frame by frame, many details of the movement become visible; in some cases, though, line drawings have to be made from the still pictures before the observer can sort out what is happening.

Where more complex and subtle movement patterns are under investigation, other techniques may be necessary. In studies of the development of jaw movement, for example, an X-ray microbeam system may be used. Radiodense markers are placed on the jaw and tracked by a low-dosage narrow beam X ray, which records the movements of the markers (Ostry, Flanagan, Feldman, & Munhall, 1991).

Technology is a part of other aspects of research on motor development, too. A movable platform can be used to study posture and balance in infants and children. The child stands on the platform, which can be moved in various directions, and sensors attached to parts of the body measure muscle change when the child adjusts her balance in response to the platform's movement. A treadmill device can be used to elicit and measure walking movements in infants who are too young to walk. These babies do not show walking movements ordinarily, but the legs move in a coordinated walking fashion when the baby is held supported with the feet on the moving belts of the treadmill. Cameras on each side of the treadmill record the movements of each leg.

Some work on motor development asks about the relationship of fetal movements to those of the newborn and older infant. Ultrasound techniques are used to record fetal movement patterns. The pregnant mother can also note her sensations as the fetus turns or kicks.

Note that the study of motor development does not focus on a completed movement alone but also looks at details of the movement. For example, a moving limb will begin to decelerate long before it changes direction (otherwise it would be stopped abruptly by the anatomical limits on movement),

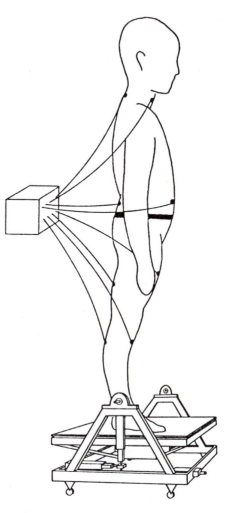

Early motor development includes the mastery of balance control, which allows the child to keep her position even when pushed off balance. The device shown here is a movable platform that can provide the desired size and direction of "push," allowing researchers to study the toddler's technique of retaining balance. (Source: Woolacott, Shumway-Cook, & Williams, 1989)

and the details of acceleration and deceleration are important to our understanding of the movement (cf. Jensen, Thelen, & Ulrich, 1989). Sensors and recorders are needed to collect information on movement velocities and changes that cannot be detected with the naked eye.

Understanding motor development also requires measurement of body proportions, changes in weight, the flexibility of the body (that is, how far a body part can be moved by the examiner's hand), and muscle tone (the amount of tension in muscles). Without these details, it would not be possible to put together a meaningful picture of motor development.

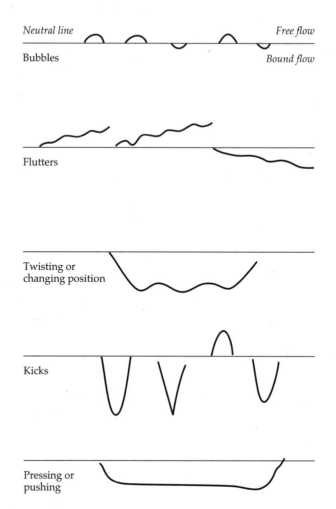

Neutral line   Free flow

Bubbles   Bound flow

Flutters

Twisting or
changing position

Kicks

Pressing or
pushing

With instruction, a pregnant woman can learn to record her unborn infant's movement patterns in a format like this one. It has been suggested that recording fetal movement can be a good way to prepare parents to know and understand their baby. (Source: Loman, 1994)

The design of research on motor development needs to deal with the possible existence of gender differences, genetic differences between ethnic groups, and even differences dependent on very early experience. Bell and Darling (1965), who tested infants of about 74 hours of age on the prone head reaction, noted that researchers "could obtain exactly opposite results by unknowingly sampling breast and bottle-fed infants in very different proportions" (p. 948). Differences in the infant's position relative to the pull of gravity may also create differences in the specific muscular work done to achieve a result like kicking.

An important point about research designs is that it is necessary to look at the variability of performance. One pattern we see in motor development is an increase in the number of ways the infant can perform a task. Averaging information from many babies or from many attempts at a task may obscure some of the variations that are so crucial to our understanding (Jensen, Thelen, & Ulrich, 1989). Longitudinal or sequential designs are certainly preferable to cross-sectional approaches.

Where older infants and toddlers are concerned, the success of the research depends in part on the observer's skill in approaching the child. A frightened or tired baby does not show us all that he or she can do. Patience is an important resource in this sort of observational work, as is an awareness of what tasks are age-appropriate in cognitive and sensory as well as motor terms.

REFLEXES, MILESTONES, AND PATTERNS

Looking for patterns in early motor development can be frustrating and confusing. In a newborn, movement is frequent, even during sleep; but it is rare to see the performance of a "task" as an adult would define it, except for sucking and swallowing food and getting a hand to the mouth. Many of the newborn's movements are stereotyped and involuntary. By age 6 months, the baby may be beginning to sit without support and to grasp bits of food to bring to the mouth. In another year, the baby will be walking, climbing, using a spoon, turning pages, petting a kitten with some degree of gentleness, and banging a drum as loudly as possible.

Does it make sense to differentiate between the involuntary movements of the newborn and the skilled voluntary movements of the toddler? Does it make sense to look for a pattern of motor development that is the same for every human infant? Does it make sense to expect each "milestone" of motor achievement, like standing alone, to occur within a normal range of ages? The answers to all these questions would once have been a definitive "yes," but this is no longer a matter of universal agreement.

continuum: a series of states that involve small variations in an orderly sequence from one extreme to another; from the Latin *continuus* (held together).

Many researchers today have abandoned the idea of reflexes as rigidly determined involuntary movements (Thelen, Ulrich, & Jensen, 1989). Instead, they think of all movements, from birth on, as part of a **continuum,** from very stable, inflexible, invariable movements at one end to very flexible and variable patterns at the other end. Rather than thinking of an unvarying sequence of development, too, modern researchers may believe that the common patterns seen in the past had more to do with frequent child-rearing practices than with basic human development (cf. Zelazo, Zelazo, & Kolb, 1972).

invariance: the absence of change; from the Latin *in-* (not), *variare* (to vary).

One important modern theme in the study of motor development is the idea that the developing infant perfects more and more ways to achieve the same motor outcome, therefore becoming capable of doing a task well under many different circumstances. Functional **invariance** (the repeated performance of the same task) goes along with movement variability (the establishment of many alternative muscle and joint movements). Trying different ways of doing things leads to an understanding of the limits on variation of movements; as Reed (1989) points out, falling is actually an important part of learning to stand.

REFLEX MOVEMENTS

Whether or not reflex movement patterns are "really" different from voluntary movements, a description of infant reflexes remains an important part of the picture of early motor development. Newborns show frequent stereotyped reflex responses to environmental stimulation. Gradually, and possibly because the cortex matures and suppresses some reflex reactions, the baby shows more clearly voluntary activity. Nevertheless, reflex reactivity remains an important part of motor functioning in infants and adults alike.

The words *reflex* and *reflexive* are so frequently misused in everyday speech that it is probably necessary to review their technical meaning. A reflex is a form of movement that fits the following criteria. A reflex movement is *involuntary*; it cannot be performed deliberately in exactly the reflex form, and people cannot deliberately keep themselves from doing it. A reflex is *unlearned* and it *does not fatigue* no matter how many times it occurs. A reflex also has a *specific form*; it involves the same muscles contracting or relaxing in the same way each time. It also has a *specific stimulus* that releases it, and no other stimulus will cause the reflex to occur. Finally, reflexes are *species-specific* and occur in the same way in all members of a species who are at a given stage of development (although a few reflexes, such as the milk ejection reflex, are found only in one sex). A movement can occur "automatically" and without conscious thought if it has been learned thoroughly and practiced often, but it is not a reflex if it does not meet these other criteria.

The newborn infant has many reflex responses, and an examination of them gives some useful clues about the baby's gestational age and physical condition. Although a neurological examination would explore the reflexes in detail, for our purposes a description of a few readily observable reflexes will be enough.

The *rooting* and *sucking reflexes* are powerful and obvious in healthy full-term babies. Rooting occurs when the hungry baby's cheek is touched. The head turns toward the touch and head and mouth carry out small "searching" movements that facilitate finding and mouthing the nipple. The sucking reflex occurs when the nipple or another object has been taken deep into the mouth so that it touches the back of the palate. The baby's lips seal around the nipple and a "chomping" movement of the jaws acts to express milk in a pattern that does not much resemble the sucking of an older child or an adult.

The *grasp reflex* is released when an object touches the palm or the sole of the foot near the toes. The fingers or toes curl tightly around the object, and the fingers hold on so strongly that the baby can be lifted in this way.

The asymmetric *tonic neck reflex* occurs when the baby is supine (lying on her back) and her head is turned to one side. If her head is turned to the right, the right arm extends and the right leg flexes while the left arm flexes and the left leg extends, rather like a fencer about to lunge. If the baby's head is turned to the left, the opposite pattern of flexion and extension occurs.

The *Moro*, or *startle, reflex* is startling and worrisome to many young parents. It is triggered by a brief sensation of loss of support, such as might occur when the parent lays the baby down on a changing table. The infant responds to the sensation first by opening his hands, extending his arms and then moving them toward each other, and then by throwing his arms outward and crying. The whole pattern happens very quickly and resembles someone grabbing for support when falling.

For various reasons, the infant begins to lose these early reflexes after a few months, and the reflex repertoire comes to look more and more like that of an adult. Within a month or so, the rooting and sucking reflexes weaken and the baby's sucking becomes more and more a voluntary act, so that she can let go of the nipple when she chooses. The Moro reflex weakens a great deal by age 3 months and disappears by 6 months (although its pattern can still be seen in the movements of an adult who is startled by a loud noise). The tonic neck reflex follows a similar pattern. The tongue-thrust reflex, which pushes out substances in the front of the mouth, diminishes as well.

The infant in the first few months is to some extent a prisoner of reflexes. He or she must follow certain movement patterns when the environment triggers certain reflexes. Surprisingly, though, if the infant is situated with the body supported so that reflexes are not released, a good deal of voluntary activity appears even in the very young infant. Amiel-Tison and Grenier (1986) have demonstrated what they call a *liberated state.* This state is achieved by maintaining a calm, quiet environment, by gently holding the baby's head from behind so that it is supported, by talking gently and maintaining eye contact with the baby, and by holding the baby in one of several special positions. These actions reduce the chances that reflexes will interrupt the baby's behavior, and they stabilize the baby's head when he cannot yet hold it steady by himself. When this liberated state is achieved, the baby shows abilities to control the body that would not usually be expected until a much greater age, such as accurate reaching and grasping at 14 days (Amiel-Tison & Grenier, 1986).

As the reflex reactions of early infancy diminish with age, the baby's passive *muscle tone,* or muscular tension when it is not actively moving, also diminishes in a cephalocaudal pattern. A normal newborn has high muscle tone, as you can see from the baby's tightly flexed position, but as he or she gets older the baby lies in a more and more relaxed position. At the same time, the baby's ability to control body movement also progresses in a cephalocaudal direction. As well as showing progress from the head end to the lower end of the body, the baby's increasing motor control follows a *proximodistal* pattern, from the midline of the body out toward the extremities.

Might there be more than one reason why reflexes diminish in the way they do? It is intriguing to question whether maturation is the only factor influencing the timing and sequence of changes. It is always possible that sequences that look to us like maturational stages might occur because babies all over the world have some similar experiences. If the experiences are

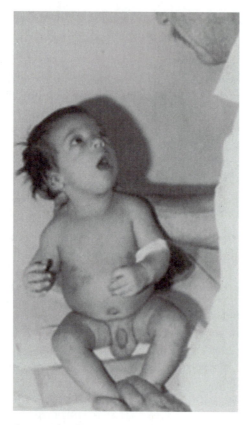

Support for the head and back frees this 1-month-old to inspect the examiner's face visually. Without such support, it would be hard to get the baby's attention.

altered, we may see altered expression of reflexes. For example, newborn babies show a walking reflex, in which stepping occurs when the baby is held upright with the feet touching a horizontal surface. Most parents do not often put the baby in this kind of position, and the baby ordinarily stops showing the reflex within a few months. The baby begins to extend the legs and step again only after 8 or 9 months, when the action becomes voluntary. But if the caregivers have frequently put the young baby in a position that brings out the walking reflex, the reflexive reaction will be prolonged long past the usual age and will merge with voluntary walking, which in turn will develop unusually early (Zelazo, Zelazo, & Kolb, 1972). Is the baby's cortex being prevented from suppressing the walking reflex? Perhaps so, but an alternative explanation (Thelen, Ulrich, & Jensen, 1989) suggests that the ordinary loss of the reflex results from increased fat on the legs, which makes them too heavy for the weak muscles to lift; the continuation of the reflex with exercise may result from increases in muscle strength that offset the increased weight.

THE "MOTOR MILESTONES"

As motor ability progresses, we see the baby manage feats of motor control such as sitting alone and pulling to a standing position. When such an achievement appears for the first time, it is referred to as a *motor milestone*. These developmental milestones give us good, quick indicators of the child's progress, but they should not be considered isolated events or skills. They indicate a continuous building process (Goldberg, 1989) and are part of an evolving balance of muscle use.

As we examine the major motor milestones, we need to keep in mind that the baby is always working against gravity to achieve motor development. She develops the ability to carry out the extension of a body part against the pull of gravity first, and only later becomes able to manage flexion of the part against gravity. The newborn's motor abilities are also affected by the great weight of her head relative to the rest of her body. We need to remember, too, that the newborn begins motor development in a state of physiological flexion of the hips, so the legs are pulled up under her body in the prone position and are drawn up toward her torso in the supine position.

The pull of gravity on the body provides a major sensory framework for movement, of course, but there is also a framework provided by vision. Information from the visual field, such as the horizontal and vertical lines of a room, gives a framework that has a strong effect on balance. Even an adult can be made to sway back and forth if the major visual coordinates of an experimental room are moved, and a toddler can be made to fall down just by such visual movement (Butterworth & Hicks, 1977). Vision is also powerfully integrated into behaviors such as reaching, where the action can be carried out only when sensory and motor events are thoroughly coordinated with each other.

Our description of the motor milestones (much of which follows that of Goldberg, 1989) will include ages at which the events are likely to be seen. It is important to realize, though, that these ages are averages and that there is a great deal of variability. In fact, the more advanced the milestone, the more age variability there is likely to be; some of the many factors that determine when a particular milestone will be achieved are discussed in a later section.

The first motor milestone to be seen soon after birth is the ability to *raise the head* when in a prone position. This would be more difficult for the baby than for an adult even if muscle control were well developed, because the baby has only a small, light body to counterbalance the heavy head.

Around 1–2 months, a second milestone is achieved. The baby's hips are less flexed and he can more effectively extend a body part against gravity; the baby can get his head and chest up while supporting his weight on the elbows and forearms, but he has to keep the elbows behind the shoulder girdle to maintain balance.

At about 3 months, the baby has progressed in her style of pushing up. Growth and a decrease in hip flexion are moving the center of gravity farther back in the body, so the elbows can come forward in line with the shoulders

APPLICATIONS & ARGUMENTS
Playpens

If a baby is confined to a crib or playpen for most of his waking hours, he is missing out on experiences that are important for both motor and cognitive development. Playpens offer quite limited motor experiences because their affordances are soon exhausted. The baby crawling on carpet must move differently than when on a polished hardwood floor or on uneven tiles, but in the playpen the surface is pretty much the same at all points. The baby who is pulling up into a standing position does so differently when holding the upholstered sofa, a kitchen chair, or drawer handles, but a mesh-sided playpen does not offer variety. From the cognitive perspective, free exploration is far superior to confinement, helping to encourage curiosity and a sense of mastery. Even the existence of minor dangers and discomforts outside the playpen provides some opportunities for learning.

Are playpens good for anything? In a run-down house that cannot be "baby-proofed," they may be an essential safety measure. When a parent has to run outdoors to rescue an older child from a tricycle accident, popping the baby in the playpen for temporary safekeeping is a great idea. And, of course, when company is coming, a playpen can hold most of the toys that are ordinarily all over the floor!

and the baby can still keep her balance. Her arms stay close to her body for stability, and this position helps stretch the muscles of the upper arm and shoulder blade. When lying on her back, the infant can keep her head in the midline; this means she can use her eyes and hands together and can play with her hands and feet.

By about 4 months, the baby can *push up on extended arms* while in the prone position if someone uses a hand to hold the baby's pelvis flat. If the baby turns his head to one side while pushing up, he may accidentally roll to the side because he still does a poor job of weight shifting to compensate for the pull of his large head.

By about 5 months, the baby's pelvis lies flatter as he extends his body more. The chest is held up better, and control of the head has also improved. The baby can shift his weight better and is less likely to roll sideways when he turns his head.

The 6-month-old lies still flatter, and her abdominal and hip muscles can now keep the pelvis more stable. The center of gravity continues to move downward, so the lower part of the body does an improved job of counterbalancing the head. The baby still has trouble shifting her weight from side to side while propped on her extended arms, so if she reaches for a toy, she may lean on one elbow and use the hand and forearm to grasp.

By 7 months, the baby has reached the milestone of sitting alone. Her legs are spread wide for stability and she leans slightly forward, but she can play using both hands while sitting. The baby is now very stable in the prone position. She can get onto all fours and rock back and forth. Some can creep or "bear-walk" on hands and feet, and they can reach for a toy in that position while shifting the head to one side to remain in a stable position while picking up the hand.

Few 7-month-olds either walk alone or show the walking reflex characteristic of much younger babies. They appear to be in some sort of limbo between reflexive and voluntary walking. However, when held with their feet touching a motorized treadmill (as described earlier), these babies demonstrate well-coordinated alternating stepping movements resembling upright walking (Thelen & Ulrich, 1991), which they never do under other circumstances. As the treadmill researchers have suggested, it may be that the way the treadmill pulls the leg backward stretches the leg muscles and stores energy that allows the leg to spring forward, thus providing a factor that combines with the baby's other abilities to show a mature movement pattern that would not emerge without help (Thelen & Ulrich, 1991).

By 8 months, the baby is likely to begin *creeping*. The baby can keep his pelvis and trunk stable while moving his legs. Some babies at this age move

This 5-month-old can sit alone for a few seconds but manages better with a stabilizing touch on the arm. The spread legs provide a base of support that compensates for the infant's lack of hip control. The hands are also used for balance.

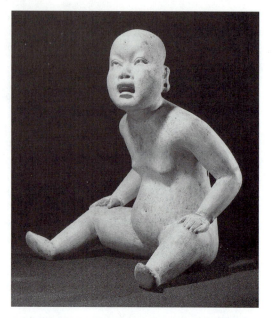

In about 1200 B.C., a sculptor among the Olmec people of Central America captured this immature sitting posture. The position and facial expression are remarkably like those of the 5-month-old in the previous illustration, though this baby looks a little older.

easily from sitting to the creeping position, whereas others do not. The baby also *pulls up* into a kneeling or standing position; he must use the strength of the arms and shoulders to pull up, because his hip muscles are not yet under good control. If someone is supporting him, the baby may bear his weight on the whole foot, but when he is holding on, his weight is thrown forward and his position is on tiptoe.

At 9 or 10 months, the baby *cruises* while holding on for support and even turns so that the movement is more like true walking. Little time is now spent in the prone position. Because the baby has much better control of the hip and trunk, she moves more easily between positions. She can sit with her legs to one side or "W-sit," with the knees in front and the lower legs pointing back at an angle on each side.

Standing without holding on to something requires increased postural control because the area supporting the body's weight is smaller than was the case with earlier positions. The center of gravity must remain over the feet for standing to be stable (Dietz & Horstmann, 1991). The baby's head, still proportionately large, creates a high center of gravity and thus some difficulty in maintaining balance in the standing position.

By 11 or 12 months, the baby may *walk alone.* The walk is more flat-footed, unlike the extended ankle of the walking reflex, and the baby steps backward in an exaggerated way to maintain his balance at times. The hands are in the "high guard" position, lifted at each side. If the baby tries to carry a toy in one hand, balance problems appear because the upper limbs are both needed to balance with. A baby who has been walking flat-footed may walk on tiptoe when carrying something, returning to the more stable stiff posture of earlier weeks.

Even new walkers show a coordination of the limbs similar to that of adults. The left leg begins its cycle of movement forward when the right is halfway through its own cycle. The coordination is more variable than it will be in a few months or in adulthood, but the new walker can be helped by holding her hands and helping her balance (Clark & Whittall, 1989). (Once again, as in the treadmill study, helping with one factor seems to allow more advanced coordination to emerge.)

Of course, during all these months, the baby is continuing to grow, and most of that growth is in the trunk and limbs. The baby's proportions are changing, and that fact as well as the increased extension of the body continues to lower the center of gravity, making the baby increasingly stable in a standing position. Nevertheless, the toddler uses a broad-based gait with the feet farther apart than an older child's, and he may bend the knees a bit, providing still more stability. He still walks with flat feet. A squatting position may be used for play. By about 24 months, the walk includes movement from heel to toe and arm swinging. Greater control of hip muscles means toddlers can jump, and they enjoy doing so.

Once again, as Goldberg (1989) has noted, motor development is a continuous building process. The baby may walk alone at 11 or 12 months, but skill at walking will go on improving for years. Motor abilities go on developing long after their "milestone" occurs. For example, the motor pattern used in crawling changes a good deal between 18 months and 4 years (Touwer, Hempel, & Westra, 1992). More efficient crawling develops, and the initially rather stiff use of the body "breaks down" into the use of parts either individually or in combinations, with smooth sequences of movements and flexibility of the trunk. The movement pattern becomes much more variable and can include head turning and other movements. Each part of the movement pattern has become **modularized** and can be used alone or in many combinations.

modularize: to master a skill so thoroughly that it can be carried out easily in combination with other functions; from the Latin *modulus* (a small measure, rhythm).

Similar changes are seen as walking advances. Adult patterns of walking may not appear until 7 to 9 years of age (Inman, Ralston, & Todd, 1981). Stable and well-balanced walking includes rotation of the shoulders in the opposite direction from pelvic movement, creating an arm swing that helps balance and smooth the individual's movement. The opposed shoulder movement and pelvic movement require trunk flexibility and well-organized sequences of movements.

REACHING AND GRASPING AND HAND PREFERENCE

So far our discussion of motor development has dealt with the milestones occurring in cephalocaudal development, but of course events also occur in a proximodistal progression. The development of *voluntary grasping and hand control* is a good example.

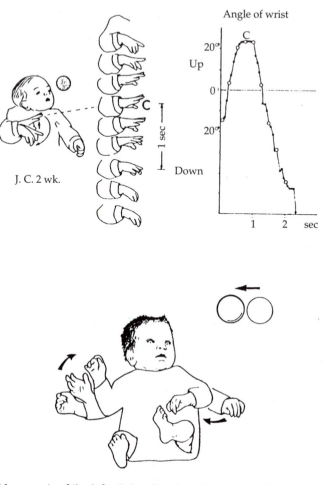

Movements of the infant's hand and wrist seem to indicate attempts to reach and grasp at just a few weeks of age. (Source: Based on Trevarthen, 1982)

The development of control over the hands is also a good example of the functional nature of motor development. When we see a young baby kick, it does not seem quite clear what the baby is doing or what those movements will ever have to do with voluntary actions. From the beginning, however, the functional nature of hand movement is obvious. Within days after birth, many babies can bring their hands to their mouth and suck them for comfort. By 3 or 4 months, grasped objects are brought to the mouth for exploration. By 6 or 7 months, the baby can bring bits of food to the mouth and can hold objects in front of the eyes for inspection.

Hand movement, even in the newborn, frequently seems to be part of a task. The baby manipulates the environment or the body itself. The hands are used in the service first of the mouth and later of the eyes (Bruner, 1969). The special function of hand movement is to bring objects near another part of the body. The coordination of hand and mouth, in particular, is apparent even at birth, when the mouth reflexively opens as the palm is pressed (the Babkin reflex).

At birth, the hands tend to be closed most of the time. Grasping is *reflexive* at this point and occurs when something touches the palms. If you pry the baby's hands open, you may find bits of blanket fuzz or the mother's hair.

Between months 2 and 4, the grasp reflex weakens and the hands are open more of the time. If you look back to other aspects of motor development, you will recall that the baby is now starting to use his hands to push up, which stretches his muscles and opens his hands still further. In accordance with proximodistal development, the palm and upper parts of the fingers come under control before the whole finger is controlled, so the 3- or 4-month-old scoops up an object with the palm and fingers. The thumb plays a very small role in the act at this point.

What the baby can do with respect to picking up an object depends in part on the object itself—the affordances the object offers. If you try to pick things up without using your thumb, you will see that you can do a fairly good job with larger objects, but it is very hard to pick up a raisin or a Cheerio this way. The same is true as the baby begins thumb use. Thus, as we watch the baby become able to pick up an object using an *opposed thumb,* we see that she can manage a 1-inch cube by about age 7 months by opposing the thumb to all the fingers together. Picking up a small pellet with a pincer grasp that uses the thumb against one or two fingers needs one or two more months of proximodistal progress, as does poking with the index finger (Ames & Ilg, 1964).

For the baby to grasp an object that is not placed directly into the hand, the baby must *reach* for the object. Reaching requires coordination of movement with visual information. As we saw earlier in our discussion of Amiel-Tison's work on the "liberated state," even a neonate may be able to reach accurately if given the appropriate position and postural support. However, without support and help, the infant does not reach well in all directions until about age 4 to 5 months.

The development of reaching for a seen object is complex and still not completely understood. It was once thought that the baby learns to reach by looking back and forth from his hand to the object as he moves his hand (the so-called Piagetian reach), but this does not seem to be the case; at least no researcher today reports observing such a thing. Modern research does show some severe early limitations on the baby's reaching ability, but the ability to reach for something on the same side as the reaching hand goes to 100% accuracy between 9 and 17 weeks (Provine & Westerman, 1979).

The improvement of directed reaching does not happen all at once. One group of researchers reported that between the ages of 3 and 4 months, infants sometimes showed apparently undirected flapping or waving, and sometimes directed or even successful attempts to touch a toy (Thelen et al., 1991). The infants had some techniques that helped them move from flapping to reaching and grasping. Sometimes they slowed the velocity of the movement, which improved accuracy; they also contracted and stiffened the shoulder joint, which stabilized the joint and prevented shoulder movement from causing extra variability in the hand's pathway.

A curious limitation on the infant's reaching involves the midline of the body. If one arm is restrained, the baby will reach across to the opposite side of the body to get an object with about 70% accuracy by 17 weeks (Provine & Westerman, 1979). Even at 7 months, though, there is a "midline barrier" (Bruner, 1969). If the baby has grasped a toy in her left hand and another toy is held on that side, her right hand does not reach across to get the toy.

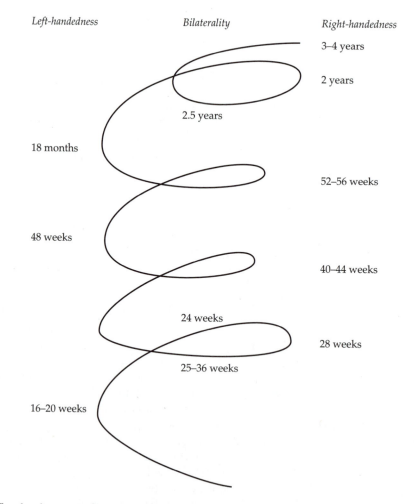

The development of a consistent hand preference takes a long time. This graph shows how a typical right-handed child went through periods of preference for the left hand before eventually settling down to right-handedness. (Source: Ames & Ilg, 1964)

Instead, her left hand tenses and the baby bangs the new toy with the clenched hand, still holding the old one.

The pattern of spontaneous reaching is coordinated with the baby's posture. Before he can sit alone, he reaches with both hands when supported; the beginning sitter uses one hand for balance while reaching with the other (Rochat & Senders, 1991). There is a relationship between postures and the occurrence of reaching with one or both hands.

What else determines which hand an infant uses? Older children and adults show a consistent hand preference, which runs parallel to the lateralization of function in the individual's brain and is thought to have developed in the course of evolution because of its advantages for tree-dwellers (Mac-Neilage, 1991). Infants, however, normally show no clear-cut hand preference for years. Instead, they alternate periods of left-handedness, right-handedness, and bilaterality. By age 2, some have established a hand preference, but others continue alternating for several more years (Ames & Ilg, 1964). In the absence of social pressure to the contrary, about 13% will be left-handed (Anderson, 1993b). However, those born with very low weight (less than 1000 grams) show about 22% of nonright-handedness; this proportion is a good deal smaller than used to be the case, and the change is probably accounted for by better early care (Powls, Botting, Cooke, & Marlow, 1996).

CONTROL OF MOUTH MOVEMENTS

Except for the term *motor mouth,* we get relatively few reminders of the motor control necessary for sucking, chewing, and speaking. These tasks actually involve complex and well-coordinated movement patterns. Jaw opening alone requires three muscle groups working together to rotate the jaw downward and move it forward (Ostry et al., 1991). A more complicated task like utterance of one syllable requires the coordination of more than 70 muscles and involves a number of body parts, all the way from the diaphragm to the lips (Thelen, 1991).

Like other motor tasks, speaking involves an unvarying outcome that may be brought about by a variety of motor combinations. Before he or she can begin to speak, the infant needs to master the components that make up all those combinations. This process of mastery is based on a variety of developmental changes, for the anatomy of the mouth and throat in the early months is rather different than it will be later. Young infants have a small mouth cavity; a large tongue that is difficult to move; small, relatively immobile lips; and fat pads in the cheeks that restrict cheek movement. Gradually, the tongue elongates and undergoes muscle development and the fat pads decrease in size. The anatomy that functions in speech is actually molded by use; sucking, crying, and swallowing with the large tongue all exert stresses on the palate and jaw, molding them into their eventual sizes and shapes (Thelen, 1991), much as pushing up in the prone position helps to stretch and open the hands.

TABLE 9.1   *Oral motor abilities help determine how and what an infant can eat at any point in development. Here are some abilities that would be expected in normally developing babies at different ages.*

Age	Usual food	Oral skills
0–4 mos.	Breast or bottle	Reflex rooting, sucking, swallowing; movement of tongue up, down, in, out; poor skill at closing lips around object
4–6 mos.	Breast, bottle; cup for milk or juice; spoon-fed cereal, strained fruit or vegetables	May still thrust tongue when drinking from cup; opens mouth for spoon but tongue thrusts when spoon is removed
6–12 mos.	Breast, bottle, cup; spoon-fed; finger foods	Moves jaw up and down; moves tongue side to side; brings upper lip down on spoon
12–18 mos.	Begins table food as well as above	Seals lips well when drinking from cup; does not cough or choke often; rotary pattern of jaw movement when chewing

Source: Based on Linder, 1990.

INDIVIDUAL DIFFERENCES AND PROBLEMS IN MOTOR DEVELOPMENT

Variation is the name of the game in motor development, as in other aspects of infant development. Babies do not all reach the same milestone at the same time, nor does a baby spend equal amounts of time in each stage. Some stages may be very brief—so brief that an observer might not even notice when a particular baby displayed them. The common belief that a baby should crawl before it walks does not take this variability into account. A baby can walk only after she has completed the development needed for walking as well as that needed for crawling, but for various reasons she may crawl only briefly or just sit around until she is ready to walk. No doubt some of the variations in motor development result from genetic differences. Others, however, result from various aspects of the infant's experience, as they combine in a dynamic action system with physical development.

There is a great deal of variation in normal development, but obviously abnormal development presents considerable deviation from the averages. Abnormal motor development can result from serious physical deformities such as malformations of hands or feet, but most motor abnormalities seen in developed countries today are the result of central nervous system damage. Such abnormalities are referred to as *cerebral palsy* (CP). CP may have occurred as a result of prenatal infection or drug use, or because of complications of premature birth, or as a consequence of postnatal problems.

Abnormal motor development can be a transactional process, in which the problem develops slowly as a result of interactions between the baby's

---

APPLICATIONS & ARGUMENTS
Baby Gyms

In recent years, a practice that has grown rapidly among middle-class parents is involvement with an infant gym program. These programs cost varying amounts and provide equipment like small trampolines and balance apparatuses. A common feature is a big silk parachute that everyone can get under or on top of. Parents and babies attend these gyms in groups, and each parent is seen as her child's teacher or coach. Baby gym programs often advertise themselves as facilitating both motor and cognitive development.

Can such programs be harmful? Probably not, as long as everyone is reasonably careful. The programs do not ordinarily try to force performance or get a baby to do more than his body can deal with. They emphasize fun and activity.

Can programs be helpful? In one sense, yes, but in another, no. Of course, babies benefit from having fun with their parents while playing physical games. Parents of infants may need opportunities to meet other parents of infants. Some parents who have had little experience with children may really need to learn how to play with their baby.

On the other hand, parents do not need to pay a fee to get these advantages. With a little investment of imagination, anything that can be done in the gym can be done at home. There are also other ways for parents to meet and learn from each other. It would be a shame for poor parents to feel that their baby was further disadvantaged because they could not afford gym fees.

---

hypotonic: with abnormally low muscle tone; from the Greek *hypo-* (under), the Latin *tonus* (tension).

experiences and his nervous processes. This process may be most obvious in babies who are **hypotonic,** or low in muscle tone. These so-called floppy babies compensate for their low tone as they develop by adopting motor habits that eventually cause functional problems and physical deformations. Whereas the normal baby in the prone position bears his weight on the face and lower legs, the floppy baby lies flat with much of the weight on the abdomen; as a result, he develops abnormal breathing patterns that can later affect speech.

Floppiness makes it much harder for the baby to push up in the prone position, so her hands are not pressed, stretched, and opened and are more likely to become inflexible and clawlike. When the floppy baby matures enough to sit alone, she has trouble controlling her head. To keep her head from flopping, the baby pulls back the shoulder blades. This keeps the head supported from the rear but makes it impossible to use the hands. As the muscles shorten from lack of use, this position becomes permanent. The baby also retracts her tongue, which alters the positions of structures in the neck and stabilizes the head (try it yourself to see what it does to your head movement) but will also interfere with speech later. The baby's later sitting may involve prolonged periods in the W position described earlier. Although this position stabilizes the body, it eventually bends the soft bones of the legs and knees and produces a knock-kneed gait, with knees together and feet apart. If this goes on long enough, the bones can be straightened only through orthopedic surgery.

As you can see, these changes for the worse were all part of a transactional process. The baby did the best things he could to breathe, sit, look around, and play in a body that had difficulty resisting the pull of gravity. Unfortunately, the actions that were most functional in the short run caused damage in the long run.

The connection between central nervous system damage and motor development means that motor functioning can be a way to evaluate nervous system functioning. A number of signs in the first few years of life should create some suspicion of brain damage (Taft, 1981). Poor sucking may indicate nervous system problems that will show up later in other motor disabilities. Early handedness (strong preference for use of one hand at age 4 or 5 months) probably indicates that something is wrong with the parts of the brain that control the other side. Early rolling over (by 6 weeks or so) indicates that one side of the body is stronger than the other, and may be a sign of cerebral palsy. **Asymmetric** crawling (pushing off with only one arm and leg), even if only temporary, may result from a problem. Persistent drooling, past age 2 or 3 years, may be caused by brain damage. Prolonged toe walking, past the age when a flat-footed gait usually develops, may indicate a problem, as may feet turning in or out. Finally, trouble climbing stairs and falling easily may result from weakness of certain muscles caused by damage to the nervous system. These effects result from damage to specific parts of the brain that are involved in motor functioning and motor learning; the cerebellum is especially important here (Raymond, Lisberger, & Mauk, 1996).

Problems in motor development are not always a result of nervous system difficulties, however. Because movement depends on the coordination of many factors in a system, a problem with any single factor can alter the outcome. For example, infants who have had early abdominal surgery may show delayed development of control over the trunk because the weakness of the healing muscles disrupts the balance between extension and flexion functions (Simon, Brady, Stafford, & Powell, 1992).

asymmetric: shaped differently on the two sides; from the Greek *a-* (not), *syn-* (with), *metron* (measure).

TREATMENT OF PROBLEMS IN MOTOR DEVELOPMENT

When infants and toddlers have cerebral palsy (CP) or problems caused by later brain damage, their motor development can often be helped by therapy. Physical therapists, occupational therapists, and speech therapists may all be involved in treatment.

Some general ideas about treatment of CP children should be kept in mind. In spite of brain damage, individuals with disabilities can learn and improve. What they can do will change over time even without treatment, but structured programs are more helpful than occasional experiences, especially if they stress motivation and the total learning experience (Goldstein, 1995). However, there are limitations to recovery, and therapy helps a child do a task in the way that is possible for her, not necessarily in the "usual" way (Farrel & Hooper, 1995).

Physical therapists in recent years have begun to consider how principles of dynamic action systems apply to their work (Heriza & Sweeney, 1994). The principle of self-organization suggests that therapy needs to work on performance of real tasks of daily living, not just isolated tasks. The principle of transition states implies that there will be periods when it is easier or more difficult to foster development of motor control, and the therapist should concentrate on the easier times. Finally, the principle of rate-limiting factors suggests that the therapist needs to look for and correct factors that may be slowing the infant's progress, such as parents' attitudes or the size and shape of a spoon (Darrah & Bartlett, 1995).

Physical therapy with infants and toddlers often involves the *Bobath method* (Spivack, 1995). With this approach, the child has half-hour individual sessions with physical, occupational, and speech therapists several times a week. Devices like wheelchairs and locking braces are used. Exercises include work on range of motion of body parts and vestibular stimulation through lying on and rolling with a large ball. Special education sessions are also provided for children in groups.

A therapy technique for cerebral palsy recently imported to the United States opens some interesting issues about testing the effects of treatment. *Conductive education* is a method developed in Hungary. This technique begins when the infant is between 6 and 12 months of age and includes work to educate the parents. It follows an educationally rather than medically based model, works with children in groups, and may take as much as 13 hours per day. Although other therapists are involved, most of the direct work with the child is done by a worker called the *conductor* (Kozma & Balogh, 1995; Spivack, 1995).

The conductor's job is to help the CP child think through and pursue the path to achievement of some developmentally appropriate goal like self-feeding or play. Verbal cues and songs help maintain the child's attention, and the rhythms of speech and music are used to guide the rhythms of the child's actions (Spivack, 1995).

As Goldstein (1995) has pointed out, many therapy programs tend to report only anecdotes and case studies as demonstrations that their methods work. A real demonstration would involve a prospective (see Chapter 2) clinical trial that would make sure that selection of subjects was unbiased, that observers were trained and reliable, and that there was an investigation of the long-term effect of the treatment on the activities of daily living. Therapists and parents both want very much to improve the functioning of infants with disabilities, and it is possible that they see what they want to see.

THE INTEGRATED BABY

Before ending this chapter, we need to think about how a baby actually uses his motor functions in the real world. After all, a baby is not just a bundle of reflexes, flexions, and extensions; he has things he wants to do and he does them as well as his body permits at any given time.

Imagine a 7-month-old baby sitting in a high chair eating pieces of banana. This behavior will continue only as long as the baby is hungry; it depends on a motivational state and is voluntary, not reflexive. It involves a sensory framework, too. The baby responds to vestibular stimulation and holds his head up against the pull of gravity. The baby can use his hand to pick up the banana because he does not need to pull his shoulder blades back to support his head. Vision and proprioception guide his hand to the piece of banana, which is big enough to be picked up by the thumb opposed to one or more of the other fingers. (This is possible in part because the hands have been stretched by the earlier activity of pushing up in the prone position.) The baby brings his hand to his mouth by flexing the arm, guiding the muscles' work by proprioception. Because he does not have the ability to release the banana easily, the baby does not just pop the piece neatly into his mouth. Instead, he rubs the banana across the mouth area, gradually letting go as more banana is pushed into the mouth and there is less left in the (now extremely sticky) hand. Once the banana is in the mouth, it remains there to be swallowed, because the tongue-thrust reflex is no longer operating; instead of pushing the food out, the tongue helps maneuver the food back to the point where it can be swallowed. After the baby has had all the banana he wants, other motor functions will come into play; pushing at the high chair tray, crying if sufficiently frustrated, lifting the arms to signal "up" to an adult. All these actions now serve as means to ends.

PROBLEMS TO CONSIDER AND DISCUSS

1. If there is a transition state in crawling before walking begins, how would you expect the baby's behavior to alter during that period?

2. How is a reflex different from a learned reaction that occurs without conscious thought? For example, how is your action in drinking through a straw different from a newborn's sucking reflex?

3. How do the infant's physical proportions affect the achievement of motor milestones?

4. How is the development of hand preference related to lateralization in the nervous system (which was discussed in an earlier chapter)?

5. How would you carry out a test of a treatment like conductive education? Could this be done as an experiment? Why or why not?

10

Cognitive Development

cognition:
thinking, knowing, remembering, processing information; from the Latin *com-* (with), *gnoscere* (to come to know).

Cognition is a rather broad term that encompasses a variety of intellectual functions. Learning, problem solving, remembering and forgetting, abstracting, thinking in categories, recognizing oneself, imitation of other people all come under the rubric of cognition. It seems that our language could use a verb "to cognize," but the closest we come to it is *recognize* (presumably, to cognize again what we cognized before). The use of language to represent objects and events is an important aspect of cognition, but it is so complex that a separate chapter is devoted to the subject.

Cognitive development involves changes in all the functions mentioned above. Simple experience is one aspect of cognitive development; an older baby has experienced and learned more and thus knows more than a younger one does. But cognitive development is more than just mastering information, because the older baby can also do more with what he knows than the younger one can.

The study of cognitive development has to find ways to discover what the baby learns and how she becomes more cognitively competent as she gets older. These questions, complex in themselves, are complicated still further by noncognitive factors that influence cognitive performance.

An adult who has to study for an exam is keenly aware that conditions affect the success of his or her efforts. Poor light, distracting noise, a disagreement with a loved one, fatigue—all these factors influence the efficiency of adult learning. It should come as no surprise, then, that similar factors encourage or discourage an infant's cognitive functioning.

1. Sensory abilities   Recall from Chapter 8 that there is a gradual development in infants' visual abilities. The infant will not learn about a visual display that is too distant or too fine-grained for her to resolve. Auditory abilities are much more mature at birth, but problems like otitis media can occur. In one study of 12- and 18-month-olds, children with chronic otitis media were especially inattentive during an episode of the ear inflammation (Feagans, Kipp, & Blood, 1994).

In addition to the changes in infants' actual sensory abilities, there are developmental changes in the senses they seem to attend to most. Before age 6 months, touch seems most important; mouthing and then fingering are preferred ways to explore. Later in the first year, there is an increase in visual examining, sometimes following the mouthing of an object (Bruner, 1969; Ruff, Saltarelli, Capozzoli, & Dubiner, 1992).

2. The nervous system   As the infant develops through the first year, the speed of processing in the nervous system increases (Rovee-Collier & Boller, 1995). The nervous system is also changing; its plasticity allows events in the environment to guide its growth. Both *long-term depression* (LTD) and *long-term potentiation* (LTP) of synapses can be mechanisms of learning. These changes can be influenced by many factors other than the practice, reward, and punishment that we usually think of as influencing learning. For example, the functioning of one neuron in the crayfish is actually influenced by whether the animal recently won or lost a fight with another crayfish (Yeh, Fricke, & Edwards, 1996). Similarly, in some neurons of monkeys who have been trained to do a task for a reward, activity is different depending on the type of reward and the way it is given (Watanabe, 1996).

The nervous system's capacity to support cognitive development is related to a number of factors discussed in Chapter 7. Genetic problems, exposure to environmental lead, infectious disease, and head injury can all have a detrimental effect on cognitive development that results from their direct effect on the brain. However, it should be noted that these factors interact with other factors, like family environment, and cognitive outcome is determined by a combination of factors (Liaw & Brooks-Gunn, 1993) that function as a dynamic action system.

3. Social and emotional development   As infants reach the second half of the first year, they begin to display fear of the unfamiliar, especially if they are alone or with strangers rather than with a familiar caregiver. Crying or looking away interferes with cognitive functioning. The fearful, distressed child may not even see well enough to take in information, much less look attentively and learn from what he sees.

4. State   The concept of *state* is important for the understanding of infant cognition. State involves a group of variables in the nervous system that determine how ready the baby is to behave in certain ways; the behaviors themselves are taken as measures of readiness (Emde, Gaensbauer, & Harmon, 1976; Prechtl, Akiyama, Zinkin, & Grant, 1968).

The following states can be noted in infants from birth on: (1) active, or REM (rapid eye movement) sleep; (2) quiet, or non-REM sleep; (3) drowsy awakeness; (4) alert awakeness; (5) fussing and high activity; and (6) crying. Of these six states, the one most conducive to learning is a quiet alert period, which may occur toward the end of a period of drowsy awakeness. Alert awakeness involves more movement and vocalization and less looking and listening, and crying or sleeping are obviously not good learning situations. When the baby is propped up (as in an infant seat) rather than supine, there seems to be greater visual attentiveness.

In the very young infant, states shift rapidly and are poorly organized, and sleep takes up a good deal of the baby's time. Older babies spend much more time in the quiet alert state that is conducive to learning.

RESEARCH METHODS

Many of the research techniques discussed in Chapters 7 and 8 are also relevant to the study of cognitive development, but some special issues and approaches need to be described.

Although past work on cognitive development generally involved painstaking observation, most modern work is experimental in nature. The researcher manipulates an independent variable, usually in the form of a visual display the baby watches, and measures dependent variables of infant behavior. Some studies in cognitive development are directed at assessing an infant's cognitive abilities, and they often involve testing many babies in order to establish norms that relate performance to age. For early intervention programs that attempt to facilitate cognitive development in infants who are at risk, research may focus on program evaluation, a particularly difficult task for the researcher.

Physiological measures of cognitive activity are an important concern for researchers working with infants, adults, and animals. Measures of activity in parts of the nervous system are available (see Chapter 7) but not necessarily easy to use with an infant while learning and thinking are in progress. Measures of heart rate are easier to carry out, and changes are considered to indicate that the infant is paying attention to a stimulus (Berg & Berg, 1987; Richards, 1987).

Behavioral measures of cognition include simple behaviors like visual scanning and preferential looking, where a baby's longer scanning or looking are considered to indicate that a stimulus is more novel or interesting to the baby than another. Measures of looking are also used in the *violation-of-expectation* method (Baillargeon, 1994), in which the baby is presented with a "possible" and an "impossible" event to look at; looking longer at the "impossible" event suggests that the baby is surprised by the unexpected.

Behavioral measures can include reinforcement techniques. For example, a very young baby can show whether she can tell differences in numbers of objects by learning to suck to get milk for one number and learning that there is no point in sucking when another number is seen. A more complex use of reinforcement is in the **mobile conjugate reinforcement paradigm** (Rovee-Collier & Boller, 1995). In this situation, a ribbon is tied to a baby's ankle while the baby looks at a mobile. Initially, the mobile is not connected to the ribbon, so a baseline measure of the baby's tendency to kick can be established. Later, the ribbon is attached to the mobile, so the baby's kicking makes the mobile move. The baby now kicks more often because the experience of making the mobile move acts as a reinforcer. The appearance of the mobile itself or of fabric surrounding the crib can be changed. Subsequent tests of the baby's rate of kicking (compared to the baseline) can indicate whether the baby is learning about particular features of the mobile; the infant's memory for the situation can also be assessed.

Some general issues about cognitive development research involve the baby's interest and her ability to do the task. Stimuli used in this work often

mobile: in this context, a toy that hangs over a baby's crib and rotates as the crib is jiggled or as the wind moves it; from the Latin *movere* (to move).

conjugate: joined, coupled; from the Latin *com-* (with), *jugare* (to join).

One approach to the study of cognitive development examines infants' responses to "possible" and "impossible" events. In both the events shown here, a hand makes a box slide along the top of another box. In the "impossible" event, the top box moves so far that we would expect it to fall off, but it does not. (Source: Baillargeon, 1994)

involve bright colors and flashing lights, which attract the infant's attention. The infant must have the ability either to control eye movements, to reach, or to pick up an object; otherwise her performance cannot reflect her actual cognitive ability. When the investigation looks at complex behaviors of older babies, such as imitation, the baby may simply refuse the task and do something else instead.

SIMPLE FORMS OF LEARNING

Learning is said to have occurred when a change in behavior follows an experience. This change in behavior lasts for a relatively long time, sometimes for one's entire life, so it is different from more temporary alterations like those due to illness or fatigue. The change that comes with learning is based on experience, so it is different from changes due to aging or physical growth.

When adults think about their own learning, they often recall academic experience and the deliberate effort required to commit information to memory. Some simple forms of learning, however, appear almost effortless. They occur because it is the nature of the organism to learn, not because there has been an attempt to practice or "study." These simple forms of learning are found in newborn infants as well as in nonhumans.

Habituation

A learned behavior change called *habituation* occurs in full-term newborns and, under some circumstances, in preterm babies. As we discussed before,

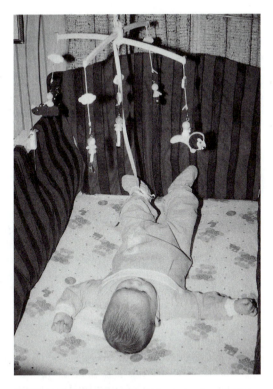

In the mobile conjugate reinforcement paradigm, the baby's ankle is tied to the mobile by a ribbon, so that kicking activates the mobile.

decrement: a reduction; from the Latin *decrescere* (to decrease).

habituation involves a response **decrement**—a reduction in behavior such as visual scanning directed toward an object.

A baby initially responds to a visible stimulus with attention and visual activity, which shows that he is looking at the stimulus. After the stimulus has been presented repeatedly, the baby will spend less time looking. The baby, at this point, is said to have habituated to the stimulus. If the now-familiar stimulus is removed and subsequently brought back again, the baby will respond with a brief period of scanning (dishabituation) and will then rapidly habituate once more. If a new stimulus is introduced that is so similar to the first that the baby cannot tell the difference, the baby will quickly reduce looking. A new and obviously different stimulus, on the other hand, will be scanned vigorously until the baby habituates to that stimulus as well.

Habituation has been spoken of as a forerunner of category formation (Rovee-Collier, 1987). The habituating infant has to pay attention to specific features of the stimulus and respond to similarities and differences—the basic task that is carried to a higher level when an object is treated as part of a category.

APPLICATIONS & ARGUMENTS
Discipline, Child Abuse, and Expectations About Cognition

Guidance and discipline are proper tasks of a parent, but they can turn into abusive treatment if the parent misunderstands an infant's cognitive abilities. The parent who assumes the baby possesses adult memory, decision, and intention is likely to judge the baby as "disobeying" when the infant actually has no idea what is going on. Repeated punishment may follow, as the parent believes that the baby is deliberately rebellious.

Adolescent parents are likely to expect a baby to be more mature in many areas than is realistic. A 2-week-old's accidental blow against the mother's face may be interpreted as deliberate, and the mother may insist that the baby "knows it hurts because I say 'ouch.'" It would not be surprising if this mother slapped her baby for his behavior—an action that many would consider abusive because of the child's age (if for no other reason).

Biting an infant or toddler would probably be classified as abusive, but it is a common reaction to a bite from a child. The parent may argue that the action is needed "to show her what it feels like." The assumption, of course, is that the baby is capable of learning, from the pain of a bite, that her own bite caused a similar experience in another person. For such learning to occur, the baby would need to have a sophisticated "theory of mind" that would recognize that other people have experiences and wishes. The infant would also need to categorize the two bites as similar enough to have the same effect. Finally, the infant would need to have a sufficient concept of the self to feel a negative social emotion such as shame or guilt after recognizing that she has hurt someone.

Classical Conditioning

contingency: an event dependent on a previous event; from the Latin *com-* (with), *tangere* (to touch).

One issue in simple learning has to do with **contingencies;** the infant learns when one event is likely to be accompanied or followed by another event. *Classical conditioning* is a form of contingency learning in which the baby learns that one event reliably follows another. The first event, in fact, comes to act as a signal that the second is to occur, and it produces a behavior that used to be produced only by the second event.

For classical conditioning to occur, certain circumstances must be in place. First, there must be a stimulus event that reliably brings about a detectable response. For example, the stimulus of a puff of air against the eye reliably brings about a reflex eye-blink reaction. The puff of air in this case is referred to as an *unconditional stimulus* because it always has the same effect and does not depend on conditions, and the eye blink is termed the *unconditional response* for the same reason.

The second set of circumstances necessary for classical conditioning involves an irrelevant stimulus, one that does not cause the eye blink (or other response under consideration). The irrelevant stimulus—a bell, for example—must now occur shortly before the unconditional stimulus on a number of occasions. (How shortly before and how many times depends on the baby's age.) After the pairing has occurred enough times, the eye blink begins to occur in response to the bell alone. Then classical conditioning has taken place, and the bell has become a *conditional stimulus*. The eye blink, somewhat reduced in magnitude, is a *conditional response*. The connection between them is conditional upon the experience of the occurrence of bell and puff in a predictable sequence. If the bell is now experienced a number of times without being followed by the puff of air, the conditioning will be extinguished. After extinction, the bell is no longer followed by the eye blink.

It is likely that emotional responses are most often classically conditioned in infants. For example, the infant sees the white coat of the doctor or nurse and soon afterward experiences the pain of a hypodermic injection, followed unconditionally by crying and distress. In the future, the sight of the white coat may be a conditional stimulus that will produce crying. The response may even generalize to white coats outside the doctor's office, so the infant shrieks at the sight of a waiter in a restaurant. (In pediatric hospitals, care is sometimes taken to have nurses who do feeding and other tasks wear very different clothing from staff members who must carry out painful procedures like changing surgical dressings.) An example of the conditioning of emotional responses even in the very immature infant comes from a study on preterm infants between 28 and 38 weeks GA. These babies experienced frequent heel-stick procedures to obtain blood samples. Over time, they began to show similar but not identical responses to a "sham" heel stick that did not draw blood and to a real heel stick (Johnson, Stevens, Yang, & Horton, 1996). The sensations of having the heel grasped and swabbed with alcohol had come to act as a conditional stimulus that produced some of the physiologically measured emotional changes previously called out by the real heel stick.

aversive: repulsive; from the Latin *ab-* (away from), *vergere* (to bend).

Classical **aversive** conditioning occurs when an irrelevant stimulus is followed by an unpleasant event. A common example in adulthood involves eating a harmless food and later vomiting for unrelated reasons; the food may become disliked and avoided even though it was well liked before. One infant was seen to refuse milk for almost a year after lifting a slightly overheated bottle and having milk squirt in his face twice within a few minutes. The milk was not hot enough to burn, but the unpleasant surprise was enough to cause him to avoid milk (juice was still accepted in a bottle). Aversive conditioning happens very quickly, sometimes after only one or two experiences. Although classical aversive conditioning has been said to occur primarily after crawling and walking begin (Rovee-Collier, 1987), it can cause problems if a very young breast-fed baby accidentally has her air supply cut off by the breast pressing against her nose. After a couple of experiences of this kind, the baby will fight and scream when held in the nursing position, and it will not be possible to breast-feed her (Gunther, 1970).

Instrumental Conditioning

Instrumental (sometimes called *operant*) conditioning is another form of contingency learning. In this case, the infant learns that certain actions of his will be followed by desirable events such as food or something interesting to see. He may also learn that this contingency holds in some circumstances but not in others.

Instrumental conditioning involves actions that a baby performs spontaneously (that is, we adult observers cannot tell why they occur). Some events that follow those actions may make them occur more frequently. When this happens, instrumental conditioning has taken place. The events that followed the actions and led to the increase in frequency are called *reinforcers*. If reinforcers are later withheld, the frequency of the behavior will gradually be reduced to its original baseline level.

A common misunderstanding about reinforcers involves the distinction between positive and negative reinforcers. The term *negative reinforcement* is commonly used in the mass media to mean the same thing as "punishment," something you do to get rid of a behavior you dislike. This is a mistake. Positive and negative reinforcers have exactly the same effect on behavior; when they follow a behavior, the behavior subsequently occurs more often. A positive reinforcer is generally an event that most of us would see as desirable or rewarding, but an angry, punishing adult may provide positive reinforcement for a child who is alone and frightened or who gets little attention. A negative reinforcer does involve an unpleasant, aversive situation, but it is the *escape* from the situation that is the reinforcer. For example, one occasionally finds a parent who will spank a toddler until he cries and then will stop spanking; crying becomes more frequent because it is negatively reinforced by the escape from spanking that follows.

Differences in the occurrences of reinforcers are important in the maintenance of instrumentally conditioned behavior; different patterns of reinforcement are called *schedules* of reinforcement. When a behavior has been reinforced every time it occurs, removal of the reinforcement is followed by rapid extinction (return of the frequency to baseline). When the behavior has been reinforced only occasionally, it will take much longer to extinguish when reinforcement no longer occurs.

Why, you may be wondering, would reinforcement occur only now and then? The answer is that situations in real life are complicated; things do not always work as they are expected to, and adults are not always paying attention. The baby who would be reinforced for grabbing the cat's tail by feeling the interesting furry sensation and seeing the animal's antics will not always make a successful grab; she may miss, or the cat may get smart and leave. When the reinforcement is the deliberate act of an adult, inattention may interfere. For example, a toddler's first successful toilet "performance" is often followed by many actions intended as reinforcers: hand clapping, enthusiastic cries of "good boy" or "good girl," telephone calls to Daddy or Grandma with the good news. As the weeks go by, however, the enthusiasm moderates. The parents may have to remind themselves to give a positive response. Finally, the day will come when a parent is talking on the phone or dealing with a leaking washing machine and there is no attempt at reinforcement whatsoever. Because the change has been gradual, however (and because there are reinforcers other than what adults give), the behavior does not return to baseline.

A real-life example of schedules of reinforcement at work involves the baby of 15 months who has begun to protest being left alone in her bed. (Please note that this example involves a 15-month-old; a much younger baby would need more immediate responsiveness to her distress.) The baby cries and calls to her parents, who go to her because they are afraid she has a real problem. After some weeks of this, the parents realize that they are spending every evening in this pursuit and that there are more calls every evening. If, like most U.S. parents, they feel the baby should "learn independence," they will be concerned and want the behavior to stop. They may realize or be told that they have been reinforcing the very behavior they object to. The parents now decide to withhold reinforcement by refusing to go to the baby no matter how she screams. For several evenings, they sit for hours with their hands over their ears while the baby cries brokenheartedly until she falls asleep. The duration of crying begins to diminish. But, perhaps on the fourth or fifth night, one of the parents breaks the resolution. There may be some concern because the baby was not well during the day, or one parent may become frustrated enough to go in and yell at the baby. It does not matter whether the parent goes to the baby for comforting or for punitive purposes; from the baby's point of view, the presence of the parent is reinforcing, and whatever behavior preceded it will become more frequent. The parents have accidentally moved from a regular to an occasional schedule of reinforcement and have set up a situation in which extinction will take much longer. The baby has essentially learned that you have to cry for four nights to get a parent to come.

Another real-life example of the effect of schedules of reinforcement is the *time-out* approach. Time-out is a temporary isolation of a young child who has been doing something the caregiver objects to. The original idea was that time-out would prevent any ongoing reinforcement of the behavior and would thus reduce its frequency. The approach is frequently suggested to parents as an alternative to physical punishment. Unfortunately, much advice on this topic simply "prescribes" a number of minutes of isolation based on the child's age, without any consideration of whether the undesirable behavior is being reinforced or whether reinforcement can be withheld. If the child experiences reinforcement during time-out (because of other people's looks or comments), the behavior will not be reduced. If the child goes straight back into the reinforcing situation after the time-out, all that has happened is a change in the schedule of reinforcement, which will in fact *strengthen* the unwanted behavior. Time-out can be a useful strategy for changing some behaviors, but its effective use requires an analysis of the situation, not a "cookbook" approach.

Although instrumental conditioning can occur in newborns, you should not imagine that it can be used to structure a baby's behavior along lines ideal for a parent. For one thing, instrumental conditioning can be used only to change the frequencies of behaviors. Generally speaking, only behaviors that actually occur can be reinforced (but see the section on intervention later in this chapter for a more complete discussion). In a newborn, reinforceable behaviors will be things like sucking, eye movement, and head turning. As the infant gets older, more varieties of behavior emerge.

A second limitation on instrumental conditioning has to do with discrimination. Instrumental conditioning often involves situational learning; the baby learns that mouth opening is followed by food when the mother has a spoon in her hand but not when she doesn't. If the baby cannot discriminate or is not interested in the events that define the situation, he or she will not show instrumental conditioning. For example, the work of Elliott Blass (described by Kolata, 1987b) started with discrimination learning involving touch. The researcher stroked a newborn's forehead and then presented a sweet solution that the baby could suck if he turned his head to the left. After a few repetitions, the baby would turn to the left as soon as he felt the touch on his forehead. When the sweet solution was withheld after the touch, the baby cried.

Further work by Blass used sounds as signals for the sweet solution, but only one type of sound—a click—led to conditioning of head turning. A "shh" sound, a "ting" sound, and a "psst" sound were also tried, but the babies did not make the connection with the availability of the sweet solution (Kolata, 1987b). Apparently, not all stimuli are equally interesting or discriminable for the very young infant.

COGNITIVE DEVELOPMENT: THEORIES AND ISSUES

Of all the things that are known about infant cognition, the most obvious is that it develops. The older baby knows more than the younger baby does and can do more with what she knows than the younger baby can. When we compare individual babies, there seem to be similarities in the sequences (if not the ages) of reaching particular cognitive abilities.

Theories of cognitive development attempt to tie together these facts into coherent frameworks. They also make some assumptions about the mechanisms of development: how and why cognitive change occurs. In addition, theories lead to specific hypotheses and research approaches.

The following discussion of theories of cognitive development is very different from one that might have been written in 1980. Since that date, there has been an extraordinary alteration in cognitive development theories and consequent changes in research in this area. An important change in orientation has been toward a stress on the "competent infant"—a concern with finding what the baby can do rather than what she cannot do (Butterworth, 1990b).

Our discussion of cognitive development theories will deal with three basic approaches: (1) traditional constructivist theory, (2) connectionist theory, and (3) dynamic systems theory (Thelen & Smith, 1994).

Traditional Constructivist Theory

For decades, the only real theory of cognitive development (as opposed to learning) was that of the Swiss psychologist Jean Piaget, whose work became available in translation in the 1950s. Piaget's work is no longer in the forefront of cognitive development theory, but it is worth attention for a number of reasons. Many of the problems dealt with by modern theorists date back to Piaget's work, and the very language used to describe events is in many cases Piagetian. In addition, approaches to intervention and early education are often based on a foundation of Piagetian terms and concepts, so you would be severely handicapped in learning more about cognitive development issues if you were unfamiliar with Piaget.

Piaget's approach to cognitive development was strongly biological and assumed that evolution had determined a sequence of developmental events that occurred in each human being. Each stage of cognitive development was a period when cognitive functioning was qualitatively different than it was at any other period. Although Piaget discussed cognitive development as it proceeded through adolescence, our emphasis will naturally be on his description of events in the first two years of life. Piaget referred to this as the *sensorimotor period;* all learning during this time was considered to result from sensory input and motor activity, rather than from experiences like verbal instruction or from abstract thought. Understanding of the world was constructed as a consequence of experience.

schema: in this context, a way of solving a problem or responding to the environment; from the Latin *schema* (arrangement).

Piaget described cognitive events in the sensorimotor period in terms of **schemas**—essentially, ways of dealing with the environment and its problems. A schema could be a simple action like sucking, or it could be a more advanced ability like uncovering something in order to see it. One important type of schema was the *circular reaction,* a stereotyped, repeated, spontaneous activity. New schemas were said to develop from old ones through two processes: (1) **assimilation,** or applying old schemas to novel situations, and (2) **accommodation,** or altering a schema so it worked better. (For example, a baby who reflexively sucks her mother's nipple can assimilate the nipple of a bottle and suck it in a similar way; she can accommodate by changing the sucking pattern so that she has two slightly different schemas, one that works well for the breast and one that works well for the bottle.)

assimilation: in this context, the application of an old schema to a new situation; from the Latin *assimilare* (to make similar).

accommodation: in this context, to alter an old schema after having new experiences; from the Latin *accommodare* (to make suitable).

Piaget described six substages within the sensorimotor period. The first stage, in the first month of life, was the *reflex* stage; all available schemas at this point were reflex reactions such as rooting or tongue-thrusting. All later schemas developed out of these as a result of assimilation and accommodation.

The second sensorimotor stage was the stage of *primary circular reactions,* from about 1 to 4 months. This period was characterized by stereotyped, repeated, spontaneous activities that were carried out for their own sake, not for reinforcement or because they had an interesting effect. Schemas like kicking or cooing were exercised simply because the baby could do them.

The third stage was the stage of *secondary circular reactions,* from about 4 to about 8 months. The baby at this point began to notice the impact of his activities, and when they caused interesting events to occur, he would keep on looking, pushing, or sucking to prolong the interesting spectacle. If the interesting event stopped, though, the baby would stop too, apparently unable to see that the interesting event could be made to start again.

The fourth sensorimotor stage was seen as a time of crucial cognitive advancement. From about 8 to about 12 months, the baby was in the stage of *coordination of secondary schemas.* Schemas from the stage of secondary circular reactions, such as looking, reaching, and grabbing, were deployed with a sequence and timing that would yield new accomplishments. A great breakthrough of this stage was the achievement of *object permanence,* the ability to remember and find a hidden object.

The fifth stage, from about 12 to about 18 months, was the stage of *tertiary circular reactions.* These repeated, stereotyped activities were directed toward initiating interesting events and tended to concentrate on the new schemas of voluntary release: dropping and throwing. Active, hands-on experimentation characterized the toddler's life at this point.

The final sensorimotor stage, from 18 to about 24 months, was clearly a bridge to more advanced cognitive abilities. It involved invention of new means through mental combinations. The baby was no longer locked into hands-on investigation of the world but was able to solve some problems by thinking. She could represent the outside world symbolically, in thought and, increasingly, by words. In Piaget's view, the infant gradually constructed an understanding of the real world, as schemas and experiences interacted.

Connectionist Theories

Connectionist theories of cognitive development have compared cognition to mechanical events rather than to biological ones. For some years, the major analogy with which connectionists worked was that cognition was like a computer program. More recently, and as some of the facts about the nervous system noted in Chapter 7 have become known, a shift to a brain metaphor has occurred (Holyoak, 1987). That is, cognitive events are thought of as following something like the rules of neural functioning rather than as a separate set of rules.

One connectionist approach uses the concept of *parallel distributed processing* (PDP) (Holyoak, 1987). PDP assumes that information processing is based on patterns of activation of neuronlike "units" that communicate via synapselike "connections." Like neural communication, this transmission of information can either excite or inhibit a unit. Input into this system is caused directly by features of the environment. Processing can involve a middle layer of units, and responses are a function of output units.

Developmental change in cognition, then, results from effects of experience (environmental input) on activation of units and connections. The probability of the activation of a unit is related to the frequency with which it has been activated before, as well as to the particular other units activated at the time; so the history of activation and the present circumstances operate together to determine what will happen at a given point in development.

Why, then, do the stages Piaget discussed seem like a reasonable description of a baby's cognitive development? If experience plays such a strong role, why is cognitive development so orderly? Babies have different experiences, so why do they not show much greater variability in developmental sequences? The answer is that babies need certain things to survive, so there are limits to the kinds of experiences they can have and still live; therefore, all living babies have had considerable similarities in experience. They also share physical growth patterns and motor development, so they may well have had more shared than different experiences at a given age. This would account for the general orderliness of cognitive change in infancy within the framework of connectionist theory.

Dynamic Systems Theory

Dynamic systems theory is a relatively recent and potentially very powerful approach to cognitive development. As we have noted before, the basic tenet of dynamic systems theory is that any system (for example, an infant, its actions, and its environment) is self-organizing. It is the nature of the dynamic action system to form a pattern and for the pattern to change; the pattern does not have to be forced on the system by a set of rules like genetic programming: "Although behavior and development appear structured, there are no structures. Although behavior and development appear rule-driven, there are no rules" (Thelen & Smith, 1994, p. 56).

Although there are "no rules," dynamic systems theory assumes that certain principles are involved in self-organization. Initially, many behavioral outcomes are possible. When one factor occurs frequently, however, it can become an *order parameter* that helps limit the number of possible outcomes. An infant's visual, auditory, and motor abilities at any given time could all be order parameters around which cognitive functioning could organize. Other order parameters could have to do with the environment. For example, a depressed mother might rarely play with the baby, so fewer opportunities than normal would be present for the baby to learn about her environment; a baby who experienced parental play with a rolling toy could learn earlier about the "collision rules" discussed later in this chapter. A baby cared for in a series of foster homes with different routines might be slower to show surprise at unusual events than would an infant for whom a stable home routine offered an order parameter of familiarity to which the unusual could be compared.

When the system self-organizes around an order parameter, it begins to follow a small number of modes of behavior that the system "prefers" over other modes (Thelen & Smith, 1994, p. 56). Such a mode is called an *attractor state*. A baby's length of waking time could function as an attractor state to help determine the occurrence of other functions like fatigue, crying, and attentiveness. When walking begins, the baby's fascination with the new ability is an attractor state that increases walking time, makes the infant less interested in being carried, and temporarily slows development of other skills, like speech. An attractor state increases the time the baby spends in a particular activity and decreases the time and energy put into other actions. Attractor states can also make other related activities more likely; the baby who smiles and vocalizes is more often approached by adults and given chances for social play.

A particular self-organization can go on functioning even though some elements change. Body temperature, for instance, is maintained within a certain range even though the environment gets quite hot or quite cold. But let the environmental temperature go beyond a certain limit, and body temperature suddenly begins to rise or fall. This sort of dramatic change in response to a small alteration is called a *phase shift.* With respect to cognitive development, a phase shift to a new level of functioning might occur when a baby had just one additional experience of a type he had had before. The result is a transition to what Piaget would call a new stage.

An important aspect of dynamic systems theory is the stress on the simultaneous functioning of all components of the organism and of the environment. Cognition is seen as arising out of perception, motor abilities, states of arousal, and all the other characteristics the infant has at a given time, as well as the events that are occurring and that have occurred in the past in the environment.

Some Issues for Cognitive Development Theories

As was mentioned earlier, the concept of a stage of development is a source of concern for theories of cognitive development. Is the stage "in" the infant, or is it in our thinking about the infant? Are stages simply artifacts of the ways we ask questions about cognitive development? Although there seem to be abrupt changes in the quality of cognitive and other behavior, we might be able to see that the change is a gradual one if we only took measurements close enough together. Where stage concepts are used, they need to take into account that it is possible when under stress to **regress** to the performance quality of an earlier stage, and that the infant may show abilities when dealing only with certain kinds of information but not with others. Piaget referred to the latter phenomenon as **décalage.**

A second problem for theorists of cognitive development involves domains of thinking. The idea here is that the mind is "compartmentalized" in such a way that thinking about human beings (for example) may follow different rules from thinking about inanimate objects (Wellman & Gelman, 1992).

Cognitive development theories also need to deal with the question of continuities and discontinuities (Rutter, 1987). The general assumption that early experience leads directly to changes that in turn directly cause other changes—that development is continuous—is not necessarily correct. Old structures or processes could be replaced by new ones, leading to reorganization and discontinuous developmental events.

Finally, theories of cognitive development need to deal with issues about timing of events. In previous chapters, we discussed the idea of critical or sensitive periods: biologically determined times when, for good or ill, events

regress: to return to an earlier stage; from the Latin *re-* (back, again), *gradi* (to go).

décalage: the operation of one cognitive stage with respect to some kinds of problems, and an earlier or later one with respect to other kinds; from the French *décalage* (displacement in space or time).

in the environment have unusually powerful effects. The idea of biological critical periods is not usually emphasized in the study of cognitive development (although we will see its relevance to language development in Chapter 11). However, there recently has been some consideration of the influence of the infant's own history of experiences on his ability to integrate new information with old. It has been suggested that a period called a *time window* helps to determine this (Rovee-Collier, 1995).

A time window is a period within which new information can be connected with experiences that occurred earlier in the same period; *connection* in this case refers to the kind of processing involved in habituation, for example, or in forming a category, or in classical conditioning of an association. The time window opens when an experience occurs and shuts again when it has been forgotten. The longer the time window is open, the more information can be connected with the initial event. Older babies have longer time windows, and events that encourage memory retention also keep time windows open for a longer period. An important idea about time windows is that events at different points in the period may have different effects, and events occurring late in the time window may have an especially powerful influence on memory: "New information that is encountered late in the time window . . . may facilitate retention of that information at the expense of other components of the original memory" (Rovee-Collier, 1995, p. 148).

ATTENTION, INTENTION, OBJECT
Past History

Traditional views of early cognitive development taught that the young infant responds to sensory stimulation but is unaware of the environment as a coherent, patterned experience. The infant was described as experiencing a disconnected series of events without discriminating which ones came from outside and which came from inside the self. Shapes, colors, sounds, pains, movement sensations, touches, and smells were all experienced separately and with equal lack of meaning. When there was a focus, it was on internal sensations; for example, the infant was thought to experience her own activity without making any connection with the sights or sounds she produced.

According to this view, the infant took many months of experience and maturation to develop an *object concept:* the understanding that an object is outside the self, that it exists permanently even when it cannot be seen (with certain exceptions), and that it is subject to particular physical laws. In Piaget's view, the concept of object permanence did not emerge until the age of 8 to 12 months, when the infant could uncover an object that had been covered while she watched. This understanding of physical laws developed during the period of tertiary circular reactions in the first half of the second year.

The traditional emphasis was clearly on what babies could not do rather than on any indication of early competence.

APPLICATIONS & ARGUMENTS
Helping the Baby Learn to Wait

When children and adults need to use their cognitive skills, one ability is almost essential: they must be able to *wait* before they do things. Impulsiveness leads to errors, but the reflective person, who thinks things over before deciding, is likely to be much more accurate. Failure to wait often interferes with problem solving, even if the problem is one the person understands perfectly well.

How does a baby learn to wait? How does he postpone the gratification of acting? Caregivers can help in the slow process of becoming reflective.

Paradoxically, waiting becomes easier when the baby is not made to wait too long. When food or comfort appear before there is great distress, the infant learns a sense of trust and confidence that his needs will eventually be satisfied. When waiting too often goes on too long, it begins to produce a sense that the goal will never be reached and a wish to grab as fast as possible at gratification. The baby who is teased and is deliberately made uncertain begins to respond to waiting with rage.

Language can provide a great deal of help for the baby who is mastering waiting. A caregiver can give verbal cues like "Wait just a minute," "Almost ready," or "We can't touch it yet." Whatever helps the development of language comprehension will thus help with waiting.

Waiting is just one example of inhibition of behavior. There are many circumstances in which a baby can learn to slow down a behavior or make it less intense. We noted in an earlier chapter that the breast-fed baby must learn not to bite her mother's nipple; the baby brings her jaws close together while sucking, but learns not to bring them too close. Learning to pat another person or a pet gently is another aspect of inhibition that is probably related to learning to wait.

Current Work: Attention and Intention

Current thinking focuses on what babies can do. From the earliest weeks, an infant displays attention to objects. The baby's attentiveness depends both on characteristics of the object itself and on the baby's experiential and developmental history. *Attention*, which is usually considered in terms of orienting or turning toward a stimulus and the subsequent visual scanning or touching, involves three phases (DeGangi & Porges, 1990). The first, *attention getting*, is a response to novel objects or to salient ones, such as food when the baby is hungry. The second, *attention holding*, involves continued scanning or touching and is a response to novel, meaningful, or complex events. Finally, *attention releasing* occurs. These attentional changes occur in response to objects, not "in a vacuum" or in response to a featureless environment. The baby acts as if his awareness of the object parallels an adult's, although of course we cannot know in any direct way what the baby is experiencing.

The infant's attention changes with age. This is especially true of the attention releasing or habituation function. Measurement of the movement of fetuses in response to sounds suggests that habituation occurs even before birth (Hepper & Shahidullah, 1992). A baby in the first month may show what has been called "obligatory attention"; she may gaze at an object for a long time and seem distressed (M. Johnson, 1993). Under the right circumstances, however, even newborns show habituation, in the reduction of their scanning of an object after attention has continued for a time (Fantz, 1964; Slater, Morrison, & Rose, 1984).

Although attention is usually thought of as involving one stimulus only, it appears that responses to other stimuli are also influenced by attentional state. In one study with 4-month-olds (Anthony & Graham, 1983), babies who were watching interesting pictures (slides of smiling faces) were more likely to blink if a flash of light was introduced than were babies who were watching "dull" blank slides.

Attention and habituation may be cognitive factors that both influence and are influenced by emotional development (DeGangi & Porges, 1990). As we will discuss in Chapter 12, one early step in emotional development is self-regulation, the ability to keep somewhat calm even when hungry or uncomfortable. The process of self-regulation involves techniques of shifting attention away from the distress—sucking the thumb or looking at the hands, for instance. The baby who remains unregulated is handicapped in later cognitive development because he is rarely calm, alert, and ready to learn. He will also be slowed in moving to later emotional development because he is rarely attentive to other people's actions.

The display of *intention* is a sticky issue. If an infant shows the intention to act in a particular way toward an object, we can infer that she understands that the object is outside her and subject to physical events. The circumstances under which we can assume that there is intention are debatable, of course (Rutkowska, 1993), but some actions of very young infants have been considered as showing intention, or at least as precursors of intention (Trevarthen, 1982). Intentionality is suggested by behavior like that of very young infants, who turn their heads and cry when it looks as though an object is approaching and will strike them (Yonas, Pettersen, & Lockman, 1979).

Inanimate Objects Versus Humans

Human beings share some but not all characteristics of inanimate objects and so may be regarded as "objects" of a specialized nature. Nevertheless, human beings follow some rules of their own, and an infant's understanding of the world will be very limited unless she comprehends this. As a matter of fact, infants show evidence of discriminating human beings from objects at an early age.

Even in the first weeks, an infant's movements shown in response to humans are different from those shown to objects (Trevarthen, 1982). The response to an object is a prereaching movement; the hand is opened and raised toward the object and swept downward while the fingers close in a grasping movement (all too fast to see unless it is slowed down on film). Responses to a person include a greeting gesture, in which the open hand is briefly raised at the baby's side, and prespeech movements, in which the tongue and lips are moved and bubbles are blown, indicating that air is traveling across the tongue.

Emotional responses to humans and to objects are different, too. For example, 3-month-olds show distress when a person in front of them looks blankly and does not respond to the babies' sociable actions. This still-face effect leads to crying and depressed, withdrawn behavior if it goes on long enough. A toy that moves and makes sounds attracts attention and leads to smiles and vocalization in 3-month-olds, too, but if the toy stays motionless and silent, no still-face effect is seen (Ellsworth, Muir, & Haines, 1993).

Although infants show particular attention to people from an early age, especially to other babies (Butterworth, 1990a), they are surprisingly late in learning to recognize their own reflections. Self-mirror-recognition does not occur until between 15 and 18 months. The technique for testing this recognition, and its relevance to emotional development, will be discussed in Chapter 12.

Rules about Objects

An understanding of how the world works is based in part on a comprehension of the many rules that govern objects. Simply understanding that an

TABLE 10.1 *Like other aspects of development, the ability to recognize the self in a mirror emerges from early steps toward understanding the nature of the self and of others.*

Age	Behavior	Achievement
3–8 months	Looks into mirror and behaves socially toward image; recognizes others in mirror; may look back and forth from other to image	Shows attraction to images of others
8–12 months	Finds objects attached to body by looking in mirror; can tell whether video image of self is performing same or different movements as self; likes to play peek-a-boo with mirror self	Is aware of self as permanent object
12–15 months	Uses mirror to find others; can tell video image of self from those of others	Differentiates self from others
15 months on	Recognizes own face; looks embarrassed when sees self in mirror; notices rouge on nose in mirror image	Recognizes own facial features

Source: Based on Butterworth, 1990.

object is outside you and has an existence of its own does not explain all that needs to be known.

Research on a number of rules about objects has shown that babies understand a good deal about the physical world, and at an earlier age than used to be thought. Evidence clearly supports a good deal of sophistication in this area by age 2 or 3 months. Some authors have asserted that the baby begins life with an advanced understanding of objects (Spelke, 1985). However, a good deal of research suggests that there is developmental change in this area during the first year or so. The following sections will describe work that has revealed the development of understanding of certain rules about objects, using the violation-of-expectation method described in "Research Methods" in this chapter.

Support rules   Older children and adults understand very well that an object will fall unless a large enough amount of its surface is on top of another object that is itself supported in some way. A box that is pushed to and beyond the edge of a platform it is resting on will certainly fall at the point where it loses all contact with the platform, and probably a good deal before that. But 3-month-olds expect a box not to fall as long as it touches the top or side of the platform. At 4½ to 5½ months, they realize that only contact with the top of the platform gives support; they also begin to understand that the amount of

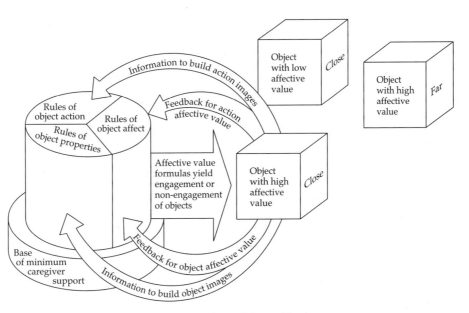

Environmental Conditions of Setting

Many factors interact to determine the infant's application of a rule at a given time.
(Source: Pierce, 1991)

the box in contact with the platform determines whether it will fall, but initially they think that as small an amount as 15% of the box in contact will keep it stable. By 6½ months, they know that the box will fall unless a large proportion of its bottom is on the platform (Baillargeon, 1994).

Collision rules   Older children and adults understand that when one object collides with another, the struck object will move unless it is much larger than the striking object. The relative size of the objects is one factor that determines what will happen. In one study (Baillargeon, 1994), a bright-colored cylinder was rolled down a ramp to hit a toy bug. Even at age 2½ months, infants expected the bug not to move unless it was hit and were surprised if the bug moved when the cylinder had been stopped by a barrier. However, it was not until 5½ to 6½ months that they were surprised when a small cylinder pushed the bug farther than a large one did.

Unveiling rules   Older children and adults know that a hidden object still exists, and they also know that the bulge a hidden object makes under its cover is related to the size of the object. At 9½ months, babies are not surprised when a large toy dog is retrieved from under a cover with a small bulge in it, but by 12½ months they expect a small toy to come out from under a cover with a small bulge (Baillargeon, 1994).

Constancy rules   Older children and adults recognize an object as having the same shape even though they see it at an angle such that the retinal image is severely distorted. For example, a saucer is recognized as circular no matter what angle it is seen from, but if it is held between a lamp and a piece of paper and rotated in various directions, someone looking at the shadow on the paper will see that the shape is constantly changing. Our ability to attend to the real shape of the object is called *shape constancy. Size constancy* is a similar ability to attend to the real size of an object even though the size of its image changes as it approaches or recedes.

Without these and other constancies, we would perceive the world as altering with every motion we made or observed—a fantastically confusing situation. It appears that young infants have both size and shape constancy (Bower, 1989). When contact with an object is not possible, however, the infant may show poor size judgement (just as adults do). Older babies enthusiastically accept the idea that one could reach for the moon; one 15-month-old explained why the moon could not be seen one night by declaring that cats had jumped up and eaten it!

Causality rules   Although older children and adults can certainly become confused about cause-and-effect relationships (as superstitions show us), they have some basic ideas about how causes can operate. One approach to the study of infants' understanding of causality involves launching events; when one object moves until it touches a second and the second then moves, an older person is likely to conclude that the touch caused the motion of the second object. Seven-month-olds seem to expect launching to occur only when the second object is actually touched by the first and when there is no delay in the movement of the second. Ten-month-olds are less rigid, however, and are not surprised when the second object moves in an ambiguous situation (Oakes, 1944). The older infant seems to accept that the rules about causality can be complex.

Numerosity rules   When most of us recall our early struggles with arithmetic, it is hard to imagine that infants have a concept of number. However, several studies have shown that some basic concepts about small numbers are present at an early age. Seven-month-olds, for example, prefer to look at pictures that show the same number of objects as the number of sounds the baby hears simultaneously; if the baby hears two drumbeats, she looks at a picture with two rather than three objects in it (Starkey, Spelke, & Gelman, 1983).

The simple recognition of patterns that could allow the baby to tell three from two has been called *subitizing*, and some research in this area has attributed infants' responses to numbers to this sort of immediate perceptual response. There does seem to be some evidence that infants have some genuine comprehension of small numbers, however. When 5-month-olds see an object added to or subtracted from other objects behind a screen and then the screen is removed, revealing the wrong number of objects, the babies show their surprise by looking at the scene for a longer time than they do when the right number is revealed (Wynn, 1992). Similarly, 5-month-olds can use the number of objects shown in a slide to find out where (left or right) the picture will appear in the next slide (Canfield & Smith, 1996).

Object Permanence and the A̅B Problem

The term *object permanence* refers to the awareness that a hidden object still exists and could reappear or be found. (This is *generally* true about objects, of course, because something might dissolve in water or be burned to ashes and no longer exist in the same form.) Object permanence has traditionally been described as occurring between 8 and 12 months and can easily be demonstrated at that point in several ways. For example, with a baby who has not yet mastered the idea of object permanence, an attempt to play peek-a-boo will fall flat. To demonstrate this, get the baby's interest, and then cover your face with your hands. If you peek between your fingers, you will see that the baby simply looks away and is no longer paying attention when you uncover your face. Another attempt a few months later will lead to fascinated, rather anxious gazing at your covered face, followed by delighted laughter when you reveal yourself.

In the same way, the reaction to a covered toy changes with age. A 7-month-old will look intently at your car keys and prepare to grab them, but if you quickly throw a scarf over them, she simply stops and turns away. Even if she accidentally dislodges the scarf and reveals the keys, she is likely not to notice them. A month or two later, though, she will probably push the scarf away and triumphantly seize the keys. When this sort of informal observation

Sequence of events

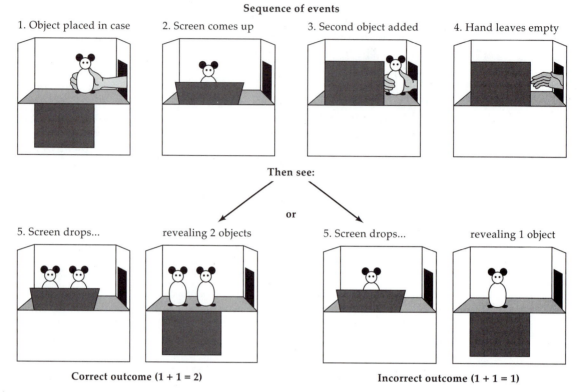

1. Object placed in case   2. Screen comes up   3. Second object added   4. Hand leaves empty

Then see:

or

5. Screen drops...   revealing 2 objects   5. Screen drops...   revealing 1 object

Correct outcome (1 + 1 = 2)   **Incorrect outcome (1 + 1 = 1)**

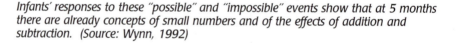

Which outcome is looked at longer?

Infants' responses to these "possible" and "impossible" events show that at 5 months there are already concepts of small numbers and of the effects of addition and subtraction. (Source: Wynn, 1992)

is used, object permanence seems to arise suddenly and dramatically. With finer measurement, however, we can see that the ability began to develop earlier and continues to refine itself for many months. (Indeed, we might question whether even adults develop perfect confidence in the existence of a person or object long unseen.)

When the baby is mature enough (at 8 months or so) to search for and find a hidden object, other tests show that his understanding is still far from complete. One of these tests, the $A\overline{B}$ (pronounced "A not B") task, may be the most researched topic in infant development. The "A" and "B" refer to two hiding places in which some interesting object can be concealed. The object is hidden under A (a bucket, perhaps) while the baby watches. As soon as she is allowed, the baby picks up the bucket and finds the toy. This is repeated several times, with the baby invariably succeeding in finding the toy. Now, the researcher takes the toy and hides it under B (a different bucket) while the baby watches. When allowed to search, the baby goes to work at once—and

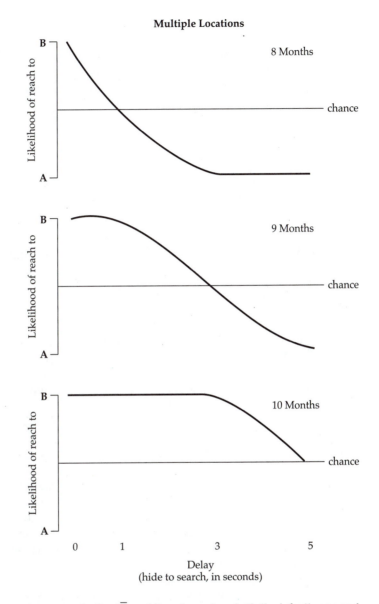

Responses to the A͞B problem depend on both the infant's age and the amount of time that passes before reaching is allowed. (Source: Thelen & Smith, 1994)

looks under A again. By 12 months, however, the baby systematically looks in the hiding place where she last saw the toy being put.

A number of factors help determine how well an infant solves the A͞B problem. One variable is the delay between the hiding and the baby's search. Even 8-month-olds sometimes solve the problem if there is no delay or if the delay is only 1 second, but they make the error if delayed for 3 or 5 seconds. As babies get older, they can deal with longer delays (Thelen & Smith, 1994).

An interesting elaboration on the A$\overline{B}$ task is A$\overline{B}$ with multiple wells (Diamond, Gruttenden, & Neiderman, 1994). Rather than having two hiding places, a larger number, arranged in a semi-circle, are used. Curiously, infants solve the A$\overline{B}$ task more often when there are many hiding places, perhaps simply because A and B are farther apart in this task.

More complex versions of the object permanence task were also worked out by Uzgiris and Hunt (1987); their variations include covering the object with more than one cover and hiding the object without letting the infant see where it was last visible. These more complicated tasks are not mastered until the preschool period.

INTERNAL REPRESENTATIONS AND PROCESSES

Unless a cognitive task is performed while a stimulus is still present, the task must involve some sort of internal representation or symbolization of events in the environment. For a baby to be surprised when an unusual event occurs implies that there must be some internal, mental representation of the familiar event to which the unfamiliar one can be compared.

Some research on cognitive development focuses on the functions of *internal representation*. The study of memory, for example, explores how long internal representations can last and under what conditions. Investigations of concepts and categories look at the infant's internal juggling and organizing of the ways in which events are represented.

Memory

The study of memory is concerned with internal representation, but, of course, it can measure only performance from which the representation can be inferred. In the study of adult memory, there are two basic types of performance: *recall*, where the learned task can be carried out at will, and *recognition*, where the learner can identify what was previously experienced. Essay tests and multiple choice tests can be examples of these types of performance. Memory can also be tested by the *savings* method, which measures how long it takes to relearn something that has been forgotten; if the second learning time is shorter than the original one, this indicates that some memory still exists even though recall is not possible.

preverbal: before speech is possible; from the Latin *prae* (before), *verbum* (word).

premobile: before movement is well developed; from the Latin *prae* (before), *movere* (to move).

Investigations of infant memories have to deal with performance that is possible for an infant. Recall is not a very likely measure for the young, **preverbal, premobile** infant because she cannot do much to show that she recalls. Savings can be demonstrated when a baby relearns an association (in classical conditioning, for example), and memory over periods of 10 days or more has been shown in this way for infants in the first month (Rovee-Collier & Boller, 1995).

Recognition can be shown in 2- to 6-month-olds by teaching them to kick using the mobile conjugate reinforcement paradigm described earlier (see "Research Methods"). The speed of learning and forgetting changes with age. Two-month-olds learn to kick to make the mobile move in 7 to 9 minutes and forget within 2 days; 3-month-olds take 4 to 6 minutes to learn and remember for 6 or 7 days; 6-month-olds take only 1 to 3 minutes to learn and remember for 15 or 16 days (Rovee-Collier & Boller, 1995). Infants 9 and 12 months and older remember for many weeks.

Memory reactivation is a technique that greatly improves the length of memory. In the case of learning to kick to move the mobile, this is simply a matter of showing the baby the mobile, or the cloth liner of the crib in which they learned, for 2 or 3 minutes on the day before they are tested. Following memory reactivation, the baby's performance can return to the level it was before forgetting, and 3-month-olds who have had two memory reactivations will remember for more than twice as long as they initially remembered. It should be noted however, that the memory does not return immediately after the reminder. At age 3 months, 8 hours must pass after the reminder before the memory begins to return, and it takes 3 days after the reminder for the memory to reach its peak of strength. By age 6 months, it takes only 1 hour for the memory to be reactivated, and the peak is reached 4 hours after the reminder (Rovee-Collier & Boller, 1995).

Young infants' memory ability depends in part on their attention to events, and this in turn is related to their emotional arousal. As we noted earlier, the baby who is upset a great deal does not have many calm, attentive periods in which to learn. In one study, 3-month-olds learned to kick to make a mobile move; all the babies remembered what they had learned after one day, but only those who did not cry at the time remembered after 7 days (Singer & Fagen, 1992). These issues about the relationship between emotion and cognition will be discussed further in Chapter 12.

Categories and Concepts

It would be hard to understand the world if we had to deal with every event as if it were utterly unique. Our comprehension, and that of infants, is based partly on thinking of similar events in similar ways. We establish categories, or groupings of events and objects that share some characteristics, and from them we develop concepts, or abstractions that consider the characteristics separately from the real events or objects. Categories and concepts can involve features and feature relations. A face, for example, could be thought of as a circle with two eyes somewhere in it or as a circle in which certain proportions of distances separated the features—or as both.

Infants initially seem to focus more on differences than on similarities and do not recognize a mobile as being the same if just one object on it has been changed (Rovee-Collier, 1995). Three-month-olds showed the same lack of reaction to a mobile that had the same features but whose feature relations (arrangement of parts) had been changed (Bhatt & Rovee-Collier, 1994).

Spontaneous behavior that involves categories and concepts does not become easily observable until the infant develops improved motor control and locomotion. One child at 10½ months, when looking at a picture of mothers holding babies, pointed at the babies successively and then put each index finger on a mother. At 12 months he pointed at his toy rabbit and then at a picture of a rabbit on the wall. A month later, his mother pointed out a picture of a house on a quilt; later, he looked out of the window and saw the neighboring house, pointed at it, then turned and pointed at the house on the quilt. The same child at 16 months found the cut-off T-shaped end of a plastic device used to hold hang-tags on garments; he grasped it by the long arm, called it "ham" (hammer) and banged things with it. These category-related behaviors would not have been observable if the child had not achieved a great deal of motor control.

Responses to the visual cliff illusion of depth (discussed in Chapter 8) show the use of categories, too. A 9-month-old who is afraid to cross the apparent drop but who is encouraged by his mother may turn around and try to "back down" the drop, treating it as if it belongs in the same category as a step.

Development of category use is a long process that is still ongoing at 5 or 6 years of age. However, its early beginning is essential to the mastery of some important skills. As we will see in Chapter 11, language development depends in part on the ability to recognize categories of sounds spoken in slightly different ways by different people and at different times (a woman shouting a word as compared to a man whispering the same word, for example).

Cross-Modal Connections

Experience in the real world often involves simultaneous stimulation in several sensory modalities. A face is seen, a voice is heard, the touch of a hand is felt, all at the same time. *Cross-modal cognition* relates and associates the internal representations of events as they occur in different sensory modalities. During the first weeks of life, cross-modal cognition already leads to expectation that certain events will go together. Two-week-olds avoid looking at their mothers' faces when they are presented together with strangers' voices, and they also avoid a stranger's face matched with the mother's voice (Carpenter, described by Bower, 1982).

Infants less than 4 days old are able to make a connection between the shape of a pacifier in their mouths and a shape seen on a screen (Kaye & Bower, 1994). They looked longer at the picture of the pacifier they were sucking in a situation in which they could control which picture appeared by their sucking behavior. (This behavior could indicate a very early capacity for categorization and concept use.)

Imitation

The capacity for *imitation* is one of the most puzzling aspects of cognitive development. How is it possible for one person to match the behavior of another unless she can see herself and the other person at the same time? How, in particular, can a baby match another person's facial expression when she rarely sees herself in a mirror and, if she did, would not even recognize the reflection as her own until well into the second year of life? Imitation must be based on internal representations of both the other person's and the infant's actions and a capacity to compare them.

Early reports that infants as young as 36 hours were able to imitate adult facial expressions (Field, Woodson, Greenberg, & Cohen, 1982; Meltzoff & Moore, 1977) were greeted with initial disbelief but have been supported by later work (Meltzoff & Moore, 1989). As we will note in Chapter 11, a less specific form of imitation can be seen in the entrainment of infant movement; in the first weeks, the rhythms of the baby's movement follow the rhythms of the adult speech they are listening to.

As the infant becomes motorically more competent, evidence of imitation can be seen in everyday life. A 6-month-old may be seen imitating an adult waving in time to music. Imitations of adult "peek-a-boo" and of gestures like

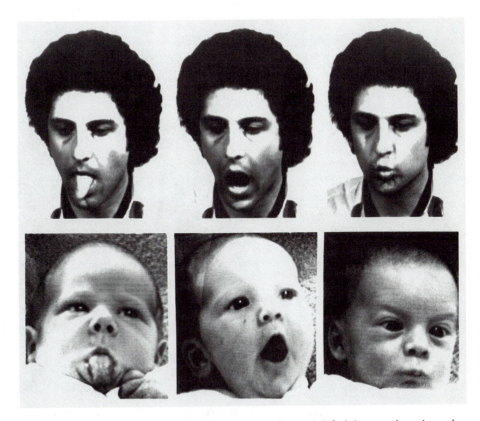

At age 2 or 3 weeks, or even earlier, infants can imitate adult facial expressions. In each of these photographs, the infant is responding to the adult facial expression shown above.

shaking the head follow in a few months, as do wordlike vocalizations in some children.

By 12 months, imitation has become quite sophisticated. Sequences of several actions are imitated in the correct order (Bauer & Mandler, 1992). At 16 months, the child not only can remember how to imitate something for a week but can select the right objects to do the action with—or equivalent objects if the exact ones are not available (Bauer & Dow, 1994). One child of this age, after a visit to the doctor, found a set of spark plug cables and used them as a stethoscope on his family.

Toddlers imitate other children as well as adults, and the imitation can occur at home even though the original event took place at the day care center (Hanna & Meltzoff, 1993). Imitation occurs on the spot as well as after a delay, and the extent to which this happens can depend on the child's other cognitive achievements. In **synchronic** imitation, toddlers play side by side, using similar objects in similar ways at the same time. This may be one of the reasons for their frequent interest in getting hold of the other child's toy. The occurrence of extensive synchronic imitation seems to depend on whether the children have achieved mirror self-recognition; it is rare when only one of a pair or neither is a self-recognizer (Asendorpf & Baudonnière, 1993).

synchronic: occurring at the same time; from the Greek *syn-* (together), *chronos* (time).

Through careful imitation of adults, the toddler learns actions that are characteristic of her cultural group.

EVERYDAY LEARNING

Some of the cognitive change we have discussed so far has involved experimental work, where the baby has been trained and tested in the laboratory. Most babies never enter a laboratory, of course, and even those who do spend little time there. Infant cognitive development occurs as a part of the baby's everyday life. The experiences that influence cognitive development are usually quite unsystematic and unplanned, but the baby is attentive, interested, and eager to learn from them.

Motivation

Why does a baby learn so eagerly? Students who are busy trying to learn what someone has assigned them to study often believe that learning has to be for an obvious purpose, that there must be some *motivation* in the form of achieving a desirable outcome or escaping an undesirable one.

Of course, infants can learn in order to get something. Our discussion of instrumental conditioning noted that babies learn a task when they are rewarded with milk or with having a parent come to them when they are frightened. But most of the tasks in the studies discussed in this chapter have not been associated with a material or even an emotional achievement. The outcome of most of the learning tasks we have discussed was getting to make something interesting happen. Infants will work hard at a task to make a mobile move or to get someone to "peek-a-boo" them. The basic motive seems to be mastery of the environment (White, 1959; Yarrow, 1981), rather than some special need to see a moving mobile.

If an infant has few experiences of mastery—if the infant's attempts at tasks are consistently frustrated or even punished—the outcome may be *learned helplessness* (Seligman, Maier, & Solomon, 1971). In this case, the normal motivation for learning and performance is replaced by an expectation of failure.

Social and emotional factors play roles in the determination of an infant's motivation to learn. As we will see in Chapter 12, an infant who has formed a secure attachment to an adult (usually after about 8 months) will explore an unfamiliar place if the adult is present, but not otherwise. In the strange place, the familiar caregiver serves as a secure base from which to explore. The infant frequently returns to or looks toward the familiar person or shows things to the adult (Maslin-Cole & Spieker, 1990).

proximal: near, in space or time; from the Latin *proximus,* (near).

The relationship between emotion and cognitive functioning is also shown in the idea of a zone of **proximal** development (Vygotsky, 1978). This "zone" is a level of performance that is new to the child and that can be achieved only when there is an affectionate, supportive adult staying near the child.

In Chapter 12, our discussion of emotional development will explore more connections with cognition, including both the role of learning in emotional growth and the role of emotion in intellectual development.

The presence of an affectionate, supportive adult is an important component of an infant's learning environment.

Play and Exploration

When an activity does not have to be done in order for the individual to be clothed, fed, sheltered, kept safe, or even loved, but a lot of energy goes into the activity anyway, we tend to describe that activity as *play.* A playful activity that focuses on examining unfamiliar objects or places is *exploration.* Together, these activities take up a great deal of an infant's "free time" (time not spent eating, sleeping, or fussing).

Play and exploration are major sources of the experiences that bring about cognitive development. The infant's spontaneous activity and the feedback she gets from her actions are better suited to provide her with information than anything an adult could design (Bertenthal, Campos, & Kermoian, 1994). The experiences the infant causes for herself occur almost by definition when she is ready to pay attention. If she were not calm and reasonably undisturbed by physical needs, she would not be playing. The infant's control over her own experiences also allows her to repeat them as often as needed and at whatever intervals best suit her cognitive abilities. The play of infants and toddlers often involves repetitions so prolonged that adults get bored (indeed, if we saw an adult whose behavior was as repetitive as an infant's, we would correctly think of him as emotionally disturbed).

Like other behaviors linked with cognition, play depends on available motor abilities. In the early months, play and exploration involve looking at distant objects and mouthing objects that can be grasped. As motor skills improve, mouthing decreases and fingering increases (Gibson, 1988). Waving and banging objects give way to dropping and throwing as voluntary release becomes possible. As walking is mastered, it is combined playfully with carrying objects (the bigger, the better, it seems) and stunts like goose-stepping with one foot.

Although play usually involves objects in some way, there is no need for them to be actual toys. As long as the baby can manipulate them safely, common household objects like pots and big spoons are very suitable for play. The toddler may use them in the "right" way for their normal functions or may adapt them to his own goals, such as hitting a ball along the floor with a comb.

Actually, the most fascinating play objects for infants are those that provide complex, multisensory stimulation and that respond to what the baby does—in other words, people. Adults are especially stimulating and responsive, but other children are attractive, too. As we noted elsewhere in this chapter, toddlers engage in synchronic activity during parallel play with their peers. Their social and cognitive skills are still too poor to allow them to play together without careful supervision, though.

Instruction and Stimulation

Parents sometimes attempt to instruct infants directly. In the earliest months, these attempts tend to focus on "helping" with motor abilities such as rolling over. Later, the instruction is often directed at very specific behaviors like waving "bye-bye" or giving a kiss. Practice of motor skills and work on specific behaviors can be effective, but it is really irrelevant to general cognitive development. (But, as we will see in Chapter 11, parents' speech is highly relevant to language development.)

Some parents, concerned about their baby's need for stimulation, aim at what has been called the "gourmet baby" (Zigler & Lang, 1986). Their child's crib is decorated with flash cards, showing black-and-white geometric figures early on and simple words (sometimes in another language) before age 1. Although it is certainly a good thing for parents to feel they are doing right by their baby, and these practices are harmless, this too is probably irrelevant to cognitive development.

What is relevant, then? What experiences in babies' lives seem to encourage early cognitive development and lead to good school performance later on? In the first half-year, plenty of physical contact with adults is important. The complex multisensory stimulation offered by the adult body draws the baby's attention and offers many possibilities for contingency learning and for cross-modal connections. Having things to look at (including faces) is also useful at this time.

In the second half-year, the baby's increased motor skills allow exploration and some improved learning about causality. The caregiver who actively

APPLICATIONS & ARGUMENTS
Cognitive Stimulation and Overstimulation

There is an excellent market for devices that are supposed to be stimulating and to encourage a baby's cognitive development. Certainly, a baby needs to learn from the environment. Much of cognitive development results from taking in information, processing it, and comparing it to what was already known.

Do babies need flash cards and classical music to foster their development? It's doubtful that these artificial additions to the environment are at all necessary. Young babies seem to learn best from the multisensory experiences—combining sounds, insights, taste, smell, and movement—that occur when they interact with human beings. Older babies learn from exploring the physical world, as well; a safe "baby-proof" house is more conducive to cognitive development than $1000 worth of educational toys.

Can an infant be overstimulated, or is more stimulation always better? Infants' behavior tells us that there are times when they have had all the stimulation they care for. The overstimulated baby may seem tense or may yawn or frown. She may suck her fingers in an attempt to calm herself and may avert her eyes, avoiding eye contact with an adult who is giving her more stimulation than she can deal with. Some fair-skinned babies can even be seen to become pale and then flush when talked to or otherwise stimulated for too long.

The baby's cues need to be read accurately, because they tell when additional stimulation will be so unpleasant that the baby will avoid it rather than learn from it. Other signals—such as smiling, reaching, looking, and vocalizing—tell when the baby is ready for more. (Mechanical stimulators like audiotapes, of course, cannot respond to the baby's cues.)

---

plays with the baby provides essential cognitive stimulation. Floor freedom—the possibility of safe exploration without much supervision—is helpful, as are having a variety of activities and a variety of objects within reach. Frequent use of playpens is associated with poor cognitive progress (White, Kaban, & Attanucci, 1979). Allowing the baby to work on self-feeding seems especially important; it involves considerable sensory stimulation, experience with physical properties and causality, and an experience of mastery. From about age 7 or 8 months, the baby's emotional attachment to familiar people makes consistent caregivers an important factor for cognitive development.

In the second year, the factors mentioned above remain important, but some others can be added. It is important for caregivers to talk and to respond to the baby's signals. There should be little restriction of what the toddler does (except for hurting himself or others, of course). A predictable environment with plenty of room and little noise or confusion is ideal.

You notice that one popular "educational device" is absent from this discussion. There is no place for television in an environment meant to encourage infant cognitive development. Educational programming is intended for children aged 3 years or older, not for infants and toddlers. Television creates noise and confusion and allows no opportunities for mastery (except for playing with the control knobs). It also distracts caregivers and makes them less responsive to the child's signals.

Child care facilities often stress their commitment to the encouragement of cognitive development. They may name themselves "schools" or "learning centers." As we will note in Chapter 14, it is common for parents to seek out child care that resembles an elementary school setting. However, we have seen that a restrictive, instruction-based style is potentially detrimental to the cognitive development of infants and toddlers. Child care facilities need to follow the same guidelines parents do to facilitate infant cognitive development. Use of appropriate guidelines is called *developmentally appropriate practice* (Gestwicki, 1995). Further guidelines for infant and toddler centers have come from the Heart Start initiative (*Zero to Three*, 1992), which stresses the role of emotional and social factors in school readiness.

A useful concept for both parents and child care facilities is called Educare. This approach, based in part on the work of Magda Gerber (Caldwell, 1991; Gonzalez-Mena & Eyer, 1980), stresses daily care routines like diapering and feeding as times for talking, making face-to-face contact, and encouraging the infant's mastery of the environment.

INTERVENTION

When an infant shows special problems or is at risk because of family factors, early intervention may be called for. A broad array of early special education programs have been developed, especially since the Individuals with Disabilities Education Act of 1986 provided for infant and toddler intervention under its Part H (also to be discussed in Chapter 15).

Early intervention programs have to be complex to be effective. A program that works with the baby alone for a few hours each week does not do much good if the family continues practices that work against cognitive development, or if the baby's physical condition interferes with learning. Effective programs also need to be individualized to meet a particular baby's and family's needs. Intervention programs start with an *individual family service plan* (IFSP), which deals with job training, parenting skills, housing, drug and alcohol problems, and nutrition, as well as with chances for cognitive progress. The IFSP may be complicated by the presence of a foster family or progress toward an adoption, as well as by the family of origin.

The strong need to individualize intervention programs makes it very difficult to assess their effectiveness. Not only is every family different, but a caregiver working with a baby needs to recognize the baby's signals, to increase or decrease the intensity of stimulation, and to know when it is time to stop or start stimulation. Fostering early cognitive development is not a simple matter of "giving a lesson."

Presumably, the basic factors that encourage cognitive development in most babies are also relevant to those with special needs. Some additional approaches for early intervention have also been suggested. For example, one approach stresses the need for an infant to learn about contingencies by actively engaging the world and experiencing success (Sullivan & Lewis, 1993). An infant with motor problems may become withdrawn and passive as a result of experiencing the environment as uncontrollable; in other words, the baby may develop learned helplessness. Similarly, an infant who has experienced the absence of social and emotional responsiveness from caregivers may give up any attempts to interact with the world. A program involving switch-activated toys may permit the child to experience mastery and learn about contingencies.

The presence of supportive, familiar caregivers may be especially important in early intervention, as the adult's presence, encouragement, and physical support make possible performance the baby could not manage alone and a consequent sense of mastery (Maslin-Cole & Spieker, 1990). Physical intervention, like supporting a baby on the lap and anticipating wobbles, can help the baby look at a face, make eye contact, and begin a social interaction that would otherwise have been impossible (Zeitlin & Williamson, 1994).

Early intervention programs need to be organized so that all the infant's experiences in the program foster development. A common problem is the handling of transition times—waiting for lunch or for the van to go home. There are situations, for instance, where babies sit in car seats for an hour while waiting for a bus to come, and they have no toys, activities, or adult involvement (Graham & Bryant, 1993). However good the intervention program is at other times, this experience fosters passivity rather than a sense of mastery.

transdisciplinary: using information drawn from a variety of branches of learning; from the Latin *trans-* (across), *disciplina* (learning).

Early intervention programs almost always need to be **transdisciplinary.** Few if any infants have a single problem that can be dealt with in a single way. Physical and occupational therapy and speech pathology are all important parts of early intervention.

Testing Cognitive Development

Tests of cognitive ability, such as intelligence tests, are not always well thought of by the public. People are concerned about labeling children on the basis of tests; about cultural biases that can cause low scores for members of minorities; and about the fact that other aspects of the individual, such as motivation, are powerful determinants of performance. Nevertheless, intelligence tests go on being used because they are very useful for school placement purposes.

Testing of infants and toddlers has different purposes from testing of school-age children. Some testing is done for research purposes, to look for connections between infants' experiences and their cognitive abilities. Assessment of the success of an early intervention program may also be a goal.

Testing is also done to make decisions about the need for early intervention. When this is the case, the process usually involves screening large groups of children to select those who may have problems, followed by an assessment with specific tests. These tests are aimed at a description of the infant's strengths and weaknesses, which can be used in designing an individualized intervention program (Hutinger, 1988).

Most tests used to assess infant cognitive development have little in common with the usual intelligence test for older children. In fact, they tend to focus on general developmental delays rather than on cognitive abilities like the $A\overline{B}$ test. At this point in our understanding of infant development, physical, motor, and social abilities in infancy give us the best predictions about how a child will do when she reaches school age (which is the real crux of our concern about cognition). Because tests for babies do not usually get directly at cognitive abilities, it may be best to consider the test as simply the starting point for an assessment that looks at a variety of factors.

An example of a commonly used test is the Bayley Scales of Infant Development (Bayley, 1969). The Bayley Scales include tests of motor as well as mental development. Mental development is evaluated on the basis of functions such as attentiveness, interaction with the examiner, meaningful play with toys (like putting an object in a cup), memory for hidden objects, and ability to follow complex directions. The Bayley Scales are standardized so that individual scores can be compared with norms developed by testing large numbers of infants at different ages. Some other scales, like the Ordinal Scales of Psychological Development (Uzgiris & Hunt, 1975) are not standardized but are *criterion-referenced*; they report specific achievements, rather than making comparisons with the abilities expected at a certain age.

A relatively new test approach, Transdisciplinary Play-Based Assessment (TPBA) (Linder, 1990), is designed to deal with two real problems of testing. The first problem is that infants and toddlers are not always willing to show their abilities; the examiner may or may not get the youngsters' cooperation, even if they perform very well at home. An unfamiliar environment and examiner disturb performance, and a child with physical disabilities may not be able to do things in exactly the form some standardized tests call for. TPBA involves play activities in which parents participate; and the assessment looks at what happens in the course of play.

The second problem of assessment emerges from the fact (mentioned in a previous section) that infants who are candidates for early intervention programs usually have multiple problems. TPBA involves observation of play by a team of assessors, including physical therapists and speech pathologists. The test does not, however, allow for comparison to age norms.

The great increase in our knowledge about cognitive development may some day make it possible for cognitive measures presently used for research to be used in assessment. Measures of infant memory would be a possibility, and habituation has been reported to be a possible key to serious cognitive problems (Hepper & Shahidullah, 1992).

Because environmental factors seem to have a strong impact on cognitive development, assessment could look at the infant's environment as well as the infant's present abilities. The Inventory of Home Stimulation, developed by Bettye Caldwell (Caldwell & Bradley, 1984), looks at items in the environment as they relate to the infant's age. The items have to do with everyday concerns like trips to the grocery store, as well as the presence of toys, pets, and houseplants.

For accuracy in assessment, testing situations and interpretations need to be considered, as well as the tests themselves. It has been suggested that testing should be done in naturalistic contexts that are familiar to the baby; that assessment should be repeated over time, rather than basing evaluation on a single occasion; and that test results should be interpreted holistically, with attention to the infant's health, emotional state, and so on. Although these suggestions were made in a discussion of assessment of motor development (Case-Smith, 1996), they also can be applied as well or better to cognitive assessment.

THE INTEGRATED BABY

What is a baby's learning and cognition like in the real world? It is almost impossible to examine this issue directly, but let us consider what a baby might learn from his experiences in the first months of being breast-fed. There is certainly some classical conditioning, and the baby comes to recognize that when his mother holds him in the right position, lifts her shirt, and unfastens her bra, feeding is about to happen. His behavior changes from fussy to anticipatory as these events occur. Cross-modal integration of information occurs as the smell and taste of milk, the smell and feel of the mother's skin, and the sound of her voice are all experienced together. Operant conditioning also occurs; the hungry young baby turns his head and nuzzles a caregiver's chest, even if the caregiver is the father or a nonlactating baby-sitter. By age 4 or 5 months, the baby will probably have learned to avoid biting the mother's nipple because such an act is followed by her screaming with pain and surprise and possibly removing his mouth from the nipple. Although the breast is usually covered when the baby is not nursing, cognitive development of object permanence will soon enable the baby to recognize that the breast is there, and he will fumble at buttons or tug at the mother's sweater to find it. The baby experiences mastery as his mother responds to his signal that he has finished with one breast and wants to switch to the other. A concept of number and memory for a sequence are displayed after he nurses at the second breast, since he does not seem to expect that a third breast will be available. As the baby gets closer to a year old, he explores the breast and the mother's face, hands, and clothing; he playfully mouths the nipple and lets go again. Far more is happening in this feeding experience than simple transfer of milk to the inside of the baby.

PROBLEMS TO CONSIDER AND DISCUSS

1. What are habituation and dishabituation, and how can they be used to test a baby's learning?
2. How is negative reinforcement different from punishment?
3. How would you decide whether a baby had shown intention to do something?
4. How is internal representation related to imitation?
5. What is the role of play in cognitive development?

11

Communication and Language

The growth of an infant's capacity for communication is a topic at the fascinating intersection of cognitive, social, and motor abilities. Communication begins at birth and culminates in mastery of spoken or signed language at about age 2. When language becomes an important part of the child's communication, infancy is left behind, for the word *infant* derives from Latin words meaning "incapable of speech."

The increasing skill the infant shows in language and other types of communication is often referred to as language development, but it is the child who does the developing. As Locke pointed out, "developing children increasingly take on and manifest the capacity for language" (1993, p. 2). Studies on this topic in the past tended to focus on samples of the speech a child produced, but the stress today is on the child's use of language and its *function* in the child's life.

Language as a specialized form of communication has a number of defining characteristics.

1. Language involves the use of symbols, whether spoken words or gestures, that represent referents in the environment.
2. The symbols are arbitrary; they have no particular link to the referent, so an orange could just as easily be called an umbrella.
3. Groups of people agree on the meaning of symbols and use them to communicate with each other.
4. A language has rules about how symbols are combined or altered to produce different meanings.

There is clearly a lot for an infant to learn about any language she hears, and the amazing thing is that so much of the learning can take place in two years.

RESEARCH METHODS

Research on early language and **communication** has tended to emphasize a longitudinal approach. Longitudinal studies give an idea of the steps the infant goes through as she moves from one communication skill level to the next.

communication: transmission of information so that it is shared by two or more people; from the Latin *communis* (common).

Early longitudinal studies in this area were attempts to record most or all of an infant's attempts at speech, usually starting at about 1 year of age. A number of data sets were established in this way and were analyzed by many researchers. More recently, the Child Language Data Exchange System (CHILDES) has become available; this is a large computerized database of transcripts from normally developing children (MacWhinney, 1994).

Naturalistic approaches, such as those just described, provide information about a toddler's spontaneous production of language. Experimental approaches present the child with a controlled stimulus and examine his response. For example, a study of a newborn's response to different vowel sounds might measure cardiac deceleration as an indication of attentiveness (Clarkson & Berg, 1983).

Studies of prespeech communication rely on videotaping or film recording to capture events that are too subtle and rapid to be picked up by an observer. They may look at events naturalistically or may experimentally alter a situation by changing the way the baby's adult partner behaves. It should be noted that work on speech or on prespeech communication may also record what the adult caregivers say and do, as one of the issues about the development of language has to do with the adult language input (Sokolov, 1993).

Clinical work with infants and toddlers has led to the development of sampling procedures that allow a child's behavior to be compared to developmental norms. Sampling procedures can involve "communicative temptations"—situations designed to entice a child to communicate. They may also use books, play, and verbal "probes" intended to give insight into the child's comprehension of language ("CSBS normed edition released," 1993). Behavioral checklists have been designed to give similar information about the prespeech period (Proctor & Murnyack, 1995).

Finally, work on communication development can include the many ways of measuring brain activity discussed in Chapters 7 and 8. Imaging techniques and methods of recording from the auditory and language areas of the brain can give important information about language development.

Not surprisingly, the use of animal models is rare in language development research. Studies of sign use and comprehension of signs or speech by chimpanzees suggest that some, though not all, language abilities are uniquely human (Cartmill, 1995). Studies of birds' song-learning are sometimes related to human language development (Locke, 1993) but are not relevant to all aspects of children's language learning.

CHANGING VIEWS OF LANGUAGE

Twenty or thirty years ago, views of the nature and origin of language stressed the roles of narrow, specific factors in the development of language functions. A major concern of those views was to try to explain how an infant could learn so much about language in such a short time, accomplishing a task that would be impossible for an adult.

One important approach to the study of language development was the *Skinnerian,* or operant conditioning, model. This approach stressed the power of environmental *reinforcement* of language behavior and the idea that it is gratifying to the child to hear himself successfully imitate his parents' speech. B. F. Skinner, the most famous of the behaviorist learning theorists, also noted that the child gets what he wants when he speaks intelligibly and that he is therefore more likely to repeat the behavior in the future (see Chapter 10 for a discussion of operant conditioning). But there were some problems with the Skinnerian approach to language development. Much early speech is not direct imitation, and toddlers say things they are not likely ever to have heard an adult say. Many of the first words are simply descriptive and are not indicative either of what the child wants or of what he gets.

A second important model, which strongly opposed Skinner's, was that of Noam Chomsky (1965). Chomsky's idea was that language is so complex that it could not possibly be learned so quickly through ordinary mechanisms of practice and reinforcement. Chomsky posited that a *module,* or brain capacity, existed that was specific to the human species and that had the ability to untangle the complexities of language experience and penetrate rapidly to the basic underlying rules of language. This Language Acquisition Device (LAD) made it possible to learn and use language in a short time, according to Chomsky. But many language researchers argued that this was not an explanation or even a good description of the events of language development. More recently, people working in this area have felt uneasy about categorizing language as a completely unique developmental form, because it seems so closely associated with other aspects of development.

A third approach to language was based on Piaget's approach to cognitive development (see Chapter 10). Although Piaget had no specific theory of language (Bates & Snyder, 1987), his ideas about symbol use and the emergence of mental representations are relevant to language development.

Modern research has linked communication before speech to the emergence of the spoken language. Neither Skinner's nor Chomsky's nor Piaget's ideas can be made to fit very well with what we now know about the beginnings of communication.

Current approaches to communication and language development stress the integration and interaction of a wide variety of skills and their contribution to gesture and speech. Locke's (1993) "biolinguistic" approach, for example, includes perceptual, social, vocal, and neural development, as well as the baby's readiness to pay attention to speech. As we will discuss in Chapter 13, some approaches to communication focus on the social interactions that culminate in language (Greenspan, 1990).

Dynamic systems approaches to language make use of some of the ideas we noted in Chapter 10. The communicating infant or toddler is seen as part of a self-organizing system, an active and adaptive part of a changing environment. The abrupt, qualitative changes we see in communication and language are considered to be phase shifts that occur when an alteration in a parameter (like the amount of experience with language the child has had)

APPLICATIONS & ARGUMENTS
Why Is a Human Baby Not Just Another Primate?

New parents are sometimes heard to contrast babies and humans: "Oh, sorry," they say, "I mean adults, of course." In many ways, babies do not seem particularly "human." The absence of fur and a tail makes them different from other higher primate infants, but they sometimes strike us as more like baby chimpanzees than like older human beings.

In a few cases, research-oriented parents have brought up their baby and an infant chimpanzee together for the first few years. The most noticeable difference at first was that the chimpanzee developed much faster; the human baby was the follower, not the leader of his chimp companion. When language came into the picture, though, the human moved farther and farther ahead.

What does the human baby have that allows language development? What is the chimp missing? Specialized brain areas are probably an important human advantage. However, there is also a behavior that seems to be peculiar to humans and that may function as the foundation of turn taking and communication. This special behavior is a sucking pattern that involves bursts of sucking interspersed with pauses. Other mammal babies suck at a regular rate, without pauses, until they have satisfied their hunger.

The human infant's sucking pattern attracts the mother's attention. Although nursing animals may be attentive to their babies, they tend to do things like clean the baby's ears rather than focus on the baby's behavior. The human mother responds to the pause in sucking and "takes a turn" stimulating the baby; she stops when it's the baby's turn. The pattern of communication is thus established: I do something, you respond, and then I respond to you.

What is the most basic characteristic of human nature? Perhaps it is simply sucking in bursts.

reaches a critical point (Kelso, 1990). Dynamic systems approaches naturally include motor, cognitive, and social factors in their consideration of language development.

THE NERVOUS SYSTEM AND LANGUAGE DEVELOPMENT

Whatever approach is taken to the study of language must take into account the facts about nervous system functioning in speech and hearing. Chapters 7 and 8 reviewed some of the developmental changes in the nervous system that are related to listening and speaking, but some specific details will be dealt with here.

temporal: in this context, having to do with the temples of the head; from the Latin *tempora* (temples).

A number of speech and hearing functions are localized in particular areas of the brain, especially in parts of the **temporal** lobe. What is particularly noticeable is that functions are lateralized as well as localized, and that one side of the brain has taken on specialized language functions even before birth (Segalowitz & Chapman, 1980). The side of the cortex where the major language functions are localized is usually the left for right-handed people, although foot preference is an even better predictor than handedness is (MacNeilage, 1991). The left planum temporale area in the temporal lobe is already larger than the right at the time of birth (Rosen & Galaburda, 1985), and it appears to play an important role in language functioning.

As we noted before, the left hemisphere does not function alone in language activity. The right hemisphere has an important language task in the processing of *pitch* information (Zatorre, Evans, Meyer, & Gjedde, 1992); as we will see later, pitch provides intonation cues that permit us to recognize questions, statements, and so on.

Brain functions related to language are not limited to the place in the brain that is activated. *Temporal* processing, the detection of tiny time differences in sounds, is a critical aspect of language comprehension and production (the relationship to the name of the temporal lobe is coincidental, by the way). Speech sounds are complex and change very rapidly over a time; the brain's processing must be able to keep up with them for comprehension to be possible. The left hemisphere seems to be particularly specialized for the rapid processing of auditory information (Tallal, Miller, & Fitch, 1993), which is especially important for detecting certain consonants. Problems with rapid information processing are associated with language impairment (Tallal, Miller, & Fitch, 1993) and have also been implicated in later reading difficulties (Galaburda & Livingstone, 1993).

expressive: carrying information outward; from the Latin *ex* (out), *premere* (to press).

receptive: taking information in; from the Latin *re-* (back, again), *capere* (to take or capture).

As we discussed in Chapter 7, brain damage during early development is less detrimental to language than similar damage in an adult would be (Huttenlocher, 1993). Damage to the nervous system from HIV infection, however, has serious and specific effects on language. **Expressive** language (speech) is significantly more affected than **receptive** language (understanding what is heard) (Wolters et al., 1995).

VOCALIZING AND SPEAKING

phoneme: the smallest sound element that, when changed, can change the meaning of a word in a particular language; from the Greek *phone* (voice, sound).

To use a spoken language, a person must have a great deal of control over the physical production of sound. He or she must be able to produce sounds through the vocal tract at the right time and to form them at will into the basic sound categories that combine to convey meaning. These basic sound categories, or **phonemes,** are complex patterns of sound energy; each phoneme involves many frequencies of sound waves, with different intensities at different times during the sound. The speaker also needs to be able to control the tempo of sound production, the overall pitch of the voice (in addition to the separate frequencies within phonemes), the overall intensity or loudness of the voice, and the separate intensities with which *stress* is given to a specific word or syllable.

Phonation

The complicated physical machinery that allows speech production has other purposes as well. Basically, the lower vocal tract is dedicated to breathing, and the upper areas—the mouth and nose—are involved in eating and drinking. Speech has to be coordinated with these more essential functions. For example, the integration of sucking, swallowing, and breathing is crucial to the automatic swallowing of excess saliva that would make speech less intelligible (Oetter, Laurel, & Cool, 1990).

In addition to coordination of functions, speech requires coordination of body parts from the diaphragm to the lips. Simply opening the jaw depends on three separate muscle groups that rotate the jaw downward and simultaneously move it forward; speaking one syllable involves the coordination of more than 70 muscles (Ostry et al., 1991; Thelen, 1991).

A further issue about the "machinery" of speech is that it undergoes considerable developmental change. The vocal tract of a newborn infant is rather different from that of an adult, and the latter is much better suited to speech. The young infant's tongue almost fills her mouth, and the larynx ("voice box") is higher and farther forward than it is in adults (Swanson & Brown, 1992). The young infant also has poor control over the tongue, with involuntary movements like the tongue-thrust reflex still dominating; she has few or no teeth to help form speech sounds; the lower jaw is still small; and fat pads inside the cheeks, which help in nursing, further reduce the space in the

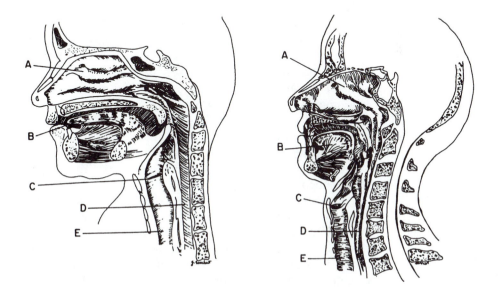

The upper airways of the adult (on the left) and the young child (on the right) are rather different, resulting in differences in breathing and sound production. (A = the turbinate bones in the nose, B = the tongue, C = the larynx, D = the esophagus, E = the trachea)

mouth. Development during the first year or so alters this situation a great deal.

phonation: the production of sound through the vocal tract; from the Greek *phone* (voice, sound).

Phonation, or sound production, occurs when air passing from the lungs over the vocal folds in the larynx causes vibration. The amount of tension in the muscular vocal folds determines the basic *frequency* of the sound produced, just as the amount of tension on a guitar string determines whether it will produce a higher or lower tone. Of course, the vibration is complex and produces more than a single frequency.

formant: one of the sound combinations that contributes to the nature of a speech sound; from the Latin *forma* (form).

resonate: to increase the amplitude of a sound wave, in this case, as a result of passing through the throat and mouth; from the Latin *re-* (back, again), *sonare* (to sound).

As we noted above, however, a phoneme is not just a single sound frequency; it is characterized by **formants,** or peaks of intensity for certain frequencies, and these change in the course of production of the phoneme. How does this come about? There is obviously more involved than a simple vibration like that of a guitar string. The entire vocal tract, including nose, mouth, and tongue, contributes to the production of a phoneme. The sound produced at the larynx **resonates**—increases in intensity—with the cavities of the vocal tract; the particular frequencies that are amplified most depend on the size and shape of the cavities at a given point (Lester, 1984). For example, holding your nose or having a cold changes your voice by altering the cavities available for resonance. The size and shape of the cavities are changed during the production of a phoneme by opening or closing the mouth and by moving the tongue against the palate, teeth, or lips to alter the flow of air out of the mouth (Wildgen, 1990). The timing of these events is crucial to accurate production of a phoneme. Fortunately, though, listeners respond to categories of sounds rather than insisting that only one sound pattern can be a given phoneme. That is why we usually understand each other when talking with food in our mouth or with a cold, and we understand the toddler who says "Chijoe" instead of "Cheerio."

The sound produced by these events can be *voiced,* if the vocal folds are rapidly opened and closed to interrupt the passage of air, or *unvoiced,* if air passes through the folds and is interrupted farther along the vocal tract (Lester, 1984); in English, "b" and "p" are examples of phonemes that have the same basic pattern, but the former is voiced and the latter is unvoiced. Both voiced and unvoiced sounds are found in the young infant's cry as well as in later sound production. Phonemes can also be considered as either vowels, where the sound can continue indefinitely, and consonants, where the sound must be stopped for the phoneme to be produced. Although there are vowellike and consonantlike sounds early on, these become much refined during the first year or so.

prosodic: in this context, relating to features of speech like pitch and tempo, rather than the words themselves; from the Greek *prosoidia* (song).

Although the production of specific phonemes is critical to intelligible speech, the baby will need to master other aspects of speech as well. Alterations in the overall *pitch* or fundamental frequency of a person's speech carry a great deal of information about emotion and social relationships; adults raise their pitch when talking to a baby, for example. *Intonation,* the changing of pitch and intensity from one word to the next, also conveys emotion. The *tempo* of speech is altered in response to a listener's information-processing needs. These are the **prosodic** elements of speech, which we will discuss in the section on nonsegmental features of speech.

Crying

The child's first vocalization occurs with the *birth cry,* a reflexive production of sound as breathing begins and air passes over the vocal cords. Crying remains the most common form of vocalization for several months.

As we will discuss later, parents tend to respond to cries as if they convey specific meaning and deliberate communication. Although the reason behind a bout of crying is not always clear, some acoustic differences among cries occur in different circumstances, and experienced parents are able to "read" these to some extent. Hunger, anger, pain, and sudden frustration lead to different tempos of inhalation, rest, crying on exhalation, rest, and so on. The "pain cry" is especially noticeable, with a sudden long, loud wail followed by an even longer rest, then an inhalation that is longer than usual, although much shorter than the rest was, and so on (Wolff, 1970).

The young infant cries frequently, and crying can take up several hours a day at about 6 weeks of age (Brazelton, 1962). How this should be handled is a vexed question for parents, and one we will discuss in Chapter 13.

Although crying is a normal occurrence, some features of the cry may allow early diagnosis of serious problems, especially problems involving the central nervous system (Lester, 1984). A normal baby's cry has characteristics different from the cry of a baby with a chromosomally caused neurological syndrome called *cri du chat* (cat's cry) syndrome; the characteristic high fundamental frequency of the *cri du chat* baby's cry can easily be seen in a sound spectrogram. Similarly, the cry of a baby with meningitis involves a great deal of variation in frequency compared to a normal baby's. Unusual cries may also help diagnose babies who have been exposed to cocaine prenatally; they produce fewer cry utterances and shorter cries, as well as fewer high frequency cries (Corwin et al., 1992).

Although noncrying sounds are produced after the baby's first 2 or 3 months, crying does not disappear. In the 4- to 8-month-old, crying has been described as discomfort sounds, or cries and whimpers accompanied by a facial expression of distress, and request sounds, which are cries and whimpers, without the "cry face" (D'Odorico, 1984).

Cooing

Between 1 and 3 months of age, the baby begins a new form of vocalization— *cooing.* This noncrying vocalization consists of long, open vowel sounds and is most frequent when the baby is quiet, awake, and alone (Locke, 1993). Cooing is very attractive to adults but does not seem to be particularly directed toward them. Instead, it seems to be primarily a form of vocal play, and as such it certainly contributes to mastery of sound production.

Consonants and the Expansion of Sounds

From age 2 to 6 months, the infant begins to increase the kinds of sounds he makes. Some consonantlike sounds appear: for example, a G-like sound is produced by closing the vocal tract. There are trills, squeals, and growls and playful experimentation with pitch and loudness. Toward the end of this period, there is the beginning of *babbling,* the production of syllables where consonantlike and vowellike sounds alternate (Locke, 1993).

During this period, growth and physical development lead to much better control over sound production. The lower jaw develops and the lower part of the face grows, creating a larger mouth cavity. Reflex use of the tongue diminishes and control improves, so the baby can voluntarily push out a disliked food or use the tongue to push the food around in the mouth and eventually swallow it. Mouthing and chomping increase as teeth begin to come in; the mouth seems to get a lot of the infant's attention, which may help in the mastery of subtle tongue and mouth movements.

Babbling and Reduplication

From about 7 to 12 months, the baby has much greater control over vowels and consonants. Syllables, consisting of consonant and vowel or consonant-vowel-consonant combinations, are produced freely. These syllables may resemble words in the language the parents speak *(ma-ma, da-da),* but they do not appear to refer to anything in particular. *Reduplicative* babbling involves the repetition of a syllable, whereas *variegated* babbling, in the last month or two of the first year, uses strings of different syllables. As we will see later, there is no sudden transition from babbling to real words. Some children already use some true words at age 10 months and mix them with babbled syllables.

Articulation

Even when true words come into the picture, often at about 12 months, pronunciation is far from mature. Toddlers manage to make themselves understood without being able to articulate many of the sounds of the adult language. Whether the child can articulate the sound depends on both the difficulty of the tongue and mouth position and whether the syllable is stressed or unstressed (Hura & Echols, 1996). At this age, children often drop consonants at the ends of words and do the same with unstressed syllables; *hat* becomes "ha" and *kangaroo* becomes "karoo." "W" and "j" sounds replace "l" and "r." Even with these alterations, a word is usually pronounced in different ways at different times. The meaning may be quite clear in the context, but it may not be as obvious what the toddler is actually trying to pronounce; one boy referred to his zippered sleeper as "sips," which could have been either "sleeper" or "zips"—or both at once.

Direct *imitation* of words lags behind other types of imitation at 10 months but becomes frequent by 21 months (Masur, 1993).

HEARING AND LISTENING

As noted in Chapter 8, hearing is quite mature at the time of birth, even in preterm babies, and stimulation by sound is experienced before as well as after birth. There are some remaining problems with newborn hearing, though, and these can certainly interfere with the baby's response to the rapid, complex sounds of the spoken language.

Infants' *sensitivity* to sounds of different frequencies is not identical to adults'. Although their abilities to detect sounds of 19,000 Hz are about the same, adults do better than infants do for 10,000-Hz sounds (Schneider, Trehub, & Bull, 1980). Speech sounds have fundamental frequencies that are much lower than either of these, but some high-frequency tones do contribute to differences between phonemes.

Tests of sensitivity to sound are done in an otherwise quiet situation, whereas real speech is often heard against a background of other noises. An infant's ability to detect sound against a noisy background is much worse than an adult's, even at age 24 months; the speech sound needs to be 10 times as loud for the infant to hear it as for an adult (Trehub, Bull, & Schneider, 1981).

Finally, infants under age 5 months seem to be affected in an immature way by the way sounds arrive at the left and right ear. Older infants and adults show a "precedence effect" when a sound arrives earlier at one ear than at the other; rather than acting as if the sounds at the two ears are separate sounds from separate sources, they act as if the sound comes from the side where it arrives earlier (Clifton, 1985). This ability could be critical in figuring out which of a great number of simultaneous sound waves came from the same source and formed a single voice.

Paying Attention to Sounds

Although the baby's hearing is not dramatically different from an adult's, her *listening* is probably a good deal different. The adult listener knows what aspects of speech to pay attention to and can focus attention voluntarily, but the young infant is unaware of meaning and is often inattentive. Fortunately, some aspects of speech catch the infant's attention and help her notice the important details.

We noted in another chapter that newborn infants pay more attention to some sounds than to others (Kolata, 1987b). What is especially important is that they pay more attention to *human voices* than to other sounds; this is particularly demonstrated in the entrainment of their movements to the rhythms of the speech they are listening to (Condon & Sanders, 1974). Newborns are not only attentive to voices, they have preferences among them, and they will suck energetically in order to hear their mothers' voices rather than those of unfamiliar women (DeCasper & Fifer, 1980).

multisensory: involving two or more sensory modalities; from the Latin *multus* (many), *sentire* (to perceive).

An important issue about infants' attentiveness to sounds is that their greatest attention is to synchronized, **multisensory** stimulation, which is just what they are likely to experience in natural interactions with other people. Infants aged 10 to 16 weeks who look at faces while hearing accompanying recordings of nursery rhymes will look more when the lip movements are synchronized with the words than when they are not (Dodd, 1979). Slightly older infants have been shown to prefer looking at a face whose lips are forming the same vowel sound the infant is listening to, rather than a different one (Kuhl & Meltzoff, 1982).

Phonetic and Phonemic Discrimination

phonetic: relating to the structure of sound wave combinations used in speech; from the Greek *phone* (voice, sound).

The **phonetic** characteristics of sounds involve a pattern of intensities and frequencies that appear in a particular order as the sound is produced. Speech sounds have a particularly complex phonetic pattern because (1) they are produced in the irregularly shaped cavities of the vocal tract, and (2) changes like the movement of the tongue alter the sound as it occurs. These complex, changing phonetic patterns are called *sound contours.*

The discrimination of phonetic characteristics is even more complex than the characteristics themselves, because certain assumptions we might make turn out not to be true. For example, we would probably assume that the events in a physical sound wave occur in the same order as we experience them, but this is not correct. The phonetic features that make "ka" sound different from "da" are not at the beginning of the syllable as they appear to be. Similarly, we might assume that the same experience (for instance, the "k" in "ka" and in "ku") must come from the same set of physical events, but this is not the case. A **spectrogram** displaying the phonetic characteristics of the "k" in "ka" looks much different from one for the "k" in "ku." We seem to treat sounds as similar not because of their phonetic characteristics but because they are made with certain tongue positions or with voicing or unvoicing at particular points (Bates, O'Connell, & Shore, 1987).

spectrogram: in this context, a visual display showing the proportions of different wave forms in a sound; from the Latin *spectrum* (appearance).

All these complexities make it especially remarkable that infants are able to make phonetic discriminations in the first weeks of their lives. Not only do they discriminate, they also respond to phonetic *categories* rather than to individual patterns (Kuhl, 1993), and this is not simply a matter of treating similar sound patterns as members of the same category. For example, the initial sounds heard in "pa" and in "ba" are different in terms of *voice onset time* (VOT), that is, whether the vibration of the vocal cords began before or after the lips were opened. The VOT could vary from voicing 150 msec *before* the lips open to voicing 150 msec *after* the lips open. A VOT of +10 msec produces a sound like "ba," whereas a VOT of +30 msec sounds like "pa"—and so does a VOT of +50 msec! The listener cannot tell the difference between +30 and +50 but hears +10 and +20 as belonging to quite different categories (Bates, O'Connell, & Shore, 1987). Infants, adults, and nonhuman mammals as well seem to respond to the phonetic characteristics of sounds with this type of categorization.

One other type of categorization is relevant to the infant's response to speech. Like adults, infants respond to *patterns* of sounds rather than to specific phonetic characteristics. For example, they recognize a melody as staying the same when all the notes are changed to different pitches but their relationships to each other are unchanged (Trehub, 1985). And they recognize a sound as belonging to the same category whether it is spoken in a male or in a female voice, in a shout or in a whisper.

In an earlier section, we discussed differences in the phonemes of spoken language. The phonemes of a language are sounds with particular phonetic characteristics that are recognized by speakers of the language as distinct and basic units of speech. Whether a sound with particular phonetic characteristics

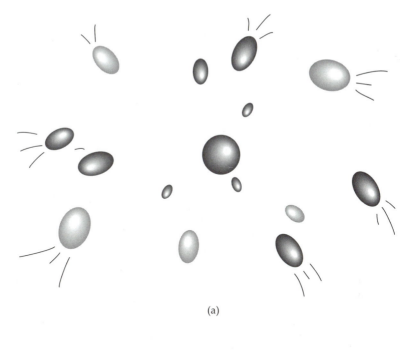

(a)

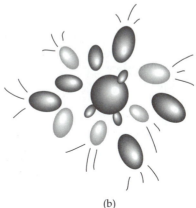

(b)

The native language magnet theory says that sounds that are similar to a phonetic prototype, as in (a), are perceived as more similar to the prototype than they really are (b). This process would exaggerate similarities among members of a phonetic category, as well as differences from other categories. (Source: Kuhl, 1993)

is a phoneme depends on the language in question. A sound that is a phoneme in one language may never be used in another, and two sounds that are regarded as separate phonemes in one language may be treated as identical in another.

Phonemes are actually functional *categories* that are only partly based on phonetic characteristics. This really has to be the case because sound patterns produced by different people or by the same person at different times are not identical. If a listener could not respond to speech sounds as members of categories, he or she would have the impossible task of analyzing patterns made up of hundreds of thousands of different sounds.

Infants initially pay attention to and discriminate among the phonemes of all the world's languages, whether they have heard them before or not. Over the first half-year, however, infants begin to lose sensitivity to the phonemes that are particular to languages they do not hear. They begin to function like adults, who "don't notice" phonemes that are not salient in their language. Unlike nonhumans, babies start to respond to some phonetic information and to ignore some.

How does this change take place? How does the infant move from his initial set of categories for sounds to a new set based on his native language? One suggestion is known as the Native Language Magnet (NLM) theory (Kuhl, 1993). The idea of the NLM is that the infant hears her caregivers speaking and develops representations in memory of the phonetic categories that are most used in the language. These representations involve whole categories, but each stresses the best example, or **prototype** of the sounds that fit the category. These prototypes act as "perceptual magnets" that make it more likely that similar sounds will be placed in the same category. If a sound category is rarely used in a language, there is no prototype and no category for it, so the older baby pays no attention to it as she tries to understand what is said. If two sounds belong to the same category in the native language, the baby will respond to them as the same; if they belong to different categories, the baby will treat them as different. In Japanese, for example, "l" and "r" are categorized as the same sound, whereas in English they are categorized as different. The process of change to a language-specific pattern of categorization is already well underway by age 6 months (Kuhl, Williams, Lacerda, Stevens, & Lindblom, 1992). Evidence that newborn infants can remember speech sounds for 24 hours suggests that the process could begin at birth (Swain, Zelazo, & Clifton, 1993).

prototype: a standard or typical example—a model on which other productions can be patterned; from the Greek *protos* (first), plus *type*.

COMMUNICATION WITHOUT WORDS

Babies listen to speech; babies make sounds, too. Nonhuman animals listen, and some, like parrots, make sounds that are identical to human words. Why, then, do we believe that the baby babbling "ma-ma" and the parrot saying "pretty boy" are not actually using language?

Elaborate sounds are not the point of language; *communication* is its basic purpose. As we look at the infant's development of language, we need to examine early capacities for communication and to see how advanced they have become before words are either spoken or understood by the infant.

Communication is basically "having something in common." When one person influences another, communication has occurred, whether it was intended or not. The infant's forms of communication are initially unintentional, but they take on intentionality as development proceeds.

Turn Taking

An example of early communication involves *turn taking* between mother and baby; one is active when the other is not, and when the first stops, the second begins activity.

The "suck-jiggle-pause" phenomenon has been considered to be a very early form of turn taking. As described earlier, this sucking pattern occurs during feeding (whether with breast or with bottle) and can be seen the first time the infant is fed. The baby sucks in short bursts, about one suck per second for 4 to 10 seconds, and then pauses for 4 to 15 seconds (Kaye, 1982a). If left to herself, the baby will resume sucking when the pause is over, but the mother responds to the pause by jiggling the baby (if asked, she may explain that she thinks this will get the baby to start sucking again). Her jiggling actually can *delay* the baby's resumption of sucking; the infant is much more likely to start to suck when the jiggle stops.

The bursts of sucking we see in human infants (but not in other mammals) may function primarily as a way for the mother to begin a turn-taking pattern (Kaye, 1982b). She does not have to interrupt the baby, but instead waits for the end of a burst of sucking and acts as if it is now her turn.

Whether or not the suck-jiggle-pause activity serves as a model for turn taking, the mother and baby of a few weeks' age engage in **protoconversations** in which turn taking occurs. The mother speaks, and then the baby vocalizes or moves his mouth in prespeech patterns (Trevarthen, 1982) that resemble the movements of an adult speaker. The two exchange eye contact and alter their facial expressions and postures in response to each other. The baby periodically averts his gaze and rests, then looks back to the mother with a brightening face. This protoconversational turn taking involves an alternation of "speaker" and "listener," who do not talk at the same time unless very excited, and there are also interconnections between turns, as each person responds to the mood and state of the other (Collis, 1985). Both mother and baby imitate head movements and mouth movements as well (Meltzoff & Moore, 1989).

protoconversation: an exchange of facial expressions, sounds, and gestures between an adult and an infant; from the Greek *protos* (first), plus *conversation*.

Joint Attention

As noted above, eye contact and *gaze aversion* are used in interactions with people, starting at a very early age. From about 6 months on, the baby's gaze is often turned toward objects of interest (Wellman, 1993).

Between 9 and 12 months, a new behavior called *joint attention* emerges. The baby looks back and forth between an object and a caregiver's eyes; she monitors the other's gaze to see where the other person is looking. The infant tries to get the adult to look at things; if the adult covers her eyes, the baby will pull her hands away or try to insert the object between the adult's hands and eyes (Wellman, 1993).

triadic: involving three people or two people and an object; from the Latin *tri-* (three).

Joint attentional behaviors are **triadic;** they involve the infant, the adult, and some third person, object, or event. Such behaviors require the ability to make a flexible, smooth transition of attention from object to person and back

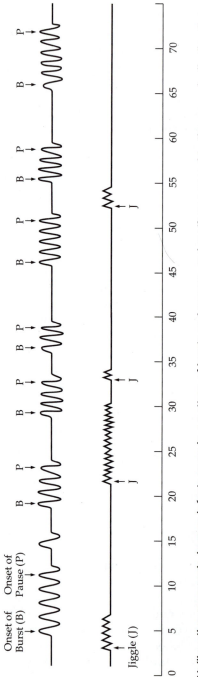

Onset of   Onset of
Burst (B)   Pause (P)

Jiggle (J)

Unlike other mammals, human infants nurse in a pattern of bursts and pauses, and mothers respond to the pause by jiggling the baby. This may form the basic model for turn taking in communication. (Source: Kaye, 1982) again. Joint attentional behaviors are not performed to get the adult to do something with the object; they apparently are simply intended as social communication about the object. These behaviors are accompanied by pleasurable emotion (Mundy, Sigman, & Kasari, 1993).

protodeclarative:
a wordless expression of information about the environment; from the Greek *protos* (first), the Latin *declarare* (to make clear).

protoimperative:
a command made without words; from the Greek *protos* (first), the Latin *imperare* (to command).

Protoimperatives

Joint attentional behaviors are sometimes called **protodeclaratives** because they seem to be primitive ways of showing or telling something, rather than requests. But it is not long before the infant shows the capacity for making **protoimperatives**—wordless requests that an adult do something. The baby persistently alternates his gaze between the object of interest and the adult's face and intensifies his activity until the goal is reached. He gestures toward the object while keeping his gaze on the adult's face. Actions like reaching and fussing, which a younger baby might direct toward a desired object, are accompanied by gazing at the adult, and they are changed in form; for example, the infant might make an open-and-shut hand gesture rather than a full reach (Bates, O'Connell, & Shore, 1987).

The mother's excitement and pleasure in joint attention are based on her relationship with her baby as much as on the interest value of the event they are watching.

Social Referencing

Joint attention and protoimperatives involve the infant's wish to send a communication, but, of course, communication can involve receiving a message from another as well. From about 6 months, infants carry out *social referencing* by looking at the parent when in an unfamiliar situation. Six- to nine-month-olds do not necessarily look at the parent's face or change their behavior in response to the parent's facial expression. Older babies do look at the parent's face specifically, and they refrain from reaching for a novel toy if the parent has a fearful expression (Walden & Ogan, 1988).

Nonsegmental Features

In addition to delivering words, voices communicate through a variety of features that do not involve phonemes. These voice characteristics, called *nonsegmental prosodic features* (the segmental features are phonemes), include overall pitch of the voice, slow or rapid tempo, rhythm, and stress on particular parts of sound patterns.

These nonsegmental features may seem to be characteristics of song rather than of speech, but if you imagine yourself talking to a variety of different people you will realize that you alter pitch, tempo, and so on to suit your view of your listener. As we will see later in this chapter, speech that adults direct toward infants is quite different in its nonsegmental features than is speech directed to other adults.

Nonsegmental features also convey the speaker's intention to ask a question, give a command, or make a statement; these sound patterns appear in infants' vocalizations at an early age, and parents respond to them as communications (Papousek & Papousek, 1987). Emotion is also implied by certain nonsegmental characteristics.

Nonsegmental prosodic features in adult speech communicate both subtle and essential distinctions. They carry information about word meanings (a light *house* keeper is different from a *light*house keeper) as well as about attitudes toward the listener. They can be used to interpret the speaker's intentions by revealing literal versus sarcastic or playful uses of words. But these complexities are far beyond the infant's or toddler's capacities to comprehend. By the end of the second year, the child can use some nonsegmental features intentionally, but she does not understand them well (Tager-Flusberg, 1993). Even a simple use like stress on one of two syllables is often done incorrectly at this age (Kehoe, Stoel-Gammon, & Buder, 1995).

Gesture

Communicative movements of the hands and body and changes of facial expression are *gestures*. Gestures are used in joint attention and in protoimperatives, where shifts in gaze direction and hand movements like pointing and grasping are essential. Gestures are not simply substitutes for speech but are an additional mode of communication that continues to be used simultaneously with speech when it emerges.

As early as the second month, infants make an open-palmed greeting gesture (similar to waving) directed toward attentive adults. This gesture is different in form from the movements shown toward moving inanimate objects (Trevarthen, 1982). By about 9 to 12 months, when joint attention appears, infants make clear gestures of pointing and "showing." The infant's intention to communicate with these gestures seems clear because "the infant will begin to point only when the other is attending to him or her, execute the point, check the other's visage, keep pointing or augment the behavior if the other is not correctly directed, and only stop when the other orients toward or comments on the object" (Wellman, 1993, p. 22). Gestures like pointing, which direct another's attention toward a particular object, are referred to as **deictic** gestures (Zinober & Martlew, 1985).

deictic: showing, or pointing out; from the Greek *deiknynai* (to show).

Although before age 10 months the infant may simply stare at someone's pointing finger instead of following it visually, she soon responds to gestures like a palm-up request to be given something. These *instrumental* gestures, intended to control the other person's behavior, are generally used by both the baby and the adult, although adults do not ordinarily have any reason to use the infant's arms-up, "pick me up" gesture.

Expressive gestures show the person's emotional state. Some of these kinds of gestures are used almost exclusively by the infant; some examples are stamping the feet in anger and flapping the hands and arms in excitement. Others are used by both parent and baby, and some, like hand clapping, are tutored by adults (Zinober & Martlew, 1985). In addition to its use in communication with others, gesture can be used as commentary or externalized thought. One 12-month-old pointed at the light his mother was about to turn out and then waved bye-bye after it was gone.

A more complex form of gesture seems to serve as communication between toddler peers. *Synchronized imitation* involves mutual copying of activities with objects; two toddlers may each hold a ball and grasp it in just the same way. The message sent by the child who imitates first may be "I am interested in you"; the reply of the other child, who imitates in turn, may mean "I am interested in you, too" (Nadel & Fontaine, 1989).

WORDS

However much the baby may communicate through gesture and nonsegmental features of vocalization, we only believe that she is developing language when she says her first word. Our problem, though, is to figure out when a sound is a word. Why would we refuse to consider the babbled "ma-ma" as a word (even though it is a word if an adult says it), but accept "kee-kah" as meaning "cat"?

The most important characteristic of a sound that is a word is that it has a *referent*; a thing or state or event must be meant by a sound in order for it to be a word. A word is a *symbol,* it is not the actual thing it stands for. But in speech or thought the word acts as a substitute for the referent; the word *means* the referent.

Words also have meaning because of their contrast with other words. They serve to point out the differences between referents that are similar to each other (for example, infant versus toddler) (McNeill, 1985). Thus, a word exists not just as a freestanding symbol but as a meaningful part of a group of symbols, agreed upon by people who use them to communicate with each other.

An entire word has a referent, but some words can be divided into smaller units of meaning. A **morpheme** is the smallest unit of language that means something and contributes to the meaning of the entire word. The word *runs,* for example, contains two morphemes: the obvious one, "run," and the ending "-s," which alters the meaning and use of the entire word. Some words, such as *run,* are single morphemes.

morpheme: the smallest group of phonemes that is a unit of meaning and, when changed, causes a change in meaning in a particular language; from the Greek *morphe* (form).

First Words

Infants are using sounds referentially (as words) when they either understand that a word-sound has a referent or when they intend to mean something. The first of these events is the beginning of receptive language and the second the beginning of expressive language.

Behavior as early as 9 months or so indicates that infants can sometimes understand that words have referents; some infants at this stage look at things that are being talked about, and some have a characteristic questioning vocalization to ask the adult to name the source of a sound—a dog barking outside, for example. By 16 months, infants tend to look longer at objects or actions that have just been named for them (Golinkoff, Hirsh-Pasek, Cualey, & Gordon, 1987).

Does the toddler know that words have meanings and that it is possible for her to discover a word's referent? In one study (Baldwin, 1993), 19- to 20-month-olds were able to use adults' speech and gazing as a way of finding a referent for an unfamiliar word, even when one object named was out of sight at the time.

First words are often spoken at about age 12 months, although there is a good deal of variability in expressive language. These first words do not necessarily have anything to do with what the child wants; after all, he has developed plenty of protoimperative skill at getting people to do things. The first words are more likely to be descriptive of interesting things in the environment—pets, people, toys. The operation of language learning as a dynamic system is shown in new studies of the kinds of words learned first in a given language. Although it was previously thought that nouns were learned before verbs, a study of infants learning Mandarin Chinese showed that, at age 22 months, more verbs than nouns were spoken (Tardif, 1996).

Word meanings quickly extend to categories rather than to a specific unique referent. One 15-month-old used his word "shop" (sharp) about knives, scissors, teeth, fingernails, and the pointed end of a plastic bag tie.

APPLICATIONS & ARGUMENTS
Reading, Singing, and Language

Exposure to language is well known as a factor that aids an infant's language development. Unfortunately, some parents feel overwhelmed by awkwardness when they try to talk to their babies. It feels ridiculous to talk to someone who can't answer, and the parent may even have been criticized by others for such silly behavior.

Reading aloud can be a way for an embarrassed parent to expose a baby to language. Of course, the reading has to be tailored to the baby, who at 6 months or so will probably want to grab and eat the book and later will want to play with pages and examine pictures. The parent should not expect to read word for word from the beginning to the end of a story. Instead, a book can be used as a way of organizing some language exposure for the baby. The adult can talk about pictures, point to them, invent a simple story, or read some or all of the actual text. The point is simply that baby and adult are doing something with language together.

A second way to provide some language experience is to sing to the baby. The words of songs follow the normal rules of the language and are even more attention-getting than speech because of their changes in pitch and intonation. One of the great pleasures of early parenthood is the discovery that the baby likes your singing, even if no one else does. Many songs for children have accompanying movements or finger plays that increase the interest and enjoyment of parent and baby both. Once again, the two are sharing language and taking pleasure in it—an ideal learning situation.

Some meanings, like that one, are clearly shared with adults, whereas others are quite idiosyncratic. The same child referred to a ceiling fan as "wud"—the same term he used for printed letters on a page—perhaps because it was X-shaped. Overextension of words is common in the second half of the second year; for example, "doggie" may be used to describe a horse, an orange may be "ball," and all men tend to be referred to as "daddy." Difficulties with articulation may confuse some of these issues, as "ban" might mean "banana" or "bannister," and "ap" could be "apple" or "lap."

Vocabulary Explosion

Somewhere around the middle of the second year, a rapid increase in vocabulary begins. This *vocabulary explosion* lasts until about age 24 months. During this period, the average child acquires understanding of 900 root words (Huttenlocher, Haight, Bryle, Seltzer, & Lyons, 1991).

CONTEXT AND COMBINATIONS

To master the use of language, the toddler needs to realize that words can have different meanings when they are in different contexts, or even in different positions in the same group of words. The situation provides cues about meaning that do not exist in the isolated word, and the arbitrary rules about position work because they are shared by a group of people, just as word meanings are shared.

Single Words and Combinations

It has been suggested that a single word used by an infant can imply a message equivalent to that of a whole sentence. Meanings can be altered depending on the context, so "baw!" could mean "oh, there's the ball, it rolled under the sideboard" or it could mean "I fell down on the ball and it hurt." Single words used in this manner to express a great deal are called **holo-phrases.** Their meaning is determined by context, nonsegmental features, gestures, and facial expression.

holophrase: a single-word utterance that carries the meaning of a whole phrase or sentence; from the Greek *holos* (whole), *phrazein* (to point out, declare).

Combinations of single words may occur before any true sentence is formed. In *vertical constructions,* the toddler adds a word to each of an adult's statements or questions. ("Do you see what you lost?" "Ball." "The ball is under the sofa." "Rug.") *Horizontal constructions,* on the other hand, have relational, sentencelike meanings that are built up one word at a time (Bates, O'Connell, & Shore, 1987). One 17-month-old produced the sequence "man-ham-bang-nay-lad-up," describing repairs to the roof, where the workman climbed a ladder with hammer and nails and proceeded to "bang." Some children also add "dummy words"—single, invented words that are combined with a one-word statement (Bates, O'Connell, & Shore, 1987). For example, one 2-year-old included the invented word "wida" with every one-word statement for some weeks, at the end of which she began to make two-word combinations (Moskowitz, 1994).

Sentences and Grammaticization

A combination of words is considered a sentence when it contains *predication:* an attribution of a state or quality to one entity, or the attribution of a relationship to two or more entities. Most children produce some word combinations that involve predication by about age 20 months (Bates, O'Connell, & Shore, 1987), but they also continue for some time to make one-word statements as well as horizontal and vertical constructions.

syntax: the rules about order of words used to convey meaning in a particular language; from the Greek *syn-* (with), *tassein* (to arrange).

Simple two-word sentences like "ride bike" and "Debbie keys" already display an understanding of the basics of grammar, because they usually conform to the word order that would be used in an expanded, adult version of the statement. *Grammaticization,* the application of appropriate grammatical rules to multiple-word statements, occurs between age 20 and 30 months. There are actually two aspects to the process. The first, **syntax,** has to do with

morphology: the study of the rules of word formation in a language, such as inflections for different tenses of a verb; from the Greek *morphe* (form).

word order and is mastered quickly. The second aspect of grammar, **morphology,** takes longer to complete. Morphology is a set of rules about suffixes, prefixes, and infixes, about changes in verb forms for different tenses, and about the use of freestanding morphemes like prepositions.

Changes in morphology are most evident in verb forms. Initially, children use the same verb form for every tense and person; "wun" covers the situation whether the running happens now or happened yesterday and whether I or she is the runner. Later, past and present are discriminated and irregular verbs like *ran* are used correctly, in exact imitation of adult use. In a third stage, however, *overgeneralization* occurs; the child tries to generate verb forms according to the rules, but he does not understand the existence of irregular verbs. He forms every past tense according to the rules and says "I runned" and "she writed." Overgeneralized verb forms may be used occasionally for many years (Bates, O'Connell, & Shore, 1987), and even adults may sometimes find themselves in difficulty with a verb like "to blow-dry."

One important consideration of grammaticization is that children seem to use much more complex grammatical information in their listening than they can manage in their expressive language. For example, if 17-month-olds hear a doll called "zav," they use "zav" as a proper name; but if they hear it called "*the* zav" or "*a* zav" they do not. If a block is referred to, however, they never think its proper name is "zav," whether they hear it called "zav," "a zav," or "the zav" (Katz, Baker, & Macnamara, 1974).

Although children of this age do not use the articles *the* and *a* in their own speech, they show a better understanding of sentences that include articles used appropriately than of sentences that do not (Gerken & McIntosh, 1993). Toddlers also act as if they know that pronouns and nouns are different, because they rarely put an adjective in front of a pronoun (Bloom, 1990).

Pragmatics

pragmatics: alterations in speech intended to convey meaning to a particular listener; from the Greek *pragma* (deed).

monologue: a speech made for the speaker's benefit, not directed to a listener; from the Greek *monos* (alone), *logos* (word).

People communicating by means of speech alter what they say to fit the context and to help guarantee that a listener will understand (or that any other purpose of the speech will be fulfilled). These efforts to tailor speech to fit a particular goal are called **pragmatics.** Pragmatics includes the choice of different types of discourse for different situations and the use of relevant information the speaker has about the listener.

Early use of pragmatics often involves *repetition* until the listener shows comprehension; the toddler's poor articulation may make dozens of repetitions necessary before even the most attentive adult understands. *Physical manipulation* of the listener or an object may also be used. The toddler thrusts an object into the listener's face, or seizes the listener's face in her hands and turns it until eye contact is made.

Not all speech is directed toward a listener. One of the functions of speech for an older toddler is as a narrative **monologue.** Carried out when she is alone, this type of speech seems to be used by the toddler to "think out loud," muse on the events of the day, and perhaps elaborate on and practice language forms. Narrative monologues may contribute to the use of verb tenses and to time concepts. For example, one 2-year-old said the following while alone in her crib: "My sleep—Mommy came—and Mommy 'get up, get up time go home'—When my slep and—Mormor came.—Then Mommy coming—then 'get up, time to go home'.—Time to go home. . . . Yesterday did that.—Now Emmy sleeping in regular bed" (Nelson, 1989, p. 302). The monologue is pragmatically different from speech directed toward a listener; it does not include attempts to ascertain that understanding has occurred. The child is not incapable of monitoring another person's comprehension, but she knows that in a monologue she does not need to do so.

INDIVIDUAL DIFFERENCES

Attempts to find a single, innate pathway for the development of language have given way to descriptions of styles of language learning. What was at one time considered to be a matter of gender differences now appears to involve individual differences.

Gender does seem to be one source of variability in language development, although some effects, like vocabulary size, are evident only at an early stage (Huttenlocher et al., 1991). As we saw in Chapter 8, some gender differences in early perceptual abilities, like sound localization, could have an effect on language learning (Muir, Clifton, & Clarkson, 1989). There also appear to be some gender differences in brain development, with adult females showing a greater density of neurons in a part of the brain related to auditory and language functions (Holden, 1995). To complicate the matter, mothers tend to treat boys and girls differently, using more verbal stimulation with boys (Weitzman, Birns, & Friend, 1985).

Birth order is another variable that seems to influence the development of language, although the differences are small. The language development of second-born children has been described as "different" rather than "disadvantaged" (Pine, 1995).

Styles of language development also apparently influence specific developmental steps. These have been described as two "strands" of development (Bates, O'Connell, & Shore, 1987). Strand 1 is more common among first-borns, females, and children from families of higher socioeconomic status, whereas Strand 2 is more characteristic of males, later-born children, and families of lower socioeconomic status. (There is much overlap, however, and it is quite possible, for example, for a first-born girl to show a Strand 2 type of development.)

Strand 1 shows *semantic*, or "meaning," differences from Strand 2. Strand 1 toddlers produce high proportions of nouns in their early speech, and their first 50 words are all single words rather than phrases. They use many adjectives, imitate labels for objects, and develop vocabulary rapidly. They are flexible in their use of single words, using a word in different contexts.

Strand 1 children also show grammatical differences. They employ "telegraphic speech" without function words like *the*. All elements of their speech are meaningful and they use novel combinations of words. They follow word-order rules with a good deal of consistency. When they imitate adult speech, they use grammar at the same level as their spontaneous speech. Strand 1 children also show better articulation, more intelligibility, and greater consistency in pronunciation. Even at the babbling stage, they use more consonants.

Strand 2 children show contrasting development in each of these areas. They show slower vocabulary development and use fewer nouns and adjectives. They use some whole phrases and formulas (like "timeforbed") in their first 50 words. Their first sentences use function words and inflected forms. They use "dummy words," described earlier. Strand 2 toddlers also use "frozen forms"—utterances containing words that are not used alone or in other combinations, such as "you have that" as a way of asking for something). Strand 2 children also use consonants less at the babbling stage and have poorer intelligibility later on (Bates, O'Connell, & Shore, 1987).

Why do these (and possibly other) "strands" exist? They may result from the interactions of the effects of gender, birth order, and socioeconomic status with aspects of parental style. For example, mothers have been described as showing either a *directive* or an *eliciting* style, no matter what child they are talking to; a more directive style may have a negative effect on early language skill (Tomasello, 1988).

INFANT-DIRECTED TALK

We have already seen that very young infants are interested in human beings, pay attention to speech, and respond to phonetic differences in much the same way that adults do. But can this account for their very rapid mastery of the spoken language? When we listen carefully to adult speech, we notice that it is ordinarily full of errors, hesitations, and unnecessary repetitions. It is also very rapid and contains few clues about where one word begins and another ends. You may have noticed, for example, that your carefully learned classroom French or Spanish is not necessarily much help in decoding everyday language in France or Spain. How does the infant make sense of English or any other language "as she is spoke"?

An important part of the answer is that a language is not "spoke" in the same way to an infant as it is to an adult. There are genuine differences between *adult-directed talk* (ADT) and *infant-directed talk* (IDT), also called *baby talk* or *motherese*. IDT is an excellent example of the adult's use of pragmatics, because its characteristics alter as the baby gets older.

IDT in general involves higher vocal pitches than ADT does. It uses *prosodic highlighting*, with unusual stress on important words, and it is often coordinated with *contextual salience*—ongoing situations that catch the child's attention (Ingram, 1995; Vihman, Kay, de Boysson-Bardies, Durand, & Sundberg, 1994). Slowing and emphasis on careful articulation are features of IDT that may help infants notice important phonemes before they have any awareness of meaning (Barinaga, 1992). IDT includes fewer errors, more complete sentences, and more repetition of salient words than does ADT.

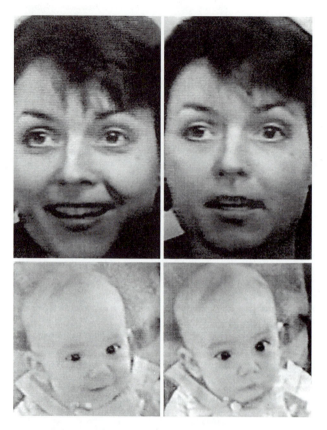

On the left, an actress pretends she is talking to a baby; on the right, she pretends to talk to an adult. Underneath are pictures of a 4-month-old's responses to video presentation of the actress's IDT and ADT. The baby's pleasure teaches adults to use IDT.

TABLE 11.1 *Some changes in vocal patterns can indicate to an infant which emotional category an adult is expressing.*

Emotional category	Vocal change
Approval	Higher pitch, less complex sound contour, longer duration
Attention	Higher pitch, more complex sound contour, shorter duration
Prohibition	Lower pitch, less complex sound contour, shorter duration
Comforting	Lower pitch, more complex sound contour, longer duration
Playing	Higher pitch, more complex sound contour, longer duration

Source: Based on Ingram, 1995.

Like ADT, IDT is accompanied by gestures and facial expressions that augment communication. Facial expressions are exaggerated, just as the intonation of IDT is exaggerated. The intent of IDT is often simply playful, rather than an attempt to communicate objective information; the goal is the exchange of positive emotional signals (Papousek & Papousek, 1987).

IDT changes as the baby gets older as part of a transactional process. Baby and caregiver influence each other, and as a result each changes and influences the other in different ways. IDT at the beginning of a baby's life is different in a number of ways from what it will be in a year or two. To understand the changes, we need to note three possible categories into which vocalizations and gestures can be placed. The first, the **perlocutionary** category, has to do with situations in which a vocalization or gesture has the *effect* of saying something whether or not it was intended to do so. The second, the **illocutionary** category, includes situations in which both speaker and listener recognize that there is an intention to communicate. The third, the **locutionary** category, is one in which words are used to communicate and they carry referential value (Austin, 1962).

McLean (1990) has described the stages of development of IDT (and of infant communication to the adult). Stage I, from birth to 2 or 3 months, is considered a *reactive perlocutionary* stage. The infant's unintentional reactions to internal and external events signal her moods and wishes to the adult, who responds to the signals as if they were intentional. IDT at this point involves nonsegmental cues such as intonation and exaggerated facial expressions, which may not have any connection to the actual content of the adult's speech. The adult may be talking about getting the car repaired, but the nonsegmental message to the baby is about pleasurable interaction and affection.

The infant's response to IDT is not the same throughout the first year. Before age 6 months, the infant's attention to IDT is primarily visual; she notices the facial expressions and movement patterns characteristic of IDT. After age 6 months, infants notice the audible aspects of IDT (Lewkowicz, 1996) and respond differently to the adult's speech as well as manner.

The caregiver at this stage (and later) may "talk for the baby," stating in an altered voice what the baby might be expected to want to say. "Talking for the baby" is often introduced by the word *say* in a less intense, lower-pitched voice. An example might be, "Say, 'I don't want my picture taken, Daddy,'" with the latter part in a louder, higher-pitched (but not otherwise babyish) voice.

The second, or *proactive perlocutionary,* stage lasts from age 2 or 3 to 8 or 9 months. The infant's communication becomes increasingly purposeful and the caregiver responds to the baby's apparent intent. Although IDT retains its special nonsegmental features, it also becomes specialized in a segmental way, as the mother emphasizes words and phrases. The baby responds to these emphasized words, especially when they are ritualized and used repeatedly in a specific situation (such as, "time for a nap!").

Stage III, the stage of *emerging illocutionary* communication, occurs between age 8 or 9 and 12 or 15 months. The baby's skills in joint attention allow

perlocutionary: relating to situations in which a vocalization or gesture conveys meaning whether it was meant to or not; from the Latin *per* (by means of), *loqui* (to speak).

illocutionary: relating to situations in which both speaker and listener know there is an intention to communicate, but words are not used; from the Latin *illatus* (brought in, inferred), *loqui* (to speak).

locutionary: using words to convey meaning; from the Latin *loqui* (to speak).

TABLE 11.2 *This list of steps in language development shows how early the process begins, but it also demonstrates how development continues for years beyond the infant period. Parents who fine-tune their language to suit the toddler's comprehension must avoid a number of constructions that a preschool child would understand but that a toddler would not.*

Age	Language comprehension ability
3–6 months	Responds to differences in sound frequencies
6–9 months	Recognizes own name, family's names; responds to "no"; seems to listen to conversations
9–12 months	Understands and responds to simple commands
12–18 months	Recognizes names of body parts
18–24 months	Understands "in" and "on"; understands complex sentences; carries out 2 or 3 steps of directions
18–24 months	Understands small numbers
24–36 months	Understands possessives, common verbs, common adjectives; understands description of functions (for example, recognizes spoon from "what you eat with")
36–48 months	Understands prepositions "next to," "behind," "in front of"
48–60 months	Understands "before" and "after" in time; prepositions "above, " "below," "at the bottom"

Source: Based on Linder, 1990.

him to direct the caregiver's attention to a referent, and he persists until understood. The baby also recognizes, responds to, and even uses some words. The mother or other caregiver continues to respond to the baby's intentions. In IDT, the caregiver now begins to fine-tune the complexity and length of utterances to make them as complex as possible but still comprehensible to the baby.

Stages IV and V, the *conventional illocutionary* and *emerging locutionary* stages, last from age 12 to 15 months to 18 to 24 months. The infant now uses conventional gestures and words to communicate, and the caregiver responds to what the baby says, rather than focusing on other aspects of intention. IDT includes expanding on and emending what is said; if the child says "car," the mother may expand ("Yes, that's Daddy's car") or correct ("No, that's a truck").

IDT remains specialized when directed at older toddlers or preschoolers. For example, when reading to children aged 18 months to 2½ years, mothers lengthened the vowels in nouns in a way they did not when reading to another adult (Swanson, Leonard, & Gandour, 1992). Fine-tuning of IDT continues as the child moves through the preschool years (Sokolov, 1993). In addition to speaking to the child at a developmentally appropriate level, the caregiver also provides *scaffolding* in the form of speech that cues more advanced responses from the child. For example, a mother asks her 20-month-old, "Do you want the dance record?" He replies, "No!" A few minutes later, she asks, "Do you want to listen to it?" and he replies with the more complex construction "No record" (Greenfield, Reilly, Leaper, & Baker, 1985). Using language playfully seems an especially important way of providing scaffolding (Norton, 1995/1996).

Motivation for IDT

Why is it that adults speak differently to infants than to other adults? The motivation must be strong, because in the United States it is common for adults to be reprimanded by others for "talking baby talk." Overhearing IDT seems anxiety-provoking for many adults.

A major reason for using IDT is that babies like it and show attentiveness and pleasure when they hear it. The infant's positive emotional reaction to IDT is clear, and adults prefer babies who show positive emotional reactions (Werker & McLeod, 1989).

Other reasons for IDT are connected with the caregiver's attitudes and expectations about the baby. Depressed mothers do not modify their behavior

---

APPLICATIONS & ARGUMENTS
Baby Talk: Good or Bad?

If you have read the text of this chapter, you are aware of the research showing that infant-directed talk is an important factor in language development. But what about other aspects of "baby talk"? What, for example, about adults who imitate the toddler's pronunciation when talking to him? What about families who retain a "baby" word for years? Obviously, it is not fair to a toddler or preschooler to fail to prepare her to talk to people outside the family, especially if the child will be in nonparental care of some kind.

Most families have some special, private words to describe elimination. These may be circumlocutions (as in the case of one boy who asked an adult to "turn on the light" as a way of requesting the assistance he needed in the bathroom), or they may be startlingly direct terms. (One couple regretted later that they had taught their sweet little girls to say "piss" and "shit," although everyone certainly knew what they meant!) Toddlers and preschoolers need to know meaningful but socially acceptable terms about elimination to use outside the family. But what about other "baby words"? Many families with quite big children still have "basketty" for dinner, and sometimes they have "meatbulbs" too. This is a private family language, almost a code, used to convey love and solidarity as well as information. Because it has no real impact on language development, I doubt that anyone has any business criticizing it.

in response to what the baby does; they are slower to respond and less likely to use exaggerated intonations in their IDT (Bettes, 1988). Fathers have been reported to speak to infants in ways that are closer to ADT than is the speech mothers use (Turbiville, Turnbull, & Turnbull, 1995). African "child nurses" of about 10 years old have been reported to talk to their infant charges significantly differently than the mothers do; the child nurses' attitudes toward the babies are undoubtedly different from those of the mothers (Nwokah, 1987).

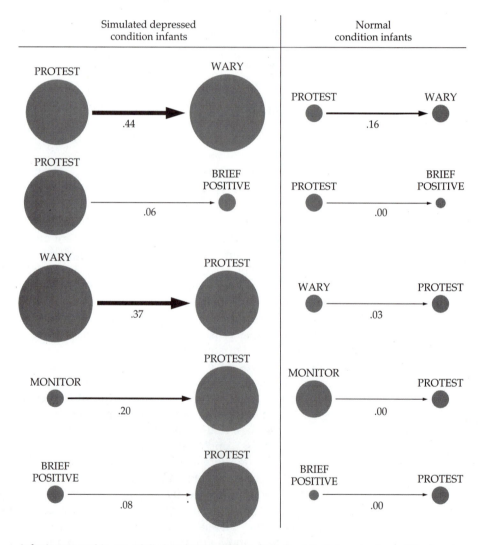

Infants exposed to an adult showing a still face (the simulated depressed condition) respond with larger amounts of protest and wariness than do infants in a normal situation. The sizes of the circles show the amount of time in each state. (Source: Cohn & Tronick, 1982)

HEARING IMPAIRMENT AND LANGUAGE DEPRIVATION

Hearing speech clearly plays an important role in the development of an infant's own spoken language. What happens if there is too little language heard? This is most likely to happen if hearing impairment is caused by genetic problems, teratogenic effects, or infections after birth. The amount of hearing impairment caused by these factors can vary from a small loss in one or both ears to complete deafness.

Otitis Media

As we noted in Chapter 8, ear infections are a common cause of hearing loss in infants and toddlers. *Acute otitis media* (AOM), often with fever and ear pain, is followed by a period of a month or more when remaining fluid in the middle ear impairs hearing. Hearing loss from otitis media (OM) can be mild to moderate, it can be in one or both ears, and it fluctuates in level from one day to the next. The child thus hears partial sounds and may miss both segmental features and nonsegmental ones, like the change in intonation that marks a question (Roberts, Wallace, & Zeisel, 1993).

The effects of OM on development can be subtle and do not necessarily show in expressive language during the infant and toddler years. Toddlers are less attentive during an OM episode (Feagans, Kipp, & Blood, 1994). They may learn to "tune out" language because they hear frequent changes in the apparent loudness of a sound. They have particular problems when there is a lot of background noise like other children talking or the television on (Feagans, Kipp, & Blood, 1994; Roberts, Wallace, & Zeisel, 1993). The difference between the language levels of some children who have had frequent OM and those who have not increases as they get older and may lead to reading problems even after hearing becomes completely normal; other children who have had OM show no problems, however (Kramer & Williams, 1993).

Profound Hearing Loss

The presence of severe hearing loss from the time of birth alters the development of prespeech vocalization, as well as interferes with spoken language. Infants with severe hearing impairments do not begin babbling until months after babies whose hearing is normal do.

The fact that the child with a hearing impairment may not speak does not indicate that she will not communicate. All other things being equal, the infant with a hearing impairment has a normal capacity for joint attention and for referential acts.

Early experience with gesture language, such as American Sign Language (ASL), makes it possible for infants with hearing impairments to reach developmental milestones of language, such as two-word combinations, at a normal pace. In fact, the time of the appearance of the "first word" (first referential sign) and the size of the vocabulary at age 1 year may be superior to those of hearing children (Meier, 1991). "Pronunciation" or articulation of signs may be clumsy initially, just as early speech is clumsy.

Language Deprivation: Feral Children

feral: developing and living outside human society; from the Latin *ferus* (wild).

Although hearing loss is the most common reason for lack of experience with the spoken language, it is also possible for a hearing child simply not to be exposed to speech. This could occur to a moderate extent because of a caregiver's depression or because of cultural differences in IDT. The more severe cases of language deprivation, however, are those of so-called **feral** children. Classically, these are children like the famous "Wild Boy of Aveyron" who have supposedly managed to survive without human care. The term has also been applied to children like "Genie," a girl who was confined to a room and heard no speech from the time she was 2 until she was rescued at age 13 (Curtiss, 1977). These children show little or no speech development initially, although some, like Genie, develop a good deal of language after their environment improves.

The difficulty with using information about feral children to improve our understanding about language development is that these children missed much more than language experience. Diet, health care, and social interaction were all abnormal. It may be the case, too, that they were abandoned or mistreated in part because of some initial abnormality.

Bilingualism

bilingual: fluent in two languages; from the Latin *bi-* (two), *lingua* (tongue).

So far in this section, we have been dealing with babies who, for one reason or another, did not have much experience hearing speech. It seems odd to include **bilingual** families under this category. Is there such a thing as hearing too much language or too many kinds of language? Some research has suggested that exposure to two languages before one has been mastered is confusing to the baby and slows language development; however, it is possible that such an effect could be due to poverty, cross-cultural conflicts, or other factors that may occur more often in bicultural families (McArdle, Kim, Grube, & Randall, 1995).

To have mastery of two languages is a great asset to an adult. But although grammar can be learned later in life, pronunciation like that of a native speaker must be acquired by the preschool or early school years. Is there some way that bilingual families can provide the benefits of language learning to their children without risking general language delays? One suggestion is the "one parent, one language" principle (Döppke, 1992): one parent, grandparent, or other caregiver uses one language, and one or more other people use the other. The child can then "decode" which language is being used by noting which person is speaking.

Increasing levels of immigration and reduction in native fertility rates (Holden, 1985) suggest that issues about bilingualism will have continuing importance for infants and toddlers in the United States. Language-minority families do not often have the choice of a child care facility where even one

Bilingual experiences in day care may give a child a foundation in the language to be used in school, while fostering continuing communication with the family.

caregiver speaks their language. Development of the home language may be reduced and even lost if most of the child's language experience is with the English-speaking caregiver; although the child will be more ready for school experience with this background in English, the effect will be at the dreadful expense of severing much communication between the child and the non-English-speaking family (Chang & Pulido, 1994).

ASSESSMENT AND INTERVENTION

A consideration of all the language-related topics we have dealt with so far will show that assessment of language development is far more than counting how many words a child can say. Assessment can begin long before any words are spoken and can look at a wide variety of communicative abilities, including receptive language, in addition to the use of speech.

Why would assessment be carried out? One reason would be the presence of risk factors, like early hearing loss, that would predict the possibility of language problems. A pediatrician may pick up some delays in the course of well-baby care, or a parent may realize that milestones of language development are not occurring as expected; the failure to produce words is most often noticed. A day care provider may call the parents' attention to problems.

Unfortunately, medical personnel and day care staff may not be aware that even children under the age of 2 can be assessed for problems of language development ("Early identification," 1993).

The goal of assessment is to guide early intervention in the hope of correcting language problems and allowing the child to catch up with peers before school entry. Children with early language problems are at serious risk of having poor academic performance (Lockwood, 1994). Impaired communication can be the first sign of mental retardation or of hearing impairment, which will require additional special care (Ogletree & Daniels, 1993).

Assessment Approaches

Assessment of language development is a complex topic on which we will touch only very briefly. Like other forms of assessment of infants and toddlers, it should involve a team approach that looks at physical and social issues as well as specific language concerns.

Language assessment needs to take into account that 15% of normally developing children show *slow expressive language development* (SELD) when tested at ages 18 to 24 months. Although they do not show the expected vocabulary size or two-word combinations, other aspects of communication are normal and they do catch up later (Paul & Jennings, 1992). The behavior of SELD toddlers may be a challenge for their parents because so much expression is nonverbal (Prizant & Wetherby, 1993).

Recent approaches to language assessment focus on the integrated development of the child and stress the role of socioemotional abilities in communication. For example, the Communication and Symbolic Behavior Scales (CSBS) look at three categories in which normally developing children show progress before they use words: (1) *behavioral regulation,* or using signals to get other people to do things; (2) *social interaction,* or using signals to attract someone's attention; and (3) *joint attention,* or calling someone's attention to an event for the purpose of sharing experience (Prizant & Wetherby, 1990). An important technique in the CSBS is the use of communicative "temptations," or engaging situations intended to entice a child to communicate. Another approach to assessment of language in the context of the child's general development is Transdisciplinary Play-Based Assessment (TPBA), discussed in Chapter 10 (Linder, 1990).

Autistic Disorders (Pervasive Developmental Disorders)

Although many disorders of language development result from hearing problems or lack of appropriate language experience, poor communication development can be an indicator of a very serious developmental disturbance. A category of socioemotional disturbance, *pervasive developmental disorders,* includes two subcategories in which problems of communication are the main features. *Autistic disorder* and *pervasive developmental disorder not otherwise specified* (PDDNOS) may both involve delay in or complete lack of development of speech or of gesture communication. However, these disorders are

TABLE 11.3 *A wide variety of communicative and symbolic abilities are assessed by tests like the Communicative and Symbolic Behavior Scales. The actual use of words is only one factor in evaluation; here are some examples of abilities that are tested.*

The proportion of communicative acts that are used for social purposes.
The use of gestural communications like pushing, pointing, waving, nodding.
The number of vocalizations that involve two or more syllables.
The number of communicative acts per minute.
Modifications of communications when a goal is not achieved.
Facial expressions showing positive emotion.
Facial expressions showing negative emotion.
Complexity of symbolic play.

Source: Based on Prizant & Wetherby, 1993.

autistic:
unresponsive to other people (relating to a category of pervasive developmental disorder); from the Greek *auto-* (self).

echolalia: speech that repeats what someone else has just said; from the Greek *echo* (echo), *lalia* (chatter).

also characterized by general impairments of social interaction and communication; lack of speech is the least of the child's problems.

In infancy, **autistic** children are impaired in early communication using gaze, facial expression, body posture, and gesture. They engage in little pretend play or social imitation. When there is speech, the autistic toddler does not succeed in conversation with others but uses language in a stereotyped or repetitive way. Some show **echolalia,** simply repeating what others say. Autistic children tend to require sameness in the environment; they want routines or rituals, and they have repetitive mannerisms of their own, like hand flapping and toe walking. (PDDNOS children do not show as extensive or early problems as autistic children do, but they are still seriously affected.)

Autism will be discussed in more detail in Chapter 12, but we should note here that it is probably biological in origin and begins before birth (Johnson, Siddons, Frith, & Morton, 1992). Although failure to develop language is usually the symptom that gets caregivers' attention, diagnosis certainly cannot be based on language problems alone. Medical and neurologic evalu-

TABLE 11.4 *Checklists can be used to elicit from parents information that could help diagnose pervasive developmental disorders at an early age. Here are some items that have been used in research on 18-month-olds.*

Parent's evaluation of whether child likes to be bounced or swung.
Parent's evaluation of whether child shows interest in other children.
Parent's evaluation of whether child likes peek-a-boo and hiding games.
Parent's evaluation of child's pretend play.
Observer's evaluation of child's eye contact.
Observer's evaluation of whether child points or responds to others' pointing for communication.

Source: Based on Baron-Cohen & Howlin, 1993.

ation as well as tests of cognitive development and other factors are essential (Freeman, 1993).

Early Intervention

Techniques used for intervention in early language development are complex and require advanced professional training, so this section will simply outline some general approaches used. Intervention involves working with the whole child and her family. Health and emotional problems must be dealt with; hearing impairment must be assessed and treated. Early language intervention is not just a matter of helping the child practice making difficult sounds.

Intervention provides an optimal listening environment. Speech is normally not a great deal louder than background noise, so the noise needs to be reduced in order to interfere less with understanding of speech. Curtains and rugs absorb echoes, and closed windows and doors exclude outside sounds. One-to-one interactions expose the child to speech under ideal conditions when the adult stays close to the child while speaking, faces the child, and stays at the child's eye level. Slow, clear speech with visual cues like facial expression and gesture helps the child listen (Roberts, Wallace, & Zeisel, 1993).

The optimal language learning environment is one in which there is plenty of talking and quick responsiveness to the child's attempts to communicate. The caregiver or therapist needs to work at the child's current level of communication rather than the stage where she "ought to be." Toddlers do not fail to speak because they are stubborn or because no one has forced them to do so to get what they want.

Multisensory information is useful in focusing the child's attention on speech or gesture. For example, Total Communication (Kouri, 1989) combines simultaneous use of sign and speech. Reading to infants and toddlers is another way to provide multisensory information and can be a good approach for caregivers who feel "silly" about talking to infants. Reading aloud is especially effective if the adult thinks about it as "book sharing" rather than as instruction (Fitzgerald & Needlman, 1991).

An optimal language learning environment also includes *motivation* of the child by "communicative temptations" (Prizant & Wetherby, 1989)—for example, activating a windup toy, letting it run down, and handing it to the child, or putting some desired food into a clear container the child cannot open and putting it in front of the child.

THE INTEGRATED BABY

The baby of 9 months responds with fascination and attention when spoken to by her mother. Sitting firmly or pulling herself into a standing position, the infant can turn body, head, and eyes to watch and listen at the same time. She can use information from both ears as well as both eyes. She notices differences among phonemes of her parents' language, and her babbled consonants stress those phonemes. Either baby or caregiver can readily draw the other into a situation of joint attention; looking at kittens playing, for example, they periodically exchange gazes and smiles.

Language directed to the infant by the caregiver uses both nonsegmental and segmental information, and the caregiver is beginning to fine-tune speech to help the baby understand. The caregiver may produce a series of comments while the baby's attention is clearly caught by the kittens; "Look at those kitty-cats! Aren't they nice kitty-cats? Look at the kitty-cats playing!" Such remarks may contain words that already have referents for the baby. When she hears those words, she may search visually for the kittens where she remembers seeing them last.

Her caregiver's language now contains some referential meaning for the infant, and the baby's cognitive ability and memory allow her to make use of the meaning. Most of her communication is still a matter of sharing emotional states with a social partner or of reaching for an object while looking to her caregiver as a request for help. But the fact that she shows some referential meaning tells us that as long as her hearing and her experience of language remain appropriate, she will soon cross the threshold to spoken language.

PROBLEMS TO CONSIDER AND DISCUSS

1. Do you think an infant could learn about language as well from television as from a real person? Why or why not?

2. Why are phonemes considered to be categories of sounds rather than specific sound patterns?

3. Do babies learn to speak to get things they want or for purposes of social interaction?

4. When is a sound a word?

5. What abilities to communicate would you expect to see in a 10-month-old?

12

Emotional Development

Like other aspects of development, social and emotional growth depends on a combination of internal and external factors. Great quantities of research have been carried out on both, because the implications of emotional development for the individual and for society are extraordinary.

The amount of information on emotional development makes it necessary to try to divide the indivisible, to separate the "basic nature" of the child from the effects of experiences with other people. This chapter will focus on some fundamentals of early emotional development. These fundamental events occur in a social context, but the stress here will be on the events themselves rather than on the social milieu. Chapter 13 will examine social experience and its impact on the child's social and emotional development.

Students of "traditional" college age sometimes have difficulty empathizing with the emotional world of the infant and toddler. The critical emotional events of the young child's world involve the development of a deep emotional connection with parents and caregivers. College students are often at a point in their lives where their greatest concern is breaking the deep connection with their own parents and reestablishing it with a potential mate. Reading and thinking about the attachment between child and parent sometimes gives students a sense of anxiety or even revulsion; it is very hard to consider these profound, almost universal emotions and not apply them to ourselves. It may help to remember the concept of developmentally appropriate practice. A set of feelings and behaviors that are appropriate at one stage of life are inappropriate or even "crazy" at another. An infant who does not develop strong feelings about some adults does not grow up to be the student who is struggling for independence. There really is a season for everything.

RESEARCH METHODS

In most subject areas we have looked at so far, research programs concentrated on experimental approaches or on carefully controlled observations in the laboratory or in the home. Studies of emotional development use those research techniques, but they may also involve clinical work, which collects information about infants or families while problems are being treated.

Clinical and experimentally oriented approaches usually have rather different flavors; they tend to follow somewhat different rules and to concentrate on different issues about development. The relationship between basic research and clinical or child care practice has diminished over the years, so today

> relative separation of basic research scientists from clinical and childcare providers has ... limited and delayed the influence of theory and research on services. ... Some service providers see researchers as investigating narrow, artificial phenomena with little direct clinical and practical value; some researchers see service providers as superstitious believers in programs and/or forms of treatment that cannot pass scientific scrutiny. (Aber & Baker, 1990, p. 427)

Nevertheless, for a complete picture of early emotional development, we need information both from the laboratory and from studies of spontaneous behavior. An understanding of the biological and genetic components of emotion is also needed.

Biological, Genetic, and Ethological Approaches

Some biological techniques noted in earlier chapters can be applied to the study of emotion. For example, structural differences in the brain can be identified through magnetic resonance imaging (Andreason et al., 1994) and compared to behavioral differences. Measurement of stress and other types of hormones, which used to require blood work, can now be done through testing of saliva (Larson, Gunnar, & Hertsgaard, 1991). Heart rates and patterns of heart rate change can be measured with little intrusion on the infant's behavior.

The study of genetic factors in emotional development usually focuses on heritability and looks at family resemblances. The more advanced techniques of genetic research (discussed in Chapter 3) are rarely applied to the study of normal emotion, although they have been used in the investigation of serious problems like schizophrenia. Do note, however, that a biological cause for an emotional characteristic does not necessarily mean the characteristic is inherited; diet, environmental pollution, injury, or illness are possible biological causes that are not transmitted genetically (Goldsmith et al., 1987).

Ethological studies of emotional development are based on the assumption that all members of our species share certain emotional patterns at particular points in development. These studies involve careful, highly detailed observation in natural settings and are most comparable to studies of animal behavior (Hinde, 1983).

Behavioral Studies

Although biological approaches can certainly look at infant behavior as well as physical and physiological factors, many studies of infant emotion are nonbiological and look only at behavior and its implications. These studies may be casual or systematic and may occur as part of deliberate hypothesis testing or simply in the course of the provision of services.

1. *Clinical infant work:* As we will discuss in detail in Chapter 14, a small number of psychotherapists work directly with infants and attempt early intervention to correct emotional problems. In the course of therapy with many infants, these clinicians collect information about special difficulties and also about emotional changes common to all their patients.

2. *Family therapy and pediatrics:* When an infant shows emotional problems, it is common for the entire family to suffer stress (either as the cause or as the effect of the infant's condition). The events during family therapy can provide information about steps in early emotional development.

Either normal or unusual emotional difficulties in a baby are often brought to the attention of the child's pediatrician, who may have a special interest in such issues.

3. *Reports of parents and caregivers:* The reports of parents and professional caregivers about infants seem to be regarded by researchers as both fascinating and untrustworthy. Caregivers, spending many hours a day with infants, have unique opportunities to see spontaneous behavior that may never occur in an unfamiliar setting. On the other hand, caregivers may not be very objective. They are rarely trained as observers and may have trouble separating their hopes or expectations from what they actually see. A caregiver is most often the only adult present with the infant, so there is little chance of comparing the caregiver's report with another adult's. Some researchers have tried to deal with these problems by using detailed questionnaires to collect information from caregivers.

4. *Observational studies and reliability:* Observations of behavior done by trained observers are usually considered a trustworthy source of information if certain steps have been followed. Professional observers need to be trained to use operational definitions of the events they are looking at, and they need to have sufficient experience in an observational task to make them accurate. To make sure that observers are doing their jobs, observations by two or more observers are correlated in order to obtain a measure of interobserver reliability. If observers do not agree on what they observe, the data they collect are not usable.

5. *Standardized testing:* A number of standardized procedures have been worked out to test specific aspects of social and emotional development. It is noticeable that research seems to follow where such procedures have been developed. For example, the Strange Situation (Ainsworth, Blehar, Waters, & Wall, 1978) is a procedure that examines an infant's emotional response to being separated from and then reunited with a parent. A child tested in the Strange Situation can be classified relative to large numbers of children who have been tested in the same way.

6. *Experimental and quasi-experimental work:* Although researchers working on emotional development have a special interest in spontaneous, everyday behavior, studies can also involve measurement of responses to a controllable stimulus. For example, the "still face" procedure looks at the child's reaction

The physical arrangement of the Strange Situation procedure allows an observer to study the infant's reactions. (Source: Based on Bretherton et al., 1979)

to an expressionless, unresponsive, adult face (Tronick, Als, & Adamson, 1979). Such experimental work often includes a quasi-experimental component, too, because of the need to understand changes with age and maturation.

Cross-Cultural Issues

Do all members of the human species undergo the same steps in early social and emotional development? We would expect them to do so, because it seems that there must have been strong evolutionary pressures for human infants to act in certain ways and attract the attention and care of adults. On the other hand, we also see that emotional expressiveness and the acceptability of some emotions in adults are different from one culture to another. These differences could result from genetic variations between groups of people or from cultural differences in infants' experiences. In either case, there is no predicting at what point in life the differences would appear.

Questions about cross-cultural differences in emotional development remain among the most difficult to answer. Adults in other cultures may not even understand certain questions the way that North Americans do. Recall the example of the mothers of the Efe group in Africa, who, when asked how their infants acted when left alone, replied that the babies did not mind. But, unlike U.S. mothers, the Efe women were assuming that *alone* meant with brothers and sisters, because they would never leave an infant in real solitude (Super & Harkness, 1986).

Some attempts are being made to develop research approaches that are specific for a given culture outside North America. For example, a Japanese temperament questionnaire (Shwalb, Shwalb, & Shoji, 1994) has been developed on the basis of free descriptions by Japanese mothers. It is hoped that this sort of instrument will make cross-cultural comparisons more possible.

INDIVIDUALITY

Everyone who has worked with many babies will confirm that they are different from birth in their individual responsiveness to the world. It is not so easy, however, to describe exactly how they are different, especially in the early months. Neither is it easy to decide when individual differences occur because of the baby's basic biological nature and when they stem from very early experience.

Temperament

temperament:
biological factors that help determine personality; from the Latin *temperare* (to mix).

Individuality in an older child presumably results from her biological nature, her experiences, and the interaction between the two. (We will explore a number of related issues in Chapter 13.) Much modern research on early individuality, however, focuses on temperament rather than on experience. **Temperamental** factors in personality are biological, constitutional characteristics of the individual that determine many behavioral responses to the environment. If a characteristic is genuinely a matter of temperament, it does not change as a result of experience (although the individual may learn to express it somewhat differently).

To be considered a temperamental factor, a characteristic must be present at birth and remain with the individual throughout life. This statement, of course, applies only to the underlying biological characteristic, not to a specific behavior. Newborn infants, 2-year-olds, and adults have dramatic behavioral differences, but the concept of temperament stresses the idea that an individual has continuity and stability in basic characteristics at all ages, even though the characteristics are quite differently expressed in behavior.

Continuity and Change

The study of *continuity and stability* in temperament is very much complicated by the fact that developmental change of all kinds is so rapid in infancy. Month by month, the baby shows dramatic alterations in the things he can do. A temperamental characteristic like activity level shows up in wiggling and restlessness in the 2-month-old but in running, jumping, and climbing in the 18-month-old. The measurement of continuity of temperament has to work with behaviors that are different at different ages but that are all assumed to show the expression of the same temperamental characteristic. A second approach in the study of continuity of temperament focuses on the behavior of an individual relative to other infants in the same age group. For example,

6-month-olds cry less than 2-month-olds do, but if the baby who cried most at 2 months was still the champion crier of the group at 6 months, this would be evidence of some continuity of temperament (McCall, 1986).

Demonstration of continuity of a temperamental characteristic depends on longitudinal studies that show similarities of the types discussed above in individuals at different ages. Not all characteristics are equally stable, and it may be that there is more continuity in a characteristic after age 6 months than there is earlier (Rothbart, 1988).

One of the difficulties in demonstrating continuity of temperament is that the infant does not develop in a social vacuum. Parents and other caregivers respond to the infant's behavior from birth on; some responses may have an impact on the behavior, making it less stable, whereas others may not affect it at all (Fish, Stiften, & Belsky, 1991).

Measuring Temperament

Attempts to measure an infant's temperament usually involve questionnaires or structured interviews with people who know the infant well. Parents or other caregivers have had many experiences with the infant's reactions and are able to summarize her usual response patterns to everyday situations. It would not be practical for a researcher to spend enough time with each infant in a study to be able to describe how he usually acts.

Although working with parent descriptions is the most practical approach to the measurement of temperament, parents are not an absolutely ideal source of information. They have great familiarity with the infant, but they also have biases and expectations that distort their reports. For example, parents who are more anxious and depressed during the pregnancy are more likely to rate the baby as fussy and difficult (Mebert, 1991).

Major Temperamental Factors

Thomas, Chess, and Birch (1970) described nine personality factors that they considered to be based on temperamental differences. The factors chosen were related to specific types of behavior noted in 2-month-olds, 6-month-olds, 12-month-olds, and 24-month-olds. Rather than noting simply whether the factors are present or absent, the researcher rates each infant on a continuum between the highest and the lowest level of a factor. Only a small number of children are found at the extremes. A child placed at an extreme on a factor may be difficult to handle, but this is simply a matter of individuality, not of pathology. The nine factors are as follows.

1. *Activity level* as a temperamental characteristic is exactly what it sounds like. A 12-month-old with a high activity level, for example, would climb onto and into everything, whereas a 12-month-old with a low activity level might allow his nails to be cut without fussing. (The term *hyperactivity* is not related to the concept of activity level as a temperamental factor, and a high activity level does not necessarily cause problems.)

2. *Rhythmicity* has to do with predictable or unpredictable physiological functioning. The baby with high rhythmicity naps for the same length of time and at about the same time every day, whereas a toddler of low rhythmicity may be hard to toilet-train because her bowel movements are at different times each day.

3. *Distractibility* involves the child's degree of concentration. A distractible hungry toddler can be coaxed to play when lunch is not quite ready, whereas the nondistractible child "wants what she wants" and will not accept substitutes.

4. *Approach and withdrawal* are the two extremes of reaction to unfamiliar situations. Most infants, of course, are not extreme in their reactions to the unfamiliar, but an extreme withdrawer, for example, tends to reject all new foods at first exposure.

5. *Adaptability* is the capacity to learn to tolerate routines and rules. For example, an adaptable 2-year-old may cry and scream when taken for his first haircut but soon adjusts and accepts the process.

6. *Attention span and persistence*, often thought of as aspects of intelligence, seem to be equally a matter of temperament.

7. *Intensity of reaction* to events may vary from intense to mild. A mild reactor may neither cry nor laugh much.

8. A *threshold of responsiveness* depends on the intensity of stimulation needed to get the child's attention. A high threshold means that a stimulus situation must be intense or very unfamiliar before it has much effect on the infant. This is not a matter of perceptual ability but of attentiveness; for example, a 12-month-old with a high threshold will eat food he dislikes if it is mixed with something he likes. A toddler with a low threshold of responsiveness may have to be tucked into bed tightly before she can fall asleep.

9. Positive or negative *quality of mood* is an aspect of the child's temperament that strongly affects other people. All infants, of course, will show a negative mood when sick, hurt, or distressed, but mood quality refers to a generally positive or negative tendency in neutral situations.

The Difficult Baby

One area stressed in the study of temperament has been the pattern of temperamental characteristics known as *difficultness*. The difficult baby presents his caregivers with a set of characteristics that make care routines especially hard to carry out. If the caregiver cannot tolerate and compensate for the baby's difficultness, the nature of their relationship may deteriorate markedly. The difficult infant shows a negative mood quality, adapts slowly, shows many withdrawal responses to new situations, and reacts intensely to the world (Thomas & Chess, 1986). Even someone who has little experience with babies can see that this pattern of characteristics will not lead to a smooth, pleasant family life.

Withdrawal and Inhibition

Probably the most-studied factor in the difficult pattern described above is the tendency to withdraw from the unfamiliar, a behavior that has also been

inhibition:
slowing or
temporarily
stopping a
response; from the
Latin *in-* (not),
habere (to have).

called **inhibition.** Inhibition has been reported as a stable, continuous temperamental factor (Kagan, Reznick, & Snidman, 1986). It is not caused by an unpleasant experience; rather, it appears to be biologically caused.

In one study by Kagan (1992), about 20% of healthy 4-month-olds showed behaviors related to inhibition when they were shown an unfamiliar, changing stimulus like a mobile. Their behavior includes "frequent, vigorous motor activity—flexing and extension of limbs, arching of the back, and occasional spasticity in the muscles—and after a few presentations of the stimulus, fretting or crying" (Kagan, 1992, p. 510). At 14 months, about half of that group showed extreme fear of unfamiliar toys, rooms and people, and stayed close to their mothers in unfamiliar situations. Of babies who reacted little to the mobile at 4 months, only about 10% showed fear at 14 months.

Implications of the Temperament Concept

The evidence for temperamental factors in individuality shows that experience is only one aspect of personality formation; however "good" or "bad" child-rearing practices may be, they do not alter the individual's basic nature.

It is important to realize that temperamental characteristics are neither good nor bad in themselves. The long-term effect of being born with a certain temperament depends on the context: parental attitudes and expectations, cultural values, even the physical environment. Rather than evaluating a temperamental pattern on its own, we need to think about how well it fits into the environment the child lives in.

Many parents and caregivers, as well as professionals who work directly with infants, have found that the temperament concept is useful for understanding individual children. For example, suppose a toddler placed in day care seems unusually distressed and is very slow to adapt to the new situation. Examination of the child's temperamental pattern may show that his reactions to the unfamiliar have always been of this type. On the other hand, if the child's temperament previously has been mild, positive, and adaptable and has shown approach to the unfamiliar, it may be a good idea to look at the new environment carefully and see whether the child is having undesirable experiences that are triggering the unusual behavior.

Adults sometimes find, to their distress, that they like some infants and toddlers better than others and they do not understand why. An examination of both the child's and the adult's temperaments can sometimes reveal the mismatch that makes a particular child less likable. Adults of low activity level may find high-activity-level children especially difficult to deal with; an adult with intense reactions may find a mildly reacting child "cool" or "aloof." It is the poor fit between the two that causes the trouble.

Sources of Temperament

By definition, a temperamental characteristic is an aspect of individuality that is determined by biology rather than by learning. But a number of biological factors could operate either directly or indirectly to create temperamental differences.

Is there a genetic factor in temperament? It seems likely that there is some degree of genetic determination of certain temperamental characteristics. A comparison of Chinese to Irish and to Bostonian 4-month-olds has shown lower levels of arousal and reactivity in the Chinese group (Kagan et al., 1994), who are also genetically different. Infants of genetically different populations who were examined soon after birth showed differences in reactivity to standard testing procedures (Freedman, 1974). Studies of twins have shown higher correlations of activity levels between monozygotic twins than between dizygotic twins (Saudino & Eaton, 1991) and apparent genetic influences for other factors, like negative mood (Emde et al., 1992).

In spite of this evidence, the role of heredity in temperament is not plain. A behavioral pattern that is genetically influenced may not show up until long after birth (Riese, 1990); an example might be development of reproductive behavior. In addition, an infant's genetic makeup may influence her behavior indirectly by stimulating adults to treat her in certain ways (cf. Scarr & McCartney, 1983). Toddlers who show high levels of inhibition tend to have parents who are somewhat shy and anxious (Rickman & Davidson, 1994). Did the toddlers acquire their characteristics genetically, did they learn inhibited behavior from the parents, or did the parents become anxious as a result of having such inhibited children?

Temperamental characteristics may accompany biological factors whose source is not clear. Infants with minor physical anomalies such as low-set ears may later show short attention spans and impulsiveness (Waldrop, Bell, McLaughlan, & Halvarson, 1978). Prenatal alcohol and drug exposure may have similar effects (Olson, 1994). It has even been suggested that postnatal experiences like circumcision without an anesthetic may have long-term behavioral effects (Richards, Bernal, & Brackbill, 1976).

An infant's capacity for sustained attention (a temperamental characteristic) has been associated with activity in the vagus nerve, shown in the heart rate pattern called *respiratory sinus arrhythmia* (RSA). Variability in the heart rate occurs at higher or lower levels in different infants. Where variability is high (that is, some periods of low heart rate and some of high), more periods of sustained attention occur (Porges, Matthews, & Pauls, 1992).

INFANT EMOTIONS

One of the biggest differences between the behavior of an infant and that of an older child or an adult has to do with the expression of *emotion*, or affect. Infants and toddlers "let it all hang out"; they cry uncontrollably, scream with terror or rage, laugh until they are near tears, and cling to those they love. Those who are temperamentally intense in their reactions are especially expressive. But emotionality is not a simple, unchanging factor in an infant's life. The causes of emotional reactions change with maturation and experience. And emotional development follows a predictable pattern.

What Is Emotion?

When adults think about their own emotional lives, they usually focus on their subjective experience of affect: sensations of anger, sadness, and so on. If subjective experience were the only component of emotion, we could not study it in infants because infants have no way of communicating their subjective experiences to us. But emotion includes other components as well: physiological responses, the motor expression of emotion through facial expression and posture, motivation or readiness to act in certain ways, and sometimes a cognitive appraisal of the situation (DeGangi & Greenspan, 1990). How these components are related to each other and to subjective experience is not completely understood; how emotion changes as cognitive development proceeds is a particularly important question.

innate: inborn, present to some extent from the time of birth; from the Latin *innasci* (to be born in).

discrete: separate from one another; from the Latin *discretus* (separate).

In recent years, students of infant emotion have returned to Darwin's idea that certain basic emotions are **innate** and universal (Izard & Malatesta, 1987). Each of these **discrete** emotions involves a set of neural processes that lead to a specific facial expression and to a corresponding specific subjective experience or feeling. The basic emotions participate in an emotions system, which relates them to each other and to events in the nervous system, as well as to physiological states of need such as pain and sexual arousal (Izard & Malatesta, 1987).

Research on infant emotion stresses the central position of affect in development. The infant's emotionality is not simply a nuisance to be coped with (by soothing the baby's crying or defusing a temper tantrum) but is a major force driving the infant's connections with the environment. Negative or positive emotional responses shape both social interactions and learning about the physical environment. *Affect* has been described as one of the critical "Four A's of Infancy"—factors whose successful development forms the foundations of later maturity. The other A's are *attention, arousal,* and *action,* all of which also have clear relations to emotionality (Lester & Tronick, 1994).

As emotion develops, expression of the baby's own feelings is accompanied by the ability to recognize and respond to other people's feelings. Emotionality comes to function in a social context as well as in isolation.

The Biology of Infant Emotion

Chapters 8 and 9 reviewed some of the factors in physical development that play a role in emotion. The abilities to hold up the head, to scan visually, and to converge the eyes are necessary for the control of attention to other people and awareness of their facial expressions. Control of the mouth and of the sequence of sucking, swallowing, and breathing are essential to voice production and expression of feeling through crying (Oetter, Laurel, & Cool, 1990).

Structures such as the limbic system, deep within the brain, are known to be related to emotionality, but they are difficult to study without intrusive methods (Locke, 1993). As a result, most of the work on brain functioning and emotion has focused on the cortex, whose activity can be measured without harming the infant (see Chapter 7 for techniques).

Studies of the cortex's role in emotional development have shown differences in the functioning of the right and left hemispheres. (Remember, however, that the brain functions as an integrated organ, contrary to popularized concepts that treat the right and left hemispheres as independent organs.) Functions of the right hemisphere (RH) apparently include face recognition, discrimination of facial expressions, and comprehension of the emotional tone of speech, as well as judgment of the positive or negative quality of affect, recall of facial expressions, and inhibition of inappropriate positive affects (such as giggling at a funeral). The left hemisphere (LH) mediates verbal labeling of emotional expressions, motor planning of facial expressions, comprehension and memory of emotionally toned stories, and inhibition of inappropriate negative affect (such as swearing at a family member who has inadvertently annoyed you). Both hemispheres are involved in "getting" the humorous content of pictures (DeGangi & Greenspan, 1990). Although this description of LH and RH functions applies to adults, some of the differences between the hemispheres have already emerged by age 1 month (de Schonen & Mathivet, 1989).

Negative and positive emotional expression has been connected with the frontal lobes of the right and left hemispheres. Greater activity of the right frontal lobe is associated with an increased tendency to cry under some circumstances, whereas the left frontal lobe is more activated in infants watching an actress showing a happy expression than a sad one (Davidson & Fox, 1982, 1989).

The autonomic nervous system (ANS), which controls internal functioning rather than cognition, is also deeply involved in emotion. Muscular changes creating different facial expressions lead to specific ANS states (Ekman, Levenson, & Friesen, 1985). Changes in heart rate and in hormone secretion accompany ANS activity.

Coordinated changes in hormone secretion and nervous system activity appear to be associated with infants' negative emotions and with calming activities. For example, the stress-related hormone cortisol is reduced in 10-month-olds after naps and car rides and is increased by separation from the mother (Larson, Gunnar, & Hertsgaard, 1991).

Examination of events that are calming to young infants suggests that there are at least two pathways in the nervous system that help reduce negative emotion (Smith, Fillion, & Blass, 1990). One pathway is activated by the taste of sucrose and seems related to the functioning of opioid drugs; the other pathway is activated by touch, such as pacifier sucking, and does not seem related to opioids. Both sugar and touch reduce crying in newborns; lactose (milk sugar) does not (Blass & Smith, 1992).

Measuring Infant Emotion

Cortisol levels, the loudness and quality of crying, and general physical activity can all be used as clues to an infant's emotional state. The most extensive research in this area, however, has focused on *facial expression* as an index of emotion.

One of the best-known systems of analyzing facial expressions of infants is the Maximally Discriminative Facial Coding System, or MAX (Izard, 1979). This system scores alterations of muscle activity in different areas of the face and assigns each expression to a particular discrete emotion on the basis of these scores. There are specific differences between an emotionally neutral face and each of Izard's basic emotional categories: anger-rage; interest-excitement; happiness-enjoyment; fear-terror; sadness-dejection; discomfort-pain; and disgust. Each facial expression is assumed to be accompanied by a matching motivational state and a matching subjective experience, so a child who looks sad feels sad, and a child who stops looking sad also stops feeling sad. As we noted in Chapter 11, gaze aversion and the maintenance of a mutual gaze also express emotional states.

As the infant grows into a toddler, additional emotional expressions can be seen. Embarrassment, and similar social emotions such as shame and pride, do not appear until about 15 to 18 months.

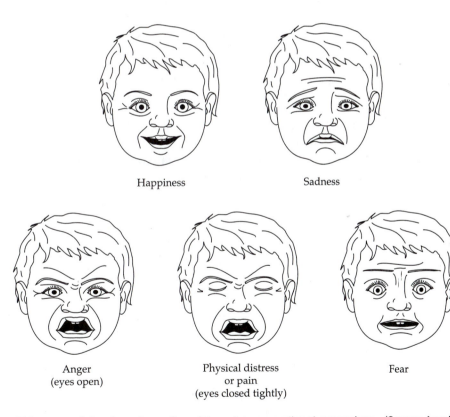

Happiness   Sadness

Anger
(eyes open)

Physical distress
or pain
(eyes closed tightly)

Fear

This group of drawings shows five of the primary emotional expressions. (Source: Izard, 1979)

The Natural History of Emotions

Although some emotions are displayed from birth onward, the infant's increasing age is accompanied by the emergence of new emotional expressiveness. This seems to occur, for the most part, according to a maturational timetable rather than because of experience.

Crying is present from the time of the reflexive "birth cry" and is a well-known feature of early behavior, increasing with age in U.S. babies until it peaks at 6 weeks with a median length of 2.75 hours per day (Brazelton, 1962). Cry patterns are different depending on the source of distress (Wolff, 1970). The rhythmical hunger cry involves a cry, a short pause, a whistling inhalation, another pause, and another cry. The cry of anger (caused, for example, by having the arms restrained) is similar in pattern but has a rough tonal quality because of the turbulence of the air passing over the vocal cords. The pain cry sounds very different; a long initial cry is followed by a long pause with held breath, an inhalation, then more cries.

Among North American infants, about 20% show a crying pattern referred to as *colic*, or *periodic irritable crying.* Spells of apparently inconsolable crying occur, especially in the early morning and in the evening; by the time the infant reaches 4 months of age, the crying has usually diminished greatly (Brazelton, 1962). Colicky crying is often thought to result from indigestion, and parents may respond to it with changes of formula. But there seems to be no reason that a food should be distressing to an infant at one time of day but not at other times. Although colicky infants seem to be suffering from stomach pains and intestinal gas, these may be the *result* of excessive crying, rather than the cause. Colicky crying may well be the result of child care practices, because it seems much less common in less industrialized cultures (Lee, 1994). (Patterns of crying also alter over the first year in response to caregiving styles, which will be discussed in more detail in Chapter 13.)

Smiling can be seen at the age of a few days but does not seem directed toward anyone or anything in particular. These *endogenous smiles,* occurring because of internal events, are often interpreted as "due to gas," or, more attractively, as "smiling at the angels." The *exogenous smile,* triggered by external factors, does not appear until about 4 to 8 weeks of age. It is initially hard to stimulate, and the baby may respond by smiling only to a very exaggerated smiling and nodding face or to an adult who looms close while opening the mouth wide. (The baby's still immature visual abilities are probably relevant here.) As the baby matures, social smiling becomes easier and easier to elicit, and 4-month-olds are rather sociable and ready to smile at all smiles they see; they also begin to chuckle at a gentle tickle. In a few months, there is laughter at "funny" noises and incongruous sights: a parent pretending to drink from a baby bottle or the cat suddenly popping its head up from behind a chair.

Anger over frustrations is apparent from an early age. Initially it is brought on by physical restrictions like holding the baby's arms to its sides (as in dressing, for instance). Later, the baby may become frustrated by her inability to carry out a desired act; the weeks before the baby creeps

Four-month-olds are often very sociable and ready to "party" with any friendly adult. In a few months, the response to unfamiliar people will change dramatically.

successfully often involve frequent angry displays. By 8 or 10 months, the baby is very aware of other people's actions and may display anger when she sees someone get a coat and go to the door, about to leave her behind. Full-fledged temper tantrums, with the child prone on the floor, screaming and jerking the arms and legs spasmodically, generally occur in the second year and result from overwhelming levels of stress and frustration.

Being startled or angered causes about 5% of infants and toddlers to have breath-holding spells (more excitingly known as **cyanotic** and pallid infantile syncope). The child will cry loudly for a few breaths, then stop breathing and possibly lose consciousness and go limp. Breathing and consciousness are usually recovered almost at once, but occasionally there is prolonged unconsciousness. There seems to be no relationship to any other problem, and the tendency is usually "outgrown" by school age (Lombroso & Lerman, 1967).

cyanotic: bluish or ashy in color because of lack of oxygen in the blood; from the Greek *kyanos* (dark-blue enamel).

Fear as a discrete emotion does not emerge clearly until 6 months or later. Before showing obvious fear, the infant may go through a month or so of *wariness*. Whereas the 4-month-old smiles at strangers, the 6- or 7-month-old inspects them solemnly and suspiciously, but finally warms up and acts friendly.

The clear expression of *fear*—stiffening or withdrawing, and crying with a fearful expression—generally begins at about 7 to 10 months and may emerge rather dramatically. Noises and events that did not bother the baby in the past may now trigger great anxiety. The weekly visit of the garbage truck is terrifying, and the rugs must either go unvacuumed or the mother must hold the baby in one arm while vacuuming with her free hand. Fearfulness at this time is especially intense in the form of stranger anxiety and separation anxiety, which will be discussed later in this chapter.

The development of the *social emotions*—empathy, embarrassment, shame, guilt, and pride—seems to depend on awareness of the self. These complex emotions result from a cognitive capacity to observe the self and others, to be aware of standards and rules, and to compare the infant's own behavior with some ideal standard (Lewis, 1992). These abilities are not present until about age 15 to 18 months.

Although the display of emotion is important in development, it is probably equally important that the infant recognize emotions displayed by others. Some remarkable research has shown that infants only 36 hours old are able to discriminate and imitate happy, sad, and surprised expressions that are modeled by an adult (Field et al., 1982). Although this certainly does not indicate that the neonate understands the meaning of the adult's expression, it shows that the infant is already paying attention to those aspects of the face that tell us most about emotion.

By the age of a few months, infants expect responses to their own facial expressions and are made anxious and depressed by an unresponsive adult. The still-face situation (described earlier), in which an adult face is oriented toward the baby but there is no eye contact or change of facial expression, leads to increasing distress and disorganized infant behavior (Tronick, Als, & Adamson, 1979). Girls are more likely than boys to be distressed by the still face (Mayes & Carter, 1990). Six-month-olds are even more likely than younger babies to look away from the mother's still face, and they also touch objects or the face and mouth while averting the gaze (Toda & Fogel, 1993).

By 7 months, infants expect the sight and sound of emotional expression to go together and spend less time looking at videos where an angry voice accompanies a happy face (Soken & Pick, 1992).

By the time an infant can crawl, she uses *social referencing* of emotion to help her understand the world. When she encounters an unfamiliar situation (the visual cliff described in Chapter 7, for example), she looks at her parent's face and acts on what she sees. If the parent looks fearful, the baby avoids the situation, but if the parent looks happy, the baby proceeds.

The development of **empathic** responses as well as recognition of others' feelings seems to depend in large part on experiences with caregivers and will be discussed in detail in Chapter 13.

empathy: awareness or vicarious experience of another's feelings; from the Greek *en-* (in), *pathos* (suffering).

SOCIAL AND EMOTIONAL DEVELOPMENTAL TASKS

Throughout infancy and toddlerhood, developmental changes occur in the child's typical social and emotional behavior. These changes are stagelike in nature; that is, they follow a predictable sequence, and there are qualitative differences at different points in the sequence. Rather than viewing the social and emotional changes as stages, however, it might be more useful for us to consider them as a series of *developmental tasks* (Havighurst, 1972). A developmental task is a job that needs to be mastered at a particular point in development in order for development to continue successfully. Social and emotional changes are not just things that happen to the baby; they are developmental tasks in the sense that the baby strives to accomplish them, and the environment can make them easier or more difficult.

Many theorists have described specific events in early social and emotional life and have attempted to link them to the larger pattern of personality development. Rather than focus on one view of early development, the following section will discuss a sequence of events whose descriptions have been chosen from the work of various authors. Most researchers who have worked on the topic of emotional development have been strongly influenced by psychoanalytic thought, so their approaches are not vastly different.

Self-Regulation

The first developmental task we will consider is worked on during the first 3 months of life, a time when it is not at all obvious that the infant has anything but a reflexive emotional life. *Self-regulation* (Greenspan, 1992a) is the ability to calm oneself when distressed or excited, rather than to be at the mercy of emotional arousal. Without this ability, the infant would have little time to watch and learn about the world, to explore or to show interest in the world. Self-regulation has been described as "a developmental task for infants [that] involves learning to modulate, tolerate, and endure experiences of negative affect" (Kopp, 1989, p. 343).

The neonate seems to be under the control of his own emotions, which run away with him unless an adult offers help. Once crying begins, unless comfort is offered, it goes on until the infant is exhausted and falls into a deep sleep. Without adult help, the infant has little calm, quiet, awake time.

In the course of the first few months, however, the well-cared-for infant begins to learn about self-regulation. Part of this learning comes about by chance, as the baby discovers her thumb and finds that sucking it is comforting; part comes as a result of adult intervention. A mother, for example, may try different positions for holding her fretful infant. As she learns what position works best, the baby does too, and in the future the baby will try to achieve that comforting position. Other self-regulating ploys the baby may use are averting the gaze, closing the eyes, looking at the hands, and rubbing or tugging at hair, clothing, or ears.

The developmental task of self-regulation is only partly achieved at the end of 3 months; indeed, we may question whether any of us as adults are ever completely able to regulate ourselves. It is certainly wrong to assume that a 3-month-old can bear the entire burden of self-comforting when hurt, sick, or hungry. However, under normal circumstances, the task of self-regulation has been partially mastered by 3 months, and the infant at this age is quite different from the completely unregulated neonate.

Attachment

After some self-regulation is achieved, the infant can spend more and more time focusing on the most interesting part of her environment: the people around her. From 2 or 3 months until 7 or 8 months, much of the infant's time is spent in play and socializing with caregivers. This activity is strongly related to the developmental task of forming an attachment to a small number of familiar people, an emotional link which is **analogous** but not identical to adult love.

analogous:
parallel or similar; from the Greek *analogos* (proportionate).

Before we go on with our discussion of attachment, a warning is in order. The popular press has created a great deal of confusion about emotional connections between parents and infants and has implied that parental love and infant love are mutual and begin at the time of birth. This is not correct. Factors influencing parental love (bonding) were discussed in Chapter 5 and will be discussed further in Chapters 13 and 14. For the time being, we are looking only at the course of the developmental task of attachment.

Attachment is the development of the infant's strong preference for a few familiar people. It occurs over a period of months and depends on the experience of social interaction with the people who will become the infant's attachment figures. At about age 7 or 8 months, the infant begins to show behavior characteristic of attachment by trying to stay close to the caregiver; she may show fear if the caregiver walks away or leaves or if an unfamiliar person approaches. This separation anxiety and stranger anxiety may act as an "invisible playpen" to keep the infant, who can crawl by now, out of trouble. The infant's fearfulness at this stage is evidence of a developmental task accomplished and is not the result of "spoiling" or mistreatment. At this time, the baby may begin to want a special blanket or other *transitional object* (Winnicott, 1953).

After the age of 8 months or so, separation and unfamiliarity have a strong impact on the infant's behavior. Alone or with a stranger in an unfamiliar place, she does not explore. The presence of a familiar adult, however, gives her a secure base for exploration; the infant makes forays into the unfamiliar room, then returns to the familiar person for "emotional refueling." The infant's behavior can be seen as the outcome of a dynamic action system that includes factors such as the infant's previous experience, the familiarity of the environment, and the presence of the adult.

Human infants seem to have a strong tendency to develop attachments if they have the opportunity to do so. If babies do not have much contact with adults (as in the traditional Israeli kibbutz), they form attachments to infants in nearby cribs (Bettelheim, 1969). Groups like the Efe of Africa, who practice multiple caretaking but whose infants sleep with their mothers, produce infants whose strongest attachment is to their mothers (Morelli & Tronick, 1991). Abusive treatment of an infant does not necessarily prevent attachment, and, sadly, an abused child in foster care may long to be returned to the abusive parent. As long as there is some minimum of social interaction with a few people over some months at the right time, attachment will probably occur.

APPLICATIONS & ARGUMENTS
Comfort Measures and Self-Regulation

A parent who is trying to soothe a crying baby is not usually aware of having a long-term goal. The intention may be to help the baby feel better, or it may be to stop the crying that is so distressing to hear, or to prevent another child from being awakened or neighbors from complaining. But the parent's comfort measures may have an important long-term effect: to help the baby develop some skill at self-regulation, one of the earliest emotional milestones.

Although some babies at birth are already able to achieve some comfort by getting their thumbs to their mouths, many cannot. Even the ones who are good thumb suckers depend a great deal on adults' efforts to calm and comfort them. Infants seem to learn from adults, as well as from trial and error, what will make them feel better. For example, an adult may try to hold the infant in different positions to see which one is most comforting. Having found a comforting position, the adult uses it again when the baby is distressed. The baby learns from this experience to try to get into that comfortable position or to signal an adult for help.

Some positions probably make it easier for the baby to get her hand to her mouth. If the infant is supine or is held facing away from the adult, her control over her hand is more difficult because the hand can move back and forth horizontally as well as up or down. The baby who is lying prone or held facing the caregiver can support her hand against the surface and simply move it up or down toward her mouth.

Rocking and rhythmic patting are comforting to the young infant, and older babies often comfort themselves with rhythmic rocking movements.

Experiencing the comfort techniques of a skillful caregiver can be a way for an infant to learn to self-regulate and calm himself.

As mentioned earlier in this chapter, attachment is probably the most studied of all events in social and emotional development. The research technique called the Strange Situation (Ainsworth et al., 1978) is a standardized approach to observation of attachment behaviors and takes about 22 minutes and 8 episodes. The infant's behavior is recorded during a reunion after separation from the mother as well as during a brief separation. (If you remember Jamal, Bobby, and Tiffany from Chapter 1, this will sound familiar.) On the basis of their behavior in the Strange Situation, 12-month-old infants are placed into one of four categories (three originally proposed by Ainsworth and her group, the fourth suggested more recently by Main and Solomon, 1986).

● **TABLE 12.1**   *Events in the Strange Situation.*

Episode	Events
1	Mother and baby enter the room with the observer, who leaves after showing the mother where to sit and to put the baby down. This takes about 30 seconds.
2	Mother puts the baby down near her chair, a few feet from some toys. Mother is not to initiate play but may respond. If the baby has not started to play after 2 minutes, the mother may take him to the toys. The episode lasts 3 minutes.
3	A stranger enters, gives a greeting, and sits quietly across from mother for 1 minute. For a second minute, the stranger converses with the mother. For the third minute, the stranger gets down on the floor and tries to initiate play with the baby. At the end of this episode, the mother leaves quietly; the baby usually notices that she goes.
4	The stranger sits on her chair and responds if the baby tries to initiate play. She tries to comfort the baby if he shows distress. If the baby is not upset, the mother stays out for 3 minutes. If the baby is upset, mother comes back early and the stranger leaves.
5	Mother calls baby's name from outside the door and then comes in. She comforts the baby if necessary and tries to get him started playing; otherwise, she sits on her chair and responds but does not initiate. After 3 minutes, she says "Bye-bye, I'll be back soon" and leaves.
6	Baby stays alone for 3 minutes. If he becomes distressed, the stranger comes back.
7	The stranger tries to comfort the baby if he is upset. Otherwise, she sits on her chair. If the baby is too distressed, the mother comes back before 3 minutes are over.
8	The mother returns as the stranger leaves. For the next 3 minutes, the mother behaves as she did in the first episode.

Source: Based on Bretherton et al., 1979.

Infants assigned to Group B are considered *securely attached*. They play and explore freely while alone with their mothers, but decrease their play slightly when the stranger enters. They cry, although not immediately, when the mother leaves the room. When the mother returns, they actively seek contact with her and are easily soothed by her. About 65% of infants are classified in this group (Teti & Nakagawa, 1990).

Infants assigned to Group A are considered *insecure-avoidant*. They are less wary of the unfamiliar person, and may not cry when the mother leaves. But the most important difference for this group occurs at the time of reunion, when they actively avoid the mother and "snub" her approaches. About 20% of infants are in this group (Teti & Nakagawa, 1990).

Group C infants are considered *insecure-ambivalent* in their attachment. They show anxiety from the beginning and have trouble using the mother as a secure base. When the mother returns, they seek her but also resist her, and she cannot soothe or "settle" them. About 15% of infants are in Group C (Teti & Nakagawa, 1990).

Group D infants are classified as showing an *insecure-disorganized/disoriented* attachment pattern (Main & Solomon, 1986). The reunion behavior of these infants is especially different from that of the other three groups and is not uniform. Group D infants may avoid the mother strongly and then immediately approach her strongly; they may show contradictory feelings by gazing away while in contact with the mother; they may show undirected expressions of fear or stereotyped rocking, or appear confused and apprehensive when the mother enters. These infants may also show behavioral stilling upon reunion; with dazed, disoriented expressions they suddenly fall prone or cease movement in depressed postures. A small proportion of infants are in Group D (Teti & Nakagawa, 1990).

What do those group classifications mean? Are these simply individual differences, or is there some implication for future development? To try to answer these questions, we need to note first that attachment is not "something inside the child." Attachment behaviors are a way of doing things within a dynamic system, so they change with context, with the people involved, and with the child's developmental status. Attachment behaviors are different at home than in a strange place and can be different with the mother than with the father or another familiar person (Main & Weston, 1981). Indeed, everyday concern about separation is reduced as the child experiences more separations and reunions (Field, 1991b). Like self-regulation, attachment is an ongoing developmental task; it is not suddenly complete at 18 months.

Nevertheless, many attachment researchers operate under the assumption that "the quality of attachment developed in infancy forms some sort of foundation for future intimate relations" (Cicchetti, Cummings, Greenberg, & Marvin, 1990, p. 11). But the outcome of various attachment patterns may depend on what is measured and when measurement occurs. For example, insecure-avoidant preschool girls have been reported to be hard to deal with and poor in peer relations (Fagot & Kavanagh, 1990), but avoidant or resistant toddlers have been described as becoming kindergarteners who are overcontrolled in their behavior (Easterbrooks & Goldberg, 1990). Group D infants are more likely to have been maltreated and to come from disadvantaged situations, so poor outcomes might be expected for them for a number of reasons (Cicchetti et al., 1990).

Mental Representations and Emotion

egocentric: in this context, believing that one's own perspective is shared by all other persons; from the Latin *ego* (I), the Greek *kentrikon* (of the center).

As we noted in Chapter 10, *mental representations* of objects and people become more mature at the end of the first year. The developing capacity for mental representation makes it possible for the infant to think not only of another person but also of what that person might think or know. Although the year-old child is still quite **egocentric** (that is, she often assumes that everyone else shares her viewpoint), she is beginning to develop a *theory of mind*. This still-primitive theory is the assumption that any person has a mind, is aware of experiences, and intends to cause events—just as the child herself does (Hobson, 1993). A theory of mind is behind intentional efforts to communicate and is related to social emotions like shame and guilt.

Where do theories of mind come from? Why does an infant not think of others as remarkable machines that can do all sorts of things but have no experience or thought? One assumption has been that human beings from the time of birth have the ability to recognize persons as such, to predict some of their actions, and to share control over their interactions. This primary **intersubjectivity** would be the basis for understanding others' feelings (Trevarthen, 1979).

More recent thinking on this topic shares the assumption that the ability to recognize something about people is a given. Hobson (1993) suggested that each fundamental emotion (discussed earlier in this chapter) is associated with a universal experience and with facial and vocal expression; the infant can therefore know that a particular expression on Daddy's face goes with the same experience the baby has when she has that expression. Cognitive and affective abilities work together as the infant uses social referencing of the parents' expressions to find out what they think about things. When the baby's and the parent's opinions are different, the baby's theory of mind develops further as she receives evidence that different persons have different minds with different thoughts.

The development of theory of mind may also be fostered by an early awareness that body movements are accompanied by specific sensations, in other people as well as in oneself. This awareness would unify "acts-as-seen and acts-as-felt into a common framework" (Meltzoff & Gopnik, 1993, pp. 340–341). The infant's theory of mind would then be advanced by the many mutual-imitation games seen at the end of the first year; 12-month-olds imitate adults, but they are also fascinated by adults who imitate them (Meltzoff, 1990).

The Self and the Social Emotions

One result of a theory of mind is an ability to be aware of the self, not only as a type of subjective experience but also as a subject of other people's evaluation. Of course, we cannot share the infant's experience of self-awareness, but we can observe some behaviors that seem to be related to his experience.

Some aspects of self-recognition are in place between about 8 and 12 months. The child can find objects attached to his body by looking at his mirror image. He is able to point to body parts when they are named even though he cannot see them, so he has some sense of some of the permanent characteristics of his body (Butterworth, 1990a).

When the infant can recognize himself in a video or in a mirror, he seems to have come to identify the self in a very specific way—that is, in terms of how he looks to other people. The ability for *mirror-self-recognition* does not

intersubjectivity: the primitive awareness that another human is a person with a capacity for experience similar to one's own; from the Latin *inter-* (between), *subjectus* (one under authority).

emerge until at least age 15 months (Lewis, 1992). Before this time, the toddler who is shown his mirror image may call it by his brother's or sister's name. Mirror-self-recognition is first apparent when the child, placed before a mirror, hangs his head and turns away smiling in an embarrassed way, and then resists looking at himself again. A more clear-cut demonstration that the child recognizes his mirror image is shown by the "rouge" technique; a dab of blush is put on the child's nose, and if he recognizes himself in the mirror, he will immediately put his hand to his nose.

Until a sense of self is present, there can be no "self-conscious" feelings. The *social emotions* derive from the consciousness of self, from the understanding of some social rules and standards, and from the ability to evaluate whether the self is meeting those standards. We would not expect these emotions to be present before about age 15 months.

One analysis of the social emotions (Lewis, 1992) considered them in terms of two factors: the sense of success or failure, and the global or specific evaluation of the self. *Shame* is a sense of failure applied globally, so that the whole self is perceived as at fault. *Hubris* (the pride that goeth before a fall, in the sense used in Greek tragedies) is a sense of success applied globally, so the

Emotions like pride and shame may be experienced only after the child begins to recognize herself in the mirror, which this baby is still too young to do.

whole self is seen as good—in an unrealistic way. *Guilt* is a sense of failure but it is specific; an action, or a part of the self, is at fault, but much of the self is still seen as worthwhile. *Pride* is a sense of specific success; unlike hubris, it does not involve the entire self.

The social emotions play a critical role in shaping the toddler's behavior. A sense of pride motivates her strongly, and she does her best to avoid or escape experiences of guilt or shame. The role these emotions play in socialization will be discussed in Chapter 13, as will development of empathic responses to others.

Autonomy and Rapprochement

autonomy: in this context, confidence that one is competent to make choices rather than depend on others' direction; from the Greek *auto-* (self), *nemein* (to distribute).

An important developmental task of the toddler and early preschool period is the achievement of a sense of **autonomy** (Erikson, 1968). Autonomy might be negatively defined as the absence of a pervading sense of shame and self-doubt. Put more positively, it is a sense of ability to make good choices without having to depend constantly on others' direction: the ability to govern the self. At first, the concept of autonomy may sound like a free rein given to selfishness and willfulness. However, a clear sense of autonomy seems to help a child cooperate and obey when necessary; the person without a sense of autonomy is so fearful of losing control that she struggles against the wishes of others even when it makes no sense to do so.

One complexity of the development of autonomy is that the emotionally healthy person (after the toddler period) can combine a sense of autonomy with a sense of connectedness to other people (Emde & Buchsbaum, 1990). The toddler period involves constant changes in emotion and behavior, as first the urge for autonomy, then the desire for affiliation, comes to the fore.

rapprochement: a period during which the toddler is deeply involved with the mother but is easily made angry by her interference or the need for her help; from the French *rapprochement* (reconciliation, reunion).

From about 15 months to 2 years, a period of behavior called **rapprochement** (Mahler, 1980) epitomizes the child's struggle to integrate the need for independence and the need for dependence. During the excitement of early walking and talking, many infants seem less involved with their mothers. As rapprochement begins, they seem to need the mother to share every new experience. They "woo" her, bring her objects, insist on showing her things. Their demanding behavior shows the frustration of the simultaneous need to do things by themselves and to have the mother share everything. One little girl whose rapprochement behavior was caught on film (Mahler, 1983) brought a musical top to her mother when she could not work it, but cried and stamped when her mother started the top spinning. When the mother offered her a simpler toy, she threw it from her.

These dramatic fights of the rapprochement period (source of the term the *terrible twos*) are aimed solely at the mother or other principal caregiver. A baby-sitter or grandparent can handle the toddler with much less fighting simply because the child's attachment is less and the autonomy conflict is not nearly as intense. The toddler fighting with his mother is working on an important developmental task, and both fighters need social support, not criticism.

APPLICATIONS & ARGUMENTS
Can Negativism Be a Positive Thing?

Well-developed toddlers begin to show behavior that resists what adults want. By about 18 months, many begin to demonstrate a level of resistance and negativism that is shocking to parents. The contrast to the compliant younger baby is a powerful one. No longer can the adult easily trade a permitted for a forbidden object or distract the child from what she wants. Angry screams and shouts of "no!" soon are daily occurrences.

It is not surprising that parents are distressed when their child shows such negative behavior. They felt much better when the baby was cheerful and happy. People outside the family may freely volunteer critical remarks. The parents are legitimately concerned that the child should be obedient, if only for safety's sake.

Is there a bright side to negativism? Looking at the larger developmental picture, there is. Imagine the difficulties of a school-age child who capitulated instantly to every nudge of peer pressure. Imagine the dangers for an adolescent who accepted every drug and every challenge to risky behavior. Imagine an adult who cannot ask for a raise or better working conditions or who must comply with every wish of a spouse. Mature skills of negotiation or resistance to others' temptations must begin somewhere, and they probably begin with the toddler's newfound recognition that she wants something different from what an adult wants.

Naturally, the toddler needs to learn some better skills; words are more desirable than screams in a social setting. But the goal should not be to stamp out resistance. Negativism in the toddler may be the foundation of the adult's independence and integrity.

PROBLEMS OF EMOTIONAL DEVELOPMENT

The vast majority of infants deal effectively with the tasks of emotional development; presumably, their biological background is sufficiently sound and their caregiving environment is good enough to support good emotional health. This healthy majority of infants may experience minor emotional problems, just as emotionally healthy adults do.

Good emotional health during the infant and toddler period is a great advantage, but it is not necessarily a guarantee that there will never be any problems. It is not possible, for instance, to diagnose attention deficit disorder, with or without hyperactivity, before age 3 years (Moffitt, 1990). Unfortunately, a small number of infants already suffer from severe difficulties in emotional development. Some of their problems can be helped, but some, sadly, do not at this time seem to be either preventable or curable.

Minor Emotional Problems

Many of the emotional manifestations that concern parents of infants and toddlers are actually a matter of temperament. For example, many parents dislike thumb sucking and are concerned about the dreamy, withdrawn state their child gets into while sucking. Some research suggests that involvement in nonnutritive sucking depends on temperament. Children who are not distractible and who are intense in their reactions seem to be more likely to persist in sucking past age 1 year (Lester, Bierbrauer, Selfridge, & Gomeringer, 1976).

Tantrums and negativism, wearing though they may be, are a normal part of toddler life and should be seen as part of the child's struggle between independence and dependence. Although these behaviors are developmentally appropriate at the toddler period, they would be expected to diminish in the preschooler.

Sleeping and eating difficulties tend to go with emotional disturbance in older persons, but they are usually just aspects of normal developmental

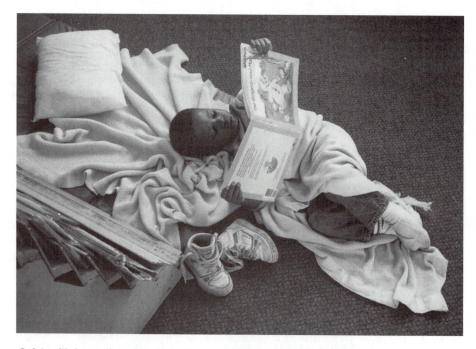

Quiet, withdrawn times are part of normal emotional development. Toddlers in day care may have a special need for opportunities to relax in this way.

change in infants and toddlers. As we will see in Chapter 13, changes in sleep patterns are ongoing for infants and toddlers. (The real problem is that parents would like to have some minimum amount of unbroken sleep.) Changes in appetite accompany the slowing of growth at about age 1 year. This is not an eating problem, but, as we will see in Chapter 13, it can be made into one by poor handling.

Fear of strangers and anxiety about separation are normal parts of attachment. Distress and grief following longer separations are also normal responses to perceived loss. As we will discuss in Chapter 13, the grieving triggered by loss takes a long time to resolve completely. A child who is too young to know that his parents have only gone away on vacation will begin to grieve as if they were dead.

APPLICATIONS & ARGUMENTS
Trying to Make a Baby "Independent"

Of all possible personality characteristics, one that people in the United States favor most is independence. A good adult is one who is seen as earning his own living, standing on his own two feet, not asking for help from anyone. In the pioneer past, these characteristics were important for survival. Even today, they can help an adult rise to life's challenges.

Unfortunately, parents may assume that the way to produce an independent adult is to force "independence" on the baby. With this goal in mind, they refuse to comfort the unhappy infant or to help the frightened one feel safe. Although it is probably less common today than it once was, parents may even deliberately frustrate or frighten the child with the stated intention of toughening him into an adult they will be proud of. (Actually, the hostility behind these acts is not very well hidden.)

Does this sort of parenting style produce a competent, independent adult? It is more likely that the result will be an angry, impulsive person who copes with anxiety by attacking others. Rather than growing up to be a pioneer hero, the baby grows to treat other people with a style much like the one he experienced from his parents.

Genuine ego strength and independence are more likely to develop when the infant experiences security, protection, and comfort and when he can explore the world gradually and without excessive anxiety. The parents' strength and protectiveness then convey to the child that it is possible to keep yourself and others strong and safe. A real ability to be independent probably stems from the experience of real dependence at the right time.

Developmental Psychopathology

psychopathology:
serious emotional
disturbance; from
the Greek *psyche*
(soul), *pathos*
(suffering).

Deciding when infant emotional development has gone seriously off track is not an easy matter. The need to make such decisions has produced a relatively new discipline, **developmental psychopathology.** The task of workers in this field is to understand normal pathways of development in order to trace significant deviations and to identify factors that cause the deviations (Sroufe, 1989). Developmental psychopathologists are also interested in factors that enable some infants to resist stress and continue on normal pathways when we might expect them to develop problems.

Diagnosis and classification of infant emotional disorders has advanced with the publication of *Diagnostic Classification: 0–3* (Diagnostic Classification Task Force, 1994), a guide to diagnosis that supplements the *Diagnostic and Statistic Manual* of the American Psychiatric Association, intended primarily for use with older patients. The following section of this chapter will highlight some of the most important diagnostic categories for infants and toddlers.

Regulatory Disorders

Our discussion of the infant's emotional developmental tasks began with the need to master self-regulation. The infant with poor self-regulation is limited in her attentiveness to the world and in the development of relationships with other people.

Infants with *regulatory disorders* are behaviorally difficult, having disturbances in sleep, feeding, self-calming, and mood control. Their irritability has the potential to lead to later poor attention skills and poor emotional control (DeGangi, Di Pietro, Greenspan, & Porges, 1991). Some infants develop inappropriate ways to self-regulate, such as rumination—regurgitation sometimes followed by rechewing and reswallowing food (Chatoor & Dickson, 1984).

One component of regulatory disorders is thought to be tactile defensiveness (Sears, 1994), or excessive reactions to the experience of touch. Tactile defensiveness can occur in the mouth, hands, trunk, or other body parts. When it is present, the ordinary soothing activities used to calm a young infant—kissing, patting, stroking, offering things to suck—are actually distressing rather than comforting. When the baby is even more distressed after the caregiver's attempts to soothe her, the caregiver may well withdraw, concluding (not unreasonably) that the baby is happier on her own. The caregiver may become depressed and doubt his or her parenting abilities, becoming less and less willing to interact with the baby, who thus has no help or guidance in achieving self-regulation.

Babies who show tactile defensiveness demonstrate negative responses to light touch. They can tolerate and enjoy deeper pressure; as older children, they may laugh if spanked. Part of their treatment, which we will discuss further in Chapter 14, involves associating light touch with experiences they do like.

Pervasive Developmental Disorders

The term *pervasive developmental disorders* (PDD) covers a number of problems of early emotional development, including the syndrome that has traditionally been called *autism*. The autistic form of PDD has been described as the "only real psychopathology of infancy" (Sigman, 1989, p. 183).

By the time an autistic child reaches school age, he or she has usually clearly shown the defining characteristics of the problem: inability to understand others' feelings, to take into account what others know, to read people's intentions, to read the listener's level of interest in one's speech, to anticipate what others might think of one's actions, to understand misunderstandings, to deceive or understand deception, or to understand the motives behind behavior. But these abilities are poor or absent in the normal infant, so how is it possible to detect autism at an early age?

Parents often bring autistic children for diagnosis at about age 2½ years because of their concern that the child is not developing language (Greenspan, 1992b). Further investigation shows that problems had already been present for many months. The human face was not interesting for these children (Klin & Volkmar, 1993), and the development of gesture communication stopped early. By age 2, autistic children are different from nonautistic children in that they show less greeting behavior, they less often share enjoyment with others, they less often coordinate their gaze and other behavior when requesting something, and they show less joint attention (see Chapter 11). They are more likely to take another person's hand and try to "make" it perform a task than to request help in a normal way (Lord, 1993). They do not show much pretend play (Leslie, 1987). When they do speak, they have abnormal tone and rhythm; they reverse pronouns, referring to themselves as "you" (Freeman, 1993). One research instrument, the Checklist for Autism in Toddlers (CHAT) (Baron-Cohen & Howlin, 1993), asks parents whether the child points to ask for or show things, whether he shows an interest in other children, and whether he brings things to show to the parent.

TABLE 12.2   *Reports and observations contributing to a diagnosis of autism in a toddler.*

Child takes no interest in other children

Child never plays pretend games, such as pretending to drink something

Child does not point in order to ask for something

Child does not point in order to indicate interest or to show parent something

Child does not really play with small toys, but mouths or drops them

Child does not make eye contact with examiner

Child does not point when asked to "show me"

Child does not look to see what examiner is pointing at

Child does not pretend to do something when examiner asks her to

Source: Based on Baron-Cohen & Howlin, 1993.

In an earlier section of this chapter, we discussed the development of a theory of mind as a developmental task of toddlers. A current view of autism suggests that children with PDD of the autistic type are lacking a well-functioning theory of mind (Baron-Cohen, 1993). They behave as if they do not know that other people have minds, intentions, and motives; for example, they treat another person's hand like a tool. Autistic children's problems with language development may stem from a lack of perceived need for communication; where there are no other minds, no communication need—or can—occur.

Neurologic Impairments

Emotional pathologies such as the ones just described are frequently accompanied by neurological problems, which may be genetically or otherwise caused. About 70% of autistic patients are also classified as mentally retarded. Fragile X syndrome may also be present (Freeman, 1993). High-functioning autistics are much less likely to have complicating conditions such as seizure disorders, possibly because they can function better in the absence of the stress created by an organic problem. There are some possible connections between neurologic abnormalities and psychopathology. There is, for example, evidence for some subtle and pervasive neurological problems in autism. Abnormalities in particular parts of the brain could keep sensory records separate and prevent integration of information; could disrupt the learning of emotional connections; and could "overprocess" information, leading to hypersensitivity. A reduction in some neurohormones could also be responsible for poor social bonding (Waterhouse, Fein, & Modahl, 1996).

THE INTEGRATED BABY

Let's consider the situation of a 10-month-old who has just started to spend his days at a baby-sitter's house after being cared for at home for most of his life. His mother carries him from the car to the house each weekday morning; although he can walk when led, he does not move quickly enough and he tends to stumble outdoors. As the door opens and the noise of other children is heard, the baby grips his mother's coat and hides his face against her. He remembers what happens at this place. The sitter comes to greet him, saying his name, but when he turns and sees her face he hides his own again. His whimpers escalate to loud crying as the sitter takes him from his mother's arms, while the latter loosens the clasp of his fingers on her coat. Mother and sitter both look serious and distressed, and the baby's social referencing of his mother's face confirms his belief that something bad is happening. He continues to cry and reach after her as she hurries out the door.

If the baby-sitter has time, she tries to soothe him, and chances are good that within 10 minutes he will have calmed a good deal. His crying and later calming are strongly influenced by his own temperament. If his reactions are intense, his mood quality is negative, and his distractibility is low, he is likely to show a good deal of distress for a long time. His mastery of self-regulation will also make a difference; techniques like sucking his thumb and averting his eyes help him make the transition more easily. Any special problem, like tactile defensiveness, will make him harder for the sitter to soothe, and she may not have the time or understanding to work with him.

In the mother's absence, exploration of the strange place is much harder for the 10-month-old. He has nobody to use for a secure base, but his favorite teddy bear may help. His language development is still too limited for him to ask for or understand information about the room or about what is happening.

Fortunately, repeated experiences of separation and reunion with the mother will help reduce the child's distress and will free him to develop a comfortable relationship with his new caregiver.

PROBLEMS TO CONSIDER AND DISCUSS

1. How do you feel when you think about a child's attachment to his parents? Do you think your feelings are related to your own stage of development?

2. What is temperament? How would you rate your own temperament in terms of the factors discussed in this chapter?

3. How is bonding on the part of a parent related to a baby's development of self-regulation? (Refer back to Chapter 5.)

4. What is a theory of mind? What experiences help an infant develop such a theory?

5. Why are a toddler's rapprochement behaviors so much more intense with the mother than with an occasional baby-sitter?

Socialization and Parenting

Socialization is the process of experience with other people through which an infant learns social rules and attitudes. What is learned may be as universal and primitive as toilet training, as unconscious and pervasive as racial prejudice, or as rule-based as table manners. Some aspects of socialization occur through imitation or through social referencing of adults, whereas others are a matter of direct instruction given to the child. Through socialization, the infant, who fits fairly well into any cultural group, becomes the toddler and preschooler whose ways are already those of her own family and culture. The well-socialized person is similar to others in her group in aggressiveness, compliance, friendliness to strangers, beliefs about sex roles, acceptance of some foods, toilet habits, and so on.

Socialization occurs within the context of a complex, ever-changing, dynamic action system. Whereas our discussion of emotional development in Chapter 12 focused on the infant alone or on the parent-infant dyad, the study of socialization needs to look at nuclear and extended families, cultural groups, and nations. Not only individual and cultural values but also economic and political concerns influence the process of socialization.

The socialization process involves dynamic action systems that work toward goals while carrying out the tasks of socializing an infant. The activities of parts of the system are organized around their goals. Systems involved in socialization also involve circular causal relationships, in which members influence each other at the same time they are influenced. Finally, a system regulates and organizes itself adaptively, so the same socialization functions can be carried out even if new factors enter the system. A new baby or a parent's broken ankle does not prevent working to help a toddler develop dressing skills, but it does mean the work must be done in a different way than before (Marvin & Stewart, 1990).

This chapter will focus on family influences and on the complex ways in which caregivers and infants "bring each other up" through mutual influences in their dynamic action system. In spite of this focus, however, we need to remember that families exist in *cultural groupings*. The appropriateness or inappropriateness of many caregiving techniques exists only with respect to the culture's rules. For example, a mother in the United States who left her 12-month-old with a 6-year-old "child nurse" would be considered negligent of both children's welfare, whereas a rural African woman who did the same thing so she could bring food from the fields would be considered a good mother. Because "right ways" and "wrong ways" of socialization and caregiving exist primarily within a cultural context, this chapter will not attempt to prescribe a single way in which socialization should be carried out. Nonetheless, neither the author nor the reader will be able to abandon their value systems about the outcome of socialization. We cannot really believe that all outcomes for infants are equally satisfactory. Perhaps the best we can manage is to accept the idea that there is more than one way for an infant to grow into the kind of adult we like best.

DOES UPBRINGING REALLY INFLUENCE DEVELOPMENT?

Does the way the twig is bent influence the way the tree grows? Gardeners tell us that the old saying is true for trees; whether the analogy holds for human infants is a question whose answer is less clear. "Everybody knows" that early experience is very important, but nobody actually has a great deal of evidence to support the idea. Even experiences of dreadful early deprivation and suffering do not necessarily lead to abnormal development if the situation is corrected (Cicchetti et al., 1990; Rutter, 1987).

The view—and what is learned—from mother's back may be rather different from the view seen from a stroller.

Understanding which causes lead to which effects is crucial if we are to know the impact of early experience, but there is little agreement on the right way to do this (Angold, 1993). Whatever formulations or predictors of development are used, they have to be complex and must take into account the individual's present circumstances as well as his early experiences (Sroufe, Egeland, & Kreutzer, 1990). The meaning and therefore the effect of any experience depend on both present and past contexts.

The modern emphasis on genetic factors in development has reduced emphasis on the effect of early experience. Evidence, for example, that the parents of inhibited children tend to be shy and anxious (Rickman & Davidson, 1994) makes it appear that the study of early experience may not be as useful as was once thought. However, we continue to need to consider how early experience and genetic factors cooperate to produce individual characteristics.

One important idea is that genetically caused characteristics of the infant lead to his being treated in certain ways, as well as to his interpretation of the treatment. Because the person is viewed as creating his own environment (Scarr, 1992), many early experiences can be considered indirect outcomes of the infant's genetic makeup. Only in truly abnormal environments would the environment have more genuine effect than the genetic background does (Scarr, 1992).

Later in this chapter, we will look at some research on parental styles and their possible effect on infants and toddlers. It is important to realize, however, that knowledge about many aspects of parenting is still so sparse that no one has any business telling a family to change except in a few very special circumstances. When such change is advisable, it can rarely be achieved just by telling the parents to change. Chapter 14 will describe some approaches to early intervention to be used when an infant's environment is outside the normal range.

RESEARCH METHODS

Research on socialization processes includes a variety of approaches, sometimes a matter of naturalistic description but often involving experimental or quasiexperimental approaches. Because socialization involves combinations of biological and experiential factors, research designs might be expected to focus on interactions, but critics have suggested that this is rarely the case (Zahn-Waxler, 1995). To some extent, researchers studying socialization are still struggling with appropriate methods for investigating their topic.

In one series of investigations, researchers used several strategies to look at early social and emotional development (Radke-Yarrow, 1986). One approach was to train mothers to make systematic observations of emotional events in their children's lives and to dictate their observations into tape recorders. A second research approach was to simulate mild emotional events like bumping someone's elbow. The third approach was to set up a homelike apartment in the laboratory where mothers and children could be observed for several days at a time.

Another useful research strategy is to use checklists to gather behavioral information. The Child Behavior Checklist for Ages 2–3 (Achenbach, Edelbrock, & Howell, 1987) looks at behavioral characteristics like sleep problems and destructive behavior. The Mother-Infant/Toddler Feeding Scale (Chatoor, 1986) is specialized to evaluate the emotionally significant feeding situation; it examines a variety of feeding events, such as the mother's forcing food into the baby's mouth or the baby's vocalizing to the mother.

Because the adult's role in socialization is a powerful one, techniques for assessing the general environment or specific adult characteristics are also relevant here. For example, the Home Observation for Measurement of the Environment (Caldwell & Bradley, 1984) examines a wide variety of environmental factors: whether there are ten books visible, whether the family has a pet, whether the parent slaps the child during the assessment visit, for example.

Some research focuses on emotional characteristics and behavior of parents. The Beck Depression Inventory (see Pickens & Field, 1993) assesses the parent's self-report about his or her mood. The Adult Attachment Interview (Fonagy, Steele, & Steele, 1991) is a standardized way to investigate a parent's view of his or her own childhood relationships. The Maternal Behavior Q-sort (Pedersen et al., 1990) looks at generally relevant child-rearing behavior such as excessive teasing or arranging one's position so the baby's signal can be perceived.

Parents and children of minority cultures may not behave according to the same rules followed by members of the majority culture. Assessment of a child's development needs to take this fact into account.

A recent addition to socialization research techniques is the ethnographic approach. Although ethnography has been used by anthropologists and ethologists for many years, it was not an approach favored by traditional infant development researchers. **Ethnography** is the observation, sometimes through videotaping, of people within their own cultural context, in their own homes, going about their daily lives. Its goal is to understand how life is seen by the individuals who are being studied (Freel, 1995/1996). Ethnographic work starts with a series of questions but may alter what is asked as information accumulates. Ethnography is a qualitative method of research and is admittedly affected by the researcher's subjective viewpoint. Finally, we may note that ethnographic work is aimed at generating rather than testing theories (Casper, 1995/1996).

ethnography: qualitative description of events in a group's everyday life; from the Greek *ethnos* (people), *graphein* (to write).

Because work on socialization usually must deal with many variables at once, computer approaches to statistical data analysis can be an essential research tool. However, many existing programs assume that the interactions between various biological and social factors are simple ones, which is probably not the case (Pickles, 1993).

SOCIALIZATION AND THE TASKS OF PARENTS

Child care is often spoken of as if it were simple and monolithic, a standard set of unchanging tasks summarized as "watching" the baby. In actuality, parenting and professional child care include a set of **heterogeneous** and constantly changing jobs, ranging from simple physical tasks like cutting fingernails to the complexities of fostering early moral development. As the infant develops into a toddler, new tasks enter the picture and old ones need to be done in different ways.

heterogeneous: mixed in composition; from the Greek *heteros* (singular, different), *genos* (kind).

It is probably wise to think of all child-rearing tasks as related in some way to socialization. Infants learn from their caregivers how things are done in their culture. At the more abstract and intellectual level, what is learned involves language. At the emotional level, it involves learning fears and other attitudes. At the level of physical functioning, the infant learns what foods are acceptable, where to eliminate, and at what times people want to sleep or to eat. Socialization also involves learning rhythms and styles of motor activity—the postures and gestures that are characteristic of one group of people and foreign to another.

Some of this learning occurs as a result of direct instruction ("we don't bite people!"). But much more comes about through imitation and social referencing. As parents go through their daily routines with infants and toddlers, socialization occurs without intention and usually without awareness.

Touch and Carrying

Some of the earliest learning from parents occurs in the context of *physical touch*. Whether the parent's physical contact with the infant is intended to soothe (an issue discussed in detail in Chapter 8) or just to dress or transport the baby, the infant is sensitive to information resulting from touch.

The caregiver's touch functions as a *Zeitgeber* ("time giver") for a very young infant. The speed and regularity of movements like breathing are communicated through touch and help set an appropriate tempo for the baby's own movements. To understand this process, we need to think of the infant in extensive physical contact with the caregiver: belly to belly, cradled against the shoulder, or sitting in the lap, not just being delicately stroked with one finger. When contact is extensive, the adult's rhythms can override the baby's tempo, calming an overexcited child or arousing a **lethargic** one.

lethargic:
abnormally drowsy or unresponsive; from the Greek *lethargos* (forgetful).

Touch often occurs in the context of carrying the infant. This may be a simple matter of transporting the infant from one place to another, but it is also used to try to soothe the crying infant. A small decrease in crying occurs when parents do more carrying (Barr, 1990).

In many parts of the world, co-sleeping is a source of touch and comfort for infants. The idea that babies should sleep in their own rooms if possible, but certainly in their own beds, is a modern Western idea that is not shared by most cultures. Middle-class Euro-Americans tend to be concerned that infants sleeping with their parents might accidentally be suffocated and that co-sleeping will lead to excessive dependency of the infant on the parents. Mayan families in rural Guatemala, on the other hand, were shocked when they were told that U.S. babies were put to bed in a separate room (Morelli, Rogoff, Oppenheim, & Goldsmith, 1992). Mayan babies had no bedtime stories or comfort objects like teddy bears; they went to sleep when the parents did, in bed with the mother or (in the case of toddlers) the father or an older brother or sister. The Mayan parents conveyed pity and disapproval about the European American custom of separate sleeping and showed that they considered the practice equivalent to child neglect.

Comforting

The many measures taken to *comfort* young infants (see above and Chapter 8) are thought to be related to the development of self-regulation (discussed in Chapter 12). The infant's developing ability to keep herself in a calm, alert state advances with the parent's skill at providing comfort. Initially, the baby depends on the parent to help regulate her degree of excitement, but she gradually learns what the parent does that makes her feel calmer. Positioning or rocking the baby, providing a pacifier or facilitating getting the thumb to the mouth, moving away from distressing sights or sounds—these are all soothing techniques the baby can learn. A tired, cranky 11- or 12-month-old may be seen sucking his thumb, twirling a bit of hair with his other hand, rocking back and forth, and humming to himself. He calms himself with techniques initially provided by a concerned, sensitive caregiver.

Social Play

Playing social games like peek-a-boo with older infants and toddlers is something most parents do "for fun" or to entertain the child and keep her from being cranky. However, *social play* seems to be the major factor in facilitating attachment. As Greenspan (1992a) points out, the good caregiver is "in love" with the infant and "woos" the infant by creating chances for pleasurable involvement. Adult and infant are both delighted by their interactions in social play, and a result is the infant's growing emotional connection with the caregiver. As the baby reaches the toddler period, some effects of attachment on socialization can be seen; the child is interested in imitating the parent and considers the parent's opinion important (although he does not always comply with it.)

Feeding

The *feeding* interaction, which occurs many times every day, is a primary situation in which socialization occurs. One aspect of this is the learning of culturally acceptable food preferences (see Chapter 8). Another is the development of expectations about where and when people eat—an expectation that leads many of us adults to clean our plates even when we are not hungry and thus gain unwanted weight.

The feeding interaction is also a situation in which the infant is socialized to expect certain attitudes and behaviors from other people. For a simple example, a caregiver's insensitivity to the child's cues that he is hungry or not hungry leads the child to expect that people do not know or care what others feel. This expectation can lead to difficulty with purposeful communication (Greenspan, 1992), which in turn is related to the child's view of the self and others and to social skills such as empathy.

If the parent pays careful attention to the baby's cues, on the other hand, the feeding interaction gives many opportunities for purposeful communication. Communications become more and more complex as the older infant and toddler begin self-feeding—still needing help at times, but deeply frustrated by parental intrusion. Again, the communicative process during feeding helps socialize views about relationships between people, especially people at different levels of power.

Toilet-Training Beginnings

Does the topic of *toilet training* belong in a book about infants and toddlers? Ninety years ago, the answer would have been "of course," but U.S. parents today usually do not make a serious conscious attempt at toilet training until their child is older than 24 months. Nevertheless, these parents begin much earlier to communicate to their infant that this aspect of socialization is of extraordinary importance. They do so in the course of everyday physical care and of ordinary interactions with the child.

The caregiver's manner, tone of voice, and facial expression during diapering are different from those shown during feeding or bathing. Even a parent who is very sensitive to a child's cues during feeding has a powerful overriding agenda when changing a soiled diaper. The parent may talk to the baby or hand him a toy to play with, but she shows a matter-of-fact concern with getting the job done. She will not let the baby roll over; she holds his feet out of the way of the dirty diaper and grabs and wipes them quickly if the baby manages to get dirty. She glances at the baby's face from time to time, but her sustained, serious gaze is directed at the bottom, not the baby's facial expression. Exceptional mess or wiggling on the baby's part may lead to muttering in a tone quite different from infant-directed talk: "Pee-yew! You are a stinker today!"—words she uses under no other circumstances. When the diapering is over, she may pat the baby on the bottom, calling attention to the focus of her interest.

As the baby begins to crawl or walk, she often shows that she is having a bowel movement by crouching quietly, perhaps after "hiding" under a chair or in a corner. The caregiver becomes aware of what is happening and communicates a response—perhaps a nervous giggle, perhaps a question like "you're going, aren't you?" The adult's behavior tells the infant that something about the situation is of special social significance.

When the baby can stand, the caregiver may begin to ask for his cooperation while changing the diaper with the baby in a standing position. She may encourage him to hold on to a chair or to lift his foot to help out in the process.

Crawling and walking babies are also exposed to siblings and parents modeling toilet use at home. Many parents tend to leave the bathroom door open when using the toilet because an older infant gets upset if there is a closed door between them, or so they can hear whether the temporarily unsupervised baby is in trouble. It is common for infants to crawl into the bathroom, pull themselves to stand with the parent's leg, and lean on the parent's knee while he or she sits on the toilet, thus witnessing socially approved techniques of elimination.

Therefore, by the time deliberate toilet training begins, many babies have already been socialized by exposure to parental attitudes and practices, if not by overt instruction.

Rules, Values, and Obedience

Socialization includes the learning of a wide set of *rules*, among which are some rules about relative power and authority. One of the jobs of parents and professional child care providers is to provide an appropriate set of rules and to guide the child to comply with the rules. Most competent caregivers begin this aspect of socialization after the child begins to walk, not before. Successful socialization about rules provides the foundation for interaction with other children, teachers, neighbors, and eventually employers and co-workers. Rules about respectful behavior toward more powerful people are especially important in school and work settings.

Of course, we would not expect an infant or toddler to say "yes, sir" or to shake hands. The social rules set for toddlers are at a much simpler level, and many of them involve prohibitions (Gralinski & Kopp, 1993). Rules about child safety include things like not touching dangerous objects. Rules about personal property, like not coloring on the walls, are common. There are rules about respect for others, such as not grabbing toys. Independence rules may include standards about walking alone rather than asking to be carried. Delay rules involve waiting for attention: not interrupting conversations or talking when mother is on the telephone. Naturally, compliance with all these rules will not be achieved by the end of the toddler period, but a start has been made. Initially, the best compliance is with safety rules and rules about others' possessions (Gralinski & Kopp, 1993).

internalization: the process of making another's values and attitudes parts of one's own thinking; from the Latin *internus* (inside).

The period during which socialization about rules and obedience begins is characterized as a time of behavioral organization, initiative, and **internalization** (Greenspan, 1992a). Ideally, the toddler does not simply obey but also internalizes rules and connects them with his own thoughts and emotions. He needs firm but tolerant and flexible guidance to achieve this outcome. Mothers are more effective in getting toddlers to comply when they give reasons for their requests or make the activity into a game, rather than shouting or using physical force (Crockenberg, 1992).

Internalization of rules and values seems to depend on the child's understanding and acceptance of the parent's message. To achieve this internalization, the parent needs to get the child's attention, to give clear, consistent messages, and to signal in a positive way how important this is to the parent. The message needs to be fitted to the child's developmental status, her temperament, and her mood. The child is more likely to internalize the message if there is a minimum threat to her autonomy—for example, when

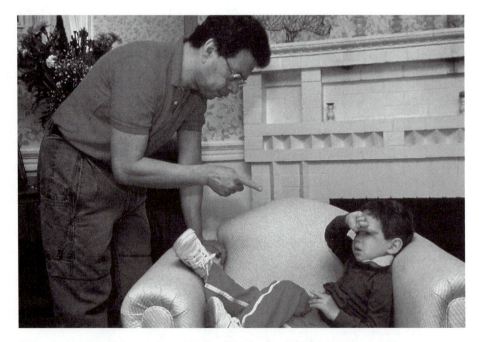

Although socialization may be subtle, it may also be direct and obvious. This parent's raised finger and serious expression are received seriously by the child.

the message is indirect and is accompanied by humor (Grusec & Goodnow, 1994; Kochanska, 1994).

Where development of empathy and helping actions is concerned, the message from the parent is partly in her modeling of such prosocial acts. The parent's demonstration of empathy when her child is hurt or needs help is probably more powerful than her instructions about helping others. It has been suggested that infants' empathic behavior before 15 to 18 months is an imitation of adult comforting behavior (Lewis, 1992).

PARENTS OF INFANTS: GENERAL CHARACTERISTICS

Emotional and intellectual changes are necessary before a human being takes on the role of parent. Instinct, however carefully we may define it, probably plays a very small role in the nurturing humans give to their babies. The conception of a child is the beginning of the process of the birth of a parent. As we noted in Chapter 5, some of the creation of a parent occurs during gestation, but much more will go on after the infant is born. The process takes time, and the early excitement often called bonding is only part of it.

The emotional component of parenting is powerful. For most people, the only emotion whose strength rivals that of parental love for an infant is adult romantic attraction. Although unusual circumstances may deaden parental feelings, the potential strength of these emotions seems to have existed throughout history and among all cultures. We know this, for example, because of poems written to lament the death of babies. The 8th-century Chinese poet, Meng Chiao, wrote:

> Don't let freezing hands play with these pearls—
> If they play with these pearls, the pearls will surely fly loose.
> Don't let the sudden frost cut off springtime—
> If it cuts off spring, no bright flowering.
> Scattering, falling, small nipple buds
> In colorful patterns like my dead baby's robes.
> I gather them—not a full hand's grasp.
> At sunset I return home in hopeless sorrow.
> ("Apricots die young," Meng Chiao, translated by S. Owen, in Liu & Lo, 1975)

It would be a mistake, however, to assume that all strong parental emotions are positive ones. Anger, frustration, even jealousy are also part of parental feeling. Parents as a group are **ambivalent** in their emotions toward their infants, and the need to handle the ambivalence is one of the sources of the vividness of parental love. Just as the toddler's deep involvement with the parent involves needs for both autonomy and connectedness, the parent struggles with the desires to protect and nurture and to escape from the child's demands.

ambivalent: experiencing two (contradictory) emotions simultaneously; from the Latin *ambo* (both), *valere* (to be strong).

The powerful emotions of parental love tend to conceal the intellectual aspects of parenting. However, parents who do a good job must reason effectively about how to care for their infant. A sense of love and connection, however strong, does not automatically provide the knowledge parents need (although it may give the motivation to learn what needs to be known).

New parents in the Western world today usually have much to learn about simple aspects of infant care. Members of small families themselves, they have rarely seen infants being cared for. They learn much from the baby's reactions, but they may also need direct instruction: how to give a bath, how to diaper, what kind of spoon or bottle to use. Well-educated parents may have a whole library of infant-care books to guide them, whereas the semiliterate mother or father seeks other people's advice or assumes wrongly that infants are just like adults.

Although information about child care is important for the parent, its real function is in combination with the parent's emotions and attitudes about the baby. This combination has been called *parental awareness* (Newberger, 1983). Parental awareness involves a person's capacity for understanding children and comprehending the tasks of becoming a parent and raising a child. Knowledge about children is part of parental awareness, but capacities for empathy and for self-awareness are critical, too. The parent uses what she has to create an organized system of thinking, to make sense of what the child does, and to create policies to guide her own actions.

Parental awareness has been described as existing at and developing through several levels of complexity (Newberger, 1983). The simplest level, the *egoistic* stage, is one in which the parent interprets the child through the parent's own needs and desires. The **egoistic** parent thinks in terms of what he or she actually does rather than the way the child may experience or interpret the actions. For example, the parent who shouts at a toddler who is crying at night thinks he has punished the child, whereas the child who is afraid of the dark may feel comforted, even by an angry parent. Parents operating at the egoistic level are more concerned with their own efforts than with their effect on the child. They may also focus on suppressing actions of the child that annoy them, rather than guiding the child's behavior.

The *conventional* level of parental awareness is more complex. Parents at the **conventional** level know that the child's needs are different from their own, but they think in terms of what *all* infants need rather than considering the uniqueness of the individual. It would be hard, for example, for a conventional-level parent to take temperamental differences into account. Parents at this level try to instill standards and values that will guide future behavior, and they are concerned that the child understand reasons for rules and punishments.

A third level, *individualistic* parental awareness, involves the understanding that a child is unique in her motives and abilities. The reasons behind a child's behavior are stressed as much as the behavior itself is. Compared to parents at the egoistic or conventional levels, these parents would have a relatively easy time, for example, adapting to a second child who is much more difficult to toilet train than the first one was.

At the highest, the *analytic* level of parental awareness, the child is seen as "a complex and ever-changing psychological self-system that interacts with

egoistic: in this context, thinking in a way that emphasizes the needs of the self; from the Latin *ego* (I).

conventional: in this context, thinking in a way that stresses actions that society in general considers right; from the Latin *convenire* (to be suitable).

the parents' systems" (Newberger, 1983, p. 73). Parents and children are seen as both autonomous and interdependent. They are also seen as constantly growing and changing—adults only slightly less than children. The child's sense of self and understanding of her own feelings are stressed. Parents at the analytic level would have a relatively easy time dealing with a 10-month-old's fearfulness, for example, because they could see the situation as a natural process of change that is part of their relationship with the baby.

The higher the level of parental awareness, the more capable the parent is of dealing with the complexities of child-rearing. As you might expect, better child development is related to higher levels of parental awareness (Pratt, Hunsberger, Pancer, Roth, & Santolupo, 1993). Although there has been little research on the topic, it is probable that the level of "parental awareness" of day care providers may also have an impact on infants and toddlers.

PARENTS OF INFANTS: DIFFERENCES IN STYLE

The concept of *parental style* is that parents can have subtle differences in their approaches to child-rearing; style is a matter of small but systematic differences, not of major deviations like abusive treatment. It is fascinating to consider the impact that differences in child-rearing style may have on infant development, but it is important to remember two things as we do so. First, we need to keep in mind that no single style is necessarily superior to another. As we noted earlier in this book, the infant just needs a "good enough mother" (Winnicott, 1953) and good enough father, not perfect parents. The issue is really one of "goodness of fit" between parent and child (Chess, 1983).

Second, we need to remember that any effect of parental style is not one-directional. Infants influence parental style as well as being influenced by it. It is critical to recall that style is part of a transactional process, not a way in which parents mold a completely plastic infant.

Given these warnings, we can look at some evidence from research on parental style.

Parents' Expectations

When parents meet their infants for the first time, the adults already have in place some *expectations* about who their babies will be. Some of the parents' expectations come from actual experiences with the unborn babies, who have already shown some differences in activity level and strength of kicking. Some expectations come from cultural beliefs about sex differences. Other expectations come from the influence of the parent's mood on his or her view of the infant. In one study, for example, mothers who were anxious or depressed during their pregnancies tended to rate their still unborn babies as fussy and difficult (Mebert, 1991). In these and similar situations, parents may especially notice the infant characteristics that are much what they expect, and they may also behave in ways that lead the baby to do what they expect (Mebert, 1991).

Parental Sensitivity and Responsiveness

Sensitive parents notice their infants' cues telling them what the infants need or want; responsive parents act in the ways suggested by the babies' signals. These two characteristics usually go together, and they are considered to be an important aspect of parental style.

Parental *sensitivity* and *responsiveness* help maintain interactions with babies. As mother and baby play socially, the baby's heart rate rises as the mother stimulates him. When the baby smiles, laughs, cries, or averts his gaze, the mother reduces the amount of stimulating she is doing. Now the baby's heart rate drops and the sequence begins again. If the mother does not reduce her activity in response to the baby's signal, the baby may avert his gaze and stop the interaction completely (Field, 1987).

Because neither partner responds perfectly to the other's cues, it is quite normal to see interactive mismatch and repair between mothers and babies. Where mismatches in interaction occur between normal mother-baby pairs, about one-third are corrected in one step, and another one-third in two steps (Tronick & Gianino, 1986). The baby's experience of frequent successful repairs of interactive mismatches seems to produce a tendency to use positive signals to get the attention of an unresponsive mother.

Parental sensitivity and responsiveness are shown in other aspects of interactions, as well, as in the use of infant-directed talk rather than adult-directed language (see Chapter 11). Another example of sensitivity is comforting infants by helping them use pacifiers or, later, blankets or stuffed animals they are attached to (Passman, 1977).

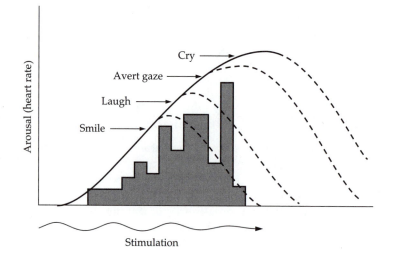

This figure shows interactions of mother and baby as they play. The curves show increasing and decreasing infant heart rates, and the bars show when the mother increases or decreases her stimulating activity (talking, making faces, tickling). (Source: Field, 1987)

The infant's experience of parental sensitivity and responsiveness may have a positive effect on cognitive development. Infants who have spent longer times in vocal turn taking with their mothers (an interaction maintained by the mothers' sensitivity) perform better on a learning task, perhaps because they have achieved an improved sense of mastery and control (Dunham & Dunham, 1990). Higher cognitive scores at age 4 years have been associated with higher maternal responsiveness in infancy (Marc Lewis, 1993).

Sensitivity and responsiveness of parents also seem to affect infant emotional development. Maternal unresponsiveness to infant boys has been associated with angry, aggressive expression of frustration at age 2 or 3 (Shaw, Keenan, & Vondra, 1994). Attachment patterns may also be related to parental sensitivity and responsiveness. Infants whose mothers were sensitive and responsive in the early months usually form secure attachments. Insecure attachments are more likely to occur when mothers are little involved, unresponsive to signals, and intrusive (try to force interaction, for example); the infant may avoid the mother as a strategy for self-protection (Isabella & Belsky, 1991).

Fathers' Styles and Mothers' Styles

By the second half of the first year, infants seem to expect men's voices to go with men's pictures and women's voices to go with women's pictures (Poulin-Dubois, Serbin, Kenyon, & Derbyshire, 1994); they are already paying attention to the social world as it is divided along gender lines. Infants tend to spend more time looking at their mothers than at their fathers when the parents' expressions give no particular signals; but when one parent has a happy and the other a fearful expression, the infant looks more at the fearful one regardless of gender (Hirshberg & Svejda, 1990). The conflicting signals are distressing to the infants, though (Hirshberg, 1990). (It is an interesting question whether in natural circumstances mothers are more likely than fathers to have fearful expressions).

It is possible that the infant's early discrimination of men and women is encouraged by his experience of different parental styles. In the early months of the baby's life, soothing behavior is somewhat more characteristic of mothers, and exciting, playful interactions are somewhat more associated with fathers. As the child reaches the toddler stage and socialization pressure begins, mothers make more control attempts than fathers do, but they also tend to be less directive. They soften their control attempts by using questions ("Wouldn't you like to have lunch now?"), bargaining, reasoning, and appeals to the idea that "everyone is going to go outside"—a communal orientation. Fathers are more often direct and assertive and exert direct pressure to comply. However, mothers are more likely to *force* compliance, for instance, by carrying a screaming child upstairs and placing him in his crib (Power, McGrath, Hughes, & Manive, 1994). These differences probably derive from different maternal and paternal child care responsibilities, as well as from gender-role differences.

Discipline Styles

Most people in the United States do not make serious attempts to discipline or socialize infants who are less than a year of age. Early attempts at training are usually directed at behaviors the adult considers dangerous, such as playing with an electrical outlet. Inner-city mothers are more likely than others to consider spanking to be an appropriate disciplinary approach (Socolar & Stein, 1995).

Experiences of severe physical punishment early in life are associated with later aggressive and even criminal behavior. The important factor seems to be the parent's attitude toward the child rather than the physical pain alone, although some studies have indicated that many murderers had experienced unusual levels of painful medical treatment in early life (Lester & Lester, 1975).

APPLICATIONS & ARGUMENTS
Nonviolent Parenting

Many parents of toddlers are heard to say, "I don't like to hit her, but what else can I do? Nothing else works!" These parents are responsibly aware of the need for socialization and that it is their job to guide and train their children. What they often do not realize is that nothing but hitting has worked because they have not really tried anything else.

There are many nonviolent (and, indeed, nonpunitive) guidance techniques that are suitable for older infants and toddlers. Supervision is a particular important approach; it involves parental awareness and careful watching when a baby may be tempted to do something undesirable. The parent simply moves in to stop the behavior as soon as it starts.

Cueing is a helpful technique when the baby has a little receptive language. A verbal reminder is given to guide behavior, but the cue comes before the behavior, not as a scolding afterward. A cue like "don't touch" or "hot" may need to be accompanied by a touch to restrain the baby's hand or guide it away from an object. Cueing may also be used to help the baby carry out a sequence of acts that is too complex to remember.

Negotiation can work well with toddlers. A command a child refuses to obey can be softened or changed to something slightly more acceptable. An attempt at negotiation often produces compliance. It is also a way for a parent to model an important social skill for the toddler.

These techniques do work to help babies learn and obey rules. They are more difficult than physical punishment, but often more effective, too. In addition, they foster a family atmosphere of competence and confidence, which is hard to achieve when physical or nonphysical punishment is frequent.

One approach to the analysis of discipline style categorizes parents as either restrictive or permissive and as either warm or hostile. Each parent's style is categorized as a combination of these factors (Becker, 1964). The warm, restrictive approach has been reported to lead to child personality characteristics of submissiveness, obedience, dependency, and a lack of friendliness and creativity. When the parenting style is warm and permissive, the outcome is said to be creativity, independence, and friendliness. A hostile and restrictive style is associated with social withdrawal, quarrelsomeness, and shyness with peers. Finally, the hostile permissive style is associated with delinquent, noncompliant, aggressive behavior.

Not only the general style of discipline but the specific demands on the child, as well, may affect development. In one study, 5-year-olds had fewer behavior problems when the early demands on them had been for **competent** action (to share, take turns, do chores) than when they had been given many social regulation demands ("keep quiet," "sit up straight," "say thank you," "tell Anne about the doll") (Kuczynski & Kochanska, 1995).

competent: able to work effectively on the environment; from the Latin *competere* (to seek together, as a prize, for example).

WHAT THE INFANT BRINGS TO SOCIALIZATION

Later in this chapter, we will look at characteristics of high-risk infants and see their effect on development. Even when we are considering normal, low-risk infants, however, we need to remember that individual differences in infants make them respond differently to socialization. Some individual differences, like temperament, may be almost impervious to social pressures. Even some characteristics that one might expect to be learned, such as sex-role orientation, may be biologically built into the individual (Gottman, 1989; Marshall, 1995).

Not only do infants respond differently to what parents do, infants may in fact influence their caregivers in individual ways. As a result, the caregivers alter their behavior with the infants, which in turn can affect the babies' development.

Infant Attractiveness

When we use the expression "a face only a mother could love," we imply that a mother can always love her baby's face, no matter how ugly someone else might consider the child. Unfortunately, mothers do seem to respond to their babies' attractiveness. In one study, babies were rated on attractiveness while still in the hospital. The mothers' attitudes toward their babies were rated at that point and again 3 months later. Mothers of less attractive babies were more likely to talk to other people or to do routine caregiving than to be playful or affectionate toward the baby (Langlois, Ritter, Casey, & Sawin, 1995).

If the baby has some physical defect (rather than simply being homely), the position of the defect is important. A defect of the face is more difficult for the parent to deal with than is one in the lower body. An infant with fetal alcohol syndrome, for example, presents a less attractive face to the mother and may thus receive less playful attention from her.

Infant Temperament

No single infant temperament factor makes for a "good" or a "bad" baby. Usually, the issue about temperament is goodness-of-fit, or the extent to which the temperaments of infant and caregiver work well together. An infant with a high activity level could exhaust a low-activity-level parent but might please and amuse one who shares a need for high activity. Differences or resemblances in temperament can either help a parent and child feel that they are "on the same wavelength" or estrange them.

Infants who are temperamentally irritable, however, may affect their mother's social behavior toward them (van den Boom & Hoeksma, 1994). Mothers seem to be systematically more positive toward nonirritable infants. Even though the irritable babies in van den Boom and Hoeksma's study became less irritable as they got to 5 or 6 months of age, the mothers' attitudes seemed to become set by their early experiences; they tried less and less to soothe the babies and decreased their responses to the babies' positive signals.

An important role that temperament plays in socialization has to do with the development of guilt and conscience. These aspects of personality are based on the child's internalization of the parent's standards and involve anxiety associated with undesirable behavior. A child's temperament helps determine whether or not a parent's attempts to instill standards are effective. Where a fearful toddler is concerned, gentle discipline that deemphasizes the parent's power seems to work best; if threats are too strong, the child may become too anxious to learn effectively. With less fearful toddlers, the encouragement of attachment seems more related to conscience than discipline approaches do (Kochanska, 1991b, 1995).

Sex Differences

Research on sex differences at this point has produced few clear-cut and reliable results. When such results have been found, it is usually quite unclear whether they are based on biological differences or differences in socialization and caregiving.

We might assume that infants a few days old would show sex differences that could not be due to differences in caregiving. In the United States, however, early sex differences are complicated by the frequency of circumcision of boys on the second or third day after birth. The operation is still most often done without anesthesia; and its stressfulness is increased by the fact that the baby is held in a restraining cradle during the procedure. In one study (Davis & Emory, 1995), circumcised newborn boys showed greatly increased heart rates under the mild stress of a later examination, as if the experience of recent acute stress had changed their reactions to other stresses. (These comments should not be taken as disapproval of circumcision, for which there are often excellent health and religious reasons, but as evidence that boy and girl infants may have quite different experiences in the early days of life.)

Some research has reported complex sex differences in movement patterns from the time of birth (Bell & Darling, 1965), whereas other work has shown no differences in areas like activity level and vigor of movement (Korner, Hutchinson, Koperski, Kraemer, & Schneider, 1981). Evidence of some sex differences in perceptual and nervous system development was discussed in early chapters.

There does not seem to be any clear picture of dramatic differences that would systematically affect how infant boys and girls respond to socialization. Any such differences would probably function in connection with parents' different expectations for boys and for girls and parents' attitudes about sex-appropriate behavior. The major exception to this statement would be toilet training, where anatomical differences require that boys and girls learn different techniques of elimination; modesty rules are associated with toilet training, too.

For older toddlers, there is evidence of sex differences in behavior that are actually contrary to the stereotype of the impulsive, rambunctious boy and the quiet, sociable girl. Groups of 1- and 2-year-olds dominated by boys have been shown to be more verbal, more likely to share, and less likely to use force in conflicts over toys (Caplan, Vespo, Pedersen, & Hay, 1991) than are groups with more girls.

There is no question that parents and toddlers alike pay close attention to sex differences. One 16-month-old boy inquired of a new friend, "Is a boy?" When he received a positive reply, the toddler commented with a happy smile, "Peter [himself] is boy too!" Before even two years have passed, we have all learned that identifying someone's sex is critical to placing him or her in the social world.

Unfortunately, there are some other reasons for our interest in sex differences. Some serious developmental problems, such as pervasive developmental disorder and dyslexia, are much more common among boys than among girls. In adulthood, men are more likely than women are to be involved in violent crimes; adult women are more likely to be depressed. How these facts can be explained in terms of biological or socialization differences remains unclear.

RISK FACTORS IN SOCIALIZATION

Risk factors are characteristics of the infant, the caregiver, or the life situation that have the potential for harming development. When risk factors are in operation, the result may be poor socialization, later problems with mental health, and poor school performance.

It is unusual to find a single risk factor operating alone in an infant's life. When risk factors exist, they generally occur in multiples, making it particularly difficult to discover the nature of their effect on the infant's development.

co-morbidity: the existence of two or more risk factors in association with each other; from the Latin *com-* (with), *morbidus* (diseased).

Certain risk factors tend to be accompanied by specific other factors, a situation termed **co-morbidity.** For example, a baby with fetal alcohol syndrome is often being cared for by a mother who continues to abuse alcohol, and the mother's negligence and abusiveness are co-morbid with the infant's physical condition. Similarly, the mother of a Fragile X baby has genetic problems of her own, which can limit her caregiving capacities (Freund, 1994).

Risk factors in the environment seem to operate in a way that is specific to a given child. Marital conflict, for instance, affects different children in a family in different ways (O'Connor & Rutter, 1996).

Risk factors function as a dynamic action system. The outcome for the infant results from the combined impact of all the risk factors in her life. It should be noted that not all the risk factors for an individual are necessarily present at birth, or even at age 2. Although early risk factors can be powerful, later events can play a very real part in determining how well a child or adult functions.

Risk Factors in the Infant

Characteristics of the infant herself help determine whether her developmental pathway will be healthy or unhealthy. Some of these characteristics, such as certain genetic syndromes, have a direct effect on social behavior. Other factors operate in an indirect way, perhaps by making the baby more difficult to care for and compromising the parent's responsiveness to her.

Physical health problems are a major risk factor for infant development and socialization. Prenatal problems and preterm birth have major impacts on the infant's social, emotional, and intellectual development (cf. Kopp, 1987). Prenatal drug exposure (discussed in Chapter 4) has received a great deal of publicity as a cause of poor emotional development, but research on this topic is so difficult that few clear conclusions can be drawn. Foster and adoptive parents hesitate to accept a "crack baby," although in fact the problems of such children may be due primarily to inadequate parenting, poverty, high stress, and exposure to violence (Lester & Tronick, 1994).

As we noted in Chapter 12, temperament can be an infant risk factor. The "difficult" infant, intense, negative, and hard to console, may be so frustrating to the caregiver that the latter spends less and less time interacting with him. If the caregiver also has certain risk factors, the outcome may be physical abuse of the child.

Poor social competence in the infant puts him at risk. The term *at risk* refers to the infant's capacity to elicit caregiving from adults. Risks are greater when the infant shows low readability (clear cues about his needs), low predictability, and low responsiveness to adults (Bromwich, 1985).

Depression in infants can be considered both a risk factor and a sign that other risk factors have been at work. Depression in infants shows itself in behaviors that are related to other aspects of development; young infants may appear listless, bland, and apathetic, whereas toddlers may have frequent temper tantrums and unusual concerns about separation (Provence, 1983). As we will see later in this chapter, depressive symptoms can result from disturbed relationships with caregivers. However, they can also operate as risk factors themselves by making the child less attractive to adults, harder to care for, and less likely to explore and learn about the world.

Infant vulnerability is a poorly understood but real risk factor. Some infants appear to be unusually strongly affected by events that would not affect a more resilient child (Werner, 1988).

Incidental Risk Factors

Some risk factors involve experiences that occur more or less by chance and can crop up in the lives of either low-risk or high-risk infants. These *incidental* risk factors may affect the infant alone or both family and infant.

Incidental risk factors involve stress for the infant. In most cases, this stress is a matter of too-rapid or too-frequent change from familiar to unfamiliar situations. The death of a parent would be an obvious and dramatic form of stress, but other events such as a mother's new pregnancy, family travel, or changes in time with a baby-sitter are also increases in stress (Elkind, 1981). Stressful events have an impact that adds up over a period of time even when each is mild, but fortunately the passage of time after each event also contributes to recovery.

The most stressful incidental risk factors involve separation after attachment has taken place. (Because very young infants have not yet become attached, separation from familiar people is far less stressful for them.) When separations are brief or gradual, attached infants may protest but are not much affected. Risk is present when the separation is abrupt and prolonged. When this occurs, infants and toddlers generally display three phases of response, which may take 6 months to a year to complete.

The initial response to an abrupt separation is *protest*. The child cries, appears anxious, and searches actively for the lost person; she may go to the door or become very alert when she hears someone coming. There is little or no play, and eating and sleeping are disrupted.

If the separation is prolonged for many days, the child enters a stage of *despair*. He appears to be mourning for the lost person and is sad and unresponsive to other people. He is unable to accept comfort from unfamiliar people. If he is reunited with the lost person at this point, he is likely to cling and to seem fearful of loss for some time; he may have trouble with sleeping alone or having the adult leave the house briefly.

If the separation continues, the child moves into a phase called *detachment*. She no longer appears to be mourning. If reunited with the adult at this point, the child shows powerful anger and ambivalence and may no longer recognize the person. Reestablishing the relationship may be difficult and time-consuming because of the child's anger and the adult's disappointment and confusion. Continued separation beyond the detachment phase culminates with the child's *resolution of grief* and her readiness to form a new attachment to a new caregiver, if one is available.

Studies of infants who have experienced abrupt and prolonged or permanent losses suggest that the experience can have a long-term effect on development (Cummings & Cicchetti, 1990). The individual may show a higher risk for depression and for suicide in adolescence and in adulthood, especially following the breakup of a love relationship or a similar loss—what has been called an "exit-type life event" (McKinney, 1985).

Like other risk factors, separation does not act independently. It combines with other risk factors to create worse problems, but, fortunately, it also interacts with buffering factors that reduce its impact. For example, infants' stress, as measured by adrenocortical responses to separation, was reduced when a substitute caregiver was warm, responsive, and interactive; this was especially the case for babies of difficult temperament (Gunnar, Larson, Hertsgaard, Harris, & Broderson, 1992). In an animal study, the effect of separation on infant monkeys' immune systems was decreased if they were in a familiar place or with familiar companions (Coe et al., 1987). The immediate effect of separation is thus buffered or reduced by familiar settings and good care; whether this also makes a difference to long-term effects is not clear.

More or less serious effects of separation are seen in many situations. Infants and toddlers who are moved into a new day care situation without familiar peers show fussing, aggressiveness, and reduced play for a time (Field, 1986). Protest, despair, and even some detachment may result when an infant's or toddler's mother is hospitalized to give birth to a new baby. Similar responses may occur when parents go on vacation alone, especially if the child is left with an unfamiliar caregiver or in an unfamiliar place. U.S. military parents who were involved in the Gulf War of 1991 returned to infants and toddlers who showed many effects of the separation.

The most serious impact of separation probably occurs when the loss results from violence or war. If the young child has seen one parent kill the other, for example, nightmares, fears, reenactment of the trauma, and aggressive behavior may result (Osofsky, 1994). Civil wars, such as the conflict between the Hutus and the Tutsi in Rwanda, produce what the Red Cross calls "unaccompanied children," some still at the infant or toddler stage. These young children may have seen their parents hacked or tortured to death or may simply have awakened to find themselves alone. They have sometimes been injured themselves and are often malnourished, but the violent and sudden loss of their parents has the greatest impact on them.

Parents' Biological Problems

Naturally, not all risk factors in socialization come from the baby or from the outside environment. Characteristics of parents can also put socialization at risk. The parental characteristics we are referring to here are not simply a subtle matter of style but deviations serious enough to have deleterious effects on infant development.

Physical problems such as partial paralysis have little effect on the parent-infant relationship, although special tools or the help of other people may be needed to carry out routine care procedures. If brain damage has occurred, there may be more difficulty, as one of the results may be problems in dealing with demanding or unfamiliar situations.

APPLICATIONS & ARGUMENTS
Worries About Separation Anxiety

When a baby first shows anxiety about separation or the approach of a stranger, the parents may be concerned about what is happening. What is going on with their fearless, sociable child? Has she been frightened or hurt in some way they don't know about? Did something happen at the day care center, and it's been kept a secret? Or can it be that the lady down the street is right, and the child has become spoiled and full of whims?

The first displays of separation concerns are an achievement that should really be ranked with milestones like the first steps or words. They show that development of emotion and cognition are on track and that the parents are providing a "good enough" environment. Perhaps someone should market a bumper sticker that brags, "My baby is afraid of strangers!" Many parents need help recognizing this development, which may well be the foundation of later social relations.

On the other hand, highly educated and sophisticated parents sometimes have the reverse concern. They know that infants are supposed to show some anxiety as attachment develops. What if their child doesn't show enough? What if she doesn't cry often or loudly, or if she warms up to strangers quickly? Is the baby attached enough? What if she is attached, but to her caregiver at the day care center instead of to her parents? Parents are always going to worry, but this particular set of worries fails to take individual differences into account. Babies are different from one another, and this will show up in their attachment behavior as well as in other ways.

Some genetic problems can lead to poor parenting, which in turn makes it difficult to pinpoint the sources of a child's symptoms. For example, a woman with Fragile X syndrome who shows some degree of impulsiveness, poor attention, and poor short-term memory will probably be impaired in her handling of her children (Freund, 1994).

Parents' Drug and Alcohol Use

Concerns with parents' use of drugs and alcohol usually concentrate on teratogenic effects of these substances. However, a woman who drinks and uses drugs during pregnancy is not very likely to stop voluntarily after the child is born. In fact, she may increase her use as she "self-medicates" against the stress of caring for a young (possibly sick and preterm) infant. Not all drug-using mothers act the same; some are easily frustrated (which is characteristic of drug users) and react with emotional detachment, whereas others tend to overstimulate the baby. Some become depressed or hostile and respond to the baby's passivity as if it were personal rejection (Freier, 1994). In addition, substance-abusing parents have what has been called "a primary commitment to chemicals, not to their children" (Howard, Beckwith, Rodning, & Kropenske, 1989, p. 8). Such parents do not function as protectors of their child's safety or consistent caregivers. Disorganized attachments are common among their children.

Mental Illness and Depression

When a caregiver has an incapacitating form of mental illness, or psychosis, his or her ability to nurture an infant is minimal. Such a person may be inattentive and neglectful or may attack the infant; psychotic adults cannot even care for themselves appropriately, much less deal with the special needs and subtle cues of a baby.

Depression is a milder form of emotional disturbance that lessens the parent's ability to interact socially with the baby, although it does not usually interfere with physical care of the infant. In Chapter 12, we noted the baby's reaction to the experimental still-face procedure and saw that a blank, unresponsive face leads to the infant's emotional withdrawal. The sad, unresponding face of the depressed caregiver probably has a similar effect on the infant.

postpartum:
soon after birth; from the Latin *post-* (after), *parere* (to produce).

The term **postpartum depression** implies that there is something about pregnancy and birth that can cause a depressive reaction. It is a good idea to try to differentiate between serious depression at a clinical level and the moderate depression that often occurs in the first months of parenthood. It is very common for a mother (particularly) to experience periods of depression, fatigue, irritability, and easy crying in the first few months of a baby's life. Although distressing, these episodes are less a matter of severe emotional disturbance than a reaction to the stress of assuming primary responsibility for a baby and adjusting to other life changes (Cohler, 1984).

The symptoms of more severe depression may be difficult to tell from the normal adjustment reactions. If the new mother is in her twenties or thirties, she may already have a history of depressive episodes that help define her problem as a more serious one. If the mother is in her teens, this may be her first episode of noticeable depression, and it may be followed by other episodes. The depressive mother's interaction with her infant is disturbed, but not all depressed mothers are withdrawn; as noted before, some are intrusive and overly stimulating (Ross, Jennings, & Popper, 1993). In either case, the mother is not "taking turns" with the infant and establishing two-way communication. The implications for the development of language (Bettes, 1988) and for emotional empathy are not good. The mother's disengagement is even more disturbing to the baby than her angry behavior is (Field, 1989).

Longer periods of maternal depression (greater than 6 months) have a more serious effect on the baby than shorter periods do (Campbell, Cohn, & Meyers, 1995). Infants and toddlers of chronically depressed mothers are likely to show insecure attachment (Teti, Gelfand, Messinger, & Isabella, 1995) and unusually inhibited behavior when approaching new places or people (Kochanska, 1991a). Their own behavior becomes depressed, and they become less good at eliciting friendly interactions from adults. [There is some disagreement as to whether this behavior is limited to reactions to the depressed mother or whether it becomes a reaction to people in general (Field, 1989)].

Why would exposure to a depressed parent lead to an infant's depression? Several reasons have been suggested. In addition to changing the patterns of interaction between mother and infant, the situation exposes the baby to depressive behavior that he may imitate. The parent's depression also increases the level of conflict and discord in the household as it influences the marital relationship (Cummings, 1995). We should remember, however, that possible genetic factors in depression could influence both mother and child.

The term *depression* is most often applied to a unipolar emotional disturbance in which unusual sadness is the most obvious symptom. However, depression may be part of a bipolar emotional disorder, characterized by swings from deep depression to an equally disturbed manic, excited state. Toddlers with bipolar caregivers show more serious problems than do those whose mothers exhibit a unipolar depression. These toddlers are more aggressive and show less sharing and helping with peers; when they are exposed to a frustrating problem, they react intensely and recover slowly, even when the problem is solved (Zahn-Waxler, Cummings, Ianotti, & Radke-Yarrow, 1984).

Parents' Issues About Attachment and Loss

In an earlier section of this chapter, we noted the impact that experiences of separation and loss had on infants. Experiences of loss can include situations in which the caregiver is physically present but is emotionally unavailable, for example, because of depression (Field, 1985). When such experiences have been severe, it is not surprising that the individual will continue to be influenced by them when he or she becomes a parent. Traumatic experiences of loss, partially forgotten but unresolved after 20 or 30 years or more, can have a serious impact on parenting behavior.

Parents who have unresolved experiences of loss of a parent through death, or who have experienced early physical or sexual abuse, are unusually likely to have toddlers whose behavior is in the D category in the Strange Situation (Main & Hesse, 1990; see Chapter 12). These children display disorganized/disoriented behavior, such as falling to the floor when reunited with the parent after an experimental separation.

It has been suggested that parents of D category toddlers are in a continual state of fear; they act frightened and are frightening to their children. Their behaviors toward their children are unusual and include sudden changes in voicing of sounds (see Chapter 11) or sudden drops in voice pitch. These parents may suddenly move an object or their own face very close to the infant's face or may suddenly move a hand across the infant's face or throat. The parent may present conflicting cues by calling to the infant while looking threatening. Paradoxically, the parent seems afraid of being rejected by the infant and may withdraw with a pleading look if the infant resists an action. Finally, in their speech and play, parents of D category toddlers show a preoccupation with fear and threat, telling the child that he might kill a (stuffed) toy. They may even act afraid of the child at times (Main & Hesse, 1990).

An early loss of a brother or sister may also influence a parent's behavior. The continuing effects of early loss in these cases have been termed *ghosts in the nursery* (Fraiberg, Adelson, & Shapiro, 1975). In these situations, the parent becomes distressed, concerned, and poor at dealing with an infant when the child approaches the age at which the parent's sibling died. If the sibling's death occurred traumatically and if the parent was only a toddler or pre-schooler at the time, the effect can be intense because the parent's emotional response has stayed at an immature level.

Although early loss seems to have an especially powerful effect on parenting, recent losses can also have an influence. This is especially true when the loss occurs within the year before the baby's birth. The process of grieving through which the parent resolves the loss of a spouse or a father or mother is thought to interfere with the capacity to make an emotional connection and bond with the new baby (Klaus & Kennell, 1982). More recent losses have a greater effect, and the most serious impact may occur when one infant in a multiple birth dies.

Adolescent Parents

Instead of "Adolescent Parents," it might be more accurate to label this section "Adolescent Mothers." Adolescent fathers are statistically unlikely to be much involved with their infants; even if they want to be involved, the young mother's parents may forbid visits. Adolescent boys who have fathered children are less likely to be the kind of partner a girl's parents would like her to have. They are significantly more likely to begin cocaine use early, to become sexually active early, to smoke cigarettes, to have a higher lifetime use of alcohol, and to have a higher lifetime number of sexual partners (Spingarn & DuRant, 1996). Adolescent mothers generally take the major role in caring for their babies. (They choose to give the baby up for adoption in only about 10% of cases.)

The level of teenage childbearing in the United States is many times higher than in most European countries, amounting to about 500,000 live births each year (Ahlburg & DeVita, 1992). Because children of adolescents are more likely to be of low birth weight (McAnarney, 1985), this group begins life with a potential for problems. Physical abuse, also more common among adolescent parents, can add more difficulties (Rogel & Petersen, 1984). To compound the problems further, adolescent mothers of infants are likely to show very inappropriate styles in interacting with their babies. The 15- to 16-year-old group of mothers have been shown to use an exceptionally high rate of assertive touch; this includes repetitive pinching and poking the baby with the fingertips, as well as pushing, shoving, and shaking (McAnarney, 1983).

For the infant, the consequences of being born to an adolescent mother involve a combination of biological and environmental factors (Thurman & Gonsalves, 1993). Adolescent mothers often have little knowledge of how infants develop and little understanding of good parenting practices. Their educational achievement is low and their emotional immaturity is exacerbated by the stress of an unplanned pregnancy (Sommer et al., 1993). They may be neglectful because they do not discriminate the child's needs from their own. For example, one adolescent mother, when asked if she had fed her baby breakfast that morning, replied, "I wasn't hungry" (Musick, 1994).

Having the support of the adolescent mother's own mother can be advantageous for the infant in some ways but not in others (Musick, 1994; Spieker & Bensley, 1994). The grandmother's insistence on her own child care approach may replicate the situation that led to her daughter's adolescent pregnancy; the teenage mother may feel she has "lost" her baby and replace the child with a new pregnancy. A nurturant grandfather's presence has been reported to have a direct positive effect on the grandchild's development (Oyserman, Radin, & Benn, 1993).

Marital Status and Parental Status

Single-parent families (of which mother-only families are by far the most common) are now almost as frequent as two-parent families. Although membership in a single-parent family (a "broken home") used to be considered a risk factor in itself, it is now recognized that co-morbidities, or associated risk factors, have a greater effect than does single-parent status alone. Single mothers are more likely than married women to be poor and to suffer problems of poverty, such as living in poor housing and violent neighborhood environments.

One of the problems with trying to study single-parent families is that they are as diverse as two-parent families are. We might do well to think of the ways in which a single parent (usually "she") might find herself in this position.

Never-married single parents fall into two major groups: those who had an unplanned first child out of wedlock early in life, perhaps in their teens, and those who planned a pregnancy when they became older and thought it unlikely that they would marry. These two groups are very different in educational level and income but are similar in that women in both are probably most likely to be rearing an infant alone. Problems of the never-married parent center around the stress of coping alone with the needs of their infants and toddlers. Loneliness for other adults and grief for their lost dreams of family life are also concerns. Potential problems of parenting emerging from this situation could include poor social interaction, neglect, and abuse (although these do not arise in the great majority of cases).

Divorced single parents of infants and toddlers include a very small number of fathers with custody. This group has experienced a high level of recent stress, as the marital breakup coincided with the pregnancy, the birth, or the infant period. They have usually experienced a simultaneous reduction in income as well. Depression and withdrawal, as well as anger, are normal parts of grieving over the divorce, but they interfere with the parent's emotional availability to the child. The noncustodial parent may visit the child or take her home for periods of time, which relieves some of the stress of constant child care but also adds to anxiety and anger involved in negotiating with the estranged spouse.

Widowed single parents are relatively rare in the Western world today. If widowhood is so recent that there is an infant or toddler in the home, the parent's grief is probably some way from resolution. If the child is more than 6 or 8 months old, his own grief and loss will have an impact on his behavior and will increase the stress in the surviving parent's life. If the parent's death was sudden or violent, the surviving parent, the infant, and other children in the family may have a great deal of trouble resolving the loss.

Adoptive and foster parents, whether married or single, may have some complex issues that help determine their relationships with the infants in their care. Some additional risks in their situations can lead to surprising numbers of disrupted adoptions as well as to rejection of foster children and abuse in both cases. Adoptive parents are particularly vulnerable because of their awareness of their own infertility. In most cases, the decision to adopt came about because no pregnancy had been achieved after years of trying and treatment. To make this decision, the adoptive parent or parents had to accept the fact of infertility and to give up the self-image of a reproductively "normal" person. Grief over the loss could take years to resolve, especially if many miscarriages had occurred. Because it is possible to be too old to adopt by the rules of adoption agencies, adoptive parents may have had to rush into the process as quickly as possible.

Foster parents have often had children of their own and are not concerned about infertility. However, the relationship with a foster child is by definition likely to be a temporary one. Foster parents are caregivers only and do not decide about a child's later placement. These facts may force foster parents to withhold deep involvement with an infant and to be less attuned and interactive with her than they might otherwise be. As we will see in Chapter 14, a special risk factor for infants and toddlers in foster care is the frequent change of caregivers.

Abusive Treatment

In Chapter 6, we discussed some aspects of physical and sexual abuse of infants. It was evident that infants with certain characteristics are more likely to be abused than others. It is also the case that some parents are more likely than others to be abusers (although it seems probable that any adult, when sufficiently stressed, can have at least the impulse to attack an infant).

The risk of abusive treatment by a mother is higher if the discipline she experienced as a child was severe, if physical discipline continued into adolescence, and if she was hit with objects and on parts other than the hands or buttocks (E. Newberger, 1983). Abusive parents are less able to understand infants' crying communication (Frodi, 1985) or their emotions in photographs (Kopp & Haynes, 1987).

In one study of abusive head trauma, fathers and mothers' boyfriends committed over 60% of the abuse, and female baby-sitters, surprisingly, were

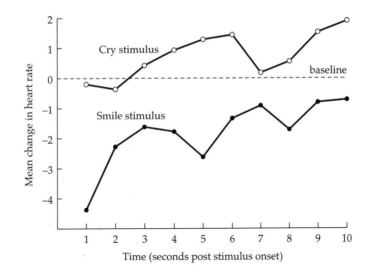

Nonabusive adults show distinctly different heart rate changes in response to infant cries and infant smiles. (Source: Frodi, 1985)

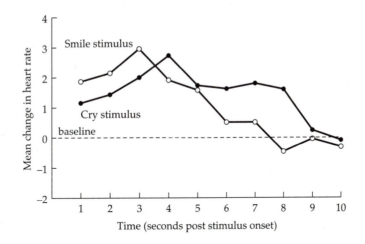

Adults with a history of abusing children show similar heart rate responses to infant smiling and crying; they react as if both behaviors were unpleasant. (Source: Frodi, 1985)

responsible for almost 20% of the cases (Starling, Holden, & Jenny, 1995). Physical (or sexual) abuse in child care centers is extremely rare.

The majority of infants of abusive parents are in the D category in the Strange Situation (see the earlier discussion) (Main & Solomon, 1990). They are less likely to be able to use the parent as a secure base, and they show reckless behavior as toddlers (Lieberman & Pawl, 1990). At school age, they are aggressive, and, significantly, are unusually likely to believe that others are hostile toward them (Weiss, Dodge, Bates, & Pettit, 1992).

THE INTEGRATED BABY

Let us consider a baby who is experiencing an environment that is not "good enough." A common way for this situation to exist today involves a single adolescent mother who is marginally involved with drugs but who has a boyfriend who is a serious member of the drug culture. This young mother's infant may or may not have been biologically affected by the mother's prenatal drug and alcohol use, and he may or may not have been influenced by the mother's poor diet and lack of prenatal care. But after birth, he finds himself with a mother who is likely to be fatigued, frustrated, depressed, and unresponsive. If the baby himself is fussy, the mother may give up very quickly any attempts she makes to soothe him, especially if her boyfriend wants her attention and tells her not to spoil the baby. With little sense of control over communication and little help with self-regulation, the baby cries more and more. As he reaches the second half of the first year, he may try to hit or bite in frustration. The crying may elicit physical punishment from the boyfriend, and the biting may prompt the mother to bite back "so he can see how it feels." The mother may expect the baby to be toilet-trained by 9 or 10 months and may resort to physical punishment when this does not happen. As a result of this hostile and restrictive environment, this child at 12 months may show the disorganized attachment pattern, looking dazed or even falling to the floor when reunited with his mother. Easy frustration and aggressive behavior will increase in the next year, whereas language and other cognitive developments will lag behind. Motor activity may be this infant's greatest pleasure and the only area where he develops freely.

PROBLEMS TO CONSIDER AND DISCUSS

1. Why is the measurement of parents' moods and attitudes considered relevant to the study of infant development?

2. In what ways does feeding play a role in socialization? (Be complete in your answer.)

3. What events in the child's experience and development need to occur before he shows signs of empathy? (Don't forget about cognition.)

4. What effects do high or low levels of sensitivity and responsiveness in mothers have on their babies? How do the babies themselves influence the mother's responsiveness?

5. How does the experience of emotional loss influence a parent's caregiving ability?

14 Infant Mental Health: Problems, Prevention, Intervention

The term *infant mental health* has a strange sound to those who are unfamiliar with it. The image evoked seems to involve infants in the situations we connect with adult psychiatric care—infants on a couch in classical psycho-analysis, infants telephoning the suicide prevention hot line, or "crazy babies" in the padded cell of the old-fashioned mental hospital.

The infant mental health movement is a recent but rapidly growing phenomenon, and of course it has nothing to do with the bizarre pictures described above. The idea behind the movement is that we can ensure good mental and emotional development of infants by primary **prevention** of problems (that is, stopping them before they start) and by early intervention when problems have already begun.

prevention: the act of hindering an event or action; from the Latin *prae-* (before), *venire* (to come).

The infant mental health movement is based on the assumption that early experience is really a good deal more important than later experience. As we have noted in earlier chapters, not all infant development researchers necessarily agree with this idea; however, it does seem clear that the resources we bring to bear on children's emotional problems when they reach school age are too little, too late, or both. Attempts at later treatment of problems that began in infancy have not been very successful, so any success, even if it has its limitations, is to be desired.

Like counseling and psychotherapy with adults, infant mental health approaches must deal with a range of problems, some apparently mild and some potentially of great severity. Again, like therapy with adults, infant mental health issues may focus on the baby, on the parents, on the family as a whole, or on other factors like the environment. The concerns may be with intellectual problems, like a parent's lack of information, or they may be concerns with serious emotional disturbances. Physical handicaps and birth defects may form part of the picture, too. In fact, most problems that require infant mental health interventions are matters of multiple risks, where a family's physical, mental, and emotional difficulties need to be treated simultaneously. Treatment does not deal with simple individual factors, but with alteration of a dynamic action system whose reorganization can lead to a better developmental outcome for an infant.

Earlier chapters of this book referred to a number of problems that may be considered to be infant mental health concerns. For example, sensory prob-

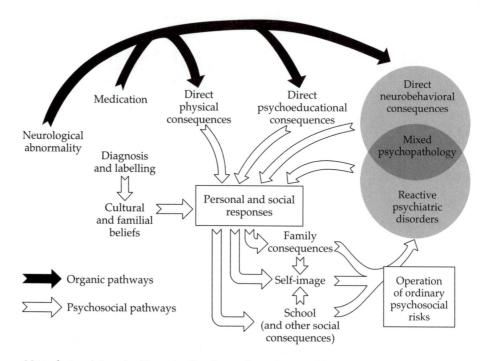

Many factors interact with each other to produce abnormal behavior. Damage to the nervous system often combines with environmental factors as a source of psychiatric disorders in childhood. (Source: Goodman, 1993)

lems, motor difficulties, and poor early language development are all related to mental and emotional development and would be treated as part of an infant mental health program.

Infant mental health concerns can also involve educating parents and facilitating their abilities to care for their infants and toddlers. Because caregivers other than parents also have a strong influence on infants, the infant mental health movement is concerned with appropriate child care settings as well as with events in the family.

The infant mental health movement has a particular concern with situations in which babies may grow up to be dangerous to themselves or to others. Emotional or physical abuse and neglect can produce an individual with strong tendencies to hurt other people. Although it is probably a mistake to think that abuse always begets abuse, early experiences of pain and terror seem to interfere with the ability to care for others.

Finally, the infant mental health movement is concerned with assuring that babies have stable, secure lives, with opportunities to form attachments to adults. As we will see in Chapter 15, current laws and policies about adoption and foster care do not necessarily work toward that goal.

RESEARCH METHODS

Earlier chapters on social and emotional development discussed a number of approaches that can be used in research on infant mental health issues. Clinical techniques are, of course, particularly important in understanding the factors that work toward or against good early development.

Do treatment approaches work? Does therapy with an infant, with a parent, or with infant and parent together make any real difference to the baby's development? If the baby seems to be doing better, would this have occurred even without therapy? These are research questions that seem to be essential ones but that are rarely answered. Unless therapy is being done as part of a research program, the therapist herself or himself is probably the person who judges whether the treatment has been effective. The question of the effectiveness of various treatment approaches is still open.

One of the most difficult but essential topics of research in infant mental health is *program evaluation.* Most programs for early intervention have as many aspects as there are sources of problems. It is almost unheard of for an early intervention program to focus on a single kind of problem. Even if this were the intention, the participating families would soon insist that other interventions be included. For example, one program for infants with adolescent parents initially worked with the babies' fathers, but the mothers made their presence felt and were also admitted into the program. The program was planned around the idea of fathers' support groups, but both fathers and mothers made it plain that they wanted individual time with counselors. That and several other requested changes were made, and the program ended with much more complex (and different) functions than had been planned.

Multiple factors in a program make it much harder to evaluate; if it works, what part is it that is making it work (Meisels, Dichtelmiller, & Liaw, 1993)? If the program, is constantly changing, the evaluation process becomes more and more challenging. As a result, there are very few reliable and valid studies of early intervention programs (Meisels, Dichtelmiller, & Liaw, 1993). The same statement applies to child care programs.

SOME MENTAL HEALTH PROBLEMS OF INFANTS

Mental health concerns about infants often focus on problems that might be expected to lead to serious emotional disturbance if not addressed early. An infant who has difficulties such as *pervasive developmental disorders* (discussed in Chapter 11) is likely to develop into an adult with little capacity for social and emotional communication.

An infant who has had many changes of caregivers or inconsistent relationships with parents may develop *attachment disorders.* For example, a toddler may be indiscriminately friendly to strangers, may be reckless and accident-prone, or may be unusually concerned about separation (Zeanah, Mammen, & Lieberman, 1993). Having an attachment disorder may negatively affect the child's development of conscience (commitment to shared social values) and other aspects of relationships.

It has recently been suggested that infants and toddlers can develop a form of *posttraumatic stress disorder* (PTSD) (Drell, Siegel, & Gaensbauer, 1993; James, 1994). This could occur as a result of experiencing an accidental injury, a terrifying event of any type, or an abusive assault. Symptoms of PTSD in children are similar to those in adults; anxiety, irritability, and **hypervigilance** (constant alert attention to the environment) are common. Physical **hyperactivity** or regressive behavior also occur. Flashbacks, the sudden memory and reliving of the trauma, may be in physical form such as vomiting. They may also involve episodes of actions the child does not remember but that appear to be repetitive reenactments of the traumatizing event (James, 1994).

Two toddler behaviors that suggest serious mental health problems are fire setting and deliberate, intense cruelty to animals—not just hugging the kitten too hard, but purposely breaking its back or stabbing it. These behaviors are not outgrown and are followed by increasingly dangerous acts as the child becomes more competent.

A child who is abused or neglected may not yet show any of these mental health problems, but the existence of abuse and neglect suggests that early treatment may be needed to prevent the development of serious problems.

hypervigilance: a pathological state of alertness which involves scanning the environment for threats; from the Greek *hyper-* (over), the Latin *vigilare* (to keep watch).

hyperactivity: a pathological level of activity, impulsiveness, and shortness of attention span; from the Greek *hyper* (over), the Latin *actum* (thing done).

INDIVIDUAL THERAPY WITH INFANTS

For anyone with even a slight experience of adult psychotherapy, it is hard to imagine how any therapeutic work could deal directly with infants. Therapy can't involve talking, and no insight will be achieved. Even play therapy with preschoolers assumes that some interpretation can be done, but surely it is not possible with infants.

In working with infants, the goal is usually to create an improved environment that will foster the child's development at all times. Working specifically with a therapist is only one part of the treatment plan. Parents, foster parents, and teachers all need to learn how best to support the child's progress.

However, there are times, especially at the beginning of intervention, when work alone with the therapist may be a primary part of the therapeutic effort. With infants and toddlers, this work is largely nonverbal in nature. Although the therapist may talk, the emphasis is on drawing the child into interactions in which communication occurs through looks, facial expressions, and movements.

Toys may be an important way to set up interactions between the infant and the therapist. Some toys, such as musical instruments, rattles, and noisy push toys, call the infant's attention to the therapist's actions. Some, like balloons and pinwheels, call attention to the adult's face. Toys like push trains or puppets help set up situations in which infant and therapist interact reciprocally. And some toys press the infant to request help from the therapist:

for example, a tightly closed jar with a snack inside or a jack-in-the-box (Prizant & Wetherby, 1989).

Dance movement therapy may also be useful for infants and toddlers. Dance therapists use movement patterns as a key to the baby's emotional experience, looking at characteristics of movement such as rhythms, enclosing or opening movements, and times of stillness and of energy (Tortora, 1994). It has even been suggested that some understanding of preferred movement patterns of the fetus can be useful for later interaction with the child (Loman, 1994).

Behavioristic therapies are less commonly used with babies than they once were. These approaches tend to focus on particular skills, such as repeating a word or putting a peg into a hole. Correct performance is rewarded by verbal praise or a small food treat.

A recent approach to therapy with infants and toddlers is called *developmental psychotherapy*, or *floor time* (Greenspan, 1992a). The theme of this approach is that the therapist actually sits on the floor with the child and tries to engage her abilities for attention and for communication (as well as some other abilities of older children). The child may be as young as 3 or 4 months.

The goal of the floor-time approach is to get the child to look at the adult, to listen, to feel calm with the adult, and to feel an emotional connection to the adult. To achieve this, the therapist must follow the child's lead, picking up cues from the baby about the things that are interesting to her. The therapist must also be patient and relaxed, rather than striving for a particular achievement. A third requirement for the therapist is that he or she needs to capture the child's emotional tone, to pick up a sense of what the child is feeling in the situation. These factors are all important in gaining the baby's attention and maintaining it as the work proceeds.

Once the baby's attention is successfully caught, the next goal is to establish intentional two-way communication. Adult or infant makes a bid for communication, perhaps by offering an object to the other person. The second person may take the object, look at it, and hand it back or do something else that elicits another action from the first person. The therapist Stanley Greenspan refers to this as "opening and closing a circle of communication" (1992a). This activity is the basis of all complex interactions between people, whether gesture, facial expression, or speech is involved. Two-way communication is the way infants learn about the organization and rules of the world, what other people intend to do, whether a situation is safe, and whether her behavior meets with approval. Such feedback lets the child learn about the relationships between her thoughts or feelings and the real world and gives some pattern to her experiences (Greenspan, 1992a).

As was the case for the earlier stage of getting the baby's attention, the therapist working toward two-way communication needs to encourage the child's initiative and assertiveness by following the child's lead. If the adult controls the action too much, the child may comply but still not achieve communication.

A warning seems to be in order against a type of "therapy" occasionally practiced with toddlers and preschoolers that involves **coercive** holding of the

coercive: dominating, compelling; from the Latin *com-* (with), *arcere* (to shut up or enclose).

child. It is sometimes called holding therapy, attachment therapy, or rage therapy, and is most often used when an adopted child does not seem to be forming a relationship with the adoptive parents (James, 1994). (These children may have been severely abused or neglected and have had many foster care placements.) Coercive holding techniques use prolonged restraint of the child, often by a number of adults; prolonged **noxious** stimulation, such as poking, tickling, and shouting in the child's face; and covering of the eyes or alternately closing off the mouth and the nose. The rationale for this approach is that the child has "repressed" rage that must be released in order for a new attachment to be formed. The child's terror is seen as a source of attachment to the parents. As one therapist has said, "We have an ethical obligation to take a strong, well-voiced position against coercive techniques. . . . These techniques have no place in our clinical **armamentarium** [emphasis added] for treating wounded children" (James, 1994, p. 94).

noxious: painful or distressing; from the Latin *noxa* (harm).

armamentarium: in this context, selection of treatment techniques; from the Latin *armamenta* (armory).

INFANT-PARENT THERAPY

Although it is informative to consider what therapists can do in their work with infants, we need to remember that such therapy is only a small part of the entire intervention. The infant is not the therapist's infant and is not going to live with the therapist. The goal of the intervention is to alter the baby's experiences so that most of them facilitate good development. A major task involves infant-parent therapy, where work with the family alters relationships so that the child's experiences with the parents are appropriate ones.

Many therapeutic approaches include parents in their work. In dynamic play therapy, for example, there is use of face-to-face games, swinging the child, peek-a-boo, and hide-and-seek (Harvey, 1994). Although these games are important for encouraging the child's communication, they may also help an adult work out problems that resulted from traumatic experiences such as rape. The adult can thus be freed for a more playful, loving, communicative relationship with the child.

Developmental psychotherapy, described above, often includes the parents in the interaction with the infant. The therapist's job may be to act as a coach and to make suggestions about what will work best with the baby. The parents are encouraged and expected to continue their floor-time sessions at home and to generalize from floor time to their other interactions with their child.

When toddlers are extremely angry and aggressive, chances are great that without intervention they will later go on to antisocial and criminal activity (Constantino, 1992). Their behavior disturbances are strongly related to problems in family relationships; they need to be treated as such, and they need to be treated early (Landy & Peters, 1991).

Floor-time sessions and similar activities are helpful in establishing interactions both parent and child can enjoy and in helping their relationship become a joyful one. But parents of aggressive toddlers need other help, too.

They may need some assistance in establishing predictable routines for family meals and bedtimes and in setting up play and other routines so the child can experience a sense of competence. Parents of aggressive toddlers often have problems dealing with their own anger and respond to the child's anger by attacking him or by ignoring his emotion. They need assistance in helping the child talk about his feelings and move back toward a more positive mood. Often parents of aggressive toddlers do not really know how to play with their children, and they need to learn how so they can **foster** communication and language development (Landy & Peters, 1991). A program like this must obviously be highly individualized for the child and the family and must constantly be fine-tuned as changes occur.

foster: to nurture; from the Old English *fostor* (food, feeding).

Infant-parent therapy sometimes extends to become *family therapy,* which assumes that all relationships in a group are affected by all other relationships. For example, one case involved a 7-month-old girl who cried persistently and had trouble sleeping (Emde, 1987). She and her single mother lived with the mother's two sisters and their parents. The grandparents' relationship turned out to be the key to the infant's problems, which were resolved when the grandparents began to go out once a week as a couple—something they had not done for years. The resulting alterations in the family relationships affected the infant as well as other family members.

When an infant or toddler is in foster care, the foster parent plays a special and challenging therapeutic role. Most young children placed in foster care have experienced abusive or chaotic environments that have made emotional interactions particularly difficult. Their capacity for self-regulation is poor and their ability for two-way communication very limited. The foster parent must try to deal with this situation while knowing that the child may be returned to the biological family. The anxiety the foster parent feels over the anticipated loss interferes with his or her emotional availability to the child. Appropriate treatment would need to include social and emotional support for the foster parent (Ghuman & Kates, 1992).

Videotaping is a useful addition to therapy with infants and parents (McDonogh, 1993). The videotaped record of the adults' interaction with their baby can be eye-opening, demonstrating to the parents that they are not necessarily behaving in the way they would prefer. When progress in therapy seems slow, videotapes of several sessions can be used to show that some changes really are taking place.

COMPREHENSIVE TREATMENT FOR INFANT MENTAL HEALTH

Our discussion of therapy involving parents and other family members has shown that successful treatment of infants must go far beyond the occasional session of individual therapy. The multiple risk factors characteristic of problems of early development require multiple treatment approaches that penetrate all areas of the infant's life. For a child with a serious problem like pervasive developmental disorder, a program might include interactive play therapy (floor time), speech therapy, and occupational therapy, each from two to five times per week, as well as parent counseling (Greenspan, 1992b).

Comprehensive treatment can include either family day care or center-based day care arrangements. One agency that manages a city's day care programs (Bemporad, 1990) carries out studies of family day care homes to ascertain which ones are best suited to deal with particular problems. The placement process also considers parents' emotional issues. A child development specialist visits the infants in the day care arrangements, while a social worker maintains contact with the parents.

Center-based day care may also form part of a comprehensive treatment for an infant or toddler. The child's poor experiences with early relationships may make it especially hard for her to adjust to the group, but, with special attention from caregivers, she may improve greatly in social competence as a result of high-quality day care (Wittmer & Petersen, 1992). She may experience positive changes in self-confidence, in trust for other people, and in prosocial skills like sharing and helping. But, especially when the child has a physical disability, caregivers must make particular efforts to bring these changes about. For example, a caregiver could let a child with problems be the first to use a new toy, thus making her a more attractive play partner for other children; or, a toddler with disabilities could be seated near another child who is very competent socially, increasing the chances of some good social interactions (Wittmer & Petersen, 1992). (People used to elementary-school children may not believe that these ploys will work, but infants and toddlers function quite differently from older children.) Treatment that includes the day care center can thus extend to social competence with peers, which would not be possible if therapy focused only on the infant in relationships with adults.

Comprehensive treatment for infants requires a team approach, with work by a mental health professional, a speech pathologist, an occupational therapist, and a special educator (Greenspan, 1992b). An appropriate early childhood care and education program, including both children with disabilities and those whose development is more typical, is also important because it provides a chance to improve the child's interactions with peers. Work on the child's interactions with his parents should also be a focus of the team (Greenspan, 1992b).

A team providing comprehensive treatment needs to work out an individualized family service plan (IFSP). The IFSP is useful not simply as a plan but also as a process in the course of which parents and professionals work out their different priorities, different values, and different views of the impact of the child's condition. Both parents and professionals need to remain flexible and open-minded during this process, but parents may have a good deal of difficulty because they are still grieving over their child's problems (see elsewhere in this chapter for a fuller discussion). Parents' participation in the planning process is different if they have voluntarily sought help than if they have been referred by a court (DeGangi et al., 1992).

The comprehensive treatment of some infants is paid for under the Individuals with Disabilities Education Act of 1991. Part H, the infant and toddler section of the act, governs delivery of comprehensive treatment to infants with disabilities and their families.

PROBLEMS OF PARENTS AND THERAPY WITH PARENTS

It is not appropriate, of course, for this book to provide a comprehensive discussion of therapy with adults. Our purpose is to consider factors that affect infant development, and to that end we can look at some special issues in psychotherapy with parents.

Such therapy is most often clearly relevant to infants' lives when the parents' negative emotions interfere with their attitudes and responsiveness toward their young children. Sometimes the problem is with grief over specific events; the events may have been in the distant or the recent past, and they may have to do with other people or with the infant herself. Another possibility is that the parent's problem is depression, a pervading sad emotional state that may be present because of experiences, biochemical processes, or a combination of the two. (Severe mental illnesses such as schizophrenia also have an impact on the infant, but they are not included here because psychotherapy is not usually considered a major aspect of their treatment.)

Grief

The emotions connected with *grieving* over a loss are complex and changing ones, including anger and fear as well as sadness. A grief cycle, the expectable sequence of emotions after a loss (Irvin, Kennell, & Klaus, 1982; Nogales, 1995), seems to occur in a wide variety of loss experiences. Initially, the person feeling the loss experiences shock and an inability to comprehend what has happened. This is followed, possibly after some days, by depression and **denial;** if the loss is due to death, the person may keep expecting the lost person to be where he usually is. Within weeks or months, depending on the individual, denial diminishes and the mourner begins to experience depression alternating with rage and feelings of guilt and shame. A sense of isolation and of bargaining (with fate or a supreme being) may occur, as the mourner prepares to accept the loss as long as nothing else bad is going to happen. Hope and finally acceptance of the loss follow. The entire process usually takes a year or more, but some personalities get "stuck" at a particular stage and are unable to go on to acceptance unaided. A loss experienced before the individual is 4 years old may not be resolved without a great deal of help (Furman, 1973).

denial: in this context, inability to be aware of an aspect of reality; from the Latin *denegare* (to deny).

Depression and rage make it extremely difficult for a parent to be adequately responsive to an infant. Preoccupation with a loss takes away energy that would otherwise be poured into the relationship with the baby.

What are some circumstances under which grief can interfere with the infant-parent relationship? The death of a loved one within the year before the infant's birth is likely to influence the parent's ability to be involved with the baby. Loss of the parent's mother or father may be followed by sad feelings about the fact that the grandparent never saw the baby or rage because the grandparent is not there to help with child care. Death of a spouse is likely to have occurred less than 9 months after the child was conceived, so the birth or at least the early months of the infant's life are likely to be well within the mourning period. The stillbirth or miscarriage of an earlier child can have a considerable impact on the parent's responsiveness to a new infant, especially if parents have followed the common advice and started a new pregnancy immediately after the loss, and so the second infant is born within a year after the death (Kennell & Klaus, 1982). The death of one of a pair of twins has a special impact on the parents as they try to establish a relationship with the surviving twin.

Divorce during or soon after the pregnancy is a situation where grief is powerful, even if the mourner is the person who initiated the separation. Completing the process of mourning over divorce is even more complex than grieving for a death, and it may be two years or more before the parent recovers normal parenting ability (Wallerstein & Kelly, 1982).

Grief is not confined to the obvious losses of death or divorce. The living infant herself may be the cause of a grief reaction if she is not like the child the parents expected and planned for. At the mildest level, perhaps a girl was born when a boy was wanted (or vice versa); a blond when a dark-haired child was anticipated; a small, quiet child when the plans were for a robust, active baby. In all these cases, there has been a loss—the loss of the infant the parents already loved in fantasy. The parents must relinquish the fantasy and involve themselves with the real baby.

At a much more serious level, the parents may experience a loss because they do not have the anticipated healthy, full-term baby. A preterm or low-birth-weight baby, or an infant with obvious birth defects or illness, means that being a parent is going to be far from the desired experience. The question may be, "Will she ever walk?" rather than, "When will she start dance lessons?" All the outcomes—even the baby's survival—may be quite unpredictable. The mother may have a sense that she has failed as a woman by giving birth to an unhealthy child. Both parents may ask themselves, "Will he live or will he die; and which is the better alternative?" (Fleischman, 1986, p. 3).

Grief that interferes with the infant-parent relationship may take on a much less obvious form when it involves a loss in the distant past. The death of a parent's sibling in early life was probably incompletely mourned because the parent was very young at the time. When an infant approaches the age at which the parent's sibling died, the parent may begin to experience anxiety that interferes with responsiveness to the baby. There is no conscious awareness that the long-past death is an issue; instead, the parent believes he or she is reacting to the present reality. Such situations, where the past loss causes infant-parent problems, have been described vividly as "ghosts in the nursery" (Fraiberg, Adelson, & Shapiro, 1975).

When fear was a large part of an experience in the distant past, the parent's reaction to the trauma may be continuing fear, rather than the sadness and rage that are usually emphasized in grief. The parent's behavior toward the infant continues to have frightened or frightening components, resulting in a confused and frightened baby. Because the parent is a source of fear and at the same time the source of consolation, the baby is disorganized (see Chapter 12) in his attachment behavior (Main & Hesse, 1990).

Depression

depression: a state of sadness and dejection; from the Latin *depressus* (pressed down).

Many readers who encounter the term **depression** with reference to parents will think immediately of postpartum depression, an emotional reaction of the mother occurring soon after birth. It is certainly very common for women to experience a mild form of the "baby blues" in the first days after the baby's birth. Physical exhaustion, hormonal changes, anxiety about new responsibilities, and concern about changes in the marital relationship can all lead to emotional ups and downs, including periods of crying. For most new mothers, there is a quick resolution of these feelings and the mother's mood becomes normal again.

For about 20% of new mothers, however, the depression lasts at least two weeks, and about half of those mothers are still depressed after a year or more (Clark, Keller, Fedderly, & Paulson, 1993). These mothers have a great deal of trouble responding to their babies. Although nondepressed mothers often "mirror" their babies' feelings in their facial expressions after they attend to and understand the feelings, depressed mothers rarely do. They seem to avoid looking into their babies' eyes. It has been suggested that they may be trying to protect the infant from the sight of their rage or that they are afraid of being engulfed by the baby's needs (Clark et al., 1993).

Women are about twice as likely as men to experience a serious depression (Weissman & Olfson, 1995); childbirth is just one of the associated factors. Marital and financial problems, stressful life events, and having a child with a difficult temperament are also implicated in depression (Goodman, Radke-Yarrow, & Teti, 1993). If these additional factors exist, the mother's capacity to deal with a baby will be still further compromised.

Therapy

therapy: treatment; from the Greek *therapeuein* (to treat).

Whether grief, fear, or depression is the problem, **therapy** is directed at the specific difficulties of a specific individual or family. Treatment is of a person, not of a diagnosis. All depressed mothers do not behave in the same way. For example, a depressed mother may be unresponsive, or she may stimulate her baby too much and without regard to his reaction. She may be very harsh as she tries to socialize a toddler, or she may avoid this difficult task. Some depressed mothers are unusually affectionate and seem to draw the child close to use him as a "comfort blanket" (Goodman, Radke-Yarrow, & Teti, 1993).

When a parent's problems disturb the relationship with an infant, chances are that parent and baby are not the only ones involved. The baby's other parent, the grandparents, and other children in the family may all be part of the work in family therapy. Relieving marital problems, for example, may

Poverty, deprivation, and emotional depression can interfere with a parent's capacity to care for her infant.

lighten the burdens that are creating the mother's depressed behavior with the baby. However, many families do not understand the complexity of the situation and believe that treatment is for the depressed or otherwise disturbed mother alone.

If grief over a recent loss is the main issue, counseling takes into account the normal course of the grief process. The events of mourning are not to be hurried, but they can be facilitated as the mourner is helped to become conscious of, to articulate, and to communicate emotions. Support groups and group therapy can be very helpful when grief has to do with an infant's illness or handicap; parents mourning under these circumstances may be able to accept help best from others in similar situations. They want people who have shared their experiences, not "more professionals" (Hoelting, Sandell, Letourneau, Smerlinder, & Stranik, 1996).

Some special factors must be considered in treatment for grief over a stillbirth or the death of a baby soon after a birth. The parents will usually benefit from seeing the baby's body, because the defects they can imagine are far worse than the reality can be. Having some time and privacy to hold the baby's body seems to be helpful; otherwise, the parents may be preoccupied with the idea that "I never even got to hold her." When one or both parents are reluctant to see the baby's body, photographs may be taken and kept for the time—perhaps months away—when the parents will feel the wish to know what their child looked like (Kennell & Klaus, 1982).

When the parent's difficulty involves "a ghost in the nursery," remembering and resolving the early loss seems to be the key to the problem. In one case, for example, a young mother living in stressful circumstances began to say that she wanted a tubal ligation and showed a great deal of anxiety about her little boy when he was about 13 months old. Her concerns turned out to be related to the death of a younger sister at age 15 months; the young mother (a preschooler at the time of her sister's death) had found her toddler sister in the bathroom, poisoned by ingesting a can of cleaner. She never saw her sister alive again and was offered no explanation for her disappearance, but she became preoccupied with the fear that she might do something wrong and that she might even have caused the sister's death. After discussing this issue with the therapist, the young woman began to realize the source of the strong doubts she had had about her capacity to care for her child (Kalmanson & Lieberman, 1982).

Treatment of depression may include antidepressant medication (a problem for breast-feeding mothers) or hospitalization (which exacerbates relationship problems by separating mother and baby). There may be a need for individual therapy combined with group therapy, as well as treatment to facilitate the infant's development. This combined approach can deal with the relationships that need improvement, as well as with the depression itself (Clark et al., 1993).

One therapeutic technique used when parents have serious emotional disturbances is called *previewing*. This technique, which can also be used with more stable parents, teaches the parent to predict how the child will soon change developmentally, to imagine how life will be at that point, and to help the baby experience the new skill. The previewing skill is especially important when a parent is emotionally disturbed, because developmental change in the infant can trigger problem behavior in such a parent (Trad, 1993).

One group of parents who are particularly in need of treatment today are immigrants. For cultural and financial reasons, it is quite unlikely that immigrant parents will seek individual therapy. What is likely is that they will bear unusual emotional burdens that will interfere with relationships with their infants. Many immigrants come from situations of grief and loss, whether because of war, terrorism, or simply separation from loved ones and familiar places. Young mothers, in particular, may miss the culturally prescribed help of their mothers, aunts, and sisters and may find themselves isolated at home. Their anxiety and depression are sufficient to affect their infants.

One program for Latino women started as an attempt to establish a support group, but the women made it clear (by not attending) that they wanted individual help rather than a group arrangement (Lieberman, 1990). Programs for immigrants cannot necessarily be tailored before they begin; instead, they may need to be developed slowly in response to the needs of the particular group as they emerge. As immigrants make up a larger and larger part of the North American population, their needs may form an important part of the infant mental health picture.

HELPING PARENTS: OTHER FACTORS IN INFANT MENTAL HEALTH

Parents: General Education and Parenting Education

A parent's cognitive development and general educational background are important determinants of his or her child-rearing ability and are especially related to the capacity to deal with stress (Sommer et al., 1993). Intellectual development of children with Down syndrome is better when their mothers have a higher educational level (Sharav, Collins, & Shlomo, 1985). Mothers who think about development in more sophisticated ways are also likely to be more responsive and supportive to their children (Pratt et al., 1993).

Over the last 20 years or so, a number of parent training programs intended for education specifically about child-rearing concerns have appeared. Some of these programs emphasize behavior change through manipulation of reinforcement (Berman, 1993), including the use of time-out and the withholding of reinforcement until extinction of a behavior occurs. Such approaches may be particularly useful in dealing with undesirable behavior like excessive temper tantrums.

Behavioral parent training programs ideally work on other aspects of parent behavior as well as on the specific use of reinforcement. For example, a parent may need to practice giving attention without giving commands or criticisms (Wierson & Forehand, 1994).

Many parent training programs, however, emphasize changes in the way a parent thinks about dealing with a problem. An example of such a cognitively oriented program is STAR Parenting (Fox, Anderson, Fox, & Rodriguez, 1991), a four-session, 8-hour course that uses group discussion as well as direct instruction of parents. STAR is an acronym for stop, think, ask, respond—actions a parent needs to take to avoid a negative cycle of interactions with a child. The parent is to *stop* rather than respond immediately to a problem behavior, unless the child is in danger. She is then to *think* about her own feelings of distress and how she can gain control of them. The third step is to *ask* herself about the problem: whether the behavior is age-appropriate, or what she wants the child to do, for example. Finally, the parent is to *respond* to the child, preferably using redirection, ignoring, or quiet time rather than physical punishment.

Other types of courses for parents may deal with factors that indirectly affect child-rearing, such as time management, involvement with day care, and family stress issues.

Education on Feeding and Breast-Feeding

The feeding situation epitomizes a basic truth of child-rearing: doing the job well is a matter of attitude and of education. However well meaning a caregiver may be, lack of information can lead to poor care, and no matter how well informed one is, negative feelings can have the same effect.

Although emotion has a strong impact on the feeding relationship, a simple lack of information often needs to be addressed. This is especially the case with respect to breast-feeding, which many new parents in the United States have never seen done. The Surgeon General's Workshop on Breast-feeding and Human Lactation in 1984 noted a national objective to be achieved by 1990: at least 75% of women should be breast-feeding when discharged from the hospital with their babies, and at least 35% should still be breast-feeding when the babies are 6 months old. This objective was not realized, particularly with respect to families who are at risk for problems and who are least likely of all to breast-feed.

One of the difficulties with influencing breast-feeding practices is that there are so few points at which communication with parents is possible. However, the period of hospitalization for childbirth is a time at which new parents are available for instruction and when they are likely to be anxiously conscious of their ignorance.

The first day or so after childbirth is the ideal time for nursing staff to guide mothers and babies in their breast-feeding and to provide informal instruction on the advantages of breast-feeding. Hospital policies at this time can also encourage breast-feeding mothers; for example, there needs to be an arrangement for the baby to be fed "on demand," and supplemental bottle feedings should not be given unless necessary. The hospital can also send the right message by refraining from putting bottles of formula in the discharge pack sent home with the baby (Axelrod, 1984).

When women are participating in programs like WIC (Supplemental Food Program for Women, Infants, and Children), there is an opportunity for encouraging breast-feeding. Projects carried on through WIC programs have included training peer counselors and establishing telephone "hot lines" to help with breast-feeding problems (MacGowan et al., 1991). Because poverty and low educational level are associated with reluctance to breast-feed, the group of women who are eligible for WIC seem very appropriate candidates for breast-feeding programs.

Volunteer groups such as La Leche League are also sources of information about breast-feeding, but they do not do much outreach to parents who are strongly opposed to breast-feeding. La Leche League volunteers are available by telephone or at meetings to help with practical breast-feeding problems. As a group, they know most of what there is to be known about feeding babies, but they are not generally in a position to reach women who have not asked directly for help.

Most parents believe that their most important choice about feeding has to do with breast versus bottle, but there are many more subtle feeding decisions to be made. Those decisions influence not only the baby's diet but her experience of her earliest relationships as well. Helping parents do a good job of feeding may be one of the most useful approaches to improving relationships and preventing mental health problems.

One tool for assessing early feeding and relationship problems is the NCAST (Nursing Child Assessment by Satellite Training) program (Farel, Freeman, Keenan, & Huber, 1991). This assessment notes, for example, whether the mother talks to the baby while feeding and whether she seems to pick up his cues that he has eaten enough. If there seems to be a need for improvement, the mother is guided to more appropriate behavior. This approach can be used while the baby is still in the hospital or at a later time if it seems needed.

Information Sources for Parents

Although some parents need to be told that they are making mistakes with their infants, a great many people are very aware of the complexity of parenting and of their need for information. They often seek information about infant development and care in an informal way, such as talking to friends or relatives. For very young parents, their own parents or grandparents are often the most trusted source of advice.

For many parents, the preferred source of information about infants is the pediatrician or pediatric nurse-practitioner. When the infant has a well-baby checkup, the parents often ask behavioral or developmental questions. Many of these questions have to do with physical concerns, but many more are about toilet training, sleep problems, and discipline.

Well-educated parents often prefer to get their information from the hundreds of specialized books and articles published each year. A recent study examined the advice given in popular publications and the way it has changed as research has discovered more about early development (Young, 1990). The information used came from the Children's Bureau publication *Infant Care* and from *Parents* magazine for the years 1955 to 1984, a period during which the scientific study of infancy advanced a great deal. These publications reflected current research in their discussion of biologically related topics like perception, but they were somewhat less complete or up-to-date in their comments about language development. Advice in other areas often reflected the assumptions of the culture rather than research evidence; for example, the emotional benefits of breast-feeding were stressed, even though there is no clear evidence to support this idea (Young, 1990).

Published advice to parents is not necessarily based on clear-cut evidence. For example, in 1994, the U.S. Public Health Service was preparing a campaign to advise parents to put babies to sleep on their backs or sides as a way to avoid sudden infant death syndrome. This decision was a result of evidence from Australia, Britain, New Zealand, and Norway that SIDS death dropped after physicians began to tell parents not to put babies down to sleep in the prone position. However, SIDS deaths in the United States already occurred at a much lower rate than in those countries (Stone, 1994a), and the role of sleeping position in SIDS deaths has been questioned by research in the United States (Klonoff-Cohen & Edelstein, 1995).

Parent Support Groups and Networks

Parent support groups can provide both information and the sharing of feelings that makes people feel less alone with their problems. During pregnancy or soon after the birth, people may feel a special need to be with others who are in the midst of similar experiences. Their own normal social network may not seem quite adequate at such times. They want to talk about and learn more about their situation, and many of their friends and relatives will be obviously bored by hearing the same topics repeatedly.

During pregnancy, classes of the type sponsored by the Childbirth Education Association are popular ways to find information and support. After childbirth, a variety of local mothers' groups and organizations, like La Leche League, can be helpful. Some organizations have a strong educational emphasis and may charge tuition; an example is P.A.C.E. (Parents After Childbirth Education), which offers a series of sessions on topics like the balancing of family and career.

When a baby is preterm or has a disabling condition, specialized parent support groups can be invaluable. Many parents of babies with disabilities believe that only someone who has had the same experience can be of any real help (Boukydis & Moses, 1995). Help can come through formal meetings of a support group or through an alternative such as telephone contacts or volunteer visitors. Adjustment to the situation takes time, and many parents feel that the whole first year is a "blackout" (Zeitlin & Williamson, 1994).

Adolescent Parents: Support and Education

Programs for adolescent parents often become enormously complicated and unwieldy as they attempt to deal with the adolescents' need for help in many forms. Emotional support, education about child-rearing, access to alternative school arrangements, medical and dental help, diapers and infant formula—these are only the beginning of the requirements. In addition to the multiplicity of their needs, adolescent parents have frequent crises and often fail to plan ahead, so the help they ask for is often help "right now."

The fact that adolescent parents may still be in the care of their own parents does not necessarily simplify their lives. The birth of a child to an adolescent mother may remind her mother and her grandmother that the girl is repeating their own adolescent experiences, complicating the whole family's emotional response to the infant. The infant's grandmother may respond to her memories by barring the child's father from the household if he tries to maintain contact with infant and mother. A program for adolescent parents needs to focus on these family issues as well as on the issues peculiar to the adolescent parent and her infant.

One special concern about adolescent mothers has to do with the low level of responsiveness the mothers show their babies; they look at the infants and talk to them less than older mothers do (Baskin, Umansky, & Sanders, 1987). One program, the Contingency Response Intervention for Infants of Adolescent Parents, used guided discovery activities such as watching the baby's reaction to a rattle shaken at various distances. The adolescent mothers were also trained to notice their babies' cues, which showed that they wanted to stop or continue a play activity, as well as to follow the baby's lead in play. The program resulted in some improvement in the mothers' responsiveness (Baskin, Umansky, & Sanders, 1987).

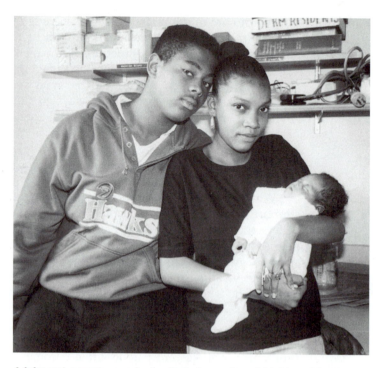

Adolescent parents may be fascinated, awed, and frightened by their baby.

Fathers

There seems to be a strange implication in putting a special section about fathers in a chapter that stresses parents' issues. There is almost a suggestion that fathers are not parents—or at least not parents in the same way that mothers are. It is certainly true that fathers are not mothers behaviorally speaking (as we discussed in Chapter 13). Although they may need just as much education and intervention as mothers do, it is quite possible that fathers will benefit most from programs that are designed especially with their needs in mind.

Fathers seem to become more involved with their children as they learn through experience to feel more confident as caregivers. They rarely take courses on parenting issues or read much on the topic; in fact, most newspaper and magazine articles about parenting are directed toward women (Palm & Palkovitz, 1988).

When a young child has a disability, the individualized family service plan (IFSP) needs to mobilize the father's contribution as much as possible. (Unfortunately, it is rather common for planners to assume that the father can be expected not to participate.) To encourage fathers to be involved, it may be necessary to pay close attention to their preferred ways of doing things. For example, fathers may be more inclined toward play-oriented activity rather than deliberate teaching of children. Fathers of children with disabilities may prefer to stay at home rather than be "visible" in public with their children. They may often prefer to interact with their children while doing something else, such as watching television. If those preferred circumstances are made available, it may be much easier to involve fathers (Turbiville et al., 1995).

Parents with Physical Disabilities

Some physical disabilities have very little real impact on a parent's capacity to care for a baby, but other physical problems can interfere noticeably with day-to-day care. Whatever the effect of the problem, the parent with a disability may have grown up assuming that sexuality and parenthood would play no part in her life, and she may find it difficult to reconcile her past beliefs with her present reality.

The parent with a disability may need help figuring out how to carry out a task like diapering when strength or dexterity is not sufficient to do it in the usual way. Special equipment may be needed; for example, a mother who has been able to walk with crutches may need a wheelchair to carry her baby (Kirshbaum, 1988).

Networking with other parents with disabilities may be particularly helpful. It has been reported that parents with disabilities manage child care by eliciting more cooperation from the child than fully functioning parents usually achieve. For example, a parent in a wheelchair may encourage a toddler to climb onto the footrest of the wheelchair in preparation for being picked up (Kirshbaum, 1988). This sort of technique would probably not be learned from watching parents without disabilities, who are more able to force the child to comply.

Family Planning

It may not seem immediately obvious that family planning is a factor in infant mental health. However, the impact of an unplanned pregnancy on the parents' marital relationship and the effect of distress on the mother's emotional availability to her child are clearly relevant to an infant's experience. An important aspect of intervention may be to provide family planning information, but information alone is not the entire solution to the problem. As Lieberman (1993) has pointed out, when a parent seems casual about unplanned pregnancies, it may be that she feels a general lack of control over her own life and hopelessness about her children's future. Until the feeling of helplessness is alleviated, information about family planning is not useful or interesting to such an individual. Assistance with family planning can thus be based just as much on the establishment of a good relationship with a counselor as on specific instruction.

Family planning can be a particularly difficult issue when parents already have a child with a disability. Genetic counseling (discussed in Chapter 3) needs to be added to family planning information in these situations. Parents need to be given options and helped to think through their own priorities and goals (Cooley et al., 1993).

Home Nursing Visits

Most Western countries in the earlier part of this century had formal visiting nurse programs. Rather than the current U.S. practice of well-baby care, where infants are given regular checkups at physicians' offices or clinics, similar checkups were done at home by visiting nurses. Although this approach did not allow ready access to infants' records or to laboratory facilities, it kept contagious babies out of contact with each other, eliminated concerns about transportation, and allowed the nurse to get some idea of the infant's home circumstances.

Would it be a good idea to reinstate home visiting as a form of regular care for U.S. babies? One program that tested the results of home visits (Olds et al., 1994) found no differences between visited and unvisited children in frequency of child abuse or intelligence at ages 2 to 4 years. However, the visited children had 40% fewer accidental injuries and ingestions, 35% fewer emergency room visits, and 45% fewer behavior problems noted by physicians. The visited mothers were rated as more involved, and (or "but"!) they punished their children more than the unvisited mothers did.

WHEN THE ENVIRONMENT IS THE PROBLEM

As we discuss parent education, psychotherapy, and developmentally appropriate practice, it is easy to forget that not all problems have to do with relationships alone. For many of the world's people, poverty, disease, and violence are the factors that interfere most with their babies' development. Sometimes these problems do their harm to children directly; sometimes they do harm by interfering with parents' abilities to nurture. In either case, our discussion of intervention is not complete without some consideration of how social and economic problems affect the very young. Much of our concern about therapy would be unnecessary if these problems could be removed.

When Parents Are Overwhelmed

In Chapter 10, we referred to the idea of learned helplessness (Seligman, Maier, & Solomon, 1971), a state of mind in which the individual gives up attempts to cope or solve problems and responds instead with passivity and lack of interest. Learned helplessness follows many experiences of painful events that cannot be predicted or controlled. For example, consider the life events of a poor inner-city mother who has survived physical abuse in childhood and adulthood, chronic ill health, constant fear, and poverty. She may be incapable of intervening when someone hurts her child or of deciding what to do for a sick baby.

At its most extreme, learned helplessness may give rise to a *lifeboat mentality,* a sense that there is no point in giving care to those who are weak. In a moving account of the despair possible to human beings, Scheper-Hughes (1993) has described poor women in a Brazilian slum and their failure to care for babies who (in their words) "don't want to live." Although many of the babies are seriously ill and could probably not be saved with any resources available to their mothers, many more are simply not fed and, as they grow weaker, are ignored more and more. The mothers' behavior, which might be seen as "unnatural" or morally reprehensible, is in fact the result of life in an environment where only the strong can survive.

When There Is War

The Geneva Convention may state that noncombatants are not to be harmed during wartime, but the words of the convention are no protection to infants. The work of organizations like Médicins sans Frontières (Doctors without Borders), the French humanitarian medical group, has come to include the treatment of children's mental suffering in wartime, as well as medical and surgical help (Moro, 1994).

Infants' and toddlers' suffering in wartime often leads to symptoms of posttraumatic stress disorder. They show disruptions of eating and sleeping, difficulties in paying attention, and fearfulness. Even if they are not old enough to speak, their behavior may show that they are reexperiencing the trauma (Drell, Siegel, & Gaensbauer, 1993).

Care for infants who are suffering from traumatic separation is critical. However, infants suffer when mothers are so absorbed with mourning for their own losses that they are not emotionally available to their children. Mothers who have been raped, tortured, or made witnesses to the deaths of husbands, parents, and children need help in rebuilding themselves so that they can foster their infants' growth (Moro, 1994). Missions to refugees in the former Yugoslavia, for instance, have tried to do this kind of work as short-term therapy in three months or less.

When Violence Is in the Community or the Home

Community violence—presently at epidemic levels in U.S. cities (Osofsky, 1994)—can result in the same posttraumatic stress disorders as war. In fact, the chances for repeated exposure, with increasing effects on the child, are probably greater in a violent community than in war.

Serious domestic violence is not only distressing but potentially harmful to the infant or toddler; seeing one parent kill the other has been described as "a catastrophic psychological trauma for the young child" (Osofsky, 1994, p. 5). Children with such experiences probably have already had some problems, but after the murder they show new symptoms such as reenactments of the experience, nightmares, fears, and aggressive behavior.

These Rwandan infants were orphaned during a civil war between tribal factions. A few of them seem curious, but others show the withdrawal state of severe emotional trauma.

When Poverty and Violence Interfere with Good Experiences

The drama of infants exposed to war and violence can make us forget that bad environments can prevent a child from having good experiences, as well as expose her to bad ones. Where poverty or violence rule, it is almost impossible for a young child to experience some aspects of the environment that are related to good development (Caldwell & Bradley, 1984). A well-organized physical environment is not usually found in a crowded, damaged living area. The only safe play area may be a dark, cramped apartment. There may be no place to keep toys; for that matter, there are probably few of the riding toys, push-pull toys, stuffed animals, books, or music considered supportive of development. Pets do not survive long in wartime or where poverty is extreme.

DAY CARE AND OTHER FORMS OF NONPARENTAL CARE

How is day care associated with infant mental health? Over the past 20 years, larger and larger numbers of U.S. babies have received much of their care from adults other than their parents. The common term *day care* has come to be used so broadly that it gives us little information about an infant's experiences. Day care does not necessarily even occur during the day; parents who do shift work may sometimes seek 24-hour care. However we define it, day care can have a strong effect for good or ill on infant mental health because it accounts for a large proportion of many infants' experiences.

Nonparental care actually comes in a wide variety of forms. Some infant care arrangements are paid for by the parents and involve professional or quasiprofessional care providers. Others are informal arrangements in which services or social obligations are bartered for care; for example, a grandmother cares for an infant and receives her own child's respect and help in exchange, or two neighbors take turns in caring for the children of both. Some child care deals with infants in groups; other arrangements have one caregiver for each baby. Most child care arrangements are outside the infant's home, in a caregiver's house (often called family day care) or in a day care center, but some are in the infant's home—a baby-sitter who comes in, or a live-in nanny or *au pair*.

Most nonparental infant care is arranged to allow parents to be employed outside the home, but there are other reasons it might occur. Parents of a toddler may feel that some group experience would be socially beneficial to their child. Social services agencies may obtain court orders to place abused or neglected infants in part-time nonparental care, with the intention of improving the infant's environment without completely separating parent and child. Finally, nonparental care may be part of a treatment program for young children with disabling conditions.

The best-known form of nonparental care is group care in formal day care centers. These arrangements are subject to licensing laws and must maintain records about attendance and finances. They are run either for profit under the ordinary business laws of their locality, or as nonprofit organizations, usually as a service of an institution such as a hospital or a university. They may also be accredited under the rules of an organization like the National Association for the Education of Young Children.

The characteristics of family day care are quite variable. Some family day care providers are members of family day care networks. They keep careful records and are accredited members of their groups, so that information about them is available. Many family day care arrangements, however, are essentially part of an underground economy about which little is known. If a family day care provider is caring for five children or fewer, he or she is probably exempt from state requirements for licensing, or even for registration, and many such providers would prefer to remain unidentified to avoid income tax issues. Others care for a larger number of children but do so illegally and without the knowledge of authorities. Informal arrangements with a grandparent or a neighbor, of course, are usually known only to the participants, and the same is true for nannies or baby-sitters.

It has been estimated that in 1990 about half of all preschool children with employed mothers were cared for by grandparents or other relatives; about a quarter were in center-based day care, 20% were in family day care, and the remainder were cared for in their homes by a nonrelative (Scarr & Eisenberg, 1993). Because more than 50% of U.S. mothers of infants work outside the home, these figures apply to very large numbers of babies (Scarr, Lande, & McCartney, 1989). It should be noted that the placement of an infant in a particular care arrangement is not necessarily the free choice of the parents, because infant and toddler care is often not as readily available as is care for older children (Hill-Scott, 1989; Muscari, 1989). Where state regulations for infant and toddler care are strict, it may be offered less frequently (Muscari, 1989). For-profit day care centers, particularly, may see infant care as an unprofitable service that is desirable only as a "feeder" of children into their preschool or after-school programs.

APPLICATIONS & ARGUMENTS
Choosing Day Care

The early entry of infants into day care often means that parents are making a difficult and important choice when they have hardly had time to adjust to parenthood. The period is one of high stress and emotionality and is not the best time to be making an informed decision. Feelings run high and tend to swamp whatever clear thinking could otherwise be done. Parents often fall back on an attempt to recreate their own childhood experiences.

Unfortunately, most of the early experiences that the parents can remember go back only to kindergarten or first grade, where groups of children sat in little desks and were supposed to keep quiet and learn as directed. Based on those memories, many parents' expectations are that a good infant care setting will be quiet and organized and will emphasize instruction.

On the contrary, good day care for infants stresses play and warm emotional involvement. Instruction is rare, except perhaps when toddlers ask questions. Although the noise level should not be deafening, a cheerful, busy hum of voices is appropriate. Caregivers use as much one-to-one interaction and as little group activity as they can manage. As much as is possible, an infant is in charge of what happens to her, and the caregiver's job is to be sensitive and responsive rather than directive. A good day care center is well-organized, but the organization is around infant needs and rhythms, rather than around adult plans and curricula.

THE EFFECTS OF NONPARENTAL INFANT AND TODDLER CARE ON DEVELOPMENT

To understand the effects of day care and similar arrangements, we need to differentiate between the effects of nonparental care on infants and the effects of poor-quality care. Most work in this area, unfortunately, has not done a very good job of this; all types and qualities of nonparental care tend to be lumped together. The unfortunate assumption that nonparental care has some special quality of its own ignores the almost universal tendency for human parents to get someone else to take care of their babies often; from the child nurses of Africa to the wet nurses of 19th-century France and on to day care, nonparental care is very much part of human parenting.

Research on effects of nonparental care has generally focused on center-based care of the *modal* (most common) rather than the *model* ideal type. Less work has looked at family day care or informal care by relatives, and still less has examined nanny care (Scarr & Eisenberg, 1993; Scarr, Lande, & McCartney, 1989).

As you might expect, outcomes of studies on the effects of nonparental care have been quite mixed. In the 1980s, reviews of research noted increased aggressiveness, noncompliance, and avoidance of adults among children who had begun day care in their first year of life (Belsky, 1986). More recent work has noted a correlation between more negative adjustment in kindergarten children and more experience of day care (Bates et al., 1994).

On the other hand, positive outcomes have also been reported. In one study, sixth-graders who had experienced stable, full-time infant and pre-school day care were more often assigned to a "gifted" group, received higher math grades, and were rated higher on emotional well-being, attractiveness, and assertiveness (Field, 1991a). A Swedish study, which controlled for home background, gender, and intelligence, found that 13-year-olds who had entered day care before age 1 performed better in school and were rated higher by their teachers on several social and emotional factors (Anderson, 1992).

Like other aspects of infant development, the effects of day care undoubtedly result from many factors working together in a dynamic system. Gender may help determine the outcome of day care experience; boys with nonparental care have been reported to be more defiant (Crockenberg & Litman, 1991). Infants who are temperamentally inhibited seem to show more difficulty adjusting to day care, seem less able to play alone in the mother's absence, and show less high-quality play with peers either at home or in day care (Broberg, Lamb, & Hwang, 1990). The child's previous experience can also have an effect; young children show less reaction to separations from their mothers as they experience more separations and reunions (Field, 1991b).

An infant's or toddler's attachment status can also influence the effects of day care experience. Securely attached children have been reported to be more involved with their teachers, who are more sensitive to these children than to those of less secure attachment status (Howes & Hamilton, 1992a,b). Toddlers whose attachment is classified as avoidant seem to show more whimpering

The transition from home to day care, or from day care to home, is often problematic for infants. A good day care center will take special pains with transition times.

and crying in the Strange Situation if they have experienced more nonparental care (Belsky & Braungart, 1991). One study of teachers' ratings of social competence and emotional health found that early experience of day care had negative effects for securely attached children but positive effects for others (Egeland & Hiester, 1995).

A major issue in nonparental care is that it involves relationships. Quality of attachment to mother and to teacher is not necessarily the same (Howes & Hamilton, 1992a,b). Nor do caregivers have the same attachment to all the infants they work with. Secure attachments are more likely when the infant is from a middle-class family and spends more time in day care, and when the caregiver is younger and plays more sensitively with the infant (Goossens & van IJzendoorn, 1990).

We remain without a clear-cut assessment of the effects of nonparental care on infant and toddler development. Nevertheless, many thousands of infants and toddlers will continue to be cared for by people other than their parents. If there are potential negative outcomes for these children, we can probably minimize problems most effectively by encouraging the children's relationships with their caregivers, reducing the total number of caregivers, reducing caregiver turnover, and making sure that caregivers are assigned to specific children in a group rather than to the group as a whole. When children move to a new group or a new day care arrangement, we need to be aware of their experience of loss and separation and to help them build new relationships that will comfort and nurture them.

ASSESSING THE QUALITY OF INFANT/TODDLER CARE

Assessment of the quality of nonparental care of infants and toddlers is not as simple as might be thought. As noted earlier, parents selecting a care arrangement often think in terms of their own childhood experience in groups, which probably did not begin until they entered kindergarten at age 4 or 5. Their model for good infant and toddler care is based on their experience of school. Indeed, day care centers often play into this concept by calling caregivers "teachers" or using names like "Little Schoolhouse" or "Learning Center."

Developmentally appropriate infant and toddler care does not resemble elementary school. It is based on relationships, not on instruction (Pawl, 1990).

Care of infants and toddlers involves a high degree of intimacy when it is done well.

A review of the earlier chapters of this book will show how early development depends on the comforting, responsive, affectionate caregiving of a small number of adults. Although group care of infants has not gone on long enough for us to know for sure, our best guess is that the events that lead to good development in the home will have the same effect in other care settings. Good care, leading to good development, is labor-intensive, and therefore expensive.

Regulation and Standards of Infant Care

Although many states have tried to establish regulations to ensure high-quality infant care, there are many reasons the regulations can remain

---

APPLICATIONS & ARGUMENTS
Should Men Work in Day Care Centers?

In the 1970s, a remarkable change in attitudes about men as caregivers for the very young came about. Draft laws exempted male teachers and thus encouraged men to teach at all levels, not just in high schools. The movement toward gender equality stressed the idea that women could do "men's jobs" and men could do "women's jobs." The father's role in development was stressed, and day care centers boasted of male caregivers who could be models for boys.

As usual, public opinion soon began to swing back to the opposite extreme. Publicity about accusations of sexual molestation forced day care centers to be concerned about the vulnerability of their staff to unjustified suspicion. Pressure from parents made it difficult to allow male caregivers to do care tasks like diaper changing. Consequently, male caregivers are rare today.

It is true that physical and sexual abuse of infants and toddlers is more likely to be carried out by men than by women. This is especially the case for sexual penetration, which can cause severe injury or death. However, it is also true that, statistically speaking, physical and sexual abuse are family matters and are rarely associated with day care.

Male caregivers have different styles of interacting with babies than females do and probably bring interesting and novel types of stimulation to infants in their care. They may be unusually able to tolerate and admire noisy and rowdy play. Some toddlers seem to regard men as especially strong, competent, and capable of keeping children safe.

There may be some slight additional risks where males are caregivers, but there are also opportunities for improvement of young children's day care experiences.

unenforced. Poorly trained caregivers hired at low wages may simply not have the capacity to do a high-quality job. The underground economy in child care means that authorities are unaware of many infant care arrangements. And, of course, parents under economic pressure are quite likely to choose a cheaper, lower-quality caregiver over a more expensive one, especially if they have little awareness of indicators of quality in care. This is especially the case among low-income parents, whose infants may already be at risk.

Although states have had some success in enforcing health and safety regulations in licensed care arrangements, the responsibility for choosing quality care remains in the hands of parents. The following discussion summarizes some important factors in quality care that are considered in accreditation by the National Association for the Education of Young Children.

1. Staff to child ratio   The most important of all considerations about infant day care involves the number of caregivers and the number of children. One adult cannot give quality care to more than a small number of infants. Parents should look for a setting in which one adult cares for no more than three infants under age 1 year or no more than five toddlers or preschoolers. In family day care, an adult who has several toddlers to care for should probably deal with only one infant.

The staff-to-child ratio is absolutely critical with respect to safety. Jessica McClure, the Texas toddler whose ordeal we all watched some years ago, was not playing in her own yard when she fell down the pipe. She was with a baby-sitter who had eight other children to care for.

2. Group size   The number of children in a group makes a major difference to a baby's experience, even when there are a number of adults present. The larger the group, the higher the noise level, general activity, and confusion. Three or 4 infants with one caregiver in a small room fare much better than do 16 infants and 5 caregivers in a large room. (This is not necessarily the case for preschoolers.)

3. Staff turnover   Infants thrive on consistent care and a chance to develop real relationships with their caregivers. In a day care center with frequent staff turnover, consistency is hard to maintain. In addition, if new staff members need training, which they usually do, a high frequency of turnover means babies are often with inexperienced caregivers.

Unfortunately, day care workers tend to leave for better-paying jobs, so staff turnover is a chronic problem. More consistency may be possible with a family day care provider who really wants to work in her home, although she too may suddenly decide to change careers. A family day care provider who has been caring for infants for a long time is probably the most likely person to continue doing so.

4. Feeding   Of all the situations infants experience in day care, feeding is probably the most critical. It is a situation that involves important health and

Infants can benefit from a lot of social stimulation, but small groups are usually considered to be more appropriate for this period of development.

safety factors while also influencing social development and learning. You can probably tell more about quality of care from the feeding procedure practiced in a day care setting than from any other single factor.

A number of specific points should be considered. First, bottles should not be propped. This common practice is actually illegal in day care centers in a number of states because of its potential for causing health problems. Cuddling and social stimulation are important components of feeding, so every baby should be held while being fed from a bottle.

Infant feeders (bottles that contain strained food) should not be used. An infant who is being fed strained food should be spoon-fed while sitting on someone's lap or in a high chair when old enough. This is a matter of emotional and mental stimulation as well as one related to the development of proper chewing and swallowing patterns.

Self-feeding and finger-feeding should be encouraged. From the age of about 6 months, most babies are interested in picking up bits of food and putting them in their mouths. They are also interested in grabbing spoons, although it will be many months before they will be able to spoon-feed themselves effectively. Permitting the baby to try some self-feeding is a necessary preparation for later self-feeding skills. In addition, the hand-mouth coordination developed in this way is a foundation for the eye-hand coordination that will follow.

APPLICATIONS & ARGUMENTS
Should the Law Forbid Physical Punishment in Day Care Centers?

Laws and policies about day care centers are not necessarily made by the parents of children who are cared for in the centers. The people who influence law and policymakers are more likely to be members of professional groups or of organized child advocacy groups than busy working parents of infants. The resulting policies may be a good deal closer to what professionals think is right for babies than to what all parents want.

For example, many parents use spanking or hand slapping as a disciplinary technique for infants and toddlers. Unless a physical injury results, this practice is not against the law. However, laws forbid the use of physical punishment by day care workers, and day care centers usually have policies against the use of physical punishment by a parent while at the center.

Some parents might very well prefer a day care center where physical punishment is used. They want some continuity between home and day care, and they may believe quite firmly that physical punishment is the foundation of character development. Although these parents are free to discipline as they think best at home, they are not free to choose a day care arrangement that follows their home rules.

So the law does not say that physical punishment is actually wrong for all infants and toddlers. Instead, the law leaves the use of spanking to the parents' discretion—except in the day care setting. This paradox has come about because parents would object strongly if legislators interfered with their child-rearing techniques, but professional groups exert more pressure than parents do on day care issues.

Good feeding practices require patience and tolerance and are a good indication to parents of how tolerant day care staff members are likely to be with babies in general.

5. Proper equipment   Family day care providers may not have cribs or high chairs, and the substitutes they use may interfere with good development. (In one case, a day care provider who had a baby napping in a carriage pushed him down every time he tried to sit up because she was afraid he would fall out.) Parents need to check the availability of equipment and help provide it if necessary.

All infants need a protected sleeping place, such as a crib, and crawlers need a place to crawl safely. Ideally, this would be a "baby-proofed room," but it should be at least of playpen size. A baby old enough to sit and finger-feed should have a safe chair with a tray or table. The freedom of movement babies gain from proper equipment is the foundation of their interest in exploring and learning.

Because day care centers are licensed, they generally have proper equipment and space for infant care. However, it is important to make sure that cribs and high chairs are used properly. Babies should not be in cribs for long periods when they are not sleeping, and they should not be confined to high chairs when they are not eating.

Only a careful visit to a day care center or home will really allow parents to evaluate the situation on the points discussed above. A center or family day care home that does not allow a long, relaxed observational visit is not a proper place for a baby. A quick guided tour or questions answered over the phone cannot substitute for seeing what really happens in the day-to-day functioning of any child care setting.

Factors behind the scenes of an infant care arrangement may also have a powerful effect on the quality of care. Caregivers for infants have a very demanding job, physically, intellectually, and emotionally. If they are to avoid "burnout," they need opportunities for consultation, help, and nurturing from other adults (Cundiff-Stith, 1995; Leavitt, 1994).

The statements about quality care discussed so far are based on research and recommendations by national accrediting groups. It would be wrong, however, to assume that they are absolute and final. Many questions about quality infant care remain, and some of the most difficult involve special concerns of specific ethnic groups. Hispanic parents have real worries about their young children's language experiences (Hill-Scott, 1989). They want child care arrangements that foster the use of Spanish as well as help prepare toddlers for an English-speaking school system. (They want to avoid the experience of one Hispanic attorney who overheard a day care worker tell another not to try to talk to the attorney's crying 15-month-old "because he doesn't speak English.") African American parents and infant care providers tend to prefer programs with heavy stress on discipline and academic achievement (Hill-Scott, 1989) rather than the exploration and socialization emphasized in many standards for accreditation. Whether these preferences actually make for a better, more appropriate care experience for Hispanic and African American infants is not known at this point.

The Frequency of Poor-Quality Care

You may have noted that, in all this discussion of quality infant care, there has been no particular reference to the prevention of abusive treatment. The real danger in infant care arrangements is of neglect, not abuse. Sexual abuse in particular tends to occur at home rather than in day care, where privacy is hard to find and the constant demands are exhausting. However, neglectful and emotionally distant treatment of infants and toddlers is a distressingly frequent component of nonparental care.

The comparison of model versus modal infant and toddler care (Wittmer, 1986) suggests that poor-quality care is the most common experience, especially for babies already at risk because of poverty. Their day care arrangements usually lack well-trained staff, individualized treatment, assessment for special services, and parent education programs. (These are likely to be part of "model child care," often found in university-connected infant care centers.) In the modal care experience, infants are often left to cry in high chairs until the whole group has finished eating. Toddlers are not picked up because "he'll always want it if you do it." Even a casual visitor hears scraps of verbal abuse ("Do you want to live till your mother gets here?"). Caregivers are overwhelmed with work, and even those who are well trained may regress under stress to the egoistic level of thinking about children described in Chapter 13. Low pay and low status add to caregivers' stress and make it likely that many

APPLICATIONS & ARGUMENTS
Interfering in Another Culture

When a baby is having developmental problems, intervention may be needed; when a family's difficulties in functioning are harming their children, the whole family may benefit from intervention. But what if a cultural group is seen as "doing something wrong"? If we try to change them, are we intervening or just plain interfering?

Unfortunately, well-meant attempts at intervention into another culture's ways may harm much more than they help. For example, indigenous peoples of the Amazon region have traditionally brewed homemade beer, which was drunk by everyone, including children. These people came under pressure from missionary groups to stop this practice, which was seen as immoral and as bad for the children. The unexpected result was the development of high levels of vitamin deficiency, for the home brew contained not only a small amount of alcohol but large quantities of B vitamins.

Within a different cultural context, the missionaries might well have had a point. Consuming alcohol can be harmful to young children. If their diets had had a different source of B vitamins, these children might have benefited from the removal of alcohol. Under the circumstances, they did not.

Policies that exert pressure for change on cultural or subcultural groups need to be based on a thorough understanding of the cultural context. A single practice is likely to be linked to many other aspects of the culture in a dynamic action system. Causing one practice to change can lead to so many other alterations that, on balance, the people concerned are harmed far more than they are benefited.

infant care workers are people who cannot get any other job. The potential impact of low-quality care on infant mental health is depressingly obvious.

PROBLEMS TO CONSIDER AND DISCUSS

1. Basing your answer on what you have learned about communication, learning, and emotional development, discuss why "following the child's lead" is considered an important aspect of psychotherapy with infants.

2. Why do foster parents have an especially difficult set of tasks when they care for infants with emotional disturbances? (Be sure to consider what you read in Chapters 12 and 13.)

3. What are some special problems of parents and infants who have fled war or terrorism?

4. How might learned helplessness and the lifeboat mentality affect a parent's ability to care for an infant?

5. What are the advantages and disadvantages of having a relative care for an infant while the parent works, rather than using a day care center? (Be complete in your answer.)

15

Law, Policy, and Ethics: Effects on Infant Development

Infants develop from conception onward in an environment whose nature is partly determined by national policies and laws. Policies help decide the availability of contraception or abortion, of prenatal health care, of well-baby care and immunization, of professional child care, and of family income and insurance. Policies and laws affect marriage and divorce, child custody, and penalties for neglect or abuse of babies.

A national policy is a chosen course of action that guides decision making. It is aimed at a goal that some part of the nation considers to be an appropriate one—whether for financial, practical, or moral reasons. Policy can be expressed through specific legislation or through enforcement or nonenforcement of existing laws. In the United States, an executive order directly from the president or from a cabinet secretary can be a way to enforce compliance with policy. Policy can also be supported by providing or denying public funding of certain actions (for example, financial help for adoptive parents or elective abortions for poor women).

Policy Making in the United States

The making of public policy in the United States reflects the deliberate fragmentation that is designed into the government. The separation of executive, legislative, and judicial powers, with their checks and balances on each other, makes it nearly impossible for one governmental branch to set policy without input from the others.

The U.S. governmental system involves a good deal of conflict among adversaries during policy making. The heterogeneity of the population, with multiple religious, ethnic, and language groups, almost guarantees that a policy suggested by a single group will not be acceptable to others. Bargaining and compromise are critical parts of the policy-making process. Policy making, like other political processes in the United States, tends to be characterized by stress on "condensational symbols" (Merrick, 1992)—emotionally loaded **stereotypes** and oversimplifications, like the "welfare queen" or the "greedy geezer."

stereotype: a standardized mental image; from the Greek *stereos* (solid), the Latin *typus* (an image).

The process of policy making is one of continual change, but there are some stages that can be identified. First, *problem identification* and *agenda formation* take place. (The events that cause the identification of a problem will

Factors that influence the poverty rate can have a profound effect on infants' development.

agenda: plans for work to be done; from the Latin *agendum* (thing to be done).

be discussed in a later section.) As one writer put it, a formal **agenda** is created when "policy makers feel compelled to act, or at least feel compelled to appear to be acting, to resolve [a] problem" (Merrick, 1992, p. 38).

A second step in policy making is *formulation.* The policy to be created and its specific statement are negotiated by branches of the federal government and by professional and special-interest groups (Merrick, 1992). (Again, the last two will be discussed in a later section.)

The third step in the making of policy is *adoption.* In this part of the process, legislation or presidential directives specify the requirements for compliance with the policy. There is still a possibility the courts will interpret the laws or directives as unacceptable in their forms. Once a policy is adopted, its *implementation* involves administrative rule making, adjudication, and law enforcement (Merrick, 1992).

A final step in policy making should be *evaluation* of the outcome of the new policy, which may or may not have the desired results. Evaluation may be very difficult, however, in part because years may pass before sufficient data can be collected and analyzed. Other events at the time of the policy change may also affect the outcomes being measured, so evaluators cannot tell what is responsible for changes that occur. For example, the reduction in highway deaths that followed setting the speed limit at 55 mph could have been caused by added safety features in cars bought at the time. Assessment of outcomes is also affected by the fact that policy implementation may go through gradual change as rules are fine-tuned and as courts interpret laws.

What Drives National Policy Change?

Policy change tends to begin with some sort of triggering event that brings an issue to the attention of the public and of governmental agencies. Sometimes the triggering events involve individual infants and their families, especially those who receive media attention because of dramatic health problems or because of involvement with the courts. Technological change that allows treatment of formerly untreatable conditions may trigger policy change as people try to decide the circumstances under which the treatment may be used.

Economic conditions such as increases in the unemployment rate may lead to policy change as their impact on infants and families becomes evident. Changes in immigration patterns, leading to new demographics and new concerns, may also trigger policy change. Similarly, social changes in the status of women and in the acceptability of single parenthood have brought about alterations in policy.

Does research lead to national policy change? If it does so at all, its effect is probably rather indirect and dependent on the extent to which researchers and interest groups make an effort to influence policy. Research on complex questions of infant development often yields conflicting results from different studies, leaving uncertainty about the direction policy should go if it is to be influenced by research at all. In recent years, a technique called meta-analysis has been used in medical research and social science. This approach, which can combine many studies and resolve their disagreements, may have the potential for guiding appropriate policy change (Mann, 1994).

Who Tries to Change Policy?

Policy changes that influence infant development may come about at the urging of special interest and professional groups whose work is related to infants, as we might expect. Other groups may also be involved; for example, religious groups may have particular interests in policy about contraception or abortion. Because infants' lives are especially closely linked with those of their mothers, groups that have particular concerns with women's issues may press for policies that will have an impact on infants as well as on women.

Concern with national policy affecting infants has been part of the work of the Children's Defense Fund and of the National Center for Clinical Infant Programs, also called Zero to Three. State groups affiliated with the World Association for Infant Mental Health have also been involved. Organizations like the Association for Retarded Citizens and the Junior League have contributed to policy change in this area, even though those groups are oriented to other issues as well.

From time to time, pressure for policy change will come from a book or article written by professionals who choose that approach to gain the attention of others in their field and of the general public. Although policy changes may follow such efforts, they do not seem to occur as rapidly as they do when the "national imagination" is caught by news stories about individuals.

Groups may oppose possible policy changes as well as advocate them. For example, tobacco companies have strongly resisted tobacco control legislation, although there is good evidence that exposure to smoking has a serious effect on infants' health, both prenatally and postnatally (Bloch, 1992).

Proposals and Attempts at Policy Change

Certain changes in U.S. policy affecting infants have been proposed repeatedly without much effect. For example, paid family leaves for childbirth, child care, and adoption have been suggested, as has a basic family allowance program providing direct grants to parents to cover the expenses of child-rearing. Programs of national health insurance have been suggested again and again. Government regulation and subsidization of infant and toddler care is a fairly recent proposal. But these programs, found in almost all other industrialized countries, have not yet come to pass in the United States.

Some suggestions about the provision of such benefits stress that employers could be made responsible for programs such as paid parental leave or subsidized child care. However, this approach is probably less efficient and less equitable than a national program paid for through taxation would be. In addition, most poor children do not live in households where employer-run programs would have much effect (Fuchs & Reklis, 1992).

Three Proposals for Policy Change

Several attempts to influence policy have involved a good deal of effort and some publicity, with varying degrees of success. The following discussion will examine three of them.

1. The principle of "the best interests of the child"   One idea that has had an impact on policy as expressed through judicial decisions is a concern with the *best interests of the child.* This term, part of the title of two books (Goldstein, Freud, & Solnit, 1973, 1979), refers to an approach to court decisions about child custody and termination of parental rights. Old English common law and past U.S. legal attitudes treated a child as essentially a piece of property whose possession was almost always a right of a biological parent; prior to 1900, that right had been primarily the father's, and in the 20th century the right was commonly assigned to the mother, especially when an infant or a young child was in question.

detrimental: harmful; from the Latin *detrere* (to impair).

Decisions made "in the best interests of the child" look for the situation least **detrimental** to the child's life and development and seek to determine this by the procedures that are least detrimental. Some guidelines were proposed to help in the selection of the least detrimental outcome. First, the decisions should take into account that a child needs continuity of relationships. Second, decisions should consider a child's rather than an adult's sense of time; whereas a year may be a short time for a court, it is immensely long for a 3-year-old. Finally, decisions need to consider the facts that the law cannot supervise interpersonal relationships and that long-range predictions are difficult to make (Goldstein, Freud, & Solnit, 1979).

The principle of the "best interests of the child" is not to be applied unless the family has ceased to do its job; when that occurs, the court temporarily takes on the role of parent. As we will see later in this chapter, some custody decisions are based on the best interests of the child, but others are not (Solnit, 1984).

2. The "Heart Start" proposals

Another attempt to influence policy can be seen in the Heart Start proposals suggested by Zero to Three (National Center for Clinical Infant Programs, 1992). These proposals are a formulation of policy to ensure that the emotional foundations of school readiness are developed in infants, toddlers, and preschoolers. The emotional foundations are confidence, curiosity, intentionality, self-control, relatedness to others, pleasure in communication, and cooperativeness. The Heart Start proposals are directed at young children's needs in the areas of health care, unhurried time with adults, responsive caregiving from parents and child care workers, and safe environments.

The Heart Start recommendations are too complex to be summarized here. However, for one goal, increasing responsiveness of child care workers, one of the emphases is on continuity of care. One recommendation is that child care programs should assign a particular caregiver to each child (although, of course, not to that child alone). Another is that programs should have caregivers "move up the age range" so that they care for the same individual children from infancy to preschool.

The Heart Start proposals have received some criticism since their publication (for example, Menzel, 1994). Child care providers are not always enthusiastic about the suggestions that affect their work. More broadly, there are questions about the extent to which child-rearing approaches should be recommended when they may conflict with the values of individual families or cultures.

3. The United Nations Convention on the Rights of the Child

So far, our discussion of policies that affect infants has focused on events in the United States, but policy changes can be international, too. In 1989, the General Assembly of the United Nations adopted a *Convention on the Rights of the Child,* intended to describe rights and freedoms that should belong to every human being under the age of 18. A number of the articles of the convention stress rights to education and are not immediately relevant to the lives of infants and toddlers. Some of the articles, however, are clearly related to infant development.

The principle of the best interests of the child is presented as the standard for legal and administrative decisions. The convention declares that both parents are responsible for their children, but that the state should ensure the provision of child care for working parents. Alternative care is to be guaranteed to children without families, and refugee children are to be assisted in reuniting with their families. Health care is to be provided, which includes work toward abolition of harmful traditional practices. Abuse, neglect, and exploitation are to be prevented, and help is be to provided for rehabilitation of victims of those practices, of torture, or of war. Adoption is to be regulated, and the abduction and sale of children are forbidden.

The convention has been signed and ratified by a large number of countries. In spite of a petition campaign by U.S. children several years ago, the United States has neither signed nor ratified—nor have Iraq, Saudi Arabia, the United Arab Emirates, or about two dozen other countries.

Although the *U.N. Convention on the Rights of the Child* was formulated as the result of years of discussion and negotiation, its language and assumptions are obviously not acceptable to all countries. The very idea of rights is a Western one that is not shared in parts of the Third World, where the stress is on the obligations of one person toward another. The specific prohibition of "harmful traditional practices" would be of concern in countries where genital mutilation of little girls is an essential part of the social fabric. Some provisions of the convention are covered by religious law and may be seen as inappropriate. And in some cultures, concerns about abuse or exploitation of children may be seen as weakening parental authority.

FAMILY LAW

The term *family law* refers to aspects of the law that are involved in the creation or dissolution of family relationships. Marriage, divorce, child custody and visitation, adoption, and inheritance are all parts of family law; so are issues about determination of paternity and about termination of parental rights.

Like other aspects of law and policy, family law changes through legislation and through judicial interpretation. These changes tend to be based on emotional responses rather than on well-thought-out analyses of consequences (Melton & Wilcox, 1989). For example, no-fault divorce was intended to reduce the emotional and material expenses of divorce, but one of its primary effects may have been to decrease income of divorced mothers with custody of their children, and to increase income of divorced noncustodial fathers (McLinden, 1987). Some family law changes, like prohibiting discrimination against "illegitimate" children, have occurred as a result of societal change. Others, like laws about surrogate parenthood, have come about as a result of technological change.

Before the 18th century, the English common law (and its offspring, U.S., Canadian, and Australian law) took little interest in infants. Children took on status as persons and had rights when they were old enough to understand the consequences of agreements they might make. Legal concerns about infants focused on their status as property and on the rights of parents or others to possess and control them (Hart, 1991). Determination of the child's

legitimacy: the state of having been born to legally married parents; from the Latin *lex* (law).

legitimacy was of special concern. Throughout the 19th century, the father was considered the "owner" of children and had custody in cases of separation or divorce, even when the children were very young. In the 20th century, the "tender years" doctrine mandated that custody be assigned to the mother, especially if the children were infants or toddlers.

In the later part of the 20th century, two new principles became prominent in family law. One (discussed earlier in this chapter) was the idea of the best interests of the child; when a family has ceased to nurture, protect, and advocate for a child, courts should make the decision that has the least detrimental effect on the child's development (Solnit, 1984). Under the principle of the best interests of the child, the custodial parent is considered to be an infant's only legitimate advocate and the natural person to make decisions about visitation with the noncustodial parent. Nevertheless, courts have tended to count the noncustodial parent's right to visitation more heavily than the child's need for visitation (Solnit, 1984).

A second principle recently introduced into family law is the idea of *psychological parenting* (Chenoweth, 1992). This concept, which has sometimes been used in judicial decisions about infants, is related to the theory of attachment (see Chapter 12) and states that development is best when the child experiences continuity of caregiving rather than abrupt changes. Thus, people who have been acting as parents become, psychologically speaking, the child's real parents, whether they are biologically related or not. (Legal discussions of psychological parenting often refer to this event as "bonding" and seem to imply that it is based on readily detectable changes in both adult and child. There seems to have been little awareness of the effect of a child's developmental level on her reaction to separation.) One legal concern about the psychological parenting principle is that parents who had sought foster care for their children during family difficulties might not be able to get them back if continuity of caregiving were the highest priority.

In addition to the guiding principles noted above, the U.S. Supreme Court has established a doctrine about *family privacy.* The family is seen as "a zone of privacy into which the state cannot enter without a compelling justification" (Melton & Wilcox, 1989, p. 1213). At the same time, however, individual rights of women and children may justify intrusion, so the privacy doctrine has limits.

The laws of the fifty states are by no means identical in their treatment of legal issues related to infants. However, there are ongoing attempts to create uniform codes about issues like child abuse. A Uniform Child Custody Jurisdiction Act has been adopted by all the states to help determine which state's laws apply in a given case (Freed & Walker, 1988).

Situations involving family law are not usually presented in federal courts. Depending on the state and county, cases may be heard in a unified family court or in a trial court. Some cases, such as those concerning abuse or neglect, may be heard either in a civil or in a criminal court, depending on the prosecutor's decision. Civil courts require proof "by a preponderance of evidence," whereas criminal courts ask for proof "beyond a reasonable doubt," so the choice of courts may have a real impact on the outcome. In most states, an infant involved in a court case will have a guardian *ad litem*, an attorney, who is appointed to make sure that the baby's interests are considered (Horowitz, 1992/1993).

Although most court cases involving infants are matters of abuse or custody, there are ongoing changes in torts (personal injury suits). Infants and toddlers may now be plaintiffs in cases requesting compensation for harm they have experienced. Courts in the past have assumed the *parental immunity doctrine*—that children could not bring tort suits against their parents—but this is no longer necessarily the case. Prenatal tort theory is a recent idea suggesting that a child could sue his mother if her behavior during pregnancy contributed to birth defects or other developmental problems; but courts have been reluctant to accept this idea. Similarly, courts have not generally accepted the idea of a wrongful life suit, in which an infant with a disability seeks compensation from a physician or a genetic counselor who failed to advise the parents to terminate the pregnancy (Horowitz, 1992/1993).

Court cases are an expensive, inefficient way to deal with issues like child custody. Many states now provide alternate dispute resolution (ADR) services as an auxiliary court service. These tend to work well in custody and visitation disagreements, except where there is a history of domestic violence (Horowitz, 1992/1993).

Custody After Divorce

custody: charge of and control over a person; from the Latin *custos* (guardian).

When a family is dissolved through divorce, decisions must be made to determine which parent will have responsibility and authority with respect to minor children. That parent is said to have **custody** of the children, and the other is referred to as the noncustodial parent. Joint custody theoretically has parents share responsibility, but children usually spend more time with one.

Most custody cases involve older children. Parents and courts alike tend to think that custody of infants and toddlers should go to the mother. There have been increasing numbers of lawsuits about infant custody and visitation, however (Horner & Guyer, 1993). When men seek custody, they must sometimes document their ability to cook and do child care (McCant, 1987).

Assignment of custody is not necessarily the end of the story. In fact, it would be realistic to expect that custody arrangements and visitation will need continued negotiation as an infant matures and as the parents' lives alter following the divorce. Although there is no single prescription for successful co-parenting after divorce, some suggestions have been made about handling an infant in this situation (Horner & Guyer, 1993).

A guideline about frequency of contact is that visitation plans for a newborn should be based on the baby's eating and sleep-wake cycle. Furthermore, if the mother breast-feeds, "the schedule of contacts must be left entirely in her hands, even if the court perceives one of her motives for breast feeding to be that of controlling contacts between the newborn and the father" (Horner & Guyer, 1993, p. 469). Nevertheless, it is desirable to keep contact with the father at more than a token level to prevent a later loss of contact. One issue between divorcing parents may involve overnight visits with the baby. A guideline on this topic suggests that infants can adjust to different sleeping places (as they do in day care), but if a breast-fed baby wakes to nurse, overnight visits should be postponed until weaning (Horner & Guyer, 1993).

A difficulty in toddler visitation arises when attachment has occurred but the child has not yet developed good language skills or a clear sense of time. Transitions from one household to another may be followed by displays of anger and distress, and each parent is likely to consider this as evidence that the other treats the toddler badly. If visits occur only at intervals of weeks, the child is especially likely to show distress. Increasing the frequency of visitation is much more likely to help than decreasing it is.

Termination of Parental Rights

Divorce means that only one parent is likely to lack custody of a child, but other legal proceedings can lead to complete termination of parental rights. When parental rights are terminated, the adult loses all of his or her rights to custody of the child, to participation in decision making about the child, and even to contact through visitation. If both parents lose their rights, or if only one parent was known to begin with, the child may then be adopted legally by another family.

If parents cooperate or have abandoned the child, termination of parental rights may be fairly simple. If the parents resist termination, however, a court will not terminate their parental rights unless it is shown that there are grounds in the statutes for termination and that termination is in the child's best interests (Horowitz, 1992/1993). The court has to decide whether the parents are capable of raising the child without causing further harm (in the form of abuse or neglect, for instance). Proof will be based on the extent of past abuse or neglect and the probability that it will continue. Only if the initial cause of harm is still present, and if it will cause continuing serious and lasting harm to the child, is termination of parental rights considered justified. If the child has been in foster care and the relationship with the foster parents is given as a reason to terminate the biological parents' rights, evidence about the relationship with the biological parents must also be considered (Chenoweth, 1992).

When biological parents resist termination of their rights, the process is time-consuming, and the child will probably pass the toddler period before he or she is free for adoption.

Foster Care and Adoption

When the biological parents have been unable to care adequately for a child, several systems of alternate care exist. For (usually) brief periods of time, newborn infants may stay as boarder babies in the hospital where they were born. Alternatively, an infant may go to the home of foster parents, who are paid by the state to care for one or more children. If the biological parents give permission or if their parental rights are terminated, the infant may go directly

APPLICATIONS & ARGUMENTS
When Do We Intervene in a Family's Life?

Laws designed to protect infants and children provide ways to intervene in a family's life when authorities decide it is necessary. With or without the parents' permission, children can be placed in temporary foster care or even be adopted by another family. Parents and children may also be ordered into treatment programs of various kinds under the threat of jail for the parent or foster care placement for the child.

Decision making about this kind of intervention is far from uniform. Whether a problem about an infant comes to anyone's attention may depend on where the family lives and whether authorities are swamped with even more serious problems. The police and social workers must use their discretion about a particular case, and decisions often depend on personal opinions or experiences. This is true of judges, too. The resources available can also play a major role in intervention decisions. If there is no foster home available to care for a baby, she will probably be removed from her parents' care only if death or serious injury seem to be possibilities.

A decision about intervention cannot follow exact rules. What needs to be done depends on the family, the baby, and the resources, and it may well be that the opinion of an experienced person is as good a guide as any. However, that decision needs to be made on the basis of a long-term perspective. If an infant goes into foster care today, are the resources available to help the parents visit and maintain a relationship? Is the baby of an age at which separation can be a devastating experience? Are there resources to help the parents reincorporate the baby into the family if they are reunited a year from now? An intervention needs to assure the infant's physical health and safety, but its long-term consequences need to be considered as well.

to adoptive parents. After the legal process of adoption is complete, the adoptive parents have the same rights and responsibilities toward the child as toward a child to whom they gave birth.

Foster parents may care for a child from an adequate home during a crisis such as loss of appropriate housing or a parent's medical treatment; the child then returns to the biological parents as soon as the crisis is over. Foster care may also be given to a child who has been abused or neglected and who has been removed from the biological parents by a protective services agency. In that case, the child will stay in foster care until the parents are considered capable of adequate child-rearing or until their parental rights are terminated. A child in foster care may also be there to await placement with an adoptive family after termination of the biological parents' rights. The fastest-growing category of children in foster care is infants under 1 year of age (Garfinkel, 1995).

Infants in foster care may have a variety of experiences. Some remain with a foster family, develop a strong relationship with them, and are eventually adopted by them. More commonly, an infant experiences many transitions: from biological parents to foster family, back to biological parents, to a different foster family, and so on. While the infant is in foster care, the biological parents (unless their rights have been terminated) are allowed supervised visits with their child, even when the foster parents believe this is harmful (Argenta, 1990). But they do not always make such visits.

Foster parents have no legal rights to a continuing relationship with a baby they have cared for (Argenta, 1990). They know this and are aware that the baby may be with them only for a short time, so they are inhibited from being totally emotionally available to the infant (Ghuman & Kates, 1992). Foster parents today often find themselves dealing with the most difficult infants: those with serious illnesses like AIDS, with severe physical handicaps, or with deep emotional disturbances.

The difficulties of foster parenting are such that changes have been needed in the foster care system. Gay and lesbian couples, once unwelcome as foster parents, are now regarded differently, in part because of their willingness to care for AIDS babies. "Kinship care," where approved relatives of the child are reimbursed for giving care, has become a major part of the foster care system in some cities (Takas, 1992/1993). Additional reimbursements have been given to foster parents to pay for homemaking services and respite care. Foster parents have also been given specialized training in dealing with medically fragile babies and are paid more for such work (De Palma, 1989).

Unlike foster care, adoption can occur only when a child's parents are dead or when parental rights have been terminated (whether voluntarily or involuntarily). The great advantage of adoption over foster care is that adoption provides both child and parent with a sense of permanency.

oblation: in this context, the custom of offering an infant to be brought up as a member of a religious community; from the Latin *oblatus* (offered).

The practice of adoption of children who were abandoned or sold by their parents goes back to before the Roman Empire. In the Middle Ages, the practice sometimes took on the religious form of **oblation,** or the giving of a child to a monastery (Boswell, 1988). Adoption in some form has been a way to care for parentless children throughout the world, although it has often been kept secret because of its implications about the adoptive parents' fertility or sexuality. In the United States, the adoption of war orphans after World War II was followed by a peak of adoptions in the 1950s and 1960s (Palmos, 1991). Because the proportion of unmarried mothers keeping their babies has increased enormously recently, there are many fewer infants available for adoption in this country, and people who wish to adopt may look abroad. (There are, however, many thousands of older children and infants with disabilities who are available for adoption but for whom no adoptive family can be found.)

A serious concern about adoption in the United States has been whether placement of a child in an adoptive family of a different ethnicity could be considered to be in the child's best interests. There are disproportionately large numbers of African American children available for adoption but disproportionately small numbers of African American adoptive families. However, there have been concerns about an African American child's loss of her ethnic heritage if she is adopted by a family of European background. The Multiethnic Placement Act of 1994 was intended to lower the barriers to interracial adoption. Under this act, states and adoption agencies could lose federal funds if they use racial differences as a reason to refuse adoptions (Jones, 1995).

Although adoption is a legal process a court must agree to, the initial steps can be pursued in two ways: through independent adoptions and through social services agencies. Before there were comprehensive adoption laws in the United States, adoption was usually independent or "direct," involving the biological parent(s), the adoptive parents, and an attorney who transferred the custody of the child according to the procedures used to transfer property (Pierce & Vitello, 1991). More than half of the adoptions in the United States in 1951 followed this pattern, but many fewer take place independently today.

Although standards for adoption agencies state that finding children for adoptive families is not their main purpose, independent adoption practitioners can legally contract to find a child for adoption. They can accept fees to represent the adoptive parents' interests rather than those of the child or the biological parents. They are not involved in screening of parents or in provision of postadoption services (Pierce & Vitello, 1991).

Adoptions are increasingly taking place through social services agencies that provide a full range of adoption services. Prospective adoptive parents are screened, the best interests of the children are considered, and postadoption services (which we will discuss later) may be provided. Agencies generally follow a Supreme Court ruling stating that in some cases unmarried fathers must be notified of adoption proceedings (Pierce & Vitello, 1991).

Adoption law is different from one country to the next, but there is a movement toward an emphasis on the child's best interests. An agreement in 1967 among 16 European countries stressed that the child's best interests would include an attempt to give an adopted child a family environment similar to his original one, a need for the biological mother's consent, and a need for a preadoption waiting period before the adoption becomes legally final (Caiani-Praturlon, 1991). U.S. adoption agencies are thus in line with international thinking on this subject.

The need for pre- and postadoption services is a critical issue for adoption policy. It is important to realize that adoption does not always work. Ten percent or more of all adoptions are *disrupted,* and the child is returned to the agency or foster home. (The greatest number of disruptions occur when the child is older or has physical or emotional problems.) Adoption is a dynamic process (Nordhaus & Solnit, 1990) in which reorganization and change can lead to a good or a poor outcome. Assessment of the prospective adoptive parents, of the child, and of their "goodness of fit" are essential preadoption services that can help prevent disruption.

After adoption, the adoptive family will probably need continued help and emotional support (Tsiantis, 1991). Adoptive parents may enter the process with severe conflicts about their own infertility; they may be longing to accept any baby and may be unrealistic about their own wishes and abilities and about the nature of parenthood (Brazelton, 1990; Hoksbergen, 1991).

As the adopted child develops, the family will need additional emotional support at particular points. The adoptive parents may encourage prolonged stranger anxiety because they need to be reassured that the child is attached to them. As the toddler begins to show increased autonomy, the adoptive parents may have trouble accepting the change; they may be fearful of the child's normal anger and aggression and feel ambivalent about setting limits (Frank & Row, 1990; Hibbs, 1991b).

If a child is adopted after the newborn period, of course, her previous experiences and the impact of separation and loss will put special demands on the adoptive parents. Similarly, a child who needs unusual physical care will create an unusual need for support and help. Stress on the family may also occur because of the adoption laws in their particular state; some set no deadlines for biological parents to appeal an adoption proceeding (Johnson, 1992), so there may be ongoing uncertainty about whether the baby will stay.

Disrupted adoptions occur because one or more factors in the dynamic action system work against rather than toward family formation. Often, the problem is that commitment to the adopted child seems to be harming commitments to other loved ones (Ziegler, 1994). Adoption policies and laws need to recognize this problem and prevent the disruption of adoption, which wrecks the life of the child as well as that of the adoptive family.

LIFE AND DEATH DECISIONS

Among the characteristics of infancy that set it apart from other times in human life are the vulnerability of the baby and the certainty of death if adult protection is withdrawn. From time to time, that protection is taken away—sometimes impulsively and sometimes after careful thought about the best decision to make.

There are two common situations in which adults decide to take actions to withdraw their protection. One is *abortion*, where the withdrawal is a matter of direct action leading to the death of the embryo or fetus. The other involves *withholding care* from a neonate, with the expectation that death will follow. Historically, this withholding occurred by exposing unwanted infants to the elements. In the industrialized world today, it involves withholding treatment for neonates who have severe impairments or are very premature and for whom current treatment holds no hope of anything beyond mere survival.

Because neither abortion nor withholding of treatment can be reversed, there is much concern about the decision-making process in most cases. State laws about abortion may mandate a waiting period or discussion with counselors. The decision to withhold treatment from a neonate would usually involve physicians and the baby's parents (and possibly other people, as we will discuss later).

Who Is a Person?

The types of decisions made about abortion or withholding of treatment are a matter of values, not of scientific knowledge. One of the most important values involved in such decisions is the definition of *personhood*, which may or may not include the unborn or the neonate. The examination of such values is usually considered the task of philosophers and ethicists.

ontology: the study of the nature of existence, especially that of a human being; from the Greek *einai* (to be), *logos* (word).

From the philosopher's point of view, being a person is not simply a matter of belonging to the human species. Personhood is a category to which a living entity is assigned on the basis of **ontological** status, that is, the nature of its existence. A living being who is categorized as a person is considered to have certain rights, the chief one, for our purposes, being the right not to be killed.

How do we determine the nature of the existence of a fetus or a neonate? Most philosophers agree that personhood requires consciousness, self-awareness, and some minimum level of rationality (Weir, 1992). It seems unlikely that a fetus has these characteristics, and, as we saw in Chapter 10, they are probably only very dimly present in a well-developed neonate.

Three basic positions attempt to relate the ontological nature of the fetus or neonate to personhood (Weir, 1992). The first states simply that fetuses and neonates are nonpersons and do not have the rights of persons. The reasoning here is that personhood requires cognitive characteristics that fetuses and neonates do not have, and having the potential for developing those characteristics is not enough to entitle the nonperson to an actual person's rights.

actual: existing in reality; from the Latin *actus* (deed, act).

A second position is that fetuses and neonates may be **actual** persons. The reasoning of this position is that the category of personhood is determined by social consensus as beginning at a particular chronological point, which (depending on the society) could be conception, or viability, or birth. Any human who is past that chronological point is a person and has all the rights of personhood, such as the right not to be killed.

potential: with the possibility but not the present reality of existence; from the Latin *potentia* (power).

A third position—and the one that is probably most emphasized in U.S. law at this juncture—is that some fetuses and most neonates are **potential** persons. Although actual personhood involves certain cognitive abilities that fetuses and even neonates do not have, they will acquire these abilities in the ordinary course of development. The potential for personhood, in this argument, wins for its possessor some of the rights of actual persons, such as the right not to be killed. The potential for personhood is considered to be seen in fetuses when their brains have already shown activity, and in neonates when they do not have severe neurological impairment.

Personhood and Other Aspects of Decision Making

Of the three positions about the personhood of fetuses just described, the first would clearly allow the acceptability of abortion for any reason and at any time during the pregnancy. The second position would assume that abortion was or was not acceptable after certain points in the pregnancy, depending on the consensus of the social group. The third would limit abortion to periods before the occurrence of measurable brain activity.

Decisions about withholding treatment from a neonate have a somewhat more complicated relationship to the idea of personhood (Weir, 1992). These decisions are influenced by views of the obligations of the medical profession and of the rights and obligations of parents. They also involve concerns about the appropriateness of sustaining life by providing food and fluids, whether or not other treatment is attempted. The issue of life-sustaining treatment has probably received the most attention from ethicists.

One position about life-sustaining treatment holds that the only appropriate time to withhold such care is when the infant is irretrievably dying. (As we

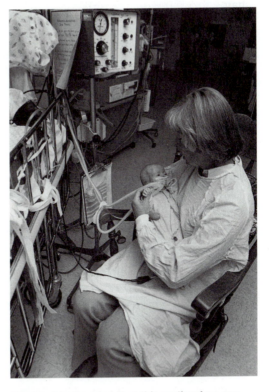

It is hard to imagine that this mother has any questions about the personhood of her tiny infant, no matter what his medical needs may be.

will see later, this view has had a powerful effect on U.S. policy and law.) A second position is that we are obliged to sustain life only for neonates who count as persons; the problem then becomes one of defining *personhood*. A third possible position on life-sustaining treatment holds that the real question is who makes the decision; under this assumption, the parents have the right to decide what to do for the infant because they stand to gain or lose most from the outcome. A fourth position stresses the quality of life (rather than its **sanctity,** as in the first position we considered). In this point of view, the quality of life the child will eventually experience is considered the most important concern, so withholding life-sustaining treatment is acceptable for cases of very severe long-term disabilities, especially of a neurological nature. A final possible position is that the decision to give or withhold treatment should be made individually, based on the best interests of the infant (Weir, 1992).

sanctity: sacred value; from the Latin *sanctus* (holy).

The positions on quality of life and on the best interests of the infant have been discussed at some length by ethicists. In both cases, multiple factors and their interactions are the foundations for decision making. One approach to making decisions based on quality of life looks at the baby's natural endowment, the degree of support for his development that can be expected in his home, and the degree of support likely to be given by society (Shaw, 1992).

The best interests standard has focused less on the social support expected for the infant and more on the infant's individual characteristics. One formulation (Weir, 1992) suggests that consideration be given to the severity of the infant's medical condition, the availability of effective treatment, the achievability of important medical goals, the presence of serious neurological impairment, the number of other serious medical problems, and the life expectancy of the infant. This approach is also concerned with the extent of the infant's suffering and the proportion of benefits of treatment compared to the harm experienced as a result of the treatment (Weir, 1992). (You may wish to review the section on pain perception in Chapter 8 as background to these last two issues.)

So far, the ethical positions we have discussed have not considered economic concerns as a factor in decisions on treatment of neonates. Unfortunately, however, such concerns are already a real part of decision making and will probably increase in importance in the coming years (Blank, 1992). The cost of the technology used in the treatment of neonates can be staggering. If an infant's life is saved but severe disabilities remain, society will have to pay for many years to sustain an individual who cannot support or even care for himself. The resources to pay for such services are withdrawn from somewhere—care for later-born infants with impairments, education of people who could provide services, health care for the elderly, the nation's defense budget, or any of our many other national needs. Unless more resources can be allocated through changes in taxation or better use of fiscal resources, a decision to care for one infant will mean that some other work will be unfunded. Understanding trade-offs of this kind may be a real part of ethical decision making, repulsive though it may be to most of us to think so.

Law and Abortion

Because of the broad range of differing opinions in the United States, our present laws about abortion do not represent any consensus about the personhood of the embryo or fetus. Instead, the most important Supreme Court decision on abortion, *Roe v. Wade* (1973), was based on the limits of government intervention into the life of the individual (Garrow, 1995).

Under *Roe v. Wade*, states are limited in their rights to regulate abortion before the limits of viability (usually considered to be about 24 weeks of gestation) but allowed to legislate greater limitations on later abortions. It is accepted that women have certain rights of control over their own bodies, but it is also recognized that states have interests in the health of their citizens and in the regulation of the practice of medicine. Since the *Roe v. Wade* decision, many attempts have been made by the strong "pro-life" lobby in the United States to make all or most abortions illegal, and constitutional amendments have been proposed to this end.

At the time of this writing, the House of Representatives had passed and the Senate was considering the Partial Birth Abortion Act of 1995, the first attempt to outlaw a specific medical procedure (Mayer, 1995). The term *partial birth abortion* refers to a technique used late in pregnancy when some very serious disabling conditions have been diagnosed in the fetus. The fetus is alive at the beginning of the procedure, in the course of which the fetus' brain is removed by suction; the reduced head size greatly simplifies delivery. One argument in favor of this procedure is that the death and decomposition of the fetus in the uterus may endanger the mother's life (Schulte, 1995), but a counterargument is that it would be safer and more humane to induce labor (Chen, 1995). The Partial Birth Abortion Ban Act may have its greatest importance in its function as a "wedge issue" to destroy the unity of support for current abortion laws and practices (Mayer, 1995) and possibly lead to some considerable changes in the legal situation.

Although specific laws about the practice of abortion have a powerful effect, they are not the only factors influencing the actual abortion rate. Access to abortion is also an economic issue because, as is true for other medical procedures, it must be paid for in some way. Private health insurance generally does not cover abortion unless there is some other serious medical issue involved. In most states, public financing for abortions for poor women has been absent for many years, nor has Medicaid provided coverage (Harris & Schulte, 1993).

Concern about the ethics of abortion has influenced some related legal and policy decisions. For example, the use of fetal tissue transplantation in medical treatment has been affected by changes in planning for a fetal tissue bank, a network organized by the federal government that would supervise collection and use of fetal tissue. These changes have been based in part on concerns that the use of fetal tissue might increase the frequency of abortion.

A fetal tissue bank was established by presidential executive order in May, 1992, and almost immediately cancelled in a clause of the 1993 National Institutes of Health Revitalization law. The reasons for establishing such a

In China, rapid population growth and crowding have led to pressure for contraception and abortion. The house in this picture had to be rebuilt after authorities tore it down because the family had a second child before the first was 4 years old.

bank would be the practical issue of providing a safe source of fetal tissue and the ethical issue of creating a "wall of separation" between those who have transplants and those who perform them (Cohen & Jonsen, 1993). Tissue from elective surgical abortions is more likely to be uninfected and genetically normal than is tissue from spontaneous abortions (miscarriages), but its use is not ethically acceptable to everyone.

It has been recommended that an ethical fetal tissue bank would separate the decision about abortion from the decision about tissue donation and would forbid sale of fetal tissue or direct donation to a designated person in need of a transplant. An ethical tissue bank would need to be a nonprofit organization. As experimental work with fetal tissue transplants continues, more issues will undoubtedly come to light (Cohen & Jonsen, 1993), but the connection with abortion will remain the most serious ethical concern.

Decisions About Care of Neonates: The Baby Doe Rules

Happily, no special decisions need to be made about the great majority of newborns—just decisions about a name and whether that nose is Grandma's or Uncle John's. Some newborns may have conditions for which treatment is available and the decision to use it is easy to make; an example would be an otherwise healthy newborn with a cleft lip.

For some newborns, however, it is difficult to decide what to do for their multiple problems. These babies may be preterm, of very low birth weight, and have genetically or teratogenically caused malformations. Surgery or

anencephalic:
without a fully developed brain; from the Greek *an-* (without), *enkephalos* (brain).

other treatment for their problems may or may not be likely to cure them. They may even be **anencephalic** and require constant treatment to remain alive at all.

In the distant past, there were no decisions to make about these babies because there were no ways to treat them. A small number lived for a while, but most died fairly soon after birth, if not at once. They were kept warm, and they were given milk or water if they could take it; this "comfort care" was intended simply to make their dying as easy as possible.

As techniques for treating the very sick neonate developed, there were times when decisions about treatment were made, usually by the parents and physicians together. Sometimes these decisions led to attempts, successful or unsuccessful, to sustain the baby's life and to correct some problems. These attempts could involve many surgical operations, and, as we noted in Chapter 8, pain relief was not considered necessary for the neonate. In other cases, the parents and physicians felt that the most humane decision was to refrain from subjecting the baby to treatment, to keep him or her as comfortable as possible, and to "let nature take its course"—a course that usually ended with the infant's death.

In 1982, changes in U.S. government policy (and later law) altered this picture to one where treatment decisions are restricted and guided by specific rules. This change followed media and governmental attention to an infant suffering from Down syndrome and multiple physical defects born in Indiana on April 9, 1982. The child's parents did not want their baby to receive treatment or intravenous feeding (because of the physical defects, feeding by mouth was not possible). In a court case to determine the legality of the parents' decision, the infant was referred to as "Baby Doe," a traditional term that keeps the family anonymous. The courts supported Baby Doe's parents and the infant died.

Within weeks, the U.S. Department of Health and Human Services (DHHS), under instruction from the White House staff, published a notice to all hospitals receiving federal funds. This notice, the first of the "Baby Doe regulations," was based on the Rehabilitation Act of 1973 and stated that it was unlawful to withhold treatment from an infant with a disability if the decision was based solely on the infant's disability; such a decision was regarded as discrimination against people with disabilities. About a year later, another directive from DHHS required hospitals receiving federal aid to post notices stating that withholding of treatment was forbidden if it was done because of handicapping conditions, as well as a toll-free hot line number so that anyone in the hospital could report violations to federal authorities. A so-called Baby Doe squad of DHHS personnel was available to investigate reports (in fact, the investigations they carried out found that they agreed with treatment decisions that had been made). In 1984, DHHS linked compliance with the Baby Doe regulations to eligibility for federal funds for fighting child abuse.

The Baby Doe regulations became law in the form of the Child Abuse Amendments of 1984 (Public Law 98-457) and made compliance a prerequisite for federal aid to state child protective services. The Child Abuse Amendments of 1984 required certain standards of care for infants with severe

chronic:
persisting over
time; from the
Greek *chronos*
(time).

disabilities. Basically, these amendments state that infants with disabilities must always receive "comfort care" (appropriate food and fluids). All babies with disabilities must also be given any other treatment their medical condition indicates, except in three situations. Other treatment may be withheld if the infant is "**chronically** and irreversibly comatose," if the treatment would simply prolong the infant's dying and would be futile in terms of survival, or if the treatment would be virtually futile and would be inhumane in terms of the suffering caused to the infant (Bopp & Nimz, 1992; Merrick, 1992). In spite of much criticism and legal action involving the Child Abuse Amendments Act of 1984, they were reauthorized in 1991 (Public Law 101-126).

The Baby Doe rules have been criticized as being too vague. The exceptions to treatment listed above are not, in fact, clear-cut and are interpreted differently by different members of the medical profession. Other criticisms have addressed the issue of government interference with family and medical decision making. It has been suggested that the regulations have led to overtreatment of neonates (Campbell, 1992) and even to "what can . . . be little more than prolonged torture" (Penticuff, 1992, p. 269). A concern with the effect of the Baby Doe rules on the rationing of health care resources has also been expressed (Blank, 1992).

As the medical technology available for treatment of high-risk newborns develops further, the Baby Doe regulations may need more than a little fine-tuning. The cases on which the rules were originally based involved spina bifida and Down syndrome, problems for which treatment has greatly advanced and where decisions are no longer as difficult as they were in 1982. Infants who are extremely premature or who have severe genetic disorders like Tay-Sachs disease (see Chapter 3) are not really the ones toward whom the original concerns were directed (Caplan, 1992), although in another 20 years those problems may seem much more treatable.

In the meantime, challenges to the Baby Doe rules continue to arise. In one case a few years ago, parents who knew their fetus was anencephalic chose to carry the baby to term, assuming that the child would be considered "brain dead" (because there was no brain) and that other infants could receive transplants of the healthy organs; but the legality of this plan was not clear (Chartrand, 1992). In another case, a hospital wanted to withhold further treatment from a 16-month-old who had only rudimentary brain structures but whose mother had insisted that the infant be kept breathing; a federal appeals court ruled that the hospital must continue treatment (Greenhouse, 1994). In one tragic case with an older infant, a 6-month-old suffered permanent, profound brain damage after inhaling part of a balloon and needed a ventilator to breathe (and was comatose as well). His father's request to take him off the ventilator was refused on the advice of the hospital's attorney. After many more requests, the father held the medical staff at gunpoint, disconnected the ventilator, and let his son die in his arms (see Weir, 1992).

In spite of these cases, there are also some questions about the extent to which many states are actually in compliance with the Child Abuse Amendments of 1984 (Bopp & Nimz, 1992). Little training about interpreting and complying with the Baby Doe rules seems to be given to nurses who will be doing intensive care with infants with disabilities (Penticuff, 1992).

One question we may ask about the Baby Doe rules is whether they are related to the late-term abortions discussed in an earlier section of this chapter. Parents who knew that their unborn child had severe disabilities, but who also knew that their wish to let the baby "die in peace" might not be granted could well choose abortion as the one way to make their own choice for the manner of their child's death.

POLICY, REGULATION, AND INFANT DEVELOPMENT

Our discussion of issues like the Baby Doe regulations or termination of parental rights shows the dramatic role law can play in an infant's life. But it should not be forgotten that policies and regulations are at work behind the scenes in quiet, constant determination of many aspects of infant experience and development. In this final section, we will examine some of these less dramatic issues that can nevertheless have a profound effect on the quality of an infant's existence and development.

Child Care Regulation

Paradoxically, although day care arrangements are much affected by laws, many important aspects of their functioning remain essentially unregulated. Like any other business, day care programs are regulated under sanitation, building, and fire safety laws. They must also comply with zoning regulations (and these may have a serious impact on family day care homes, which can be zoned out of some towns). Day care programs may also have to meet licensing requirements set by the states. These requirements usually involve adult-child ratios, staff training, aspects of the physical environment like floor space and number of exits, and health and safety concerns (Willer, 1989). The specific requirements should be different for children of different ages; for example, there needs to be a much smaller ratio of infants to adults than of preschoolers to adults. Day care programs associated with religious organizations often have these licensing requirements waived (Kendall, 1989). In any case, many of the standards are not particularly stringent (Griffin, 1991).

Family day care homes are regulated only when they are intended for more than a minimum number of children (often 5). Some states require licensing for family day care programs, whereas others request simple registration with the state. In either case, it is relatively easy for an unlicensed or unregistered family day care home to operate undetected. Family day care providers who care for only a small number of children are often unregulated by law. There is probably a considerable "underground economy" in family day care, where caregivers prefer to be unregistered, to be paid under the table, and to avoid reporting income to tax authorities. To try to offset this tendency, states offer benefits to those who register, such as surplus food for snacks. (Actually, caregivers would probably benefit financially from reporting their incomes, because many of their expenses would be tax-deductible.)

Accreditation of day care centers is sometimes done through state programs, but is not generally required for licensing. Accreditation may also be granted by groups like the National Academy of Early Childhood Programs, which is part of the National Association for the Education of Young Children. Family day care homes may go through an accreditation process if they join certain family day care networks. Accreditation serves as a statement that the day care program meets higher standards than those required for licensing or registration alone.

Regulation of staff training and salaries can be an essential part of maintaining high quality in day care. Although most states require a check on the criminal background of day care employees, few require much in the way of training about infant development. Care of infants still tends to be regarded as a custodial, nonprofessional task. This attitude is matched by salary scales for caregivers, which tend to be lower than those paid to zoo workers (Noble, 1993). Although there has been pressure for higher wages from groups like the Worthy Wage Coalition, it may not be possible for most parents to pay the higher fees that would support higher wages. The answer to this problem may be government subsidies for infant care, like those provided by most European countries.

One attempt to encourage better training of caregivers is the Child Development Associate National Credentialing Program. This credential (CDA), required by some state regulations, involves assessment of the caregiver by a representative of the Child Development Associate Consortium and includes observation for 3 hours during the course of a day. The assessment follows at least 640 hours of experience in child care, some courses or workshops, and consultation with an advisor. It should be noted that 98% of caregivers pass the assessment (Arnett, 1989), but it is probably true that they ask to be assessed only when they are reasonably well trained.

Why is there no federal regulation of child care programs? One real issue is that parents are not in agreement about the need for regulation (Kendall, 1989). Americans as a group tend to stress their right to rear children as they see fit, without government interference. The national emphasis on individualism creates particular opposition to rules that appear to impose value structure on child care settings. Parents want freedom of choice in child care; paradoxically, however, they also want careful regulation that will guarantee children's health and safety and protect them against physical or sexual abuse. In different geographical regions and among different cultural groups, different standards are desired. In spite of efforts such as the Federal Interagency Day Care Requirements and the Act for Better Child Care, it seems unlikely that states will achieve uniform standards or that standards will go beyond the simplest health and safety issues.

Although many European countries offer a government-run and subsidized child-care system, the cultural diversity of the people of the United States may make such a solution impossible. A system that will work here may need to involve a full range of choices (see Miller, 1989) because different religious and ethnic groups may have quite distinct preferences about value orientations, discipline goals and techniques, modesty training, and the socialization of sex roles. If we allow parents to spank infants and toddlers at home, for example, it follows that we should allow them to choose a day care setting where spanking is used, if they prefer it.

Insurance, Government Regulation, and Infant Development

One of the great concerns of any business in operation today is the maintenance of adequate insurance coverage. Without insurance, a business such as a day care center may find itself paying out enormous sums to an injured employee or customer. Individuals, too, look for jobs whose benefits include health insurance to prevent them from financial disaster if they or their children suffer catastrophic illness.

Insurance companies sell a service and they do so to make a profit. If they insure more businesses or individuals who have claims than those who do not, that profit will not be achieved. This fact can affect infants in a number of ways.

Some changes in biotechnology have altered the traditional insurance picture in a way that has special relevance to infants. An insurance company used to sell policies and trust to fortune that more of the purchasers would stay healthy than would become sick; now it is possible through genetic testing to predict some serious illnesses to come for newborns or even for fetuses (Marshall, 1994c). It is certainly not to the benefit of an insurance company to provide a policy for a person who will almost certainly need years of expensive treatment, but how does a family pay for the treatment out of their pockets?

Current practice, except where state laws specifically forbid it, allows insurance companies to use genetic discrimination and to refuse coverage for a person known to have certain genetic defects. Some state laws that forbid discrimination against people with sickle cell anemia were passed because of the existence of insurance discrimination. There are presently no federal laws against genetic discrimination by health insurance companies. One policy suggestion made would prohibit insurance companies from limiting coverage or altering their rates on the basis of genetic information; companies would also be forbidden to request genetic information or to release what they have without the insured individual's authorization (Hudson, Rothenberg, Andrews, Kahn, & Collins, 1995).

Insurance issues also affect the medical care available to newborns. Because insurance companies began to pay for hospital care on the basis of diagnosis-related groups (DRGs), reimbursement has been limited to shorter and shorter hospital stays for apparently healthy newborns; in some cases, reimbursement was given for no more than a 24-hour stay (see Chapter 4), leading to concerns that an infant would be taken home before problems were diagnosed. Although state laws may mandate payment for a 48-hour hospital stay, they cannot regulate payments by companies based in a different state. A federal law passed in 1996 requires guaranteed payment for a 48-hour stay (Johnson, 1995).

Insurance is a critical factor in the functioning of day care. Medical bills for an injured child or employee could rapidly bankrupt any day care center. Lawsuits related to accusations of abusive treatment would be astronomically expensive to fight, whether the abuse had really occurred or not. In family day care arrangements, a lawsuit could take all of a family's assets and might attach future earnings as well (homeowner's insurance does not usually cover home-run businesses like day care).

A crisis in the insurance industry in 1985 had notable ill effects on day care centers and family day care providers, particularly in California. Policies were cancelled, new policies were unavailable, and rates rose by a factor of 4 in some cases. Companies would not write policies for centers that served "special needs" children or where pet animals were kept because in these situations the chances of accidents and claims are slightly higher. Infant programs and family day care providers were especially affected (Kalemkiarian, 1989).

The results of this insurance crisis were multiple. Because most centers could not raise their fees without losing their clientele, they had to pay for insurance fees with money that could have gone to other expenses like staff training. Some centers had to close, and new projects were slowed or stopped. Children from poor families were especially likely to attend uninsured care programs.

Insurance continues to be an issue with serious implications for the quality and availability of child care. Federal regulation of the insurance industry, which has hardly existed for many years, is a possible solution to the problem. No-fault insurance policies and changes in laws about personal injury suits have also been suggested (Kalemkiarian, 1989).

Child Abuse and Neglect Laws: Changing Attitudes

Policies governing abuse or neglect of infants and toddlers have changed considerably during the 20th century. The term *battered child* was not introduced until the 1960s. Neither abuse nor neglect has a clear-cut definition at this point, reflecting the differences in attitudes among different groups of people and of changes in attitudes as they have occurred over time. Almost everyone would agree that an infant who suffers nonaccidental extensive bruising or broken bones at the hands of an adult has been abused, but only a small number of people would say that any and all physical punishment of an infant is abusive. The laws allow sufficient room for interpretation to compensate for these differences.

Laws about reporting abuse vary and have undergone a great deal of change in the last 20 years. Physicians are generally required to report suspected abuse when a child receives medical attention. Private citizens may also be required to report to child protective agencies when they suspect abuse, but such a law is very difficult to enforce. Dramatic changes may be seen in a state's reported number of abuse cases when reporting procedures are changed (Williams, 1980).

One of the special problems of enforcement of child abuse laws is that there may be no better place for an infant or toddler than her own home, even if abusive treatment occurs there. Separation from the parents may have an impact as great as or greater than that of being abused. There is no guarantee that a foster home will not also be abusive, and in any case entrance into foster care may be only the beginning of a cycle of separations and transitions. Removing the child from the home—the great threat that law enforcement agencies have for parents—may not be in the child's best interests at all.

Some policy recommendations aimed at preventing child abuse have included the provision of leadership by governmental leaders from the president down; the generation and dissemination of more knowledge about child abuse; and an increase in human resources (U.S. Advisory Board on Child Abuse and Neglect, quoted by Zigler, Hopper, & Hall, 1993).

Child abuse statutes were generally written with the intention of protecting children after their birth. Recent attempts, however, have been made to apply the laws to unborn babies. In the late 1980s, several women were prosecuted on the grounds that they had delivered drugs to a minor by using drugs while pregnant. In one case, the Connecticut Supreme Court ruled that use of cocaine several hours before childbirth, resulting in the birth of a traumatized, oxygen-deprived infant, was not child abuse because a fetus is not a child until birth (Johnson, 1992). (Incidentally, the court also ruled that although this infant had been with a foster family for two years, the lack of a parental relationship could not be used to prevent return to the biological mother because the separation had been due entirely to a state action.)

A number of writers have spoken out against punishing pregnant women for drug use on the grounds that it would make pregnant drug users even less likely to seek prenatal care (Garrity-Rokous, 1994; Johnson, 1992; Neuspiel & Hamel, 1991). Sanctions for drug use during pregnancy have also been criticized as unconstitutional (Garrity-Rokous, 1994).

Entitlements of Infants and Toddlers

entitlement: the legal right to a benefit; from the Latin *intitulare* (to have a right or title).

Every industrialized nation today is committed to a set of **entitlements** for infants and toddlers: services or financial supports that are legally guaranteed to some or all of the country's babies. The particular set of guarantees varies widely from country to country. As this chapter was being written early in 1996, the U.S. government was in a state of conflict, as the branches struggled with each other to achieve their differing goals about entitlements. At one extreme, the goal was to remove almost all entitlements in the hope of balancing the budget and removing any encouragement of unmarried parenthood. At the opposite extreme, the goal was to increase and reorganize entitlements in the hope of improving the health and academic achievement of U.S. children.

One of the special problems about understanding the entitlements of U.S. babies is that the guarantees involve a patchwork of federal, state, and local services, with dozens of funding sources. A second complicating issue is that services and money are often given to an infant via the family, rather than directly; the infant, of course, cannot cash a check or apply for food stamps, but the involvement of the family can bring in concerns such as the parents' marital status. Some services, like counseling for parents, have an indirect but real effect on infant development.

Direct payments to poor families may occur in the form of Aid to Families with Dependent Children (AFDC), a provision of the Social Security Act. At this time, AFDC-eligible families may also be able to receive child care reimbursement if one or both parents participate in employment or training (Pizzo, 1990). States may decide how to apply some AFDC funds. For example, in 1992, New Jersey decided that an AFDC-recipient adult who had another baby while receiving benefits would not be eligible for additional AFDC benefits. Whether or not this policy has resulted in fewer births to AFDC recipients remains unclear, and indeed too short a time has passed to detect any change.

When a family is eligible for AFDC because of poverty and unemployment, its infants and toddlers are eligible for Medicaid services. This may also be true for babies of working families with low incomes. Medicaid-eligible children may receive developmental assessment through the Early and Periodic Screening, Diagnosis and Treatment (EPSDT) program. Transportation to medical and dental services may also be paid for if it is provided through child care or other programs (Pizzo, 1990). The Child Care Food Program provides federal funds to pay for nutritious meals and snacks for eligible children in nonprofit day care centers, and in some cases in other programs (Pizzo, 1990).

Although poverty can be the single reason for providing government-funded services for a baby, disabling conditions may also entitle the infant to help. Public Law 99-457, the Education of the Handicapped Act Amendments of 1986, provides for family-centered services to children who have disabilities or are at risk of developing them. Part H of P.L. 99-457 was particularly directed at help for infants and toddlers, and this intention was reauthorized as part of the Individuals with Disabilities Education Act (IDEA) in 1991. Part H provided for early intervention services for children under age 3 who have problems with physical, cognitive, language, and psychosocial development. An unusual aspect of Part H is its encouragement of coordination of services and most particularly its involvement of parents as advocates, coordinators, and decision makers (Hausslein, Kaufmann, & Hurth, 1992).

Some provisions of services and funds for handicapped babies have altered over the years as a result of judicial and agency interpretation. Supplemental Security Income (SSI) is a federal cash assistance program for low-income children with certain disabilities or chronic illnesses. Many children with disabilities born in the 1970s and 1980s were denied SSI because the list of eligible conditions did not include problems such as autism and Down syndrome (Schulzinger, 1992/1993). In a case heard before the U.S. Supreme Court (*Sullivan v. Zebley*, 1990), the Court ruled that the Social Security Administration's handling of SSI violated the agency's own statutes. Following the Zebley case, the Social Security Administration revised the evaluation process, added mental and emotional disabilities to the eligibility

Public policy in the U.S. may be one of the causes of high child poverty rates compared to other industrialized countries. (Source: Luxembourg Income Study)

list, and included the failure to achieve developmental milestones and lack of age-appropriate behavior. Special provisions for infants and toddlers have been added, replacing the old approach that deferred decisions until standardized testing could be done (Schulzinger, 1992/1993).

Unfortunately, the families who are most in need may be least likely to seek entitlements for themselves or their babies. Those who cannot read or speak English well and those who are easily intimidated may not even apply for food stamps (Frank, Allen, & Brown, 1985), much less go through the more complicated process of seeking SSI. Once again, the parents' educational and social conditions have a profound effect on infants' access to the resources they need. Policy and law may make some guarantees to babies, but family circumstances can still lead to deprivation.

PROBLEMS TO CONSIDER AND DISCUSS

1. What do you see as the advantages and disadvantages of federal nationwide family policies and laws in the United States? Keep in mind the increasing diversity of the population.

2. Why do you suppose the United States has not yet ratified the *U.N. Convention on the Rights of the Child*?

3. Discuss why a toddler might show anger and distress after a visit to a noncustodial parent. (Review Chapters 12 through 14 for ideas.)

4. What are the advantages and disadvantages of independent adoptions, as compared to those arranged through social services agencies?

5. What is your opinion of the personhood of a neonate? Give reasons for your answer.

Afterword: Changes and Challenges

Many chapters (and probably many weeks) ago you began this book by meeting Jamal, Bobby, and Tiffany as they experienced the Strange Situation. In the ensuing chapters, you learned a great deal that helps to explain the differences among those three babies—their physical and motor development, their speech, and their responses to their mothers. Still, you are probably well aware that you have not mastered all there is to know on those topics. I hope you are also aware that even the most knowledgeable people in the infant development field remain, at bottom, humble students. The study of infant development still has far to go.

Change has been an important theme of this book: changing demographics, changing technology, changing attitudes and beliefs, accumulating information—all have been noted as relevant to the study of infant development. There is no doubt that these changes will continue. But what will be their impact on our understanding of infancy? What *should* the impact be?

In an article on the future of the social and behavioral sciences (Smith & Torrey, 1996), two policy specialists suggested five general challenges to be considered. Although intended to have broad general significance for all social and behavioral sciences, these challenges speak clearly to the future of the study of infancy.

The first challenge is to integrate current data sets—to bring together, coordinate, and make available information that is already in existence. As we noted in Chapter 11, students of language development have begun this process with the CHILDES system (MacWhinney, 1994), which allows researchers access to many examples of early language.

The second challenge is to improve the coverage of longitudinal surveys. This is especially important from a dynamic systems perspective because longitudinal information helps us understand transitions such as phase shifts. More work is now being done longitudinally in areas such as motor development, which used to be studied primarily from a cross-sectional viewpoint. A special concern involves the resilience of infants.

A third challenge is to investigate new methodologies to study dynamic systems. Recent techniques such as video recording and MRI studies have already been helpful in providing information about rapid, subtle, but orderly events. An increased use of ethnography will also help place events within the cultural contexts that influence them.

A fourth challenge is to develop comparable international research to study behavioral and social phenomena. Cross-cultural comparisons are badly needed in many areas of infant development, and at this point the field is progressing very slowly. Work like the reports on caregiving among the Efe (Morelli & Tronick, 1991) is needed to keep us from being too bound by our own cultural perspective. We need to remember, too, that there are cross-cultural differences within a nation and that it would be a grave mistake to assume that all children in the United States are culturally the same.

The fifth challenge discussed by Smith and Torrey suggests the need to integrate qualitative and quantitative research methods more systematically, with the goal of advancing new theory. Qualitative information such as history should contribute to work on infant development. Qualitative approaches such as ethnography function to generate hypotheses (Casper, 1995/1996). At this point, however, infant development research tends to be haphazard at best in making the connections between qualitative and quantitative work.

A sixth challenge for future work on infant development may be to work more effectively toward practical applications of what is known. Education of the public and influences on law and policy are two types of practical applications. When pregnant women do not understand why drinking alcohol is a problem, when courts make unpredictable judgments about custody of infants, when adoptions are disrupted for lack of help—in all these circumstances, we see the need for effective application of what we already know about infant development.

In the final analysis, we may know that we have fully understood infant development when we can guide Bobby and his family to cope better with their lives and help Tiffany and her mother overcome the effects of the past trauma that still haunts them.

References

Abel, E. (1989). *Behavioral teratogenesis and behavioral mutagenesis.* New York: Plenum.

Abel, E., & Sokol, R. (1991). A revised conservative estimate of the incidence of FAS and its economic impact. *Alcoholism: Clinical and Experimental Research, 156,* 514–524.

Aber, J., & Baker, A. (1990). Security of attachment in toddlerhood: Modifying assessment procedures for joint clinical and research purposes. In M. Greenberg, D. Cicchetti, & E. Cummings (Eds.), *Attachment in the preschool years* (pp. 427–462). Chicago: University of Chicago Press.

Abramov, I., Gordon, J., et al. (1982). The retina of the newborn human infant. *Science, 217,* 265–267.

Abrams, B., & Laros, R. (1986). Prepregnancy weight, weight gain, and birth weight. *American Journal of Obstetrics and Gynecology, 154,* 503–508.

Achenbach, T., Edelbrock, C., & Howell, C. (1987). Empirically based assessment of the behavioral/emotional problems of 2- and 3-year-old children. *Journal of Abnormal Child Psychology, 15,* 629–650.

Adams, R., Maurer, D., & Davis, M. (1986). Newborns' discrimination of chromatic from achromatic stimuli. *Journal of Experimental Child Psychology, 41,* 267–281.

"A 'declaration of intent.' " (1987). *Pediatrics, 79*(3), A38.

Adler, N., David, H., Major, B., Roth, S., Russo, N., & Wyatt, G. (1990). Psychological responses after abortion. *Science, 248,* 41–44.

Adler, N., Keyes, S., & Robertson, P. (1991). Psychological issues in new reproductive technologies: Pregnancy-inducing technology and diagnostic screening. In J. Rodin & A. Collins (Eds.), *Women and new reproductive technologies* (pp. 111–134). Hillsdale, NJ: Erlbaum.

Ahlburg, D., & DeVita, C. (1992). New realities of the American family. *Population Bulletin, 47*(2), 1–44.

Ainsworth, M., Blehar, M., Waters, E., & Wall, S. (1978). *Patterns of attachment.* Hillsdale, NJ: Erlbaum.

Aitken, D., Wallace, E., Crossley, J., Swanston, I., van Pareren, Y., et al. (1996). Dimeric inhibin A as a marker for Down's syndrome in early pregnancy. *New England Journal of Medicine, 334*(19), 1231–1236.

Aldhous, P. (1993). Disease gene search goes big science. *Science, 259,* 591–592.

Aldhous, P. (1994). A booster for contraceptive vaccines. *Science, 266,* 1484–1486.

Allen, D., Banks, M., & Norcia, A. (1993). Does chromatic sensitivity develop more slowly than luminance sensitivity? *Vision Research, 33,* 2553–2562.

Allen, M. (1992). Developmental implications of intrauterine growth retardation. *Infants and Young Children, 5*(2), 12–28.

Als, H. (1985). Reciprocity and autonomy: parenting a blind infant. *Zero to Three, 5*(5), 8–10.

Altemeier, W., O'Connor, S., Sherrod, K., Yeager, T., & Vietze, P. (1985). A strategy for managing non-organic failure to thrive based on a prospective study of antecedents. In D. Drotar (Ed.), *New directions in failure to thrive* (pp. 211–222). New York: Plenum.

Altman, J. (1970). Postnatal neurogenesis and the problem of neural plasticity. In W. Himwich (Ed.), *Developmental neurobiology* (pp. 197–240). Springfield, IL: Charles C Thomas.

Altman, J. (1971). Nutritional deprivation and neural development. In M. Sterman, D. Mc Ginty, & A. Adinolfi (Eds.), *Brain development and behavior* (pp. 359–368). New York: Academic Press.

Altman, L. (1993, June 6). At AIDS talks, science confronts daunting maze. *New York Times,* p. 20.

American Academy of Pediatrics and American Society of Anesthesiologists Statement on Neonatal Anesthesia. (1987). *Pediatrics, 80,* 446.

Ames, L., & Ilg, F. (1964). The developmental point of view with special reference to the principle of reciprocal neuromotor interweaving. *Journal of Genetic Psychology, 105,* 195–209.

Amiel-Tison, C., & Grenier, A. (1986). *Neurological assessment during the first year of life.* New York: Oxford University Press.

Anand, K., Brown, M., Christofides, N., Bloom, S., & Aynsley-Green, A. (1985). Can the human neonate mount an endocrine and metabolic response to surgery? *Journal of Pediatric Surgery, 20,* 41–48.

Anders, T. (1975). The sleep of infants and children. *Sandorama, 3,* 20–23.

Anders, T., Halpern, L., & Hua, J. (1992). Sleeping through the night: A developmental perspective. *Pediatrics, 90,* 554–590.

Anderson, B. (1992). Effects of day-care on cognitive and socioemotional competence of thirteen-year-old Swedish schoolchildren. *Child Development, 63,* 20–36.

Anderson, C. (1993a). Healy stays, fetal tissue ban goes. *Science, 259,* 591.

Anderson, C. (1993b). Long live the lefties. *Science, 259,* 1118.

Anderson, J. (1972). Attachment behavior out of doors. In N. Jones (Ed.), *Ethological studies of child behavior* (pp. 199–216). Cambridge: Cambridge University Press.

Anderson, K. (1995). One signal, two body axes. *Science, 269,* 489–490.

Andreasen, N., Arndt, S., Swayze, V., Cizadlo, T., Flaum, M., O'Leary, D., et al. (1994). Thalamic abnormalities in schizophrenia visualized through magnetic resonance imaging. *Science, 266,* 294–297.

"A new prenatal screening program." (1987). *Harvard Medical School Health Letter, 12*(4), 6–8.

Angold, A. (1993). Why do we not know the cause of depression in children? In D. Hay & A. Angold (Eds.), *Precursors and causes in development and psychopathology* (pp. 265–292). New York: Wiley.

Anthony, B., & Graham, F. (1983). Evidence for sensory-selective set in young infants. *Science, 220,* 742–744.

Antonini, A., & Stryker, M. (1993). Rapid remodeling of axonal arbors in the visual cortex. *Science, 260,* 1819–1821.

Anzalone, M. (1993). Sensory contributions to action: A sensory integrative approach. *Zero to Three, 14*(2), 17–20.

Argenta, D. (1990). And baby makes two: Adoption and the single parent. *Zero to Three, 10*(5), 9–12.

Arnett, J. (1989). Issues and obstacles in the training of caregivers. In J. Lande, S. Scarr, & N. Gunzenhauser (Eds.), *Caring for children: Challenge to America* (pp. 241–256). Hillsdale, NJ: Erlbaum.

Artal, R., Wiswell, R., Romem, Y., & Dorey, F. (1986). Pulmonary responses to exercise in pregnancy. *American Journal of Obstetrics and Gynecology, 154,* 378–383.

Asendorpf, J., & Baudonnière, P. (1993). Self-awareness and other-awareness: Mirror self-recognition and synchronic imitation among unfamiliar peers. *Developmental Psychology, 29,* 88–95.

Aslin, R. (1977). Development of binocular fixation in human infants. *Journal of Experimental Child Psychology, 23,* 133–150.

Aslin, R. (1993). Commentary: The strange attractiveness of dynamic systems to development. In L. Smith & E. Thelen (Eds.), *A dynamic systems approach to development: Applications* (pp. 385–399). Cambridge: MIT Press.

Athey, J., & Kavanagh, L. (1991). Childhood burns: The preventable epidemic. *Zero to Three, 11*(5), 8–13.

Atkinson, J., & Braddick, O. (1981). Acuity, contrast sensitivity, and accommodation in infancy. In R. Aslin, J. Alberts, & M. Petersen (Eds.), *Development of perception: Vol. 2. The visual system* (pp. 245–278). New York: Academic Press.

Austin, J. (1962). *How to do things with words.* New York: Oxford University Press.

Avery, M., & Fletcher, B. (1974). *The lung and its disorders in the newborn infant.* Philadelphia: Saunders.

Axelrod, D. (1984). Breast-feeding: New York State's infant health strategy. In C. Koop (Ed.), *Report of the Surgeon General's Workshop on Breast-feeding and Human Lactation* (pp. 52–55). U.S. Department of Health and Human Services.

Baillargeon, R. (1994). How do infants learn about the physical world? *Current Directions in Psychological Science, 3*(5), 133–140.

Bairstow, P., & Laszlo, J. (1981). Kinaesthetic sensitivity to passive movements and its relationships to motor development and motor control. *Developmental Medicine and Child Neurology, 23,* 606–616.

Balaban, M. (1995). Affective influences on startle in five-month-old infants: Reactions to facial expressions of emotion. *Child Development, 66,* 28–36.

Baldwin, D. (1993). Early referential understanding: Infants' ability to recognize referential acts for what they are. *Developmental Psychology, 29,* 832–843.

Banks, M. (1982). The development of spatial and temporal contrast sensitivity. *Current Eye Research, 2,* 191–198.

Banks, M., & Salapatek, P. (1978). Acuity and contrast sensitivity in 1-, 2-, and 3-month-old infants. *Investigative Ophthalmology and Visual Science, 17,* 361–365.

Banks, M., & Salapatek, P. (1981). Infant pattern vision: A new approach based on the contrast sensitivity function. *Journal of Experimental Child Psychology, 31,* 1–45.

Banks, M., & Shannon, E. (1993). Spatial and chromatic visual efficiency in human neonates. In C. Granrud (Ed.), *Visual perception and cognition in infancy* (pp. 1–46). Hillsdale, NJ: Erlbaum.

Barglow, P. (1987). Some further comments about infant day-care research. *Zero to Three, 7*(5), 26–28.

Barinaga, M. (1991). The nose knows: Olfactory receptor cloned. *Science, 252,* 209–210.

Barinaga, M. (1992). The brain remaps its own contours. *Science, 258,* 216–220.

Barinaga, M. (1993a). Carbon monoxide: Killer to brain messenger in one step. *Science, 259,* 309.

Barinaga, M. (1993b). Death gives birth to the nervous system. But how? *Science, 259,* 762–763.

Barinaga, M. (1994). Looking to development's future. *Science, 266,* 561–564.

Barinaga, M. (1995). Shedding light on blindness. *Science, 267,* 452–453.

Barnes, D. (1986). Brain function decline in children with AIDS. *Science, 232,* 1196.

Baron-Cohen, S. (1993). From attention-goal psychology to belief-desire psychology: The development of a theory of mind, and its dysfunction. In S. Baron-Cohen, H. Tager-Flusberg, & D. Cohen (Eds.), *Understanding other minds* (pp. 59–82). New York: Oxford University Press.

Baron-Cohen, S., & Howlin, P. (1993). The theory of mind deficit in autism: Some questions for teaching and diagnosis. In S. Baron-Cohen, H. Tager-Flusberg, & D. Cohen (Eds.), *Understanding other minds* (pp. 228–291). New York: Oxford University Press.

Barr, R. (1990). Reduction of infant crying by parent carrying. In N. Gunzenhauser (Ed.), *Advances in touch* (pp. 105–116). Skillman, NJ: Johnson and Johnson.

Baskin, C., Umansky, W., & Sanders, W. (1987). Influencing the responsiveness of adolescent mothers to their infants. *Zero to Three, 8*(2), 7–11.

Bates, E., O' Connell, B., & Shore, C. (1987). Language and communication in infancy. In J. Osofsky (Ed.), *Handbook of infant development* (pp. 149–203). New York: Wiley.

Bates, E., & Snyder, L. (1987). The cognitive hypothesis of language development. In I. Uzgiris & J. Hunt (Eds.), *Infant performance and experience* (pp. 168–206). Urbana: University of Illinois Press.

Bates, J., Marvinney, D., Kelly, T., Dodge, M., Bennett, D., & Pettit, G. (1994). Child-care history and kindergarten adjustment. *Developmental Psychology, 30,* 690–700.

Bates, P., Reese, H., & Nesselroade, J. (1977). *Life-span developmental psychology: Introduction to research methods.* Pacific Grove, CA: Brooks/Cole,.

Bateson, G., & Mead, M. (1942). *Balinese character.* New York: New York Academy of Sciences.

Battle, J. (1994). Facts on: Adolescent substance abuse. *N.J. Alcohol/Drug Resources Center and Clearinghouse, Fact Sheet No. 26.*

Bauer, J., Shimojo, S., Gwiazda, J., & Held, R. (1986). Sex differences in the development of binocularity in human infants. *Investigative Ophthalmology and Visual Science, 27* (Suppl. 3), 265.

Bauer, P., & Dow, G. (1994). Episodic memory in 16- and 20-month-old children: Specifics are generalized but not forgotten. *Developmental Psychology, 30*, 403–417.

Bauer, P., & Mandler, J. (1992). Putting the horse before the cart: The use of temporal order in recall of events by one-year-old children. *Developmental Psychology, 28*, 441–452.

Bayley, N. (1969). *Scales of infant development.* New York: Psychological Corporation.

Becker, W. (1964). Consequences of different kinds of parental discipline. In M. Hoffman & L. Hoffman (Eds.), *Review of child development research* (Vol. I, pp. 169–208). New York: Russell Sage Foundation.

Beebe, S., Britton, J., Britton, H., Fan, P., & Jepson, B. (1996). Neonatal mortality and length of hospital stay. *Pediatrics, 98*(2), 231–235.

Beeghly, M., & Tronick, E. (1994). Effects of prenatal exposure to cocaine in early infancy: Toxic effects on the process of mutual regulation. *Infant Mental Health Journal, 15*, 158–175.

Behnke, M., & Eyler, F. (1994). Issues in prenatal cocaine use research: Problems in identifying and choosing an appropriate comparison group. *Infant Mental Health Journal, 15*, 146–157.

Bell, R., & Darling, J. (1965). The prone head reaction in the human newborn: A relationship with sex and tactile sensitivity. *Child Development, 36*, 943–949.

Belsky, J. (1986). Infant day care: a cause for concern? *Zero to Three, 6*(5), 1–7.

Belsky, J., & Braungart, J. (1991). Are insecure-avoidant infants with extensive day-care experience less stressed by and more independent in the strange situation? *Child Development, 62*, 567–571.

Bemporad, S. (1990). Promoting and safeguarding early relationships in child care: The Child Care Dallas Family Day Home System. *Zero to Three, 10*(1), 10–11.

Benson, A., & Lane, S. (1993). The developmental impact of low-level lead exposure. *Infants and Young Children, 6*(2), 41–51.

Berg, W., & Berg, K. (1987). Psychophysiological development in infancy: State, startle, and attention. In J. Osofsky (Ed.), *Handbook of infant development* (pp. 238–317). New York: Wiley.

Berman, B. (1993). Difficult and challenging behaviors in young children: A neurodevelopmental perspective for assessment and intervention. *Infants and Young Children, 6*(1), 26–84.

Berman, C. (1992). Part H coordinators: Stresses, satisfactions, and supports. *Zero to Three, 12*(1), 13–18.

Bernstein, N. (1967). *The coordination and regulation of movements.* New York: Pergamon.

Bertenthal, B., Campos, J., & Kermoian, R. (1994). An epigenetic perspective on the development of self-produced locomotion and its consequences. *Current Directions in Psychological Science, 3*(5), 140–145.

Bettelheim, B. (1969). *The children of the dream.* New York: Macmillan.

Bettes, B. (1988). Maternal depression and motherese: Temporal and intonational features. *Child Development, 59*, 1089–1096.

Bhatt, R. & Rovee-Collier, C. (1994). Perception and 24-hour retention of feature relations in infancy. *Developmental Psychology, 30*, 142–150.

Birch, L., & Marlin, D. (1982). I don't like it; I never tried it: Effects of exposure on two-year-old children's food preferences. *Appetite, 3*, 353–360.

Bittles, A., Mason, W., Greene T, & Rao, N. (1991). Reproductive behavior and health in consanquineous marriages. *Science, 252,* 789–794.

Black, F. (1992). Why did they die? *Science, 258,* 1739–1740.

"Black infant mortality still more than whites'." (1994, April 30). *The Press of Atlantic City,* p. A10.

Blakemore, C. (1989). Principles of development in the nervous system. In C. von Euler, H. Forssberg, & H. Lagerkrantz (Eds.), *Neurobiology of early infant behavior* (pp. 7–18). New York: Stockton Press.

Blank, H. (1989). Child care: Issues at the state level. In J. Lande, S. Scarr, & N. Gunzenhauser (Eds.), *Caring for children: Challenge to America* (pp. 139–152). Hillsdale, NJ: Erlbaum.

Blank, R. (1992). Rationing medicine in the Neonatal Intensive Care Unit (NICU). In A. Caplan, R. Blank, & J. Merrick (Eds.), *Compelled compassion* (pp. 155–184). Totowa, NJ: Humana.

Blass, E. (1989). Opioid and nonopioid influences on behavioral development in rat and human infants. In C. von Euler, H. Forssberg, & H. Lagerkrantz (Eds.), *Neurobiology of early infant behavior* (pp. 237–248). New York: Stockton Press.

Blass, E., & Smith, B. (1992). Differential effects of sucrose, fructose, glucose, and lactose on crying in 1- to 3-day-old human infants: Qualitative and quantitative considerations. *Developmental Psychology, 28,* 804–810.

Bloch, M. (1992). Tobacco control advocacy: Winning the war on tobacco. *Zero to Three, 13*(1), 24–27.

Bloom, P. (1990). Syntactic distinctions in child speech. *Journal of Child Language, 17,* 343–356.

Bopp, J., & Nimz, M. (1992). A legal analysis of the Child Abuse Amendments of 1984. In A. Kaplan, R. Blank, & J. Merrick (Eds.)., *Compelled compassion* (pp. 73–104). Totowa, NJ: Humana Press.

Boswell, J. (1988). *The kindness of strangers.* New York: Vintage.

Boukydis, C., & Moses, L. (1995). Establishing and maintaining a parenting network for parents of premature/high risk infants. *Infants and Young Children, 7*(4), 77–87.

Bower, T. (1982). *Development in infancy.* San Francisco: Freeman.

Bower, T. (1989). *The rational infant.* New York: Freeman.

Brams, J., & Coury, D. (1985). Exploring some "myths" of failure to thrive: A brief guide for diagnosis and management. *Zero to Three, 5*(3), 21–22.

Braun, S. (1996). New experiments underscore warnings on maternal drinking. *Science, 273,* 738–739.

Bray, D., & White, J. (1988). Cortical flow in animal cells. *Science, 239,* 883–888.

Brazelton, T. (1962). Crying in infancy. *Pediatrics, 29,* 579–588.

Brazelton, T. (1984). *Neonatal Behavioral Assessment Scale.* (Spastics International Medical Publications). Philadelphia: Lippincott.

Brazelton, T. (1990). On adoption. *Zero to Three, 10*(5), 5–8.

Bredberg, G. (1985). The anatomy of the developing ear. In S. Trehub & B. Schneider (Eds.), *Auditory development in infancy* (pp. 3–20). New York: Plenum.

Broberg, A., Lamb, M., & Hwang, P. (1990). Inhibition: Its stability and correlates in sixteen- to forty-month-old children. *Child Development, 61,* 1153–1163.

Bromwich, R. (1985). "Vulnerable infants" and "risky environments." *Zero to Three, 6*(2), 7–12.

Brown, S., & Valluzzi, J. (1995). Do not resuscitate orders in early intervention settings: Who should make the decision? *Infants and Young Children, 7*(3), 13–27.

Bruner, J. (1969). Eye, hand, and mind. In D. Elkind & J. Flavell (Eds.), *Studies in cognitive development: Essays in honor of Jean Piaget* (pp. 223–236). New York: Oxford University Press.

Brunner, H., Nelen, M., Breakefield, X., Ropers, H., & van Oost, B. (1993). Abnormal behavior associated with a point mutation in the structural gene for monoamine oxidase A. *Science, 262,* 578–580.

Brunswik, E. (1955). Representative design and probabilistic theory in a functional psychology. *Psychological Review, 62,* 193–217.

Buchwald, J. (1987). A comparison of plasticity in sensory and cognitive processing systems. In N. Gunzenhauser (Ed.), *Infant stimulation.* Skillman, NJ: Johnson and Johnson.

Bundey, S., Hardy, C., Vickers, S., Kilpatrick, M., and Corbett, J. (1994). Duplication of the 15q 11-13 region in a patient with autism, epilepsy, and ataxia. *Developmental Medicine and Child Neurology, 36,* 736–742.

Burke, B. (1989, Nov. 5.). A moral burden (letter). *New York Times,* Section H, p. 3.

Burton, B., Schulz, C., & Burd, L. (1993). Spectrum of limb disruption defects associated with chorionic villus sampling. *Pediatrics, 92,* 989–993.

Butterfield, E. (1981). Behavioral assessment of infants' hearing. In D. Radcliffe (Ed.), *Development disabilities in the preschool child* (pp. 16–19). New York: SP Medical and Scientific Books.

Butterworth, G. (1990a). Self-perception in infancy. In D. Cicchetti & M. Beeghly (Eds.), *The self in transition* (pp. 119–138). Chicago: University of Chicago Press.

Butterworth, G. (1990b). On reconceptualizing sensorimotor development in dynamic systems terms. In H. Bloch & B. Bertenthal (Eds.), *Sensory-motor organizations and development in infancy and early childhood* (pp. 57–74). Dordrecht, Netherlands: Kluwer.

Butterworth, G. (1993). Dynamic approaches to infant perception and action: Old and new theories about the origins of knowledge. In L. Smith & E. Thelen (Eds.), *A dynamic systems approach to development: Applications* (pp. 171–188). Cambridge, MA: MIT Press.

Butterworth, G., & Hicks, L. (1977). Visual proprioception and postural stability in infancy: A developmental study. *Perception, 6,* 255–262.

Butz, A., Fosarelli, P., Dick, J., Cusack, T., & Yolken, R. (1993). Prevalence of rotavirus on high-risk fomites in day-care facilities. *Pediatrics, 92,* 202–205.

Caiani-Praturlon, G. (1991). Inter-country adoption in European legislation. In E. Hibbs (Ed.), *Adoption: International perspectives* (pp. 205–214). Madison, CN: International Universities Press.

Caldwell, B. (1991). Educare: new product, new future. *Developmental and Behavioral Pediatrics, 12,* 199–204.

Caldwell, B., & Bradley, R. (1984). *Manual for the Home Observation for Measurement of the Environment.* Little Rock: University of Arkansas Press.

Caldwell, M., Fleming, P., & Oxtoby, M. (1992). Estimated number of AIDS orphans in the United States. *Pediatrics, 90*, 402.

Calem, R. (1993, April 18). Working at home, for better or worse. *New York Times,* Section 3, pp. 1, 6.

Calvin, M., Lester, B., Sepkoski, C., McLaughlin, S., Kayne, H., & Golub, H. (1992). Effects of in utero cocaine exposure on newborn acoustical cry characteristics. *Pediatrics, 89*, 1199–1203.

Campbell, A. (1992). Baby Doe and forgoing life-sustaining treatment. In A. Caplan, R. Blank, & J. Merrick (Ed.), *Compelled compassion* (pp. 207–236). Totowa, NJ: Humana.

Campbell, S., Cohn, J., & Meyers, T. (1995). Depression in first-time mothers: Mother-infant interaction and depression chronicity. *Developmental Psychology, 31*, 349–357.

Campos, R. (1988). Comfort measures for infant pain. *Zero to Three, 9*(2), 6–13.

Canfield, R., & Smith, E. (1996). Number-based expectations and sequential enumeration by 5-month-old infants. *Developmental Psychology, 32*(2), 269–279.

Caplan, A. (1992). Hard cases make bad law. In A. Caplan, R. Blank, & J. Merrick (Eds.), *Compelled compassion* (pp. 105–122). Totowa, NJ: Humana.

Caplan, M., Vespo, J., Pedersen, J., & Hay, D. (1991). Conflict and its resolution in small groups of one- and two-year-olds. *Child Development, 62*, 1513–1524.

Carney, P., Freeman, R., Mc Murrain, D., Slavin, M., & Ueland, K. (1980). Working in pregnancy. *Contemporary Ob/Gyn, 16*, 154–166.

Cartmill, M. (1995). Significant others (book reviews). *Natural History, 104*(6), 74–77.

Case-Smith, J. (1996). Analysis of current motor development theory and recently published infant assessments. *Infants and Young Children, 9*(1), 29–41.

Casey, P., Collie, W., & Blakemore, W. (1985). Zinc nutrition in children who fail to thrive. In D. Drotar (Ed.), *New directions in failure to thrive* (pp. 77–86). New York: Plenum.

Casper, V. (1995/1996). Making familiar unfamiliar and unfamiliar familiar. *Zero to Three, 16*(3), 14–20.

Chang, H., & Pulido, D. (1994). The critical importance of cultural and linguistic continuity for infants and toddlers. *Zero to Three, 15*(2), 13–17.

Changeux, J. (1985). *Neuronal man.* New York: Pantheon.

Charleza-McGoldrick, M. (1994). Dilation and curettage (D and C). In M. Gulanick, M. Puzas, D. Gradishar, & K. Gettrust (Eds.), *Obstetric and gynecologic nursing* (pp. 115–119). Albany, NY: Delmar.

Chartrand, S. (1992, March 29). Legal definition of death as challenged in Florida infant case. *New York Times,* p. 12.

Chatoor, I. (1986). *Mother-infant/toddler feeding scale.* Washington, DC: Children's Hospital Medical Center.

Chatoor, I., & Dickson, L. (1984). Rumination: A maladaptive attempt at self-regulation in infants and children. *Clinical Proceedings, Children's Hospital National Medical Center, 40*, 107–116.

Chatoor, I., Schaefer, S., Dickson, L., & Egan, J. (1985). A developmental approach to feeding disturbances: Failure to thrive and growth disorders in infants and young children. *Zero to Three, 5*(3), 12–16.

Chen, E. (1995, Nov. 1). Ban on late-abortion method eyed. *Philadelphia Inquirer.*

Chenoweth, P. (1992, July 6). Two cases seek to clarify use of psychological-parenting theories. *New Jersey Law Journal, 131,* 37–41.

Chess, S. (1983). Basic adaptations required for successful parenting. In V. Sasserath (Ed.), *Minimizing high-risk parenting* (pp. 5–10). Skillman, NJ: Johnson and Johnson.

Child Abuse Amendments of 1984, Pub. L. No. 98–457, 98 Stat. 1749 (codified in scattered sections of 42 U.S.C.).

Child Abuse Prevention Challenge Grants Reauthorization Act of 1989, Pub. L. No. 101–126 (codified as amended in scattered sections of 42 U.S.C.).

Chomsky, N. (1965). *Aspects of the theory of syntax.* Cambridge, MA: MIT Press.

Chung, A. (1979). Breast-feeding in a developing country: The People's Republic of China. In D. Raphael (Ed.), *Breast-feeding and food policy in a hungry world* (pp. 81–86). New York: Academic Press.

Cicchetti, D., Cummings, E., Greenberg, M., & Marvin, R. (1990). An organizational perspective on attachment beyond infancy. In M. Greenberg, D. Cicchetti, & E. Cummings (Eds.), *Attachment in the preschool years* (pp. 3–50). Chicago: University of Chicago Press.

Cioni, G., & Castellacci, A. (1990). Development of fetal and neonatal motor activity: Implications for neurology. In H. Bloch & B. Bertenthal (Eds.), *Sensory-motor organizations and development in infancy and early childhood* (pp. 135–144). Dordrecht, Netherlands: Kluwer.

Cioni, G., & Prechtl, H. (1989). Development of posture and motility in preterm infants. In C. von Euler, H. Forssberg, & H. Lagercrantz (Eds.), *Neurobiology of early infant behavior* (pp. 69–78). New York: Stockton Press.

Clapp, J. (1985). Fetal heart rate response to running in midpregnancy and late pregnancy. *American Journal of Obstetrics and Gynecology, 153,* 251–252.

Clark, A. (1979). Application of psychosocial concepts. In A. Clark, D. Affonso, & T. Harris (Eds.), *Childbearing: A nursing perspective* (pp. 323–344). Philadelphia: Davis.

Clark, R., Keller, A., Fedderly, S., & Paulson, A. (1993). Treating the relationships affected by postpartum depression: A group therapy model. *Zero to Three, 13*(5), 16–23.

Clark, T., & Whittal, J. (1989). Changing patterns of locomotion: From walking to skipping. In M. Woollacott & A. Shumway-Cook (Eds.), *Development of posture and gait across the life span* (pp. 128–154). Columbia: University of South Carolina Press.

Clarkson, M., & Berg, W. (1983). Cardiac deceleration and vowel discrimination in newborns: Crucial parameters of acoustic stimuli. *Child Development, 54,* 162–171.

Clarkson, R., Vohr, B., Blackwell, P., & White, K. (1994). Universal infant hearing screening and prevention: The Rhode Island program. *Infants and Young Children, 6*(3), 65–74.

Clavedetscher, J., Brown, A., Ankrum, C., & Teller, D. (1988). Spectral sensitivity and chromatic discriminations in 3- and 7-week-old human infants. *Journal of the Optical Society of America, 5,* 2093–2105.

Clifton, R. (1985). The precedence effect: Its implications for developmental questions. In S. Trehub & B. Schneider (Eds.), *Auditory development in infancy* (pp. 85–100). New York: Plenum.

Coe, C., Rosenberg, L., Fischer, M., & Levine, S. (1987). Psychological factors capable of preventing the inhibition of antibody responses in separated infant monkeys. *Child Development, 58,* 1420–1430.

Cohen, C., & Jonsen, A. (1993). The future of the fetal tissue bank. *Science, 262,* 1663–1665.

Cohen, J. (1996a). Does nature drive nurture? *Science, 273,* 577–578.

Cohen, J. (1996b). Likely HIV cofactor found. *Science, 272,* 809–810.

Cohen, J. (1992). Pediatric AIDS trials set. *Science, 258,* 1568–1570.

Cohen, M., & Roessmann, V. (1994). *In utero* brain damage: Relationship of gestational age to pathological consequences. *Developmental Medicine and Child Neurology, 36,* 263–268.

Cohler, B. (1984). Parenthood, psychopathology, and child care. In R. Cohen, B. Cohler, & S. Weissman (Eds.), *Parenthood* (pp. 119–147). New York: Guilford.

Cole, J., Begish Duddy, A., Judas, M., & Jorgensen, K. (1990). Changing the NICU environment: The Boston City Hospital model. *Neonatal Network, 9*(2), 15–23.

Collis, G. (1985). On the origins of turn-taking: Alternation and meaning. In M. Barrett (Ed.), *Children's single-word speech* (pp. 217–230). New York: Wiley.

Committee on Psychosocial Aspects of Child and Family Health, 1985–1988. (1988). *Guidelines for health supervision II.* Elk Grove, IL: American Academy of Pediatrics.

Condon, W., & Sanders, L. (1974). Neonate movement is synchronized with adult speech: Interactional participation and language acquisition. *Science, 183,* 99–101.

Constantino, J. (1992). On the prevention of conduct disorder: A rationale for preventive efforts in infancy. *Infants and Young Children, 5*(2), 29–41.

Cook, M., & Birch, R. (1984). Infant perception of the shapes of tilted plane forms. *Infant Behavior and Development, 7,* 389–402.

Cooley, L., & Therkauf, W. (1994). Cytoskeletal functions during drosophila oögenesis. *Science, 266,* 590–596.

Cooley, W., Andrew, C., Berg, S., Fisher-Sass, T., et al. (1993). Family planning and disability: Issues in family-centered care. *Zero to Three, 13*(6), 12–17.

Corwin, C., Lester, B., Sepkoski, C., McLaughlin, S., Kayne, H., & Golub, H. (1992). Effects of in utero cocaine exposure on newborn acoustical cry characteristics. *Pediatrics, 89,* 1199–1203.

Courage, M., Adams, R., Reyno, S., & Kwa, P. (1994). Visual acuity in infants and children with Down syndrome. *Developmental Medicine and Child Neurology, 36,* 586–593.

Court, J., Perry, E., Johnson, M., Kerwin, J., Perry, R., & Ince, P. (1993). Regional patterns of cholinergic and glutamate activity in the developing and aging human brain. *Developmental Brain Research, 74,* 73–82.

Cox, M., Owen, M., Lewis, J., & Henderson, V. (1989). Marriage, adult adjustment, and early parenting. *Child Development, 60,* 1015–1024.

Cratty, B. (1981). Sensory-motor and perceptual-motor theories and practices: An overview and evaluation. In R. Walk & H. Pick (Eds.), *Intersensory perception and sensory integration* (pp. 345–374). New York: Plenum.

Crawford, M., Smith, E., Harwerth, R., & van Noorden, G. (1984). Stereoblind monkeys have few binocular neurons. *Investigative Ophthalmology and Vision. Science, 25,* 779–781.

Crease, R. (1993). Biomedicine in the age of imaging. *Science, 261*, 554–561.

Crockenberg, S. (1992). How children learn to resolve conflicts in families. *Zero to Three, 12*(4), 11–13.

Crockenberg, S., & Litman, C. (1991). Effects of maternal employment on maternal and two-year-old child behavior. *Child Development, 62*, 930–953.

Cross, J., Werb, Z., & Fisher, S. (1994). Implantation and the placenta: key pieces of the development puzzle. *Science, 266*, 1508–1519.

"CSBS normed edition released" (1993). *ECOletter, 3*(1), 1, 7–8.

Cumming, D., Vickovic, M., Wall, S., Fluker, M., & Belcastro, A. (1985). The effect of acute exercise on pulsatile release of luteinizing hormone in women runners. *American Journal of Obstetrics and Gynecology, 153*, 482–485.

Cummings, E. (1995). Security, emotionality, and parental depression: A commentary. *Developmental Psychology, 31*, 425–527.

Cummings, E., & Cicchetti, D. (1990). Toward a transactional model of relations between attachment and depression. In M. Greenberg, D. Cicchetti, & E. Cummings (Eds.), *Attachment in the preschool years* (pp. 339–374). Chicago: University of Chicago Press.

Cundiff-Stith, D. (1995, Jan.). Overcoming feelings of isolation. *Scholastic Early Childhood Today, 28*, 28.

Curtiss, S. (1977). *Genie: A psycholinguistic study of a modern-day "wild child."* New York: Academic Press.

Darrah, J., & Bartlett, D. (1995). Dynamic systems theory and management of children with cerebral palsy: Unresolved issues. *Infants and Young Children, 8*(1), 52–59.

Davidson, R., & Fox, N. (1982). Asymmetrical brain activity discriminates between positive versus negative stimuli in human infants. *Science, 218*, 1235–1237.

Davidson, R., & Fox, N. (1989). Frontal brain asymmetry predicts infants' response to maternal separation. *Journal of Abnormal Psychology, 98*, 127–131.

Davis, M., & Emory, E. (1995). Sex differences in neonatal stress reactivity. *Child Development, 66*, 14–27.

DeCasper, A., & Fifer, W. (1980). Of human bonding: Newborns prefer their mothers' voices. *Science, 208*, 1174–1176.

DeGangi, G., Di Pietro, J., Greenspan, S., & Porges, S. (1991). Psychophysiological characteristics of the regulatory disordered infant. *Infant Behavior and Development, 14*, 27–50.

DeGangi, G., & Greenspan, S. (1990). Affect/interaction skills. In C. Royeen (Ed.), *Neuroscience foundations of human performance.* Rockville, MD: American Occupational Therapy Association.

DeGangi, G., & Porges, S. (1990). Attention/alertness/arousal. In C. Royeen (Ed.), *Neuroscience foundations of human performance.* Rockville, MD.: American Occupational Therapy Association.

Dekaban, A. (1970). *Neurology of early childhood.* Baltimore: Williams & Wilkins.

DeMause, L. (1974). The evolution of childhood. In L. DeMause (Ed.), *The history of childhood* (pp. 1–74). New York: The Psychohistory Press.

de Michelena, M., Burstein, E., Lama, J., & Vasquez, J. (1993). Paternal age as a risk factor for Down syndrome. *American Journal of Medical Genetics, 45*, 679–682.

De Palma, A. (1989, Dec. 3). New incentives offered to foster parents. *New York Times,* Section 11, p. 4.

de Schonen, S., & Mathivet, E. (1989). First come, first served: A scenario about the development of hemispheric specialization in face recognition. *Cahiers de Psychologie Cognitive, 9*(1), 3–44.

de Schonen, S., & Mathivet, E. (1990). Hemispheric asymmetry in a face discrimination task in infants. *Child Development, 61,* 1192–1205.

Diagnostic Classification Task Force, Zero to Three (National Center for Clinical Infant Programs). (1994). *Diagnostic classification: 0–3.* Arlington, VA: National Center for Clinical Infant Programs.

Diamond, A., Gruttenden, L., & Neiderman, D. (1994). $\overline{AB}$ with multiple wells: 1) Why are multiple wells sometimes easier than two wells? 2) Memory or memory + inhibition? *Developmental Psychology, 30,* 195–205.

Diamond, J. (1991). Pearl Harbor and the emperor's physiologists. *Natural History, 12*(1), 2–7.

DiDomenico, C. & Asuni, J. (1979). Breast-feeding practices among urban women in Ibadan, Nigeria. In D. Raphael (Ed.), *Breast-feeding and food policy in a hungry world* (pp. 51–58). New York: Academic Press.

Diefendorf, A., Reitz, P., & Cox, J. (1992). The Joint Committee on Infant Hearing 1990 position statement: A closer look. *Infants and Young Children, 5,* v–xi.

Dienske, H. (1984). Early development of motor abilities, daytime sleep, and social interactions in the rhesus monkey, chimpanzee, and man. In H. Prechtl (Ed.), *Continuity of neural functions from prenatal to postnatal life* (pp. 126–143). Philadelphia: Lippincott.

Dietz, V., & Horstmann, G. (1991). Afferent control of posture. In J. Requin & G. Stelmach (Eds.), *Tutorials in Motor Neuroscience* (pp. 209–222). NATO ASI series. Series D: Behavioral and Social Sciences (Vol. 62). Dordrecht, Netherlands: Kluwer.

Dix, D. (1990). Infants and children with acquired immunodeficiency syndrome: Placement in adoption and foster care. *Pediatrics, 85,* 388.

Dixon, S. (1994). Neurological consequences of prenatal stimulant drug exposure. *Infant Mental Health Journal, 15,* 134–145.

Dobbing, J. (1970). Undernutrition and the developing brain. In W. Himwich (Ed.), *Developmental neurobiology* (pp. 241–261). Springfield, IL.: Charles C Thomas.

Dobson, V. (1993). Commentary: Extending the ideal observer approach. In C. Granrud (Ed.), *Visual perception and cognition in infancy* (pp. 317–332). Hillsdale, NJ: Erlbaum.

Dobson, V., & Teller, D. (1978). Visual acuity in human infants: A review and comparison of behavioral and electrophysiological studies. *Vision Research, 18,* 1469–1483.

Dodd, B. (1979), Lip reading in infants: Attention to speech presented in- and out-of-synchrony. *Cognitive Psychology, 11,* 478–484.

D'Odorico, L. (1984). Nonsegmental features in prelinguistic communications; an analysis of some types of infant cry and noncry vocalizations. *Journal of Child Language, 11,* 17–27.

Döppke, S. (1992). *One parent, one language.* Philadelphia: Benjamins.

Dorozynski, A. (1991). Privacy rules blindside French glaucoma effort. *Science, 252,* 369–370.

Dreher, M., Nugent, K., & Hudgkins, R. (1994). Prenatal marijuana exposure and neonatal outcomes in Jamaica: An ethnographic study. *Pediatrics, 93,* 254–260.

Drell, M., Siegel, C., & Gaensbauer, T. (1993). Post-traumatic stress disorder. In C. Zeanah (Ed.), *Handbook of infant mental health* (pp. 291–304). New York: Guilford.

"Drinking, female sexuality, and AIDS: Cultural beliefs and research" (1994). *N.J. Collegiate Bulletin, 3*(4), 1–2.

"Drug abuse's most innocent victims" (1989, May). *CDF Reports,* 4–5.

Dubowitz, L., Dubowitz, V., & Goldberg, C. (1970). Clinical assessment of gestational age in the newborn infant. *Journal of Pediatrics, 77,* 1–10.

Duncan, B., Ey, J., Holberg, C., Martinez, F., & Taussig, L. (1993). Exclusive breast-feeding for at least 4 months protects against *otitis media. Pediatrics, 91,* 867–872.

Dunham, P., & Dunham, F. (1990). Effects of mother-infant social interactions on infants' subsequent contingency task performance. *Child Development, 61,* 785–793.

"Early identification of children at risk: An interview with Amy Miller Wetherby." (1993). *ECOletter, 3*(1), 1–2, 10, 16.

Easterbrooks, M., & Goldberg, W. (1990). Security of toddler-parent attachment. In M. Greenberg, D. Cicchetti, & E. Cummings (Eds.), *Attachment in the preschool years* (pp. 221–244). Chicago: University of Chicago Press.

Eckholm, E., & Tierney, J. (1990, Sept. 16). AIDS in Africa: a killer rages. *New York Times,* sec. 1, p. 1.

Egeland, B., & Hiester, M. (1995). The long-term consequences of infant day-care and mother-infant attachment. *Child Development, 66*(2), 474–485.

Einfeld, S., & Hall, W. (1994). When is a behavioral phenotype not a phenotype? *Developmental Medicine and Child Neurology, 36,* 467–470.

Ekman, P., Levenson, R., & Friesen, W. (1985). Autonomic nervous system activity distinguishes among emotions. *Science, 221,* 1208–1210.

Elias, M., Nicolson, N., Bora, C., & Johnston, J. (1986). Sleep/wake patterns of breast-fed babies in the first two years of life. *Pediatrics, 77,* 322–329.

Elkind, D. (1981). *The hurried child.* Reading, MA.: Addison-Wesley.

Ellison, P., & Lager, C. (1986). Moderate recreational running is associated with lowered salivary progesterone profiles in women. *American Journal of Obstetrics and Gynecology, 154,* 1000–1003.

Ellsworth, C., Muir, D., & Haines, S. (1993). Social competence and person-object differentiation: An analysis of the still-face effect. *Developmental Psychology, 29,* 63–73.

Emde, R. (1987). Infant mental health: Clinical dilemmas, the expansion of meaning, and opportunities. In J. Osofsky (Ed.), *Handbook of infant development* (pp. 1297–1320). New York: Wiley.

Emde, R., & Buchsbaum, H. (1990). "Didn't you hear my mommy?" Autonomy *with* connectedness in moral self emergence. In D. Cicchetti & M. Beeghly (Eds.), *The self in transition* (pp. 35–60). Chicago: University of Chicago Press.

Emde, R., Gaensbauer, T., & Harmon, R. (1976). Emotional expression in infancy: A biobehavioral study. *Psychological Issues, 10,* No. 1.

Emde, R., Plomin, R., Robinson, J., Corley, R., De Fries, J., Fulker, D., Resnick, J., et al. (1992). Temperament, emotion, and recognition at 14 months: The MacArthur Longitudinal Twin Study. *Child Development, 63,* 1437–1455.

Erikson, E. (1968). *Identity, youth, and crisis.* New York: Norton.

Erwin, E. (1994). Social competence in young children with visual impairments. *Infants and young children, 6*(3), 26–33.

Estok, P., & Rudy, E. (1984). Intensity of jogging: Relationship with menstrual/reproductive variables. *Journal of Obstetric, Gynecologic, and Neonatal Nursing, 13,* 390–399.

Evans, L. (1990). Impact of infant massage on the neonate and the parent-infant relationship. In N. Gunzenhauser (Ed.), *Advances in touch* (pp. 71–79). Skillman, NJ: Johnson and Johnson.

Faden, R. (1991). Autonomy, choice, and the new reproductive technologies: The role of informed consent in prenatal genetic diagnosis. In J. Rodin & A. Collins (Eds.), *Women and new reproductive technologies* (pp. 37–48). Hillsdale, NJ: Erlbaum.

Fagot, B., & Kavanagh, K. (1990). The prediction of antisocial behavior from avoidant attachment classification. *Child Development, 61,* 864–872.

Fantz, R. (1964). Visual experience in infants: Decreased attention to familiar patterns relative to novel ones. *Science, 146,* 668–670.

Farel, A., Freeman, V., Keenan, N., & Huber, C. (1991). Interaction between high-risk infants and their mothers: the NCAST as an assessment tool. *Research in Nursing and Health, 14,* 109–118.

Farrel, P., & Hooper, C. (1995). Biological limits to behavioral recovery following injury to the central nervous system: Implications for early intervention. *Infants and Young Children, 8*(1), 1–7.

Farr, C., & Goodfellow, P. (1992). Hidden messages in genetic maps. *Science, 258,* 49.

Feagans, L., Kipp, E., & Blood, I. (1994). The effects of otitis media on the attention skills of day-care-attending toddlers. *Developmental Psychology, 30,* 701–708.

Feinberg, E. (1992). The long aftermath: Ethical dilemmas in resource allocation posed by the care of medically fragile young children. *Zero to Three, 12*(3), 27–31.

Fenichel, E. (1992). Editor's note. *Zero to Three, 13*(2), 3.

Field, T. (1985). Attachment a psychobiological attunement: Being on the same wavelength. In M. Reite & T. Field (Eds.), *The psychobiology of attachment and separation* (pp. 415–454). New York: Wiley.

Field, T. (1986). Affective responses to separation. In T. Brazelton & M. Yogman (Eds.), *Affective development in infancy* (pp. 125–144). Norwood, NJ: Ablex.

Field, T. (1987). Affective and interactive disturbances in infants. In J. Osofsky (Ed.), *Handbook of infant development* (pp. 972–1005). New York: Wiley.

Field, T. (1989). Maternal depression effects on infant interaction and attachment behavior. In D. Cicchetti (Ed.), *The emergence of a discipline: The Rochester Symposium on developmental psychopathology* (Vol. I, pp. 139–164). Hillsdale, NJ: Erlbaum.

Field, T. (1991a). Quality infant day-care and grade school behavior and performance. *Child Development, 62,* 863–870.

Field, T. (1991b). Young children's adaptations to repeated separations from their mothers. *Child Development, 62,* 539–547.

Field, T. (1993). Infant massage. *Zero to Three, 14*(2), 8–12.

Field, T., & Goldson, E. (1984). Pacifying effects of nonnutritive sucking on term and pre-term neonates during heelstick procedures. *Pediatrics, 74,* 1012–1015.

Field, T., & Schanberg, S. (1990). Massage alters growth and catecholamine production in preterm newborns. In N. Gunzenhauser (Ed.), *Advances in touch* (pp. 96–104). Skillman, NJ: Johnson and Johnson.

Field, T., Schanberg, S., Scafidi, F., Bauer, C., Vega-Lahr, N., Garcia, R., Nystrom, J., & Kuhn, C. (1986). Tactile/kinesthetic stimulation effects on pre-term neonates. *Pediatrics, 77*(5), 654–658.

Field, T., Woodson, R., Greenberg, R., & Cohen, D. (1982). Discrimination and imitation of facial expressions by newborns. *Science, 218,* 179–181.

Fildes, V. (1988). *Wet nursing.* New York: Blackwell.

Finney, J., Brown, G., & Syme, S. (1992). *Conceptual and methodological issues for behavioral pediatrics and the facilitating environment.* New York: International Universities Press.

"First pre-pregnancy Tay-Sachs screened baby born." (1994, Feb. 24.) *The Press of Atlantic City.*

Fish, M., Stiften, C., & Belsky, J. (1991). Conditions of continuity and discontinuity in infant negative emotionality: Newborn to five months. *Child Development, 62,* 1525–1537.

Fitzgerald, K., & Needlman, R. (1991). Reach Out and Read: A pediatric program to support emergent literacy. *Zero to Three, 10*(4), 17–20.

Flamm, F. (1993). Why map Y? *Science, 261,* 679.

Fleischman, A. (1986). The immediate impact of the birth of a low birth weight baby on the family. *Zero to Three, 6*(4), 1–5.

Fogel, A. (1990). Sensorimotor factors in communicative development. In H. Bloch & B. Bertenthal (Eds.), *Sensory-motor organizations and development in infancy and early childhood* (pp. 75–88). Dordrecht, Netherlands: Kluwer.

Fonagy, R., Steele, H., & Steele, M. (1991). Maternal representations of attachment during pregnancy predict the organization of infant mother attachment at one year of age. *Child Development, 62,* 891–905.

Forest, M., Cathiard, A., & Bertrand, J. (1973). Evidence of testicular activity in early infancy. *Journal of Clinical Endocrinology and Metabolism, 37,* 148–150.

Forge, A., Li, L. Corwin, J., & Nevill, G. (1993). Ultrastructural evidence for hair cell regeneration in the mammalian inner ear. *Science, 259,* 1616–1619.

Fox, R., Anderson, R., Fox, T., & Rodriguez, M. (1991, Sept.). STAR parenting: A model for helping parents effectively deal with behavioral difficulties. *Young Children,* 54–60.

Fraiberg, S., Adelson, E., & Shapiro, V. (1975). Ghosts in the nursery: A psychoanalytic approach to the problems of impaired infant-mother relationships. *Journal of the American Academy of Child Psychiatry, 14,* 387–421.

Frank, D., Allen, D., & Brown, J. (1985). Primary prevention of failure to thrive. In D. Drotar (Ed.), *New directions in failure to thrive* (pp. 337–358). New York: Plenum.

Frank, E., & Rowe, D. (1990). Preventive-intervention groups with adoptive parents and their babies: Minimizing the risks to emotional development in the first three years. *Zero to Three, 10*(5), 19–25.

Frasier, L., Bachman, V., & Alexander, R. (1992). Physical and behavioral signs of sexual abuse in infants and toddlers. *Infants and Young Children, 5*(2), 1–12.

Freed, D., & Walker, T. (1988). Family law in the fifty states: An overview. *Family Law Quarterly, 21*, 417–572.

Freel, K. (1995/1996). Finding complexities and balancing perspectives: using an ethnographic viewpoint to understand children and their families. *Zero to Three, 16*(3), 1–7.

Freeman, B. (1993). The syndrome of autism: Update and guidelines for diagnosis. *Infants and Young Children, 6*(2), 1–11.

Freedman, D. (1974). *Human infancy: An evolutionary perspective.* Hillsdale, NJ: Erlbaum.

Freier, K. (1994). In utero drug exposure and maternal-infant interaction: The complexities of the dyad and their environment. *Infant Mental Health Journal, 15*, 176–188.

Freund, L. (1994). Diagnosis and developmental issues for young children with fragile X syndrome. *Infants and Young Children, 6*(3), 34–45.

Fried, M., & Duffy, P. (1996). Adherence of *Plasmodium falciparum* to chondroitin sulfate A in the human placenta. *Science, 272*, 1502–1504.

Friedl, E. (1992). Moonrose watched through a sunny day. *Natural History,* August, 34–44.

Frodi, A. (1985). Variations in parental and non-parental response to early infant communication. In M. Reite & T. Field (Eds.), *The psychobiology of attachment and separation* (pp. 351–368) New York: Wiley.

Frost, B., & Nakayama, K. (1983). Single visual neurons code opposing motion independent of direction. *Science, 220*, 744.

Fuchs, V., & Reklis, D. (1992). America's children: Economic perspectives and policy options. *Science, 255*, 41–46.

Furman, R. (1973). A child's capacity for mourning. In E. Anthony & C. Koupernik (Eds.), *The child in his family* (Vol 2, pp. 225–232). New York: Wiley.

Galaburda, A., & Livingstone, M. (1993). Evidence for a magnocellular defect in developmental dyslexia. In P. Tallal, A. Galaburda, R. Llinás, & C. von Euler (Eds.), *Temporal information processing in the nervous system. Annals of the New York Academy of Sciences* (Vol. 682, pp. 70–82). New York: New York Academy of Sciences.

Garfield, R., & Daniel, E. (1977). Gap junctions: Their presence and necessity in myometrium during parturition. *Science, 198*, 958.

Garfinkel, R. (1995, Aug. 20). Biological parents aren't better—it's a myth that hurts kids. *Philadelphia Inquirer,* p. E5.

Garrity-Rokous, F. (1994). Punitive legal approaches to the problem of prenatal drug exposure. *Infant Mental Health Journal, 15*, 218–237.

Garrow, D. (1995). *Liberty and sexuality: The right to privacy and the making of Roe vs. Wade.* New York: Macmillan.

Gazzaniga, M. (1989). Organization of the human brain. *Science, 245,* 947–952.

Georgopoulos, A., Schwartz, A., & Kettner, R. (1986). Neuronal population coding of a movement direction. *Science, 233,* 1416–1419.

Gerken, L., & McIntosh, B. (1993). Interplay of function morphemes and prosody in early language. *Developmental Psychology, 29,* 448–457.

Geschwind, N., & Galaburda, A. (1987). *Cerebral lateralization: Biological mechanisms, associations, and pathology.* Cambridge, MA: MIT Press.

Gestwicki, C. (1995). *Developmentally appropriate practice.* Albany, NY: Delmar.

Ghuman, J., & Kates, W. (1992). Approaches to the development of social communication in foster children with pervasive developmental disorder. *Zero to Three, 12*(4), 27–31.

Gibbons, A. (1994). Children's vaccine initiative stumbles. *Science, 265,* 1376–1377.

Gibson, D., Sheps, S., Schechter, M., Wiggins, S., & McCormick, A. (1989). Retinopathy of prematurity: A new epidemic? *Pediatrics, 83,* 486–492.

Gibson, E. (1988). Exploratory behavior in the development of perceiving, acting, and the acquiring of knowledge. *Annual Review of Psychology, 39,* 1–41.

Gibson, E. & Walk, R. (1960). The "visual cliff." *Scientific American, 202,* pp. 64–71.

Gibson, J. (1962). Observations on active touch. *Psychological Review, 69,* 477–491.

Globus, A. (1971). Neuronal ontogeny: Its use in tracing connectivity. In M. Sterman, D. Mc Ginty, & A. Adinolfi (Eds.), *Brain development and behavior* (pp. 253–264). New York: Academic Press.

Gluckman, P., & Williams, C. (1992). When and why do brain cells die? *Developmental Medicine and Child Neurology, 34,* 1010–1014.

Goldberg, C. (1989). Normal motor development. In J. Tecklin (Ed.), *Pediatric physical therapy* (pp. 1–15). Philadelphia: Lippincott.

Goldsmith, H., Buss, A., Plomin, R., Rothbart, M., Thomas, A., Chess, S., Hinde, R., & McCall, R. (1987). Roundtable: What is temperament? *Child Development, 58,* 505–529.

Goldstein, J., Freud, A., & Solnit, A. (1973). *Beyond the best interests of the child.* New York: Free Press.

Goldstein, J., Freud, A., & Solnit, A. (1979). *Before the best interests of the child.* New York: Free Press.

Goldstein, M. (1995). Perspective. Conductive education: An overview. *Infants and Young Children, 8*(1), vi–vii.

Golinkoff, R., Hirsh-Pasek, K., Cualey, K., & Gordon, L. (1987). The eyes have it: Lexical and syntactic comprehension in a new paradigm. *Journal of Child Language, 14,* 23–45.

Gomi, H., & Kawato, M. (1996). Equilibrium-point control hypothesis examined by measured arm stiffness during multi-joint movement. *Science, 272,* 117–120.

Gonsalves, S., & Mercer, J. (1993). Physiologic correlates of painful stimulation in preterm infants. *Clinical Journal of Pain, 9,* 88–93.

Gonzales, N. (1963). Breast-feeding, weaning, and acculturation. *Journal of Pediatrics, 63,* 577–581.

Gonzalez-Mena, J., & Eyer, D. (1980). *Infancy and Caregiving.* Palo Alto, CA: Mayfield.

Goodman, R. (1993). Brain abnormalities and psychological development. In D. Hay & A. Angold (Eds.), *Precursors and causes in development and psychopathology* (pp. 51–85). New York: Wiley.

Goodman, S., Radke-Yarrow, M., & Teti, D. (1993). Maternal depression as a context for childrearing. *Zero to Three, 13*(5), 10–15.

Goossens, F., & van IJzendoorn, M. (1990). Quality of infants' attachments to professional caregivers: Relation to infant-parent attachment and day-care characteristics. *Child Development, 61*, 832–837.

Gorer, G., & Rickman, J. (1962). *The peoples of Great Russia.* New York: Norton.

Gottlieb, G. (1971). Ontogenesis of sensory function in birds and mammals. In E. Tobach, L. Aronson, & E. Shaw (Eds.), *The biopsychology of development* (pp. 67–128). New York: Academic Press.

Gottman, J. (1989). Children of gay and lesbian parents. *Marriage and Family Review, 14*, 177–196.

Graham, M., & Bryant, D. (1993). Developmentally appropriate environments for children with special needs. *Infants and Young Children, 5*(3), 31–42.

Gralinski, J., & Kopp, C. (1993). Everyday rules for behavior: Mothers' requests to young children. *Developmental Psychology, 29*, 573–584.

Grandin, T. (1995). *Thinking in pictures.* New York: Doubleday.

Granrud, C., Yonas, A., & Pettersen, L. (1984). A comparison of monocular and binocular depth perception in 5- and 7-month-old infants. *Journal of Experimental Child Psychology, 38*, 19–32.

Grant, J. (1987). *The state of the world's children 1987.* New York: Oxford University Press.

Greenberg, J. (1991). Environmental risks to the infants and toddlers of migrant farmworkers. *Zero to Three, 11*(5), 22–23.

Greenfield, P., Reilly, T., Leaper, C., & Baker, N. (1985). The structural and functional status of single-word utterances and their relationship to early multiword speech. In M. Barret (Ed.), *Children's single-word speech* (pp. 233–268). New York: Wiley.

Greenhill, J., & Friedman, E. (1974). *Biological principles and modern practice of obstetrics.* Philadelphia: Saunders.

Greenhouse, L. (1994, Feb. 20). Court order to treat baby with partial brain prompts debate on costs and ethics. *New York Times,* p. 20.

Greenough, W., Black, J., & Wallace, C. (1993). Experience and brain development. In M. Johnson (Ed.), *Brain development and cognition* (pp. 319–322). Oxford: Blackwell.

Greenspan, N. (1991). Infants, toddlers, and indoor air pollution. *Zero to Three, 9*(5), 14–21.

Greenspan, S. (1990). Introduction to this issue. *Zero to Three, 11*(1), 3.

Greenspan, S. (1992a). *Infancy and early childhood.* Madison, CT: International Universities Press.

Greenspan, S. (1992b). Reconsidering the diagnosis and treatment of very young children with autistic spectrum or pervasive developmental disorder. *Zero to Three, 13*(2), 1–9.

Griffin, A. (1991). State regulations concerning toddlers in child care. *Zero to Three, 11*(3), 11–12.

Gross, S., Slagle, T., D'Eugenio, D., & Mettelman, B. (1992). Impact of a matched term control group on interpretation of developmental performance in preterm infants. *Pediatrics, 90,* 681–687.

Grossman, F., Pollack, W., Golding, E., & Fedele, N. (1987). Affiliation and autonomy in the transition to parenthood. *Family Relations, 36,* 263–269.

Gruenwald, P. (Ed.) (1975). *The placenta.* Baltimore: University Park Press.

Grusec, J., & Goodnow, J. (1994). Impact of parent discipline methods on the child's internalization of values: A reconceptualization of current points of view. *Developmental Psychology, 30,* 4–19.

Guiard, Y. (1991). Several effectors for a single act: coordination and cooperation. In J. Requin & G. Stelmach (Eds.), *Tutorials in motor neuroscience* (pp. 297–304). NATO ASI Series. Series D: Behavioral and Social Sciences (Vol. 62). Dordrecht, Netherlands: Kluwer.

Gunn, A., Gunn, T., Rabone, D., Breier, B., Blum, W., & Gluckman, P. (1996). Growth hormone increases breast milk volumes in mothers of preterm infants. *Pediatrics, 98*(2), 279–282.

Gunnar, M., Larson, M., Hertsgaard, L., Harris, M., & Broderson, L. (1992). The stressfulness of separation among nine-month-old infants: Effects of social context variables and infant temperament. *Child Development, 63,* 290–303.

Gunther, M. (1970). Infant behavior at the breast. In B. Foss (Ed.), *Determinants of infant behavior* (Vol. I, pp. 37–39). London: Methuen.

Gussler, J. (1979). Village women of St. Kitts. In D. Raphael (Ed.), *Breast-feeding and food policy in a hungry world* (pp. 59–66). New York: Academic Press.

Gwiazda, J., Bauer, J., & Held, R. (1989). From visual acuity to hyperacuity: A 10-year update. *Canadian Journal of Psychology, 43,* 109–120.

Gwiazda, J., Bauer, J., Thorn, F., & Held, R. (1986). Meridional amblyopia *does* result from astigmatism in early childhood. *Clinical Vision Sciences, 1,* 145–152.

Hagg, C., King, C., Ukiyama, E., Falsafi, S., Hagg, T., Donahue, P., & Weiss, M. (1994). Molecular basis of mammalian sexual determination: Activation of Müllerian inhibiting substance gene expression by SRY. *Science, 266,* 1494–1500.

Haith, M., Bergman, T., & Moore, M. (1977). Eye contact and face scanning in early infancy. *Science, 198,* 853–855.

Hanna, A., & Meltzoff, A. (1993). Peer imitation by toddlers in laboratory, home, and day-care contexts: Implications for social learning and memory. *Developmental Psychology, 29,* 701–710.

Harris, I., & Schulte, N. (1993). Should taxpayers fund abortions for poor women? *Zero to Three, 13*(6), 18–24.

Hart, S. (1991). From property to person status: historical perspective on children's rights. *American Psychologist, 46,* 53–59.

Harvey, S. (1994). Dynamic Play Therapy: An integrated expressive arts approach to the family treatment of infants and toddlers. *Zero to Three, 15*(1), 11–17.

Hata, Y., & Stryker, M. (1994). Control of thalamo-cortical afferent rearrangement by postsynaptic activity in developing visual cortex. *Science, 265,* 1732–1735.

Hausslein, E., Kaufmann, R., & Hurth, J. (1992). From case management to service coordination: Families, policymaking, and Part H. *Zero to Three, 12*(3), 10–12.

Havighurst, R. (1972). *Developmental tasks and education.* New York: David McKay.

Hayflick, L. (1992). Fetal tissue banned . . . and used (letter). *Science, 257*, 1027.

Heinrichs, C., Munson, P., Counts, D., Cutler, G., & Baron, J. (1995). Patterns of human growth. *Science, 268*, 442–445.

Held, R. (1981). Development of acuity in infants with normal and anomalous visual experience. In R. Aslin, J. Alberts, & M. Petersen (Eds.), *Development of perception.* Vol. 2. *The visual system* (pp. 279–297). New York: Academic Press.

Held, R. (1989). Development of cortically mediated visual processes in human infants. In C. von Euler, H. Forssberg, & H. Lagerkrantz (Eds.), *Neurobiology of early infant behavior* (pp. 155–164). New York: Stockton Press.

Held, R. (1993a). Binocular vision—behavioral and neuronal development. In M. Johnson (Ed.), *Brain development and cognition* (pp. 152–158). Oxford: Blackwell.

Held, R. (1993b). What can rates of development tell us about underlying mechanisms? In C. Granrud (Ed.), *Visual perception and cognition in infancy* (pp. 75–90). Hillsdale, NJ: Erlbaum.

Held, R., Shimojo, S., & Gwiazda, J. (1984). Gender differences in the early development of human visual acuity. *Investigative Ophthalmology and Visual Science, 25* (Suppl. 3), 220.

Hendrickson, A., & Yuodelis, C. (1984). The morphological development of the human fovea. *Ophthalmology, 91*, 603–612.

Hepper, P. & Shahidullah, S. (1992). Habituation in normal and Down's syndrome fetuses. *Quarterly Journal of Experimental Psychology, 44B(3/4)*, 305–317.

Herbert, V. (1994). Fetal supplements should be appropriately labeled to protect customers. *Pediatrics, 93*, 694–695.

Heriza, C., & Sweeney, J. (1994). Pediatric physical therapy: Part I. Practice scope, scientific basis, and theoretical foundation. *Infants and Young Children, 7(2)*, 20–32.

Herrgard, E., Luoma, L., Tuppurainen, K., Karjalainen, S., & Martikainen, A. (1993). Neurodevelopmental profile at 5 years of children born at ≤ 32 weeks gestation. *Developmental Medicine and Child Neurology, 35*, 1083–1097.

Heymann, S. (1995). Patients in research: Not just subjects, but partners. *Science, 269*, 797–798.

Hibbs, E. (1991a). Introduction. In E. Hibbs (Ed.), *Adoption: International perspectives* (pp. 1–14). Madison, CT: International Universities Press.

Hibbs, E. (1991b). Parental responses to the developmental stages of adopted children. In E. Hibbs (Ed.), *Adoption: international perspectives* (pp. 15–26). Madison, CN: International Universities Press.

Hill-Scott, K. (1989). No room at the inn: The crisis in child care supply. In J. Lande, S. Scarr, & N. Gunzenhauser (Eds.), *Caring for children: Challenge to America* (pp. 197–216). Hillsdale, NJ: Erlbaum.

Himwich, W. (1972). Biochemical processes of nervous system development. In E. Tobach, L. Aronson, & E. Shaw (Eds.), *The biopsychology of development* (pp. 173–194). New York: Academic Press.

Hinde, R. (1983). Ethology and child development. In M. Haith & J. Campos (Eds.), *Handbook of child psychology* (Vol. 2, pp. 27–94). New York: Wiley.

Hirshberg, L. (1990). When infants look to their parents: II. Twelve-month-olds' response to conflicting parental emotional signals. *Child Development, 61*, 1187–1191.

Hirshberg, L., & Svejda, M. (1990). When infants look to their parents: I. Infants' social referencing of mothers compared to fathers. *Child Development, 61,* 1175–1186.

Hobson, P. (1993). Understanding persons: The role of affect. In S. Baron-Cohen, H. Tager-Flusberg, & D. Cohen (Eds.), *Understanding other minds* (pp. 204–227). New York: Oxford University Press.

Hoelting, J., Sandell, E., Letourneau, S., Smerlinder, J., & Stranik, M. (1996). The MELD experience with parent groups. *Zero to Three, 16*(6), 9–18.

Hoffman, M. (1991). How parents make their mark on genes. *Science, 252,* 1250–1251.

Hoksbergen, R. (1991). Understanding and preventing "failing adoptions." In E. Hibbs (Ed.), *Adoption: International perspectives* (pp. 265–278). Madison, CT: International Universities Press.

Holden, C. (1985). Debate warming up on legal migration policy. *Science, 241,* 286–290.

Holden, C. (1986). High court says no to administration's Baby Doe rules. *Science, 232,* 1595–1596.

Holden, C. (1991). Pediatrician kicks sacred cow. *Science,* 1063.

Holden, C. (1993). The hazards of estrogen. *Science, 260,* 1238–1239.

Holden, C. (1995). Sex and the granular layer. *Science, 268,* 807.

Holden, C. (1996). The brain as orchestra. *Science, 273,* 1051.

Holyoak, C. (1987). A connectionist view of cognition (book review). *Science, 236,* 992–996.

Holzman, C., Paneth, N., Little, R., Pinto-Martin, J., et al. (1995). Perinatal brain injury in premature infants born to mothers using alcohol during pregnancy. *Pediatrics, 95,* 66–73.

Hooper, S., & Moulins, M. (1989). Switching of a neuron from one network to another by sensory-induced changes in membrane properties. *Science, 244,* 1587–1589.

Horner, T., & Guyer, M. (1993). Infant placement and custody. In C. Zeanah (Ed.), *Handbook of infant mental health* (pp. 462–479). New York: Guilford.

Horowitz, R. (1992/1993). Families, infants and the justice system. *Zero to Three, 13*(3), 1–7.

Howard, J., Beckwith, L., Rodning, C., & Kropenske, V. (1989). The development of young children of substance-abusing parents. *Zero to Three, 9*(5), 8–12.

Howes, C., & Hamilton, C. (1992a). Children's relationships with caregivers: Mothers and child care teachers. *Child Development, 63,* 859–866.

Howes, C., & Hamilton, C. (1992b). Children's relationships with child care teachers: stability and concordance with parental attachments. *Child Development, 63,* 867–878.

Hubel, D., & Wiesel, T. (1963). Binocular interaction of striate cortex of kittens reared with artificial squint. *Journal of Neurophysiology, 28,* 1041–1059.

Hudson, K., Rothenberg, K., Andrews, L., Kahn, M., & Collins, F. (1995). Genetic discrimination and health insurance: an urgent need for reform. *Science, 270,* 391–393.

Hull, V. (1985). Breast-feeding, birth spacing, and social change in rural Java. In V. Hull & M. Simpson (Eds.), *Breast-feeding, child health and child spacing* (pp. 78–108). Dover, NH: Croom Helm.

Hunt, C. (1995). Sudden infant death syndrome and subsequent siblings. *Pediatrics, 95*, 430–432.

Hunter, J., Zwischenberger, J., & Bhatia, J. (1992). Neonatal extracorporeal membrane oxygenation: Neurodevelopmental outcome of survivors. *Infants and Young Children, 4*(4), 63–76.

Hunter-Duvar, I. (1985). Introductory comment on the anatomy and physiology of the developing auditory system. In S. Trehub & B. Schneider (Eds.), *Auditory development in infancy* (pp. 47–50). New York: Plenum.

Hura, S., & Echols, C. (1996). The role of stress and articulatory difficulty in children's early productions. *Developmental psychology, 32*(1), 165–176.

Hurley, L. (1980). *Developmental nutrition.* Englewood Cliffs, NJ: Prentice-Hall.

Hutinger, P. (1988). Linking screening, identification, and assessment with curriculum. In J. Jordan, J. Gallagher, P. Hutinger, & M. Karnes (Eds.), *Early childhood special education: Birth to three* (pp. 29–66). Reston, VA: The Council for Exceptional Children and its Division for Early Childhood.

Huttenlocher, P. (1993). Morphometric study of human cerebral cortex development. In M. Johnson (Ed.), *Brain development and cognition* (pp. 112–124). Oxford: Blackwell.

Huttenlocher, P., Haight, W., Bryle, A., Seltzer, M., & Lyons, T. (1991). Early vocabulary growth: Relation to language input and gender. *Developmental Psychology, 27*, 238–246.

Hutton, N., & Wisson, L. (1991). Maternal and newborn HIV screening: Implications for children and families. In R. Faden, G. Geller, & M. Powers (Eds.), *AIDS, women, and the next generation* (pp. 105–120). New York: Oxford University Press.

Ingram, D. (1995). The cultural basis of prosodic modifications to infants and children: A response to Fernald's universalist theory. *Journal of Child Language, 22*, 223–233.

Inman, V., Ralston, H., & Todd, F. (1981). *Human walking.* Baltimore: Williams & Wilkins.

Irvin, N., Kennel, J., & Klaus, M. (1982). Caring for the parents of an infant with a congenital malformation. In M. Klaus & J. Kennell (Eds.), *Parent-infant bonding* (2nd ed.) (pp. 227–258). St. Louis: C.V. Mosby.

Isaacson, R. (1987). Brain plasticity after damage. In N. Gunzenhauser (Ed.), *Infant stimulation* (pp. 12–20). Skillman, NJ: Johnson and Johnson.

Isabella, R., & Belsky, J. (1991). Interactional synchrony and the origins of infant-mother attachment: A replication study. *Child Development, 62*, 373–384.

Izard, C. (1979). *The Maximally Discriminative Facial Coding System (MAX).* Newark, DE: University of Delaware Instructional Resources Center.

Izard, C., & Malatesta, C. (1987). Perspectives on emotional development. I. Differential emotions theory of early emotional development. In J. Osofsky (Ed.), *Handbook of infant development* (pp. 494–554). New York: Wiley.

Jacobs, R., & Fraser, S. (1994). Magnetic resonance microscopy of embryonic cell lineages and movements. *Science, 263*, 681–684.

Jacobson, M. (1970). *Developmental neurobiology.* New York: Holt, Rinehart & Winston.

James, B. (1994). *Handbook for treatment of attachment-trauma problems in children.* New York: Lexington.

Jensen, J., Thelen, E., & Ulrich, B. (1989). Constraints on multi-joint movements: From the spontaneity of infancy to the skill of adults. *Human Movement Science, 8*, 393–402.

Jitsukawa, M., & Djerassi, C. (1994). Birth control in Japan: Realities and prognosis. *Science, 265*, 1048–1051.

Johnson, C. (1993). Developmental issues: Children infected with the human immunodeficiency virus. *Infants and Young Children, 6*(1), 1–10.

Johnson, C., Stevens, B., Yang, F., & Horton, L. (1996). Developmental changes in response to heelstick in preterm infants: A prospective cohort study. *Developmental Medicine and Child Neurology, 38*, 438–445.

Johnson, K. (1992, Aug. 18). Child abuse is ruled out in birth case. *New York Times*, p. B1.

Johnson, L. (1995, Dec. 12). Legislators seeking help on newborn law. *Philadelphia Inquirer*, p. S4.

Johnson, M. (1993). Cortical maturation and the development of visual attention in early infancy. In M. Johnson (Ed.), *Brain development and cognition* (pp. 167–194). Oxford: Blackwell.

Johnson, M., Siddons, F., Frith, U., & Morton, J. (1992). Can autism be predicted on the basis of infant screening tests? *Developmental Medicine and Child Neurology, 34*, 316–320.

Jones, R. (1995, Nov. 25). Race issue fuels debate on adoption. *Philadelphia Inquirer*, p. A1, A16.

Jusczyk, P., Pisoni, D., Reed, M., Fernald, A.,& Myers, M. (1983.) Infants' discrimination of the duration of a rapid spectrum change in nonspeech signals. *Science, 222*, 175–177.

Kagan, J. (1992). Behavior, biology, and the meaning of temperamental constructs. *Pediatrics, 90*(3, Part 2), 510–513.

Kagan, J., Arcus, D., Snidman, N., Feng, W., Hindler, J., & Greene, S. (1994). Reactivity in infants: A cross-national comparison. *Developmental Psychology, 30*, 342–345.

Kagan, J., & Greenspan, S. (1986). Milestones of development: A dialogue. *Zero to Three, 6*(5), 1–9.

Kagan, J., Reznick, S., & Snidman, N. (1986). Temperamental inhibition in early childhood. In R. Plomin & J. Dunn (Eds.), *The study of temperament: Changes, continuities, and challenges* (pp. 53–66). Hillsdale, NJ: Erlbaum.

Kahn, P. (1994). Genetic diversity project tries again. *Science, 266*, 720–722.

Kaiser, J. (1996). New yeast study finds strength in numbers. *Science, 272*, 1418.

Kalemkiarian, S. (1989). Insuring child care's future: The continuing crisis. In J. Lande, S. Scarr, & N. Gunzenhauser (Eds.), *Caring for children: Challenge to America* (pp. 181–196). Hillsdale, NJ: Erlbaum.

Kalmanson, B., & Lieberman, A. (1982). Removing obstacles to attachment: Infant-parent psychotherapy with an adolescent mother and her baby. *Zero to Three, 3*(1), 10–13.

Kamal, H. (1975). *Encyclopedia of Islamic Medicine.* Cairo: General Egyptian Book Organization.

Kandel, E., & O'Dell, T. (1992). Are adult learning mechanisms also used for development? *Science, 258*, 243–245.

Kaplan, P., Normandin, J., Wilson, G., et al. (1990). Malformations and minor anomalies in children whose mothers had prenatal diagnosis: Comparison between CVS and amniocentesis. *American Journal of Medical Genetics, 36,* 366–370.

Karpen, G., Le, M.-H., & Le, H. (1996). Centric heterochromatin and the efficiency of achiasmatic disjunction in *Drosophila* female meiosis. *Science, 273,* 118–122.

Katz, N., Baker, E., & Macnamara, J. (1974). What's in a name? A study of how children learn common and proper names. *Child Development, 45,* 469–473.

Kaye, K. (1982a). *The mental and social life of babies.* Chicago: University of Chicago Press.

Kaye, K. (1982b). Organism, apprentice, and person. In E. Tronick (Ed.), *Social interchange in infancy* (pp. 183–196). Baltimore: University Park Press.

Kaye, K., & Bower, T. (1994). Learning and intermodal transfer of information in newborns. *Psychological Science, 5*(5), 286–288.

Kehoe, M., Stoel-Gammon, C., & Buder, E. (1995). Acoustic correlates of stress in young children's speech. *Journal of Speech and Hearing Research, 38,* 338–350.

Keller, B., & Sandelski, M. (1994). Newborn assessment from birth to two hours of life. In M. Gulanick, M. Puzas, D. Gradishar, & K. Gettrust (Eds.), *Obstetric and gynecologic nursing* (pp. 414–422). Albany, NY: Delmar.

Kelso, J. (1990). Phase transitions: Foundations of behavior. In H. Haken & M. Stadler (Eds.), *Synergetics of cognition* (pp. 249–268). New York: Springer-Verlag.

Kendall, E. (1989). Enforcement of child care regulations. In J. Lande, S. Scarr, & N. Gunzenhauser (Eds.), *Caring for children: Challenge to America* (pp. 167–180). Hillsdale, NJ: Erlbaum.

Kennell, J., & Klaus, M. (1982). Caring for the parents of a stillborn or an infant who dies. In M. Klaus & J. Kennell (Eds.), *Parent-infant bonding* (pp. 151–266). St. Louis: C.V. Mosby.

Keohane, N., & Lacey, L. (1991). Preparing the woman with gestational diabetes for self-care. *Journal of Obstetric, Gynecologic, and Neonatal Nursing, 20*(3), 189–193.

Keverne, E., Levy, F., Poindron, P., & Lindsay, P. (1983). Vaginal stimulation: An important determinant of maternal bonding in sheep. *Science, 219,* 81–83.

"Key facts about children." (1996). *CDF Reports, 17*(2), 5.

Kinney, H., Filiano, J., Sleeper, L., Mandell, F., Valdes-Dapena, M., & White, W. (1995). Decreased muscarinic receptor binding in the arcuate nucleus in sudden infant death syndrome. *Science, 269,* 1446–1450.

Kirshbaum, M. (1988). Parents with physical disabilities and their babies. *Zero to Three, 8*(5), 8–15.

Klass, P. (1992, Dec. 13). Treating problems we thought we solved. *New York Times Magazine.*

Klaus, M. & Kennell, J. (1982). Labor, birth, and bonding. In M. Klaus & J. Kennell (Eds.), *Parent-infant bonding* (pp. 22–98). St. Louis: C.V. Mosby.

Klin, A., & Volkmar, F. (1993). The development of individuals with autism: Implications for the theory-of-mind hypothesis. In S. Baron-Cohen, H. Tager-Flusberg, & D. Cohen (Eds.), *Understanding other minds* (pp. 317–334). New York: Oxford University Press.

Klonoff-Cohen, H., & Edelstein, S. (1995). A case-control study of routine and death scene sleeping position and sudden infant death syndrome in Southern California. *Journal of the American Medical Association, 273*(1), 790–794.

Knauer, M. (1985). Breast-feeding and the return of menstruation in urban Canadian mothers practicing "natural mothering." In V. Hull & M. Simpson (Eds.), *Breast-feeding, child health and child spacing* (pp. 187–212). Dover, NH: Croom Helm.

Knoppers, B., & Chadwick, R. (1994). The human genome project: Under an international ethical microscope. *Science, 265,* 2035–2036.

Kochanska, G. (1991a). Patterns of inhibition to the unfamiliar in children of normal and affectively ill mothers. *Child Development, 62,* 250–263.

Kochanska, G. (1991b). Socialization and temperament in the development of guilt and conscience. *Child Development, 62,* 1379–1392.

Kochanska, G. (1994). Beyond cognition: Expanding the search for the early roots of internalization and conscience. *Developmental Psychology, 30,* 20–22.

Kochanska, G. (1995). Children's temperament, mothers' discipline, and security of attachment: Multiple pathways to emerging internalization. *Child Development, 66,* 597–615.

Koh, J.-Y., Suh, S., Gwag, B., He, Y., Hsu, C., & Choi, D. (1996). The role of zinc in selective neuronal death after transient global cerebral ischemia. *Science, 272,* 1013–1016.

Kojima, H. (1986). Becoming nurturant in Japan: Past and present. In A. Fogel & G. Melson (Eds.), *Origins of nurturance: Developmental, biological, and cultural perspectives on caregiving* (pp. 123–140). Hillsdale, NJ: Erlbaum.

Kolata, G. (1983). First trimester prenatal diagnosis. *Science, 221,* 1031.

Kolata, G. (1987a). Panel urges newborn sickle cell screening. *Science, 236,* 259–260.

Kolata, G. (1987b). What babies know, and noises parents make. *Science, 237,* 726.

Kolata, G. (1991, Aug. 25). U.S. rule on fetal studies hampers research on AZT. *New York Times,* p. 20.

Kolata, G. (1992, Jan. 5). In late abortions, decisions are painful and options few. *New York Times,* pp. 1, 16.

Kolb, B. (1993). Brain development, plasticity, and behavior. In M. Johnson (Ed.), *Brain development and cognition* (pp. 338–356). Oxford: Blackwell.

Koop, C. (1984). *Report of the Surgeon General's Workshop on Breast-feeding and Human Lactation.* Washington, DC: U.S. Department of Health and Human Services.

Kopp, C. (1987). Developmental risk: Historical reflections. In J. Osofsky (Ed.), *Handbook of infant development* (pp. 881–912). New York: Wiley.

Kopp, C. (1989). Regulation of distress and negative emotions: A developmental view. *Developmental Psychology, 25,* 343–354.

Kopp, C., & Haynes, O. (1987). Abusive and non-abusive mothers' ability to identify general and specific emotion signals of infants. *Child Development, 58,* 187–190.

Korner, A. (1984a). Interconnections between sensory and affective development in early infancy. *Zero to Three, 5*(1), 1–6.

Korner, A. (1984b). The many faces of touch. In C. Brown (Ed.), *The many facets of touch* (pp. 107–113). Skillman, NJ: Johnson and Johnson.

Korner, A., Hutchinson, C., Koperski, J., Kraemer, H., & Schneider, P. (1981). Stability of individual differences of neonatal motor and crying patterns. *Child Development, 52,* 83–90.

Kouri, T. (1989). How manual sign language relates to the development of spoken language: A case study. *Language, Speech, and Hearing Services in Schools, 20*(1), 50–61.

Kozma, I., & Balogh, E. (1995). A brief introduction to conductive therapy and its application at an early age. *Infants and Young Children, 8*(1), 68–74.

Kramer, S., & Williams, D. (1993). The hearing-impaired infant and toddler: Identification, assessment, and intervention. *Infants and Young Children, 6*(1), 35–49.

Kristof, W. (1993, April 25). China's crackdown on births: a stunning, and harsh, success. *New York Times,* pp. 1, 12.

Kuczynski, L., & Kochanska, G. (1995). Function and content of maternal demands: Developmental significance of early demands for competent action. *Child Development, 66,* 616–628.

Kuhl, P. (1993). Developmental speech perception: Implications for models of language impairment. In P. Tallal, A. Galaburda, R. Llinás, & C. von Euler (Eds.), *Temporal information processing in the nervous system. Annals of the New York Academy of Sciences,* (Vol. 682, pp. 248–263). New York: New York Academy of Sciences.

Kuhl, P. & Meltzoff, A. (1982). The bimodal representation of speech in infancy. *Science, 218,* 1138–1141.

Kuhl, P., Williams, K., Lacerda, F., Stevens, K., & Lindblom. B. (1992). Linguistic experience alters phonetic experience in infants by 6 months of age. *Science, 225,* 606–608.

Lagerkrantz, H. (1989). Neurochemical modulation of fetal behavior and excitation at birth. In C. von Euler, H. Forssberg, & H. Lagerkrantz (Eds.), *Neurobiology of early infant behavior* (pp. 19–30). New York: Stockton Press.

Lamont, P., Sachinwalla, T., & Pamphlett, R. (1995). Myelin in SIDS: Assessment of development and damage using MRI. *Pediatrics, 95*(3), 409–413.

Lampl, M., Cameron, N., Veldhuis, J., & Johnson, M. (1995). Patterns of human growth (response to Heinrichs et al.). *Science, 268,* 445–447.

Lander, E., & Schork, N. (1994). Genetic dissection of complex traits. *Science, 265,* 2037–2048.

Landers, C. (1990). Child-rearing practices and infant development in South India. In N. Gunzenhauser (Ed.), *Advances in touch* (pp. 42–51). Skillman, NJ: Johnson and Johnson.

Landers, D., & Sweet, R. (1996). Reducing mother-to-infant transmission of HIV—the door remains open. *New England Journal of Medicine, 334*(25), 1664–1665.

Landesman, S., Kalish, L., Burns, D., Minkoff, H., et al. (1996). Obstetrical factors and the transmission of human immuno-deficiency virus type 1 from mother to child. *New England Journal of Medicine, 334*(25), 1617–1623.

Landy, S., & Peters, R. (1991). Understanding and treating the hyperaggressive toddler. *Zero to Three, 11*(3), 22–31.

Langlois, J., Ritter, J., Casey, R., & Sawin, D. (1995). Infant attractiveness predicts maternal behaviors and attitudes. *Developmental Psychology, 31,* 464–472.

Larson, M., Gunnar, M., & Hertsgaard, L. (1991). The effects of morning naps, car trips, and maternal separation on adrenocortical activity in human infants. *Child Development, 62,* 362–372.

Lawrence, R. (1984). Human lactation as a physiologic process. *Report of the Surgeon General's Workshop on Breast-feeding and Human Lactation* (pp. 9–13). (DHHS Publication No. HRS-D-MC 84-2). Washington, DC: U.S. Government Printing Office.

Lawson, J. (1988). Standards of practice and the pain of premature infants. *Zero to Three, 9*(2), 1–5.

Leavitt, R. (1994). *Power and emotion in infant-toddler day care.* Albany, NY: SUNY Press.

Lee, D., & Aronson, E. (1974). Visual proprioceptive control of standing in human infants. *Perception and Psychophysics, 15,* 529–532.

Lee, F. (1993, March 7). The scythe of AIDS leaves a generation of orphans. *New York Times,* p. 18.

Lee, K. (1994). The crying pattern of Korean infants and related factors. *Developmental Medicine and Child Neurology, 36,* 601–607.

Lefebvre, D., Giaid, A., Bennett, H., Larivière, R., & Zingg, H. (1992). Oxytocin gene expression in rat uterus. *Science, 256,* 1553–1555.

Leslie, A. (1987). Pretence and representations: The origins of "theory of mind." *Psychological Review, 94*(4), 412–426.

Lester, B. (1984). A biosocial model of infant crying. In L. Lipsitt & C. Rovee-Collier (Eds.), *Advances in infancy research* (Vol. III, pp. 168–212). Norwood, NJ: Ablex.

Lester, B., Als, H., & Brazelton, T. (1982). Regional obstetric anesthesia and newborn behavior: A reanalysis toward synergistic effects. *Child Development, 53,* 687–692.

Lester, B., & Tronick, E. (1994). The effects of prenatal cocaine exposure and child outcome. *Infant Mental Health Journal, 15,* 107–120.

Lester, D., & Lester, G. (1975). *Crime of passion: Murder and the murderer.* Chicago: Nelson-Hall.

Lester, G., Bierbrauer, B., Selfridge, B., & Gomeringer, D. (1976). Distractibility, intensity of reaction, and nonnutritive sucking. *Psychological Reports, 39,* 1212–1214.

Lewis, M. (1992). *Shame: The exposed self.* New York: Free Press.

Lewis, M. (1993). Early socioemotional predictors of cognitive competency. *Developmental Psychology, 29,* 1036–1043.

Lewkowicz, D. (1996). Infants' responses to the audible and visible properties of the human face: 1. Role of lexical-syntactic content, temporal synchrony, gender, and manner of speech. *Developmental Psychology, 32*(2), 347–366.

Li, C., Windsor, R., Perkins, L., Goldenberg, R., & Lowe, J. (1993). The impact on infant birth weight and gestational age of criterion-validated smoking reduction during pregnancy. *Journal of the American Medical Association, 269*(12), 1519–1524.

Liaw, F. & Brooks-Gunn, J. (1993). Patterns of low-birth-weight children's cognitive development. *Developmental Psychology, 29,* 1024–1035.

Lieberman, A. (1990). Infant-parent intervention with recent immigrants: Reflections on a study with Latino families. *Zero to Three, 10*(2), 8–11.

Lieberman, A. (1993). Family planning as a clinical issue. *Zero to Three, 13*(6), 1–5.

Lieberman, A., & Birch, M. (1985). The etiology of failure to thrive: An interactional developmental approach. In D. Drotar (Ed.), *New directions in failure to thrive* (pp. 259–278). New York: Plenum.

Lieberman, A., & Pawl, J. (1990). Disorders of attachment and secure base behavior in the second year of life. In M. Greenberg, D. Cicchetti, & E. Cummings (Eds.), *Attachment in the preschool years* (pp. 375–398). Chicago: University of Chicago Press.

Linder, T. (1990). *Transdisciplinary play-based assessment.* Baltimore: Paul H. Brookes.

Liu, W., & Lo, I. (Eds.) (1975). *Sunflower splendor: Three thousand years of Chinese poetry.* Garden City, NY: Anchor.

Locke, J. (1993). *The child's path to spoken language.* Cambridge, MA: Harvard University Press.

Lockwood, C., Senyei, A., Dische, M., Casal, D., Shah, K., Thung, S. et al. (1991). Fetal fibronectin in cervical and vaginal secretions as a predictor of preterm delivery. *New England Journal of Medicine, 325*(10), 669–674.

Lockwood, S. (1994). Early speech and language indicators for later learning problems: Recognizing a language organization disorder. *Infants and Young Children, 7*(2), 43–51.

Lois, C., & Alvarez-Buylla, A. (1994). Long-distance neuronal migration in the adult mammalian brain. *Science, 264,* 1145–1148.

Loman, L. (1994). Attuning to the fetus and the young child: Approaches from dance/movement therapy. *Zero to Three, 15*(1), 20–26.

Lombroso, C. & Lerman, P. (1967). Breathholding spells (cyanotic and pallid infantile syncope). *Pediatrics, 39,* 563–581.

Long, S. (1996). Early and accurate detection of infection with human immuno-deficiency virus type 1 in vertically exposed infants. *Journal of Pediatrics, 129*(2), 189–191.

Lord, C. (1993). The complexity of social behavior in autism. In S. Baron-Cohen, H. Tager-Flusberg, & D. Cohen (Eds.), *Understanding other minds* (pp. 292–316). New York: Oxford University Press.

Lou, H. (1989). Brain circulation and neurodevelopmental disorders. In C. von Euler, H. Forssberg, & H. Lagerkrantz (Eds.), *Neurobiology of early infant behavior* (pp. 331–336). New York: Stockton Press.

Lovegrove, W. (1993). Weakness in the transient visual system: a causal factor in dyslexia. In P. Tallal, A. Galaburda, R. Llinás, & C. von Euler (Eds.), *Temporal information processing in the nervous system. Annals of the New York Academy of Sciences* (Vol. 682, pp. 57–69). New York: New York Academy of Sciences.

Low, H., Hansen, D., Nordentoft, M., Pryds, O., Jensen, F., Nim, J., & Hemmingsen, R. (1994). Prenatal stressors of human life affect fetal brain development. *Developmental Medicine and Child Neurology, 36,* 826–832.

Lucey, J. (1984). The sleeping, dreaming fetus meets the intensive care nursery. In C. Brown (Ed.), *The many facets of touch* (pp. 75–83). Skillman, NJ: Johnson and Johnson.

MacGowan, R., MacGowan, C., Serdula, M., Lane, J., et al. (1991). Breast-feeding among women attending Women, Infants, and Children Clinics in Georgia, 1987. *Pediatrics, 87,* 361–366.

MacNeilage, P. (1991). The "postural origins" theory of primate neurobiological asymmetries. In N. Krasnegor, D. Rumbaugh, R. Schiefelbusch, & M. Studdert-Kennedy (Eds.), *Biological and behavioral determinants of language development* (pp. 165–188). Hillsdale, NJ: Erlbaum.

MacWhinney, B. (1994). Using CHILDES to study language disorders. *Journal of Communication Disorders, 27,* 67–70.

Mahler, M. (1980). Rapprochement subphase of the separation-individuation process. In R. Lax, S. Bach, & J. Burland (Eds.), *Rapprochement: The critical subphase of separation-individuation* (pp. 3–22). New York: Aronson.

Mahler, M. (1983). *The psychological birth of the human infant* [Film]. Franklin Lakes, NJ: Mahler Foundation Film Library.

Main, M., & Hesse, E. (1990). Parents' unresolved traumatic experiences are related to infant disorganized attachment status: Is frightened and/or frightening behavior the linking mechanism? In M. Greenberg, D. Cicchetti, & E. Cummings (Eds.), *Attachment in the preschool years* (pp. 161–184). Chicago: University of Chicago Press.

Main, M., & Solomon, J. (1986). Discovery of an insecure-disorganized/disoriented attachment pattern. In T. Brazelton & M. Yogman (Eds.), *Affective development in infancy* (pp. 95–124). Norwood, NJ: Ablex.

Main, M., & Solomon, J. (1990). Procedures for identifying infants as disorganized/ disoriented during the Ainsworth Strange Situation. In M. Greenberg, D. Cicchetti, & E. Cummings (Eds.), *Attachment in the pre-school years* (pp. 121–160). Chicago: University of Chicago Press.

Main, M., & Weston, D. (1981). The independence of infant-mother and infant-father attachment relationships: Security of attachment characterizes relationships, not infants. *Child Development, 52,* 932–940.

Mann, C. (1994). Can meta-analysis make policy? *Science, 266,* 960–962.

Mantovani, J. (1994). Brain imaging in children with neurodevelopmental disorders. *Infants and Young Children, 7,* 60–68.

Marks, P. (1993, Feb. 14). Shots are often free, but many children miss immunizations. *New York Times,* pp. 1, 52.

Marshall, E. (1993). A tough line on genetic screening. *Science, 262,* 984–985.

Marshall, E. (1994a). Genetic testing set for takeoff. *Science, 265,* 464–467.

Marshall, E. (1994b). New law brings affirmative action to clinical research. *Science, 263,* 602.

Marshall, E. (1994c). Rules on embryo research due out. *Science, 265,* 1024–1026.

Marshall, E. (1995). NIH's "gay gene" study questioned. *Science, 268,* 1841.

Martinez, G. (1984). Trends in breast-feeding in the United States. *Report of the Surgeon General's Workshop on Breast-feeding and Human Lactation* (pp. 18–22). (DHHS Publication No. HRS-D-MC 84-2). Washington, DC: U.S. Government Printing Office.

Marvin, R., & Stewart, R. (1990). A family systems framework for the study of attachment. In M. Greenberg, D. Cicchetti, & E. Cummings (Eds.), *Attachment in the preschool years* (pp. 51–86). Chicago: University of Chicago Press.

Marx, J. (1989). The cystic fibrosis gene is found. *Science, 245,* 923–925.

Marx, J. (1993). Cell communication failure leads to immune disorder. *Science, 259,* 896–897.

Marx, J. (1995). Cell cycle inhibitors may help brake growth as cells develop. *Science, 267,* 963–964.

Marx, J. (1996a). Chromosome *(sic)* yield new clue to pairing in meiosis. *Science, 273,* 35–36.

Marx, J. (1996b). New methods for expanding the chromosomal paint kit. *Science, 273,* 430.

Maslin-Cole, C., & Spieker, S. (1990). Attachment as a basis for independent motivation. In M. Greenberg, D. Cicchetti, & E. Cummings (Eds.), *Attachment in the preschool years* (pp. 245–272). Chicago: University of Chicago Press.

Mason, J. (1992). From the Assistant Secretary for Health, U.S. Public Health Service: A national agenda for women's health. *Journal of the American Medical Association, 267*(4), 482.

Massaro, D. (1987). Information-processing theory and strong inference: A paradigm for psychological inquiry. In H. Heuer & A. Sanders (Eds.), *Perspectives on perception and action* (pp. 273–300). Hillsdale, NJ: Erlbaum.

Massery, M. (1993). Innovative concepts in neurological rehabilitation: A pulmonary focused therapeutic exercise approach. Unpublished lecture notes. N.J. American Physical Therapy Association.

Masten, A. (1989). Resilience in development: Implications of the study of successful adaptation for developmental psychopathology. In D. Cicchetti (Ed.), *The emergence of a discipline: Rochester symposium on developmental psychopathology* (pp. 261–294). Hillsdale, NJ: Erlbaum.

Masur, E. (1993). Transitions in representational ability: Infants' verbal, vocal, and action imitations during the second year. *Merrill-Palmer Quarterly, 39,* 437–456.

Matthews, K. (1996). The whole lactose repressor. *Science, 271,* 1245–1246.

Mayer, J. (1995, Dec. 4). A harder choice. *New Yorker,* pp. 5–6.

Mayes, L. (1994). Neurobiology of prenatal cocaine exposure effect on developing monoamine systems. *Infant Mental Health Journal, 15,* 121–133.

Mayes, L., & Carter, A. (1990). Emerging social regulatory capacities as seen in the still-face situation. *Child Development, 61,* 754–763.

Mayes, L., Granger, R., Bornstein, M., & Zuckerman, B. (1992). The problem of prenatal cocaine exposure: A rush to judgment. *Journal of the American Medical Association, 267*(3), 406–408.

McAnarney, E. (1983). The vulnerable dyad: Adolescent mothers and their infants. In V. Sasserath (Ed.), *Minimizing high-risk parenting* (pp. 39–43). Skillman, NJ: Johnson and Johnson.

McAnarney, E. (1985). Adolescent pregnancy and childbearing: New data, new challenges. *Pediatrics, 75,* 973–975.

McArdle, P., Kim, T., Grube, C., & Randall, V. (1995). An approach to bilingualism in early intervention. *Infants and Young Children, 7*(3), 63–73.

McCall, R. (1986). Issues of stability and continuity in temperament research. In A. Plomin & J. Dunn (Eds.), *The study of temperament: Changes, continuities, and challenges* (pp. 13–26). Hillsdale, NJ.: Erlbaum.

McCall, R. (1987). The media, society, and child development research. In J. Osofsky (Ed.), *Handbook of infant development* (pp. 1199–1255). New York: Wiley.

McCant, J. (1987). The cultural contradiction of fathers as nonparents. *Family Law Quarterly, 21,* 127–143.

McCauley, E., Kay, T., Ito, J., & Treder, R. (1987). The Turner syndrome: Cognitive deficits, affective discrimination, and behavior problems. *Child Development, 58,* 464–473.

McConnell, S., Ghosh, A., & Shatz, C. (1989). Subplate neurons pioneer the first axon pathway from the cerebral cortex. *Science, 245,* 978–982.

McDonogh, S. (1993). Interaction guidance. In C. Zeanah (Ed.), *Handbook of infant mental health* (pp. 414–426). New York: Guilford.

McDowell, R. (1979). The dairy industry in less developed countries. In D. Raphael (Ed.), *Breast-feeding and food policy in a hungry world* (pp. 105–114). New York: Academic Press.

McGrath, P. (1990). *Pain in children.* New York: Guilford.

McKinney, W. (1985). Separation and depression: biological markers. In M. Reite & T. Field (Eds.), *The psychobiology of attachment and separation* (pp. 201–222). New York: Wiley.

McLean, L. (1990). Communication development in the first two years of life: A transactional process. *Zero to Three, 11*(1), 13–19.

McLinden, J. (1987). Separate but unequal: The economic disaster of divorce for women and children. *Family Law Quarterly, 21,* 351–409.

McNeill, D. (1985). Holophrastic noun phrases within grammatical clauses. In M. Barrett (Ed.), *Children's single-word speech* (pp. 269–286). New York: Wiley.

Mead, M., & Métraux, R. (Eds.). (1953). *The study of culture at a distance.* Chicago: University of Chicago Press.

Meaney, M., Aitken, D., Bhatnagar, S., Bodnoff, S., Mitchell, J., & Sarrieau, A. (1990). Neonatal handling and the development of the adrenocortical response to stress. In N. Gunzenhauser (Ed.), *Advances in touch* (pp. 11–21). Skillman, NJ: Johnson and Johnson.

Meaney, M., Aitken, D., Bodnoff, S., Iny, L., Tatarewicz, J., & Sopolsky, R. (1985). Early, postnatal handling alters glucocorticoid receptor concentrations in selected brain regions. *Behavioral Neuroscience, 99,* 760–765.

Mebert, C. (1991). Dimensions of subjectivity in parents' ratings of infant temperament. *Child Development, 62,* 352–361.

Mednick, S., Machon, R., Huttunen, M., & Bonnett, D. (1988). Adult schizophrenia following prenatal exposure to an influenza epidemic. *Archives of General Psychiatry, 45,* 189–192.

Meier, R. (1991). Language acquisition by deaf children. *American Scientist, 79,* 60–70.

Meisels, S., Dichtelmiller, M., & Liaw, F. (1993). A multidimensional analysis of early childhood intervention programs. In C. Zeanah (Ed.), *Handbook of infant mental health* (pp. 361–385). New York: Guilford.

Meister, M., Wong, R., Baylor, D., & Shatz, C. (1991). Synchronous bursts of action potentials in ganglion cells of the developing mammalian retina. *Science, 252,* 939–943.

Meizner, I., & Bar-Ziv, J. (1985). Dorsiflexion of the big toe—a sign of impending fetal micturition. *American Journal of Obstetrics and Gynecology, 1985, 152,* 722.

Mello, N., Bree, M., Mendelson, J., & Ellingboe, J. (1983). Alcohol self-administration disrupts reproductive function in female macaque monkeys. *Science, 221,* 677.

Melton, G., & Wilcox, B. (1989). Changes in family law and family life. *American Psychologist, 44,* 1213–1216.

Meltzoff, A. (1990). Foundations for developing a concept of self: The role of imitation in relating self to other and the value of social mirroring, social modeling, and self practice in infancy. In D. Cicchetti & M. Beeghly (Eds.), *The self in transition* (pp. 139–164). Chicago: University of Chicago Press.

Meltzoff, A., & Gopnik, A. (1993). The role of imitation in understanding persons and developing a theory of mind. In S. Baron-Cohen, H. Tager-Flusberg, & D. Cohen (Eds.), *Understanding other minds* (pp. 335–366). New York: Oxford University Press.

Meltzoff, A., & Moore, M. (1977). Imitation of facial and manual gestures by human neonates. *Science, 198,* 75–78.

Meltzoff, A., & Moore, M. (1989). Imitation in newborn infants: Exploring the range of gestures imitated and the underlying mechanisms. *Developmental Psychology, 25,* 954–962.

Melzack, R., & Wall, P. (1965). Pain mechanisms: A new theory. *Science, 150,* 971–979.

Mennella, J., & Beauchamp, G. (1993). Early flavor experiences: When do they start? *Zero to Three, 14*(2), 1–7.

Menzel, B. (1994, Fall). Comment. *The Phoenix,* p. 2.

Mercer, J., & Gonsalves, S. (1992). Parental experience during treatment of very small preterm infants. *Illness, Crises, and Loss, 2*(3), 70–73.

Mercer, J., & McMurdy, C. (1985). A stereotyped following behavior in young children. *Journal of General Psychology, 112,* 261–266.

Mercer, J., & Russ, R. (1980). Variables affecting time between childbirth and establishment of lactation. *Journal of General Psychology, 102,* 155–156.

Merrick, J. (1992). Conflict, compromise, and symbolism. In A. Caplan, R. Blank, & J. Merrick (Eds.), *Compelled compassion* (pp. 35–72). Totowa, NJ: Humana.

Merzenich, M. (1984). Functional "maps" of skin sensations. In C. Brown (Ed.), *The many facets of touch* (pp. 15–21). Skillman, NJ: Johnson and Johnson.

Merzenich, M., Schreiner, C., Jenkins, W., & Wang, X. (1993). Neural mechanisms underlying temporal integration, segmentation, and input sequence representation: Some implications for the origins of learning disabilities. In P. Tallal, A. Galaburda, R. Llinás & C. von Euler (Eds.), *Temporal information processing in the nervous system: Special reference to dyslexia and dysphasia* (pp. 1–22). Annals of the New York Academy of Sciences, Vol. 682.

Migeon, B. (1995). Maleness and femaleness [Review of the book *Sex determination, differentiation, and intersexuality in placental animals*]. *Science, 270,* 113.

Miller, G. (1989). Crafting the future of child care. In J. Lande, S. Scarr, & N. Gunzenhauser (Eds.), *Caring for children: Challenge to America* (pp. 129–138). Hillsdale, NJ: Erlbaum.

Modlin, J., & Saah, A. (1991). Public health and clinical aspects of HIV infection and disease in women and children in the U.S. In R. Faden, G. Geller, & M. Powers

(Eds.), *AIDS, Women, and the next generation* (pp. 29–58). New York: Oxford University Press.

Moffitt, T. (1990). Juvenile delinquency and Attention Deficit Disorder: Boys' developmental trajectories from age 3 to age 15. *Child Development, 61,* 893–910.

Money, J., & Ehrhardt, A. (1972). *Man and woman, boy and girl.* Baltimore: Johns Hopkins University Press.

Moore, M. (1972). *The newborn and the nurse.* Philadelphia: Saunders.

Moore-Ede, M., Sulzman, F., & Fuller, C. (1982). *The clocks that time us.* Cambridge: Harvard University Press.

Morelli, G., Rogoff, B., Oppenheim, D., & Goldsmith, D. (1992). Cultural variations in infants' sleeping arrangements: questions of independence. *Developmental Psychology, 28,* 604–613.

Morelli, G., & Tronick, E. (1991). Efe multiple caretaking and attachment. In J. Gewirtz & W. Kurtines (Eds.), *Intersections with attachment* (pp. 41–54). Hillsdale, NJ: Erlbaum.

Moro, M. (1994). Psychiatric interventions in crisis situations: working in the former Yugoslavia. *The Signal 2*(1), 1–4.

Morrell, V. (1993). The puzzle of the triple repeats. *Science, 260,* 1422–1423.

Morrell, V. (1994). Rise and fall of the Y chromosome. *Science, 263,* 171–172.

Morris, S. (1989). Development of oral-motor skills in the neurologically impaired child receiving non-oral feedings. *Dysphagia, 3,* 135–154.

Moskowitz, B. (1994). The acquisition of language. In V. Clark, P. Escholz, & A. Rosa (Eds.), *Language* (pp. 85–112). New York: St. Martin's Press.

Muir, D., Clifton, R., & Clarkson, M. (1989). The development of a human auditory localization response: A U-shaped function. *Canadian Journal of Psychology, 43,* 199–216.

Mukherjee, A., & Hodgen, G. (1983). Maternal ethanol exposure induces transient impairment of umbilical circulation and fetal hypoxia in monkeys. *Science, 218,* 700.

Mullis, A., Mullis, R., & Normandin, D. (1992). Cross-sectional and longitudinal comparisons of adolescent self-esteem. *Adolescence, 27,* 51–61.

Mullis, R., Smith, D., & Vollmers, K. (1983). Prosocial behaviors in young children and parental guidance. *Child Study Journal, 13,* 13–22.

Mundy, P., Sigman, M., & Kasari, C. (1993). The theory of mind and joint-attention deficits in autism. In S. Baron-Cohen, H. Tager-Flusberg, & D. Cohen (Eds.), *Understanding other minds* (pp. 181–203). New York: Oxford University Press.

Murphy, L., & Small, C. (1991). Toddlers: themes and variations. *Zero to Three, 11*(3), 1–5.

Murray, A. (1992). Early intervention program evaluation: numbers or narratives? *Infants and Young Children, 4*(4), 77–88.

Muscari, A. (1989). Aims, policies, and standards of for-profit child care. In J. Lande, S. Scarr, & N. Gunzenhauser (Eds.), *Caring for children: Challenge to America* (pp. 233–240). Hillsdale, NJ: Erlbaum.

Musick, J. (1994). Grandmothers and grandmothers-to-be: Effects on adolescent mothers and adolescent mothering. *Infants and Young Children, 6*(3), 1–9.

Myers, B., Olson, H., & Kaltenbach, K. (1992). Cocaine-exposed infants: Myths and misunderstandings. *Zero to Three, 13*(1), 1–5.

Nadel, J., & Fontaine, A. (1989). Communicating by imitation: A developmental and comparative approach to transitory social competence. In B. Schneider, G. Attili, J. Nadel, & R. Weissberg (Eds.), *Social competence in developmental perspective* (pp. 131–144). Dordrecht, Netherlands: Kluwer.

Naeye, R., Burt, L., Wright, D., Blanc, W., & Tatter, D. (1971). Neonatal mortality: The male disadvantage. *Pediatrics, 48*, 902–906.

Nalbandov, A. (1964). *Reproductive physiology.* San Francisco: Freeman.

National Center for Clinical Infant Programs (1992). *Heart Start: The emotional foundations of school readiness.* Arlington, VA: Zero to Three.

Nelson, K. (1989). Monologue as the linguistic construction of self in time. In K. Nelson (Ed.), *Narratives from the crib* (pp. 284–308). Cambridge, MA: Harvard University Press.

Nesselroade, J., & Baltes, P. (1984). Sequential strategies and the role of cohort effects in behavioral development: Adolescent personality as a sample case. In S. Mednick, M. Harway, & K. Finello (Eds.), *Handbook of longitudinal research.* New York: Praeger.

Neuspiel, D., & Hamel, S. (1991). Cocaine and infant behavior. *Developmental and Behavioral Pediatrics, 12*, 55–64.

Newberger, C. (1980). The cognitive structure of parenthood: Designing a descriptive measure. In R. Selman & R. Yando (Eds.), *New directions for child development* (Vol. 7, pp. 45–68). San Francisco: Jossey-Bass.

Newberger, C. (1983). Stages of parental understanding in child abuse and neglect. In V. Sasserath (Ed.), *Minimizing high-risk parenting* (pp. 69–74). Skillman, NJ: Johnson and Johnson.

Newberger, E. (1983). When the injury is a symptom: interrelations among the pediatric social illness. In V. Sasserath (Ed.), *Minimizing high-risk parenting* (pp. 65–68). Skillman, NJ: Johnson and Johnson.

Nickel, R. (1992). Disorders of brain development. *Infants and Young Children, 5*(1), 1–11.

Nishi, R. (1994). Neurotrophic factors: Two are better than one. *Science, 205*, 1052–1053.

Noble, B. (1992, May 3). When a white collar unravels. *New York Times*, Section 3, p. 25.

Noble, B. (1993, April 18). Worthy child-care pay scales. *New York Times*, Section 3, p. 25.

Nogales, H. (1995). Perspective. *Infants and Young Children, 7*(4), v–vii.

Nordhaus, B., & Solnit, A. (1990). Adoption, 1990. *Zero to Three, 10*(5), 1–4.

Norton, D. (1995/1996). Early linguistic interaction and school achievement: An ethnographical, ecological perspective. *Zero to Three, 16*(3), 8–14.

Nowak, R. (1993). Draft genome map debuts on Internet. *Science, 262*, 1967.

Nowak, R. (1994a). Moving developmental research into the clinic. *Science, 266*, 567–568.

Nowak, R. (1994b). Smoke in hamster oviducts. *Science, 263*, 31.

Nowakowski, R. (1993). Basic concepts of CNS development. In M. Johnson (Ed.), *Brain development and cognition* (pp. 54–92). Oxford: Blackwell.

Nüsslein-Volhard, C. (1994). Of flies and fishes. *Science, 266,* 572–574.

Nwokah, E. (1987). Maidese vs. motherese—is the language input of child and adult caregivers similar? *Language and Speech, 30*(3), 213–238.

O'Brien, J. (1970). Lipids and myelination. In W. Himwich (Ed.), *Developmental neurobiology* (pp. 262–286). Springfield, IL: Charles C Thomas.

O'Connor, T., & Rutter, M. (1996). Risk mechanisms in development: Some conceptual and methodological considerations. *Developmental Psychology, 32*(4), 787–795.

Oakes, L. (1994). Development of infants' use of continuity cues in their perception of causality. *Developmental Psychology, 30,* 869–879.

Oetter, P., Laurel, M., & Cool, S. (1990). Sensorimotor foundations of communication. In C. Royeen (Ed.), *Neuroscience foundations of human performance.* Rockville, MD: American Occupational Therapy Association.

Ogletree, B., & Daniels, D. (1993). Communication-based assessment and intervention for pre-linguistic infants and toddlers: Strategies and issues. *Infants and Young Children, 5*(3), 22–30.

Ohzawa, I., de Angelis, G., & Freeman, R. (1990). Stereoscopic depth discrimination in the visual cortex: neurons ideally suited as disparity detectors. *Science, 249,* 1036–1041.

Olds, D., Henderson, C., & Kitzman, H. (1994). Does prenatal and infancy home visitation have enduring effects on qualities of parental caregiving and child health at 25 to 50 months of age? *Pediatrics, 93,* 89–98.

Oller, D. (1990). Tactile hearing for deaf children. In N. Gunzenhauser (Ed.), *Advances in touch* (pp. 117–124). Skillman, NJ: Johnson and Johnson.

Olson, C., & Freeman, R. (1980). Profile of the sensitive period for monocular deprivation in kittens. *Experimental Brain Research, 39,* 17–21.

Olson, H. (1994). The effects of prenatal alcohol exposure on child development. *Infants and Young Children, 6*(3), 10–25.

Olson, H., Burgess, D., & Streissguth, A. (1992). Fetal alcohol syndrome (FAS) and fetal alcohol effects (FAE): A lifespan view, with implications for early intervention. *Zero to Three, 13*(1), 24–29.

Oppenheim, R. (1984). Ontogenetic adaptations in neural and behavioral development: Toward a more "ecological" developmental psychobiology. In H. Prechtl (Ed.), *Continuity of neural functions from prenatal to postnatal life* (pp. 16–30). Philadelphia: Lippincott.

Osofsky, H. (1983). Coping with pregnancy and parenthood. In V. Sasserath (Ed.), *Minimizing high-risk parenting* (pp. 33–38). Skillman, NJ: Johnson and Johnson.

Osofsky, J. (1994). Introduction. In J. Osofsky & E. Fenichel (Eds.), *Caring for infants and toddlers in violent environments: hurt, healing, and hope* (pp. 3–6). Arlington, VA: Zero to Three.

Ostry, D., Flanagan, J., Feldman, A., & Munhall, K. (1991). Human jaw motion control in mastication and speech. In J. Requin & G. Spelmach (Eds.), *Tutorials in motor neuroscience* (pp. 535–546). NATO ASI Series. Series D: Behavioral and Social Sciences (Vol. 62). Dordrecht, Netherlands: Kluwer.

Oyama, S. (1987). *The ontogeny of information.* Cambridge: Cambridge University Press.

Oyserman, D., Radin, N., & Benn, R. (1993). Dynamics in a three-generational family: Teens, grandparents, and babies. *Developmental Psychology, 29,* 564–572.

Palca, J. (1991a). Fetal brain signals time for birth. *Science, 256,* 1360.

Palca, J. (1991b). HIV risk higher for first-born twins. *Science, 256,* 1729.

Palca, J. (1992a). Infection with selection: HIV in human infants. *Science, 257,* 1069.

Palca, J. (1992b). Agencies split on nutrition advice. *Science, 257,* 1857.

Palm, G., & Palkovitz, R. (1988). The challenge of working with new fathers: Implications for support providers. *Marriage and Family Review, 12,* 357–376.

Palmos, P. (1991). Preface. In E. Hibbs (Ed.), *Adoption: International perspectives* (pp. xi–xii). Madison, CN: International Universities Press.

Papousek, H., & Papousek, M. (1987). Intuitive parenting: A dialectic counterpart to the infant's integrative competence. In J. Osofsky (Ed.), *Handbook of infant development* (pp. 669–720). New York: Wiley.

Passman, R. (1977). Providing attachment objects to facilitate learning and reduce distress. *Developmental Psychology, 13,* 25–28.

Paul, R., & Jennings, P. (1992). Phonological behavior in toddlers with slow expressive language development. *Journal of Speech and Hearing Research, 35,* 99–107.

Pawl, J. (1990). Infants in day care: Reflections on experiences, expectations and relationships. *Zero to Three, 10*(3), 1–6.

Peabody, R. (1981). Intervention strategies for the visually impaired. In D. Radcliffe (Ed.), *Developmental disabilities in the preschool child* (pp. 7–9). New York: SP Medical and Scientific Books.

Pear, R. (1992, Sept. 13). U.S. orders testing of poor children for lead poisoning. *New York Times,* p. 6.

Pederson, D., Moran, G., Sitko, C., Campbell, K., Ghesquire, K., & Acton, H. (1990). Maternal sensitivity and the security of infant-mother attachment: A Q-sort study. *Child Development, 61,* 1974–1983.

Pennisi, E. (1996). Studly sheep by non-Mendelian means. *Science, 272,* 1099–1100.

Penticuff, J. (1992). The impact of the Child Abuse Amendments on nursing staff and their care of handicapped newborns. In A. Caplan, R. Blank, & J. Merrick (Eds.), *Compelled compassion* (pp. 267–284). Totowa, NJ: Humana.

Pettit, M., & Schwark, H. (1993). Receptive field reorganization during temporary denervation. *Science, 262,* 2054–2059.

Phillips, C., & Cooper, R. (1992). Cultural dimensions of feeding relationships. *Zero to Three, 12*(5), 10–13.

Phillips, K. (1993, January 10). Down and out: Can the middle class rise again? *New York Times Magazine,* p. 16, 20, 32–33.

Pickens, J., & Field, T. (1993). Facial expressivity in infants of depressed mothers. *Developmental Psychology, 29,* 986–988.

Pickles, A. (1993). Stages, precursors, and causes in development. In D. Hay & A. Angold (Eds.), *Precursors and causes in development and psychopathology* (pp. 23–49). New York: Wiley.

Pierce, W., & Vitello, R. (1991). Independent adoptions and the "baby market." In E. Hibbs (Ed.), *Adoption: International perspectives* (pp. 131–144). Madison, CN: International Universities Press.

Pine, J. (1995). Variation in vocabulary development as a function of birth order. *Child Development, 66*(1), 272–281.

Pinholster, G. (1995). Multiple "SIDS" case ruled murder. *Science, 268,* 494.

Piper, M., Junos, V., Willis, D., Mazer, B., Ramsey, M., & Silver, K. (1986). Early physical therapy effects on the high-risk infant: A randomized controlled trial. *Pediatrics, 78,* 216–224.

Pipes, P. (1977). *Nutrition in infancy and childhood.* St. Louis: C.V. Mosby.

Pirchio, M., Spinelli, D., Fiorentini, A., & Maffei, L. (1978). Infant contrast sensitivity evaluated by evoked potentials. *Brain Research, 141,* 179–184.

Pizzo, P. (1990). Whole babies, parents, and pieces of funds: Creating comprehensive programs for infants and toddlers. *Zero to Three, 10*(1), 24–28.

Platt, B., & Ginn, S. (1938). Chinese methods of infant feeding and nursing. *Archives of Disease in Childhood, 13,* 343–354.

Plotkin, S. (1994). Vaccines for varicella-zoster virus and cytomegalovirus: Recent progress. *Science, 265,* 1383–1385.

Porges, S. (1993). The infant's sixth sense: Awareness and regulation of bodily processes. *Zero to Three, 14*(2), 12–16.

Porges, S., Matthews, K., & Pauls, D. (1992). The biobehavioral interface in behavioral pediatrics. *Pediatrics, 90,* 789–797.

Porter, B. (1993, April 11). I met my daughter at the Wuhan Foundling Hospital. *New York Times Magazine,* pp. 24–27.

Poulin-Dubois, J., Serbin, L., Kenyon, B., & Derbyshire, A. (1994). Compliance and self-assertion: Young children's responses to mothers versus fathers. *Developmental Psychology, 30,* 980–989.

Power, T., McGrath, M., Hughes, S., & Manive, S. (1994). Compliance and self-assertion: Young children's responses to mothers versus fathers. *Developmental Psychology 30,* 980–989.

Powls, A., Botting, N., Cooke, R., & Marlow, N. (1996). Handedness in very-low-birthweight (VLBW) children at 12 years of age: In relation to perinatal and outcome variables. *Developmental Medicine and Child Neurology, 38,* 594–602.

Pratt, M., Hunsberger, B., Pancer, S., Roth, D., & Santolupo, S. (1993). Thinking about parenting: Reasoning about developmental issues across the lifespan. *Developmental Psychology, 29,* 585–595.

Prechtl, H. (1984a). Continuity and change in early neural development. In H. Prechtl (Ed.), *Continuity of neural functions from prenatal to postnatal life* (pp. 1–15). Philadelphia: Lippincott.

Prechtl, H. (1984b). Epilogue. In H. Prechtl (Ed.), *Continuity of neural functions from prenatal to postnatal life* (pp. 245–247). Philadelphia: Lippincott.

Prechtl, H. (1990). Qualitative changes of spontaneous movements in fetus and preterm infant are a marker of neurological dysfunction. *Early Human Development, 23,* 151–158.

Prechtl, H., Akiyama, Y., Zinkin, P., & Grant, D. (1968). Polygraphic studies in the full-term newborn. I. Technical aspects and qualitative analysis. In M. Bax & R. McKeith (Eds.), *Studies in infancy* (pp. 1–21). London: Heinemann.

Preston, J. (1993, February 15). Third World, Second class. Part 2. *Washington Post,* pp. A1, A32–A33.

Prezant, T., Shohat, M., Jaber, L., Pressman, S., & Fischel-Ghodsian, N. (1992). Biochemical characterization of a pedigree with mitochondrially inherited deafness. *American Journal of Medical Genetics, 44,* 465–472.

Prizant, B., & Wetherby, A. (1989). Enhancing communication: From theory to practice. In G. Dawson (Ed.), *Autism: New perspectives on diagnosis, nature, and treatment* (pp. 282–309). New York: Guilford.

Prizant, B., & Wetherby, A. (1990). Assessing the communication of infants and toddlers: Integrating a socioemotional perspective. *Zero to Three, 11*(1), 1–12.

Prizant, B., & Wetherby, A. (1993). Communication and language assessment for young children. *Infants and Young Children, 5*(4), 20–34.

Proctor, A., & Murnyack, T. (1995). Assessing communication, cognition, and vocalization in the prelinguistic period. *Infants and Young Children, 7*(4), 39–54.

Profet, M. (1992). Pregnancy sickness as adaptation: A deterrent to maternal ingestion of teratogens. In J. Barkow, L. Cosmides, & J. Tooby (Eds.), *The adapted mind* (pp. 327–366). New York: Oxford University Press.

Program Analysis and Evaluation Branch, Office of Program Planning and Management. (1968). *Mental Health Program Reports 2.* (Public Health Service Publication No. 1743).

Provence, S. (1983). Depression in infancy? *Zero to Three, 3*(4), 1–4.

Provine, R., & Westerman, J. (1979). Crossing the midline: Limits of early eye-hand behavior. *Child Development, 50,* 437–441.

Radbill, S. (1945). Child hygiene among the American Indians. *Texas Reports on Biology and Medicine, 4,* 419–512.

Rader, N., Bausano, M., & Richards, J. (1980). On the nature of the visual-cliff-avoidance response in human infants. *Child Development, 51,* 61–68.

Radetsky, P. (1994). Stopping premature births before it's too late. *Science, 266,* 1486–1488.

Radke-Yarrow, M. (1986). Affective development in young children. In T. Brazelton & M. Yogman (Eds.), *Affective development in infancy* (pp. 145–152). Norwood, NJ: Ablex.

Raff, M., Barres, B., Burne, J., Coles, H., Ishizaki, Y., & Jacobson, M. (1993). Programmed cell death and the control of cell survival: Lessons from the nervous system. *Science, 262,* 695–699.

Raloff, J. (1992). Infant growth: A sporadic phenomenon. *Science News, 141,* 102.

Ramsay, M., & Gisel, E. (1996). Neonatal sucking and maternal feeding practices. *Developmental Medicine and Child Neurology, 38,* 34–47.

Raphael, D., & Davis, F. (1985). *Only mothers know: Patterns of infant feeding in traditional cultures.* Westport, CT: Greenwood.

Rathlev, M. (1994). Universal precautions in early intervention and childcare. *Infants and Young Children, 6*(3), 54–64.

Raymond, J., Lisberger, S., & Mauk, M. (1996). The cerebellum: A neuronal learning machine. *Science, 272,* 1126–1131.

Reed, E. (1989). Changing theories of postural development. In M. Woollacott & A. Shumway-Cook (Eds.), *Development of posture and gait across the life span* (pp. 3–24). Columbia: University of South Carolina Press.

Reisen, A. (1971). Problems in correlating behavioral and physiological development. In M. Sterman, D. McGinty, & A. Adinolfi (Eds.), *Brain development and behavior* (pp. 59–70). New York: Academic Press.

Reite, M. (1990). Effects of touch on the immune system. In N. Gunzenhauser (Ed.), *Advances in touch* (pp. 22–34). Skillman, NJ: Johnson and Johnson.

Reuben, R. (1981). Clinical appraisal of vision. In D. Radcliffe (Ed.), *Developmental disabilities in the preschool child* (pp. 5–6). New York: SP Medical and Scientific Books.

Richards, J. (1987). Infant visual sustained attention and respiratory sinus arrhythmia. *Child Development, 58,* 488–496.

Richards, M., Bernal, J., & Brackbill, Y. (1976). Early behavioral differences: Gender or circumcision? *Developmental Psychobiology, 9,* 89–95.

Richardson, L. (1993, May 2). Nannygate for the poor. *New York Times,* p. 52.

Rickman, M., & Davidson, R. (1994). Personality and behavior in parents of temperamentally inhibited and uninhibited children. *Developmental Psychology, 30,* 346–354.

Riese, M. (1990). Neonatal temperament in monozygotic and dizygotic twin pairs. *Child Development, 61,* 1230–1237.

Roberts, J., Wallace, I., & Zeisel, S. (1993). Otitis media: Implications for early intervention. *Zero to Three, 13*(4), 24–28.

Roberts, L. (1991a). Does egg beckon sperm when the time is right? *Science, 252,* 214.

Roberts, L. (1991b). FISHing cuts the angst in amniocentesis. *Science, 254,* 378–379.

Roberts, L. (1992a). Anthropologists climb (gingerly) on board. *Science, 258,* 1300–1301.

Roberts, L. (1992b). Two chromosomes down, 22 to go. *Science, 258,* 28–30.

Robson, K. (1967). The role of eye-to-eye contact in maternal-infant attachment. *Journal of Child Psychology and Psychiatry, 8,* 13–25.

Rochat, P. (1987). Mouthing and grasping in neonates: Evidence for early detection of what hard and soft substances afford for action. *Infant Behavior and Development, 11,* 261–278.

Rochat, P., Blass, E., & Hoffmeyer, L. (1988). Oropharyngeal control of hand-mouth coordination in newborn infants. *Developmental Psychology, 24,* 459–463.

Rochat, P., & Senders, S. (1991). Active touch in infancy: Action systems in development. In M. Weiss & P. Zelazo (Eds.), *Newborn attention: Biological constraints and the influence of experience* (pp. 412–442). Norwood, NJ: Ablex.

Roe v. Wade, 410 U.S. 113 (1973).

Rogel, M., & Petersen, A. (1984). Some adolescent experiences of motherhood. In R. Cohen, B. Cohler, & S. Weissman (Eds.), *Parenthood* (pp. 85–102). New York: Guilford.

Romond, J., & Baker, I. (1985). Squatting in childbirth: A new look at an old tradition. *Journal of Obstetric, Gynecologic, and Neonatal Nursing, 14,* 406–411.

Rosen, G., & Galaburda, A. (1985). Development of language: A question of asymmetry and deviation. In J. Mehler & R. Fox (Eds.), *Neonate cognition* (pp. 307–326). Hillsdale, NJ: Erlbaum.

Ross, S., Jennings, K., & Popper, S. (1993). Identifying maternal depression in an early intervention setting. *Infants and Young Children, 5*(3), 12–21.

Rothbart, M. (1988). Temperament and the development of inhibited approach. *Child Development, 59,* 1241–1250.

Roush, W. (1995). Embryos travel forking path as they tell left from right. *Science, 269,* 1514–1515.

Roush, W. (1996a). Guarding against premature birth. *Science, 271,* 1126–1131.

Roush, W. (1996b). Putting the brakes on bone growth. *Science, 273,* 579.

Rovee-Collier, C. (1987). Learning and memory in infancy. In J. Osofsky (Ed.), *Handbook of infant development* (pp. 98–148). New York: Wiley.

Rovee-Collier, C. (1995). Time windows in cognitive development. *Developmental Psychology, 31,* 146–169.

Rovee-Collier, C., & Boller, K. (1995). Current theory and research on infant learning and memory. *Infants and Young Children, 7*(3), 1–12.

Rubenstein, J., Martinez, S., Shimamuru, K., & Puelles, L. (1994). The embryonic vertebrate forebrain: The prosomeric model. *Science, 266,* 578–580.

Ruff, H., Saltarelli, L., Capozzoli, M., & Dubiner, K. (1992). The differentiation of activity in infants' exploration of objects. *Developmental Psychology, 28,* 851–861.

Rutkowska, J. (1993). *The computational infant.* Hemel Hempstead: Harvester Wheatsheaf.

Rutter, M. (1987). Continuities and discontinuities from infancy. In J. Osofsky (Ed.), *Handbook of infant development* (pp. 1256–1296). New York: Wiley.

Ryan, C., & Finer, N. (1994). Changing attitudes and practices regarding local analgesia for newborn circumcision. *Pediatrics, 94,* 230–233.

Sameroff, A. (1983). Factors in predicting successful parenting. In V. Sasserath (Ed.), *Minimizing high-risk parenting* (pp. 16–24). Skillman, NJ: Johnson and Johnson.

Sandford, M., Kissling, G., & Joubert, P. (1992). Neural tube defect etiology: New evidence concerning maternal hyperthermia, health, and diet. *Developmental Medicine and Child Neurology, 34,* 661–675.

Sary, G., Vogels, R., & Orban, G. (1993). Cue-invariant shape selectivity of macaque inferior temporal neurons. *Science, 260,* 995–997.

Saudino, K., & Eaton, W. (1991). Infant temperament and genetics: An objective twin study of motor activity level. *Child Development, 62,* 1167–1174.

Scarr, S. (1992). Developmental theories for the 1990s: Development and individual differences. *Child Development, 63,* 1–19.

Scarr, S., & Eisenberg, M. (1993). Child care research: Issues, perspectives, and results. *Annual Review of Psychology, 44,* 613–644.

Scarr, S., Lande, J., & McCartney, K. (1989). Child care and the family: Complements and interactions. In J. Lande, S. Scarr, & N. Gunzenhauser (Eds.), *Caring for children: Challenge to America* (pp. 1–22). Hillsdale,NJ: Erlbaum.

Scarr, S., & McCartney, K. (1983). How people make their own environments: A theory of genotype-environment effects. *Child Development, 54,* 424–435.

Schaal, B., Montagner, H., Hertling, E., Bolzoni, D., Moyse, A., & Quichon, R. (1980). Les stimulations olfactives dans les relations entre l'enfant et la mère. *Réproduction, Nutrition, Développement, 20,* 843–858.

Schanberg, S., Field, T., Kuhn, C., & Bartolome, J. (1993). Touch: A biological regulator of growth and development in the neonate. *Verhaltenstherapie, 3* (Supplement 1), 15.

Schanberg, S., Kuhn, C., Field, T., & Bartolome, J. (1990). Maternal deprivation and growth suppression. In N. Gunzenhauser (Ed.), *Advances in touch* (pp. 3–10). Skillman, NJ: Johnson and Johnson.

Scheibel, M., & Scheibel, A. (1971). Selected structural-functional correlations in postnatal brain. In M. Sterman, D. McGinty, & A. Adinolfi (Eds.), *Brain development and behavior* (pp. 1–22). New York: Academic Press.

Scheper-Hughes, N. (1993). Lifeboat ethics: Mother love and child death in Northeast Brazil. In C. Brettel & C. Sargent (Eds.), *Gender in cross-cultural perspective* (pp. 31–37). Englewood Cliffs, NJ: Prentice-Hall.

Schneider, B., Trehub, S., & Bull, D. (1980). High-frequency sensitivity in infants. *Science, 207,* 1003–1004.

Schoendorf, K., & Kiely, J. (1992). Relationship of Sudden Infant Death Syndrome to maternal smoking during and after pregnancy. *Pediatrics, 90,* 905–908.

Schrag, E. (1984). Infant and toddler care in the states: the comparative licensing study and beyond. *Zero to Three, 4*(3), 8–11.

Schulte, B. (1995, Nov. 9). Senate defers action on a late-abortion ban. *Philadelphia Inquirer,* p. A19.

Schulzinger, R. (1992/1993). Infants, toddlers, and SSI: Changing the rules, reaching the children. *Zero to Three, 13*(3), 27–30.

Schwartz, M., & Goldman-Rakic, P. (1987). Development and plasticity of the association cortex. In N. Gunzenhauser (Ed.), *Infant stimulation* (pp. 30–42). Skillman, NJ: Johnson and Johnson.

Seabrook, J. (1994, March 28). Building a better human. *The New Yorker,* pp. 109–114.

Seachrist, L. (1994). Allergy gene nothing to sneeze at. *Science, 264,* 1533.

Sears, J. (1994). Recognizing and coping with tactile defensiveness in young children. *Infants and Young Children, 6*(4), 46–53.

Segalowitz, S., & Chapman, J. (1980). Cerebral asymmetry for speech in infants: A behavioral measure. *Brain and Language, 9,* 281–288.

Seligman, M., Maier, S., & Solomon, R. (1971). Unpredictable and uncontrollable aversive events. In F. Brush (Ed.), *Aversive conditioning and learning* (pp. 347–401). New York: Academic Press.

Service, R. (1994a). An anti-HIV vitamin? *Science, 265,* 315.

Service, R. (1994b). Contraceptive methods go back to the basics. *Science, 266,* 1480–1481.

Service, R. (1994c). Triggering the first line of defense. *Science, 265,* 1522–1524.

Sever, J. (1983). Maternal infections. In C. Brown (Ed.), *Childhood learning disabilities and prenatal risk* (pp. 31–37). Skillman, NJ: Johnson and Johnson.

Shapiro, B. (1994). The environmental basis of the Down syndrome phenotype. *Developmental Medicine and Child Neurology, 36,* 84–90.

Sharav, T., Collins, R., & Shlomo, L. (1985). Effect of maternal education on prognosis of development in children with Down syndrome. *Pediatrics, 76,* 387–391.

Shaver, S. (1979). Maternal physiologic adaptations to nurture the fetus. In A. Clark, D. Affonso, & T. Harris (Eds.), *Childbearing: A nursing perspective* (pp. 123–138). Philadelphia: Davis.

Shaw, A. (1992). Baby Doe and me. In A. Caplan, R. Blank, & J. Merrick (Eds.), *Compelled compassion* (pp. 185–206). Totowa, NJ: Humana.

Shaw, D., Keenan, K., & Vondra, J. (1994). Developmental precursors of externalizing behavior: Ages 1 to 3. *Developmental Psychology, 30,* 355–364.

Shea, S., Fox, R., Aslin, R., & Dumais, S. (1980). Assessment of stereopsis in human infants. *Investigative Ophthalmology and Visual Science, 19,* 1400–1404.

Shinefield, H., Ribble, J., Borrs, M., & Eichenwald, H. (1963). Bacterial interference: Its effect on nursery-acquired infection with *Staphylococcus aureus.* I. Preliminary observations on artificial colonization of newborns. *American Journal of Diseases of Children, 105,* 146–154.

Shwalb, B., Shwalb, D., & Shoji, J. (1994). Structure and dimensions of maternal perceptions of Japanese temperament. *Developmental Psychology, 30,* 131–141.

Sidel, R. (1973). *Women and child care in China.* Baltimore: Penguin.

Sigman, M. (1989). The application of developmental knowledge to a clinical problem: The study of childhood autism. In D. Cicchetti (Ed.), *The emergence of a discipline: Rochester symposium on developmental psychopathology* (pp. 165–188). Hillsdale, NJ: Erlbaum.

Silverman, W. (1992). Overtreatment of neonates? A personal retrospective. *Pediatrics, 90,* 971–976.

Simon, N., Brady, N., Stafford, R., & Powell, R. (1992). The effect of abdominal incisions on early motor development of infants with necrotizing enterocolitis. *Developmental Medicine and Child Neurology, 34,* 49–53.

Simpson, M. (1985). Breast-feeding, infant growth and return to fertility in an Iranian city. In V. Hull & M. Simpson (Eds.), *Breast-feeding, child health and child spacing* (pp. 109–138). Dover, NH: Croom Helm.

Singer, J., & Fagen, J. (1992). Negative affect, emotional expression, and forgetting in young infants. *Developmental Psychology, 28,* 48–57.

Slater, A., Morrison, V., & Rose, D. (1984). Habituation in the newborn. *Infant Behavior and Development, 7,* 183–200.

Slater, P. (1970). *Views of children and of child rearing during the early national period: A study in the New England intellect.* Unpublished doctoral dissertation, University of California, Berkeley.

Smith, B., Fillion, T., & Blass, E. (1990). Orally mediated sources of calming in 1- to 3-day-old human infants. *Developmental Psychology, 26,* 731–737.

Smith, P., & Torrey, B. (1996). The future of the behavioral and social sciences. *Science, 271,* 611–612.

Socolar, R., & Stein, R. (1995). Spanking infants and toddlers: Maternal beliefs and practice. *Pediatrics, 95,* 105–111.

Soken, N., & Pick, A. (1992). Intermodal perception of happy and angry expressive behaviors by 7-month-old infants. *Child Development, 63,* 787–795.

Sokol, S. (1982). Infant visual development: Evoked potential estimates. In I. Bodis-Wollner (Ed.), *Evoked potentials. Annals of the New York Academy of Sciences* (Vol. 388, pp. 514–525). New York: New York Academy of Sciences.

Sokolov, J. (1993). A local contingency analysis of the fine-tuning hypothesis. *Developmental Psychology, 29*(6), 1008–1023.

Solnit, A. (1984). Parenthood and child advocacy. In R. Cohen, B. Cohen, & S. Weissman (Eds.), *Parenthood* (pp. 227–238). New York: Guilford.

Soltesz, M., & Brockway, N. (1989). The high-risk infant. In J. Tecklin (Ed.), *Pediatric physical therapy* (pp. 40–67). Philadelphia: Lippincott.

Sommer, K., Whitman, T., Borkowski, J., Schellenbach, C., Maxwell, S., & Keogh, D. (1993). Cognitive readiness and adolescent parenting. *Developmental Psychology, 29,* 389–398.

Spelke, E. (1985). Perception of unity, persistence, and identity: Thoughts on infants' conceptions of objects. In J. Mehler & R. Fox (Eds.), *Neonate cognition* (pp. 89–114). Hillsdale, NJ: Erlbaum.

Spieker, S., & Bensley, L. (1994). Roles of living arrangements and grandmother social support in adolescent mothering and infant attachment. *Developmental Psychology, 30,* 102–111.

Spinelli, D. (1987). Plasticity triggering experiences, nature, and the dual genesis of brain structure and function. In N. Gunzenhauser (Ed.), *Infant stimulation* (pp. 21–29). Skillman, NJ: Johnson and Johnson.

Spingarn, R., & DuRant, R. (1996). Male adolescents involved in pregnancy: Associated health risks and problem behaviors. *Pediatrics, 98*(2), 262–268.

Spivack, F. (1995). Conductive education perspectives. *Infants and Young Children, 8*(1), 75–85.

Sroufe, L. (1989). Pathways to adaptation and maladaptation: psychopathology as developmental deviation. In D. Cicchetti (Ed.), *The emergence of a discipline: Rochester symposium on developmental psychopathology* (pp. 13–40). Hillsdale, NJ: Erlbaum.

Sroufe, L., Egeland, B., & Kreutzer, T. (1990). The fate of early experience following developmental change: Longitudinal approaches to individual adaptation in childhood. *Child Development, 61,* 1363–1373.

Stanovich, K. (1992). *How to think straight about psychology.* New York: Harper Collins.

Starkey, P., Spelke, E., & Gelman, R. (1983). Detection of intermodal numerical correspondences by human infants. *Science, 222,* 179–181.

Starling, S., Holden, T., & Jenny, C. (1995). Abusive head trauma: The relationship of perpetrators to their victims. *Pediatrics, 95,* 259–262.

Stiehm, E., & Fulginiti, V. (1973). *Immunologic disorders in infants and children.* Philadelphia: Saunders.

Stone, R. (1992a). Can a father's exposure lead to illness in his children? *Science, 258,* 31.

Stone, R. (1992b). Polarized debate: EMFs and cancer. *Science, 258,* 1724–1725.

Stone, R. (1993a). Sandoz adds brainchild to brood. *Science, 259,* 299.

Stone, R. (1993b). The hazards of frequent flying. *Science, 262,* 979.

Stone, R. (1994a). Controversial SIDS advice may get government imprimatur. *Science, 263,* 1079.

Stone, R. (1994b). Environmental estrogens stir debate. *Science, 265,* 308–310.

Streissguth, A. (1983). Smoking and drinking. In C. Brown (Ed.), *Childhood learning disabilities and prenatal risk* (pp. 49–55). Skillman, NJ: Johnson and Johnson.

Stryker, M. (1994). Precise development from imprecise rules. *Science, 263,* 1244–1245.

Stryker, M., Sherk, H., Leventhal, A., & Hirsch, H. (1978). Physiological consequences for the cat's visual cortex of effectively restricting early visual experience with oriented contours. *Journal of Neurophysiology, 41,* 896–909.

Sullivan, M., & Lewis, M. (1993). Contingency, means-end skills, and the use of technology in infant intervention. *Infants and Young Children, 5*(4), 58–77.

Sullivan v. Zebley, 493 U.S. 521 (1990).

Sumits, T., Bennett, R., & Gould, J. (1996). Maternal risks for very low birth weight infant mortality. *Pediatrics, 98*(2), 236–241.

Sun, M. (1985). The vexing problems of vaccine. *Science, 227,* 1013.

Super, C., & Harkness, S. (1982). The infant's niche in rural Kenya and metropolitan America. In L. Adler (Ed.), *Cross-cultural research at issue* (pp. 47–56). New York: Academic Press.

Super, C., & Harkness, S. (1986). Temperament, development, and culture. In R. Plomin & J. Dunn (Eds.), *The study of temperament: Changes, continuities, and challenges* (pp. 131–150). Hillsdale, NJ: Erlbaum.

Swain, I., Zelazo, P., & Clifton, R. (1993). Newborn infants' memory for speech sounds retained over 24 hours. *Developmental Psychology, 29,* 312–323.

Swanson, C., & Brown, M. (1992). Understanding children with chronic lung disease: Part I. Lung function. *Infants and Young Children, 5*(2), 68–77.

Swanson, L., Leonard, L., & Gandour, J. (1992). Vowel duration in mothers' speech to young children. *Journal of Speech and Hearing Research, 35,* 617–625.

Taft, L. (1981). Clinical appraisal of motor functions. In D. Radcliffe (Ed.), *Developmental disabilities in the preschool child* (pp. 25–27). New York: SP Medical and Scientific Books.

Tager-Flusberg, H. (1993). What language reveals about the understanding of minds in children with autism. In S. Baron-Cohen, H. Tager-Flusberg, & D. Cohen (Eds.), *Understanding other minds* (pp. 138–157). New York: Oxford University Press.

Takas, M. (1992/1993). Kinship care: Developing a safe and effective framework for protective placement of children with relatives. *Zero to Three, 13*(3), 12–17.

Tallal, P., Miller, S., & Fitch, R. (1993). Neurobiological basis of speech: A case for the preeminence of temporal processing. In P. Tallal, A. Galaburda, R. Llinás, & C. von Euler (Eds.), *Temporal information processing in the nervous system. Annals of New York Academy of Sciences* (Vol. 682, pp. 27–47). New York: New York Academy of Sciences.

Talley-Lacy, M., & McCarthy, M. (1994). Premature labor (tocolysis). In M. Gulanick, M. Puzas, D. Gradishar, & K. Gettrust (Eds.), *Obstetric and gynecologic nursing* (pp. 506–515). Albany, NY: Delmar.

Tamarkin, L., Baird, C., & Almeida, O. (1985). Melatonin: A coordinating signal for mammalian reproduction. *Science, 227,* 714–720.

Tanaka, K. (1993). Neuronal mechanisms of object recognition. *Science, 262,* 685–688.

Tanner, J. (1978). *Foetus into man.* Cambridge, MA: Harvard University Press.

Tardif, T. (1996). Nouns are not always learned before verbs: Evidence from Mandarin speakers' early vocabularies. *Developmental Psychology, 32*(3), 492–504.

Taubes, G. (1995). Use of placebo controls in clinical trials disputed. *Science, 267,* 25–26.

Taussig, H. (1968). The thalidomide syndrome. In G. Hardin (Ed.), *Thirty-nine steps to biology* (pp. 301–307). San Francisco: Freeman.

Teller, D., Morse, R., Borton, R., & Regal, D. (1974). Visual acuity for vertical and diagonal gratings in human infants. *Vision Research, 14,* 1433–1439.

Teti, D., Gelfand, D., Messinger, D., & Isabella, R. (1995). Maternal depression and the quality of early attachment. *Developmental Psychology, 31,* 364–376.

Teti, D., & Nakagawa, M. (1990). Assessing attachment in infancy: The strange situation and alternate systems. In E. Gibbs & D. Teti (Eds.), *Interdisciplinary assessment of infants* (pp. 191–214). Baltimore: P.H. Brookes.

Thatcher, S., & DeCherney, A. (1991). Pregnancy-inducing technologies: Biological and medical implications. In J. Rodin & A. Collins (Eds.), *Women and new reproductive technologies* (pp. 27–36). Hillsdale, NJ: Erlbaum.

Thelen, E. (1991). Motor aspects of emergent speech: A dynamic approach. In N. Krasnegor, D. Rumbaugh, R. Schiefelbusch, & M. Studdert-Kennedy (Eds.), *Biological and behavioral determinants of language development* (pp. 339–362). Hillsdale, NJ: Erlbaum.

Thelen, E., Jensen, J., Kamm, K., Corbetta, D., Schneider, K., & Zernicke, R. (1991). Infant motor development: Implications for motor neuroscience. In J. Requin & G. Stelmach (Eds.), *Tutorials in motor neuroscience* (pp. 43–58). NATO ASI Series. Series D: Behavioral and Social Sciences (Vol. 62). Dordrecht, Netherlands: Kluwer.

Thelen, E., & Smith, L. (1994). *A dynamic systems approach to the development of cognition and action.* Cambridge, MA: MIT Press.

Thelen, E., & Ulrich, B. (1991). Hidden skills: A dynamic systems analysis of treadmill stepping during the first year. *Monographs of the Society for Research in Child Development, 56,* (1, Serial No. 223).

Thelen, E., Ulrich, B., & Jensen, J. (1989). The developmental origins of locomotion. In M. Woollacott & A. Shumway-Cook (Eds.), *Development of posture and gait across the life span* (pp. 25–47). Columbia: University of South Carolina Press.

Thomas, A., & Chess, S. (1986). The New York Longitudinal Study: From infancy to early adult life. In R. Plomin & J. Dunn (Eds.), *The study of temperament: Changes, continuities, and challenges* (pp. 39–52). Hillsdale, NJ: Erlbaum.

Thomas, A., Chess, S., & Birch, H. (1970). The origin of personality. *Scientific American,* August, 106–107.

Thompson, C. (1996). Can some infants beat HIV? *Science, 271,* 441.

Thompson, L. (1992). Harkin seeks compassionate use of unproven treatments. *Science, 258,* 1728.

Thompson, L. (1993). Gene therapists jump ship. *Science, 259,* 303.

Thorson, S. (1994). Perspective. *Infants and Young Children, 6*(3), vi–viii.

Thurman, S., & Gonsalves, S. (1993). Adolescent mothers and their premature infants: Responding to double risk. *Infants and Young Children, 5*(4), 44–51.

Toda, S., & Fogel, A. (1993). Infant response to the still-face situation at 3 and 6 months. *Developmental Psychology, 29,* 532–538.

Tomasello, M. (1988). The role of joint attentional processes in early language development. *Language Science, 10*(1), 69–88.

Tortora, S. (1994). Join my dance: The unique movement style of each infant and toddler can invite communication, expression, and intervention. *Zero to Three, 15*(1), 1–10.

Touchette, N. (1994). Finding clues about how embryo structures form. *Science, 266,* 564–565.

Touwer, B., Hempel, M., & Westra, L. (1992). The development of crawling between 18 months and four years. *Developmental Medicine and Child Neurology, 34,* 410–416.

Trad, P. (1993). Previewing: An intervention strategy for psychiatrically ill parents of infants and toddlers. *Zero to Three, 13*(5), 24–29.

Travis, J. (1994). Watching new developments—live. *Science, 263,* 610.

Trehub, S. (1985). Auditory pattern perception in infancy. In S. Trehub & B. Schneider (Eds.), *Auditory development in infancy* (pp. 183–196). New York: Plenum.

Trehub, S., Bull, D., & Schneider, B. (1981). Infants' detection of speech in noise. *Journal of Speech and Hearing Research, 24,* 202–206.

Tretter, F., Cynader, M., & Singer, W. (1975). Modification of direction selectivity of neurons in the visual cortex of kittens. *Brain Research, 84,* 143–149.

Trevarthen, C. (1979). Communication and cooperation in early infancy: A description of primary intersubjectivity. In M. Bullowa (Ed.), *Before speech* (pp. 321–348). Cambridge: Cambridge University Press.

Trevarthen, C. (1982). Basic patterns of psychogenetic change in infancy. In T. Bever (Ed.), *Regressions in mental development* (pp. 7–46). Hillsdale, NJ: Erlbaum.

Tronick, E., Als, H., & Adamson, L. (1979). Structure of early face-to-face communicative interactions. In M. Bullowa (Ed.), *Before speech* (pp. 349–372). Cambridge: Cambridge University Press.

Tronick, E., & Gianino, A. (1986). Interactive mismatch and repair. *Zero to Three, 6*(3), 1–6.

Tronick, E., Morelli, G., & Ivery, P. (1992). The Efe forager infant and toddler's pattern of social relationships: Multiple and simultaneous. *Developmental Psychology, 28,* 568–577.

Tsiantis, J. (1991). Assessment of parental care capacity in the context of adoption. In E. Hibbs (Ed.), *Adoption: International perspectives* (pp. 57–72). Madison, CT: International Universities Press.

Turbiville, V., Turnbull, A., & Rutherford, H. (1995). Fathers and family-centered early intervention. *Infants and Young Children, 7*(4), 12–19.

Turrigiano, G., Abbott, L., & Marder, E. (1994). Activity-dependent changes in the intrinsic properties of cultured neurons. *Science, 264,* 974–977.

Tversky, A., & Kahneman, D. (1974). Judgment under uncertainty: Heuristics and biases. *Science, 185,* 1124–1131.

Tychsen, L., Rastelli, A., Steinman, S., & Steinman, B. (1996). Biases of motion perception revealed by reversing gratings in humans who had infantile-onset strabismus. *Developmental Medicine and Child Neurology, 38,* 408–422.

U.S. Department of Health and Human Services. (1980). *Infant care.* Washington, DC: Author.

U.S. Department of Health, Education, and Welfare, Children's Bureau. (1945). *Your child from one to six.* Washington, DC: Author.

U.S. Department of Labor. (1924). *Infant care.* (Children's Bureau Publication No. 8). Washington, DC: U.S. Government Printing Office.

Uzgiris, I., & Hunt, J. (1975). *Assessment in infancy.* Urbana, IL: University of Illinois Press.

Uzgiris, I., & Hunt, J. (Eds.). (1987). *Infant performance and experience: New findings with the ordinal scale.* Urbana, IL: University of Illinois Press.

Valaes, T., Petmezaki, S., Henschke, C., Drummond, G., & Kappas, A. (1994). Control of jaundice in preterm newborns by an inhibitor of bilirubin production: Studies with tin-meso-porphyrin. *Pediatrics, 93,* 1–11.

van den Boom, D., & Hoeksma, J. (1994). The effect of infant irritability on mother-infant interaction: A growth-curve analysis. *Developmental Psychology, 30,* 581–590.

Van Dyke, D., & Lin-Dyken, D. (1993). The new genetics, developmental disabilities, and early intervention. *Infants and Young Children, 5*(4), 8–19.

Van Essen, D., Anderson, C., & Felleman, D. (1992). Information processing in the primate visual system: An integrated systems perspective. *Science, 255,* 419–423.

van Esterik, P. (1985). The cultural context of breast-feeding in rural Thailand. In V. Hull & M. Simpson (Eds.), *Breast-feeding, child health and child spacing* (pp. 139–161). Dover, NH: Croom Helm.

Varner, D., Cook, J., Schenck, M., McDonald, M., & Teller, D. (1985). Tritan discriminations by 1- and 2-month-old human infants. *Vision Research, 25,* 821–831.

Veille, J., Hohimer, A., Burry, K., & Speroff, L. (1985). The effect of exercise on uterine activity in the last eight weeks of pregnancy. *American Journal of Obstetrics and Gynecology, 151,* 727–730.

Vihman, M., Kay, E., de Boysson-Bardies, B., Durand, C., & Sundberg, U. (1994). External sources of individual differences? A cross-linguistic analysis of the phonetics of mothers' speech to 1-year-old children. *Developmental Psychology, 30*(5), 651–662.

Vinter, A. (1986). The role of movement in eliciting early imitations. *Child Development, 57,* 66–71.

von Hofsten, C. (1990). Development of manipulation action in infancy. In H. Bloch & B. Bertenthal (Eds.), *Sensory-motor organizations and development in infancy and early childhood* (pp. 273–284). Dordrecht, Netherlands: Kluwer.

Von Noorden, G. (1973). Experimental amblyopia in monkeys. *Investigative Ophthalmology, 12,* 721–726.

Von Noorden, G., & Maumenee, A. (1968). Clinical observations on stimulus deprivation amblyopia *(amblyopia ex anopsia). American Journal of Ophthalmology, 65,* 229–234.

Vortkamp, A., Lee, K., Lanske, B., Segre, G., Kronenberg, H., & Tabin, C. (1996). Regulation of rate of change of cartilage differentiation by Indian hedgehog and PTH-related protein. *Science, 273,* 613–622.

Vygotsky, L. (1978). *Mind in society: The development of higher psychological processes.* Cambridge, MA: Harvard University Press.

Waddington, C. (1971). Concepts of development. In E. Tobach, L. Aronson, & E. Shaw (Eds.), *The biopsychology of development* (pp. 17–26). New York: Academic Press.

Wagner, R., Maguire, M., & Stallings, R. (1993). *Chromosomes: A synthesis.* New York: Wiley-Liss.

Walden, T., & Ogan, T. (1988). The development of social referencing. *Child Development, 59,* 1230–1240.

Waldrop, M., Bell, R., Mc Laughlan, B., & Halvarson, C. (1978). Newborn minor physical anomalies predict short attention span, peer aggression, and impulsivity at age 3. *Science, 199,* 563–565.

Wallerstein, J., & Kelly, J. (1982). The father-child relationship: Changes after divorce. In S. Cath, A. Gurwitt, & J. Russ (Eds.), *Father and child* (pp. 451–466). Boston: Little, Brown.

Wang, H., Wysocki, C., & Gold, G. (1993). Induction of olfactory receptor sensitivity in mice. *Science, 260,* 998–1000.

Warchol, M., Lambert, P., Goldstein, B., Forge, A., & Corwin, J. (1993). Regenerative proliferation in inner ear sensory epithelia from adult guinea pigs and humans. *Science, 259,* 1619–1622.

Watanabe, M. (1996). Reward expectancy in primate prefrontal neurons. *Nature, 382*(6592), 629–632.

Waterhouse, L., Fein, D., & Modahl, C. (1996). Neurofunctional mechanisms in autism. *Psychological Review, 103*(3), 457–489.

Watson, J., & Raynor, R (1920). Conditioned emotional reactions. *Journal of Experimental Psychology, 1920, 3,* 1–14.

Wei, S. (1974). Nutritional aspects of dental caries. In S. Fomon (Ed.), *Infant nutrition* (pp. 338–358). Philadelphia: Saunders.

Weir, R. (1992). Life-and-death decisions in the midst of uncertainty. In A. Caplan, R. Blank, & J. Merrick (Eds.), *Compelled compassion* (pp. 1–34). Totowa, NJ: Humana.

Weiss, B., Dodge, K., Bates, J., & Pettit, G. (1992). Some consequences of early harsh discipline: Child aggression and maladaptive social information processing style. *Child Development, 63,* 1321–1335.

Weiss, R. (1992). Measles battle loses potent weapon. *Science, 258,* 546–547.

Weissman, M., & Olfson, M. (1995). Depression in women: Implications for health care research. *Science, 269,* 799–801.

Weisz, J. (1989). Culture and the development of child psychopathology: Lessons from Thailand. In D. Cicchetti (Ed.), *The emergence of a discipline: Rochester symposium on developmental psychopathology* (pp. 89–118). Hillsdale, NJ: Erlbaum.

Weitzman, N., Birns, B., & Friend, R. (1985). Traditional and nontraditional mothers' communication with their daughters and sons. *Child Development, 56,* 894–898.

Wellman, H. (1993). Early understanding of mind: The normal case. In S. Baron-Cohen, H. Tager-Flusberg, & D. Cohen (Eds.), *Understanding other minds* (pp. 10–39). New York: Oxford University Press.

Wellman, H., & Gelman, S. (1992). Cognitive development: foundational theories of core domains. *Annual Review of Psychology, 43,* 337–375.

Welsh, M., Pennington, B., Ozonoff, S., Rouse, B., & McCabe, E. (1990). Neuropsychology of early-treated phenylketonuria: Specific executive function deficits. *Child Development, 61,* 1697–1713.

Werker, J., & McLeod, P. (1989). Infant preference for both male and female infant-directed talk: Developmental study of attentional and affective responsiveness. *Canadian Journal of Psychology, 43*, 230–246.

Werler, M., Mitchell, A., & Shapiro, S. (1992). First trimester maternal medication use in relation to gastroschisis. *Teratology, 45*, 361–367.

Werner, E. (1988). Individual differences, universal needs: A 30-year study of resilient high risk infants. *Zero to Three, 8*(4), 1–5.

Werner, J., & Wooten, B. (1979). Human infant color vision and color perception. *Infant Behavior and Development, 2*, 241–274.

Wertheimer, M. (1961). Psychomotor coordination of auditory and visual space at birth. *Science, 134*, 1692.

White, B., Kaban, B., & Attanucci, J. (1979). *The origins of human competence.* Lexington, MA: Lexington Books.

White, R. (1959). Motivation reconsidered: The concept of competence. *Psychological Review, 66*, 297–323.

Whiting, J., & Child, I. (1953). *Child training and personality.* New Haven: Yale University Press.

Wierson, M., & Forehand, R. (1994). Parent behavioral training for child noncompliance: Rationale, concepts, and effectiveness. *Current Directions in Psychological Science, 3*(5), 14–149.

Wiesel, T., & Hubel, D. (1963). Single-cell responses in striate cortex of kittens deprived of vision in one eye. *Journal of Neurophysiology, 26*, 1003–1017.

Wiggins, J. (1979). *Childbearing: Physiology, experiences, needs.* St. Louis: Mosby.

Wilcox, B., & Naimark, H. (1991). The rights of the child: Progress toward human dignity. *American Psychologist, 46*, 49–65.

Wildgen, W. (1990). Basic principles of self-organization in language. In H. Haken & M. Stadler (Eds.), *Synergetics of cognition* (pp. 415–426). Berlin: Springer-Verlag.

Willer, B. (1989). Licensing and accreditation of child care facilities. In J. Lande, S. Scarr, & N. Gunzenhauser (Eds.), *Caring for children: Challenge to America* (pp. 153–166). Hillsdale, NJ: Erlbaum.

Williams, G. (1980). Child abuse and neglect: Problems of definition and incidence. In G. Williams & J. Money (Eds.), *Traumatic abuse and neglect of children at home* (pp. 483–497). Baltimore: Johns Hopkins University Press.

Williams, J. (1994). Prostaglandin-induced abortion. In M. Gulanick, M. Puzas, D. Gradishar, & K. Gettrust (Eds.), *Obstetric and gynecologic nursing* (pp. 73–81). Albany, NY: Delmar.

Williamson, G. (1988). Motor control as a resource for adaptive coping. *Zero to Three, 9*(1), 1–7.

Williamson, W., & Demmler, G. (1992). Congenital infections: Clinical outcome and educational implications. *Infants and Young Children, 4*(4), 1–10.

Wills, C. (1994, June). Putting human genes on the map (book review). *Natural History*, pp. 82–85.

Winick, M. (1980). Nutrition and brain development. *Natural History, 89*(12), 6–13.

Winnicott, D. (1953). Transitional objects and transitional phenomena. In D. Winnicott, *Playing and reality* (pp. 1–25). Middlesex, England: Penguin.

Winston, R., & Handyside, A. (1993). New challenges in human *in vitro* fertilization. *Science, 260*, 932–936.

Wittmer, D., & Petersen, S. (1992). Social development and integration: Facilitating the prosocial development of typical and exceptional infants and toddlers in group settings. *Zero to Three, 12*(2), 14–20.

Wittmer, S. (1986). Model versus modal child care for children from low-income families. *Zero to Three, 6*(5), 8–10.

Wivel, N., & Walters, L. (1993). Germ-line gene modification and disease prevention: Some medical and ethical perspectives. *Science, 262*, 533–538.

Wolff, P. (1970). The natural history of crying and other vocalizations in early infancy. In B. Foss (Ed.), *Determinants of infant behavior* (Vol. IV, pp. 81–110). London: Methuen.

Wolters, P., Brouwers, P., Moss, H., & Pizzo, P. (1995). Differential receptive and expressive language functioning of children with symptomatic HIV disease and relation to CT scan brain abnormalities. *Pediatrics, 95*, 112–119.

Woollacott, M., Shumway-Cook, A., & Williams, H. (1989). The development of posture and balance control in children. In M. Woollacott & A. Shumway-Cook (Eds.), *Development of posture and gait across the life span* (pp. 77–96). Columbia, SC: University of South Carolina Press.

WuDunn, S. (1993, April 25). Births punished by fine, beating, or ruined home. *New York Times*, p. 12.

Wynn, K. (1992). Addition and subtraction by human infants. *Natural, 358*, 749–750.

Wynn, R. (1975). Principles of placentation and early human placental development. In P. Gruenwald (Ed.), *The placenta* (pp. 18–34). Baltimore: University Park Press.

Yakovlev, P., & Lecours, A. (1967). The myelogenetic cycles of regional maturation of the brain. In A. Minkowski (Ed.), *Regional development of the brain in early life* (pp. 3–70). Oxford: Blackwell.

Yarrow, L. (1981). Beyond cognition: the development of mastery motivation. *Zero to Three, 1*(3), 1–5.

Yazigi, R., Odem, R., & Polakoski, K. (1991). Demonstration of specific binding of cocaine to human spermatozoa. *Journal of the American Medical Association, 266*, 1956–1959.

Yeh, S.-R., Fricke, R., & Edwards, D. (1996). The effect of social experience on serotonergic modulation of the escape circuit of crayfish. *Science, 271*, 366–369.

Yonas, A., Granrud, C., & Pettersen, L. (1985). Infants' sensitivity to relative size as information for distance. *Developmental Psychology, 21*, 161–167.

Yonas, A., Pettersen, L., & Lockman, J. (1979). Young infants' sensitivity to optical information for collision. *Canadian Journal of Psychology, 33*, 268–276.

Young, K. (1990). American conceptions of infant development from 1955 to 1984: What the experts are telling parents. *Child Development, 61*, 17–29.

Young, M., & Yamane, S. (1992). Sparse population coding of faces in the inferotemporal cortex. *Science, 256*, 1327–1331.

Young, W. (1996). Spinal cord regeneration. *Science, 273*, 451.

Yuodelis, C., & Hendrickson, A. (1986). A qualitative and quantitative analysis of the human fovea during development. *Vision Research, 26*, 846–855.

Zahn-Waxler, C. (1995). Introduction to special section: Parental depression and distress: Implications for development in infancy, childhood, and adolescence. *Developmental Psychology, 31*, 347–348.

Zahn-Waxler, C., Cummings, E., Ianotti, R., & Radke-Yarrow, M. (1984). Young children of depressed parents. *Zero to Three, 4*(4), 7–12.

Zatorre, R., Evans, A., Meyer, E., & Gjedde, A. (1992). Lateralization of phonetic and pitch discrimination in speech processing. *Science, 256*, 846–847.

Zeanah, C., Mammen, O., & Lieberman, A. (1993). Disorders of attachment. In C. Zeanah (Ed.), *Handbook of infant mental health* (pp. 332–349). New York: Guilford.

Zeitlin, S., & Williamson, G. (1994). *Coping in young children: Early intervention practices to enhance adaptive behavior and resilience.* Baltimore: Paul H. Brookes.

Zelazo, P., Zelazo, N., & Kolb, S. (1972). "Walking" in the newborn. *Science, 176*, 314–315.

Zepeda, M. (1982). Selected maternal-infant care practices of Spanish-speaking women. *Journal of Obstetrical, Gynecologic, and Neonatal Nursing, 11*, 371–374.

Zero to Three. (1992). *Heart Start: Emotional foundations of school readiness.* Arlington, VA: Zero to Three (National Center for Clinical Infant Programs).

Ziegler, D. (1994). Adoption and attachment. In B. James (Ed.), *Handbook for treatment of attachment-trauma problems in children* (pp. 256–266). New York: Lexington.

Zigler, E., & Lang, M. (1986). The "gourmet baby" and the "little wildflower." *Zero to Three, 7*(2), 8–12.

Zigler, E., Hopper, P., & Hall, N. (1993). Infant mental health and social policy. In C. Zeanah (Ed.), *Handbook of infant mental health* (pp. 480–492). New York: Guilford.

Zinober, B., & Martlew, M. (1985). The development of communicative gestures. In M. Barrett (Ed.), *Children's single-word speech* (pp. 183–216). New York: Wiley.

Name Index

Subject Index

Credits

This page constitutes an extension of the copyright page. We have made every effort to trace the ownership of all copyrighted material and to secure permission from copyright holders. In the event of any question arising as to the use of any material, we will be pleased to make the necessary corrections in future printings. Thanks are due to the following authors, publishers, and agents for permission to use the material indicated.

Chapter 2
34: Figure from "Making a Model of Development and Its Implications for Working with Young Infants," by F. Horowitz, December 1985, *Zero to Three*, 6(2), pp. 1–6. Copyright © 1985 ZERO TO THREE: National Center for Infants, Toddlers, and Families (formerly known as National Center for Clinical Infant Programs). Reprinted by permission.

Chapter 3
59: Figure reprinted by permission from Jane Gitschier. **71:** Family Health History form copyright © 1994 March of Dimes Birth Defects Foundation, 1994. Reprinted by permission.

Chapter 4
84: Figure from *Children in a Changing World*, by E. Zigler and M. Finn Stevenson, p. 119. Copyright © 1993 Brooks/Cole Publishing Company. **85:** Figure adapted from *Before We Are Born: Basic Embryology and Birth Defects*, Fourth Edition, by K. L. Moore. Copyright © 1993 by W. B. Saunders. Adapted by permission. **103:** Graph from *Maternal Nutrition and the Course of Pregnancy*, Washington D.C.: Committee on Maternal Nutrition/Food and Nutrition Board, National Research Council, National Academy of Sciences, 1970. Reprinted by permission.

Chapter 5
135: Translation of "A Declaration of Intention" reproduced by permission of *Pediatrics*, 79(3), p. A38, Copyright 1987.

Chapter 6
143: Charts reproduced by permission of *Pediatrics* from "Composite International and Interracial Graphs," by G. Nelhaus, 1968, *Pediatrics, 41*, p. 106. Copyright © 1968 American Academy of Pediatrics. **156:** Figure from *Report of the Surgeon General's Workshop on Breastfeeding & Human Lactation*, presented by the U.S. Department of Health & Human Services in cooperation with the University of Rochester Medical Center, 1984. DHHS Publication No. HRS-D-MC 84-2.

Chapter 7
179: Graph from "Effect of Experimental Undernutrition on Development of the Nervous System," by J. Dobbing. In N. Scrimshaw and J. Gordon (Eds.), *Malnutrition, Learning, and Behavior*. Copyright © 1968 MIT Press. Reprinted by permission. **188:** Graph from "Lead Exposure: The Commonest Environmental Disease of Childhood," by H. Needleman, July 1991, *Zero to Three*, 11(5), pp. 1–6. Copyright © 1991 ZERO TO THREE: National Center for Infants, Toddlers, and Families (formerly known as National Center for Clinical Infant Programs). Reprinted by permission. **192:** Figure from *Sensation & Perception*, Fourth Edition, by E. B. Goldstein, p. 44. Copyright © 1996 Brooks/Cole Publishing Company.

Chapter 8
204: Figure from "Ontogenesis of Sensory Function in Birds and Mammals," by G. Gottlieb. In E. Tobach, L. Aronson, and E. Shaw (Eds.), *The Biopsychol-*

PHOTO CREDITS

Chapter 1
3: © Paul Griffin/Stock Boston. **9:** © Robin L. Sachs/PhotoEdit. **12:** © Corbis-Bettmann.

Chapter 2
21: From Conception to Delivery by Sono Kochi Hasegawa/National Library of Medicine, Bethesda/Courtesy of Natural History Magazine. **23:** © Hildegard Adler. **40:** © North Wind Picture Archives. **43:** © Elizabeth Crews/The Image Works.

Chapter 3
50: Photo courtesy of Elwyn, Inc. **58:** © Science Photo Library/Photo Researchers, Inc.

Chapter 4
93: © Ted Wood. **109:** © 1993 Will & Deni/Photo Researchers, Inc.

Chapter 5
119: Dumbarton Oaks Research Library and Collections, Washington, D.C. **130:** © M. Kathryne Jacobs, PhD. **133:** © Elizabeth Crews/Stock Boston.

Chapter 6
152: Courtesy of the University Affiliated Cincinnati Center for Developmental Disorders/Children's Hospital Medical Center/The University of Cincinnati. **161:** © Peter Menzel/Stock Boston. **164:** © Marilyn Nolt.

Chapter 7
189: From A. Dekaban (1970) *Neurology of Early Childhood* (Baltimore: Williams & Wilkins), p. 405. **195:** © Tony Freeman/PhotoEdit.

Chapter 8
212: © Barbara Rios, 1991/Photo Researchers, Inc. **214:** Courtesy of Pediatric Basics, Vol. 65 © 1993 Gerber Products Company. **227:** Courtesy of Gordon Williamson.

Chapter 9
231: Lois Murphy and *Zero to Three*. **240:** From C. S. Amiel-Tison & A. Grenier (1986) *Neurological Assessment During the First Year of Life* (New York: Oxford University Press). **243:** © Michael Newman/PhotoEdit. **244:** © 1996 John Bigelow Taylor, NYC.

Chapter 10
259: Courtesy of Professor Carolyn Rovee-Collier/Rutgers University. **281:** Reprinted with permission from A. N. Meltzoff & M. K. Moore (1977), "Imitation of Facial and Manual Gestures by Human Neonates," *Science, 198,* 75–78. Copyright 1977 American Association for the Advancement of Science. **282:** © Elizabeth Crews/The Image Works. **284:** © Elizabeth Crews/Stock Boston.

Chapter 11
307: © Michael Dwyer/Stock Boston. **316:** From J. F. Werker & P. J. McLeod (1989), "Infant Preference for Both Male and Female Infant-Directed Talk: A Developmental Study of Attentional and Affective Responsiveness," *Canadian Journal of Psychology, 43,* 230–246. **323:** © Elizabeth Crews/Stock Boston.

Chapter 12
341: © Michael Newman/PhotoEdit. **349:** © Elizabeth Crews/The Image Works. **352:** © Elizabeth Crews/Stock Boston.

Chapter 13
359: © Cathy Cheney/Stock Boston. **361:** © Robert Brenner/PhotoEdit. **366:** © Robert Brenner/PhotoEdit.

Chapter 14
398: © Christiana Dittmann from Rainbow. **404:** © Susan Kuklin 1990/Photo Researchers, Inc. **412:** © Ursula Markus/Photo Researchers, Inc. **413:** © Paul Conklin/PhotoEdit. **416:** © Laima Druskis/Photo Researchers, Inc.

Chapter 15
422: © John Lei/Stock Boston. **435:** © Jeffry W. Myers/Stock Boston. **438:** © Sheryl Wudunn/NYT Pictures.

TO THE OWNER OF THIS BOOK:

I hope that you have found *Infant Development: A Multidisciplinary Introduction* useful. So that this book can be improved in a future edition, would you take the time to complete this sheet and return it? Thank you.

School and address: _____

Department: _____

Instructor's name: _____

1. What I like most about this book is: _____

_____

_____

2. What I like least about this book is: _____

_____

_____

3. My general reaction to this book is: _____

_____

4. The name of the course in which I used this book is: _____

_____

5. Were all of the chapters of the book assigned for you to read? _____

   If not, which ones weren't? _____

6. In the space below, or on a separate sheet of paper, please write specific suggestions for improving this book and anything else you'd care to share about your experience in using the book.

_____

_____

_____

_____

_____